The Adagio of Samuel Barber

CMS SOURCEBOOKS IN AMERICAN MUSIC
No. 8

To David.
From Michael
Christmas 2013

CMS Sourcebooks in American Music

No. 1 — Larry Starr: The Dickinson Songs of Aaron Copland
No. 2 — Neil Minturn: The Last Waltz of The Band
No. 3 — Gene H. Anderson: The Original Hot Five Recordings of Louis Armstrong
No. 4 — Paul Laird: The Chichester Psalms of Leonard Bernstein
No. 5 — Frank Tirro: The Birth of the Cool of Miles Davis and His Associates
No. 6 — Mark Zobel: The Third Symphony of Charles Ives
No. 7 — Thomas DeLio: The Amores of John Cage

Monographs & Bibliographies in American Music

No. 1 — Charles Schwartz: George Gershwin: A Selective Bibliography and Discography
No. 2 — Hans Nathan: William Billings: Data and Documents
No. 3 — Donna K. Anderson: Charles K. Griffes: An Annotated Bibliography-Discography
No. 4 — H. Earle Johnson: First Performances in America to 1900: Works with Orchestra
No. 5 — Irving Lowens: Haydn in America
No. 6 — Wilma Reid Cipolla: A Catalog of the Works of Arthur Foote, 1853-1907
No. 7 — John G. Doyle: Louis Moreau Gottschalk (1829-1869): A Bibliographical Study and Catalog of Works
No. 8 — James R. Heintze: American Music Studies: A Classified Bibliography of Masters Theses
No. 9 — William Phemister: American Piano Concertos: A Bibliography
No. 10 — Edward Brookhart: Music of American Higher Education: An Annotated Bibliography
No. 11 — Ernst C. Krohn: Music Publishing in St. Louis
No. 12 — Thomas E. Warner: Periodical Literature on American Music, 1620-1920: A Classified Bibliography with Annotations
No. 13 — Kenneth Graber: William Mason (1829-1908): An Annotated Bibliography and Catalog of Works
No. 15 — David P. DeVenney: Source Readings in American Choral Music: Composers' Writings, Interviews, & Reviews
No. 16 — James R. Heintze and Michael Saffle, eds.: Reflections of American Music: The 20th Century and the New Millennium
No. 17 — Michael J. Budds, ed.: Jazz & The Germans: Essays on the Influence of "Hot" American Idioms on 20th-Century German Music
No. 18 — James Mack Burk: A Charles Ives Omnibus
No. 19 — Bill F. Faucett: Music in America, 1860-1918: Essays, Reviews, & Comments on Critical Issues
No. 20 — Franco Sciannameo: Phil Trajetta (1777-1854): Patriot, Musician, Immigrant
No. 21 — Keith C. Ward: For the Parlor and the Concert Stage: A Guide to Recent Collections of American Piano Music from the Classic and Romantic Era
No. 22 — James R. Briscoe, ed.: *Vitalizing* Music History Teaching
No. 23 — Kathy H. Brown: Lotte Lehmann in America: Her Legacy as Artist Teacher
No. 24 — Matthew J. Cooper: Duke Ellington as Pianist

CMS Sourcebooks
in American Music

The Adagio of Samuel Barber

by WAYNE C. WENTZEL

Edited by Michael J. Budds

The College Music Society
Missoula, Montana

Library of Congress Cataloging-in-Publication Data

Wentzel, Wayne C. (Wayne Clifford), 1942-
The Adagio of Samuel Barber / Wayne C. Wentzel, Michael J. Budds.
pages cm. -- (Sourcebooks in American music)
Includes bibliographical references and index.
ISBN 978-1-881913-62-7 (alk. paper)
1. Barber, Samuel, 1910-1981. Quartets, no. 1, op. 11, Adagio. strings, B minor. 2. Barber, Samuel, 1910-1981. Quartets, no. 1, op. 11, Adagio; strings, B minor. arranged I. Budds, Michael J., 1947- II. Title.

ML410.B23W46 2013
784.7'189--dc23

2013015505

From the Series Editor

The College Music Society can boast of a proud tradition of contributions to the study of American music with its series *Monographs and Bibliographies in American Music*. For many years, volumes disseminated under this banner were rather lavishly produced and fell into the category of reference works, the majority of which were devoted to individual—and sometimes neglected—musical figures. In more recent times, the Society has determined to intensify its efforts by considering a greater range of topics and formats and by making available publications in paperback editions at reasonable prices.

In this spirit, The College Music Society has initiated a correlative series titled *CMS Sourcebooks in American Music*. The new venture was conceived to underscore the remarkable diversity in our nation's musical expression and to call attention to both landmark and representative achievements in its evolution. Whether the subject is a concert or stage work communicated through a notated score, a virtual performance frozen in time by modern technology (such as a film score or a recording), or some other mode of preservation not yet invented or standardized, the goal is the same: to gather materials for study, to reconsider and synthesize existing commentary and criticism, and to offer a fresh assessment or appreciation. Although a canonizing tendency is implicit in any selection process, every attempt has been made to address as many strands in the fabric of American music as possible.

These texts should not be perceived as ends in themselves, moreover, but as educational resources directed to teachers of music, students of music, and other lovers of music. Each author has been advised to take the benefit of primary sources of various kinds as well as the generous body of relevant scholarship and to place his or her subject in contexts most meaningful to contemporary readers. Although there is no intent to provide scholastic tracts of the most exacting rigor, these studies have been carefully and engagingly written and fully documented. Whenever possible, a compact disc featuring performances of historical importance has been attached to the volume as both a convenience and an added value.

It is always prudent to question the feasibility of yet another series of music publications. This is so especially now—when the fruits of the "Information Age" overwhelm the most curious, voracious, or dedicated reader and when the capacity and immediacy of the Internet challenge traditional practice. And yet it is never foolhardy to respond to the needs of an honorable profession in the service of a glorious art.

Michael J. Budds
Columbia, Missouri

I am pleased to acknowledge the assistance of Jacob Anthony Hallman in the production of this volume from the beginning of the project through its completion. His problem-solving skills, his curiosity, and his judgment all contributed to the excellence of the finished product; just as importantly, his reliability and wit made my work easier.

From the Author

> It sometimes happens . . . that a piece of music appears whose content is so consistently expressive, its climaxes so telling, its proportions so just, its entire facture so clear and convincing, that the discriminating musical public accepts it at once and wholeheartedly, and musicians wonder why so striking yet simple an idea waited so long to be born. Such a piece is the noble slow movement of the String Quartet, Op. 11, much better known as the Adagio for Strings.
>
> —Nathan Broder, *Samuel Barber* (New York: G. Schirmer, 1954), 74.[1]

This observation by Barber's first biographer sums up what many listeners feel about *Adagio for Strings*. I use the word "feel" because many not only accept *Adagio* as a lovely, well-constructed piece of music but also embrace it on an emotional level. It is accepted and embraced, moreover, not only by the "discriminating musical public," but it reaches the hearts and minds of many who have no background or interest in classical music. In this book I will attempt to present aspects of *Adagio* from many different viewpoints, looking at it from various angles and showing how and why it has become such a beloved piece of music.

I began this project, like all those interested in Barber's music, with the composer's two biographies: Nathan Broder, *Samuel Barber* (New York: G. Schirmer, 1954); and Barbara B. Heyman, *Samuel Barber: The Composer and His Music* (New York: Oxford University Press, 1992). Broder's early work is a slim volume with only a moderate amount of information about the composer's music in general and very little on *Adagio for Strings* itself. On the other hand, Heyman's monograph is more recent and far more comprehensive, with discussions on the origin of the string quartet and the genesis of the string orchestra version. I have cribbed unmercifully from her accounts but have fleshed them out with information from other sources. For bibliographic information I have relied on Don Hennessee's *Samuel Barber: A Bio-Bibliography* (Westport, Conn.: Greenwood, 1985), and my own update of that work, *Samuel Barber: A Research and Information Guide*, 2nd ed. (New York: Routledge, 2010).

[1]Nathan Broder, *Samuel Barber* (New York: G. Schirmer, 1954), 74.

Armed with this and other information, I formulated the second and third chapters, dealing with the String Quartet and its transformation into the orchestral *Adagio*. In my *Guide to Research* I had listed several *Adagio* arrangements, notably William Strickland's organ version, Barber's own Agnus Dei, and several others. Such arrangements are the subject of Chapter 4, which I have titled, "*Adagio* for . . . Just about Everything," because I am hard pressed to think of any instrumental combination for which the work has not been transcribed or arranged.

Chapter 5 began as a survey of dances choreographed to *Adagio*. The only commercially available performance on DVD is the Kirov *pas de deux*. Recently Julio Bocca presented a different dance to *Adagio* on a program for his Ballet Argentino. Seeing it gave me a chance to compare and contrast the two interpretations. Newspaper accounts of additional choreographies as well as interviews and correspondences informed me about performances that I did not have the opportunity to watch. This chapter also extends beyond dance into other performing areas: the use of *Adagio* in drama productions, figure skating, drum and bugle corps, even the circus. This music also extends into the worlds of visual arts and literature, the topic of Chapter 6. Some paintings or sculptures are either called "Adagio" or are inspired by it. In addition, *Adagio* is often referred to in novels, short stories, and poetry, either as a significant feature or as a passing remark by one of the characters, sometimes reflecting the author's own admiration for the work.

Other chapters deal with *Adagio* in movies, television, and the pop music world. In 2002 I presented a paper at the First International Samuel Barber Symposium at Virginia Commonwealth University. Two other papers were particularly interesting, informative, and relevant. Julie McQuinn, then a graduate student at Northwestern University and now a member of the faculty of Lawrence University, presented "Filmic Counterpoint: Barber's *Adagio for Strings* as a Voice in a Time of War," dealing with the use of the work in *Platoon* and *Les Roseaux sauvages*.[2] Although I had never seen *Platoon,* I was aware that *Adagio* figured prominently in it. Her paper (which she generously sent me later) revealed how the work set a mood and helped tell a story. I had never heard of *Les Roseaux,* in which *Adagio* was used quite differently but effectively. The brief film clips that she provided in her presentation whetted my appetite

[2]McQuinn has recently published a revised version of this paper, adding insights into other movies: "Listening Again to Barber's *Adagio for Strings* as Film Music," *American Music* XXVII/4 (Winter 2009), 461-99. I recommend reading it in connection with my own discussion of films in Chapter 8.

to watch the entire movies. In preparing the film and television chapter I watched them and many others to see not only how McQuinn's concepts might apply, but how I might formulate some of my own ideas. Articles and interviews by directors or film score composers helped me understand why and how *Adagio* was incorporated in their movies.

I also investigated *Adagio*'s presence in television shows. Unlike most films, which can easily be rented, television series are more elusive, unless they have been issued on videotape or DVD. Consequently, seeing some of them was hit or miss, as in soap operas where episodes from earlier years are seldom rebroadcast. The Museum of Television and Radio in New York City (now known as the Paley Center), a huge repository of broadcast material, however, had both episodes of *One Life to Live* that featured *Adagio*. I watched them, trying to see how lines of dialogue matched the music. A surprising aspect of *Adagio* in some movies and television was its use as parody. How could such an intense, serious piece of music be played for laughs? Yet that is one of *Adagio*'s most recent and slightly disturbing manifestations. Could I catch the right episodes of *Seinfeld* or *The Simpsons* when they were being rerun? Luck was with me, and I was able to see most of them, sometimes thanks to current or former students who often informed me about these telecasts. Finding episodes of British television series is even more of a hit or miss situation. When series have played on American cable channels, I could watch several episodes (*e.g.*, *Spaced* and *At Home with the Braithwaites*), but for some I have had to rely on other, sometimes hearsay, evidence.

Another significant paper at the Barber Symposium was "Whose Adagio? The Pop-Culture Repercussions of Barber's *Adagio for Strings*" by Luke Howard, then from the University of Missouri-Kansas City and now associate professor at Brigham Young University.[3] It was extremely revealing. Because I am basically a classical music junkie with little interest in popular music, I did not recognize any of his musical examples. I had heard of a rap artist called Puff Daddy but had no idea what his music was like or that he had borrowed a bit of Barber's Agnus Dei for one of his songs. Howard's paper became the point of departure for the chapter on *Adagio* in popular music, in which I have tried to sort out the many different pop (and jazz) versions and their relationship, not only to Barber's original, but also to each other. In the meantime Howard

[3]He also presented the paper in Seattle at the Pop Music Studies Conference (April 2002) and in Melbourne, Australia, at the Symposium of the International Musicological Society at Monash University (July 2004). An abstract is available at www.emptive.com.

published a revised version of his paper titled "The Popular Reception of Samuel Barber's *Adagio for Strings.*"[4] I had completed virtually all my own research before the article came out, but it was reassuring to find that he has come to many of the same conclusions that I have.

In addition to the area of pop music, *Adagio* has entered into other areas of pop culture, the most recent and most prominent of which is the incredible phenomenon called *YouTube*. Started in February 2005 by Chad Hurley, Steve Chen, and Jawed Karim, it has become an immense storehouse of videos, both amateur and professional. Some with *Adagio for Strings* are personal downloads of varying quality while others are taken directly from televised programs. Where else could I view clips that I otherwise missed, such as David Blaine's use of Agnus Dei for his escape trick or Puff Daddy's performance on the MTV awards?

Beginning with some of its early performances, *Adagio* is often associated with tragedy and death. One chapter of this book is devoted to such associations. Although it was not played at the funerals of Franklin Delano Roosevelt and John F. Kennedy, it has been performed at other funerals or memorial services and was also played frequently at the time of the 9 / 11 tragedies. Some people feel a sense of sadness in *Adagio* because of this association with death. Or is it an intrinsic part of the music?

The last main chapter, "The Legacy of *Adagio*," places the work in different contexts, such as computer game, ringtones, and greeting cards. *Adagio* even figures into education and laboratory-controlled psychology experiments. The work has also influenced the music of other composers, not only in the concert hall repertoire but also in movie and television soundtracks. In the concluding chapter I attempt to sort out some of *Adagio*'s most meaningful aspects. Is it American? Modern? Sad? Gay? Trite? With its constant use and (perhaps) abuse, is it getting on our nerves? Everywhere one turns, it seems to seek us out. *Adagio* is truly all around us.

In this day of technology the Internet has become the principle source of information. Printed documents, while still valuable, do not provide nearly enough data on *Adagio*. Therefore I have "googled" just about every conceivable combination of *Adagio for Strings* and other promising terms, sometimes with amazing results. Many fully-texted articles and

[4]Luke Howard, "The Popular Reception of Samuel Barber's *Adagio for Strings*," *American Music* XXV/1 (Spring 2007), 30-60.

newspaper reviews are available, fully on line. One can even read large chunks of published books on Google Books Search. In addition, *Wikipedia* has been a good place to turn for information on popular culture, such as Japanese anime cartoons, descriptions of trance dance terminology, and video games. Because amateur writers rather than professionals provide this information, it may not always be accurate, but coordinating it with other sources can often clear up discrepancies. Moreover, because the material is constantly being updated, there is hardly a more current source. One Internet realm I have generally avoided is chat-room conversations. Not only are people often misinformed about *Adagio*, they may also perpetuate other people's misinformation. I have cited chat-room comments only to get a sense of public opinion about the music. Many bloggers, for instance, have commented favorably about the use of Agnus Dei in the computer game *Homeworld*; others have decried its appearance in trance dance music. Such opinions are often as relevant and interesting as professional, critical reviews.

ACKNOWLEDGMENTS

In many respects, human resources are still the most valuable source of information. I am indebted to many people who have helped in the preparation of this study, most of all to Michael Budds for guidance in the final structure of the manuscript, which often required shifting around material from one part of the book to another. I am grateful for his patience and aid in turning the book from a dry catalogue into what I hope is a good read. In addition I would like to reiterate his thanks to Jacob Anthony Hallman for his invaluable service in the preparation of this book. He was especially patient in the handling of small but very important details. I am also pleased to acknowledge that I had the benefit of the expertise and generosity of Barbara B. Heyman, Luke Howard, and Judith A. Mabary who served me and The College Music Society as pre-publication reviewers.

I have been gratified by the responses, usually by email, to questions that I have posed to many of the conductors and performers of *Adagio*. Painters, sculptors, poets, and authors have also provided information about their works, often confessing how *Adagio* has inspired them. The following is a list of many of those who provided me with such details. Many of their names are cited in relevant footnotes, but others may not get the credit they deserve. I begin with those with whom I have had interviews or conversations:

Eldar Aliev (ballet dancer)
Timothy Brimmer (music coordinator)
Richard Auldon Clark (conductor)
Larry Coryell (guitarist)
Kathleen Dixon (author)
James Finnie (steel drum director)
Margaret Jones (violinist)
Phyllis Kirk (handbell choir director)
Raymond Leppard (conductor)
Scott Pfizinger (librarian)
Kevin Schussler (band director)

The following have provided me with important information by email:

Philip Aaberg (pianist)
Glenn Alexander (guitarist)
John Alfieri (marimbist)
Charlotte Blake Alston (storyteller)
Jordan Beckman (student arranger)
Julio Bocca (ballet dancer)
Rolf Boon (composer)
Carter Burwell (composer)
Troy Cady (actor)
James R. Cassidy (conductor)
Tony Cirrone (percussion director)
L. Bennett Crantford (double bassist, arranger)
Robert Genn (painter)
David Gerrold (author)
Richard Gibson (choreographer)
Jeffrey Gold (composer)
Gregory Hancock (choreographer)
Deborah Hay (choreographer, dancer)
Harry Hayfield (body-building instructor)
Barbara B. Heyman (Barber scholar)
Homer Hickam, Jr. (author)
Shelly Hocknell (artist)
Holly Hofmann (flutist, arranger)
Jamie Howarth (composer)
David M. Ice (harpist)
Mark Jarman (poet)
Nigel Keale (composer)
John Kennedy (conductor)
Kosta (video game player)
Bert Lams (guitarist)
Kevin Lavine (librarian)
Larry McDonough (jazz musician)
John Matthias (poet)
Julie McQuinn (film scholar)
John Meehan (choreographer)
Antonio MillàN (deejay)
Brent Miller (radio show host)
Dan Moore (steel drum director)
Michael J. Nelson (TV host)
Charles Noble (violinist)
Volkan Orhon (double bassist)
George Parker (author)
Matthew Parkison (student)
M. R. M. Parrott (poet)
Peggy Person (ice skating enthusiast)
Robert Pinsky (poet)
Scott Pollard (marimbist)
Stephanie Poxon (librarian, Barber scholar)
Cynthia Pratt (choreographer)

Ted Richer (poet)
Larry Riggs (aid in translation)
Matthew J. Savoie (ice skater)
Daniel Scott (dance manager)
James Sewell (choreographer)
Neil Shepard (poet)
Chris Snidow (composer)
Sheridan Stormes (music librarian)
Robert Stumpf II (Stokowski Society)
Milon Townsend (sculptor)
J. Rigbie Turner (librarian)
Linda Versprille (bell choir director)
Jonathan Wacker (marimbist)
James Westwater (photographer)
Thomas Wilkins (conductor)
Bekki Williams (musician)
John Wright (play director)
Fred Yaniga (aid in translation)

Finally I would like to thank those friends and students on "*Adagio* Alert," who have steered me in the right direction, often telling me, with unanticipated glee, about their latest *Adagio* sightings:

Stephen Asunto
Jordan Beckman
Victoria Benton
Susan Berger (librarian)
Cara Dobie
Frank Felice
William "Skip" George
Elizabeth Leatherberry
David McCollough
Michael Schelle
Joshua Southard
Zack Stachowski
Michael Swope
Christopher Tracy
Angel Velez
Matthew Vest
Joseph Weber
Linda M. Willem

Whether by interview, email, or simple word of mouth, all those listed above have made an enormous contribution to this book, for which I am extremely grateful.

Wayne C. Wentzel
Professor Emeritus
Butler University
Indianapolis, Indiana

Contents

Musical Examples

Tabular Information

Illustrations

Concerning Documentation

The author of this book has taken full advantage of the current spectrum of information sources. Providing standard documentation for those that are traditional in nature, *e.g.*, books, essays, journal articles, and newspaper reports, present few problems. In addition, he has—by means of email correspondence—made direct inquiries of a large number of public figures with connections to Barber's *Adagio* and has supplied appropriate facts about these exchanges. But others, now a vitally important part of the contemporary information explosion, pose serious challenges to the painstaking scholar trained in identifying consulted sources in considerable detail for the reader's benefit. I am referring, of course, to information sites on the Internet: home pages and blogs; websites reprinting published or broadcast materials; even, in several instances, chat rooms. By its very nature the Internet lacks the reassuring qualities of permanence and predictability that have conditioned scholarship until recent times. Relevant, highly instructive information accessible one day may be gone the next. A perfect example of this transitory dilemma concerns the visual contributions that are disseminated on *YouTube*. Unfortunately the shelf-life of individual postings cannot be controlled by the intrepid scholar. Nor is it reasonable to pretend that, once a video was conceived, was disseminated, and was later withdrawn, it never existed nor communicated important ideas.

As a result of this quandary and with my full approval, the author has provided as much relevant documentation as was available to him. For example, references to newspaper accounts reprinted on the Internet often lack the expected pagination of the original. Page numbers are no longer relevant to the inquisitive reader who will undoubtedly look up the information on-line rather than scroll through microfilm copies or browse through old, yellowed printed originals. Typing in the name of the author or first words of the title will automatically locate the whole article. While this information is likely to remain available for the foreseeable future, others, once accessible by URL, may already be impossible to find, so-called "dead" links. Therefore the author and I have also agreed to omit reporting the date he first accessed a site for two reasons: that fact, considering the ephemeral sensibility of information in cyberspace, is relatively meaningless in the grand scheme of things, and its inclusion tended to clutter footnote citations to no real advantage. Readers will need to trust the author when he reports on matters that no longer can be verified independently.

Introduction: *Adagio for Strings*—(Almost) Everyone's Favorite

CHAPTER 1

Man, oh man, does this piece grab you!

—Conductor Thomas Wilkins, *St. Petersburg Times* (6 May 1994).[1]

Why *Adagio for Strings*? What exactly is it about this composition of American composer Samuel Barber (1910-1981) that makes it attractive to so many people representing so many different ways of life and attuned to such different musical aesthetics? From famous conductors to provocative rap artists, from successful authors to dedicated video game players, from notable poets, choreographers, and sculptors to competitive bodybuilders and ice skaters, *Adagio* has sex appeal! Almost everyone responds in a positive manner to this nine-minute work that unfolds at a leisurely pace. Many absolutely love it. It, indeed, "grabs" many individuals.

It may take the remainder of this book to answer these questions—and even then there may still be lingering uncertainties, some intangible elements that the most strenuous efforts of scholarship cannot seem to pin down. Is *Adagio* worth all the effort? Is it worth the time to listen to it? Is it worth studying its history, its construction, its reception, and its many manifestations? I firmly believe so. But, please, do not take my word for it. Many of Barber's fellow composers as well as present-day concert artists, conductors, pop musicians, actors, and others are ready to attest to its merits.

Testimonials and Endorsements

COMPOSERS

For a BBC radio broadcast on 23 January 1982, the first anniversary of Barber's death, Aaron Copland was one of several American composers asked to evaluate the significance of *Adagio for Strings*.

> It's really well felt, it's believable you see, it's not phony. He's not just making it up because he thinks that would sound well. It comes straight from the heart, to use old-fashioned terms. The

[1]Thomas Wilkins, quoted in John Fleming, "Humor, and a Resident Conductor, in Debut," *St. Petersburg* [Fla.] *Times* (6 May 1994), B: 6.

> sense of continuity, the steadiness of the flow, the satisfaction of the arch that it creates from beginning to end.[2]

William Schuman, a colleague and friend of Barber, expressed a similar opinion: "I think it works because it's so precise emotionally. The emotional climate is never left in doubt. It begins, it reaches its climax, it makes its point, and it goes away. For me it's never a war-horse; when I hear it played, I'm always moved by it."[3]

While composer and writer Ned Rorem has often been dismissive of the music of Barber, he, too, has commented (somewhat) favorably on this particular composition:

> As the most performed "serious" piece by an American, the *Adagio* dispels two notions of conventional wisdom, that what is popular is necessarily junk, and the late improves upon the early. . . . Forever weaving and reweaving their web around our globe, what do *Adagio*'s strings sing to us if not a sad, brief perfection.[4]

Further assessments by these and other composers will be introduced at various stages throughout this book.

PERFORMERS

For his recently published collection of Barber memories Peter Dickinson recorded the opinions of esteemed concert artists. When he asked superstar soprano Leontyne Price if she had a favorite instrumental piece among Barber's compositions, she unhesitatingly replied: *Adagio for Strings*. "I'd like it played at my funeral. . . . There's nothing ever written like it. I . . . associate it with Sam as the most beautiful thing he's written. I mean, the strings just kill you. It tears you apart."[5] Pianist John Browning also holds the work in high regard: "It's very Bachian in a way—the

[2]Aaron Copland, BBC broadcast (23 January 1982), quoted in Barbara B. Heyman, *Samuel Barber: The Composer and His Music* (New York: Oxford University Press, 1992), 174.

[3]William Schuman, quoted in Peter Dickinson, *Samuel Barber Remembered: A Centenary Tribute* (Rochester, N.Y.: University of Rochester Press, 2010), 103. Dickinson's interview with Schuman is dated 14 May 1981.

[4]Ned Rorem, *A Ned Rorem Reader* (Harrisonburg, Va.: R. R. Donnelly and Sons, 2001), 238.

[5]Leontyne Price, quoted in Peter Dickinson, *Samuel Barber Remembered*, 130. Dickinson's interview with Price is dated 14 May 1981.

tremendous admiration Sam had for Bach comes out, I think, very strongly. And yet there's this tremendously lush texture . . . ; it's very, very lush."[6] It is likely that many others, if approached for this purpose, would echo these sentiments.

CONDUCTORS

The epigram by Thomas Wilkins at the head of this chapter announces his view of *Adagio for Strings*. Other conductors have raved about it as well. If he or she is resolutely dedicated to it, a conductor will probably lead a better performance. Richard Auldon Clark, of the Manhattan Chamber Orchestra, has declared it "the pinnacle of American string writing of the 20th century—and beyond. No other string piece comes close to it. It has a spiritual quality to it, almost a prayer, but not an elegy. Instead it is uplifting."[7] Director of the Cincinnati Orchestra Paavo Järvi has described the work as "one of the most touching and deeply felt pieces of music by an American composer."[8] Leonard Slatkin, conductor of the National Symphony Orchestra and other orchestras in America and abroad, became acquainted with Barber at a very young age: "My parents played his String Quartet, so I heard "Adagio for Strings" as a quartet piece before I knew it as a string orchestra work."[9] He was drawn to it because of its long melodic lines and "classical restraint."[10] When he began his conducting career in 1964, it was the first piece he conducted publicly. From a more philosophical and ethereal viewpoint comes a comment by Gustavo Dudamel, the rising young Venezuelan conductor and newest director of the Los Angeles Philharmonic Orchestra, who has emphasized *Adagio's* atmospheric quality: "*Adagio for Strings* is a very special piece because for me it is not about time, only space. It is like when you are out of the [Earth's] atmosphere. It comes from—I don't know where—the sound is coming like magic. *Adagio* is always floating in space."[11]

[6]John Browning, quoted in Peter Dickinson, *Samuel Barber Remembered*, 140. Dickinson's interview with Browning is dated 13 May 1981.

[7]Richard Auldon Clark, interview (3 May 2005) with the author.

[8]Paavo Järvi, quoted in "Don't Let Them Win," *Cincinnati Post* (13 September 2001).

[9]Leonard Slatkin, quoted in Mark Styker, "A Chat with Composer Leonard Slatkin," [Detroit] *Free Press* (27 September 2009); reprinted www.freep.com.

[10]Leonard Slatkin, quoted in Scott Timberg, "A Coda for Samuel Barber," *Los Angeles Times* (21 November 2004), E: 40.

[11]Gustavo Dudamel, interview (10 January 2009) with Phillip Huscher [radio broadcast].

After years of interest in avant-garde music there has been a swing back to tonality, and Barber is once again fashionable. Noting such changes in musical politics, Slatkin summarized the composer's new status: "He's not looked at as a throwback any more but a visionary."[12] Sam would be surprised and pleased.

OTHER CELEBRITIES

Many are swayed by the opinions of celebrities. Many care which political party so-and-so is supporting. As a result, the views of notable actors on the virtues of Barber's *Adagio for Strings* become matters of some interest.[13]

Sean Hayes, best known for playing the flighty but loveable Jack McFarland on *Will and Grace,* is a classically trained pianist and believes his musical background has helped him in his acting career. He pointed out that the "the art and creativity of music and the creativity of acting" have been compared many times "because there are beats and pauses, especially in comedy. The tone of your voice is musical."[14] After working with actor Morgan Freeman on the film *Bucket List* (2007), he compared Freeman's acting style to *Adagio for Strings*, a work he greatly admires: "You can be as simple and sustainable as [*Adagio*] in your vocal tone when you are acting. He doesn't need anything but to use his voice to act."[15]

Another partisan is Leonardo DiCaprio, who, after his success in *Titanic* (1997), starred in the movie *The Beach* (1999). Because DiCaprio appeared shirtless in nearly every scene, director Andrew MacDonald hired a personal trainer, Cornel Chin, to shape him up. Chin observed, "Leo was in pretty good shape, he plays a lot of sport. But to get the lean look required for the role, we had to do a lot of aerobic exercise with him and resistance exercise."[16] As they worked out, they played many kinds of music, *e.g.*, Pink Floyd and the Doors. But Leo also insisted they listen

[12]Leonard Slatkin, "A Coda for Samuel Barber," *Los Angeles Times* (21 November 2004), E: 40.

[13]For additional comments by various figures prominent in the realm of popular culture, please see Appendix 1.

[14]Sean Hayes, quoted in Susan King, "Musical Training Helps 'Will and Grace' Actor on the Big Screen," *Los Angeles Times* (30 December 2007).

[15]*Ibid.*

[16]Cornel Chin, quoted in Chloe Hague, "Pumped Up after Training Leo for His Beach," *New Shopper* (19 December 1999); reprinted www.thaistudents.com/the beach/archives_12_99.html.

to Bach's Air (Suite No. 3) and Barber's *Adagio for Strings.* According to Chin, "They're both really moving pieces of music, and it made a refreshing change from having the usual dance beat I'd use while I work out."[17]

Television personality David Soul, who starred in the series *Starsky and Hutch*, connected to this music in a completely different context:

> The *Adagio* was played in one of the best films about Vietnam called *Platoon.* I was part of that antiwar movement that basically said this war is wrong and we are not going. When my friends started coming home dead, I felt angry about not having been there. The *Adagio* sort of brings some peace to that idea; some comfort, to me, personally.[18]

His special bond with this piece was conditioned, in part, by non-musical events and associations. And yet the actor found soothing comfort in the music of Barber in spite of the anger he felt over losing his friends.

Whenever Kenneth Plume interviews actors for *FilmForce* magazine, he always asks them ten questions, one of which is "what is your favorite piece of music?" *"Adagio for Strings"* was the response of the following individuals:

Billy Boyd—Scottish actor, known mainly as Pippin Took in the *Lord of the Rings* movies
David Cross—comic, actor, writer, and star of HBO's *Mr. Show*
Anthony Stewart Head—British actor, known primarily as Rupert "Rippen" Giles, in the television series *Buffy the Vampire Slayer*
Tom Wilson—actor, best known as Coach Fredricks in *Freaks and Geeks*[19]

[17] *Ibid.*

[18] David Soul, "Music for Film and TV," *Maestro* [BBC television series], telecast 2008.

[19] Billy Boyd, *FilmForce* (5 March 2003); David Cross, *FilmForce* (1 May 2002); Anthony Stewart Head, *FilmForce* (12 January 2002); Tom Wilson, *FilmForce* (19 May 2004); reprinted www.uk.ign.com/articles/.

Desert Island Choices: A Loaf of Bread, a Jug of Wine, and *Adagio for Strings*

One of the BBC's longest running radio shows is *Desert Island Discs,* where celebrity guests, suitably called castaways, identify eight records that they would want with them were they were stranded on the proverbial desert isle. Former host Sue Lawley remembered some of her guests' choices: "people choose music for all sorts of reasons, from nostalgia to sadness. . . . [They] often choose *Adagio for Strings.* It is very moving."[20]

A sampling of the castaways and their comments, when available, is highly instructive. Two singers from dramatically different professional backgrounds—operatic soprano Maggie Teyte and World War II Era pop music artist Vera Lynn—selected *Adagio.*[21] Actor-musician John Reed confessed that it was his "mood music to sit a long time to think and remember things."[22] In the 1980s both photo-journalist Don McCullin and actor Bob Hoskins selected it. McCullin listened to the Barber in his darkroom while he developed his own photographs, often shots of tragic events. He admitted that, "when I play this music, I inject a lot more of 'me' into the pictures."[23] Hoskins regards *Adagio* as the most religious music he has ever heard. This comes from a man who usually does not consider religion to be important, but after hearing it he confessed, "well, you never know!"[24] If he had to narrow his eight selections down to only one, the Barber piece would be the one. In 1996 British Prime Minister Tony Blair told Lawley that he had listened to it while writing that year's emotional Labour Party conference speech: "It is a wonderful and inspirational piece of music."[25] In explaining his choices comedian Bob

[20]Hugh Davies, "Presenter of Desert Island Discs Decides to Quit after 19 Years," *Daily Telegraph* (13 April 2006); reprinted www.telegraph.co.uk/news/main.jhtml=/news/2006/04/13/ndid13.xml.

[21]The Teyte broadcast occurred on 30 May 1951; the recording was one of the few then available: the Boyd Neel Orchestra. Lynn's broadcast occurred on 3 September 1989; she chose the Philadelphia Orchestra with conductor Eugene Ormandy.

[22]John Reed, quoted in pinafore.www3.50megs.LOM|castaway.html. On 23 September 1972 he too chose the recording by the Philadelphia Orchestra with Ormandy conducting.

[23]Don McCullin, quoted in *Desert Island Discs,* www.bbc.uk/radio4/features/desert-island-discs. His choice on the 10 March 1984 broadcast was Bernstein's recording with the Los Angeles Philharmonic.

[24]Bob Hoskins, quoted in *Desert Island Discs,* www.bbc.uk/radio4/features/desert-island-discs. He preferred the recording by Neville Marriner and Academy of St. Martin in the Fields during the 17 November 1988 broadcast.

[25]Tony Blair, quoted in Tim Moynihan and David Cracknell, "Blair Would Take His Parents' Top Tunes to Desert Island," *Press Association* (24 November 1996). His choice was the recording by the Scottish Chamber Orchesta under the baton of Jukka-Pekka Saraste.

Monkhouse noted that *Adagio* has a "melody that I find entrancingly sad but uplifting."[26] In February 2003 actor Ian McKellen revealed to Lawless that, if stranded, "I'd like to indulge my melancholic mood occasionally, and this will certainly help."[27]

When Lawley stepped down as host in 2006, her replacement Kirsty Young carried on the tradition. Foreign correspondent Robert Fisk, one of her first guests, named *Adagio* because it is music "of utter conviction. If you listen to this, you understand the meaning of real tragedy. . . . It is absolutely devastating."[28] In 2012 former rugby player Brian Moore selected *Adagio* partly because he remembered its performance at the funeral of a friend who had died of a drug overdose. Sometimes he cannot listen to it because it brings back painful memories. He commented, "It is a stunning piece of music, it touches my soul. I think it's sublime."[29] In addition to those who preferred the orchestral version, scholar and critic George Steiner named Agnus Dei, the composer's own choral rendition. His favorite recording is the one by the Trinity College Choir—a classic American composition performed by a quintessentially British chorus. In his view, this is a work in which "American and English truths meet in a completely unique way."[30] Because the show remains on the air (as of 2012), it is likely that more celebrities will name Barber's *Adagio* among their "Desert Island Discs."

Meanwhile, back in the United States, singer-songwriter Billy Joel decided to play the game himself and compiled his own eclectic list called, appropriately, "Billy Joel's Desert Island Discs" with such pop music choices as the Beatles's album *Rubber Soul* (1965), the Rolling Stones's compilation *Hot Rocks, 1964-1971* (1971), and Dave Brubeck's

[26]Bob Monkhouse, quoted in *Desert Island Discs*, www.bbc.uk/radio4/features/desert-island-discs. On the 20 December 1998 broadcast he selected the recording by the Philharmonia Orchestra with conductor Geoffrey Simon.

[27]Ian McKellen, quoted in *Desert Island Discs*, www.bbc.co.uk/radio4/factual/desertislanddiscs_20030209.shtml. In January 2002 BBC Music released the album *Desert Island Discs: Sue Lawley Presents Classics in Paradise*, a compilation of many of the celebrities' choices over the years.

[28]Robert Fisk, quoted in *Desert Island Discs*, www.bbc.uk/radio4/features/desert-island-discs. On the 15 October 2005 broadcast he named the City of London Sinfonia recording conducted by Richard Hickox.

[29]Brian Moore, quoted in *Desert Island Discs*, www.bbc.uk/radio4/features/desert-island-discs. Moore's preference on 26 February 2012 was the recording by the London Symphony Orchestra with conductor André Previn.

[30]George Steiner, quoted in Miranda Sawyer, "Luxury Items and Duck Walks," *The Observer* (22 October 2006).

jazz classic "Take Five" (1959). Because of Joel's appreciation of classical music, it is no surprise that *Adagio for Strings* (Bernstein with the New York Philharmonic) should make his list (see Chapter 7). Joel considers *Adagio* "one of the most emotional pieces ever written."[31]

I've Got a Little List: *Adagio* and the Not So Rich and Famous

If testimonials by famous musicians and celebrities are not convincing, what about opinions held by members of the general public? How, in fact, do ordinary mortals react to *Adagio,* and how much do average persons want it as part of their daily lives?[32] Barber's biographer Nathan Broder observed that its "expressive content does not have to hurdle any stylistic obstacles to reach the average audience."[33] And members of the general audience love it, as can be confirmed by polls taken by radio stations around the world.

THE NPR TOP 100

In 1999 National Public Radio received a grant from the National Endowment for the Arts to compile a list of the most important American musical works of the twentieth century. NPR officials invited a group of music producers, editors, critics, and scholars to nominate works that they thought were "exceptionally beautiful or broke new musical ground or had a major effect on American culture and civilization." An initial list of 300 pieces was eventually narrowed down to 100, with music covering a wide range of idioms from classical to rock and roll. *Adagio for Strings* was one of only seven classical pieces (eight, if counting the crossover "Mack the Knife" by Kurt Weill).

When one of the judges, Joe Robinson, principal oboist of the New York Philharmonic, was a guest on *All Things Considered* on 3 January 2000, he proposed for the list *Adagio,* one of his favorite pieces: "I think Samuel Barber has written some of the most beautiful music written by any

[31]Billy Joel, quoted in "Take the Billy Joel Challenge," www.turnstiles.org/articles/Pulse11-89.html.

[32]For a sample of the average person's reaction to *Adagio*, see the site on *Facebook*, "I Love Samuel Barber's Adagio for Strings," which also allows for discussion of his choral version, Agnus Dei. In addition, there are similar blog sites, for example, one on *Twitter*.

[33]Nathan Broder, *Samuel Barber* (New York: G. Schirmer, 1954), 58-59. In a personal communication (9 August 2013), Barbara B. Heyman has reported to me that Barber did not have much confidence in Broder's writing.

American in the 20th Century."[34] The program then featured an *Adagio* sound bite. On a later occasion Murray Horowitz, NPR Vice President of Cultural Programming, offered his opinion of *Adagio:* "Wow . . . it's just so gorgeous. I mean, it's just as beautiful a work as anything composed in the 20th century. . . . And it's really in the American consciousness."[35]

As the year unfolded, each piece was presented on the show, with commentary. Critic John W. Barker, however, was dismayed that so few classical pieces made the list: "When it came the turn of the Barber piece, instead of devoting more than a few words to the composer and the music itself, the treatment focused on how it had been used as background in a highly successful war movie!"[36] While this is true, separate conversations presented on the segment with David Lynch, director of *The Elephant Man* (1980), and Oliver Stone, director of *Platoon* (1986), are quite revealing, nevertheless, and are valuable resources for understanding their decisions to add *Adagio* to their films.

OTHER RADIO STATIONS

Independent radio stations across the country have occasionally presented their own lists of favorite pieces. Table 1.1 enumerates some of the stations whose listener preferences favored either Barber's *Adagio* or Agnus Dei or both.

Table 1.1. Selected Radio Station Compilations

WCRB [Boston]: A List of 102.5 Essential Classics
KING [Seattle]: Classical Favorites
KPBS [Portland, Ore.]: Classical Listeners' Top 100
CPE [Raleigh-Durham, N.C.]: Top 100
KBYU [Brigham Young University]: Top 20
NPR [Miss.]: Top 25
KFUO [St. Louis, Mo.]: Top 99 Countdown

[34]Joe Robinson, quoted in "Analysis: Best Songs of the 20th Century" [transcript], *All Things Considered* [National Public Radio] (14 March 2001).

[35]Murray Horowitz, quoted in "Analysis," *All Things Considered* [National Public Radio] (14 March 2001).

[36]John W. Barker, quoted in "Critical Convictions: On Pop and Dumbed-Down Classical," *American Record Guide* (January / February 2003), 57. NPR released several compact discs of the one-hundred selections grouped by the years when they were written or first performed. *Adagio* is provided on *NPR 100: 1938-1939* (NPR, 20021203, 2001).

Is there any difference between the sexes regarding the popularity of *Adagio*? In 2005 station KBYU-FM of Brigham Young University separated its Top 40 poll according to male and female responders. While *Adagio* placed seventh among women, it was a more distant fifteenth among men. Are women more responsive to its plaintive, serene sounds than men? Because this may be the only survey to judge musical favorites by gender, it is doubtful that the results have any real significance. Most of the top twenty picks by both sexes were the same.[37]

Since the mid-1990s the BBC's *Radio Times* magazine, in conjunction with Channel 4 and Classic FM, has conducted a poll to determine its readers' favorite pieces of classical music under the "naff" title, "Hall of Fame." Barber's *Adagio* always makes the list, often in the top ten. In some years both it and Agnus Dei appear, but, as critic Michael White pointed out, "that's only because Classic FM's music staff haven't woken up to the fact that it's the same piece by another name."[38] Another critic, Bill Coles, has noted a trend in the selections: rather than being vigorous and rousing, the pieces tend to be sad or contemplative. He considered the list a "set of chocolate box tunes that could be fairly packaged up under the title: Classic pieces that make us blub."[39] While works like Elgar's *Pomp and Circumstance* are favorites in public concerts, "in the privacy of our own homes, us uptight, repressed Brits like to give full reign to our emotions as we listen to another tearjerker like Barber's *Adagio for Strings*"[40]

In 2001 the Australian Broadcasting Corporation's similar station, ABC-Classic FM, conducted its own contest to identify the classic 100 with Barber's *Adagio* coming in at a respectable 36. The network later produced compact disc sets of all 100 items, with the recording by Jorge Mester and the Melbourne Symphony Orchestra. On that same station Margaret Throsby presided over her own music-and-interview program where guests supply favorite recordings for discussion (somewhat like the "desert island" format, discussed earlier). In 2004 ABC-Classic issued a

[37]Full results were published in [Salt Lake City] *Deseret News* (5 June 2005).

[38]Michael White, quoted in "Classical Music: 'Vanessa' Goes on a Diet," [London] *Independent* (17 January 1999), 7.

[39]Bill Coles, quoted in "Death by Classical Selection," *Scotsman* (23 April 2003).

[40]*Ibid.* In 2004 Classic FM issued a disc of various pieces called *Popular Music: Hall of Fame 2000* with Barber's *Adagio*. Note that the title means "popular classical favorites" rather than songs in the pop music tradition.

tenth anniversary collection of some of these pieces. Several well-known celebrities in Australia (but not exactly household names in America) requested *Adagio for Strings* for that album.[41]

NUMBER OF PERFORMANCES, RECORDED AND LIVE

One reasonable way of assessing the popularity of a piece of music is to determine how many different performances become available on recordings. While many listeners consider Aaron Copland their favorite twentieth-century American composer, if executives at record companies were asked, they would probably put him on a par in sales with Barber. A list of recordings of both composers can be found on the Internet website, *ArkivMusic.com*, a source that is the most current as well as one that is constantly updated. Both composers' compositions appear on a great number of recordings. Barber (650) currently outdistances Copland (648), each exceeding any other twentieth-century American composer except George Gershwin (1,023).[42] But if narrowing the search to individual pieces, the number of recordings of *Adagio for Strings* far outstrips them all, with the exception of *Rhapsody in Blue*. The Barber piece can be heard on at least 212 different compact discs produced by over seventy different record labels. Some of these performances are duplicates (record companies love to recycle their music for different buyers) or arrangements (for sundry instrumental combinations), but the number of recordings of the original orchestral *Adagio* by different orchestras totals about fifty-four, plus another thirty-three of Agnus Dei, appearing on seventy-six different compact discs. In contrast, Copland's most recorded work, *Fanfare for the Common Man,* appears on eighty-six albums, performed by thirty-five different groups. Some composers, such as Charles Ives or Leroy Anderson, are represented by a great many recordings, but they cover many different works, with no single musical composition predominating. There is no question that *Adagio* is a favorite among record collectors.

[41]In 2005 Radio Telefis Éireann (RTÉ), Ireland's public service broadcaster, listed the "Top 100 Most Requested Pieces." *Adagio for Strings* placed 102. Only the Irish can figure that one out!

[42]Consult the statistics provided on www.arkivmusic.com. All of these statistics from Arkiv were current in September 2013. One might also add the nine different performances of the String Quartet movement, each on a different record label.

Table 1.2. Orchestras Featuring *Adagio for Strings* (July-November 2007)

Date	Orchestra
4 July	Boston Pops Orchestra
7 July	Ridgefield [N.Y.] Symphony Orchestra (outdoor concert)
17 July	University of Redlands [Calif.] Ensemble
4 Aug	Orchestra of the Mozart Festival
18 Aug	Central City [Colo.] Opera Festival Orchestra (tribute to Gian Carlo Menotti)
27 Aug (?)	Adrian [Mich.] Symphony Orchestra
2 Sept	Scottish Chamber Orchestra (with fireworks)
4 Sept	Montreal Symphony Orchestra
11 Sept	Columbus [Ohio] Symphony (in memoriam, U.S. Rep. Paul Gillmor)
13 Sept	Grand Rapids Symphony
24 Sept	Utah Symphony
29 Sept	Newport [Ore.] Symphony Orchestra
30 Sept	New Bedford [Mass.] Symphony Orchestra
6 Oct	Roanoke [Va.] Symphony Orchestra
25 Oct	Langley High School Orchestra [Great Falls, Va.]
27 Oct	Salem [Ore.] Youth Orchestra
5 Nov	Dubuque [Iowa] Community String Orchestra
7 Nov	Royal Scottish National Orchestra ("Classic Bites")
10 Nov	Oregon Symphony Orchestra (memorial in a church)

Another way of evaluating a work's popularity is the number of times it is programmed around the world. In Great Britain the Performing Right Society, responsible for collecting royalties for performers, writers, and artists, announced in September 2008 that *Adagio for Strings* "has been broadcast or performed live more than any other classical piece in the past year."[43] While it may not be quite that popular in the United States and other parts of the world, *Adagio* is found frequently on orchestra programs. Table 1.2 is a list of orchestral concerts over a span of about five months

[43]Ben Spencer, "Platoon Tune Is a Classic Choice," *Glasgow Daily Record* (12 September 2008), www.dailyrecord.co.uk. Note the reference to *Adagio* as the tune from a movie, the place many listeners first heard it.

in mid-2007, which I believe to be reasonably representative.[44] According to this information, no major orchestra played *Adagio* during this period, but it was performed by several smaller city orchestras, by a community orchestra, and by orchestras at a high school and a university. Two performances were given in Scotland. Two were memorial tributes; one was the result of orchestra members selecting favorite pieces; and two were played outdoors, one of which was accompanied by fireworks. The circumstances of such performances are, indeed, varied and far ranging. (Some specific instances will be discussed in the next chapter.)

In addition to the full orchestra and chamber orchestra performances identified in Table 1.2, others during this same period are cited in Table 1.3. Among those listed there are two of Barber's choral arrangement, Agnus Dei, his own third step beyond the string quartet movement. Another is the organ transcription by Barber's friend William Strickland, a project that Barber sanctioned. A version for four cellos was contrived after Barber's death. Who knows whether he would have approved of it or of the many other unusual versions of his beloved orchestral work.

Table 1.3. Other Performances (June-November 2007)

Date	Performance
22 June	A choral performance of Agnus Dei: Cathedral Choral Society, Washington, D.C.
2 July	A dance performance of Agnus Dei: Scott Leo "Taye" Diggs
20 July	Felix Hall, organ transcription, Portland, Ore.
4 Aug	Ying String Quartet, Syracuse, N.Y.
11 Aug	Northwest Dance Project, Portland, Ore.
11 Sept	The Portland Cello Project [Ore.]

Agnus Dei and Other Treatments

Because *Adagio for Strings* has appealed to so many people over the years, it has become a source of countless transcriptions and arrangements. Barber's Agnus Dei has been performed and recorded by many choral groups (some of which are mentioned in Chapter 4). Radio stations around the United States and Great Britain also programmed Agnus Dei (*e.g.*, WFME, WGBH, WKAR) mainly around 11 September 2001 as part of the

[44]Google provides an "alert" service that sends an email when a website or newspaper mentions a specific term. I am on an "Adagio alert," which emails me whenever that work is scheduled on a program. Such messages may be announcements of upcoming performances or reviews of recent ones.

World Trade Center memorial.[45] Brent Miller has featured the piece three times on his show *Choral Colors* (WICR, Indianapolis). In his opinion "it is a marvelous work. I have studied the score and have sung it in two different ensembles. It is difficult to sing, but well worth the effort."[46]

In addition, many diverse versions have come into existence because someone—often the director or a member of an ensemble—appreciates it and tries it out with the group. Such an endeavor, however, succeeds in the repertoire only if it goes over well with an audience. Discussed in Chapter 4, for example, are those for a single double bass (plus tape), a guitar trio, a marimba ensemble, and a steel drum band. Scott Pollard of the marimba group Attacca asserts that the feedback from the audience to its arrangement has been outstanding: "Most people love the piece to begin with and are shocked at how well it works for marimba. It's really something else and still gives me chills every time we do it."[47] Volkan Orhon, who has arranged it for solo double bass, remarked, "I was always a huge fan of *Adagio* so I decided to try this piece as an experiment. . . . People enjoy it and get really fascinated by the whole process."[48] In his performance he plays the main melody live along with a pre-recorded sound track of his playing of the other parts. Bert Lams, a member of the California Guitar Trio, is pleased with the way listeners respond to its arrangement: "In my experience, *Adagio* is one of the most captivating pieces of music I have ever played for an audience."[49] Jimmie Finnie, the percussion instructor at Indiana State University, has rehearsed Al O'Connor's steel drum arrangement with a small group of students: "It has been one of my favorite pieces for years, ever since I was a freshman at college"; he has never thought the piece was sad, but instead, uplifting —"music for heaven."[50] The Cainhoy Steel Tigers Steel Drum Band has also played O'Connor's arrangement. According to its director Linda Versprille, the audience goes "wild over it."[51]

[45]WFME (30 August 2001); WGBH (11 September 2001); WKAR (12 September 2001).

[46]Brent Miller, email (20 January 2006) to the author.

[47]Scott Pollard, email (9 August 2004) to the author.

[48]Volkan Orhon, email (22 June 2005) to the author.

[49]Bert Lams, email (19 August 2004) to the author.

[50]Jimmie Finnie, interview (5 August 2004) with the author.

[51]Linda Versprille, email (30 April 2007) to the author.

Dance and Other Performing Arts

Choreographers need appropriate music to accompany their creations, whether ballet, modern dance, or post-modern dance, and many have selected the Barber work. In some cases a choreographer may have considered *Adagio* for a long time but needed to find a suitable occasion to stage it. Edward Morgan and Daniel Scott of the MorganScott Ballet revealed that they had always wanted to create a dance to *Adagio* but felt they had to wait for the right concept and the right moment. Scott believes that its "perfect build to the climax . . . makes it possible to be moved by it again and again."[52] He and Morgan realized its simplicity was ideal for their dance *Earthly Love, Heavenly Spirits* (1999). Likewise, when Mikhail Baryshnikov was preparing to stage his version of *HeartBeat:mb* (1998), he considered the Adagio movement from Barber's String Quartet but remained somewhat hesitant. He asked one of his musicians, Margaret Jones, to listen to a recording of it while he played a videotape of his dancing. Because it was so perfect, she admonished him not to consider another option.[53] James Sewell, head of the Sewell Dance Company, had known the Barber Agnus Dei for years. When he was choreographing "Suspended Breath," a component of *Good Mourning* (1997), he heard it again in the context of the "emerging movement, and discovered that it is very effective, sets a very strong tone, and supports [the dance] in several ways."[54]

Other choreographers heard *Adagio* during performances by other dancers and decided that they also wanted to dance to it. When Julio Bocca, director, lead dancer, and choreographer of Ballet Argentino, saw Mauricio Wainrot's dance set to *Adagio,* he asked permission to perform it with his own company. Bocca reported, "I always liked Barber's *Adagio* and, when I saw Mauricio's *pas de deux,* I liked it even more."[55] Deborah Hay, a post-modern dance choreographer, decided on the movement from Barber's Quartet for one of her works after she heard it in a dance by a colleague. She recalled, "the music so moved me that each time she performed I became more convinced that my greatest challenge as a

[52]Daniel Scott, email (11 February 2006) to the author.

[53]Margaret Jones, interview (21 May 2004) with the author.

[54]James Sewell, email (25 October 2005) to the author.

[55]Julio Bocca, email (3 April 2004) to the author. [Translation by Linda M. Willem]

choreographer would be to use . . . *Adagio* for my new dance."[56] Other choreographers may have decided on *Adagio for Strings* for similar reasons.

If *Adagio* can support a dance, then why not introduce part of it in a theatrical production? Several stage directors have incorporated the familiar work in their dramas, often discovering it in a roundabout way. Vern Slater, the director of a 2001 production of *The Diary of Anne Frank* (1955), had not planned on adding music but ultimately determined that Barber's composition served as fitting counterpoint to the climactic scene where the Franks await the arrival of the Nazis.[57] He concluded, "we never would have been able to obtain the level of emotion we attained had we not utilized Barber's lovely Adagio for Strings."[58] Coincidently, *Adagio* also enhanced another production of that same play. The director was about to cut the final scene because she felt it was "anti-climactic" but promised she would reconsider if the right kind of music could be found to accompany it.[59] When a cast member brought in a recording of *Adagio* and played it for the company, everyone knew that this was what the scene needed.

Adagio for Strings in a dance or drama is logical—but in a drum and bugle corps exhibition? Yet it was featured in the Star of Indiana's hit show, *Blast II: Shockwave* (2002). One of the group's founders, Jim Mason, confided, "I just pick music that I like, that touched me or moved me when I was younger or pieces that I always wanted to do."[60] Many regarded the *Adagio* segment a highlight of this particular show. Another drum and bugle corps, the Santa Clara Vanguard, presented an excerpt in its *Age of Reverence* (2000). Not originally a part of the program, it was substituted for a more challenging piece. Besides, choreographer Myron Rosander and director Jim Casella were "kinda dying to do" *Adagio* sometime anyway. Rosander realized that "When you take a piece of music with this emotional caliber, you really have to be very cautious that you do it justice. This is a once in a lifetime opportunity to do Barber's

[56]Deborah Hay, *My Body, the Buddhist* (Hanover, N.H.: Wesleyan University Press, 2000), 7.

[57]The play, which was produced on Broadway, was written by Frances Goodrich and Albert Hockett.

[58]Vern Slater, "Bird Soup and Hummus," *The Play's the Thing* (30 June 2003); quoted in www.geocities.com/vernslater/annefrank.html.

[59]Troy Cady, email (17 June 2005) to the author.

[60]Chip Chandler, "Musicians Become Athletes," *Amarillo* [Tex.] *Globe-News* (26 January 2003).

Adagio."[61] In addition to these diverse performances, *Adagio* has been heard in a circus, in a body building competition, and in an escape artist's trick!

Visual Arts and Literature

Artists and authors have often been inspired by listening to *Adagio for Strings* while they work. When Robert Genn was painting his canvas *Autumn Pattern* (2001), *Adagio* was playing on the radio. He believes that his painting was affected by the music. Likewise, Milon Townsend listened to the Barber piece as he worked on his sculpture *Mourn* (2001), admitting that "It takes me out of who 'I' am. *Adagio* always moves me."[62] Other artists such as Austin Davies, Thompson Lehnert, and Fiona Taylor have actually titled their works *Adagio for Strings*. Such a practice implies that the music has gone beyond inspiration—that it has become embedded in their creations.

The Barber composition has inspired authors as well. Some have played it to enhance their creative processes. When Mara Purl, author of the "Milford-Haven" novels, was asked which music most inspired her to write or what she liked to listen to while writing, she mentioned *Adagio.*[63] Likewise, Alan Furst, writer of spy novels such as *Night Soldiers* (1988), uses music for stimulation and listens to *Adagio* when he is working on "elegiac scenes."[64]

When *Adagio* is referenced in poetry, it may be the focus of the whole work as in John Matthias's "A Note on Barber's Adagio" (2000), which tells the story (probably apocryphal) of Barber hearing his music on the radio on the day of John F. Kennedy's assassination. The music may also be linked in the poet's memory to an almost forgotten incident, as in Neil Shepard's "Listening to Samuel Barber's Adagio for Strings" (1988). This piece of music is among those elements that compare and contrast bonds between him and his lover. On the other hand, John Brian Perkins's poem, "A Little Annoying Night Music" (2003), shows that the narrator's view of

[61]Myron Rosander, quoted in *Age of Reverence*, perf. Santa Clara Vanguard, cond. Jim Casella, *DCI* [Drum Corps International] *2000 World Championships* [DVD], Audio Track 3.

[62]Milon Townsend, email (14 December 2005) to the author.

[63]Mara Purl, "Amazon.com Talks to Mara Purl," www.amazon.com/exec/obidos/show-interview/p-m-urlara/102-5595833-9487359.

[64]Richard Dyer, "Cloak and Typewriter Spy Master Alan Furst Explores Moral Choice in His Period Novels," *Boston Globe* (27 March 2001), E: 1.

Adagio changes after his lover has gone. While he once enjoyed it, he ultimately complains that "Barber's strings are now terribly annoying."[65]

When cited in a short story or novel, *Adagio* usually plays a lesser role than in a poem. Whether a character hears the work at a concert, as in Valerie Christie's *The Mysterious Affair at Redfield* (2002), or hears it on the radio or on a recording, as in Jerry Flesher's *Tomorrow I'll Miss You* (2005), the piece often conjures up memories of the past, either pleasant experiences or slightly disturbing incidents. A character's view of the work sometimes mirrors that of the author. Like Hunter, a character in his novel *The Atomic Kid: Adventures in the Antiworld* (2004), author George Parker has felt that *Adagio* has "tugged long forgotten memories from my heart and my mind . . . and lifted me from one imagined plateau of existence up to another."[66]

The World of Popular Music

> Most modern composers avoid
> Old methods we've always enjoyed,
> But no grudge do I harbor
> For Samuel Barber:
> He's almost as good as Pink Floyd.
>
> —Graham Lester, *The Omnificent English Dictionary in Limerick Form*.[67]

Not only do classical musicians, conductors, and choreographers (so-called "serious" performers) appreciate and love *Adagio for Strings,* but many pop musicians, as wide ranging as Billy Joel and The Cure's Robert Smith, respond with comparable enthusiasm. For example, when Joel thought about the tragedy of 11 September 2001, he reflected that "nobody can describe the depths of emotions that people are having right now. I listened to the Barber 'Adagio for Strings' and I wept, and it made me feel better."[68] He once introduced one of his songs at a concert with a

[65]John Brian Perkins, "A Little Annoying Night Music," *The Fruit of Falling Down* (Bloomington, Ind.: Xlibris, 2003), 47.

[66]George Parker, email (27 January 2006) to the author.

[67]Graham Lester, Limerick #11253, *OEDILF [The Omnificent English Dictionary in Limerick Form]*, www.oedilf.com/db/Lim.php.

[68]Billy Joel, quoted in Andrew Druckenbrod, "'Piano Man' Composes for Solo Piano as New CD Goes Beyond Pop," *Pittsburgh Post-Gazette* (3 October 2001), E: 1.

brief improvisation on *Adagio*. In a similar way, when Robert Smith wanted to begin a concert on The Cure's 2000 "Dream Tour" with music "that would get both us and the audience in the same right mood at the start of every show," he thought *Adagio* would do it,—"(and I love it!)."[69]

Three individuals who completely transmuted *Adagio for Strings* into a dance-floor anthem—William Ørbit, Ferry Corsten, and Tiësto —all appreciated it long before they started working with it. Ørbit, who produced an elegant version for synthesizer, has declared that Barber's original is "a great piece of music. . . . It gets me every time. . . . Adagio is beautiful."[70] Corsten, who gave Ørbit's version a dance beat, agreed: "I loved the original piece of music";[71] it is "just a piece of art and it was a dream of mine to work with something as beautiful as that."[72] His colleague, Tiësto, who also transformed Ørbit's arrangement into a dance hit, confessed that "I really like classical music, and *Adagio* was always one of my favorite pieces."[73] Inasmuch as all three admire the Barber composition, they do not intentionally abuse it but attempt to transfer some of its character into newly formed pieces of music.

Other musicians who have never introduced it into their own works have at least been inspired by it. Jim Creeggan, vocalist and bass player for Barenaked Ladies, has acknowledged that he tried to give his song "War on Drugs" on the album *Everything to Everyone* (2003) an *Adagio for Strings* quality:

> *Adagio for Strings* is [one of] the most emotive string pieces I know. I love how it patiently staggers each part around a simple recurring theme. For me it creates an image of someone slowly

[69]Robert Smith, interview (14 July 2001) with Craig Parker, "Chain of Flowers Interview with Robert Smith," www.chainofflowers.com/robertint.html.

[70]Nick Coleman and William Ørbit, "Record Producer and Musician, William Ørbit on Samuel Barber's Adagio for Strings," [London] *Independent* (3 March 1995), 26.

[71]Ferry Corsten, interview (15 May 2004) with Aldrin Tan, www.trancerepublic.com.

[72]Glittergirl, "Interview: Ferry Corsten," *Groovanauts* (21 December 2003); reprinted www.groovanauts.com/board/articles.php?article_id=80.

[73]Sean O'Neal, "One Moment in Time," *Philadelphia Citypaper*; reprinted www.citypaper.net/articles/2004-09-23/music.shtml.

> fighting the force of gravity, like a rock climber climbing without a rope.[74]

When some pop musicians admire *Adagio for Strings,* they compare it to songs of the culture in which they live and work. For instance, vocalist Pam Rose has contended that "I never thought there was much difference between Taj Mahal blues and Samuel Barber's *Adagio for Strings.* I think they are equally evocative."[75] Paul Schneider, bass player for the heavy metal group Freudian Slip, expressed this view:

> I like Samuel Barber's *Adagio,* probably one of the most intense pieces I've ever heard in my life. Musically, I could compare it to nobody. But you can also compare that feeling to a Fred Green song or something. Fred Green might be more of a hip-hop, rock, funk thing, but I could compare that intensity of feeling.[76]

When producer and deejay[77] Les Hemstock was asked to identify his favorite all-time top five tracks, recordings that have changed him and his music, his list consisted of only two pieces: Frankie Goes to Hollywood's "Relax" (1983) and Barber's *Adagio.*[78]

When pop musicians try to put into words the reason they like *Adagio* so much, the three factors that arise most often are tears, goosebumps, and transcendence. That is, the very experience of hearing *Adagio* can result in crying, can produce an indescribable thrill, or can create a state of other-worldly ecstasy.

[74]Jim Creeggan, "Strings Attached," *BNL Blog* (23 May 2003), www.bnlblog.com/entry.asp?dDate=5/23/2003.

[75]Pam Rose, "Pamela Rose: Morpheus," *Independent Music,* www.mattgalligan.com/genre_New_Age/genre_Healing/album_PAMELA_ROSE_Morpheus.html.

[76]Paul Schneider, quoted in Gilbert Garcia, "Rocks Off: It Ain't Heavy, It's the Unclassifiable Thunder of Freudian Slip," *Phoenix New Times* (3 July 1997).

[77]I use this form of the term to distinguish between the traditional disk jockey who selects the music for a radio show and a deejay (DJ) who makes foreground contribution to the dance music in nightclubs and rave events.

[78]"Interview with Les Hemstock," *Megamind Magazine, Nordic Clubbing and DJ Culture* (19 May 2003); reprinted www.megamind.se/page.php?id=231.

TEARS (WITHOUT BLOOD OR SWEAT)

Some perceive an inherent sadness in *Adagio*, notably the following musicians who candidly expressed such a personal response. In his 2002 commencement address at Boston's Berklee School of Music singer and guitarist Sting spoke of his emotional reaction to *Adagio*:

> How is it that some music can move us to tears? Why is some music indescribably beautiful? I never tire of hearing Samuel Barber's "Adagio for Strings" or Fauré's "Pavane" or Otis Redding's "Dock of the Bay." These pieces speak to me in the only religious language I understand. They induce in me a state of deep meditation, of wonder. They make me silent.[79]

Glenn Alexander, whose own guitar arrangement is discussed in Chapter Seven, made a similar confession: "The piece is so incredible to me and simply moves me, sometimes to tears, with its extraordinary beauty."[80] Tom Philips of the doom band While Heaven Wept reflected, "If you listen to Henryk Górecki's 'Symphony No. 3' or Samuel Barber's *Adagio for Strings,* chances are very high your eye will not stay dry."[81] When singer Cynthia Clawson was asked which songs she wanted performed at her funeral, she named her favorite hymn, "O Love That Will Not Let Me Go," and added: "And I think I want them to play Samuel Barber's *Adagio for Strings*, because everybody cries when they hear that, and I want them to cry a lot."[82]

A CHILL UP YOUR SPINE OR THE GOOSEBUMP EFFECT

Adagio may move some listeners to tears but to others it is a thrilling experience. Guitarist Steve Trovato reported that, when he heard Barber's music in *Platoon* (see Chapter 8), it gave him goosebumps because "it

[79]Sting, quoted in *The Berklee History Series* (26 September 2002), www.berklee.edu/html/ab_sting.html.

[80]Glenn Alexander, email (28 June 2004) to the author.

[81]Tom Philips, quoted in Orion, "While Heaven Wept Interview" (May 2003), www.blooddawn.de/interviews/while heavenwept.htm.

[82]Cynthia Clawson, quoted in Marv Knox, "Deep in the Heart of Texas," *Baptist Standard* (7 May 2001); reprinted www.baptiststandard.com/2001-5.

was so moving and sad."[83] For others it is one of the dance (trance) versions that elicits this chilling effect. Dutch deejay Menno de Jong considered Corsten's *Adagio* remix one of his favorites: "I don't think I need to tell you guys why this song is so incredible. It just gives me goose bumps every single time I hear it."[84] For Tiësto it is not his own remix that thrills him but his audience's reaction to it. At a 2003 concert in Greece 4,000 spectators screamed and danced while he played it. "I had goosebumps all over! Moments like that remind me of the reason why I want to be a deejay."[85] Many of his fans have expressed in chat-room discussions that his remix gives them goosebumps as well. Nonetheless, another trance fan still preferred Corsten's version: "damn—I'm getting goosebumps just humming it."[86]

OUT OF THIS WORLD

Other musicians attribute a transcendent or otherworldly quality to this music, one that takes them beyond everyday experiences. For instance, Richard Wileman, founder of the British rock group Karda Estra, believes that Barber has the power to "get over the more transcendental beauty of the pieces I particularly love such as *Adagio for Strings*."[87] Sherman Holmes, of the Holmes Brothers, admitted, "I love tones more than I like music itself, and [*Adagio for Strings*] just takes me into a world by myself. I can just get lost in the music."[88] And when songwriter and performer George Sarah was asked, "what is your favorite song of all time?" he replied, "I truly believe [*Adagio for Strings*] is being performed and composed throughout the universe."[89] Once when singer and songwriter Steve Perry, best known as lead singer for Journey, heard a string quartet

[83]Steve Trovato, quoted in Jim Walk, "Steve Trovato Interview–Part 2," *AFG Sound Hole* 15 (Fall 2002); reprinted www.social.rr.com/feltenmichelle/trovato2.htm. AFG is the acronym for the Association of Fingerstyle Guitarists.

[84]Menno de Jong, quoted in Mista, "Interview with Menno de Jong," *Trance Inc.* (12 June 2004), www.trance-inc.com/?page=articles&article_id=3.

[85]DJ Tiësto, "Petite Déclaration de Tiësto," *Trance Addict Forums–Europe–France* (16 September 2003), www.tranceaddict.com/forums/showthread/t-129204.html.

[86]*Rapture TV Forum*. This blog is no longer maintained.

[87]Richard Wileman, quoted in "Progfreak.com's Interview with Karda Estra's Richard Wileman," *Progfreaks.com* (22 October 2001), www.progfreaks.com/Interviews/KardaEstra/Interviewptone.htm.

[88]Sherman Holmes, quoted in "Pop: Brother to Brother," *Barnes and Noble*, www.bn.com.

[89]George Sarah, quoted in Bret Miller, "Interview with George Sarah," *Highwire Daze*; reprinted www.members.tripod.com/tildebretthehitman/georgesarah.html.

performing at a restaurant, he requested *Adagio for Strings*. He claimed, "I could not remember the title so I sang the melody and they knew it immediately. I personally feel the arch of my whole life in that piece. It covers all the things that have happened and all that has yet to happen."[90]

Movies and Television

One reason that *Adagio for Strings*'s immense popularity extends beyond the concert hall is its association over the last few decades with well-received movies. Inserting classical music in a feature film may be the quickest way to reach a general audience today. How it ends up in a film may come about in several ways, but ultimately it is the director's decision. Not all have explained their musical decisions publicly, but two of them—David Lynch of *The Elephant Man* (1980) and Oliver Stone of *Platoon* (1986)—have described in print and in radio interviews how *Adagio* became an important part of their movies. When Lynch heard it on the radio, "It washed over me. It was just so unbelievably beautiful and so perfect for the ending of the film."[91] Stone warmed to *Adagio* when he used it as a "temp track," music that is temporarily added for editing purposes. But when he kept hearing that particular music in various scenes, he decided that its status should change from temporary to permanent: "I fell in love with it, and it was such a strong counterpoint to the brutality and savagery of the [film's] imagery."[92]

Some people, other than classical music buffs, first heard *Adagio* as they viewed *Platoon* and have never forgotten its impact. Guitarists Glenn Alexander and Steve Trovato admitted that hearing it in the movie theater eventually led to their own interpretations. Carla Bley remembered *Adagio* in *Platoon* when she arranged it for Charlie Haden's Liberation Orchestra. She got the idea when she recalled the dead bodies in that film and the list of names read on television of soldiers who died in Iraq: "It represents the sadness of people dying for political reasons."[93] Likewise, Chris Snidow,

[90]Steve Perry, quoted in *Fan Asylum* (4 January 2007), www.fanasylum.com/steveperry/.

[91]David Lynch, quoted in Marie Pohl, "David Lynch on Meditation," *Süddeutsche Zeitung* (13-14 May 2006); reprinted www.businessportal24.com/de/a/30092.

[92]Oliver Stone, quoted in "Profile: Samuel Barber's Adagio for Strings," [transcript], *All Things Considered* [National Public Radio] (13 March 2000); rebroadcast www.npr.org/2000/03/13/1071551/barbers-iconic-adagio-for-strings.

[93]Carla Bley, quoted in Dan Ouellette, "Charlie Haden and Carla Bley: 'Maybe We Should Take Machine Guns Out and Shoot Everyone in the Audience,'" *Downbeat* (January 2006); reprinted www.downbeat.com.

who arranged *Adagio* for synthesizer, has confided that he was "deeply enchanted" with it ever since he first heard it in *Platoon*.[94]

Adagio for Strings also plays an important role in Christoffer Boe's film *Reconstruction* (2003). Boe not only directed the film but also wrote the screenplay and may have had *Adagio* in mind while he was preparing it. When he sent a copy of the script to his leading actor, he included a compact disc of music to accompany each scene. It seems likely that *Adagio* was provided on that recording. Although Boe wanted *Adagio* in his movie, most film score composers, such as John Morris of *The Elephant Man* and George Delerue of *Platoon*, would prefer not to have it compete with their original music, but John Barry was the one who suggested that Barber's Agnus Dei be used in his music for *The Scarlet Letter* (1995). He had heard a recording and thought it was "just gorgeous," that it would be "so wonderful over the long sermon and a few other places."[95] Barry got his wish.

It is relatively easy to determine who selects the music for movies, but it is more difficult for television shows. Usually many people are involved: writers, producers, and directors; seldom do any of them discuss their decisions in the public arena. *Adagio* may be added simply because it fits the mood of the action on the screen, as in Jacob Bronowski's *Ascent of Man* (1973), where it accompanies the moment when a baby stands up and walks. In a different situation, on the soap opera *One Life to Live*, the full *Adagio for Strings* precisely fits the length of the scene in which it is heard. Moreover, because the climax of the dialogue exactly coincides with the climax of the music, this score was chosen first and the dialogue written to fit with it.

These referenced movies and television shows are, of course, devised by professionals, but amateur filmmakers or videographers also consider *Adagio for Strings* appropriate for their creative efforts. New video clips are posted on *YouTube* every day, and it is amazing to see how many adopt a form of *Adagio* as the soundtrack. Some people got to know the work from its various trance-dance music versions, especially Tiësto's. Yet the orchestral *Adagio* is also selected frequently, sometimes in obvious situations: photographs of war, the death of an actor. But what prompts

[94]Chris Snidow, email (2 November 2004) to the author.

[95]Michael Schelle, *The Score: Interviews with Film Composers* (Los Angeles: Silman-James Press, 1999), 36.

someone to pair it to slow-motion clips of a French football match or kung fu scenes from a Jet Li movie?

In Memoriam

Because many consider *Adagio*'s subtext to be one of sadness, it has been heard at numerous funerals and memorial concerts. Sometimes it is chosen because it merely seems appropriate, as in a tribute to violinist and teacher Josef Gingold, but other times it is selected because the deceased favored it. For instance, it was performed at the funerals of both Princess Grace and Prince Rainier of Monaco because it was their personal request. The string quartet adagio movement was played at the funeral of Gian Carlo Menotti; the orchestral *Adagio* was featured at a later memorial concert. Although he may not have commented favorably about the work, he and Barber, nevertheless, were living happily in an Austrian village when Barber conceived it. The composer, on the other hand, expressly instructed several friends that he did not want this particular composition to be performed at his own funeral; his wishes were honored.

To play *Adagio* in association with the 11 September attacks seems like an obvious decision. Leonard Slatkin, who conducted it shortly after the incident, made the following comment: "The intensive emotion of [*Adagio*] has come to mean something very special, not just for Americans but, I think, for everyone. It is our music for grief."[96] At one of these performances, he addressed the audience: "If one piece of music is said to reflect our feelings during this time, it's the piece we are about to play, Samuel Barber's *Adagio for Strings*."[97] In September of 2001 when Billy Joel was emotionally affected by the attacks at the World Trade Center, he related that these events were "so sad, there are no words to describe it, only music . . . like Samuel Barber's *Adagio for Strings* or Beethoven's Third Symphony."[98]

Adagio has also seemed appropriate at other concerts that honor the dead, such as victims of disasters, genocides, and other tragedies. It has been featured on Memorial Day concerts, Veterans Day concerts, and even at a usually joyous holiday celebration, such as Independence Day.

[96]Leonard Slatkin, quoted in "Sombre Proms Reflect Public Grief," *BBC News* (15 September 2001); reprinted www.news.bbc.co.uk/2/hi/entertainment/1546547.stm.

[97]*Ibid.*

[98]Billy Joel, quoted in Mitchell Fink, "When There Are No Words," *New York Daily News* (25 September 2001), 57.

Off and Running!

In light of my introductory overview, it seems clear that few pieces of music of any time or any place have been welcomed in such diverse circumstances, have crossed so many arbitrary boundaries, or have solicited deep admiration by such a wide cross-section of humanity as Barber's *Adagio*. I trust that the documentation provided in the following chapters will be regarded as a compelling testament to the power of a single composition, one, I enthusiastically argue, that is worthy of our attention. It may be a short work, but it casts a long shadow. *Adagio* is truly all around us!

From String Quartet to Orchestral *Adagio*

CHAPTER 2

> I have just finished the slow movement of my quartet today—it is a knockout! Now for a finale.
>
> —Samuel Barber, letter to Orlando Cole (19 September 1936).[1]

Origins and Early History of the String Quartet

CD Track 1

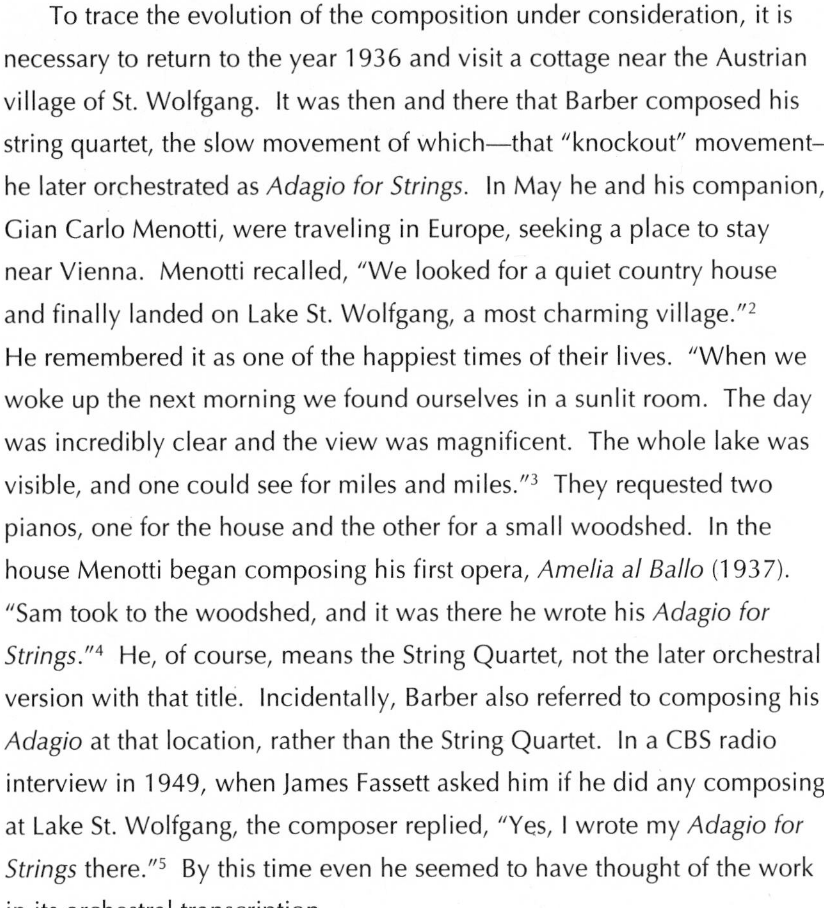

To trace the evolution of the composition under consideration, it is necessary to return to the year 1936 and visit a cottage near the Austrian village of St. Wolfgang. It was then and there that Barber composed his string quartet, the slow movement of which—that "knockout" movement—he later orchestrated as *Adagio for Strings*. In May he and his companion, Gian Carlo Menotti, were traveling in Europe, seeking a place to stay near Vienna. Menotti recalled, "We looked for a quiet country house and finally landed on Lake St. Wolfgang, a most charming village."[2] He remembered it as one of the happiest times of their lives. "When we woke up the next morning we found ourselves in a sunlit room. The day was incredibly clear and the view was magnificent. The whole lake was visible, and one could see for miles and miles."[3] They requested two pianos, one for the house and the other for a small woodshed. In the house Menotti began composing his first opera, *Amelia al Ballo* (1937). "Sam took to the woodshed, and it was there he wrote his *Adagio for Strings*."[4] He, of course, means the String Quartet, not the later orchestral version with that title. Incidentally, Barber also referred to composing his *Adagio* at that location, rather than the String Quartet. In a CBS radio interview in 1949, when James Fassett asked him if he did any composing at Lake St. Wolfgang, the composer replied, "Yes, I wrote my *Adagio for Strings* there."[5] By this time even he seemed to have thought of the work in its orchestral transcription.

[1]Samuel Barber, letter (19 September 1936) to Orlando Cole, quoted in Barbara B. Heyman, *Samuel Barber: The Composer and His Music* (New York: Oxford University Press, 1992), 153.

[2]Gian Carlo Menotti, quoted in John Gruen, *Menotti: A Biography* (New York: MacMillan, 1978), 27.

[3]*Ibid.*

[4]*Ibid.*

[5]Samuel Barber, quoted in James Fassett, interview (1949) with Samuel Barber for CBS Radio (Washington, D.C.: Motion Picture, Broadcasting, and Recorded Sound Division of the Library of Congress).

Illustration 2.1. Gian Carlo Menotti and Samuel Barber at a Regatta, Lake St. Wolfgang, Austria, September 1937

Courtesy of the Library of Congress and the Estate of Samuel Barber

Because Barber was such a stalwart letter writer, his correspondence can be used to patch together the evolution of the quartet. In May 1936, when composing at the American Academy in Rome, he wrote to his friend Orlando Cole, cellist of the Curtis Quartet: "I have vague quartettish rumblings in my innards and need a bit of celestial Ex Lax to restore my equilibrium."[6] He confided to his teacher Rosario Scalero: "I have started a string quartet: but how difficult it is! It seems to me that because we have so assiduously forced our personalities on Music—on Music, who never asked for them!—we have lost elegance; and if we cannot recapture elegance, the quartet form has escaped us forever. It is a struggle."[7] This sense of elegance may have its roots in the works of Schubert, a composer much on his mind during his writing of the quartet, as he admitted to Cole in a letter.[8] Admiring the music of the Viennese master, he once remarked, "how much Schubert . . . can say to us!"[9] Although the slow movement of the String Quintet in C Major is quite different in form and texture from Barber's adagio movement, its sense of serenity is similar. This—or, perhaps, other Schubert movements—may have inspired him.

[6]Samuel Barber, letter (6 May 1936) to Orlando Cole, quoted in Barbara B. Heyman, *Samuel Barber* (1992), 150. The Curtis Quartet resided at the Curtis Institute, Barber's alma mater.

[7]Samuel Barber, letter (5 August 1936) to Rosario Scalero quoted in Barbara B. Heyman, *Samuel Barber* (1992), 153.

[8]Samuel Barber, letter (6 February 1937) to Orlando Cole, referenced in Barbara B. Heyman, *Samuel Barber* (1992), 154.

[9]Samuel Barber, letter (17 July 1952) to his family, quoted in Barbara B. Heyman, *Samuel Barber* (1992), 331.

Barber hoped that the Curtis Quartet could introduce the new piece during its European tour that summer but alerted Cole that it was "coming along slowly, but will not be ready in time. The best thing will probably be for me to have it tried out by the Rome quartet [the Pro Arte Quartet] in rehearsal, and then I can send it over to you from Rome."[10] Shortly after this, he made his famous "it is a knockout!" comment. When the members of the Curtis Quartet began their European tour, they stopped off in Rome to visit Barber at the American Academy. By then he must have completed most of the quartet because Cole remembered having a great time playing the new work, "and there was a great deal of interest."[11] Decades later Cole acknowledged that Barber "knew he had a hit."[12]

During the summer Barber had written of his recent effort to his uncle and confidant, the composer Sidney Homer. His response was emphatic:

> I am happy you are writing a string quartet. There is just one thing that counts and that is finished work, and by finished I mean of a quality that is beyond dispute. . . . Send me a few bars of the movements of the Quartet. They will make me hunger for the rest.[13]

When the quartet was completed, Homer was indeed impressed: "You make the four instruments sound gigantic. I also want from you the greatest intimacy in spirit. If Mozart could trust and love his listener, so can you."[14] Homer continued his encouragement throughout the quartet's evolution.[15]

[10]Samuel Barber, letter (31 August 1936) to Orlando Cole, quoted in Barbara B. Heyman, *Samuel Barber* (1992), 153.

[11]Orlando Cole, interview with Eliza Ann Viles (20 May 1983), quoted in Eliza Ann Viles, *Mary Louise Curtis Bok Zimbalist: Founder of the Curtis Institute of Music and Patron of American Arts* (Ph.D. dissertation, Bryn Mawr College, 1983), 107.

[12]Samuel Barber, letter to Orlando Cole, quoted in Tim Janof, "ICS Exclusive Interview!!! Conversation with Orlando Cole," *Internet Cello Society* (14 June 2002); reprinted "Conversation with Orlando Cole," Tim Janof, www.cello.org/Newsletter/Articles/cole.htm. Cole recently donated the letter to the Curtis Institute.

[13]Sidney Homer, letter (17 August 1936) to Samuel Barber, quoted in Barbara B. Heyman, *Samuel Barber* (1992), 151-52.

[14]Sidney Homer, letter (6 February 1937) to Samuel Barber, quoted in Barbara B. Heyman, *Samuel Barber* (1992), 154.

[15]For a timeline of selected *Adagio for Strings* performances, notably the ones cited in this chapter, see Appendix 2.

Illustration 2.2. Facsimile of the Sketch of the Opening Phrase of the String Quartet Movement, 1936

Courtesy of the Library of Congress and the Estate of Samuel Barber

The String Quartet Manuscript

There is only one brief sketch for the slow movement of the String Quartet, found in a sketchbook at the Library of Congress and dated by the Library as "begun 1933."[16] It contains the opening musical phrase of the first violins (see Illustration 2.2 after the bar line, top two staves), with the lower parts written as chords on a single staff below it. While neither staff has a clef sign, treble and bass clefs are easily inferred. No key signature is used, but appropriate flats appear before most relevant notes, except for the Ds. This could mean one of two things: either Barber conceived of the melody as being more "majorish" (unlikely) or simply neglected to include the flats (more likely). After all, a sketch is just a sketch, not a definitive musical statement. The passage is notated without bar lines, making it difficult to know what the intended meter will be. Perhaps most significantly, the note values are basically half that of the later holograph score, discussed below. That is, Barber used flowing eighth notes rather than the quarter notes that will occur in the manuscript and eventually the printed score.

The holograph of the slow movement of Barber's String Quartet seems to be a fair copy: it contains little in the way of corrections; no measures

[16]Barbara B. Heyman, *Samuel Barber: A Thematic Catalogue of the Complete Works* (Oxford: Oxford University Press, 2012), 178. Heyman lists this sketch as Item E, holograph sketch (1930s), page 64. The Library of Congress numbers it as page 66. The sketch, as well as the entire notebook, is available on line at www.lcweb2.loc.gov/diglib as the sidebar. See also the attached short article: James Wintle, "Samuel Barber at the Library of Congress."

are crossed out; it bears no traces of a "working out" process typical of sketches.[17] It is written in pencil on Alberto de Santis manuscript paper, which Barber probably bought in Rome during his stay there. The Adagio is the only movement from the quartet that he donated to the Library of Congress; a note on the bottom of page 13 states "Gift—Samuel Barber, December 28, 1954." Does this late December date mean a last-minute tax write-off? Barber could be an extremely practical man.

The main differences between this manuscript and the final published score are those of articulation and dynamics. Barber designated the tempo as simply "adagio," not "molto adagio," and designated a metronome marking of 𝅗𝅥 = 54, the only time that I know of that he made any kind of metronomic suggestion, otherwise allowing performers to project an ideal tempo and duration. When he omitted the metronome marking and added "molto" to the published score, however, one might presume (or not) that his concept of the movement changed to a slightly slower, more sustained tempo. His expression instruction at the beginning is simply "espr."—not the "espr. cantando" that he later added, probably no significant change. He surely had the concept of a "singing" style in mind from the beginning but decided to make it more explicit. There are also a few minor alterations in dynamics. In the second measure he indicated a crescendo from the opening *pp* up to *p* but has later crossed out the *p*. For the coda he changed his original marking *p* to *mf* in the published score. He may have decided that, after the climax, the music achieves a stronger effect with *mf,* whereas the quieter *p* might have weakened the ending.

Early Performances and Recordings

Three string quartets gave the earliest performances of the piece in 1936 and 1937: the Pro Arte, the Curtis, and the Gordon.[18] Although Barber had the Curtis Quartet in mind when he wrote the work, the Pro Arte group gave the first performance, which took place at the Academy in Rome on 14 December 1936. Then, during the following March, the Curtis Quartet gave the American première at the Curtis Institute of Music, but only the first two of the three movements were programmed. A critic from the *Philadelphia Evening Bulletin* complained that the work seemed

[17]Library of Congress, microfilm Music 1907.

[18]The Pro Arte Quartet: Alphonse Onnou and Laurent Halleux, violins; Germain Prévost, viola; Marcel Maas, cello; the Curtis String Quartet: Jascha Brodsky and Charles Jaffe, violins; Max Aronoff, viola; Orlando Cole, cello; and the Gordon Quartet: Jacques Gordon and David Sackson, violins; William Lincer, viola; and Naoum Benditzky, cello.

"unduly pretentious, and in the opening allegro, Barber seemed to be seeking effects better suited to orchestral expression. The slow movement succeeded in evoking mood, but suffered from repetitiousness."[19] Later that year the Gordon Quartet prepared to perform the work at the Library of Congress in Washington, D.C. By March Barber had sent the first two movements to Oliver Strunk, chief librarian of the Music Division, who replied that there was no real hurry for the third. By not sending the third movement Barber was implying that at this stage he had doubts about the efficacy of the finale. Once he submitted it, the Gordon Quartet set to work and performed the new composition in April.

On 14 March 1938, the day before its New York Town Hall recital, the Curtis String Quartet performed the complete work at the Curtis Institute. This is probably the performance heard by critic Arthur Cohn when he formed this opinion: "No one can deny the technical equipment of this young man, but one may inquire whether he realizes that the year is 1938 and things are not so placid as his carefully tailored quartet would make us believe."[20] This, however, might say as much about the hovering specter of the Second World War as the contemporary music scene in general. In this performance, preserved on an archive tape at the Library of Congress, the players make a diminuendo on the high chord at the climax right before the pause.[21] Most groups sustain the chord or even make a slight crescendo, pushing through to the cutoff. This is, incidentally, the only recording I am aware of with the original third movement: "Andante mosso, un poco agitato—Allegro molto, alla breve," the one that Barber later withdrew.[22]

The very next day the Curtis ensemble played the work at Town Hall, where *New York Times* critic Howard Taubman heard it for the first time and hoped that it would not be the last. He regarded the Adagio movement as "the finest of the work; it is deeply felt and written with economy, resourcefulness and distinction. Mr. Barber writes in a romantic vein; he does not try to be what he is not. The total effect, taking

[19]"Composer's Evening: Program of Music by Samuel Barber Given at Casimir Hall," *Philadelphia Evening Bulletin* (8 March 1937), quoted in Barbara B. Heyman, *Samuel Barber* (1992), 154.

[20]Arthur Cohn, "How News Comes to Philadelphia," *Modern Music* XV (May-June 1938), 237.

[21]Library of Congress, Tapes LWO 8575, R15B4, and R16A1, and West Hill Radio Archives, CD-WHRA-6039.

[22]String parts are held in the Orlando Cole Collection at the Curtis Institute of Music. A facsimile of the first page is reproduced in Barbara B. Heyman, *Samuel Barber* (1992), 159.

Illustration 2.3. The Curtis String Quartet (Charles Jaffe, Jascha Brodsky, Orlando Cole, Max Aronoff), ca. 1937

Courtesy of the Curtis Institute of Music Archives

Image by Alix Williamson

weaknesses into account, is impressive."[23] Despite these words of praise, Cohn and Taubman already intimated that *Adagio*'s romantic nature may represent a drawback, a reproof leveled by other critics over the years.

Later that summer the Curtis Quartet played the work on the radio. Barber and Menotti were driving through a small town in Vermont when they stopped at a grocery store and, by chance, heard the performance. Barber later told Cole:

> There surrounded by hams, sausages, and flour I heard your performance and very clearly. A couple of Green Mountain boys were hanging around, listened with some curiosity and launched a few well-aimed shots, during the *Adagio,* at a corner spittoon. All very rural![24]

When, on 3 October 1938, the group performed the work on *Monday Afternoon Concerts from the Curtis Institute* (broadcast by CBS Radio), its members reverted to playing only the first two movements. The composer

[23]Howard Taubman, "Samuel Barber Work Heard," *The New York Times* (16 March 1938), 20.

[24]Samuel Barber, letter (ca. August 1938) to Orlando Cole, quoted in full in Barbara B. Heyman, *Samuel Barber* (1992), 157.

had probably decided to eliminate the third movement but had not yet completed the new recapitulatory finale. This performance is splendid, with the adagio movement just a bit quicker than their earlier rendition. The string playing is also better, with Cole's cello sound especially rich and warm.[25]

Later, in 1938, the Curtis ensemble did finally perform the quartet in Europe. While Glasgow critics were impressed with the work in general, they particularly responded to the slow movement. One reported that "It is music I want to hear again, for I doubt if anything recently has given me as much pleasure as the adagio movement of this quartet"; another observed that "the slow movement (always the most difficult to compose) is quite distinguished in its writing."[26] After its performance by the same musicians at Bowdoin College in Brunswick, Maine, critic Moses Smith noted its "suave sonorities and platitudes."[27] Years later he seems to have recalled more of the platitudes than the suave sonorities; he admitted, "I have been prejudiced against Barber ever since the time years ago when I heard a gooey indiscretion for quartet."[28] For some, the romanticism of the quartet was beginning to cloy.

During the next twenty years several ensembles offered the quartet in concerts at the Elizabeth Sprague Coolidge Auditorium of the Library of Congress. The Budapest String Quartet gave three performances: in 1945, 1951, and 1961. Among others were the Alexander, Boston, Cleveland, Emerson, Miró, and New Music.[29]

While many public performances of the work took place during the 1940s, no commercial recording was issued until 1951, when string players associated with Stradivari Records produced and released it in the new LP format.[30] This disc (Stradivari STR 602) remained the only

[25]Library of Congress Archive Tape LWO 8575 R21 B3.

[26]The first quotation is taken from the *Glasgow Evening Citizen*; the second, from the *Glasgow Evening News*. Both are reprinted in "In Memoriam: Jascha Brodsky (1907-1997)," *Temple University Museletter* (Fall 1997).

[27]Moses Smith, "Bowdoin College Series," *Modern Music* XVI/4 (May-June 1939), 261.

[28]Moses Smith, "Americans and Shostakovich in Boston," *Modern Music* XXI (May-June 1944), 252.

[29]These performances can be found in the Recorded Sound Reference Center of the Library of Congress. Tapes of live performances of the work have been featured on NPR's *Performance Today*, notably The Audubon String Quartet at Wilshire Ebell Theatre, Los Angeles (1995); The Emerson String Quartet at Aspen Music Festival, Colorado (6 May 1997) and at Portland State University (18 April 2001); and The Shanghai String Quartet at Scottsdale Center for the Arts, Arizona (19 January 1999).

[30]Arnold Eidus, Louis Graeler, violins; David Mankowitz, viola; and George Ricci, cello.

available recording for the next decade. Barber himself donated a copy to the American Academy and Institute of the Arts in New York City; he apparently approved of the performance.

In general, critics approved as well. Arthur Berger referred to the performance as being of "the finest quality and musicianship" but did not care for the "big, resonant orchestral sound" that may be trying to compete with the orchestral *Adagio*.[31] Carter Harman believed that the musicians performed the work with "vigor and resourcefulness" and that the record itself has "great resonance but not quite optimal brilliance," sometimes giving the strings a "glassy and almost muted quality."[32] Harold C. Schonberg included the recording in his *Music Guide to Long-Playing Records* (1955), observing that the work, conservative and "full of promise," is well played by the Stradivari group. For him, the piece commanded respect because of its "seriousness of purpose" but did not have "as strong a profile" as some of Barber's later pieces.[33] It is a clear performance without any extremes of vibrato; the cello variation is quite subdued. Yet the quarter-note motion at the beginning seems deliberate rather than flowing.

While various groups played Barber's String Quartet during the next decades, few recordings were made. (Some of these will be discussed in the next chapter.) This state of affairs can be explained primarily by the very existence of Barber's orchestrated version of the slow movement. *Adagio for Strings* became so popular that it completely outstripped the original version, leaving the String Quartet as a kind of poor relation.

The Genesis of *Adagio for Strings*

The journey began in August 1933, when Barber and Menotti visited Arturo Toscanini at his villa on Isolino di San Giovanni (in Lago Maggiore). Barber wrote to his family about their meeting: "my heart still beats faster at the thought. Soon he appeared . . . and greeted us. He was the nicest thing you could imagine, took us around to a terrace with a heavenly view,

[31]Arthur Berger, "Spotlight on the Moderns," *Saturday Review* XXXIV (26 January 1952), 54.

[32]Carter Harman, "Other Reviews: Barber Quartet," *The New York Times* (18 November 1951), 2: 6.

[33]Harold C. Schoenberg, *Music Guide to Long-Playing Records: Chamber and Solo Instrumental Music* (New York: Knopf, 1955), III, 21-22.

and there we sat and talked."[34] What actually transpired at this meeting is speculative, generating various rumors. For instance, Bill McLaughlin, on his radio show *ExploringMusic*, attributed an explicit *Adagio for Strings* request to the Italian maestro: "Toscanini asked [*sic*] Barber, 'make me a string orchestra arrangement of your wonderful Adagio from your string quartet, and I'll go play it with my new orchestra, the NBC Symphony Orchestra.'"[35] Such a specific request is impossible. This meeting occurred three years before Barber wrote a single note of his quartet. Toscanini may have told Barber that he was interested in conducting one of his works, but the formation of the NBC Symphony was also years down the road. Heyman noted that at the time Toscanini told the young composer that he would like to perform one of his works.[36] The exact impetus for the *Adagio* orchestration may never be known, but it cannot stem from this meeting.

Nonetheless, when Sidney Homer heard of Toscanini's interest, he urged his nephew to take advantage of the opportunity:

> The thing now is to write something for Toscanini that expresses the depth and sincerity of your nature. . . . You know as well as I do that the Maestro loves sincere straightforward stuff, with genuine feeling in it and no artificial pretense and padding.[37]

Apparently, Barber took his uncle's advice to heart, for all the qualities that Homer suggested for a new orchestral work were soon to emerge instead in the string quartet movement. These same qualities are retained, of course, in the orchestrated version. In fact, when critics later described and praised *Adagio for Strings*, they often used the same words: "sincere," "feeling," and "without pretense." For example:

> Olin Downes: "an impression of a beauty and sincerity lamentably lacking in the smart score and the overworked and by now very

[34]Samuel Barber, letter (11 August 1933) to his family, quoted in Nathan Broder, *Samuel Barber*, 24-25, and Barbara B. Heyman, *Samuel Barber* (1992), 163.

[35]Bill McLaughlin, *ExploringMusic* (first aired 20 March 2007; repeated 5 August 2008).

[36]Barbara B. Heyman, *Samuel Barber* (1992), 162-64.

[37]Sidney Homer, letter (15 January 1934) to Samuel Barber, quoted in full in Barbara B. Heyman, *Samuel Barber* (1992), 164. The emphasis on "write" is mine.

banal musical jests of Dimitri Shostakovich." It has a "genuine and noble feeling . . . which is unfortunately rare today."[38]

> Henry-Louis de La Grange: "an incomparable and engaging sincerity."[39]

> David Hall: "it is music of great lyric intensity and sincere feeling."[40]

Some of Barber's composer colleagues expressed similar views:

> Aaron Copland: it "makes you believe in the sincerity which he obviously put into it."[41]

> Vincent Persichetti: "there is real mood and restraint, and a sincerity of expression."[42]

> Reginald Smith Brindle: "the result is powerfully emotive and all the more telling because of its simplicity and guileless directness."[43]

> William Schuman: "You are not aware of any technique at all. . . . It seems quite effortless and natural."[44]

Even Jean Sibelius considered *Adagio* "excellent" and "good art"; he liked especially its simplicity.[45]

[38]Olin Downes, "Barbirolli Offers American Music," *The New York Times* (26 January 1940), 12.

[39]Henry-Louis de La Grange, "D'Amérique: Un compositeur américain indépendent," *Contrepoints* (May-June 1946), 67. ["*une sincérité parfaite autant qu'attachante.*"]

[40]David Hall, *The Record Book* (New York: Citadel Press, 1948), 281.

[41]Aaron Copland, BBC broadcast (23 January 1982), quoted in Barbara B. Heyman, *Samuel Barber* (1992), 174.

[42]Vincent Persichetti, "Philadelphia Takes a Flier," *Modern Music* XXI/2 (January-February 1944), 105.

[43]Reginald Smith Brindle, "Memory Hither Come," *The Musical Times* CXXXIX (Summer 1998), 3.

[44]William Schuman, BBC Broadcast (23 January 1982), quoted in Barbara B. Heyman, *Samuel Barber* (1992), 175.

[45]Jean Sibelius, RCA press release, quoted in Howard Pollock, "Samuel Barber, Jean Sibelius, and the Making of an American Romantic," *The Musical Quarterly* LXXXIV/2 (Summer 2000), 186.

During the next several years Barber composed his Symphony in One Movement (1937), which Artur Rodzinski conducted at the 1937 Salzburg Festival. At that time he told the composer that Toscanini was forming "an orchestra in New York," which, or course, became the NBC Symphony Orchestra. "Maestro really liked your symphony; why not do something for him and his new orchestra?"[46] Decades later, on the television show "Happy Birthday, Samuel Barber," the composer explained his response: "so, I got busy and I wrote one piece, Essay for Orchestra, and also arranged the *Adagio* of a string quartet for orchestra and submitted those to Toscanini. I waited for about a year, and I heard nothing about it."[47] This annoyed him so much that he decided not to visit Toscanini that summer as planned. When Menotti, who did pay a call to the maestro, made the excuse that Barber was ill, Toscanini replied: "he's perfectly well; he's just angry with me, but he has no reason to be—I'm going to do both of his pieces."[48] Rodzinski's widow Halina later recalled, "in this way the justly celebrated *Adagio for Strings* was born."[49] To the comment of James Tocco, the host of the cited television program, "not bad for a twenty-six or twenty-seven year old composer," Barber replied, "no, that helped me considerably. I have had the luck to have my compositions played by very famous performers, so they became known rather quickly."[50] Of course, all the major orchestras around the world have now performed *Adagio*.

On the Road to *Adagio for Strings*: A Paper Trail

While the chronology of the manuscripts for *Adagio for Strings* may be somewhat uncertain, I propose the following order:

1. Manuscript in pencil at the Pierpont Morgan Library
2. The holograph, in ink, that Barber donated to the Library of Congress

[46]Artur Rodzinski, quoted in Halina Rodzinski, *Our Two Lives* (New York: Charles Scribner's Sons, 1976), 167.

[47]Samuel Barber, "Happy Birthday, Samuel Barber" [Videotape], telecast on the CBS Sunday morning cultural program *Camera Three* (3 March 1977). Copies are available at the Paley Center, New York City, and at the Library of Congress.

[48]Arturo Toscanini, quoted in Robert Sherman, interview (30 September 1978) with Samuel Barber (New York: WQXR).

[49]Halina Rodzinski, *Our Two Lives*, 167.

[50]Samuel Barber, "Happy Birthday, Samuel Barber" [Videotape].

3. The copy prepared for publication, with editorial additions and corrections by Barber and / or the editor at Schirmer, currently housed at the Eastman School of Music

CD Track 2

Once Barber decided to orchestrate the slow movement of his String Quartet, he was obligated to make the inevitable decisions regarding the distribution of parts. The earliest result of this process is likely to be the manuscript in the Department of Music Manuscripts and Books of the Pierpont Morgan Library in New York City.[51] It is inscribed "To my friend Henry-Louis de La Grange, Souvenir of Capricorn, April 7, 1947," obviously not the date of the manuscript itself but the date when Barber gave it to La Grange, who was visiting him at his and Menotti's home, Capricorn.[52] Here, the work is entitled "Essay for Strings." Barber had either just completed or was working on his *Essay for Orchestra* (1938). Probably realizing that the term "essay" better suited that work, he consequently renamed his orchestrated string quartet movement.

The manuscript (pencil, six pages) is basically the same as the final published score but lacking any tempo indications, dynamics, expression marks, or rehearsal numbers. This is not surprising because Barber was working here as an orchestrator, not as a composer; he was simply determining when the double stops of the original should become *divisi,* where double basses are appropriate, and other such accommodations. The dynamics and phrase indications were already designated in his string quartet, which he could add later; he never got around to it. Therefore he probably considered this manuscript expendable, not worthy of the Library of Congress collection. Why not give it to a friend as a memento?

The next likely version is the score that the composer donated to the Library of Congress, a part of the Barber manuscript collection (microfilm, Music 1907, Item 20). The ink holograph, on Schirmer manuscript paper No. 5., is now officially re-titled *Adagio for Strings.* Microfilmed with it is a copy of the composer's note to Harold Spivacke, chief librarian at the Music Division of the Library of Congress in the 1940s:

[51]Robert Owen Lehman Deposit: ID 114177.

[52]La Grange and Barber visited each other and corresponded frequently until 1973. La Grange became the definitive biographer of Gustav Mahler. At some point this particular manuscript ended up at La Scala Autographs, Inc., in Pennington, New Jersey; La Grange may have sold it. Robert Owen Lehman bought it there and, in June 1986, donated it to the Pierpont Morgan Library. I am grateful to Rigbie Turner, the Mary Flagler Curator of Music and Manuscripts and Books at the Morgan Library, for this information and for a photocopy of the manuscript.

> I am glad . . . to know that you received the score. It might interest you to know that it was used by Toscanini at the first performance of the work and some of the red markings inside are his, from Pfc. Samuel Barber, Gift of composer July 29, 1943.[53]

One of Toscanini's recommendations, "but without hurrying," is an instruction that Barber must have considered unnecessary; this reminder does not appear in the published score. To the orchestrations worked out in the Pierpont Morgan manuscript, he has carried over from the quartet the appropriate tempo indications, slurs (with a few minor variants), and other expression marks. (A piece of trivia: the composer ran out of room on the final page of the music paper and drew staff lines into the margin to accommodate the last measure of the piece.)

The final step was a score prepared for publication, a copy (currently at Eastman School of Music) to be sent between the editor(s) at G. Schirmer and Barber.[54] *Adagio for Strings* is five pages long, written in black ink, also on Schirmer Style 5 manuscript paper, with the composer's name printed in green ink and signed in black ink. On the page adjacent to the first is the note: "First performance November 5, 1938, by the National Broadcasting Company Orchestra, Arturo Toscanini, conductor at New York, NY." Slurs, phrasing marks, and notes to the engraver are added in red pencil. Parts contain the initials "WJW," presumably the copyist, and the date, "2-27-39." There are two pages each for the two violins, viola, and cello, but only one page is necessary for double bass. The parts are stamped "Feb 25, 1939" and initialed "C. D." (another copyist?). Names of the string instruments are added in red ink at the left of each line, whereas ties and slurs are written in regular and blue pencil. The phrase, "with increasing intensity," is added in pencil seven measures after [3]; it had been marked in the string quartet but was inadvertently omitted from the orchestral score. Because the second violin line needs to be split onto two staves somewhere after [4], Barber told the editor "you may start the 2 braces now for violin II here or at any point before, accommodating your

[53]Samuel Barber, letter (28 July 1943) to Harold Spivacke. The letter is [Spiv 6] in Wayne C. Wentzel, *Samuel Barber: A Research and Information Guide*, 2nd ed. (New York: Routledge, 2010), 406. A facsimile of a manuscript page is provided in Barbara B. Heyman, *Samuel Barber* (1992), 169.

[54]Discussed in Wayne C. Wentzel, *A Research and Information Guide*, 2nd ed., 330. The *Adagio* score and other Barber works are on loan to the Eastman School of Music. Box 1, M2A. 1, 4-2,3; Folder 1/6 contains *Adagio for Strings*.

layout." The phrase, "sordine poco," appears at [5] and "tutti con sordine" at the coda. Barber must have reconsidered these particular instructions because they do not appear in the published score; instead, at the start of the coda (Tempo I) Barber suggested "sord. ad lib." Also at the coda he has crossed out "non troppo lento." Had he retained that expressive direction, listeners might have been spared those extra-slow endings in some performances and on some recordings.

For scholars interested in pursuing the evolution of such a famous work, these three manuscripts may seem disappointing. There are only minor changes, no unusual decisions of orchestration, no additions, no cuts, nothing that would show a compositional process. But, as noted earlier, a composer is not at work here, merely an orchestrator. Schirmer published the score of *Adagio for Strings* in 1939, and during the 1940s the company placed advertisements in several music journals promoting it, including half-page ads in several issues of *The Musical Times* from 1945 through 1948, with comments on the composer but not *Adagio* itself. Schirmer initiated a two-year advertising blitz in *The Music Journal* in May 1947 with a full-page notice for the works of Barber, including *Adagio*. In the 1946 Music Library Association publication *Notes*, the Schirmer ad asked, "does your library have these important works by Samuel Barber?"[55] *Adagio for Strings* is listed and is priced at $1.25.

A Curtis Run-Through and Toscanini's Première

Some time after orchestrating *Adagio* Barber invited the members of the student orchestra at the Curtis Institute of Music to read through it. Russell Brodine, a bass player in the orchestra at the time, remembered the occasion:

> A thrilling experience was participating in the first rehearsal of a new work, *Adagio for Strings* by Samuel Barber, a talented recent graduate of Curtis. It was in manuscript and was, I believe, being run through for the first time. Since then it has entranced millions of listeners.[56]

[55]Advertisement for Schirmer, *Notes* IV/1 (December 1946), 16.

[56]Russell V. Brodine and Virginia Warner Brodine, *Fiddle and Fight* (New York: International Publishers, 2001), 25.

He did not give the date of this run-through, but it was likely to have happened in late 1937 or early 1938. Fritz Reiner was the conductor of the Curtis orchestra in those days, but it is not certain whether he presided over the rehearsal. It is possible that Barber himself led the group to learn if any last minute changes were needed. *Adagio for Strings* was now ready for an official première.

The Saturday evening broadcast of *Adagio for Strings* on 5 November 1938 was part of the NBC Symphony's second season of radio programs, originating in Studio 8H. Deems Taylor announced before the concert began that two new orchestral works by "the young American composer Samuel Barber" would be receiving their world premières: Essay for Orchestra and "an Adagio for Strings." Note that the article "an" makes it seem to be a generic title designated by tempo.[57] In fact, in those early days, there seemed to be a question about its official title. In line with Taylor's announcement, an advertisement for the performance in *The New York Times* listed it as "an adagio for strings." (Because I wrote down the Taylor title from a recording of the concert, I do not know whether his script capitalized any of the words. It might have been the same as *The New York Times*.) Further complicating matters are the titles provided for a performance at Lewisohn Stadium in the summer of 1940: "Adagio for string orchestra" and, in a review of that performance, "Adagio for String Orchestra." As late as 2006 Barbara Heyman inexplicably referred to the piece this way on a radio program about the Toscanini performance (see below).

The performance was fairly brisk, taking about 6 and 3 / 4 minutes, yet it never sounds rushed; it is indeed played "without hurrying." Barber fondly remembered it: "Imagine! Primrose was the first violist then, and Alfred Wallenstein was the principal cellist. Wallenstein has always said to me that he felt this was one of Toscanini's greatest performances. What luck for a young composer to have such a first performance."[58] Significant individuals in Barber's life, as well as the composer himself, attended this landmark event. In the audience were his composition teacher, Rosario Scalero; his mentor, Mrs. Mary Louise Curtis Bok, the head of the Curtis

[57]The British seem to prefer this designation; the authors of many articles and reviews, especially in *The Musical Times*, refer to it this way. Another British title preference is "Adagio for strings," with the last word uncapitalized, implying that the title is only "Adagio" and "for strings" merely the performance medium. The same problem still occurs with Debussy's "Suite" pour le piano.

[58]Samuel Barber, quoted in John Ardoin, "Samuel Barber at Capricorn," *Musical America* V (March 1960), 4-5, 46.

Institute; and Menotti. After the performance of his second piece, the Essay for Orchestra, Barber was called to the stage twice for bows. Friends in Philadelphia listening to the performance on the radio later commented, "We have heard the Adagio before in its original string quartet form. In its new dress it is lovelier than ever."[59] This may already be a premonition that *Adagio for Strings* would soon become more popular than the quartet movement.

Reviews were generally favorable, resembling those for the string quartet. *New York Times* music critic Olin Downes agreed that Barber was fortunate to have such a high caliber performance, especially with Maestro Toscanini on the podium:

> The Adagio is a work of true talent with rapidly increasing skill. It is not pretentious music. Its author does not pose and posture in his score. He writes with a definite purpose, a clear objective and a sense of structure. . . . This is the product of a musically creative nature, and an earnest student who leaves nothing undone to achieve something as perfect in mass and detail as his craftsmanship permits.[60]

Goddard Lieberson, however, was not as impressed:

> There is but a fraction of the whole which even suggests an individual technic [*sic*]; and instead of melodic creativeness and harmonic invention, Mr. Barber has substituted his wealth of experience in listening to the works of other composers. . . . Very little of the score suggests an individual technique.[61]

In 2006 archivists at the Library of Congress, under the direction of James H. Billington, placed this historic radio performance on a list of fifty diverse recordings being preserved as a part of the National Recording Registry, records that are "culturally, historically or aesthetically important

[59] *Overtones* [Newsletter of the Curtis Institute of Music] (December 1938), quoted in Barbara B. Heyman, *Samuel Barber: A Documentary Study of His Works* (Ph.D. dissertation, City University of New York, 1989), 257.

[60] Olin Downes, "Toscanini Plays Two New Works," *The New York Times* (6 November 1938), 48.

[61] Goddard Lieberson, "Over the Air," *Modern Music* XVI (November-December 1938), 65.

and / or inform or reflect life in the United States."[62] Most would agree that Toscanini's recording of *Adagio for Strings* fits all those categories and deserves to be honored in this manner. This list was discussed on 11 April 2006 during National Public Radio's *All Things Considered*, when a brief sound bite of *Adagio* was played. Several months later, in November, NPR selected the recording for discussion on *Weekend Edition* with authors Joe Horowitz, Barbara Heyman, and Mortimer Frank. Heyman observed that, because Toscanini did not perform much contemporary or American music, his decision to broadcast these compositions was "extraordinary."[63] Frank contended that his selection of *Adagio* might, at first, seem out of character. Although the maestro is considered:

> the most dynamic, the most intense, overwhelming, and arresting conductor of his time, [he was also] capable of a wonderful delicacy, tenderness, and gentleness. He knew how to deal with a piece like this, which essentially is a lyrical, gentle piece in so many ways. It is presented directly, without sentimentality, without excess, without making it sound overly sweet and cloying.[64]

Compared to later recordings and performances by other conductors, which occasionally border on the sentimental, the excessive, and the cloying, the approach here is refreshing and has held up well over the years.

In 1940 Toscanini introduced *Adagio* into the repertoire for the NBC Symphony Orchestra's tour of South America. *The New York Times* reported that it would be played in every city the orchestra visited, yet it was programmed on only the Buenos Aires concert on 27 June 1940.[65] After the tour he conducted it again during an NBC broadcast on 13

[62]Carl Hartman, "Library of Congress Goes on the Record," Associated Press (12 April 2006); reprinted "Library of Congress Preserves 50 Diverse Recordings | Houston Music | Chron.com – Houston Chronicle," Carl Hartman, www.chron.com/disp/story.mpl/ent/music/3786902.html. The archive recording at the Library of Congress is LWO 8575 R26 A3, but it has recently been commercially released; the entire concert can be heard online at Pristine Classical Recordings, PASC088.

[63]Barbara B. Heyman, *Weekend Edition* [National Public Radio] (4 November 2006).

[64]Mortimer Frank, *Weekend Edition* [National Public Radio] (4 November 2006).

[65]"Opera and Concert," *The New York Times* (16 June 1940), X: 5.

December 1941.[66] With this occurring only a few days after the Pearl Harbor attack, the program was presented by the Treasury Department to help sell defense bonds and stamps. All of these performances, plus the later RCA recording, have been preserved on record or tape and are remarkably similar. Such consistency is typical of Toscanini's approach to the music he conducted.

The Toscanini Recording

Arturo Toscanini recorded *Adagio for Strings* with the NBC Symphony Orchestra in Carnegie Hall on 19 March 1942.[67] Barber told author and music critic John Ardoin that he particularly liked this recording but not quite as much as the original radio broadcast: "To me the Carnegie recording seems to have less surge of powerful crescendo, as Toscanini had to repeat it several times in order to get the crescendo on one side of a 78-record."[68] And yet he wrote to his friend, poet Katherine Garrison Chapin Biddle, shortly after the recording session (which he attended) and expressed his pleasure that *Adagio* was the first piece of American music that Maestro Toscanini had recorded.[69] He later sent her a copy. Critic Howard Taubman cited this recording in his article on the most memorable albums of contemporary music in 1942.[70] In 1947 Barber recommended it to the American Academy in Rome to be part of a "start-off" for a record collection of his works.[71] As the only one available at the time, however, it was a choice by default.

Peter Hugh Reed, in one of the earliest published reviews of the recording, considered *Adagio* to be an "expressive work": "Toscanini plays the music with obvious affection; its long melodic lines are smoothly and rarely molded. This is a disc that deserves to be in every American record

[66]Paley Center, New York City, Tape R: 84:0030.

[67]Wayne C. Wentzel, *A Research and Information Guide*, 2nd ed., 246 [Item 803]. Victor V-11 8287 (78RPM) 1942; then RCA Victor Gold Seal 60307 (LP).

[68]Samuel Barber, quoted in Barbara B. Heyman, *Samuel Barber* (1992), 170.

[69]Samuel Barber, letter (22 March 1942) to Katherine Garrison Chapin Biddle. The letter is located in the Francis and Katherine Biddle Papers, Special Collections Division at Georgetown University, Box 28, folder 13, item 1. For a brief description of this and other letters to Barber in the collection, see Wayne C. Wentzel, *A Research and Information Guide*, 2nd ed., 351 [Bid 4]. Toscanini himself may have considered his *Adagio* recording as one of his best. It was played, among other recordings, at his seventy-fifth birthday celebration in March 1944.

[70]Howard Taubman, "Records: Our Own Time," *The New York Times* (20 December 1942), X: 6.

[71]Wayne C. Wentzel, *A Research and Information Guide*, [Rome 12].

library."[72] When the recording was released in the United Kingdom (His Master's Voice DB 6180), music critic Geoffrey N. Sharp wrote that the work is "warm, lyrical music with a strong sense of direction which leads us to expect great things of Mr. Barber in the future." He called the performance "superb," but the recorded sound was "not good enough." Nevertheless, he gave it a strong recommendation.[73] His colleague, William McNaught, offered the following appraisal:

> This work has come to the front for good reason. Though it shows no eagerness to gain the ear by fluent or striking melodies or by colourful progressions, yet it makes a direct appeal by a quality best described by calling it deeply musical. Moreover, it holds the attention by steady growth and plan: not many composers put such faith in sustained equable strength and responseful movement. At a first hearing you may not think it an eventful piece, except near the climax at the end of side 1; but on better acquaintance it takes shape as a long drawn single event, with an unhurried rise and fall and growing in cogency by its patient unfolding.[74]

These references to the climax at the end of side one bring up a rather frustrating problem for listeners in the 1940s, who had to contend with the short performance sides of 78 RPM recordings. McNaught lamented:

> The break from side 1 to side 2 is a little unfortunate, for it comes at the moment when tension is suddenly relaxed: a high pitched *forte* phrase (side 1) is echoed by the same phrase low down and *piano* (side 2). Such a moment of drama needs as much precision of timing as the notes of a melody; it would have been better, therefore, to make the break about a half-an inch earlier.[75]

[72]Peter Hugh Reed, "Fascinating Novelties in New Records," *The Etude* LXI (January 1943), 31.

[73]Geoffrey N. Sharp, "Gramophone Records," *Music Review* VI (1945), 123.

[74]William McNaught, "Gramophone Notes: Adagio for Strings," *The Musical Times* LXXXVI (May 1945), 149.

[75]*Ibid.*

A little unfortunate? Just imagine getting up out of a comfortable chair at the height of the climax to flip the disc over for the calm resolution. Yet at which point in the piece would be a better interruption? Where would a half-inch backward take us? Wherever that place may be, it would halt the inevitable flow of the music. Later generations with long-playing recordings and compact discs have been indeed fortunate not to have to face this infuriating situation.

By the second half of the 1940s the recording was listed in two rather important discographies: David Hall's *The Record Book* (1946) and Irving Kolodin's *New Guide to Recorded Music* (1950). According to Hall, "As might be expected Toscanini gives it everything he's got (which is plenty) and is backed up by superb playing and fine recording. Put this down as a 'must.'"[76] Kolodin concurred: "there is sound reason why this was the first work by an American that Toscanini chose to record; its predominantly conservative patterns are warmly reflected in the eloquence of his playing."[77] Listeners in the twenty-first century still cherish this landmark recording.

Near Misses: Sevitzky and Koussevitzky

Before Toscanini scheduled his performance of *Adagio,* Barber was naturally apprehensive, admitting that the "tentative performance with Toscanini was so uncertain."[78] Fearing that Toscanini would reject the work, he looked about for other conductors who might be willing to perform it, two of whom were John Barbirolli and Eugene Ormandy. Once Toscanini committed himself to the première, Barber was forced to ask both Barbirolli and Ormandy to "release" their performances and return their scores.

An unfortunate incident, however, occurred with conductor Fabien Sevitzky. Unbeknownst to Barber, Anis Fuleihan, an agent at Schirmer, had sent Sevitzky a score and had arranged for a performance by the conductor's Philadelphia Chamber String Sinfonietta. Because this would also have violated the Toscanini contract, Barber was obligated to apologize to Sevitzky about the incident:

[76]David Hall, *The Record Book* (New York: Citadel, 1946), 281.

[77]Irving Kolodin, *New Guide to Recorded Music* (Garden City, N.Y.: Doubleday, 1950), 35. This recording has been re-issued several times over the last decades, now on CD PHS 49.

[78]Samuel Barber, letter (24 October 1938) to Fabien Sevitzky (Washington D.C.: Library of Congress). See Wayne C. Wentzel, *A Research and Information Guide*, 2nd ed., 404 [Sev 1].

> I am sure you will understand my surprise . . . to hear that Fuleihan had booked a performance with you when I did not even know he possessed a score! You see I am not completely to blame. I regret exceedingly the annoyance this must have caused you, and repeat my apologies for this unfortunate misunderstanding.[79]

Before replying to Barber, Sevitzky had other business to transact with Fuleihan and, in a letter, informed him, "I received a very nice letter from Barber with apologies. I do not think that he is altogether to be blamed, although somehow I am still holding one strike on him."[80] Sevitzky then replied to the composer, accepting his apology, "I was quite disturbed by what happened with your Adagio for Strings for my Sinfonietta concert, but the matter is closed now and I am pleased with your kind letter of explanation." He added, "unfortunate things happen so often in our life, sometimes one more does not make any difference."[81] Although Sevitzky may have never conducted *Adagio*, he remained interested in Barber's music, for in the early 1940s he programmed his Essay for Orchestra (No. 1) with the Indianapolis Symphony Orchestra several times.

Barber had also hoped that Serge Koussevitzky (Sevitzky's uncle) might conduct *Adagio for Strings*. A week after Barber apologized to Sevitzky, he wrote to Koussevitzky: "I admire you and your orchestra so much, and hope that someday you will play something of mine."[82] He offered to send him several works, including *Adagio*. Koussevitzky's reply sounded promising: "although my programmes for the actual season (1939-40) are completed, I would be interested to examine the score of your *Adagio for Strings*."[83] Barber instructed Schirmer to send Koussevitzky a score, but nothing ever came of this. He conducted other Barber works over the next few years, but not *Adagio*.

[79] *Ibid.*

[80] Fabien Sevitzky, letter (1 November 1938) to Anis Fuleihan (Washington D.C.: Library of Congress). See Wayne C. Wentzel, *A Research and Information Guide*, 2nd ed., 404 [Sev 2].

[81] Fabien Sevitzky, letter (7 December 1938) to Samuel Barber (Washington D.C.: Library of Congress). See Wayne C. Wentzel, *A Research and Information Guide*, 2nd ed., 404 [Sev 3].

[82] Samuel Barber, letter (16 December 1938) to Serge Koussevitzky, quoted in Barbara B. Heyman, *Samuel Barber* (1992), 145.

[83] Serge Koussevitzky, letter (21 December 1938) to Samuel Barber, quoted in Barbara B. Heyman, *Samuel Barber* (1992), 145.

After Toscanini: Some Early Performances

It is impossible to trace the entire performance history of *Adagio for Strings* after Toscanini's broadcast within the scope of this book. A survey of some early performances—with various conductors presenting the work, usually for the first time—shows, nonetheless, how it entered the repertoire of prominent orchestras and gained popularity among the audiences of symphonic music.

After Toscanini's première *Adagio* caught on rather quickly, being performed by both large orchestras and smaller chamber ensembles. From what I can tell, Otto Klemperer conducted the next performance, with the Los Angeles Philharmonic on 3 March 1939. It was one of several American works that he conducted that season. He had promised the Philharmonic Board to provide the best American music he could find.[84] But many of the pieces were considered too tame for some critics; like Toscanini, he was accused of scheduling only easy and accessible works. He may not have conducted *Adagio* again. A few months later, on 15 July 1939, Vladimir Golschmann conducted the Chicago Symphony Orchestra in a performance at the Ravinia Festival.[85]

Among the earliest chamber music performances are two by all female orchestras. In early May 1939 the Orchestrette Classique, a thirty-member orchestra of women conducted by Frédérique Petrides, performed *Adagio* at the Carnegie Chamber Music Hall. Barber attended the concert and "acknowledged the applause of the audience"; a *New York Times* reporter referred to this as the "first concert hall performance."[86] He was either unaware of the Klemperer performance a few months earlier, or he meant only in the New York area. Almost a year later, in March of 1940, William Durieux presented *Adagio* at New York's Town Hall with even smaller forces: the Durieux Chamber Music Ensemble, a group consisting of only eleven women string players. (All-female orchestras were a fad in the 1930s and 1940s and may have been inspired by Phil Spitalny and His All-Girl Orchestra, a favorite on the radio at the time.) Thus, even in its early

[84]Peter Heyworth, *Otto Klemperer, His Life and Times*, 2 vols. (Cambridge: Cambridge University Press, 1988), II, 78-79.

[85]*Adagio* returned to that venue in 2009 as part of a salute to the composer in his centennial year. Golschmann's recording of *Adagio*, with the Symphony of the Air, recorded twenty years later on the Vanguard label, is now considered a classic.

[86]"Orchestrette Is Heard," *The New York Times* (2 May 1939), 33.

history, *Adagio for Strings* was performed by both large and small string ensembles.[87]

Adagio's long association with the New York Philharmonic began in June 1939, when Massimo Freccia introduced it as part of the summer concert season at Lewisohn Stadium.[88] The following September Barber sent a copy of *Adagio* to John Barbirolli, its principal conductor. Barbirolli conducted it for the first time in January of 1940. After Leonard Bernstein became assistant conductor of the orchestra, he led *Adagio* at Lewisohn Stadium in the summer of 1945, perhaps his earliest performance of the work.

Adagio for Strings also made an immediate impact on the British public. Commentator and composer Harry Dexter remarked, "Barber, of all American composers, is the one most likely to appeal to English ears"; he cited the "emotional stability" and "controlled enthusiasm" in Barber's music, traits that he considers to be typically English.[89] One of the earliest performances of *Adagio* in Great Britain, on 14 June 1943, was given during a United Nations Day Concert at Philharmonic Hall in Liverpool by the Hallé Orchestra with Louis Cohen conducting.

Meanwhile, back in the United States, other notable events took place. Eugene Ormandy conducted the Philadelphia Orchestra in his first performance of the work in 1943 as a part of a United Nations Series.[90] Subsequently, from 1943 to 1985, his orchestra then performed *Adagio* at eighty-five concerts.[91] Charles Munch presided over *Adagio* at a pair of concerts of the Boston Symphony Orchestra in February 1953; this represented not only his first time conducting the work but the "first performance at these concerts." It seems odd that it would take nearly fifteen years for the Boston orchestra to program the work. After Munch conducted it at the orchestra's summer home at Tanglewood, Barber wrote

[87]A list of significant performances between 1936 and 2004 of both quartet and orchestral versions is given in Appendix 2.

[88]The stadium on the campus of City College of New York in upper Manhattan was the venue of outdoor orchestra concerts for many years.

[89]"Samuel Barber and His Music," *Musical Opinion* LXXII (March 1949), 285.

[90]Vincent Persichetti, "Philadelphia Takes a Flier" *Modern Music* XXI/2 (January-February 1944), 104.

[91]Barbara B. Heyman, *Samuel Barber* (1992), 173.

to him, "I keep the touching memory of the *Adagio* in the Berkshires."[92] Munch conducted it there again in July 1956 and in Boston in December 1958, which according to program notes was only its second performance in Symphony Hall.

Barber as Conductor of *Adagio for Strings*

Conducting was a short phase of Barber's career. He was never seriously interested in it as a student nor gained much pleasure from it in later years. In 1932, during his student days in Fritz Reiner's conducting class at the Curtis Institute, the maestro noted on Barber's permanent record card that this student would "never make a conductor."[93] In 1943, nevertheless, Barber conducted the première of his *Commando March* with the Army Air Force Technical Training Command Band and later that year with the Goldman Band. After a few lessons with George Szell, he conducted a program of various orchestral works in Vienna and Chicago and *Adagio* in Prague with the Czech Radio Orchestra. While he may not have had much confidence in his abilities as a conductor, he must have been at least adequate. In September 1946, when he conducted *Adagio* with the London Symphony Orchestra in Hereford, England, one reviewer was impressed:

> History has recorded cases of composers unable to obtain satisfactory interpretations of their own compositions. But that was decidedly not the case at this year's Three Choir Festival; here the completely satisfying moments came when composers were in charge of their own works: Barber's sensitivity and command of his forces will indeed long live in the memory of those who were present at this performance of a beautiful work.[94]

During Barber's conducting stint in England, *Adagio for Strings* was his most requested composition. It became, in his words, "my stock piece."[95]

[92]Samuel Barber, letter (14 October 1953) to Charles Munch, quoted in Genevieve Honegger, *Charles Munch: Un chef d'orchestre dans le siecle* (Strasbourg, France: Nuée Bleue, 1992), 252-53. ["Je garde un souvenir ému de l'Adagio aux Berkshires."]

[93]Fritz Reiner, quoted in Barbara B. Heyman, *Samuel Barber* (1992), 311.

[94]Tancred, "The Three Choirs Festival: Hereford, Sept 8-14," *The Musical Times* LXXXVII (October 1946), 315.

[95]"Of Two Composers," *The New York Times* (10 November 1946), X: 7.

When he conducted it with the Hallé Orchestra at the Edinburgh Festival in 1949, one audience member was overheard to remark, "How well that Barbary [*sic*] man conducts his own work."[96] He conducted *Adagio* in Berlin and Frankfurt in 1951, but thereafter he gave up the baton, confessing, "I had about as much projection as a baby skunk. Projection, nerves—and I got bored of rehearsing my own music. Some composers just adore it, but I don't find it very interesting."[97] It is disappointing that he did not record at least one *Adagio* performance. It might have been accepted as the definitive version.

Anecdotes: From Kostelanetz to Rattle

For many years conductor André Kostelanetz and author James A. Michener were close friends. They often met socially and discussed classical music, including one such occasion a few days before a concert when Kostelanetz told Michener:

> I want to cut a record of my favorite encores, but if we call an extra practice to rehearse them, the cost will be terrific. However, if we play the seven encores after the concert on Saturday night, legitimately, then that practice time is paid for by the organization sponsoring the concert. Can you raise enough applause to keep us onstage for seven encores?[98]

Seven? Michener acknowledged that it would be difficult, but he would try. The audience applauded spontaneously after the first four encores, but, when Kostelanetz began the fifth one, *Adagio for Strings* (one of Kostelanetz's and Michener's "great favorites"), a critical moment came. Michener recalled, "There was a substantial movement toward the exits. I halted this with a frenzied burst of clapping interspersed with shouts of 'More, more!' which others took up, and we were saved."[99] It became increasingly more difficult to keep the ovation going, but Kostelanetz managed to squeeze in all seven encores. Was this encore album ever

[96]W. R. Anderson, "The Edinburgh Festival," *The Musical Times* XC (October 1949), 364.

[97]Samuel Barber, quoted in Alan Kozinn, "Samuel Barber: The Last Interview and the Legacy," *High Fidelity* XXXI (June 1981), 46.

[98]James A. Michener, *The World Is My Home: A Memoir* (New York: Random House, 1992), 163. Michener did not provide the date.

[99]*Ibid.*, 163-64.

issued? There was an album, *Kostelanetz in Wonderland: Golden Encores,* but *Adagio for Strings* is not on it.[100] I have yet to encounter a Kostelanetz recording of *Adagio.*

While Leopold Stokowski may have presided over several memorable performances of *Adagio for Strings,* the one that stands out most clearly occurred in Moscow in May 1958. At the end of *Adagio* the audience was so enthusiastic that it demanded an encore, so Stokowski repeated it. At the conclusion of the program the audience still wanted more and, according to Stokowski's biographer, Oliver Daniel, "Stoki obliged by again repeating the Adagio."[101] Three times on the same concert! Surely that is unique in the history of music and should go into the *Guinness Book of World Records.*[102]

Barber himself was fond of telling an unusual tale regarding Eugene Ormandy's performance in Moscow. He did not indicate exactly when this transaction took place, probably during the Philadelphia Orchestra's summer tour of 1958. At the time Barber's scores were difficult for Russian musicians to obtain. After one particular performance, a group of Russians approached the visiting conductor about *Adagio,* which they wanted to choreograph. Barber related, "He offered to loan them the score if they would return it the next day. They took the score and spent all night copying it so that they might have the music."[103] They presumably returned the score to Ormandy and that Russian audiences benefited from a newly choreographed dance to the Barber music. If so, it is among the earliest dances set to *Adagio for Strings.*

Klaus Tennstedt's relationship with *Adagio for Strings* is, perhaps, one of the strangest. While conducting it with the Philadelphia Orchestra in November 1985, "he felt a tickle in his throat"; a doctor who examined him the next day diagnosed throat cancer.[104] After this, Tennstedt's conducting career deteriorated. Later, when conducting a program in London for the Proms Concerts, he became ill just before he was to take the podium to conduct *Adagio.* Norman Lebrecht concluded, "ever

[100]*Kostelanetz in Wonderland: Golden Encores,* cond. Andre Kostelanetz (Columbia, CS 8878, 1963).

[101]Oliver Daniel, *Stokowski: A Counterpoint of View* (New York: Dodd, Mead, 1982), 683.

[102]For another memorable Stokowski *Adagio* performance, see Chapter 10.

[103]Samuel Barber, quoted in John Ardoin, "Samuel Barber at Capricorn," *Musical America* V (March 1960), 5.

[104]Norman Lebrecht, *The Maestro Myth: Great Conductors in Pursuit of Power* (New York: Birch Lane Press, 1991), 240.

superstitious, he blamed the final disaster on the Barber, the piece he had been performing when his cancer was diagnosed."[105]

Among the most momentous performances of *Adagio for Strings* was given on 31 January 2004, when Simon Rattle conducted the Philadelphia Orchestra in a concert commemorating the ensemble's 147th anniversary. He selected *Adagio* because the evening needed some "emotional contrast to a program of mostly 'up' tunes."[106] But what followed was a series of circumstances that no one could have foreseen. About halfway through *Adagio* a woman yelled to come to the aid of a man in distress. Critic Peter Dobrin described the scene:

> As the orchestra played on, she called out for a doctor, and the Barber became the soundtrack to a disturbing drama as people rushed to the man's side. Eventually Rattle stopped the music, and the man, suffering from apparent heart trouble, was helped out of the hall.[107]

Yet that is only half the story. Rattle restarted the work, getting to the last few notes, when another person became ill and was carried out of the hall as the piece ended. Dobrin speculates: was it "something in the air? Was the Barber, combined with Rattle's dedicatory words, causing mass psychosomatic hysteria? (It seems this second victim simply had too much to drink and was dehydrated.)"[108] David Booth, a violinist in the orchestra commented, "In my 35 years of giving concerts, I've never seen anything like this."[109] Critic David Stearns wrote that not since Oliver Stone used *Adagio* in *Platoon* had "that soulful music been linked with a series of distressing events."[110] The remainder of the program went smoothly.[111]

[105] *Ibid.*, 242.

[106] Simon Rattle, quoted in Peter Dobrin, "An Academy Anniversary Concert Both Ominous and Luminous," *Philadelphia Inquirer* (2 February 2004).

[107] Peter Dobrin, "An Academy Anniversary Concert Both Ominous and Luminous," *Philadelphia Inquirer* (2 February 2004).

[108] *Ibid.*

[109] David Booth, quoted in David Stearns, "The Curse of Barber's Adagio," *BBC Music Magazine* (1 April 2004).

[110] David Stearns, "The Curse of Barber's Adagio," *BBC Music Magazine* (1 April 2004).

[111] Two other memorable Slatkin performances of *Adagio* are described in Chapter 10, "*Adagio*: In Memoriam."

After Toscanini's performances and recording, Samuel Barber's *Adagio for Strings* became an audience favorite. Little did its composer realize how much members of the public would grow to love this "knockout" quartet movement in its orchestral guise. For his program notes for Guido Cantelli's performance of *Adagio* by the New York Philharmonic in 1955, Irving Kolodin placed the work in greater perspective: "as an augury of the musicality and sense of design the composer has manifested in many larger works since, it is a landmark as well as a signboard pointing to the future."[112]

[112] Irving Kolodin, "Program Notes," *The Philharmonic Symphony Society of New York* (20-21 January 1955), 3.

> Even as you read these words, somewhere in the world Samuel Barber's *Adagio for Strings* is being played. . . . If Barber later aimed higher, he never reached deeper into the heart.
>
> —Ned Rorem, *A Ned Rorem Reader* (2001).[1]

In this chapter I will approach *Adagio for Strings* from a variety of angles and seek to address fundamental questions about its nature. Does anything truly anticipate the piece? Is it possible to identify predecessors, both in the music of other composers or in earlier works by Barber himself? What about the size of the orchestra? Is there an ideal complement of instrumentalists necessary for a satisfactory performance? How should its tonality, its formal structure, and its melodic shapes be most meaningfully described and analyzed? Is there an ideal tempo? I will conclude with a consideration of *Adagio's* context on the radio and television and in the concert hall. Which other pieces complement an *Adagio* performance?

Possible Predecessors

Did *Adagio for Strings*—in its original string quartet guise—suddenly spring into Barber's imagination, or are there specific earlier works, by him or by predecessors, that anticipate its structure, texture, and mood? Several composers who might have influenced him have been suggested: namely, Jean Sibelius (1865-1957), Gabriel Fauré (1845-1924), Ruth Crawford Seeger (1901-1953), and Ralph Vaughan Williams (1872-1958).

Barber admired Sibelius. Barber's analysis of Sibelius's Seventh Symphony (1924) can be found among the sketches for his own Symphony in One Movement (1936).[2] Barbara Heyman noticed that both works are "generated from themes presented at the onset" and strongly suggests that the Sibelius symphony is the model Barber used for his own work.[3] In much the same way, all the thematic material in *Adagio for Strings* is generated at the onset. Several writers have heard a Sibelian influence in Barber's music. For instance, in his thesis John McAlexander compared

[1]Ned Rorem, *A Ned Rorem Reader* (Harrisonburg, Va.: R. R. Donnelly and Sons, 2001), 238.

[2]See Wayne C. Wentzel, *Samuel Barber: A Research and Information Guide*, 2nd ed. (New York: Routledge, 2010), especially Item 43, "An Old Sketchbook."

[3]Barbara B. Heyman, *Samuel Barber: The Composer and His Music* (New York: Oxford University Press, 1992), 175. The diagram in Barber's sketchbook confirms that this was his model.

Adagio to Sibelius's Fifth Symphony (1915, revised 1916 and 1919),[4] and Arthur Berger observed that Barber's music prior to his Second Symphony (1944, revised 1947) leans towards "the broad symphonic traditions of composers like Sibelius."[5] Howard Pollack identified several Sibelian traits in the introduction to Barber's String Serenade (1928): its "somewhat lugubrious tone, its smooth, stepwise voice leading, its rhythmic pliancy, and its piquant chromatic and modal ambiguities resolved by a conventional harmonic cadence."[6] According to Pollack, *Adagio* "more decidedly" suggests Sibelius's influence.[7] Critic Howard Taubman, nonetheless, was not convinced on this point: "Though those who are always hunting for reminiscences rather than marks of individuality speak of the influence of Sibelius, Mr. Barber's music can stand on its own feet."[8]

Example 3.1. Comparison of Similar Opening Statements

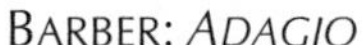

FAURÉ: PRELUDE FROM *PELLÉAS ET MÉLISANDE*

SCHREKER: INTERMEZZO FROM KLEINE SUITE

Yet some critics have found similarities between *Adagio* and the works of others. In Arthur Berger's opinion *Adagio* recalled the Prelude to Fauré's *Pelléas et Mélisande* (1898), both of which begin with a long sustained note followed by a wandering line of eighth or quarter notes.[9]

[4]John McAlexander, *A Stylistic Analysis of the First Symphony (in One Movement), Op. 9 by Samuel Barber* (M.M. thesis, Texas Tech University, 1976).

[5]Arthur Berger, "Spotlight on the Moderns," *Saturday Review of Literature* XXXIV/21 (26 May 1951), 62.

[6]Howard Pollack, "Samuel Barber, Jean Sibelius, and the Making of an American Romantic," *The Musical Quarterly* LXXXIV/2 (Summer 2000), 187.

[7]*Ibid.*

[8]Howard Taubman, "Records: Barber Adagio," *The New York Times* (1 November 1942), X: 6.

[9]Arthur Berger, "Spotlight on the Moderns," *Saturday Review of Literature,* 61.

The beginning of *Adagio* also resembles a movement of Franz Schreker's Kleine Suite for chamber orchestra (1930). While Barber may have been familiar with Fauré's prelude, it is unlikely that he would have known Schreker's intermezzo. The three melodies are aligned in Example 3.1; their "family resemblance" is probably coincidental.

Richard Taruskin claimed that the Andante for String Orchestra (1931) of Ruth Crawford Seeger "strongly resembles" the nearly contemporaneous *Adagio*. Was Barber familiar with this piece or with her work in general? (Neither Broder nor Heyman mentioned her music.) Taruskin elaborated on the comparison:

> Both works are arrangements of slow movements from string quartets, and both follow a trajectory (at once formal and expressive) from a darkly plaintive low register to a plangent high. The difference is that Crawford Seeger's piece was pervasively "dissonated" . . . in obedience to the norms of maverick manliness, while Barber, a male composer with a solid conservatory education and good connections, was confident enough to withstand the pressure.[10]

Barber may occasionally "dissonate" his music to modernize his romantic tone, but seldom in *Adagio*. Yet, despite Taruskin's comparison, to me the two works seem light years apart. Barber's piece has a memorable melody shifted from one instrument to another whereas Seeger's has no discernible melody at all, just a series of static dissonant harmonic effects. The only aspect the two have in common is their general form: both start quietly, build to a climax near the end, then pause for a quiet coda. Neither composer needed to be aware of the other's work to arrive at such a structure.

Paul Wittke, former senior editor at G. Schirmer, compared *Adagio* to Vaughan Williams's *Fantasia on a Theme by Thomas Tallis* (1910, revised 1913 and 1919):

> Both composers weave a web of stately, melancholy sound. Vaughan Williams' modal score specifically creates the world of Tudor England; yet in spite of its expressivity there is an impersonal and remote air about it. Barber, on the other hand, is more enigmatic. . . . *Adagio*'s power lies in being a work

[10]Richard Taruskin, "Music: Corralling a Herd of Musical Mavericks," *The New York Times* (23 July 2000), AR: 1.

> whose tragic atmosphere is both subjective and universal—it resonates in each of us a personal note of somber thought. We bring to it our own meaning.[11]

The stylistic link between the two works is tenuous. Barber might have been influenced in general by Vaughan Williams, whom he met in the early 1930s shortly before he composed *Adagio.* Vaughan Williams had commented favorably on *Dover Beach* (1931),[12] which is closer to the English composer's style than is *Adagio.*

Precedence in Earlier Barber Works

Prior to his string quartet, Barber wrote several works involving solo strings: the early Violin Sonata (1928), the Cello Sonata (1932), *Dover Beach* for baritone and string quartet, and the Serenade for String Quartet. Do any of them foreshadow *Adagio?* Critic Ellen Pfeifer suggested that the melodic contours of the Cello Sonata anticipate the work.[13] The introduction ("Un poco adagio") to the first movement of the Serenade begins like *Adagio*: a single sustained note in one part, followed by a full chord, but the violin melody is more angular, much less memorable. Howard Pollack reported that the harmonies, with modal ambiguities, "anticipate Barber's mature harmonic language at its most characteristic."[14] Another relationship is strictly visual; the 4 / 2 meter, another possible Sibelius trait, gives the score a "white-note" look, similar to *Adagio.*

Writer and critic Walter Simmons suggested that Interlude I for piano (1932) might be considered a predecessor "in Barber's much beloved early style that pianists and audiences have long wished for—the pianist's answer to the *Adagio for Strings,* so to speak."[15] The tempo marking is similar, "Adagio, ma non troppo"; the music is cast in one of those "rich keys" with many flats, E-flat minor; and the piece exhibits a long, arching melody. The main difference is the Interlude's bass-line, which presents a rhythmic ostinato unlike the cello line in *Adagio.* Yet the resulting sound

[11]Paul Wittke, *Samuel Barber: An Improvisatory Portrait* (New York: G. Schirmer, 1994), 12-13.

[12]Philip Ramey, liner notes to *Songs of Samuel Barber and Ned Rorem,* perf. Donald Gramm, Phyllis Curtin, Ned Rorem, Samuel Barber, *et al.* (New World Records, NW229, 1978).

[13]Ellen Pfeifer, "Music Review: Laurence Lesser," *Boston Globe* (25 March 2000), A: 12.

[14]Howard Pollack, "Samuel Barber, Jean Sibelius, and the Making of an American Romantic," *The Musical Quarterly* (2000), 177.

[15]Walter Simmons, review of *Barber: Complete Published Solo Piano Music,* perf. Daniel Pollack (Naxos, 8.559015, 1998), *Fanfare* XXII/5 (July-August 1999), 109.

may not be all that different. Because the piano, even with pedal, does not possess the sustaining power of bowed strings, this rhythmic device may be only meant to convey a low sustained bass support. Both pieces, moreover, reach a climatic point before settling down to a quiet ending. Heyman hears a "thrust of melancholy characteristic of Barber's personal voice."[16] Melancholy is often associated with *Adagio for Strings*.

Despite references to works by Sibelius, Fauré, Seeger, and Vaughan Williams, *Adagio for Strings* seems to me to be a world apart. After going back and re-listening to the String Serenade, the piano Interlude, and the slow movement of the cello sonata, I am convinced that none of these pieces, as lovely as they are, sounds remotely like *Adagio for Strings*. If I were pressed to answer the question whether this piece came to life on its own, without previous influence, I would be tempted to respond "yes." It is a musical "knockout" without precedence, a work that no one could have anticipated, one with a sound all its own.

For How Many and Which Kind of Strings?

When Barber transformed his string quartet movement, he obviously had the full sound of the NBC Symphony Orchestra in mind. Most other performances are also recorded by large orchestras: *e.g.*, the Philadelphia Orchestra with Ormandy, the Boston Symphony Orchestra with Munch, and the New York Philharmonic with Bernstein. Reviewing some of the recordings by these orchestras, Alan Kozinn commented on the "facile lushness" of Ormandy's performance, the "velvety, flawless string tone" of both the Toscanini and Munch recordings, and the "thick string sound" of Bernstein with the New York Philharmonic.[17]

Yet it may be possible to go overboard with the string sound. One author contended that the strings of the Philadelphia Orchestra "almost glut the listener with continuous lush sounds and sweet harmonies."[18] To avoid this pitfall, perhaps a chamber orchestra is the answer. What such an orchestra lacks in "thick string sound," it may compensate by giving *Adagio* a more intimate character, thereby preserving some of the chamber quality of the original quartet movement. Among the first chamber groups to record *Adagio* was the Italian ensemble I Musici. With individual string parts more exposed, the playing here has less "facile lushness." Reviewer

[16]Barbara B. Heyman, *Samuel Barber* (1992), 78.

[17]Alan Kozinn, "Samuel Barber: The Recordings," *High Fidelity and Musical America* XXXII (June 1981), 67.

[18]"Orchestra Potpourri," *The New York Times* (21 May 1961), X: 13.

William Youngren pointed out the group's "sustained eloquence, and a sheer tonal beauty that brings tears to one's eyes."[19] A chamber music performance may also reduce the amount of sentimentality that may creep into large orchestra performances. Critic Roger Hecht evaluated the sound of the thirteen-member I Musici de Montreal as having an "exuberant, bright" tone and producing one of *Adagio*'s "less sentimental and more life-affirming performances."[20] Some critics miss the large string sound in such performances, however. Two cited a lack of warmth in the recording by I Musici de Montreal: Peter J. Rabinowitz found it "surpassingly cool,"[21] and Richard Burke referred to the "strangely cold climax to the work."[22] Similar criticisms have been leveled at the I Solisti di Zagreb's recording: it "lacks body and intensity";[23] the effect is "somewhat pale and wan compared with a full symphony string sound."[24]

CD Track 3

The Smithsonian Chamber Players (ten violins, five violas, five cellos, and three basses) presented *Adagio* on "period instruments," with gut strings, as was typical up through the first part of the twentieth century.[25] The gut string sound and less vibrato give the performance a somewhat antiquated tint, almost as if John Dowland's consort of viols were time-shifted into the middle of the last century. As critic Raymond Tuttle observed, "gut gives the strings a more cutting tone, a buzz or serrated edge if you will, that suits the intensity of the Barber . . . very well."[26] Yet the sound, to my ears, is warm and rich, enhanced by several *portamenti* that were in vogue during the first half of the twentieth century.

Another unusual version is played by the Hutchins Consort, a group that performs not only Medieval and Renaissance music but also some twentieth-century pieces. This string octet is comprised of instruments, all in the violin family with some invented by member Carleen Hutchins. The instruments are the first attempt "to create an acoustically balanced set

[19]William Youngren, "Ensemble," *Fanfare* IV (November 1980), 223-24.

[20]Roger Hecht, "New York Composers," *American Record Guide* MXIV/3 (May 2001), 200-01.

[21]Peter J. Rabinowitz, "Record Reviews," *Fanfare* XI (November 1987), 294.

[22]Richard Burke, "Collections: Orchestral," *Fanfare* XXIV (May 2001), 276.

[23]David Hall, "In Brief," *HiFi / Stereo Review* X (June 1963), 70.

[24]Enos E. Shupp, "Chamber Music," *New Records* (April 1963), 2.

[25]*Metamorphosis: Music of Richard Strauss, Edward Elgar, and Samuel Barber*, perf. Smithsonian Chamber Players, cond. Kenneth Slowik (BMG / Deutsche Harmonia Mundi, 0 5472 77343 2, 1996). Also available in the anthology *Adventures in Early Music* (DHM, CD A ADVE D 92).

[26]Raymond Tuttle, "Review," *Fanfare* XIX (January 1996), 411.

that can sound truly like violins across the entire range of written music."[27] They extend from the treble violin, an octave higher than a standard violin, down to the contrabass violin, an octave lower than a cello. Listening to the arrangement by contrabassist Joe McNalley represents an introduction to a distinctive string sound, one unlike any ever heard before.[28]

Two performances take a decidedly imaginative approach and turn *Adagio for Strings* into a quasi-concerto. In the first, Jenny Oaks Baker performed an arrangement by Greg Hansen, in which she plays some phrases on solo violin while a small string orchestra, supplemented unexpectedly but not inappropriately by a harp, plays the full score. At times, however, engineers in the recording studio enhanced the solo violin sound to the point that it loses the contrast required to bring off this kind of realization.

In the other, the intriguing idea is to combine aspects of the string quartet with the orchestral version, transforming it into a kind of concerto grosso. For a performance by the Kentucky Symphony Orchestra in March 2006 conductor James R. Cassidy devised the procedure of beginning *Adagio* in its original string quartet format and gradually adding more and more strings until it becomes the familiar string orchestra rendition. He gave the second violinist, violist, and cellist the first page of the quartet as the double stops are different from the orchestral version. "I added (and then deleted) by single players in each section so as to make the shift from the quartet to full strings fairly imperceptible."[29] The orchestral strings prevailed up through the climax, after which they slowly disappeared until only the string quartet remained at the end. Thus the intimate chamber sound occurred in quieter moments, whereas the full orchestra supported the climb to the climax. Cassidy explained that this method of performing *Adagio* was meant more as a pedagogical tool than a new way of playing the piece:

> The program on which I added the Barber *Adagio* was originally intended as an education concert and recruitment ploy for string programs in the schools. My approach to the Barber was to show that out of the original string quartet grew possibly the most popular American-composed piece of the 20th century.

[27]See *The Hutchins Consort*, www.hutchinsconsort.org.

[28]For a view of these instruments, held up for the audience to see, but not played, see "Hutchins Consort Part 1," *YouTube* (20 May 2006), posted by swocehtevol.

[29]James R. Cassidy, email (3 April 2006) to the author.

> Given the educational point of what I was trying to do with this program, I think this is a good way to present the piece.[30]

He maintained that, if he were to program *Adagio* on a regular concert, he would revert to the traditional orchestral version. Yet considering how many times and how many ways *Adagio* has been arranged for other instrumental combinations (see the next chapter), a version that integrates the string quartet with the orchestra seems like a reasonable performance possibility, suitable even for adult audiences.

Bowing: Let's Get It Together or I Did It My Way

When G. Schirmer published *Adagio for Strings*, the score featured bowings in the individual string parts. It is not clear whether Barber himself specified them or if he was even concerned about such matters. (There were no bowings in the individual parts in the published String Quartet edition.) Orchestra conductors, therefore, may either follow these indications or devise their own. Eugene Ormandy (apparently) decided on his own bowings, which can be seen in the string parts donated to the University of Pennsylvania.[31] Yet are they truly intended for Ormandy performances? The opening passage of the first violin part is marked, "parts are bowed July 1980," the year Ormandy retired as music director. If they are his bowings, why were they not entered much earlier? John Bewley concluded that "the bowings . . . presumably reflect the style of bowing favored by Ormandy."[32] They may be intended for later conductors who want to obtain an Ormandy-like sound. According to Gabriel Braverman, violist and copyist for the Orchestra, Ormandy preferred frequent changes of bowing: "Instead of putting eight notes on a bow, it would be only four notes to give a more heightened sound. All the strings had to bow alike, and it had to be put into the parts for the players so that each part, each stand, would have these bowings."[33] Indeed,

[30]*Ibid.*

[31]Van Pelt Rare Book and Manuscript Collection, MS. Coll 60, Box 17. The collection contains either photocopies of Barber's manuscripts or printed scores, with notations by Ormandy and / or Barber, intended for performance by the Philadelphia Orchestra. For contents and comments, see Wayne C. Wentzel, *A Research and Information Guide*, 341-44.

[32]John Bewley, "Marking the Way: The Significance of Eugene Ormandy's Score Annotations," *Notes* LIX/4 (June 2003), 828f.

[33]Gabriel Braverman, Ormandy Oral History Collection, transcript 10, quoted in John Bewley, "Marking the Way," *Notes*, footnote 16.

the first violin part shows far more frequent changes of bow than in the Schirmer edition. Bowings have been altered fourteen times during the first twelve measures with many changes from up-bow to down-bow and vice versa.[34] Such changes may result in a different concept of phrasing, which might (or might not) be audible to some listeners. Bowing changes may be a common feature of *Adagio* scores in orchestral libraries around the world. For instance, the first violin part in the Indianapolis Symphony Orchestra library shows bowings different from both the Schirmer and the Philadelphia scores.

Specific bowing indications imply that all players should bow the same way, a uniformity that not all conductors desire. Some prefer free bowing. Videotapes of orchestras playing *Adagio* are the best way to learn if players bow in a uniform manner or not. In the performance of the Philadelphia Orchestra, under the direction of Luis Biava (recorded for telecast in 1996), bowing is uniform within each orchestral section, but only a more discerning eye than mine can determine whether they are using the "Ormandy bowings" (I think they are), the original Schirmer bowings, or another system. A video posted on *YouTube* shows that members of the Hong Kong Philharmonic Orchestra, directed by Zhang Xian, all bow together.[35] The same is true for the strings of the orchestra I Virtuosi Italiani, as can be seen in a videotape of their performance for the 2000 Jubilee at the Duomo Monza (near Milan).[36]

On the other hand, Leopold Stokowski preferred free bowing. In a rehearsal of *Adagio* with the American Symphony Orchestra, he told the musicians, "Do not change bows together. I know some conductors like the opposite. Give them what they ask. Give me what I ask, please."[37] William Ander Smith contended that free bowing is part of the Stokowski string sound:

> With Stokowski leading a free-bowing orchestra, string players could avoid running out of bow should the maestro request greater volume of sound or alter the tempo for poetic effect

[34]John Bewley, "Marking the Way," *Notes*, 835.

[35]"Barber: Adagio for Strings (by HKPO)," *YouTube* (25 September 2008), posted by hongkongclassics.

[36]*Enrico Castiglione Presents the Jubilee Concerts: From Duomo of Monza* [DVD], perf. I Virtuosi Italiani and Cecilia Gasdia (Trinidad Entertainment, TE 9798, 2000).

[37]Leopold Stokowski, quoted in "Rehearsal: Leopold Stokowski," *Fanfare* (telecast 15 August 1971). Thanks to Robert Stumpf II for providing me a tape of this program, a production of NET in cooperation with the CBC.

.... Stokowski was free to ask what he wished for in color, intensity, phrasing and volume without the constraints posed by tradition.[38]

Smith suggested that listening to Stokowski's recordings of various string orchestra pieces, including *Adagio for Strings,* is the best test for his ideas about free bowing and the responses of the string players.[39] When observing the tape of the rehearsal mentioned earlier, one can see the variation in bowing from one string player to another. At one point the maestro also calls for "more bow. You play like misers."[40]

Is one system of bowing better than the other? While there may not be a clear audible difference, there is certainly something to commend the visual appearance of uniform bowing. It seems to convey more of a sense of calm than seeing all those bows moving in a seemingly haphazard way. This is especially true for a piece like *Adagio for Strings.* Yet sometimes there can be a compromise. I attended a performance at a music festival at Indiana University in the summer of 2008. At the beginning, when the piece was at its calmest, I noticed the violins all bowing in unison, but by the time the piece reached the climax I saw all kinds of free bowings. Apparently conductor Lawrence Renes felt that a change to free bowing allowed for more sound to build through that climactic section. The orchestra reverted to uniform bowing for the coda, so that the peaceful atmosphere could return. Richard Auldon Clark, the conductor of the Manhattan Chamber Orchestra, preferred a similar approach: "I have some very specific bowings that vary depending on the size of the string section; at the loud climax I use free bowing for maximum sound."[41]

Some Analytical Observations

A QUESTION OF TONALITY

When writers criticize *Adagio* as being too conservative for twentieth-century tastes, they often berate its simplistic tonal orientation. Yet is its tonal center all that obvious? The five flats in the signature imply a key

[38]William Ander Smith, *The Mystery of Leopold Stokowski* (Cranbury, N.J.: Associated University Presses, 1990), 65.

[39]*Ibid.*

[40]Leopold Stokowski, quoted in "Rehearsal: Leopold Stokowski," *Fanfare* (telecast 15 August 1971). "Barber 'Adagio for Strings'–Stokowski Rehearsal," *YouTube* (7 December 2012), posted by adam28xx.

[41]Richard Auldon Clark, email (30 November 2011) to the author.

of B-flat minor, but the first cadence (m. 19) is the only one in the entire piece that ends on the tonic chord, and even that is plagal. I am never fooled into thinking that the piece is over at that point. Other cadences end on chords consistent with B-flat minor: F-major, the dominant (mm. 8, 35, and 64), and B-flat major (m. 28), a twentieth-century version of a Renaissance *tierce de picardie.* The final cadence adds further doubts; instead of ending on a tonic chord, it appears to end on the dominant. But does it? Some may believe so. In fact, a student of mine once told me that he mentally completes the cadence by hearing a B-flat chord in his mind. Writing about *Adagio* in his master's thesis, Steven Besedick admits that the final chord could be a dominant but suggests another possibility: "Although it would not be incorrect to label the final cadence as a half cadence in B-flat minor . . . [it] can represent a modulation to F major as well. The long duration afforded the final F major chord . . . can have the effect of establishing a sense of "tonic-arrival."[42] Is he correct? The discussion of various aspects of the coda (see page 72) may help determine that possibility.

This work occupies a territory somewhere between modality and tonality.[43] Howard Pollack refers to the whole piece as a "phrygian *Adagio,* an F-centered work with a key signature of five flats,"[44] indeed the signature of the Phrygian mode when transposed upward from E to F. Moreover, at the beginning, most notes of the melody and chords in the accompaniment use pitches from this mode. The pull of the opening E-flat minor seventh chord to an F-major triad may bolster this view. Yet there is no typical Phrygian cadence anywhere in the piece. If F is, in fact, the tonal center, there would be no need to justify a modulation to that key at the end. While a Phrygian *Adagio* is an intriguing possibility, most of the following discussion, with the exception of the coda, will be based on the more traditional view that the tonality is B-flat minor. I doubt that Barber was concerned about whether *Adagio* was modal, tonal, or something else.

MELODY AND FORM

When commenters or performers discuss the melody of *Adagio for Strings,* they are likely to refer to it as "lyrical." In pianist John Browning's

[42]Steven Besedick, *Samuel Barber's Cantilena Slow Movements: A Study of Textural Relationships* (M.M. thesis, Florida State University, 1986), 51.

[43]This is a view expressed by Kenneth Nott (see footnote 55), cited in Barbara B. Heyman, *Samuel Barber: A Thematic Catalog of the Complete Works* (Oxford: Oxford University Press, 2012), 179.

[44]Howard Pollack, "Samuel Barber, Jean Sibelius, and the Making of an American Romantic," *The Musical Quarterly* (2000), 191.

opinion, "there is an innate lyricism in no matter what instrument [Barber] wrote for, there's always that feeling of vocal line. . . . At all times the vocal persuasiveness is there."[45] If this is true, then this lyricism might imply that Barber conceived *Adagio*'s theme in vocal terms, especially considering his skill as a songwriter. Yet he would deny it. After writer and composer Philip Ramey asked him if he ever thought of the voice when he wrote for another medium, Barber replied:

> Never. Any melody I write is just abstract music coming out of my head and has nothing at all to do with the voice. I think only of whatever instrument or ensemble I happen to be writing for at the time. If I found it necessary to think of the voice when writing an orchestral work, I would have to consider myself rather limited as a composer.[46]

The length of the melody, moreover, with its constant winding around would be difficult to sing.

The melody can be thought of as cast in four phrases, presented initially in the first violin, next in the viola, and then in the cello. The composer extends the cello statement in order to build to the climax through a series of stretto presentations of the first phrase. A "quiet chord" passage separates all of this from a final statement that functions as a coda.[47]

The main four-phrase statement itself can be handily divided into two balanced halves. The first two phrases are similar to an antecedent-consequent setup. The first emphasizes a short motive functioning as an ornamental resolution of a 4 - 3 suspension (B-flat - A - B-flat - C - A), but, instead of settling into it, the line continues to wind around in sequences, alternating between consonant and dissonant notes against the harmonies until it arrives on C. Barber creates tension when he refuses to allow any dissonance to resolve for long, preventing any resolution to register in the mind of the listener, a process that carries through each time the main theme appears. This upward motion gives a sense of striving, which is

[45]John Browning, quoted in Peter Dickinson, *Samuel Barber Remembered: A Centenary Tribute* (Rochester, N.Y.: University of Rochester Press, 2010), 140. Dickinson's interview with Browning is dated 13 May 1981.

[46]Samuel Barber, quoted in Philip Ramey, "Samuel Barber at Seventy," *Ovation* I/3 (March 1980), 19.

[47]This is my characterization of this passage. I have indicated so by placing the term in quotation marks at its first appearance. When I reference these chords later in the text, this term will not be set off by quotation marks.

then followed by the second phrase, where the motion is downward, which communicates more of a sense of resignation. If one presumes that the key is B-flat minor, then the antecedent phrase ends on the remote chord of A-flat major, a pause rather than a cadence, while the resultant phrase cadences on F-major, the dominant. Thus, despite the fact that this pair of phrases is cast in the minor mode, the tonic chord never appears, and, in fact, the most prominent harmonies are all major chords: F-major, A-flat major, and G-flat major. The third phrase begins as a repeat of the first, arriving at the same note of C, but then the stepwise motion suddenly gives way to dramatic leaps with a pair of tritones and their downward resolution into fourths (see Example 3.2). Just when listeners become accustomed to a smooth flowing, stepwise melodic style, Barber suddenly jolts them with these leaps. The phrase reaches its highest note of C-flat (m. 12). Phrase four, back in the range of the earlier phrases, follows immediately without pause, ending with a plagal cadence in B-flat minor.

Example 3.2. Third Phrase of the Main Theme (mm. 11-13)

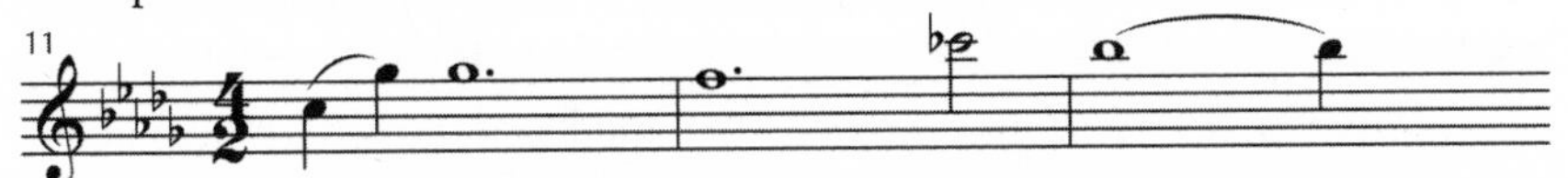

The apex of the four-phrase construction occurs in the twelfth out of nineteen measures, almost exactly at the phi point of the Fibonacci golden section, 61.8% into the passage. Barber may not have calculated this exactly (as Bartók might have), but his musical instincts led him in this direction; whatever way it came about, it seems right. (Consult Example 3.4 on page 71.) The same melodic structure occurs in the viola (transposed down a fifth) and the cello (down an octave), with each starting before the previous statement ends. Table 3.1 illustrates how the phrases overlap. Because the viola statement is somewhat hidden within the texture, some listeners may not be aware of its presence; they may still be concentrating on the continuation of the violin melody, especially if it is emphasized in the performance. On the other hand, the cello statement is usually clearly defined.

Table 3.1. Overlapping of Phrases

mm.	1	4	8	12	13	15	19	24	28	31	35	40	44
Violin 1:	[1]--	[2]--	[3]---------		[4]-----------		new material						
Viola:				[1]---------		[2]--	[3]--	[4]-----------		new material			
Cello:									[1]--	[2]--	[3]--	[4]------	new material

When the viola and cello each reach the climactic note of the third phrase (m. 23 and m. 39, respectively), all the parts have a sense of arrival, forming a "mini-climax." Before the cello starts its fourth phrase, the other parts intrude with a stretto version of phrase [1], all of which push the movement upward to *Adagio*'s huge, main climax—shown in Table 3.2.

Table 3.2. Distribution of Parts at Climax (mm. 39-56)

mm.	39	40	42	44	46	47	50	53
Violin 1:	[1]---------------------|					[1]------|	--climax---|	
Violin 2:				[1]--------------------|			--climax---|	
Viola:					[1]-----------------|		--climax---|	
Cello:		[4]-incomplete-|					--climax---|	

As the table indicates, the successive entries of [1] get closer together, a typical feature of strettos. The top line of the climactic passage first ascends quickly with rising fourths, as shown in Example 3.3. (Compare with the climbing tritones of Example 3.2.) The line then meanders in quarter-note motion, reaching a high B-flat, the highest pitch in the piece. Although the climax occurs later than the golden section (ca. 74% rather than 61.8%), the buildup to that moment starts precisely at the phi point, but to the listener the exact moments of these events are not all that significant. Performances, after all, vary a great deal in tempos, rubatos, and pauses between phrases. This high note is harmonized with the tonic B-flat minor chord, but the next sounds transport it far from that tonal center, culminating on a remote and surprising F-flat major chord. The buildup is so strong and its arrival so overwhelming that only a pause can relieve the tension. Yet, despite this dramatic culmination, the music should not sound conclusive (there are those who disagree; see page 78). This pause is just as crucial to the continuity of the music as the passages surrounding it.[48]

Example 3.3. Climbing Fourths in Top Line of Climactic Passage (mm. 45-47)

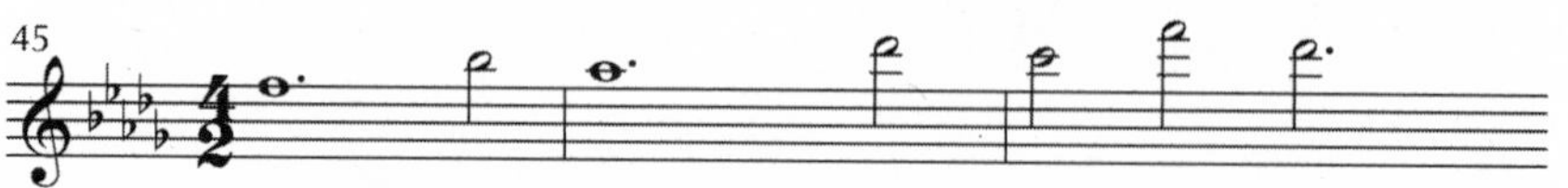

[48]Like silent moments in other pieces of music, the effectiveness could be undermined by coughs from the audience or, even worse, the ringing of a cell phone, as unfortunately happened in a performance by the Bach Society Orchestra in Cambridge, Massachusetts in October 2006.

Example 3.4. Violin I Part with Schenkerian-style Reduction (mm. 1-20)

The ensuing quiet chord passage functions in two ways: it brings the listener down psychologically from the intensity of the climax but also initiates a tonal return after going so far astray. (See Example 3.5.) Although the chords themselves move slowly, their harmonic rhythm is fast, and their juxtaposition produces a sound that at first seems ambiguous but is actually quite logical. The first two chords repeat the last two chords of the climax (C-flat major 7 —> F-flat major); the same progression is then transposed down a step (A-major 7 —> D-major); then three chords end the passage with a V / V to V in B-flat minor (B-minor —> C-major —> F-major). This cadence foreshadows the tonicization of the F-major chord at the end of the piece.

Example 3.5. The "Quiet Chords" Passage (mm. 53-56)

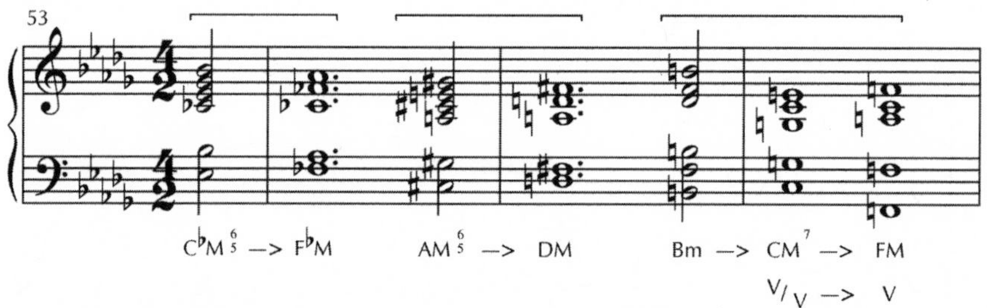

THE CODA: DETERMINATION AND RESOLUTION

The coda begins like the opening, but the violas now double the melodic line an octave lower. In most performances the two parts are balanced, but in others it sounds either like the violas are reinforcing the violins from below or the violas are being reinforced by overtones in the violins. This latter effect is apparent in the video recording of the Hong Kong Philharmonic performance mentioned earlier. Barber suggests "sordino ad lib." for all but the double basses. Stokowski called for mutes here but also liked to begin the piece with them. In a rehearsal with the American Symphony Orchestra he has the musicians play with mutes until the cello entry, which needed more sound. After the climax he urged the players to put mutes back on for the coda whenever they could.[49]

In the coda Barber now changes the second phrase of the melody for the only time in the piece. In Example 3.6 the phrase as seen at its first appearance (mm. 4-8) is aligned with this new version (mm. 60-64). The second phrase is essentially an inversion of the first: curving upward and over rather than downward and under, with the two coinciding at the end. Some listeners, at least at first, may not notice this change, but its rise to

[49]Leopold Stokowski, quoted in "Rehearsal: Leopold Stokowski," *Fanfare* (telecast 15 August 1971).

higher notes adds more pathos, even more poignancy to the phrase. The dynamic signs are placed a little differently, with the loudest part now coinciding with and reinforcing the rise to the new high G-flat.

Example 3.6. Phrase Alignment (mm. 4-8 and mm. 60-64)

Is there a psychological difference between these two phrases? Can any emotional content be imparted to them? Many listeners hear sadness in *Adagio,* whether it is intentional or not. Is there anything in the music itself that can lead to that conclusion? An author who believes in such ideas is Deryck Cooke, who, in *The Language of Music,* attributed different emotions to music based on specific melodic motives. His ideas were controversial when the book was first published (1959) and remain so today. While he did not provide excerpts from *Adagio* as illustrations, his principles can be employed to determine how they might apply to these two phrases.

The two chief segments of the first version of the melody are the small rising curve (1 - 2 - 3 - 1) in B-flat minor (the idea used motivically in the first phrase), followed by the descending scale passage, from the tonic to the dominant (8 - 7 - 6 - 5). Cooke maintained that the minor third is a "depressed" form of the major third and that "composers throughout the centuries . . . have expressed painful emotions by bringing the minor third into prominence."[50] In the exact form of this motive

> only moving out as far as the minor third, and returning immediately, is to "look on the dark side of things" in a context of immobility, neither rising up to protest, nor falling back to accept. Composers have frequently used this progression to express brooding, an obsession with gloomy feelings, a trapped fear, or a sense of inescapable doom.[51]

[50]Deryck Cooke, *The Language of Music* (London: Oxford University Press, 1959), 57-58.

[51]*Ibid.*, 140.

Extending this further, he commented about the descending scale:

> To fall from the tonic to the dominant, taking in the "mournful minor seventh" and "anguished minor sixth" is clearly to express an incoming painful emotion, an acceptance of, or yielding to grief; passive suffering; and the despair connected with death.[52]

Therefore Cooke's interpretation of the combination of motives in this phrase might be that it first arrives at a gloomy, immobile state but then yields to grief and despair. His comments expand the concept of resignation that I mentioned earlier into a more highly charged emotional territory.

By changing the second phrase the composer altered this emotional interpretation. The phrase begins with a variant of the "immobile" minor third motive (1 - 3 - 2 - 1) but then climbs upwards, stepwise, from tonic to dominant, curving over the sixth scale degree and descending again (1 - 2 - 3 - 4 - 5 - 6 - 5). Cooke claimed that this configuration (in the minor mode) "clearly expresses a powerful assertion of fundamental unhappiness —the 'protest' of 1 - 3 - 5 being extended into the 'anguish' of 5 - 6 - 5."[53] He particularly emphasized the 5 - 6 - 5 segment:

> The chief and almost only expressive function of the minor sixth is to act as an *appoggiatura* on to the dominant, giving the effect of a burst of anguish . . . one can hardly find a page of "grief" music by any tonal composer of any period without encountering it several times.[54]

If these views are accepted, then the first version of the phrase, so early in the piece, implies a passive complicity in accepting painful emotions (*i.e.*, resignation), but after such a wrenching musical climax, such complicity is no longer tenable. The second version now actively "protests" (*i.e.*, "determination") against the pain and the "despair connected with death."

Added to the feeling of determination are the two partial restatements of the composition's first phrase at the end of the coda. The first falls in the

[52]*Ibid*,. 162-63. Cooke printed examples that contain this descending passage, such as in Dowland's "Flow My Tears," where the text reinforces the sad context, and a theme from the final movement of Tchaikovsky's *Symphonie Pathétique*, where words are unnecessary to convey the tragic mood.

[53]*Ibid.*, 156. Here his examples are not as convincing, such as the main theme of Smetana's *Vltava* (*Moldau*) and the Israeli national anthem, *Hatikva*.

[54]*Ibid.*, 146.

same range and rhythm as the beginning, but the second is shifted down an octave and is rhythmically augmented. This double statement provides a sense of closure, a gesture that either produces Besedick's tonicization or reinforces Pollock's view of a Phrygian tonic. It is, at long last, a resolution of the ornamental 4 - 3 suspension that began the work.

The cadence is similar to one that ends many choral compositions by Palestrina and other Renaissance composers. In one form or another, it continued into the seventeenth century, concluding several string fantasias of Henry Purcell and even persisted into the nineteenth century, as in the ending of Robert Schumann's song "Auf einem Berg" from *Liederkreis,* Op. 37 (1840). While Barber's letters do not reveal a specific affinity to Palestrina, Kenneth Nott has discovered that the composer studied Purcell's fantasias around the time that he composed *Adagio*.[55] In addition, Barber admired nineteenth-century *lieder;* he undoubtedly knew and, perhaps, sang this particular Schumann song.[56] Example 3.7 compares the ending of *Adagio* with the final cadences of Palestrina's *Missa O sacrum convivium* (1593) and the Schumann song. While the ornamental resolutions are slightly different, all three allow the B-flat to move downward to the A, the third in the final chord.

Because it is textless, a Purcell fantasia obviously has no extra-musical connotation attached to the cadence. (Not illustrated here, it is virtually the same as Palestrina's.) Likewise, Palestrina's cadence, with its "Amen" stating "let it be," is still relatively textually neutral, a standard ending for sacred music that, in contrast to madrigals, does not attempt to depict the words (see, however, page 77). On the other hand, Schumann's cadence enhances the emotional meaning of Eichendorff's last line, "und die schöne Braut, die weinet" [and the beautiful bride weeps], with the concluding word coinciding with the resolution. Those who know this song may subconsciously carry over the weeping aspect into the ending of *Adagio,* something Barber himself may have thought of but would probably never admit.

[55]This cadence occurs at the end of Fantasias 3, 5, 9, plus in a few internal cadences. It also appears in Fantasia 2, in which a few missing notes were supplied by the editor Peter Warlock. Kenneth Nott describes several other similarities in "'Italian Primitives' and the Formation of Samuel Barber's Early Style," an unpublished paper delivered at a meeting of the Society of Seventeenth-Century Music (30 April 1994). Because this paper was not available for me to study, I am grateful to Barbara B. Heyman for pointing out some of Nott's findings.

[56]On a recital from December 1938, he sang "In der Fremde," the first song in this cycle (now available on CD: *Leontyne Price and Samuel Barber: Historic Performances*) and a few years earlier had memorized both the voice and piano accompaniment to Schumann's entire song cycle, *Dichterliebe*, Op. 48. See Barbara B. Heyman, *Samuel Barber* (1992), 103.

Example 3.7. Comparison of Closing Statements from Palestrina's *Missa O sacrum convivium*, Schumann's "Auf einen Burg" from *Liederkreis*, and Barber's *Adagio*

PALESTRINA: CREDO FROM *MISSA O SACRUM CONVIVIUM*

SCHUMANN: "AUF EINEN BURG," *LIEDERKREIS*, OP. 37

BARBER: *ADAGIO*

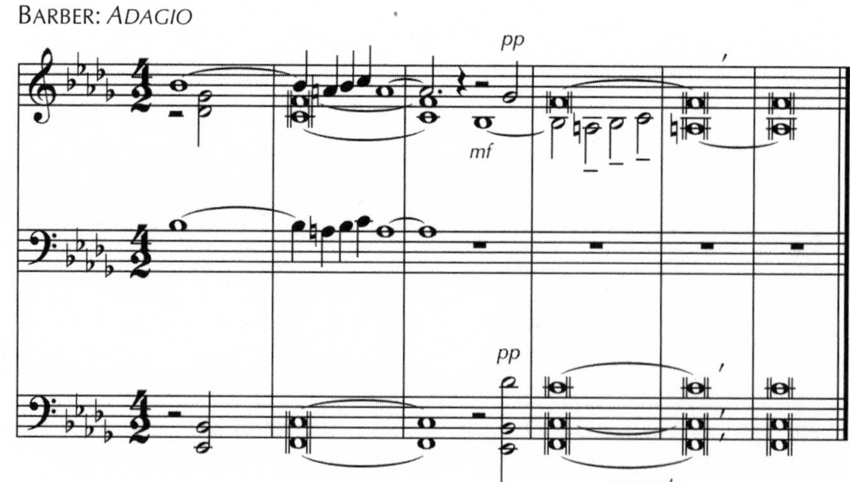

This double-phrase statement is also like the final sounds of the last movement of Gustav Mahler's Ninth Symphony, as shown in Example 3.8. Both composers take a short motive and augment it for its last statement. While Barber repeats the notes exactly, Mahler rearranges them, yet the effects are similar. Each composer emphasizes individual notes within the final phrase, Barber with *tenuto* marks and Mahler with accents. And finally, both composers let the phrase die away: Barber indicates his with *morendo,* and Mahler with *erstebend* on the final chord. Of course, Barber reaches his cadence after eight or nine minutes, whereas Mahler takes about a half an hour. As similar as these ending may be, it is unlikely that Barber cribbed from the Viennese master. Because Mahler's music was not especially in vogue during the 1930s when *Adagio* was composed, Barber may not have been aware of this or other of his works. To the best of my knowledge, there are no references to Mahler in any of Barber's correspondence, nor do Broder or Heyman ever mention him in their biographies. Two diverse composers from different times and countries probably allowed their romantic spirit to produce a similar sighing resolution.

This lower, broader transformation of the phrase enhances its sense of finality, and the *tenuto* mark on each note resembles a speaker's emphasis on the last words of a speech. It is no small wonder that, when storyteller Charlotte Blake Alston read passages from Martin Luther King's "I Have a Dream" speech to a performance of *Adagio* by the Philadelphia Orchestra, with conductor Thomas Wilkins on 12 January 2004 (and in later years), she articulated the last four words, "So - let - it - be," by making them coincide with these last four notes (see Chapter 10). While I may be reading too much into it, even without these words there seems to be a feeling of "Amen" at the end, just like the Palestrina example. The quasi-religious ending of *Adagio* later became a true religious ending in his Agnus Dei transcription, not with the word "Amen" but with "pacem," both words of quiet resignation. According to conductor Leonard Slatkin, *Adagio* is a "singing and searching piece. I feel as if it's a struggle for the melody to continually come out and when the work is over, you feel there's been a resolution to the melodic struggle that's gone on."[57] John Knight compared the ending to the curtain coming down at the end of a play.[58] Thomas Wilkins called it "the great exhalation," as if the audience

[57]Leonard Slatkin, "African-American Muslims," WBUR [Boston University] (broadcast 17 December 2001).

[58]John Knight, "Lessons in Interpretation from Toscanini," *Instrumentalist* XLVIII (December 1993), 20.

had been holding its collective breath through most of the piece.[59] Barbara Heyman summed up the impact of *Adagio* with this explanation: "it has a melodic gesture that reaches an arch like a big sigh . . . then exhales and fades off into nothingness."[60]

Example 3.8. Comparison of the Ending of Barber's *Adagio* and the Ending of Movement IV of Mahler's Ninth Symphony

BARBER: *ADAGIO*

MAHLER: SYMPHONY NO. 9, MOVEMENT IV

DIGRESSION: NOT WITH A WHIMPER BUT A BANG

Yet despite what most people consider a convincing final cadence, others feel a sense of closure earlier in the piece. For instance, when some pop musicians borrow *Adagio* for their own purposes, an extraordinary decision is occasionally made: some ignore the coda and finish with the conclusion of the climax, on that F-flat major chord, of all things! Two such instances are found in Steve Trovato's guitar arrangement and in Chris Snidow's synthesizer version (both are discussed in Chapter 7). I do not know Trovato's reason, but, when I asked Snidow why he ended his performance there, he replied, "I cut it off at the climax, just as a different approach; after all, it is the climax, and many people are not even aware

[59]Thomas Wilkins, email (25 January 2006) to the author.

[60]Barbara B. Heyman, *All Things Considered* [NPR] (broadcast 4 November 2006).

that there is a coda. I just wondered what kind of power it might evoke (or not) arranged like that."[61] He gives extra weight to his ending by adding a bass note to the final chord. I am still not convinced, however.

My first encounter with this musical abortion was a student dance performance at Butler University in Indianapolis. I did not attend the live performance, but, when I watched the videotape of it, I saw the solo dancer reach out ecstatically at the end of the climax as the lights quickly dimmed. I presumed that, when the lights came back up, I would hear the quiet chords and coda and would see her low to the ground in an introspective, inward position. But no, the next sight was the dancer taking her bows to the audience's applause. My jaw dropped. Whoever made this decision, student or supervising teacher, must have felt that this loud climactic chord, so far removed from the tonal center, sounded final. Neither this nor the other performances were confined by any time constraints; they could easily have continued to the end of the piece. Above all, ending at the climax completely contravenes the concept of the golden section, where the remainder of the piece allows the music to settle in before the conclusion. I think Barber would be appalled.

Do some people truly think that the piece is over at the climax? In live performances, do some members of the audience begin to applaud there? This is implicit in a comment from the musician known as Horse MacDonald, who remembers performing *Adagio* in a concert with the Scottish Chamber Orchestra in Glasgow when the audience applauded before the piece was over (she does not say exactly where). It seems not to have bothered her:

> But that's okay; it was the audience's spontaneous emotional response; and we shouldn't always be so rigid. And it is interesting to note that at first the orchestra and the conductor were a little irritated, but then they were actually rather pleased.[62]

Yet I doubt that the Australian choreographer Simon Hoy was pleased when a smattering of the audience attending his ballet *Submerged* at the Melbourne Ballet Company in August 2008 started to applaud after

[61]Chris Snidow, email (2 November 2004) to the author.

[62]Horse McDonald, "The Voice: Horse McDonald" (20 October 2002), www.lespres.de.102002/texte 102002/ horse.html. Thanks to Fred Yaniga for translation suggestions: "Was ich aber völlig okay finde, schließlich ist dies ein spontaner Gefühlsbeweis der ZuhörerInnen, den wir nicht unbedingt und immer reglementieren sollten. . . . Und interessanterweise war das Orchester, bzw. der Dirigent, zunächst ein wenig irritiert, dann aber höchst erfreut!"

the climax. Nothing in the choreography indicated that the dance had ended.[63]

In order to prevent this from happening, leaders of two performing organizations decided to stage a preemptive strike. For a performance of *Adagio* by the Imperial Symphony Orchestra, conductor Robert Whalen, fearing the possibility of applause after the climax, told a reporter, "I'm going to tell the audience beforehand, don't clap then. People think it's over, but it ends like it began."[64] In a similar way, for a performance of Agnus Dei, Barber's choral transcription of *Adagio*, by the Floral Park Long Island Sound, the announcer informed the audience that, after the climax on the word "*pacem*," there will be a grand pause. "We ask that you do not clap when this happens, for the music will continue."[65] He assured them, however, that they may applaud as much as they like when the director stepped down from the podium. Conductors can convince their listeners that more music awaits them, nonetheless, by their movement or lack of it on the podium. If they relax too much or pause too long, the audience will think the piece has ended.

In addition, conductors can maintain a certain tension in their bodies and, perhaps, move their arms slowly in preparation for the downbeat of the quiet chords, so the audience will realize that more music is yet on the way. Conductor Richard Auldon Clark explains: "I do keep my arms in the air to make everything freeze—any motion disrupts the drama."[66] Conductor John Larry Granger gave this cue directly to members of the audience at a performance by the Santa Cruz County Symphony in March 2010. Before the music began, he cautioned them to applaud only when his arms were "fully lowered"; as critic Phyllis Rosenblum noted in her review, "the music thus ebbed and flowed uninterrupted."[67] In a similar situation the members of a string quartet can convey to the audience that the Adagio movement is not yet complete by the way they hold their bows at the end of the climax. This is precisely what occurred in a performance by four members of the string section of the New York Philharmonic for the tenth anniversary commemoration of the 9 / 11 attacks. The pause

[63]"Submerged_Part 2," *YouTube* (27 August 2008), posted by simdhoy.

[64]Robert Whalen, quoted in Cary McMullen, "Masterworks Honors NASA's 50th Anniversary," *The* [Lakeland, Fla.] *Ledger* (16 March 2008).

[65]"Samuel Barber Agnus Dei Adagio for Strings," *YouTube* (26 May 2008), posted by Metsthr.

[66]Richard Auldon Clark, email (30 November 2011) to the author.

[67]Phyllis Rosenblum, "Symphony Soloist Shines in Tchaikovsky Piece," *Santa Cruz* [Calif.] *Sentinel* (1 April 2010).

after the climax was longer than usual, but no one in the audience was tempted to clap because the musicians held their bows stationary in preparation for the quiet chords.[68]

Applause following the climax may occur because of extenuating circumstances, as in the Wilkins-Alston performance mentioned earlier. Wilkins, who coordinated the Martin Luther King readings with the music, timed the performance so that the line, "free at last" would occur during the silence after the climax. Alston recalled, "it had such power that the audience burst into applause and shouts even though the piece was not over."[69] This must have happened the following year as well; Alston remembers: "once again the audience (and, I later found out, stage hands) got swept up in the emotional energy of the *Adagio* and text and were on their feet before we even finished."[70] In a different situation, when the Santa Clara Vanguard, a California drum and bugle corps, presented parts of *Adagio* in its performance, fans broke out in wild cheers at that climactic chord. That was primarily due, however, to how long they held the chord and the intensity with which they played it (see Chapter 5).

Such a view of *Adagio* also carries over into other aspects of pop culture. One favorite medium these days is *YouTube*, a website where aspiring videographers can devise their own images set to whatever music they want. When Barber's *Adagio for Strings* is used, it is sometimes presented only up through the climax. Like the performances mentioned above, these videographers must feel that the music's climax provides a perfectly fine ending. Again, there is no real time constraint; the full *Adagio* is well within *YouTube*'s time limitation.[71]

Why do these things happen? Is it because we usually want music to end on a big bold sound? We have all attended concerts when some members of an audience begin to applaud when they think a piece is over, often incurring scowls from others who know better. Applauding at the end of an internal movement of a symphony is somewhat the same, (e.g., the end of the third movement of Tchaikovsky's *Pathétique* Symphony), but at least that is more excusable because the individual movement itself

[68]See "Insights Series: In Times of Strife: Music Responds (Part 6)," *YouTube* (12 September 2011), posted by NewYorkPhilharmonic.

[69]Charlotte Blake Alston, email (13 October 2005) to the author.

[70]Charlotte Blake Alston, email (17 January 2006) to the author.

[71]See "Cold Bed Time Lapse Digital Painting Workshop," *YouTube* (5 February 2007), posted by PimpOfPixels; "Supernatural–Adagio for Strings," *YouTube* (23 January 2007), posted by nya1121; "Pegasus: A Tribute to the Beast," *YouTube* (24 October 2006), posted by usmc1944; and "Metal Gear Solid 3–Horrors of War," *YouTube* (30 September 2006), posted by Dielon241.

sounds conclusive. Of course, audiences watching an opera or ballet clap any time they feel like it, whether it is appropriate or not.[72]

METER AND TEMPO: JUST HOW SLOW IS ADAGIO?

The meter for *Adagio* is mainly 4 / 2, plus an occasional measure of 5 / 2 or 6 / 2. While these metric changes may make the score look more "modern," the tempo is slow enough that most listeners are not aware of them. Rather than producing a Coplandesque irregular rhythm, these metric changes, especially the 5 / 2 measures, merely build in pauses. Barber's choice of the half note as the beat, with quarter-note subdivisions, however, sometimes causes tempo problems. Why did Barber notate the movement with the half note as the beat rather than the quarter note, as he had established in his brief sketch?[73] Orlando Cole, cellist in the Curtis String Quartet and the artist who premièred Barber's Cello Sonata, may have had the answer. He recalled that Barber liked the look of long-note values on the page, especially a constant stream of quarter notes. Barber may have admired that look in some of the "early music" compositions he had studied, *e.g.*, in Josquin motets and Purcell fantasias and in the then recent symphonies of Sibelius.[74] Cole had encountered a similar situation with Barber's Cello Sonata, a work that he had premièred shortly before Barber began composing the quartet. While preparing his master's thesis, Igor Scedrov interviewed the cellist and asked him if he ever made any suggestions to Barber during the composition of the Cello Sonata. Cole referred to a change from manuscript to final print:

> He originally wrote the Scherzo movement in 12 / 4 time. I said to him, "it is so hard to read when you get something like this. If it is all quarter notes, you don't know where the beat is." And it also makes it look as if half notes would be quite slower than they

[72]Both situations applied to the performance of Mahler's Second Symphony at the 9 / 11 Memorial Concert of the New York Philharmonic (11 September 2011). Some members of the audience applauded not only at the end of the first movement but also about three-quarters of the way through because they thought the piece had ended. The music was merely beginning the recapitulation. Because of this, however, the tonal movement had returned to the tonic, making this *faux pas* somewhat more understandable. Some sense of tonal closure must have registered in the minds of these attendees. On the other hand, applauding after the F-flat major chord in Barber is basically inexcusable.

[73]See Chapter 2.

[74]Most modern editions of Josquin's mensural music are transcribed in half-note beats. Warlock's transcription of Purcell's fantasias are largely cast in 4 / 2 meter. And Barber's analysis of Sibelius's Seventh Symphony, occurring earlier in the same sketchbook containing the Adagio fragment, shows several flowing quarter-note passages.

would be, of course. So, in the original manuscript I changed them to eighth notes, and he followed that suggestion.[75]

At first Barber protested, "the quarter notes looked so pretty, just a whole string of [them]." But Barber took Cole's advice and in the published score, changed the meter to 12 / 8 with a string of eighth notes replacing the quarters. Barber may have had this "pretty" string of quarter notes in mind when he notated *Adagio*. If someone such as Cole had suggested a 4 / 4 meter, with streams of eighth notes rather than quarters, the composer might have complied by simply returning to his earlier notational concept. It might have spared listeners some of those slow tempos often heard in performances. On the other hand, the 4 / 2 meter may contribute to what Howard Pollack calls "an elusive sense of downbeat," giving the "impression of a spacious unmetered flow."[76] It is tempting to treat the quarter note as the beat rather than the half note, that is, to think in "8" rather than "4." For that reason, some arrangements of *Adagio* (e.g., Rosen's piano version) halve the meter into 4 / 4 with the quarter note as the beat and eighth notes as the subdivision.[77]

The best performances are those in which the conductor keeps the half note as the beat, which was Toscanini's approach. The beginning tempo on his commercial recording is approximately 𝅗𝅥 = 44-48, close to Barber's own metronome marking in his string quartet manuscript: 𝅗𝅥 = 54. John Knight observed that this tempo "allows the music to breathe with only subtle fluctuations. To enhance the 4 / 2 meter, Toscanini used a legato four-beat conducting pattern instead of the subdivided four-beats that many conductors use today."[78]

Adhering to this approach is conductor John Kennedy. When he led *Adagio* at a memorial concert for Gian Carlo Menotti at the 2007 Spoleto Festival in Charleston, South Carolina, he maintained a flowing half-note pulse in the performance. He asserted, "While the tempo marking is Molto adagio, because the root tempo is the half note (in 4 / 2), the quarter note

[75]Orlando Cole, quoted in Igor Scedrov, *A Study of the Reciprocal Relationship between the Composer and Performer in Selected Works for the Cello by Samuel Barber, Elliott Carter, and Charles Wuorinen* (D.M.A. thesis, Temple University, 1994), 12. In *Samuel Barber: A Thematic Catalog* (2012), 116-17, Barbara B. Heyman illustrates both the original manuscript versions and the copy in which Cole has added beams to the quarter notes.

[76]Howard Pollack, "Samuel Barber, Jean Sibelius, and the Making of an American Romantic," *The Musical Quarterly* (2000), 195.

[77]Samuel Barber, *Adagio for Strings*, arr. Lawrence Rosen (New York: G. Schirmer, 1987).

[78]John Kennedy, "Lessons in Interpretation from Toscanini," *Instrumentalist* XLVII (December 1993), 16.

theme is therefore not glacial but has an internal movement that wants to exert motion and elegance."[79] Others prefer to conduct the quarter note as the beat, which is evident on some video recordings, such as Jose E. Iglesias presiding over the Carnot Chamber Orchestra. There the tempo is indeed "glacial."[80] A quarter-note pulse may even be detected on audio recordings when the playing seems stodgy. Yet that may be more the musicians' fault than the conductor's. Sometimes a compromise can be worked out. In the video clip of Leonard Slatkin directing *Adagio* for his *Concert for America* (see Chapter 9), he conducts mostly by the half note but reverts to the quarter note at the end of some phrases, probably to achieve smoother cadences. As Richard Auldon Clark expressed it: "Most of the piece should be conducted by the half note, but there are just a few moments when a subdivision of the beat provides better clarity and ensemble precision."[81]

Naturally the tempo affects the total length of the performance. In the published score to *Adagio,* Barber suggested a timing of seven to eight minutes. Yet it is amazing, even astounding, to learn the range of times on many recordings of the work.[82] Barber would probably be pleased that almost half the performances listed in Appendix 3, including Toscanini's, meet his suggested range of timing, but he might be surprised, as many are, that over half do not. He might consider the short recordings by Mario Bernardi (ca. 5:52) and Antonio Janigro (5:57) "rushed," whereas he might think Bernstein's long performances (ca.10:00) "draggy." Alan Kozinn referred to the Bernstein reading as "flabby and distended," with a tempo at "a snail's pace."[83]

How can there be such a wide variation in tempo? Bernstein's is almost twice as slow as Bernardi's, but considering the former's emotional temperament, it is not unexpected that he would stretch out the work and make the most of every nuance of phrasing. In addition, a conductor's tempo may be a result of the circumstances of the performance; that is, a slow tempo might reflect the solemnity of a particular occasion. Critic John Ditsky suggested, for instance, that Bernstein's performance of *Adagio* with the Los Angeles Philharmonic was intended as a personal tribute to

[79]John Kennedy, email (18 June 2007) to the author.

[80]"Adagio for Strings Samuel Barber," *YouTube* (10 June 2007), posted by maurogofreedom.

[81]Richard Auldon Clark, email (30 November 2011) to the author.

[82]See the table of performance durations by forty-three ensembles in Appendix 3.

[83]Alan Kozinn, "Samuel Barber: The Recordings," *High Fidelity*, 67.

Barber shortly after his death—"to convey his so-longs to Sam."[84] While this may warrant a slow tempo, no such occasion justifies the same tempo with the New York Philharmonic a decade earlier. Bernstein apparently viewed *Adagio* as slow and sustained whether he meant it as a memorial or not. Ditsky was convinced that this dragging out process "almost causes the rhythm and texture to evaporate before our ears."[85] It sounds as if Bernstein was "challenging the orchestra to prevent the sundering of Barber's splendid score into its discrete pieces."[86] Luckily, the orchestra succeeded, but just barely, in preventing this from happening. Composer / conductor John Adams is highly critical of Bernstein's tempo, which he considers "murderously drawn out," making *Adagio* into "something it emphatically is not."[87] When conductors take such an extremely slow tempo, they—in Adams's words—"think they can say something special about the music. But more often than not, they are only saying something uncomfortably revealing about themselves."[88] Those who agree with Adams may take the viewpoint that this is Bernstein's *Adagio* rather than Barber's.

Likewise, when Leonard Slatkin performed *Adagio* with the BBC Symphony Orchestra shortly after the 11 September 2001 tragedies, he matched his tempo to the solemn occasion; it was considerably slower than the first recording he made with the St. Louis Symphony Orchestra. In fact, the BBC *Adagio,* lasting nearly ten and a half minutes, may be the slowest performance ever, three minutes longer than his earlier St. Louis recording. Yet his second recording with the same orchestra from 1988 was already nine minutes long (as was his performance with the National Symphony Orchestra, only a few days after his BBC performance). Rather than the specific occasion determining the tempo, perhaps Slatkin has rethought the work, preferring to emphasize the long, sustained lines.

On the short side is Ormandy's recording with the Philadelphia Orchestra (6:20), which is somewhat surprising because it never sounds rushed; neither do the performances by Stokowski (6:25 and 6:34). The fastest tempo for *Adagio* that I have ever heard in a live performance was one at Hunter College in 1999 by the New York Virtuosi Chamber

[84]John Ditsky, "Record Reviews," *Fanfare* VII (November 1983), 183.

[85]*Ibid.*

[86]*Ibid.*

[87]John Adams, "Do as I Say, Not What I Do (or Maybe Not)," *Hell Mouth* (13 May 2010), www.earbox.com/post/82.

[88]*Ibid.*

Symphony, directed by Kenneth Klein, as part of a Barber Festival. As I was there simply to enjoy myself, I did not time the performance, but it could not have lasted more than five minutes or so. Critic Alan Kozinn approved of the tempo: "the Adagio, in particular, was taken at a pace brisk enough to avoid the danger of mawkishness."[89] No danger of that, but what about being over-eager ("haste makes waste"), brash ("let me catch my breath for a second"), or even perfunctory ("let's get it over with")? It was a cold, emotion-starved whirlwind that left me exhausted and unsatisfied when it was over.

On the Radio

Adagio for Strings is so popular that radio stations constantly schedule it in their daily programming, apparent from the various playlists provided on the Internet. One reason it is heard so often is that it meets the criteria for an ideal radio piece. Dave Bunker, who has spent many years as a program director at public stations, gave a rationale for choosing classical music.[90] One goal is maximum variety within greater unity. A diversity of musical texture, period, and scale must occur "within a greater unity of selections that are consistently melodic, accessible and immediately pleasurable to the average music listener."[91] This is virtually a catalogue description of *Adagio*. Its melodic quality and broad popularity attest to its accessibility and the pleasure it gives to both the sophisticated and the average listener. Another rule of thumb is "use the short stuff." About one-third of the pieces on Bunker's "morning" playlist are shorter than five minutes, and another third are under twelve. Short pieces mean more programming and possibly more variety. "In the morning," moreover, implies that people want something short early in the day, perhaps while driving to work. *Adagio,* with its average length of seven or eight minutes, falls neatly into this category. I am not certain, however, that I would feel comfortable stranded in a traffic jam when *Adagio* reaches that climatic phrase.

These criteria may contribute to the frequency with which *Adagio* is heard on classical radio. In the Introduction I provided a brief list of the work's presence on several stations during the period of just a few weeks. The following discussion addresses its radio play in special circumstances,

[89]Alan Kozinn, "Critic's Notebook; Listeners Love Samuel Barber? Well, So What," *The New York Times* (8 June 1999), E: 1.

[90]Dave Bunker, "Music That Changes the Day–for *Enough* Listeners," *Current* (20 September 1999); reprinted www.current.org/rad/rad917b.html.

[91]*Ibid.*

primarily national broadcasts, beyond its status as a classical disc jockey's filler. Some programs offer either a live performance of *Adagio,* taped for broadcast, or a foreign recording not usually marketed in the United States. For instance, in May 1995 National Public Radio's *Performance Today* presented an "American-German musical cooperative venture" with a performance taped in Germany by the Saarbrücken Radio Symphony Orchestra conducted by Joseph Swensen. Another performance occurred on 19 January 2001 with Ransom Wilson leading the Solisti New York Chamber Orchestra. Similar tapes of live *Adagio* performances were selected for two BBC radio shows designed for insomniacs or other late night listeners: *Through the Night* (Radio 1) and *Euroclassic Notturno* (Radio 3). From 2004 through 2006, both shows featured performances by the Netherlands Radio Symphony Orchestra with conductor Richard Dufallo, the Bulgarian National Radio Symphony Orchestra with conductor Milen Nashev, and I Cameristi Italiani.

Adagio for Strings has been given a prominent place on what might be termed a "Barberfest," where a program or series of programs provides many or all of the composer's recorded works in historical perspective. The most ambitious of these efforts comes from the Harvard University radio station, WHRB. For decades this station has broadcast *A Musical Orgy*® during reading and exam periods, honoring many composers by playing recordings of their complete works in chronological order. Barber was finally given his own "musical orgy" on 23 May 2005. (This may also have occurred years earlier but programming details that far back are sketchy.) The station played all of his works for nineteen continuous hours from 5:00 A.M. to around midnight. All three versions of *Adagio* were aired: the String Quartet by the Emerson String Quartet (ca. 7:00 A.M.), *Adagio for Strings* by Bernstein and the New York Philharmonic (ca. 8:30 A.M.), and Agnus Dei by Robert Shaw (shortly before 9:00 P.M.). To the general listener who may consider Barber a "one-hit wonder" because of the popularity of *Adagio,* the other works probably came as a revelation.

In a similar but less thorough manner is Bill McGlaughlin's *Exploring Music* (nationally syndicated from Chicago's WFMT radio station), where he assigns a whole week (one hour per day, Monday through Friday) to a specific topic, sometimes the music of a single composer. During the week of 19-23 March 2007 he devoted the show to the music of Samuel Barber. A one-minute excerpt from *Adagio for Strings* (the New York Philharmonic with Bernstein) began the first show as general introduction. In a voice-over McGlaughlin told his listeners that, "even if you don't go to concerts very much, you probably know *Adagio* from motion pictures."[92] In a promo for the program he indicated that the title of the series, *The World of Samuel Barber,* implies that the composer wrote many more pieces than *Adagio for Strings.* In other words, his "world" encompasses a wide variety of music, stretching far beyond *Adagio.* Then for the five-episode program, he scheduled many works (some neglected), essentially in chronological order, but never the full orchestral version. The complete String Quartet, interpreted by the Emerson String Quartet, however, was played on the second show. Near the end of his introduction McGlaughlin declared that Barber "left us a marvelous body of wonderful, lyrical, Romantic pieces of music, which somehow seem a little out-of-tune with the more dissonant times in which Barber lived."[93]

In a narrower context Barber's *Adagio* has often been heard in single-episode "theme shows," where it fits a specific topic. Occasionally Karl Haas featured the work on his long-running program *Adventures in Good Music.* Each month he presided over "Name the Composer" (otherwise known as the "Mystery Composer Quiz"), where he played pieces by a single composer and invited the audience to guess his or her identity. The gimmick was to start with a composer's least known or least characteristic piece and proceed until the compositions became more familiar. One month, when the composer was Barber, Haas started with the waltz from *Souvenirs* (1952), not a very typical piece, and then logically concluded with *Adagio* (Academy of St. Martin in the Fields). The score also began another episode, "Lest We Forget," the Memorial Day program of 2004, and was programmed again on "A Sigh of Belief," an episode devoted to slow movements of works that "tend to make us believe that there is a better world out there." Another time it appeared on "Twentieth Century Surprises," with compositions from that century that "actually"—and "surprisingly"—have a melody! In a similar way, after playing *Adagio* on "Liberty and the Pursuit of Notes" Haas reiterated, "Who said the twentieth century didn't produce any melodies?" This is a patronizing approach because, despite the show's title, Haas rarely played any work remotely adventurous. On another program, "Self-contained Dependence," he offered the Adagio from the String Quartet as an example of a movement from a multi-movement work that can stand on its own.[94]

[92]Bill McGlaughlin, *Exploring Music* [WFMT Chicago] (broadcast 19 March 2007). The five-show series was repeated in August 2008.

[93]*Ibid.*

[94]"Lest We Forget" and subsequent shows were broadcast on ABC Classic FM as early as 28 May 2001; "A Sigh of Belief" as early as 14 May 1997; "Twentieth Century Surprises" as early as 2 June 1999;

In addition to presenting a full week of Barber's music on *Exploring Music,* Bill McGlaughlin has included both *Adagio for Strings* and the slow movement from the String Quartet on individual theme week shows. One week his topic was "An Intelligent Conversation," tracing the evolution of the string quartet.[95] He derived the title from a comment by Goethe, who proposed that listening to a string quartet was like listening in on an intelligent conversation. By the final episode, the program had reached the twentieth century, which included the Adagio from Barber's Quartet (again, by the Emerson String Quartet). McGlaughlin contended that it expresses something that cannot be put into words, echoing a phrase from J. Peter Burkholder's liner notes for the Emerson recording: "A sense of suspension or slowed down time creates an impression of deep feeling that can scarcely be born, like inexpressible grief."[96] A passage from Adagio was played during McGlaughlin's closing comments. The host also turned to the orchestral *Adagio* (Ormandy and the Philadelphia Orchestra) for his show during the week titled "I Hear America Singing" (first aired, July 2005, and again in 2006 and 2007), featuring not only vocal works by American composers but also instrumental works of a lyrical nature. Again, *Adagio for Strings* fit the show's theme.

A brief excerpt from *Adagio* has been featured with commentary on *Composers Datebook,* a daily public radio "filler" germane to a specific date in music history. Each program observes "significant or intriguing musical events" with "appropriate and accessible music related to each." For example, *Adagio* appeared on 5 November 2001, the sixty-third anniversary of its première (the program has been recycled for the same date in other years). Inexplicably, a performance by Semyon Bychkov and the Berlin Philharmonic was featured instead of the Toscanini recording. Host John Zech mentioned, erroneously, that *Adagio* was played at Roosevelt's funeral and, correctly, that it appeared in *Platoon.* He then quoted Ned Rorem: "If Barber later aimed higher, he never reached deeper into the heart."[97] With the program lasting only two minutes, obviously only a few phrases could be played. On the program for 6 August 2002 *Adagio* was paired with Krzysztof Penderecki's *Threnody for the Victims*

"Liberty and the Pursuit of Notes" as early as 13 March 1998; "Self-contained Dependence" as early as 4 March 1999.

[95]First broadcast in March 2005, and rerun several times after that.

[96]J. Peter Burkholder, liner notes to *American Originals: Ives & Barber, String Quartets*, perf. Emerson String Quartet (Deutsche Grammophon, 435 864-2, 1993).

[97]Ned Rorem, *A Ned Rorem Reader*, 238.

of Hiroshima (1960). Although both are written for string orchestra, they could hardly be further apart in style. For the anniversary of the bombing of Hiroshima, the Penderecki piece makes sense, but why *Adagio?* Zech considered it a "threnody for America's war dead."[98] Thus both pieces, in this context, were regarded as sharing a similar goal.[99]

With Narration

In addition to full performances of *Adagio for Strings,* sometimes a portion of it is adopted as background music, *i.e.* underscoring narratives. This is its role in a radio commentary near the end of an episode of Tom Ashbrook's *On Point* on 17 December 2001. Guest Leonard Slatkin explained why "in times of tragedy" many ensembles play it:

> I suspect it has to do with the solemn nature of the music. . . . There's a simple melodic line that goes on the top. There's no complexity of counterpoint at all; it's simply one melodic line played with chordal structure of a very conservative nature underneath. But the bottom line is that the work is filled with emotion. . . . So the work itself in being thought of for sobering occasions has the feeling of struggle, but at the same time resolution, which is something we all seem to need.[100]

Adagio was played throughout the segment, through the climax but not through the coda. (To stop there was probably not Slatkin's decision.)

On another occasion, *Adagio* accompanied Wilfred Owen's moving anti-war poem "Dulce et decorum est" on *Sound and Spirit,* a radio series from WGBH (Boston). The episode "To End All War," broadcast on 2 November 2003, anticipated the upcoming commemoration of Armistice Day (now known as Veterans Day), 11 November 1918, the date that World War I officially ended. As narrator Ellen Kushner read the second half of the poem, the quiet chord passage (Lawrence Foster and the Orchestre Philharmonique de Monte Carlo) faded in and continued through the coda. Its war association (e.g., as music in *Platoon*), made it

[98]John Zech, *Composers Datebook* (6 November 2002).

[99]On 14 December 2003, and again on 2006, the program, "Barber in Rome," marked the anniversary of the first performance of Barber's String Quartet, by playing the Tokyo String Quartet recording. *Adagio* has also appeared on NPR's *SymphonyCast* and *America in Concert.*

[100]Leonard Slatkin, quoted in "African-American Muslims," WBUR [Boston]. Transcripts from an audio file can be found on www.wbur.org/special/specialcoverage/diaries.asp. The Slatkin segment has nothing to do with the main topic of Ashbrook's radio show and is simply an addendum.

an appropriate and effective backdrop for Owen's brutal depiction of the Western Front. He conveys in vivid, unforgettable phrases that, if one could watch "white eyes writhing," "blood come gargling from the froth-corrupted, obscene lungs," and "incurable sores,"

> My friend, you would not tell with such high zest
> To children ardent for some desperate glory,
> The old lie: Dulce et decorum est
> Pro patria mori.[101]

The Latin phrase is taken from one of Horace's odes. "It is sweet and proper to die for your country" is a platitude once taught to British school children, which Owen now realized is blatantly untrue. (The phrase out of context does not do justice to Horace's original thought, however. He continued, "it is even sweeter to live for your country.") The reality of war changed Owen's perspective: nothing was sweet or proper about the gruesome reality he witnessed. Ironically, after being wounded several times, he died just seven days before the armistice was signed. "Dulce et decorum est," especially when enhanced by *Adagio,* is a moving anti-war polemic.

In 2004 former commander of the United Nations Assistance Mission in Rwanda, Lieutenant-General Roméo Dallaire, testified at the war crimes trial of Theoneste Bagasora, the man accused of masterminding the 1994 genocide in Rwanda. That month CBC radio devoted its *Dispatches* to an interview with him, entitled *"Adagio for Strings* and Genocide." What is the connection? In a passage from his book *Shake Hands with the Devil: The Failure of Humanity in Rwanda,* Dallaire linked the atrocities and the music:

> As I write these words I am listening to Samuel Barber's Adagio for Strings, which strikes me as the purest expression in music of the suffering, mutilation, rape and murder of 800,000 Rwandans, with the help of the member nations of the only supposedly impartial world body: the United Nations.[102]

[101]Wilfred Owen, "Dulce et decorum est," *War Poems* (New York: New Directions, 1963), 55.

[102]Roméo Dallaire and Brent Beardsley, *Shake Hands with the Devil: The Failure of Humanity in Rwanda* (New York: Carroll & Graf, 2004), 322.

The show's producers, perhaps at Dallaire's suggestion, accompanied these words with an excerpt from the Barber piece. Later, when he read another passage from his book about his encounter with leaders of the group responsible for most of the killings, the Interhamwe militia, *Adagio* was again played in the background:

> I had my first meeting with the leaders of the Interhamwe. Arriving at the [Diplomat] Hotel I took the bullets out of my pistol just in case the temptation to shoot them was too extreme. The three young men introduced to me had no particular distinguishing features. I nearly lost my composure when I noticed that the middle guy's open-collared, white shirt was spattered with dried blood. There were more small flecks on his right arm, as we shook hands. What a sick event![103]

At the end of the meeting he confided, "I felt I had shaken hands with the devil." Because he had expressed his views on *Adagio* earlier, it made sense to insert a segment of it to intensify the impact of these words.

A few months later *The Connection* (WBUR Boston) presented two programs on 21 and 22 April 2004 about the Rwandan Genocide. This time *Adagio* was never actually mentioned but functioned as introduction, interludes, and conclusion. The first program, "Roméo Dallaire," began with the opening of the piece while host Dick Gordon talked about the genocide. Much of the program was devoted to his interview with Dallaire, plus listener call-ins. Twice Gordon stopped the conversation for a break, with *Adagio* fading in and out. The show concluded with *Adagio*'s climactic phrase. The second program, "The Women of Rwanda," related their plight during the genocide and addressed their determination and courage. Gordon quoted from Dallaire's book describing "the death masks of the raped and sexually mutilated girls and women; women who died in a position of total vulnerability."[104] *Adagio* functioned in this program in the same way as the first.[105] Would Barber have approved of the use of his music for such horrific associations?

[103]*Ibid.*, 345-47. This is an abridged account from his book. The radio program is archived at cbc.ca/dispatches/thisseason.html.

[104]*Ibid.*, 430.

[105]Both programs are available on www.theconnection.org/shows/2004/04/20040421_b_main.asp. *Adagio* also appears at the beginning of the 2005 documentary film, *Shake Hands with the Devil: The Journey of Roméo Dallaire*, based partly on his book but with footage of his return to Rwanda ten years later. See Chapter 8.

In August 2004 the presidential campaign was heating up, especially concerning John Kerry's Vietnam War record. Due to its association with the movie *Platoon, Adagio* resumed its Vietnam War status by closing the final portion of the NPR news show, *Here and Now.* Host Robin Young had asked writers Tim O'Brien and Stanley Karnow why they thought that "Vietnam's ghosts still wander the campaign trail."[106] Closing the segment with *Adagio* was not only logical, it needed no explanation. Even twenty years after *Platoon,* for many people *Adagio* signifies music for the Vietnam War.

On the Television

The Barber *Adagio* is programmed frequently on classical radio stations because of their dependency on recordings to fill out many hours of broadcasting, often twenty-four hours a day. Classical music on television is another matter entirely. The main networks used to telecast classical music concerts and operas during the 1950s and 1960s but then relegated that task to educational television, National Education Television (NET) and its successor Public Broadcasting Service (PBS). At one time, cable channels, such as A&E and Bravo, showed promise to supplement the presentation of classical music but have since capitulated to commercial interests. Even on PBS, classical music has been reduced to a few concerts a year. With such hit or miss telecasting, *Adagio* has not fared well in this environment. Out of all the years of concerts on television, I can find only three that featured it: one in rehearsal and two in the circumstances of a recorded performance.[107]

Leopold Stokowski conducts the American Symphony Orchestra in "Rehearsal: Leopold Stokowski," a program telecast on the NET series *Fanfare* (15 August 1971), the second of two parts devoted to a few days in the life of the famous maestro in early 1968. He talks to people, travels around New York City, and rehearses the orchestra in preparation for a concert in Madison Square Garden. On the program he rehearses several works, including *Adagio for Strings.* As is usual in rehearsals, he frequently starts and stops the piece to advise the musicians and to strive for the sound he wants. The orchestra has its shaky moments and late entrances, but the viewer can hear how the piece begins to take shape in his hands. After several interruptions, however, he allows the orchestra to play

[106]Robin Young, *Here and Now* [NPR], www.here-now.org/shows/2004/08/20040826.asp.

[107]Other performances of *Adagio* on television—for drama or comedy—will be discussed in Chapter 8. Its contribution to a dance performance on CBS's *Camera Three* will be cited in Chapter 5.

through to the end. Naturally, this read-through lacks the polish and continuity of one of his recordings, but it does give a glimpse of what a Stokowski performance might be like. At the end he tells the musicians "not very good. Do better tomorrow." The orchestra must have improved in time for the concert (2 February 1968) because according to critic Harold C. Schonberg, "everything went smoothly."[108]

A complete performance of *Adagio* can be found on a program by the Philadelphia Orchestra conducted by Luis Biava, its resident conductor in the 1990s. It was telecast live from the newly restored Media Theater in Media, Pennsylvania on 18 October 1996. The announcer introduces the performance by declaring, "Considered by many as a romantic gem, the *Adagio* has a deep emotion under the surface that touches the heart as well as the spirit. But its directness and unaffected pathos could only have been captured by an American."[109] The performance itself is lovely and worthy of the string sound for which the Philadelphia Orchestra is so celebrated.

NEBRASKAland Symphony: The Road Home is a "chamber of commerce" type concert celebrating the state of Nebraska, produced by Nebraska Educational Television (NET) and telecast over KUON, the local PBS station in Lincoln during the 2000 season.[110] It consists of American music, coordinated with vintage photographs and old film clips related to the landscape and people of Nebraska. The Lincoln Symphony Orchestra, under Edward Polochick, establishes various stages of a thematic journey with music: The Land (an excerpt from Dvořák's "New World" Symphony), The Dream (movements from Copland's *Rodeo*), Disillusionment (a full performance of *Adagio for Strings*) and The Road Home (a reprise of the "New World" Symphony as well as music by Leroy Anderson). Dressed in a casual sweater and sitting in a comfortable armchair, then Senator Robert Kerrey delivers the narration.[111] Because it is so often associated with sad occasions, *Adagio* functions in the "disillusionment" segment, fittingly depicting the Depression of the 1930s and Nebraska's struggle during the "dust bowl." A generous portion of the narrative was taken

[108]Harold C. Schonberg, "Music: In Caverns Echoless to Man," *The New York Times* (3 February 1968), 21. The television program is not commercially available on tape or DVD.

[109]The entire concert including an intermission feature is available on VHS tape as *Bridging the Silence* as well as the audio portion on compact disc.

[110]The program was videotaped for television broadcast but has not become commercially available. I was able to view it via inter-library loan from Doane College. Another copy is located at the University of Nebraska at Kearney.

[111]Kerrey served as governor of Nebraska (1983-1987) and represented the state as a United States senator (1989-2001).

from the works of Willa Cather (1873-1947), but in order to introduce the *Adagio* segment Kerrey reads passages written by American author and photographer Margaret Bourke-White (1904-1971).[112] The passage accompanying the opening of Barber's music describes the dust storms:

> Vitamin K they call it—the dust which sifts under the door sills, and stings in the eyes, and seasons every spoonful of food. The dust storms have distinct personalities, rising in formation like rolling clouds, creeping up silently like formless fog, approaching violently like a tornado. Where has it come from? It provides topics of endless speculation. Red, it is the topsoil from Oklahoma; brown, it is the fertile earth of western Kansas; the good grazing land of Texas and New Mexico sweeps by as a murky yellow haze. Or, tracing it locally, "My uncle will be along pretty soon," they say: "I just saw his farm go by."[113]

The final phrase of this passage appears to be a common joke during the period, not originating with Bourke-White. Because it is more ironic than funny, no one in the audience laughed.

The photographs and film clips shown during the *Adagio* performance vividly portrayed this tragic time in mid-America during the 1930s: images of dry, arid land, stunted corn stalks, sad faces at soup kitchens, and anti-Hoover demonstrations. This was no time for upbeat Copland music; only Barber's *Adagio* was suitable. The audience applauded at the end of all other pieces of music on the program but remained reverently silent for *Adagio*'s conclusion. Barber wrote this music during the time of the dust bowl but was geographically distant and emotionally detached from it. The music, nonetheless, almost seems as if it had been composed for a depiction of this bleak era specifically.

In addition to these American performances, *Adagio for Strings* has also been heard on at least two European television networks, one French and the other British. During 2007 it was selected for the French program *Presto* (France 2) featuring Orchestre les Siècles under the direction of François Xavier Roth. During the performance the narrator Pierre Charvet gives a running commentary. The score itself, nevertheless, is strangely

[112]Philip Heckman, credited as narration editor, presumably selected the various passages.

[113]Margaret Bourke-White, "Dust Changes America," *The Nation* CXL/3646 (22 May 1935), 597-98. She was one of the leading news reporters of the twentieth century but is known today primarily for her photographs, many of which appeared in *Life* (magazine). "Vitamin K" is not the vitamin identified in the 1920s but the term some people gave to dust blowing in from Kansas.

edited. The music skips from the tenth measure to rehearsal [2], and the coda is totally wrong! It begins simply as a repeat of the opening two phrases from the beginning, which, of course, eliminates the newer added sound of the violas doubling the melody. But more importantly, it ignores the significant recasting of the second phrase, discussed earlier. The piece, nonetheless, proceeds to the final cadence as usual. Such shameful editing seems completely unnecessary and certainly unwarranted because the performance itself is rich and warm and, if left alone, would be a pleasant listening experience.[114]

In 2008 the British Broadcasting Corporation telecast six episodes of *Maestro*, in which famous guests got a chance to fulfill a secret desire to conduct an orchestra. On the episode "Music for Film and TV," actor David Soul (Hutch of *Starsky and Hutch*) conducted an "extract" from Barber's *Adagio for Strings*. In addition to the live conducting of the music, the show also supplied clips of the rehearsals. During one of these, Soul commented: "I have to stay on top of the technique and give the space and room and the invitation to the players so that the reaction is felt with an audience."[115] He then conducted his passage. The performance was a bit shaky—one judge recalled a "train wreck"—but Soul managed to get through it. Critical evaluation and comments by the judges were generally favorable; they liked the sound that he created and his connection with the piece. And yet one thought that his conducting interfered with the music. His score (22 points) was insufficient to keep him on the program.

In the Concert Hall

ADAGIO AS PART OF A THEME PROGRAM

There need not be a specific justification to include *Adagio for Strings* on an orchestral concert. On a generic program, it might function as the token twentieth-century work—a short, easy-to-digest piece for audiences too timid to accept the more dissonant sound of Ives or Bartók. *Adagio*, nevertheless, may be selected to satisfy a general theme, such as an all-American program or part of a commemoration.

All-American concerts are often scheduled around the time of national holidays, as part of a feel-good patriotic spirit. For instance, the New York Philharmonic performed *Adagio for Strings* on its post-Independence Day celebration in 2006. On one occasion Leonard Slatkin included it on a

[114]"Adagio of Barber," *YouTube* (5 May 2009), posted by goldmund55.

[115]David Soul, quoted in "Music for Film and TV," *Maestro* [BBC] *Television*, 2008.

concert of American music in 1991, during the tense time of the Persian Gulf War. In a remark to the audience he suggested that the program was not only intended to honor worthy American composers but also to send "red blood coursing through the veins of patriots."[116] In July 2004 Charles Ansbacher conducted the Boston Landmarks Orchestra in "Landmarks of Freedom: Of the People, By the People, For the People," a gala featuring primarily American works, including *Adagio*. The orchestra performed this program at six different venues around the Boston area; the one at Harvard University was designated as part of the Democratic National Convention.

Adagio has also been invoked to celebrate diverse anniversaries—from the founding of the United Nations to the establishment of the city of Williamsbsurg, Virginia to an observance of the new millennium. In August 1995 the strings of the Asia Youth Orchestra performed *Adagio* on a program as a "prayer to peace for the 50th Anniversary of the United Nations." The orchestra consisted of musicians from Hong Kong, China, Japan, Taiwan, Korea, Vietnam, and other countries—"places that 50 years ago, and since, have been at war. Yet today they are making music together."[117] Reporter Victoria Finley recalled, "there was, as requested, no applause when [they] laid down their bows at the end of Samuel Barber's haunting *Adagio for Strings* . . . just awestruck silence . . . as shivers ran down the spines of many of the people assembled . . . the symbolic element was touchingly clear."[118]

On 1 May 1999 Leonard Slatkin conducted the National Symphony Orchestra in a concert at the College of William and Mary, celebrating the 300th anniversary of the founding of the city of Williamsburg, Virginia. The event consisted of several American pieces, notably Barber's *Adagio*. For once there was no funereal tinge to this performance, but instead a spirit of celebration generated by one of the most beloved pieces of American music. In this instance, *Adagio* represented both a part of a celebration and an example of American music.

I Virtuosi Italiani, a string ensemble of about fifteen performers from Modena, played a concert at the Duomo di Monza in Milan, one of several that the Pope sponsored for Jubilaeum 2000 to celebrate the

[116]Donal Henahan, "Review/Music; A Rousing, All-American Program to Stir the Blood," *The New York Times* (6 April 1991).

[117]Victoria Finley, "Asia's Symphony to Peace," [Hong Kong] *South China Morning Post* (27 August 1995), 2.

[118]*Ibid.*

millennium. It began with *Adagio,* directed, but not conducted by Philip Murton.[119]

ADAGIO GOES POP

Adagio for Strings has become such a favorite among both serious concert-goers and popular music lovers that it now sometimes is chosen for pops concerts. *Adagio*'s contemplative mood is often a respite among the other livelier pieces. For instance, in June 2000, Giancarlo Guerrero conducted the Cabaret Pops of the Minnesota Orchestra in "Classical Thunder 2000," with *Adagio* taking its place alongside Mussorgsky's *Night on Bald Mountain* (1867) and Wagner's "The Ride of the Valkyries" (1856).

Great Britain's Royal Philharmonic Concert Orchestra found its own way to upgrade the pops concert tradition by presenting "Here Come the Classics." No pop tunes at all, just "classic" pops pieces (*i.e.*, classical warhorses) ranging from the Overture of Rossini's *Guillaume Tell* (1829), which invariably begins such a program, to Ravel's *Boléro,* (1928), which usually ends it. *Adagio* is often included somewhere in between.

The Dallas Symphony Orchestra has taken the classics approach a step further by presenting its "Choose the Music" concerts. Each year for its Audi Pops Series, conductor Richard Kaufman asks the orchestra's patrons to select the repertoire. In 2003 he received hundreds of requests. The list was first narrowed to fifteen selections and then to seven with *Adagio for Strings* among them.

Just as some compact disc recordings are devoted to classical music in the movies, so are concerts where people can hear their favorite movie music live, an ideal theme for a pops concert, such as "Music from the Movies" (June 1992) by the Texas Music Festival Orchestra, and the Chamber Orchestra of Philadelphia (February 2002), both of which included *Adagio.*[120] The Buffalo Philharmonic often presents the series "Jeans and Beer," coupling a program of casual classics with casual attire. In May 1994 *Adagio* was part of a film music program "Jeans and Beer Goes to the Movies." For a costume party afterwards, people came as favorite movie characters, *e.g.*, Scarlett O'Hara and the Tin Man. I wonder if anyone dressed in army fatigues as Charlie Sheen in *Platoon.*

At least two orchestras coordinated its movie theme selections with movie footage projections: the Honolulu Symphony Orchestra, conducted by Sam Wong, in "Masterworks: Film Style" (November 2002), and the

[119]*Enrico Castiglione Presents the Jubilee Concerts* [DVD].

[120]For additional performances of this nature, see Appendix 3.

Utah Symphony, conducted by Kurt Bestor, in "Night at the Movies" (2003). Critic Carma Wadley wrote that the Utah performance made one long for the days when live orchestras accompanied films and reflected, "it made you appreciate what music does for film and how very visual sound can be."[121] In both cases audience members could be reminded of their experience seeing *Platoon* for the first time by watching appropriate scenes during the performance of *Adagio for Strings*.

BARBER WITH STRANGE—AND NOT SO STRANGE—BEDFELLOWS

The most logical companions to *Adagio for Strings* on concerts are other Barber works, resulting in a mini-Barberfest. They are typically presented as separate pieces, but for a concert by the Pittsburgh Symphony Orchestra, Leonard Slatkin devised a "pseudo-symphony" consisting of an opening movement, the familiar and popular Overture to *The School for Scandal* (1931), followed by *Adagio* as the requisite slow movement, and ending with *Medea's Dance of Vengeance* (1956) as its dramatic finale. The reaction of audience members was confusing: they were confused, and they applauded at the end of each "movement" as if they were separate pieces (which, of course, they are).

When *Adagio* is played at an all-American concert, its most constant comrade is Copland's *Fanfare for the Common Man* (1942), a work so far removed from Barber's in terms of orchestration and aesthetics that the pairing produces a contrasting and formidable "odd couple."[122] An even less likely companion is the Ives *Unanswered Question* (1906), a pairing that conductor David Robertson made on his Memorial Day Concert in May 2009. Yet, as critic Alan Kozinn observed, both works are "thoughtful scores that promote sober introspection."[123] The Ives work led directly into Barber's without a pause for applause. Kozinn concluded that the "nebulous, piannissmo string writing at the heart of the Ives . . . seemed to melt into Barber's more sumptuous textures."[124] The conjunction of this even odder couple (Barber = Felix; Ives = Oscar), furthermore, might have caused Barber great consternation. He once complained, "I can't bear Ives. . . . In my opinion he was an amateur, a hack, who didn't put

[121]"Bestor's 'Night at the Movies' Is a Hit," [Salt Lake City, Utah] *Deseret News* (17 May 2003).

[122]Neil Simon's *The Odd Couple* (1965) was a Broadway hit, a feature film (1968), and a television situation comedy (1970-1975) featuring two divorced men living as roommates in a Manhattan apartment.

[123]Alan Kozinn, "Stately Works Befitting the Fallen," *The New York Times* (26 May 2009). The concert took place at the Cathedral of St. John the Divine in New York City.

[124]*Ibid.*

pieces together well."[125] Yet, despite potential posthumous objections on Barber's part, this melting together of two generally accepted American masterpieces proved to be, in Kozinn's words, "a brilliant touch."[126]

On such All-American programs *Adagio* tends to be flanked by "serious" works, such as these compositions by Copland and Ives. At New York's Bottom Line nightclub on 8 February 1983, however, David Amram presented a combination concert-seminar on American music, "Americana —from Gershwin to Monk," where *Adagio*'s companions were works from the world of pop music and jazz.[127] Amram has long advocated giving equal artistic weight to classical, jazz, pop, and ethnic music. He led a performance of *Adagio* along with his own "Brazilian Memories," Scott Joplin rags, and jazz interpretations of tunes by George Gershwin. How might Barber have reacted to the inclusion of his Adagio in this jazz-pop conglomeration? He seems not to have made observations on Joplin's music, but his opinion of Gershwin is revealed after attending a concert in Vienna at the Musikvereinsaal, where he was invited to "hear an entire evening arranged by the American government of Gershwin—a highly overrated composer who only sounded childish in these surroundings."[128] As for jazz, he once wrote, it "is not really supposed to be edifying. You listen to jazz with feet or snapping fingers, not so much the ear."[129] There may be, however, hints of Joplin in Barber's *Souvenirs* (1953) and a touch of Gershwin in the *Excursions* (1944), and one might be tempted to snap one's fingers at the beginning of *A Hand of Bridge* (1959). On the other hand, *Adagio for Strings* is very much "ear" music and indisputably edifying.

Sometimes *Adagio* is assigned to the same program with a highly contrasting piece of music, such as Morton Gould's *Tap Dance Concerto* (1952) or an orchestrated version of Anton Webern's early Five Movements for String Quartet, Op. 5 (1929).[130] But that simply makes for a diversified listening experience, not a meaningful pairing. More significant is the deliberate matching of *Adagio* with another specifically chosen work,

[125]Samuel Barber, quoted in Philip Ramey, "Samuel Barber at Seventy; The Composer Talks about His Vocal Music," *Ovation* I/3 (March 1980), 18-19.

[126]Alan Kozinn, "Samuel Barber at Seventy," *Ovation* I/3 (1980), 19.

[127]This nightclub was a venerable venue for all kinds of music in New York City for thirty years.

[128]Samuel Barber, letter (8 March 1951) to Sidney Homer, quoted in Barbara B. Heyman, *Samuel Barber* (1992), 232 (footnote).

[129]Samuel Barber, quoted in Barbara B. Heyman, *Samuel Barber* (1992), 238.

[130]For additional performances of this nature, see Appendix 3.

where each member of the pair reinforces the other, and the sum is greater than the parts. Such is the case in two clever pairings on programs led by Andreas Delfs.

Delfs, Milwaukee Symphony Orchestra's music director, is known for inventive programming. To "challenge and enlighten his audience," he played Arnold Schoenberg's *A Survivor from Warsaw* (1947) twice on a program on 18 September 1998 with *Adagio for Strings* "sandwiched between."[131] Schoenberg's work for orchestra and men's chorus requires a narrator, in this performance, the experienced actor and opera singer Monte Jaffe. Schoenberg's text, depicting the tragedy of Jews in the Warsaw Ghetto during World War II, uses material from original letters and memoirs. Delfs stated that *Survivor* was "too intense to digest in one hearing. I want people to get something out of it."[132] He evidently considered *Adagio,* with its various war associations, complementary to that work. For a transition from the first playing of *Survivor* into *Adagio,* Delfs composed a short klezmer-style transition passage for solo clarinet. This passage is an extension of the final part of *Survivor,* "Sh'ma Yisrael, Adonai Eloheinu" [Hear, O Israel, the Lord is our God], the Jewish prayer that the prisoners sing on their way to the gas chamber. Critic Tom Strini observed that the clarinetist "made of its bent tones the dying protest of a crushed soul; if Job played the clarinet, it would have sounded like this."[133] Strini is aware that *Adagio* can be a "real tearjerker, but Delfs and the MSO strings brought to it a sublime calm. Its overwhelming climax was not a cry of pain and anguish but a transcendent vision of light."[134] Another critic, Melinda Bargreen, observed that *Adagio* seemed like an "extended meditation" by Schoenberg's narrator / witness.[135]

In 2004 Delfs brought this concept to the Seattle Symphony, where *Adagio* was again placed between two performances of *A Survivor from Warsaw,* but this time the second playing was staged differently. The narrator, again Monte Jaffe, appeared in traditional tails for the first rendition, but for the second "I walked up a short stairway to the stage as if emerging from the audience, wearing an off-the-rack grey suit, white

[131]Robert Croan, "Good Ideas and Insights Are All Around," *Pittsburgh Post-Gazette* (9 March 1999), D: 4.

[132]Tom Strini,"Symphony to Fill '98-99 with Harmonic Convergences," *Milwaukee Journal Sentinel* (14 February 1998).

[133]Tom Strini, "Survivor from Warsaw a Triumph," *Milwaukee Journal Sentinel* (19 September 1998).

[134]*Ibid.*

[135]"Seattle Symphony Returns with Solemn, Timely Concert," *Seattle Times* (10 April 2004).

shirt and yarmulke and spoke the words again."[136] It is as if the narrator now recollects in old age, the events of the Holocaust from his youth; after fifty years he still remembers and is still a survivor.

Jaffe considers it an honor to be a part of this "powerful" combination of musical works. In his opinion:

> While Barber's *Adagio* conveys innocence and naïve beauty, it also expresses the unbearable pain and sorrow caused by man's inhumanity to man. Schoenberg's *A Survivor from Warsaw* is almost too powerful to perform. I am a Jew and was born in the United States. Had I been born in Europe, this work could have been about me. It is certainly about my family and about all victims regardless of race or religion. It is the sound of murder and horror but also the sound of courage and, even in dying, an unshakable belief in God.[137]

Stories told by the surviving members of Jaffe's family about the Holocaust undoubtedly contributed to the emotional way he recited Schoenberg's words.[138]

Critics were impressed with the results. Indeed, Tom Strini called the performances "gripping, and the juxtapositions left us with much to think about. Like this program or not, it was impossible to sit through and drift; it had to be engaged."[139] Philip Kiraly concluded, "the whole was intensely moving, and orchestra and chorale responded to Delfs by performing with all the emotion he requested."[140] If there were any Holocaust survivors in the audience, they were probably moved to tears.

What might Barber have thought of the pairing of such seemingly contrasting works? He did not hold a high opinion of Schoenberg's music in general. After hearing a 1955 concert featuring works by the Viennese composer (he does not specify which), Barber wrote in his travelogue that his style was "a little middle-aged and flaccid."[141] It is difficult to imagine,

[136]Monte Jaffe, telephone interview (23 July 2006) with the author.

[137]Monte Jaffe, email (23 June 2006) to the author.

[138]Monte Jaffe, telephone interview (23 July 2006) with the author.

[139]Tom Strini, "Cue Review '98: 10 Music and Dance Shows to Remember," *Milwaukee Journal Sentinel* (24 December 1998).

[140]Philip Kiraly, "Symphonie's Superb Program Incites the Emotions," *Seattle Post-Intelligencer* (10 April 2004).

[141]Samuel Barber, Travelogue (1955), quoted in Barbara B. Heyman, *Samuel Barber* (1992), 356.

nonetheless, that Barber would describe *A Survivor from Warsaw* as being flaccid. He might even have approved of this dramatic juxtaposition. No one will ever know.

Delfs continued his inventive programming in June 2005 by placing *Adagio* between two Gustav Mahler songs. Bass Eric Owens performed "Revelge" (1899) and "Der Tamboursg'sell" (1901) from *Das Knaben Wunderhorn,* in which "jaunty military accompaniment rings bitterly ironic against the ghastly events related in these old German poems."[142] Delfs interpolated *Adagio* between the songs because, as Strini puts it, "it has taken on a pacifist aura" ever since it appeared in *Platoon*. *Adagio* and the songs were also compatible musically: both songs are in a minor mode, with "Der Tamboursg'sell" emphasizing a rising minor third motive much like *Adagio*. The *Adagio* portion was intensified by a slide show by Sean McBryde with pictures of protagonists of non-violent protest, such as Mahatma Gandhi, Martin Luther King, Jr., Nelson Mandela, and Lech Walesa. This enhancement "drove the point home and turned the *Adagio* into background music."[143] As in the Schoenberg-Barber juxtaposition, this pairing undoubtedly made an emotional impact on the audience.

ADAGIO FOR A WORTHY CAUSE

The somber, meditative nature of *Adagio* makes it appropriate for programs that promote various causes, such as awareness and education about AIDS and the remembrance of those who have lost their lives. "ARTcetera '90" was an art auction by the AIDS Action Committee of Boston in November 1990 at which a candlelight ceremony honored members of the arts whose deaths were AIDS related. While *Adagio* played, Liz Page, one of the auction's founders, read many of their names, including photographer Robert Mapplethorpe, fashion designer Halston, and choreographer Choo San Goh. A concert featuring gay composers was dedicated to the memory of founding member Michael Dash.[144]

Adagio has been selected on several programs for the homeless. In February 1996 the Arlington [Va.] Symphony performed it on a benefit for the Arlington-Alexandria Coalition for the homeless. In December 2001 Catholic University and the National Shrine for the Immaculate Conception sponsored a charity concert at the Basilica of the National Shrine to help New Endeavors, an organization that supports homeless

[142]Tom Strini, "4 Famous Notes Are Just the Beginning," *Milwaukee Journal Sentinel* (17 June 2005).

[143]*Ibid.*

[144]For additional performances of this nature, see Appendix 3.

women in the Washington, D.C., area. Piotr Gajeski led The Catholic University Symphony in a performance of various pieces, among them, *Adagio for Strings*. In December 2003 Larry McDonough played a jazz piano arrangement of *Adagio* on 18 December 2003 at the nineteenth "Annual Homeless Memorial Service" for the Simpson Housing Service of the Minneapolis area. During the candle-lighting segment names of the 101 homeless people who had died in Minnesota during the past year were read, and people shared memories of them.

ADAGIO IN CONTEXT AND THE STRING QUARTET REDUX

While Barber's String Quartet remained in the repertoire of some ensembles over the years, it was not performed nearly as often as the orchestral transcription. Nathan Broder argued, "The popularity of this movement in the version for string orchestra has resulted in an undeserved neglect of the Quartet."[145] During the 1950s the only recording available was the one by the Stradivari Quartet. In fact, when later releases came out, reviewers often had to remind readers that the Adagio movement was the initial version of the work they knew and loved as *Adagio for Strings*. Now that *Adagio* has become even more popular due to its use in movies, memorial services, and other endeavors, there has also been a renewed interest in the original version. More recordings have recently become available, and many string quartets now program it.[146]

Many critics and record reviewers agree that it is good—or at least interesting—to hear *Adagio* in its quartet setting. For instance, when Conrad Wilson heard the Lindsay String Quartet's performance of the entire work, he concluded, "for all its fame as an elegiac morceau, Barber's *Adagio* makes its strongest impression in the place where it belongs—inside his early string quartet, where its textures sound less soupy, and the other movements, both of them fast and edgy, throw its rueful serenity into high relief."[147] In his notes to the Duke String Quartet recording, Robert Maycock points out the significance of the Adagio movement as it is placed between the outer two. Adagio is

> the contemplative response to a highly dramatic opening movement in which vigorous and lyrical themes struggle for

[145]Nathan Broder, *Samuel Barber*, 74.

[146]A list in Appendix 3 identifies recordings—first in the LP format, then in the CD format—of either the complete String Quartet or only the Adagio movement.

[147]Conrad Wilson, "Eloquence Restored Lindsay String Quartet, Queen's Hall, Edinburgh," *The* [Glasgow] *Herald* (15 November 1994), 24.

> supremacy without finding more than a temporary answer. And the slow movement itself turns out to lead straight into a resumption of battle, revisiting some of the initial thoughts as though in the light of experience, and accelerating towards a terse resolution.[148]

Yet not all critics are convinced. Richard D. Freed admitted that the Adagio movement, as played by the Beaux-Arts Quartet, "tends to overshadow the substantial allegro that precedes it and the tiny one that follows it."[149] Royal S. Brown is even less persuaded, as he expressed in his review of the Cleveland Quartet recording:

> It would be nice to be able to report that the outer sections of Barber's String Quartet are worthy of the famous Adagio movement. Unfortunately, this is not the case . . . the first movement comes on basically as a choppy mishmash of pedestrian rhythmic figures and surprisingly ordinary (for Barber) themes, while the final movement . . . does little but restate the material in an even more perfunctory manner. In this setting, the gloriously flowing, long-phrased, and decidedly melancholic Adagio stands out even more strongly for the masterpiece it is.[150]

Robert Croan, reviewing a Tokyo String Quartet performance, takes a somewhat middle position:

> It was pleasant to hear the adagio as the composer first conceived it—sparsely but no less forceful in its emotional message. The allegro movements that surround it are not quite so inspired, but the present rendition was at times exciting, at other times, eloquent. The outer movements contained high drama, setting off the reposeful adagio in high relief.[151]

[148]Robert Maycock, liner notes to *The Duke Quartet*, perf. The Duke String Quartet (Collins Classic, CDC 1386-2, 1993).

[149]Richard D. Freed, "Diamond Comes Home," *The New York Times* (26 December 1965), B: 21.

[150]Royal S. Brown, "Classical," *High Fidelity* XXVI (October 1976), 110.

[151]Robert Croan, "Tokyo Quartet: Adept and Predictable," *Pittsburgh Post-Gazette* (19 April 1994), D: 2.

The problem with hearing the full quartet is not that the Adagio movement relieves the tension of the opening jarring material, it is the return of some of that material that nullifies the relief. It is just as if a tranquilizer has suddenly worn off and returns a person to his or her previous nervous, agitated state. Commenting on the "furious and violent" aspects of the first movement, Steven Ritter queried, "after the sublime Adagio, who wants to be bothered with all that again? I have always felt that this is [the quartet's] primary weakness."[152] What if Barber had retained his original third movement? His dissatisfaction with it is well known, but its lighter, more dance-like atmosphere might have been a better alternative. Or he might have tried harder to come up with a more gratifying ending.

One frequent solution is to play or record only the Adagio movement, the part audiences want to hear. It allows listeners to enjoy a favorite piece in the chamber music setting minus the "extraneous" movements that surround it. In 1990 the Emerson String Quartet recorded the entire work for their album, *American Originals*, but included only the adagio movement on their later album, *Emerson Encores*. Of course, it is the nature of that kind of album to excerpt single movements from works on previous albums. It is almost as if the string quartet movement is now considered a chamber music arrangement of the orchestral piece. In fact, one reviewer, writing a critique of a string quartet performance got things backwards: "while deeply moving, the original arrangement for a larger group—a string orchestra—seems to work better than this one for quartet, however."[153] For that author, the cart comes before the horse and the chicken before the egg.

[152]Steven Ritter, a review of *The Philadelphia Connection*, perf. 1807 & Friends (Direct to Tape Recording, DTR 9303, 1999), "Guide to Records," *American Record Guide* (March-April 2000), 70. In 2010 the Ying Quartet resurrected and performed the original third movement instead of Barber's short recapitulation-style coda.

[153]Mel Wilhoit, "Choral Arts Remembers" (30 October 2006), www.chatanoogan.com/articles/article95687.asp. The performance was given by the Chattanooga Symphony and Opera Strings Quartet.

Adagio for . . . Just about Everything: Transcriptions, Arrangements, and Other Transmogrifications

> On the one hand, Barber's masterpiece is so perfectly written for strings it's difficult to hear it another way. On the other hand, what's wrong with some first-rate musicians . . . having a go at one of classical music's most sacred works?
>
> —Tom Manoff, on the NPR program, *All Things Considered* (4 October 2001).[1]

This judgment illustrates the typical dilemma of how musicians view a transcription or an arrangement: for some it is an abomination; for others, an opportunity. For better or worse, *Adagio* has been re-invented for many different performing forces, pushing it beyond the confines of the string quartet or string orchestra. In the case of transcriptions the piece remains very much intact, indeed as a re-instrumentation. This often means a change of key, and occasionally it requires an instrument to play one or more of Barber's phrases in a different octave. The piece as a whole, however, remains basically the same. In an arrangement the music is altered, if only slightly. In some of the following examples *Adagio* is considerably shortened. Yet there is often a fine line between the results of these two approaches to adaptation. For the last examples addressed in this chapter, in which the work is radically transformed, I reserve the term "transmogrification." In 1967 Barber himself contributed to the transcribed repertoire with his own choral treatment, Agnus Dei for mixed chorus and optional piano or organ.

Agnus Dei

THE TRANSFORMATION

Author and critic Walter Simmons described the orchestral *Adagio for Strings* as a "pseudo-Renaissance motet" containing a motif that is developed "pseudo-polyphonically" with dissonances derived primarily from suspensions, appoggiaturas, and cross relations.[2] With a similar

[1]Tom Manoff, review of a recording of *Adagio* on *Daydream*, perf. The Washington Saxophone Quartet, *All Things Considered* [National Public Radio] (4 October 2001).

[2]Walter Simmons, *Voices in the Wilderness: Six American Neo-Romantic Composers* (Lanham, Md.: Scarecrow Press, 2004), 274.

viewpoint Harper Garson, in his notes for the Stradivari String Quartet album, suggested that the slow movement creates "an almost liturgical atmosphere."[3] By adding a Latin text the composer has transformed his *Adagio* into an even grander pseudo-motet with an even more prominent and emphatic "liturgical atmosphere": an amalgamation of sixteenth- and twentieth-century details. He may, indeed, have been influenced by Renaissance motets and Masses, a repertory he knew from his conducting a madrigal group at the Curtis Institute, for which he transcribed an "Ave Maria" by Josquin des Prez.[4] In his master's thesis Stephen T. Besedick observed that the melodic movement in *Adagio* is primarily stepwise while leaps are often countered by movement in the opposite direction, highly reminiscent of the vocal style of Renaissance Masses and motets, those by Palestrina particularly.[5] This describes the Agnus Dei as well.

CD Track 4

For his choral setting Barber [P] retained the original meter and key signature and suggested with a footnote in the score that, "if the chorus is large and expert enough, the piece may be sung *a cappella*."[6] If not, he provided an organ or piano accompaniment, which is strictly a transferal of all the vocal parts, neither a reduction of the texture nor an independent keyboard part. While this accompaniment is feasible for the piano and might be practical for rehearsals, it is almost impossible to play on the organ, even with the bass line relegated to the pedals. Although Barber did not specifically state it, he presumed that the organist would use both an 8′ and 16′ stop for the pedals at the beginning of the work but did note that the 16′ stop must come off at Figure [3], when the basses have the melody. During this passage the tenors are singing below the basses (just as the violas are sounding below the cellos in the orchestral version); a 16′ stop would ruin the texture. As for the manuals, two hands cannot possibly grapple with all the doublings and wide stretches that the score requires. As a result, the organist faces an enormous task and is obligated

[3]Harper Garson, liner notes to *Stradivari String Quartet* (Naxos Classical Archives, 9.80942, 1951).

[4]Barbara B. Heyman, *Samuel Barber: The Composer and His Music* (New York: Oxford University Press, 1992), 180.

[5]Stephen T. Besedick, *Samuel Barber's Cantilena Slow Movements: A Study of Textural Relationships* (M.M. thesis, Florida State University, 1986), 33.

[6]Samuel Barber, *Agnus Dei* (New York: G. Schirmer, 1967), 2. For the sake of expedience, the details concerning the recordings and publications cited in this chapter can be referenced in Appendix 4. The presence of the code [P] indicates that the music under discussion has been published. The code [R] indicates the availability of a recorded performance on compact disc. The reader is invited to consult that appendix for details concerning published scores and a classified discography.

to make many compromises, working out all kinds of details well ahead of time. If accompaniment by organ is needed, why not utilize Strickland's solo organ transcription—it is cast in the right key and meter—and then make a few adjustments? (Strickland's version is discussed later in this chapter.) The first phrase of Barber's accompaniment, Strickland's more practical organ transcription, and my own stab at simplification are aligned for comparison in Example 4.1.

Example. 4.1. Comparison of Accompanimental Figures

Pity the poor organist who must fumble for all those keys in the second measure of Barber's version. Actually, even Strickland's transcribed lines could be further simplified. Because he wanted the melody to stand out, he assigned it to the right hand, playing on the "Great" manual; the rest of the chord must be played with the left hand on the "Choir," which has a more subdued registration. In Barber's choral scoring, an organ, providing only an accompaniment for a choir, need not make this distinction; two voices can be played on the Great, and the other two on the Choir, as illustrated in my hypothetical example. I have not heard a performance or recording with organ accompaniment, perhaps because of the logistical difficulties, but, if the problems could be solved, the combination of choral and organ sonorities might be highly effective.

When Barber conceived the work for strings, he faced no worries about sustaining long notes, but for a choral setting he realized that voices are limited in this ability. He therefore advised that, again by means of a footnote in the score, "the various individual singers on each part should breathe at different places, especially in the long phrases and held notes, in order to achieve a more sustained quality."[7] This concept of "staggered breathing," so often necessary in choral singing, is best achieved if the choir is a large one. When the Milwaukee Symphony Chorus performed Agnus Dei, reviewer Rick Walters commented that "It helps to have nearly 200 singers when tackling the forever-long phrases."[8] Those phrases were also smoothly tackled by the Mormon Tabernacle Choir (ca. 330 voices) during its 1998 European tour in a performance at the Basilica at the palace of El Escorial just outside of Madrid, Spain.[9]

For smaller groups those forever-long phrases could pose problems. The Cambridge University Chamber Choir [R], led by Timothy Brown, is normally a group of twenty-eight singers; when it recorded Agnus Dei, each section was augmented to bring the total up to forty-one. Brown must have realized that he needed more singers to sustain the sound.

One group that bravely attempted the work with eight unaccompanied vocalists is the Waverly Consort in its program "Revelation 1000-2000: Music for the Millennium." The intimate chamber sound makes it more closely resemble a Renaissance motet, an admirable goal for a group that normally performs "early music." On the occasions when this approach succeeded, critics and audiences alike approved of the chamber sound. One critic observed that "the ensemble singing was gorgeous throughout,

[7]*Ibid.*.

[8]Rick Walters, "Seat Time," *Shepherd Express* (4 November 1999); reprinted www.shepherd-express.com/shepherd/20/45/night-and-day/in-review.html.

[9]Mormon Tabernacle Choir, "Barber: Agnus Dei," *YouTube* (8 March 2007), posted by jrtapia.

notably in the sustained harmonies of Barber's Agnus Dei."[10] Yet there must have been shaky moments in some performances, for another critic complained that the eight voices "were either not enough or the singers didn't make effective use of staggered breathing. As a result, depth and poignancy were lost in choppy sounds and weak dynamics."[11] Yet staggered breathing is hardly a viable option for eight singers. In many of its pieces the Waverly Consort employs Medieval and Renaissance instruments; perhaps adding them to Agnus Dei would not only have supported the vocal sound but would also have put an interesting "early music" spin on their performance.

Yet, even for mid-size ensembles who sing the piece *a cappella*, this choral rendition still presents many difficulties and is more challenging to sing than audiences realize. Dale Warland, who has directed his singers in the work, explained:

> In 1967, Barber recast [*Adagio for Strings*] and, though he chose not to, could have called it "Adagio for Voices." In this choral transcription, Barber mostly gave the individual string parts to their appropriate vocal counterparts—for instance, the first violin line to the sopranos—shifting the parts where necessary to avoid vocal strain. That said, though, this is a tremendously difficult work. The violinist can draw the melody unbroken throughout, but the singer obviously has to breathe. The challenge is not to lose the tensile melodic pull that is the heart of this music. It is a high-wire act, demanding steel lungs, extraordinary control, and faultless confidence.[12]

Mitzi Westra, a singer in Warland's ensemble at the time, conceded that it would have helped if each member "had an extra pair of lungs."[13]

Range is another problem. Although the shifting of range of some parts and the creation of certain doublings are handled reasonably well, there are a few awkward places. Of course, because the string version

[10]Marc Shulgold, "Ensemble an Enticing Blend of Old, New," *Rocky Mountain News* (4 March 2000), A: 64. Mormon Tabernacle Choir, "Barber: Agnus Dei," *YouTube* (8 March 2007), posted by jrtapia.

[11]S. L. Guthrie, "Waverly Consort Program Excites Millennium Fever," *Anchorage Daily News* (16 November 1999), D: 4.

[12]Dale Warland, liner notes to *Cathedral Classics* [R].

[13]Mitzi Westra, conversation (6 May 2006) with the author.

goes much too high for any group of voices, Barber occasionally shifted phrases down an octave, especially at the ascent to the climax. If the organ is used, two low pedal notes support the climax well. He may have borrowed this effect from Strickland. Realizing that a phrase with a high C-flat (m. 12) is beyond the range of most choral soprano sections, he assigned it to a soloist who has to sneak in and then disappear almost as quickly, merging back into the soprano section. (There are some programs and recordings that actually give this singer a solo billing!) The recording by the Crouch End Singers [R] employs enough high sopranos that, instead of relegating the top line to a soloist, the soprano section is divided into two parts. The first sopranos contend bravely with the phrase, but with rather uneven results. In Spain the Mormon Tabernacle Choir, which could easily subdivide the sopranos, still retains a soloist at that point.[14]

Frankly, I tend to get somewhat nervous at this point when I hear an Agnus Dei performance. I have yet to hear a soprano who successfully negotiates this challenge; it is always a bit of a strain. Even after this phrase the first sopranos must eventually rise to high A-flats and B-flats, belting out that climatic cadence. Good luck! In notes for the recording with the New College Choir, Oxford [R], conductor Edward Higginbottom admitted that "the setting pushes the voices to the limits, not only of their range but also of their expressive endurance."[15] Transposing the piece downward might have solved some of these problems, but then the poor basses, who already have to sing a low D-flat, would have to contend with even lower notes. Any resolution would probably have meant a complete rewriting of the whole texture. Such vocal problems are not typical of Barber's choral music in general. When he composed music originally intended for choir, such as *Reincarnations* (1940) or *Prayers of Kierkegaard* (1954), he wrote much more logical and singable vocal lines that seldom require special techniques or laborious vocal efforts.

Keeping the pitch constant is difficult in any performance. As critic Steve Schwartz noted, "strings have less of a problem sustaining pitch while holding notes. They also don't confront the problems of breath the way singers must, so the phrases tend to stretch out."[16] Westra confided

[14]Luke Howard, email (13 September 2013) to the editor. According to Howard, conductor Craig Jessop was following a practice established by his mentor Robert Shaw.

[15]Edward Higginbottom, liner notes to *Agnus Dei* [R].

[16]Steve Schwartz, "Cathedral Classics," *Classical Net Review*, www.classical.net/music/recs/reviews/a/amc00120a.php.

to me that, when the Warland group recorded the work, its members had to do it in short segments because their pitch kept going flat, due to a lack of stamina.[17] When Terry Edwards recorded his rendition with London Voices [R], he devised a clever way to maintain the pitch: "Nearly all of the record was performed by singers using headphones into which we were feeding a keyboard instrument, so that intonation problems were minimized."[18] Musicians, of course, cannot resort to such subterfuge in live performances.

Robert Spano, who recorded the work with the Atlanta Symphony Chorus [R], acknowledged that the long phrases and high notes "can be intimidating."[19] Yet performers just have to "go for it" with a "kind of fearlessness, the willingness to attempt something knowing that you can fall down."[20] Such an attitude, however, is more plausible during a recording session when more takes and splicings can compensate for various problems. He did not comment on how many takes or splicings were required to produce the final product. He does concede that a live performance is another matter: "but nothing ventured, nothing gained."[21] The audience should therefore be prepared for either success or failure.

THE AGNUS DEI TEXT AND TEXT PLACEMENT

When Barber decided to transform *Adagio* into a choral work, he first needed to select the kind of text that would reinforce the mood already established in the listener by the orchestral adaptation. The slow tempo obviously suggests a serious text, but why one from the Roman Catholic Mass? Although the composer did not conceive of the original string quartet Adagio or its orchestral alternative as appropriate for funerals or memorials, he must have inevitably become reconciled to that association. Because the Agnus Dei text (in slightly modified form) is also a part of the Requiem Mass, he may have had this in mind when he chose the words. Moreover, the wandering melodic line of the original *Adagio* has reminded listeners of plainsong; a choral setting simply takes this one step further. In

[17]Mitzi Westra, interview (6 May 2006) with the author.

[18]Terry Edwards, email (6 November 2006) to the author.

[19]Robert Spano, quoted in David Srebnik, "Virtuoso Voices: Treading Fearlessly into the Unknown and the Up High," KUAR [NPR] (26 January 2010).

[20]*Ibid.*

[21]*Ibid.*

his program notes for the San Diego Chamber Orchestra, Eric Bromberger claimed, "Barber's noble melody almost has something in common with medieval choral music."[22] This may not be a coincidence because Barber truly admired chant and once wrote to his parents of hearing a choir of Benedictine monks in Rome: "The simplicity and sincere style with which they sang this overwhelming music warmed all the corners of my heart."[23] He later professed to his friend Charles Turner that the early Catholic monophonic tradition "for me is the only religious music."[24] Furthermore, he told his uncle, Sidney Homer, that such melodies "satisfy something in my soul and help me believe that 'all is right with the world' and that the truth is just as simple and straightforward as a Gregorian Chant."[25] His Agnus Dei may convince listeners on an emotional level that all *is* right with the world. But there may be one other, subtle reason for the text selection. Earlier in the year, when Barber wrote his transcription, he had completed *Mutations from Bach* (1968), his own treatment of the Lutheran chorale "Christe, du Lamm Gottes." Although these words are never sung in this instrumental arrangement, the "Lamb of God" may have entered his subconscious mind and emerged as "Agnus Dei."

Yet the structure of the Agnus Dei text created problems when Barber tried to impose it on his pre-existent music. When composers write an Agnus Dei from scratch, they usually observe the traditional tripartite form of the text by delineating three clearly defined sections:

> Agnus Dei, qui tollis peccata mundi,
>   miserere nobis.
> Agnus Dei, qui tollis peccata mundi,
>   miserere nobis.
> Agnus Dei, qui tollis peccata mundi,
>   dona nobis pacem.

[22]Eric Bromberger, "Program Notes, San Diego Chamber Orchestra"; reprinted www.sdco.org/Season 2003-04/ProgramNotes/MythsMeditationsCelebrations.html.

[23]Samuel Barber, letter (10 January 1951) to his parents, quoted in Barbara B. Heyman, *Samuel Barber* (1992), 348.

[24]Samuel Barber, letter (Spring 1953) to Charles Turner, quoted in Barbara B. Heyman, *Samuel Barber* (1992), 348.

[25]Sidney Homer, letter (30 April 1953) to Samuel Barber, quoted in Barbara B. Heyman, *Samuel Barber* (1992), 349. Barber made use of this admiration of chant by incorporating his own interpretation of the style in the opening movement of his *Prayers of Kierkegaard* in 1954.

This pattern is apparent in chants and polyphonic settings from Machaut through Stravinsky—and later. Because this is not the form of the original *Adagio,* Barber tried to compensate by imposing incessant text repetitions. The tripartite structure of the text can never be grafted onto the music.

Equally problematic is the issue of text placement. The words need to fit already composed contrapuntal lines, which makes the text appear to be placed at random and results in syllables coming in at unexpected places and melismas at even more unexpected places. Several factors imply that Barber may have prepared this piece in a hurry. Many passages of the score look just like the orchestral version with words stuck under the string parts. As Steve Schwartz wryly observed, "the words stick to the music like Post-its."[26] Barber did not even alter his long phrase markings to accommodate the text, which is uncharacteristic of a musician who usually was meticulous with regard to prosody. Normally a composer will put slurs over a group of notes that are sung to the same syllable, but not here. To my mind, the result is much like the English dubbing of a Japanese film: there the words have to match lip movements; here they have to match pre-composed rhythms. It is also somewhat like those "singable" English translations of opera arias that nobody wants to hear (except for a few diehard voice teachers). The director of publications at G. Schirmer, Hans Heinsheimer, either chose to ignore such textual deficiencies or decided to put the relationship of text to music in the best mercantile mode when he wrote that both the Latin and English texts fit the music "like the proverbial glove."[27] (One wonders where he did his haberdashery shopping!)

There are signs of textual problems right from the start of the piece. Already as the first phrase ends, the second (unaccented) syllable of *Dei* occurs not only on the downbeat of a measure but at the culmination of the whole phrase. Whereas instrumentalists can emphasize this arrival, singers will have to be cautioned to back away from that last note. The composer, moreover, was not always consistent in his text placement in similar phrases. For instance, he underlays *qui tollis peccata mundi* two different ways, as shown in Example 4.2 on the following page. All in all, the second version is better than the first: the accented syllable of "pec-CAT-ta" occurs on the downbeat. The tenor version in the coda is already

[26]Steve Schwartz, "Cathedral Classics," *Classical Net Review*, www.classical.net.

[27]Hans Heinsheimer, "The Composing Composer: Samuel Barber," *ASCAP TODAY* II/3 (December 1968), 7.

like the alto version. If I were conducting the work, I would direct the sopranos, and later the basses, to change their underlay of syllables to match that of the altos. (*Pace,* G. Schirmer!) This would at least be more consistent than Barber's erratic text placement.

Example 4.2. Comparison of Text Setting in Soprano (mm. 4-8) and Alto (mm. 15-19)

There are additional anomalies. At one point the second sopranos are forced to sing the partial word, *misere,* an incomplete doubling of the alto part, which has the entire word. Of course, it is hidden within the texture and probably would not be noticed. A moment where text and music seem to work well together occurs during the rise to the climax, culminating in the phrase *dona nobis pacem.* In this intense passage the phrase becomes a demand for peace, perhaps even a scream for it. Then the quiet chords reiterate the phrase in a more subdued manner, as if the supplicant regretted the previous emotional outburst. Unfortunately, Barber is again faced with a textual dilemma: he must stretch these six syllables over seven chords and must change the usual grouping of chords in order to do it.[28] Then, in the coda, the sopranos are forced to sing the absurd phrase, *Dona Miserere,* a juxtaposition of words that probably has never before occurred in an Agnus Dei. Finally, when the altos, at last, get to sing a perfectly placed *dona nobis pacem,* why, oh why, does Barber have the lower parts sing *miserere nobis,* when that line of text is long past its original liturgical significance? It creates a needlessly jarring dotted rhythm, the only actual rhythmic change in the whole setting. Could not the musicians at least be allowed to sing *dona* or *pacem* in a smoother two-quarter-note rhythm? Ironically, proper declamation, normally a

[28]For some reason Barber did not carry over the slur marks of his String Quartet into the orchestral *Adagio* at that point, but I believe that is merely an oversight rather than a change of concept. Orchestral conductors would do well to consult the String Quartet score to advise players for that passage. That, of course, is of no help to a choral performance.

desirable objective for choral performances, could actually exacerbate all of these problems.[29]

Yet some find the text not only feasible, but ideal. Program annotator Andrew Stewart determined that "economy of means and beauty of sound lie at the heart of Samuel Barber's Agnus Dei. . . . The overt emotion of the original work perfectly fits the mood of the Latin prayer."[30] Reviewer David Bond referred to the "glorious combination of text and music where the rising line and harmony lifts the spirit and exudes a spirit of peace."[31] American conductor Gilbert Levine believes that Barber transcribed his *Adagio* for voices to make the work "more directly spiritual," to transform it into a "heartfelt religious hymn," and "to evoke a higher power."[32] Yet, despite technical flaws, this religious hymn suitably fits the mood of the text and lifts the spirit. In the right setting and proper atmosphere, hearing a live performance of Agnus Dei may be close to a spiritual experience. One avowed Christian, Professor Peter Dodson, recalled hearing the work at King's College Cambridge, sung by its famed choir: "I just about had an out of body experience. As tears stained my cheeks I was literally speechless."[33] Negative, technical factors should not stand in the way of enjoying *Adagio for Strings* bathed in choral sound.

Barber seems not to have confided in anyone the reason he wrote this adaptation. Did one or more prominent choral directors, such as Robert Shaw, express a desire to perform such a transcription? Did someone from his publisher suggest it? Hans Heinsheimer (from G. Schirmer) made no such connections but noted that the composer "amuses himself (and us)" by making choral arrangements of some of his earlier works "just to while

[29]Mormon Tabernacle Choir, "Barber: Agnus Dei," *YouTube* (8 March 2007), posted by jrtapia. The Goeyvaerts Ensemble produced a spirited, quick performance (7:05) with much rubato conducted by Marc Michael de Smet at the 2004 Musica Sacra International in Marktoberdorf, Germany. See "Goeyvaerts Ensemble, Belgium; Barber: Agnus Dei," *YouTube* (20 April 2007), posted by DolfRabus. There is also a brief excerpt (starting at 1:16) by the S. F. X. Boys' Choir of St. Francis Xavier College, Liverpool from the Votivskirche: "S.F.X. BOYS' CHOIR, LIVERPOOL," *YouTube* (8 February 2007), posted by FernandoAlonoso123. At least two postings coordinate a recording of the work with either religious paintings or scenes from movie versions of the passion story. For other uses of Agnus Dei on *YouTube*, see Chapter 9.

[30]Andrew Stewart, liner notes to *Lux Aeterna* [R].

[31]David Bond, "Guide to Records," *American Record Guide* LXI/6 (November 1998), 91. This statement comes from a review of the Cambridge University Chamber Choir's recording,

[32]Gilbert Levine, *Europamusicale,* www.europamusicale.de.

[33]Peter Dodson, "Leading a Life of Faith in the Secular Academy," *As Leaven in the World: Catholic Perspective on Faith, Vocation and the Intellectual Life,* ed. Thomas M. Landy (Franklin, Wis.: Sheed and Ward, 2001), 417.

away the time between major projects."[34] Whatever the catalyst may have been, in 1967 Schirmer published both Agnus Dei as well as the alternate version with the English translation, Lamb of God. While most choral organizations prefer the Latin text, a few amateur choirs and student groups have performed and recorded the work in English.[35] When they sing this text, choirs have to face the problematic flat vowel in "Lamb," which, because it is sung on a long melisma, could come out sounding like bleating sheep (a little more text painting than desired). To achieve a more mellifluous sound, the first phrase is likely to come out "Lumb of Gawd."[36]

LENGTH AND TEMPO

As with recordings of *Adagio for Strings* itself, performance timings of Agnus Dei vary a great deal.[37] One might suspect that smaller groups, due to more exposed problems of breath support, might take a somewhat faster pace, but—in general—tempo does not seem to be related to the size of the ensemble. True, the Ormond College Choir [R], with twenty-two members, has one of the shortest, whereas the Robert Shaw Festival Singers [R], a very large group, has the longest. But tempos in between do not support the premise that the smaller the group, the faster the tempo. For instance, the Sixteen [R], one of the smallest ensembles, has a fairly average length of a little over eight minutes, while the Handel and Haydn Society Choir [R] of sixty singers is a minute shorter.

On two of the albums cited in the list of durations in Appendix 4 both Agnus Dei and *Adagio for Strings* are recorded. The choral version is considerably shorter than the orchestral one in both cases, as shown in Table 4.1. This is, perhaps, another indication of the singers' more limited breath control. Note that Spano's performances of both works are more leisurely than Lawrence's and Alsop's. If, indeed, he used all 200

[34]Hans Heinsheimer, "The Composing Composer: Samuel Barber," 7.

[35]Such groups include the National Lutheran Choir (Heritage: A New Song, NLCA, 2000), the Moody Chorale of Chicago's Moody Bible Institute; the Chorale of the Boston Conservatory of Music (1998), Bethel Choir of Bethel College in St. Paul, Minnesota, and a recording made in 1972 at the Pennsylvania Music Educators Association Northeast District Chorus Festival.

[36]Opera singer George Dyer has recorded the work singing the English text as a solo aria with a chorus "ooh-ooh-ing" the other parts in the background. This performance is found on his album *A New Song*, perf. George Dyer (Salt Lake City, Utah: Deseret Book Company, 2004).

[37]In Appendix 4 I have provided a classified discography with their timings, from shortest to longest, with the name of the director, the name of the choir, the number of ensemble members, the album title, the record label, the catalog number, and the year of release.

members of the Atlanta Symphony Chorus for his recording (all members are listed on the chorus' website), it would be easier to obtain and sustain a slower tempo than Lawrence's much smaller group.

Table 4.1. Comparison of Durations

On *Samuel Barber: Choral Music* (Naxos, 2006) and *Eternal Barber* (Naxos, 2008)

5:45	Douglas Lawrence, Agnus Dei, Ormond College Choir (22)
7:41	Marin Alsop, *Adagio for Strings*, Royal Scottish National Orchestra

On *Transmigration* (Telarc, 2009)

7:41	Robert Spano, Agnus Dei, Atlanta Symphony Chorus (≈ 200)
8:54	Robert Spano, *Adagio for Strings*, Atlanta Symphony Orchestra

Like those aspects of its orchestral counterpart, the length and tempo of choral performances may depend on whether the beat is taken by the half note or quarter note, as can be observed first hand by watching video clips on *YouTube*, such as those by the Goeyvaerts Ensemble and the Mormon Tabernacle Choir.[38] One reason that the Goeyvaerts Ensemble performance is so quick and that even the Mormon Tabernacle Choir performance achieves a moderate tempo is the fact that both directors take the half note as the beat.

PACKAGING AND PROGRAMMING AGNUS DEI

Agnus Dei appears on many recordings, often aimed at quite different audiences for various purposes, as is frequently indicated by album titles. For instance, it is sometimes intended to produce a tranquil atmosphere: *e.g.*, *Peace* (Handel and Haydn Society) [R], *Renaissance: Music for Inner Peace* (The Sixteen) [R], and *Serene Journeys* (Denver St. John's Episcopal Choir) [R]. Some recordings emphasize heavenly connections: *Music from Heaven* (Choir of Ormond College) [R], *Heaven to Earth* (Westminster Choir) [R], and *A New Heaven* (Ex Cathedra) [R]. Others lead the listener to related religious references: *Images of Christ* (Cambridge Singers) [R] and *À la Gloire de Dieu* (also by The Sixteen) [R]. Only a few stress

[38]See footnote 29 for details of these *YouTube* postings.

sadness: *Melancolie* (Accentus) [R] and *More Tears from Heaven* (Cambridge Trinity College Choir) [R].[39]

One way to avoid the hazards of Barber's text placement is to sing a choral version of *Adagio for Strings* as a vocalise, that is, without words. This is the approach of Terry Edwards's group, London Voices [R], on *Choral Adagios*. His arranger, Daryl Runswick, did not merely erase the words from the choral score but based his edition on the orchestral score. It was, in fact, several years after the recording session that Edwards learned that the composer had written his own choral transcription.[40] The three Celtic Tenors [R] also perform *Adagio* as a vocalise on their album *So Strong*. In his note to the recording one of the tenors, James Nelson, expressed the hope that listeners would embrace this "wordless adaptation for three tenors in six parts," which probably means that each of the three men overdubbed a second line.[41] Staggered breathing, which allows choirs a more leisurely approach, will not work here. The tempo is quick, and much of the middle section is omitted, resulting in a rendition that lasts only a little over four minutes. Because the cut is so skillfully handled, some listeners may not realize that part of the piece is missing. How would this piece be sung in a live performance? Perhaps it never is. The singers could play a tape of the lower three voices and perform the upper parts live, or they might enlist the aid of three guests, preferably baritones, to sing the lower parts.

A clever bit of programming is performing both *Adagio for Strings* and Agnus Dei on the same concert. For instance, in March 2003 at the St. John the Evangelist Church in Kitchener, Ontario, Leonard Enns first conducted the Waterloo Chamber Players in a performance of the orchestral work. The Da Capo Chamber Choir then sang the choral version to close the program. On another concert, in November 2002 in Geisling, Germany, Norbert Herrmann first conducted The Ansbacher Kämmerorchester in *Adagio,* which was followed by an intervening work before Gerhard Klump directed the Geislinger Singkreis in Agnus Dei.

[39]Accentus, "Excerpt from Agnus Dei," *YouTube* (25 July 2008), posted by musicca75.

[40]Terry Edwards, email (6 November 2006) to the author. Other vocalise arrangements include Russian Chamber Chorus of New York, cond. and arr. by Nikolai Kachanov, *Adagio for Strings* (18 November 2011); and Sounds Wicked [sixteen-voice chamber choir], cond. by Andrew Macmillan, *Adagio* [transcribed from *Adagio for Strings*], (16 March 2002). See www.soundswicked.org.

[41]The other two tenors are Niall Morris and Matthew Gilsenan. "Backing vocals" are listed for other songs on the album but not for *Adagio.*

Another performance possibility is accompanying Agnus Dei with the orchestral *Adagio* rather than the printed keyboard score. At the Spoleto Festival USA in May 2003 Joseph Flummerfelt directed the Westminster Choir in his arrangement with the Spoleto Festival Orchestra doubling the choral parts. Critic Jack Sullivan thought it was wise to program a chamber orchestra (two violins, two violas, cello, and double bass) to prevent overpowering the choir:

> In this brisk, lucid performance (Flummerfelt is never lugubrious, even in funereal music), the strings did not gum up the vocal texture, but provided velvet cushions of shimmering overtones to the voices. It was an eerie and gratifying experience, like hearing both versions of the work at once. It also illustrated Flummerfelt's constant search for new sonorities, even in familiar material.[42]

One reviewer wondered why it was necessary for a string orchestra to supplement the singers: "The decision can't have been taken because the choir required any support since manifestly they don't. I can only think that the idea was to enrich the texture but that seems a trifle unnecessary. That said, the strings are fairly unobtrusive."[43] On the positive side, critic David Venier felt that the string enhancement was "very effective not only in adding desirable fullness and color to the sound, but also in moderating the usual vocally strained passages in this extremely taxing piece."[44] The Azusa Pacific University Choir [R] also used an orchestra to accompany its performance of Agnus Dei in 2007. This fine performance, which can be seen and heard on *YouTube*, illustrates several of the points mentioned: the strings merely support the choir and never get in the way; the tempo is brisk (6:49) to avoid taxing the singers; and the director clearly conducts

[42]Jack Sullivan, "A Spoleto Farewell: Flummerfelt's 30 Years: A Powerful Legacy," *American Record Guide* (September 2003).

[43]John Quinn, "Heaven to Earth," *Music Web International*, www.musicweb-international.com/classrev/2004/Aug04/Heaven_to_Earth.htm.

[44]"Heaven to Earth," *Naxos Web Radio*, www.classicstoday.com.

the half-note as the beat.[45] An unusual choral-instrumental performance of the work took place in April 2007 at the University of North Alabama, where the Chamber Choir was accompanied by the university percussion ensemble, consisting primarily of vibraphones and marimbas. Such a combination was unexpectedly successful, except, perhaps, during the climax, when the music became a bit too percussive.[46]

AGNUS DEI ON THE RADIO

Like the orchestral *Adagio,* Barber's Agnus Dei often can be found on classical radio stations' daily schedules, as is shown by their Internet playlists for any given week. This is surprising because a classical radio disc jockey colleague of mine once told me that his bosses insisted that he avoid solo vocal and choral music. Yet Dave Bunker, the compiler of criteria for suitable classical programming (see Chapter 3), observed in the section "No Forbidden Categories" that "some of the pieces that pull in most of the calls and letters, and favorable comments from upstairs [*i.e.*, management], now come from the vocal repertoire," with Barber's Agnus Dei an "outstanding example."[47] While this is encouraging, that work's popularity may derive not so much from its choral status but from listeners' familiarity with the orchestral version. That is, they are willing to put up with the choral sound as long as they can recognize the piece from a more familiar performance medium.

Agnus Dei is sometimes incorporated into "theme shows" or programs devoted completely to Barber's music. As previously mentioned, it was included in WHRB's Musical Orgy® as a part of a presentation of the composer's complete works. A similar series in Great Britain is *Composer of the Week* (BBC Radio 3), showcasing music of a single composer Monday through Friday for an hour each day. Barber was featured in July 2006, but, instead of playing the String Quartet or the orchestral *Adagio* for the 1930s segment (Tuesday), the show presented Agnus Dei by Dunedin

[45]Azusa Pacific University Choir, "Agnus Dei," *YouTube* (28 February 2007), posted by sc0tlas. A performance of this work can be found on their compact disc *Alleluia.* A similar doubling may be part of the arrangement of Agnus Dei that Barlow Bradford designed for his group, The Utah Chamber Artists, which they performed in Salt Lake City in October 2004. The Seattle Bach Choir, directed by Gregory Vancil, has also performed Agnus Dei with a string ensemble and in 2002 used clarinets on the second violin and viola parts.

[46]Chamber Choir, University of North Alabama, "Adagio for Strings" *YouTube* (24 April 2007), posted by nifrederick.

[47]Dave Bunker, "Music That Changes the Day—for *Enough* Listeners," *Current* (20 September 1999); reprinted www.current.org/rad/rad917b.html.

Consort [R]. Perhaps the producers thought the earlier versions had been overplayed on their network. Yet, because many choral groups in Great Britain perform Agnus Dei, it may be the most popular version among British classical radio listeners.

The choral score sometimes logically appears on series devoted specifically to sacred choral music. For instance, it was heard several times on *Choral Colors* on WICR in Indianapolis. Host Brent Miller selects the repertoire each week, usually planned around a theme. The episode on 23 May 2004, "Writing for a Transcript," consisted of choral pieces that originated in other genres. Barber's Agnus Dei was an inevitable choice.

For his show *Compact Discoveries* on WXEL-FM in West Palm Beach, Florida, host / producer Fred Flaxman concocts programs with a specific, sometimes unusual theme. In 2006 he included Agnus Dei on "Music for Insomniacs," concentrating on "soft, beautiful, hypnotizing music."[48] Before introducing the recording of the Robert Shaw Festival Singers [R], he cautioned, "American composers can put you to sleep with the best of them. Better set your alarm"; after it was over, he added, "if that piece doesn't help insomniacs fall asleep, I don't know what will."[49] Yet surely some of them awoke during the climatic section before being lulled back to sleep during the coda.

Choral conductors may have mixed feelings about this particular Barber work. Craig Hella Johnson, director of the choral group Conspirare, is torn between two views:

> It's such a physically and musically demanding work, and it can be hard to pull off. I go between this being one of my favorite pieces of choral music and my worst nightmare to rehearse. But it is certainly one of the most important pieces in the American choral repertoire."[50]

[48]Fred Flaxman, *Compact Discoveries Contents*, www.compactdiscoveries.com/CompactDiscoveries Scripts/46MusicforInsomniacs.html. Agnus Dei was also heard once on *Great Sacred Music* (WCPE, Wake Forest, N.C.) and twice on *The Sacred Concert* (KDFC, San Francisco).

[49]*Ibid.*

[50]Jeanne Claire van Ryzin, "Three Questions with Craig Hella Johnson," *Austin* [Tex.] *American-Statesman* (31 January 2008).

And yet its great number of recordings—by a variety of groups—and the many performances—both here and abroad—attest to its importance and its popularity.

Other Transcriptions and Arrangements

Adagio for Strings has become a fruitful resource for all kinds of other adaptations, ranging from keyboard to woodwinds, from selected strings to other more unanticipated ensembles. Some have been published—many by G. Schirmer—while others are devised with specific performing groups in mind, often in an "ad hoc" mode. Even if a published score does not exist, a group may have made a recording available to the general public. For versions that are neither published nor recorded, the imagination is necessary; at the very least, such endeavors reveal the work's amazing potential and its ability to withstand an incredible amount of tampering.

FOR STUDENT ORCHESTRA

Jamin Hoffman [P], a well-established conductor in the Milwaukee area, simplified *Adagio* for an intermediate string ensemble (Grades 3-4), with an optional organ part. This reconsideration involved lowering the key down a half step (to avoid all those nasty flats that might frighten high school students) and altering some of the meter changes that might confuse the counting of beats. For example, Hoffman reduced the prevailing meter from 4 / 2 to 4 / 4 and in the process eliminated the five-beat measures: he divided them into 6 / 4 + 4 / 4.[51] Most radical of all, Hoffman abridged the piece drastically. After the opening phrases in which the first violins play the melody, this edition immediately jumps to the cello entry—here played by violas—that then leads quickly to the climactic passage, where Hoffman transposed the ultra-high violin lines down an octave. An editor's review posted on the Internet calls attention to its virtues: this arrangement "now makes this landmark work accessible to advancing groups" and enables student musicians to play "one of the most important pieces of our time."[52]

[51]Other arrangers at G. Schirmer had already made many of these changes for similar reasons. See my commentary on the treatments of Rosen on page 126 and of Lanning on page 127.

[52]See halleonard.com under *Adagio for Strings (Hoffman).*

FOR KEYBOARD: SOLO ORGAN

CD Track 5

In the late 1940s G. Schirmer became interested in issuing an organ version of *Adagio for Strings*. When Barber remembered that his friend and colleague William Strickland [P] had shown him his transcription a few years earlier, he suggested that Strickland submit it to that publishing company. The composer confided to his friend, "Although I know little about the organ, I'm sure your arrangement would be best."[53] Shortly after it was issued in 1949, reviewer William Lester called it "one of the most inspired products of this prominent composer, well reset for the organ by an expert in that line. The result is a meditative lyrical movement of real beauty well worthy of attention and hearing."[54] In notes to his own 1994 recording, Todd Wilson [R] compared the arrangement (closer to a transcription) favorably with the one for string orchestra: "the organ is perhaps the only other musical medium which can provide the drawn-out lines and enormous dynamic palette required of this powerful music."[55] While an organ lacks the subtlety of gently caressed string phrasing in the orchestral treatment, it certainly gains in the ability to achieve monumental power, especially during the climax.

Strickland gave registrations for both the standard pipe organ and the Hammond organ, a popular electronic instrument of the time. The fairly generic pipe organ registration requires three manuals: Great 8′; Swell 8′ 4′; Choir 8′ 4′, plus pedal 16′ 8′, with various couplings. Organists with a two-manual instrument can registrate the piece to suit their purposes. The Hammond organ is a two-manual instrument with registration controlled by "drawbars," capable of creating various combinations of tones and overtones electronically. Both pipe organ and Hammond registrations are intended to emulate the original string sound.

The staves for the manuals contain the passages originally assigned to the violins and violas. The pedal part corresponds through most of the piece to the lines for cellos and double basses, including the passage (m. 28) where the cellos carry the melody. At this point the organist needs to remove the 16′ stop; otherwise the melody would sound below the bass line being played by the left hand. (This is much the same situation as

[53]Samuel Barber, letter (15 August 1945) to William Strickland, quoted in Barbara B. Heyman, *Samuel Barber* (1992), 175. Note that the composer did not distinguish between the terms "transcription" and "arrangement" as I do in this discussion.

[54]William Lester, "New Music for Organ," *Diapason* XL (1 November 1949), 28.

[55]Todd Wilson, liner notes to *In a Quiet Cathedral,* perf. Todd Wilson, organ (Delos, 3145, 1994).

in the choral version, discussed earlier.) Some less-than-average church organists may be daunted by the prospect of such a significant, exposed pedal line.[56] Because some models of the Hammond organ have a shorter pedal range at the top, it may be required to play some passages an octave lower. When the cello melody exceeds the pedal range of even the largest instrument (around m. 39), Strickland moves it to the manuals. For the climactic passage the full organ sound is remarkably effective, perhaps even more so than when strings are playing in their highest range. To reinforce the effect, he designates optional low pedal notes for the last two chords (mm. 48-53). Listeners accustomed to hearing this strictly in the high strings may be surprised by this bass reinforcement, but the writing is quite idiomatic for a climactic organ passage. I cannot imagine an organist resisting the temptation to bolster this climax.[57] In the coda, where violas double the violins, Strickland gives the following instruction: "8′ solo with 16′ coupler," which results in an automatic doubling of the melody. This transcription has proven its worth over the years, frequently appearing on organ recitals all over the world.[58]

FOR KEYBOARD: SOLO PIANO

Lawrence Rosen [P] transcribed *Adagio for Strings* for solo piano, with the note after its title, "Featured in The Orion Pictures Release 'Platoon,'" undoubtedly issued so that those who enjoyed the music in the movie could play it themselves on their pianos at home. It is no coincidence, therefore, that this keyboard version was published in 1987, a year after the release of the film. Rosen, who might be considered Schirmer's resident simplifier, transposed the piece down a half step and reduced the meter from 4 / 2 to 4 / 4, not only preventing the pianist from playing it too slowly (a risk for any piece in 4 / 2 meter) but probably making the

[56]See "Barber, "Adagio for Strings" (Organ)," *YouTube* (31 July 2008), posted by joenwayne. An organist, Wayne Burcham-Gulatta has posted his performance of *Adagio*. This video provides a close-up of the pedal-board when it has the melody. This is not the only way the melody can be performed, but it might give organists a guideline on how to play the passage.

[57]On the recordings I have heard of this arrangement all three organists take the optional low notes: Willibald Guggenmos [R], David Pizarro [R], and Todd Wilson [R]. Postings on *YouTube* also have the pedal reinforcement.

[58]The ABC news program, *World News Tonight* (7 June 2003), included a brief passage of *Adagio for Strings* on a segment about the pipe organ and its resurgence in popularity.

counting easier. He also translated Barber's "molto adagio" into "very slowly," for a beginner unfamiliar with Italian tempo markings.[59]

The texture is thinner than most other adaptations (*e.g.*, few low notes for left hand); therefore a pianist might miss the characteristic resonance of the string versions. Because the version seems to be designed more for pleasure at home than for professional performances, a pianist can easily double some of the bass line in octaves. The absence of damper pedal indications requires that each pianist must decide where and how much pedaling should be done. On the other hand, because all the parts fit comfortably under the hands, this could be effective for electronic keyboard or synthesizer. Such instruments are more likely than pianos to be found in American homes these days, and Rosen may have had this in mind when he made the arrangement. A synthesizer's string setting could even emulate the orchestra. Now even an average pianist can produce his own "Ørbit" synthesized performance.[60]

FOR VIOLIN AND PIANO

For his transcription for violin and piano prolific arranger Jerry Lanning [P], like Rosen, also transposed *Adagio* down a half step and changed the meter to 4 / 4. After all, Barber had basically sketched out the melody in 4 / 4 meter before he altered it to 4 / 2. These musicians could argue theoretically that they were merely returning to the composer's original concept of the meter, except that it is unlikely that they were aware of it. In fact, Lanning may have adapted Rosen's for his own version. For the most part, the violin plays the same line as the first violin in the original string quartet, with one main exception: during the cello statement the violin plays the cello line in its low range for the first and third phrases (mm. 28-31 and 35-38). The second phrase (mm. 31-35) lies too low in range for the violin; therefore, Lanning assigned it to the piano. Because the piano part contains more octaves in the left hand than Rosen's edition, judicious pedaling must be applied. Such doublings could be omitted if the pianist plays the accompaniment on an electronic keyboard.[61]

[59]In addition to his simplification of *Adagio,* Rosen has whittled down a piano arrangement of "Under the Willow Tree" from *Vanessa* and performed similar operations on other composers' works in the G. Schirmer catalogue.

[60]For an explanation of this reference, see Chapter 7. Rosen's transcription as well as other piano arrangements of *Adagio for Strings* are listed in Appendix 4.

[61]The first page of the score and much of the solo violin part are provided at the "Look Inside" feature at the *Sheet Music Plus* website: www.sheetmusicplus.com/pages.html.

FOR ACCORDION ORCHESTRA

Contemplating *Adagio for Strings* being played by an ensemble of accordions boggles the mind, but this is only one of many modifications designed for unusual instrumental combinations. Harmonica is a prize-winning youth accordion (not mouth organ) orchestra from St. Petersburg, Russia, under the direction of Vladimir Kazantsev. Its repertoire contains an arrangement of the piece, possibly by Sergé Latchev, a former leader of the group. It may be the same arrangement played by his newer group, Netherlands Ensemble, Orchestra Alphen Opus 2. He is the only member of the ensemble who plays the bajan, a Russian variant of the accordion, which has buttons for the right hand rather than a keyboard.[62] Although neither of these arrangements is commercially available for purchase, the duo "M-Elodie" (a clever pun on the names of the two performers, Maxim Fedorov and Elodie Soulard) have posted their duet collaboration on *YouTube*.[63]

CD Track 6

FOR FLUTE AND SYNTHESIZER

Purists may wince at an *Adagio* arrangement for synthesizer, and yet Hiro Fujikake [R], one of Japan's foremost composers and arrangers, demonstrated admirable restraint in the electronic effects of his treatment of the number with flute and synthesizer. In the late 1980s he collaborated with James Galway on an album comprising his compositions for that combination, which in turn led to an album of arrangements of familiar classical pieces.[64] At the beginning of *Adagio,* the sound from Fujikake's Roland synthesizer comes close to a string orchestra, more so than William Ørbit's solo synthesizer version (see Chapter 7). The usual problems ensue when a solo instrument is involved. In the original, Barber shifted the melody around from one instrument to another. Which line should the flute play? Obviously, at the beginning it plays the original violin melody, but at [1], where the viola had the melody, the synthesizer mimics an alto flute while Galway's flute continues with the first violin part. At [3], where

[62]The group has performed *Adagio* in several Dutch cities. Ralf Gscheidle has arranged *Adagio* for his accordion group [P], a community orchestra in Strümpfelbach; it was advertised as "ein Stück zur Meditation." See *Handharmonika-Club Strümpfelbach*, www.hhc-struempfelbach.fto.de/kirche2002.htm.

[63]Elodie Soulard and Maxim Fedorov of the Bajan Duo, "Samuel Barber–Adagio for Strings / M-Elodie Duo," *YouTube* (27 April 2010), posted by maksimum80.

[64]The earlier album was *The Enchanted Forest* (RCA, 7893, 1990); *Adagio* appears on *The Lark in the Clear Air* [R]. The *Adagio* arrangement is also found on *Barber's Adagio* [R].

the melody was initially heard in the cello part, however, the flute now plays it an octave higher, completely altering the texture. It remains on this line even through much of the climactic phrase but logically returns to the first violin for the coda. In this setting the ending is more abrupt: while the last phrase is still taken down an octave, it is speeded up to match the rhythms of the preceding phrase, and the final chord is not repeated. As a result, the piece loses its Mahleresque ending (as described in Chapter 3).

FOR WOODWINDS AND BRASS: FULL BAND

Schirmer publishes two full band arrangements of *Adagio for Strings.* Noted for many orchestra and band arrangements, Calvin Custer [P] adapted the work in 1992 for a fairly large concert band, with many saxophones and brass instruments. He retained the original key and meter. The opening is scored for woodwinds with the first clarinet given the melody. Paul Jennings [P], who has written and arranged many band works for this publishing company, produced in 1991 his *Adagio for Young Concert Band* for a smaller ensemble, with fewer woodwinds and horns but with the additional part for percussion. One online retailer, J. W. Pepper and Sons, recommends it as a "medium easy" piece for "developing bands" in line with the qualifier "young" in the title.[65] Both publications supply multiple copies of some parts, allowing various doublings, and a string bass part. In advertisements Schirmer describes both publications in glowing terms: "with careful attention to detail" each of these important editions is a "superb choice for groups seeking literature that demands expressive playing and musicality."[66]

Editions Marc Reift (EMR) publishes a band adaptation of *Adagio* by John Glenesk Mortimer [P], titled *Platoon: Adagio for Strings,* a curious title, considering that it was first issued in 1978, eight years before the movie. Presumably, either Mortimer or others at EMR decided later to add this reference to capitalize on the music's popularity after the movie was released. He stated his intentions: "I have tried in this arrangement to achieve the seamless legato of the string version."[67] As with some other arrangers, he retained the original key but reduced the meter from 4 / 2 to 4 / 4. His scoring requires a large ensemble of winds and brass, as many

[65] *Sheet Music at J. W. Pepper*, jwpepper.com.

[66] Publicity available at the website of G. Schirmer's distributor: www.halleonard.com.

[67] John Glenesk Mortimer, *Platoon: Adagio for Strings* (Crans-Montana, Switzerland: Editions Marc Reift, 1978).

as sixty-five players, but many are optional doublings. With such a large ensemble at his disposal, Mortimer is able to present the melody on a great variety of instruments. For example, at the beginning, the clarinets have the first two phrases, followed by the next phrases on trumpets, flute, and oboe. The horns begin the "viola" statement. Slurs are deliberately staggered among the different instruments, along with the suggestion that each player may breathe "anywhere between the slurs." He altered the dissonance in measure 24 (G-flat against G-natural) because it "sounds harsher on brass than on strings" but designates the original in the score in small notes within brackets in case the conductor wants to retain the original sound.[68]

Several European bands like to play their own versions of Barber's *Adagio*. Particularly popular is an arrangement of medium difficulty by Rieks van der Velde [P].[69] It has been recorded by several groups, notably Brighthouse and Rostrich Band [R] and Brass Band de Wâldsung [R]. Among other groups that have added it to their repertoire are L'elite de Cressier Brass Band and The Amesbury Town Band.

Another band instrumentation can be found on the album *Beyond the Stars: 16 Fantastic Film Themes*, performed by the DUT Yorkshire Imperial Rothwell Band [R] with conductor Simon Godfrey Wood. In addition to the usual brass, the instrumentation is enhanced by a soprano cornet, euphonium, and flugel horn. Because this arrangement lasts only for 4:46, it is evidently drastically abridged. One reviewer concluded, "While some of the arrangements are good, *Adagio* doesn't work for the obvious reason." Obvious to whom? He reported the director was responsible for "some of the clever arrangements," but I do not know if that pertains to the Barber work.[70]

FOR MIXED WOODWINDS: FLUTES OR CLARINETS

In addition to full band alternatives, there are others conceived for smaller wind ensembles. The 1967 transcription by John O'Reilly [P] for a large woodwind choir is one of several that he has prepared for G.

[68]The first two pages of the score are provided at the EMR website: www.reift.ch/accueil.php?=search. A performance conducted by Marc Reift [R] is available.

[69]One can see the thirty-eight measures of the score and hear an audio sample on the Bernaerts website: www.bernaertsmusic.com.

[70]www.4barsrest.com/reviews/cds/cd042.asp#.UK-2P64TAs0. Other band arrangements include Rieks van der Velde, for large concert band [P]; Bill Gordon, for brass band [R]; and J. R. Young, for the Royal Lancers Band [R].

Schirmer. The instrumental range is dramatic: from piccolo to contrabass clarinet and baritone saxophone. It has been rated for grades 5-6.

Flutist and teacher at several institutions in the New York City area, Rië Schmidt [P] has transposed her straightforward flute arrangement of *Adagio* up a whole step. While the flutes I and II, alto flute, and bass flute basically follow the roles of the original strings, some adjustments are necessary to accommodate their ranges. For practical reasons she did not double the melody in octaves in the coda. Her version has been performed by at least two ensembles: Flute Force [R], of which she is a member, on its 1993 compact disc *Pastorale*, and Flutes Fantastique [R], on its 1999 self-titled album.[71] The woodwind ensemble Tetrawind has re-orchestrated her arrangement for flute, oboe, clarinet, and bassoon. Several adjustments were necessary, particularly at the climax.[72]

For his album *Andy Findon–Tracked* [R], this versatile British flutist [P] scored *Adagio* for a fairly large flute choir, consisting of two "regular" flutes, three altos, a bass, and a contrabass, plus optional parts for clarinet and bass clarinet if the two lowest flutes are unavailable. Reviewer David Kidman referred to this *Adagio* as being "festooned with a forest of flutes." According to Findon, "Its long melody lines and dense, moving harmonies create a very warm sound for flutes. The climax takes all parts into the high register, inviting quite dramatic overtones."[73] For this passage flutes I and II must switch to piccolos; flute I returns for the quiet chords. In her review Ingrid Culliford commented that Findon spins the music's long melody with "simplicity and breadth," but Julian Coward reported that "this slightly tremulous performance conveyed only some of the restrained, noble passion of the original."[74] I have not heard this arrangement, but I suspect that the sound must be rather piercing. Not as piercing, however, as the sound produced by an ensemble of five ocarinas [!] as posted on *YouTube*.[75]

[71]The other three flutists in Flute Force are Wendy Stern, Gretchen Pusch, and Sheryl Henze. Members of Flutes Fantastique are Mary Garrison, Victoria Jicha, Nancy Fencl, and Adriana Greisman.

[72]"Tetrawind–Barber's Adagio for Strings (Arr. Rie Schmidt)," *YouTube* (27 June 2008).

[73]The entire score, available online, may be downloaded at www.andyfindon.com/albums.htm. A sample from the coda may be heard there.

[74]"Tracked: Andy Findon," *Newsletter of the New Zealand Flute Society* (n.d.); and "Andy Findon: Tracked," *Pan Magazine* (June 2007). Both are reprinted on Findon's website, cited in footnote 73.

[75]5 Ogawa Ocarinas, "サミュエル・バーバー 弦楽のためのアダージョ Op. 11 練習中," *YouTube* (31 May 2010), posted by ocahzbach.

CD Track 7

Richard Stoltzman and the Kalmen Opperman Clarinet Choir [R] perform an arrangement of *Adagio* for clarinets I and II, alto clarinet, bass clarinet, and contrabass clarinet. Opperman, the conductor of the group, may have either arranged the piece himself or may have adapted one of the Schirmer publications.[76] Because of drastic cuts, his version lasts only four and a half minutes. It starts at the beginning, proceeds through the cadence at [3], but then leaps ahead to the coda, skipping the intervening twenty-eight measures, thereby excluding the buildup to the climax.

Composer and clarinetist Lucien Cailliet [P], "the father of the clarinet choir," has scored *Adagio* for a clarinet ensemble, including an A-flat sopranino. In a note to the score (which, unlike the Opperman version, is complete), he advised that his arrangement may be performed with any number of players per part, "provided a well-balanced instrumentation is maintained." His own recording [R] features an ensemble with many doublings. The author of the liner notes compared the resulting sound of this ensemble to that of a great organ, but to my ears it is a cross between an accordion and a synthesizer. He suggested that, if no A-flat sopranino is available, another E-flat soprano could be used. This substitution was made in his own recording and also for a performance by the Indiana University Clarinet Choir on 16 November 2000. The latter was a large ensemble, with three to five on a part, including four contrabass clarinets.[77]

One arrangement for clarinets is possible only on recording. For his album *Monochrome,* clarinet virtuoso Bryan A. Crumpler [R] modified Cailliet's arrangement. He first prerecorded all the lower parts and then improvised the melody on a B-flat clarinet rather than the A-flat sopranino that Cailliet calls for. His reaction to that instrument: "YUCK!" He thought it made "a nasty piercing sound"; with the B-flat clarinet, he "warmed it up a bit . . . and added a little personal flavor to it in the middle. What would another Barber *Adagio* be without a little personality to it?"[78] Reviewer S. James Wegg, nevertheless, was not enthusiastic. He is convinced that

[76]To celebrate Stoltzman's 55th birthday in 1997 as well as his 65th birthday in 2007, Fred Child featured the recording of *Adagio* by Stoltzman and the Kalmen Opperman Clarinet Choir on his NPR radio program *Performance Today.*

[77]The entire Cailliet performance can be heard online at the Michlin Music Audio Archives: michlinmusic.com/audio.html. The Indiana University performance is available on a DAT at the IU Music Library. Other groups that have performed Cailliet's arrangement are the Capriccio Clarinet Orchestra and the Tamworth Clarinet Choir.

[78]Bryan S. Crumpler, "Background on 'Monochrome,'" *Bryan's CD Store.* An excerpt of his improvisation can be found at www.whosthatguy.com/clarinet-cds.asp?cd=1.

Crumpler's offering "brings new meaning to the notion of 'I did it my way'; considering the album as a whole "a tremendous achievement," he noted, nonetheless, that the result is "not without its problems."[79]

> The most significant *faux pas* is Barber's famed *Adagio.* Crumpler simply cannot match the legato of strings. His numerous finger slaps belie the mystery and magic of the original and arranger Lucien Cailliet's spurious additional notes for the "solo" clarinet are as trite as they are unwelcome. The famous stratospheric crisis / climax is shrill rather than intense—no collection of diaphragms and single reeds can possibly match the dramatic angst of fully drawn bows and into-the-string left hands. Still, the last gasp is marvelously exhaled.[80]

The criticism that clarinets cannot achieve what strings can might just as well apply to other woodwind versions—or to any non-string arrangement for that matter.

FOR WOODWINDS AND BRASS: OTHER WINDS

There are several arrangements of *Adagio* for saxophone ensemble. On its compact disc *Blow!–Saxophone Music from America,* the Aurelia Saxofoon Kwartet performs a quartet arrangement by its soprano sax player, Johan van der Linden [R]. It stays fairly close to the texture of the original string quartet, with a few adjustments due to the more limited range of the instruments. I am convinced that the most effective part of the piece occurs when the baritone sax has the melody, the section where the cello originally played it. Somehow, Willem van Merwijk's tone quality gives the melody an even more plaintive sound than the original. In addition to Aurelia, the venerable Washington Saxophone Quartet [R] plays van der Linden's arrangement [P] on its recording *Daydream.* Schirmer published another one by Michael Warner [P],

[79]S. James Wegg, "One-Man Band Worth a Listen," *James Wegg Review (JWR)* (29 November 2005).

[80]*Ibid.* This statement implies that Cailliet added the solo notes, but they are Crumpler's additions. In the 1970s the Champaign-Urbana Junior Clarinet Choir [R] performed Harvey Hermann's arrangement of *Adagio.* In 2003 Craig Davis arranged *Adagio* for a clarinet quintet at Furman University. The Stockholm Clarinet Choir has an uncredited arrangement in its repertoire.

which the Jean Yves Formeau Saxophone Quartet [R] offers on its album *The Art of the Jean Yves Formeau Saxophone Quartet.*[81]

For a program on 16 May 1992 in Springfield, Illinois, Quartet Bassoon 4 (Cathy McGuire, Jane Holt, Karen Strohmeyer, and Evelyn Archer) featured a performance of *Adagio* for three bassoons and one contrabassoon, appropriately re-titled *Adagio for Bassoons.* The unlisted arranger may be one of the four members of the group.

British flautist Andy Findon [R], who arranged the composition for flute ensemble, has also arranged it for panpipes, one of the few classical pieces on his modestly titled album, *The Best Panpipes Album in the World . . . Ever.* An uncredited panpipe performance (perhaps Findon's) is posted on *YouTube*, along with landscape photographs. His presentation tries to emulate the orchestral *Adagio* with the pipes playing whatever it can. At the beginning it has the melody, but when that shifts to the viola and cello parts, it is as if the panpipe does not know what to do. It drops out for a while, then re-enters with incidental passages. Logically, it must play an octave lower during the climax but builds nicely to the final notes. It returns to the melody in the coda.[82]

CD Track 8

FOR BRASS ENSEMBLES: BRASS QUINTET

Stephen McNeff [P] has arranged *Adagio* for brass quintet—two B-flat trumpets, horn, trombone, and tuba—as part of the *Canadian Brass Ensemble Series* (1986). The writer of the accompanying commentary to the score reported that it was created for the Canadian Brass [R]. The transposition down a fourth accommodates the range of brass instruments. Unlike the original string version and others for like instruments (*e.g.*, all clarinets, all saxophones), a brass quintet can provide different sounds or "colors" throughout the piece. For instance, the melody at the beginning is assigned to the horn with the harmonies surrounding it rather than supporting it from below. At other points the melody is taken by the trumpet, horn (again), and trombone. As the piece pushes toward its climax, the melody in the first trumpet is transposed down an octave.

[81]"Adagio–Samuel Barber arr. Johan van der Linden," *YouTube* (23 July 2008), posted Johan van der Linden. The Washington group's performance can be previewed at www.wsaxq.com/audio/Daydream8.mp3. Other groups, such as the Veya Saxophone Quartet, the Vienna Saxophone Quartet, the Los Angeles Pierce Symphonic Winds, and the Illinois Wesleyan University Saxophone Quartet, have all performed Warner's arrangement. William Marr has also arranged *Adagio* for saxophone ensemble. Other saxophone groups that play *Adagio* arrangements that are not clearly identified include the Amstel, McInerney, New Art, Red Line, and Paragon (formerly Saxploitation) Saxophone Quartets.

[82]"Adagio for Strings," *YouTube* (18 March 2007), posted by Bernieken.

The score calls for mutes at the coda, as Barber suggests in the orchestral *Adagio,* a welcome change of color. The Canadian Brass has performed this arrangement at several concerts, including a program on 8 August 2000 at the Music Academy of the West in Santa Barbara, California, where it was enhanced with interesting staging and lighting effects. One critic observed: "Standing in a row, facing a different direction at various points in the piece, it was an effective presentation, particularly when the lights dimmed to darkness at the end."[83]

In November 2007 the Italian quintet, Gomalan Brass [R], led by first trumpet player Marco Pierobon, recorded *Adagio* for their album, *Movie Brass.* Although the arrangement is uncredited, it sounds like the one Stephen McNeff wrote for the Canadian Brass, but without the benefit of mutes in the coda. The group posted a video on *YouTube* of its recording session in Cremona, Italy.[84]

FOR BRASS ENSEMBLES: HORNS OR TROMBONES

The horn sections of the Dallas and Houston orchestras got together in 2008 to record an album titled *Texas Horns.* For one of the tracks Roger Kaza scored the *Adagio for Strings* for this horn choir [R]. In general, the reviewers were favorable; one described the presentation as "particularly beautiful."[85] The brief sample that I have heard seems warm and mellow.

In 1994 Eric Crees [R], the principal co-trombonist for the London Symphony Orchestra arranged *Adagio* for sixteen trombones, which was recorded for the album *The London Trombone Sound* by members of seven English orchestras.[86] Reviewing the recording, Peter Oram, the trombonist in the BBC Scottish Symphony Orchestra, considered this arrangement and the ensemble's performance to be "superb," probably his favorite track on the album. He added, "In reality, the performance must have been very tiring on the lip muscles, but no hint of that can be

[83]Jessica Wood, "Canadians with a Lot of Brass and Good Humor," *Santa Barbara News-Press* (12 August 2000). Other groups that play unspecified brass arrangements are The English Brass Quintet, Sterling and Brass, London Orphean Brass, Das Renn Quintet, Valve Job, and Five Star Brass.

[84]The audio of *Adagio* can be streamed on the group's website: www.gomalanbrass.com or can be downloaded to mp3 at www.trumpetguild.org and other sites. Hans Zellner has also arranged *Adagio* for brass quintet [P].

[85]"Editorial Reviews," *Amazon*, www.amazon.com/Texas-Dallas-Houston-Symphonies-sections.

[86]The participating ensembles were the London Symphony Orchestra, Academy of St. Martin in the Fields, BBC Symphony Orchestra, Royal Opera House Covent Garden Orchestra, English Chamber Orchestra, Philharmonia Orchestra, and London Sinfonietta.

heard by this listener. (Rather you than me, guys!)"[87] In 2000 Crees was appointed principal trombonist for the Royal Opera House Orchestra at Covent Garden. In September of the following year he conducted his arrangement but increased the ensemble to thirty trombones, as a "warm-up" program for the opening night of The Royal Opera.[88]

Tony Boorer, a member of the low brass section of the KwaZulu-Natal (KZN) Philharmonic Orchestra has posted a performance of *Adagio* on *YouTube*.[89] While he usually plays in a quartet with three other trombonists of the orchestra, he apparently multi-tracked all the parts himself for his *Adagio* arrangement. He boasted, "It works so well for trombones that I couldn't resist giving it a go."[90] Given the potential problems of breathing and breath support, he takes the piece at a surprisingly slow tempo; it lasts over eight and a half minutes.

Even without cohorts or multi-tracking, the amazing musician Bill Watrous can play *Adagio* all by himself on a single trombone by using multiphonics! This technique, the simultaneous sounding of two or more notes on a single instrument, has been in use since at least the 1960s. Fellow trombonist Dan Maslowski recalled hearing Watrous play his *Adagio* at a clinic: "I thought I was listening to an orchestra; it was the most accomplished multiphonic presentation I had ever heard."[91] This probably does not constitute an "arrangement" in the traditional sense of the term because few musicians, other than Watrous, could actually manage to perform it. He, in fact, may only play a short excerpt merely to demonstrate this virtuoso technique.

FOR BRASS ENSEMBLES: A TROOP OF TUBAS

Robert Wilkinson [P] scored *Adagio* for tuba quartet—two euphoniums and two tubas—and has transposed the piece down a minor third. As with

[87]"The London Trombone Sound," *British Trombone Society*, www.trombone-society.org.uk/resources/reviews/London.php.

[88]Other trombone arrangements include James Pugh, *Adagio* for the Penn State Trombone Choir with The East Carolina University Trombone Choir; an unlisted arrangement, The Munich Trombone Quartet [R]; Charles DePaolo, trombone octet; James Williamson, trombone octet; and Jason Akai, trombone quintet.

[89]"Barber Adagio for 'Trombone' Quartet–Audio Slide Show," *YouTube* (6 November 2007), posted by tboorer. The audio portion can be found at www.babulous.com/profile.jhtml?user_id+6324. KwaZulu-Natal is a province of South Africa.

[90]*Ibid.*

[91]Dan Maslowski, *Trombone Digest*, www.trombone.org/trombone-l/archives/0202/020219_2306.txt.

the "low" arrangement for four double basses (see below), the sonorities sound full without the need for the *divisi* of the string orchestra version, yet one or two chords lack an important pitch.[92] Kenyon D. Wilson has also arranged *Adagio* for a quartet of low brass. According to *Guide to the Tuba Repertoire,* "there are two possible endings: one with the final phrase performed as *divisi* tubas, and the other which includes euphoniums if there is only one on a part," implying that the version may be played either as a strict quartet or as a larger ensemble.[93] Another arrangement by David Spies [P] is conceived for tuba sextet: three euphoniums, two bass tubas, and contrabass. Another example of large ensembles occurred when students at London's Guildhall School of Music and Drama played an arrangement of *Adagio* for twelve horns and four Wagner tubas at the 17th British Horn Festival (1996).[94] The performance might have impressed (or annoyed) both Wagner and Barber.

FOR PERCUSSION ENSEMBLES

A percussion ensemble as the performing medium for *Adagio for Strings* seems at first to be an odd choice. After all, the piece requires the utmost sustaining power to bring off its lyrical nature; therefore the use of percussion instruments would appear to counteract this intention. Yet well-planned arrangements performed by skillful players can retain the work's inherent sense of sustained lyricism.

Tony Cirone, chair of the percussion department at Indiana University has scored it for his "keyboard percussion orchestra" of xylophone, two vibraphones, five marimbas, and a bass marimba. He justified his addition of marimbas in the group with these remarks:

> The marimba has the unusual characteristic of projecting the softest quality over long phrases (of course like the organ, we don't breathe) and the extremely exciting quality of rapid single

[92]The first page of the score appears on www.windmusicplus.safeshopper.com.

[93]*Guide to the Tuba Repertoire*, ed. R. Winston Morris and Daniel Peratoni (Bloomington: Indiana University Press, 2006), 292.

[94]Allyn Lindsey [P] issued another arrangement for brass.

> stroke rolls at quite loud dynamics. This many marimbas rolling at the climax of this work is something special.[95]

He arranged *Adagio* because he considers it "one of many beautiful works for orchestra that percussionists would never get to perform."[96]

Cirone's comments also apply to *Adagio* arrangements conceived only for marimbas, such as Robert Hohner's [R] version for ten of them. In an ensemble this large, the individual tremolos usually blend into a smooth, seamless sound, especially in the lower parts. The tremolo effect is quite obvious in the melody, which needs to stand out from the rest of the texture. Yet by the time the piece reaches the climax, all marimbas get louder, and as a result, tremolos predominate in all parts.

A program by the Indiana University Percussion Ensemble on 16 November 1998 featured a transcription by Luther Schmidt for five marimbas, including a bass. The restriction to only five performers resulted in a far more "percussive" sound.[97] Pat Peringer's arrangement of *Adagio* for the Kamiakin High School Quartet (on two marimbas) is also percussive because the melody is played in single notes rather than "rolled" tremolos. When the performers change mallets immediately after the climax, the pause before the quiet chord passage is quite long.[98]

FOR PERCUSSION ENSEMBLES: THREE ON ONE MARIMBA

The trio Attacca (Marc Dinitz, Adam Green, Scott Pollard) performs in several musical styles and in many concert settings. Pollard has arranged *Adagio for Strings* for all three players to perform on a single, five-octave marimba. To "facilitate smoother connection of the notes," he transposed it down a half step.[99] He believes that rolling from black to white notes (which would have happened in the original key) can be "shifty sounding."

[95]Tony Cirone, email (17 Febrary 2007) to the author. Cirone's *Adagio* arrangement appeared on a program given by the Indiana University Percussion Ensemble (10 November 2003); on tape at the Indiana University Music Library (IUCD 139767 03-11-10).

[96]*Ibid.*

[97]During this live performance one marimbist missed some crucial accidentals, probably causing some members of the audience to cringe. See IU Music Library (DAT 139767 98-11-16).

[98]Kamiakin High School Quartet, performance at the 2007 Washington State Solo and Ensemble Contest, "Adagio for Strings," *YouTube* (24 October 2007), posted by KaHSdrummer. In April 2008 senior Allison Moucheron conducted the Lebanon Valley College Percussion Ensemble in a seven-marimba version.

[99]Scott Pollard, email (19 August 2004) to the author.

Illustration 4.1. Attacca Marimba Ensemble (Marc Dinitz, Adam Green, Scott Pollard), Kennedy Center, Washington, D.C., August 2005

Courtesy of Attacca Marimba Ensemble

Image by Jennifer Mendiola

The trio performs the piece from memory. Pollard explained:

> The arrangement involves several logistical concerns with mallets and bodies crossing and getting in the way, and it's much easier to get emotionally and physically involved without staring at the music. There's definitely a choreographic element that the audience also appreciates more without music stands in the way.[100]

It is sometimes difficult for a single marimba to yield enough sound, especially during the climax when the loudest sounds must be produced on the least resonant part of the instrument. Pollard acknowledges the problem:

> We've experimented at length to find the right mallets for that passage, while also not destroying the profound effect of the ensuing silence by switching mallets while we move back down

[100] *Ibid.*

the instrument. Fortunately, the soft bass chords that follow are a nice reward for all the flailing away.[101]

According to Pollard, that particular passage is the only place in *Adagio* that may not sound best on a single marimba; others seem like they were written for it, especially in the low register. "In the lower two or three octaves, you can barely hear the multiple strokes of the mallets—just waves of sound coming from the resonators."[102]

Attacca has performed *Adagio* many times, and audience feedback has been outstanding. Critic Gail Weil considered this arrangement "convincing" but observed, however, that "the execution didn't quite fully capture the stirring emotional value of the piece."[103] Pollard was surprised by such a critique: "Most people love the piece to begin with and are shocked at how well it works for marimba. It's really something else and still gives me chills every time we do it."[104] Performers' enthusiasm and audience responses typically outweigh the complaints of reviewers.

Just how many marimbas can gather together to play *Adagio*? A student at the University of North Texas thinks a 1996 performance in which he was involved set a world record. He and sixty-one others all "piled onto a stage" and played a ten-part arrangement with fifty-eight marimbas and four bass marimbas. He recalled, "That many of them playing like strings sounded like a choir of angels. Go see a marimba choir if you every get the chance."[105]

FOR PERCUSSION ENSEMBLES: STEEL DRUMS

In 1992 G. Allan (Al) O'Connor [P] arranged *Adagio for Strings* for the steel drum band at Northern Illinois University. A note in the published score contained the following promise: "this emotional piece from one of

[101]*Ibid.*

[102]*Ibid.*

[103]Gail Weil, "Attacca Percussion Group," *Washington Post* (11 July 2005), C: 5. Attacca has performed *Adagio* at schools, at music festivals, and at the 2004 Percussive Arts Society International Convention. See "Vic Firth Concert Percussion Podcast: Attacca Percussion Group Plays Adagio for Strings," *YouTube* (19 April 2009), posted by drummerboy1138. This video was recorded at Robert E. Lee High School, Fairfax County, Virginia. Nancy Zeltsman [R] has arranged *Adagio for Strings* for "Madam Rubio: Marimba Duo," consisting of Zeltsman and Janis M. Potter. The observant reader may notice that "Madam Rubio" is an anagram for "marimba duo."

[104]Scott Pollard, email (19 August 2004) to the author.

[105]Scott Pollard, quoted in *Alpheus*, www.Everthing2.com/index.pl?nodeid=927516.

America's great contemporary composers will provide a show-stopping number for your band."[106] Although listed as "medium difficulty," some groups might find the arrangement problematic. In fact, James Finnie, director of the steel drum band at Indiana State University, ran into trouble when he rehearsed it with his own group. "Al would probably have had numerous players per part; ours was more of a chamber ensemble of eight performers," too small a group for a public performance.[107] The primary problem occurs during the climax, where the range goes very high for the tenor pans; it sounds too "percussive." Finnie tried to mitigate this effect by using softer mallets, but that did not produce enough sound.

An arrangement of *Adagio* was to be performed by the PanAmerican Steel Band at the University of Iowa on 8 May 2004, but, according to its conductor Dan Moore, the ensemble members ran out of rehearsal time and could not realize a polished performance. Like Finnie's group, his ensemble encountered difficulties: "As you can imagine the challenge of this piece is the continuous rise of pitch level, dynamics, and intensity. For the steel band this section goes out of range of the bass pans at just the point when you need the most sonic reinforcement."[108]

In 2007, when Linda Versprille decided to perform O'Connor's *Adagio* arrangement with her group, The Cainhoy Steel Tigers, a sixteen-member steel drum band, she made a few adjustments. She also experienced problems at the climactic section at first but came up with a clever solution by switching to staccato tips. "I directed the students to make their pans 'scream.'"[109] To prepare them for rehearsal, she asked them to listen to the album *Barber's Adagio* [R], which contains a variety of arrangements, "to help determine tone color for their instruments."[110] At a recent concert a man swore he heard a French horn! What is the audience reaction? "They go wild over it."[111]

[106]"Adagio for Strings by Samuel Barber, arr. Al O'Connor (Panyard)," *Lone Star Percussion*, www.lonestarpercussion.com.

[107]James Finnie, interview (5 August 2004) with the author.

[108]Dan Moore, email (11 August 2004) to the author.

[109]Linda Versprille, email (30 April 2007) to the author.

[110]*Ibid.*

[111]*Ibid.*

FOR PERCUSSION ENSEMBLES: HAND CHIMES

A fifteen-member handbell and chime ensemble, Embellishments, performs bi-annual concerts in the Birmingham, Alabama area. *Adagio for Strings* is one of director Phyllis Kirk's favorite classical pieces and, in her opinion, "one of the most moving."[112] When she found no published arrangement for either handbells or chimes, she decided to arrange it herself for her ensemble. Due to the vast seven-octave range of the chimes, she was able "to emulate the beautiful and flowing lines"[113] played by the strings. "Although hand chimes are percussive in nature (but mellower than handbells), by using gentle wrist snaps and mallets on the lowest chimes, we were able to attain the marvelous sustained quality of the music."[114] After playing it on their 2006 Christmas program "there was a moment of silence and then thunderous applause. Even more important was the feeling that we had succeeded in conveying the beauty and feelings inherent in *Adagio for Strings*."[115] The work seems to be able to withstand even the most extreme ranges of instrumentation.

ADAGIO FOR (SOME) *STRINGS*

Although I have not encountered *Adagio* arranged for only violins, there are arrangements for cohorts of violas, cellos, or double basses. Four violists of the Oregon Symphony organized a quartet, logically called Four Violas. Because there are few pieces specifically composed for their particular medium (are there any?), virtually the ensemble's entire repertoire must consist of arrangements. Charles Noble, a member of the group, characterizes his transcription of *Adagio for Strings* as somewhat straightforward. "The viola parts are taken down an octave where register problems become an issue, and the cello part is taken up an octave where the notes fall below the range of the viola."[116] Otherwise it is close to the original string quartet.

The work has also been scored for various numbers of cellos. A four-membered group simply called Cello [R] featured Paula Kimper's

[112]Phyllis Kirk, email (17 February 2007) to the author.

[113]*Ibid.*

[114]*Ibid.*

[115]*Ibid.*

[116]Charles Noble, email (6 September 2004) to the author. The other three violists are Mara Lise Gearman, Brian Quincy, and Joël Belgique. See www.thefourviolas.com/home.htm.

arrangement on some of its concerts. Maureen McDermott, one of the members, wondered how to expand the boundaries of classical music: "We wanted to reach out and grab some new audiences. . . . There's not a lot of original music that's written for four cellos."[117] Critic Charles McCardell thought their "excellent" *Adagio* arrangement had "absolutely no trace of shrill pathos": it showcased the scope of the group and its "ability to cover almost the full range of a string quartet."[118] A group known as The Portland Cello Project (a.k.a. Celli or Cellodarity) includes in their repertoire Noah Seitz's *Adagio* arrangement for four cellos, which the ensemble scheduled on concerts in 2007. The YST Cello Choir from the Yong Siew Conservatory of Music, a part of the National University of Singapore, plays an *Adagio* transcription by Nella Hunkins, principal cellist with the Singapore Symphony Orchestra.[119] In May 2000 the Northern Ohio Cello Choir toured with a program that offered an arrangement of *Adagio* for eight cellos. With such an expanded ensemble, the opportunity arises to project a warmer string sound than with a quartet. Yet larger ensembles may push things a bit too far. For instance, in April 2005 Northwestern University presented a "Monster String Concert" as a part of its "Rite of Strings Festival," featuring a group of seventy cellos playing *Adagio*. This was probably a one-time "gimmick" presentation.

Even rarer are original pieces for four double basses, a comparable lacuna that can be assuaged by the preparation of suitable arrangements. To this end bass player Norman Ludwin scored the Barber *Adagio* for double bass quartet. While its sound resonates primarily in the deep bass register, bass I, which introduces the melody at the beginning, is required to play in a fairly high range. In a few places, the direction of an interval in the melody is reversed, *e.g.*, a tritone may move down rather than up. In this arrangement double stops, so important in the original quartet, are not necessary because harmonies sound full enough without them. In fact, they would thicken the texture adversely. According to a note in the catalogue, "it is a great crowd pleaser."[120]

[117]Aaron Davis, "Hello, Cello: String Quartet Takes Singular Approach to Chamber Music," *The Record* [Stockton, Calif.] (21 October 2004). The other four members are Maria Kitsopoulos, Laura Koehl, Maureen McDermott, and Caryl Paiser.

[118]Charles McCardell, "Cello: Four of a Good Thing," *Washington Post* (25 June 1994), G: 3. The recorded performance by Cello has been played several times on the radio show, *Hearts of Space*.

[119]"Barber Adagio for Strings by YST Cello Choir," *YouTube* (16 August 2008), posted by Celloheaven.

[120]L. Bennett Crantford, *Music with Double Bass in Mind*, www.ludwinmusic.com.

Dissatisfied with Ludwin's solution for string bass quartet, L. Bennett Crantford [R], a member of Outer Bass, prepared his own alternative for the album also called *Outer Bass*.[121] He felt that the Ludwin version was too easy to play and was "too low to make for pleasant sonorities."[122] (I agree: the melody, played by the cello in the original, is much too low in the range of the instrument; this whole passage sounds thick and muddy.) Crantford's initial response, given the "musical strength and popularity of the original," was that re-inventing the piece for only double basses was "borderline heresy," but, after relistening to Barber's quartet, he became determined to make his version "as pure as possible," and he maintained the key signature because "the color was too unique to change."[123] His ultimate product is, in his own words, "very difficult and demanding" for the players, especially at the climax. There the high tessitura does not lend itself well to the instruments. At first, his colleagues were somewhat concerned about audience reaction, but their first performances were greeted with compliments for the rich sonority.

> After hearing the Outer Bass recording, most listeners will find that it successfully portrays the values of Barber's work, but this is due mainly to the intrinsic properties of the piece itself. Yet in order for a listener to have a positive experience with any transcription, it is necessary to have the discipline to make some disconnection from the original.[124]

While some might consider such tinkering borderline heresy, others will put prejudices behind them and welcome a double bass version of *Adagio* with an open mind.

Can you imagine *Adagio for Strings* for just one double bass? Virtuoso bass player Volkan Orhon [R] has come up with a unique solution. For his album *Multiplicity* (2002) he recorded all the tracks separately and then combined them into a kind of "one-man" ensemble. He was inspired by a colleague, Scott Metcalfe, who was teaching a course on multiple track recording techniques. Orhon remarked, "I was always a huge fan of

[121]Crantford considers his adaptation the only one sanctioned by G. Schirmer.

[122]L. Bennett Crantford, email (13 March 2012) to author.

[123]*Ibid.*

[124]*Ibid.*

Adagio so I decided to try this piece as an experiment."[125] He began with the Ludwin arrangement but made a few adjustments. He recorded the top line and used it as a guide for building the rest of the parts from the bottom up. He acknowledged that it was no easy accomplishment, especially controlling the rubatos: "it was a challenge to feel the landings and cutoffs of each chord."[126] Wearing headphones, which were "half-on, half off,"[127] allowed him to match his live playing to his previously recorded tracks. He occasionally performs *Adagio* in concert by playing a soundtrack of the lower parts while delivering the top part live. For such a performance a few additional adjustments must be made. For instance, when the melody switches to the cello part in the original, Orhon moves down to that part. Because the top part has nothing but rests during this passage, he would otherwise be standing there with bow in hand and nothing to do. When the top part re-enters to build to the climax, he switches back. The listener, however, may be surprised that a few of the quiet chords are slightly different than in the original. In the coda he logically takes the lower of the two octaves for the melody. He is pleased that "People seem to enjoy it and get really fascinated by the whole process."[128]

FOR OTHER STRINGS:
SOLO HARP, GUITAR ENSEMBLE, MANDOLINS, AND ERHU

The term "string sound" typically implies the bowed instruments of the orchestra, but obviously harps, mandolins, and guitars fall into this category. Not surprisingly, *Adagio* has been arranged for those instruments as well. In his arrangement for solo harp David Ice has modified Strickland's organ version. Although he retained the original key, like several others, he reduced the meter from 4 / 2 to 4 / 4. He has argued that "the piece lends itself well to the harp, in terms of sonorities, accidentals, and fingerings."[129] The harp's lack of sustaining power, nonetheless, created some problems when the music approached the climax. He opted for a chromatic glissando: "It does change the flavor

[125]Volkan Orhon, email (22 June 2005) to the author.

[126]*Ibid.*

[127]*Ibid.*

[128]"Volkan ORHON–Samuel Barber's Adagio for Strings," *YouTube* (7 May 2007), posted by VulkanOrhon. This live performance was given at a benefit concert for September 11th Terrorist Attack Victims.

[129]David Ice, email (15 December 2007) to the author.

Illustration 4.2. California Guitar Trio (Hideyo Moriya, Paul Richards, Bert Lams), The State Room, Salt Lake City, Utah

Courtesy of the California Guitar Trio

Image by Paul Galbraith Photography

a bit, but it maintains the huge sound and the drama of the moment."[130] Ice conceded that the harp arrangement takes on a totally different character than the original for bowed string: "It sort of loses the 'angst' of the original and sounds, surprisingly 'Spanish guitar-ish.'"[131] He has performed it at a few concerts as well as at weddings when brides have specifically requested it. The audience response has been positive. He confessed, "I have always appreciated and respected Adagio. I have always felt it was the perfect musical expression of the primal scream, 'WHY?' and as such it IS beautiful."[132] Perhaps his chromatic glissando at the climax adds power to that primal scream.

CD Track 9

The California Guitar Trio has an eclectic repertoire because each guitarist brings his own background: Paul Richards, rock and jazz; Bert Lams, classical; and Hideyo Moriya, surf music. Prolific composer and guitarist Stan Funicelli arranged Barber's piece for their three custom-made acoustic guitars, which have special tunings to allow extensions above and below the usual range. Lams [R] later reworked Funicelli's arrangement: "I really got carried away for several days and came out with something I think is good: Stan is like a fourth member of the CGT. He encourages us with new ideas all the time."[133] One result is a guitar-trio *Adagio*.

After hearing the group perform live, reviewer Mac Randall admitted that he appreciated it more than the recording, which struck him as being somewhat cold: "but live, the majestically swelling lines featured all the pathos you could want. . . . When all three guitarists played full chords,

[130]*Ibid.*

[131]*Ibid.*

[132]*Ibid.*

[133]Bert Lams, "CGT Update from Bert Lams," *California Guitar Trio* (13 September 1997); reprinted www.cgtrio.com/upd0997.htm.

you'd think you were listening to someone with a few extra fingers on each hand attacking a giant, ultrasonic harpsichord."[134] Such a harpsichord reference may seem odd, but that is sometimes the sound suggested when the three instruments combine. Also, one or two notes and an occasional chord do not correspond to the original, which might surprise those who already know the piece.

The most remarkable aspect of the performance is the distribution of notes among the three guitars, in a technique known as "circulating melodies." Lams explained: "Each player passes on a note to the next in succession. Underneath the circulations I divided the harmonies for each player. Taken individually the parts do not seem to make sense, but when played together they fit together like a puzzle."[135] This represents a kind of musical "pointillism" that allows notes of a melody to connect smoothly throughout a phrase. Normally, if a single guitarist plays a melody, the fingers moving up and down the fret-board cut off a note before the next one is played. This new "circulating" technique is somewhat like the use of a damper pedal on a piano, allowing slight overlaps between notes. The players learned the technique from their mentor, Robert Fripp, who originated it as an exercise in "quality of attention" for a large group of guitarists. After participating in one of these sessions, Lams recalled: "If you can imagine a group of 20-30 players in a circle passing a note around, from player to player, you may have a faint idea of what this means."[136] When the trio appeared on the NPR program, *All Things Considered* on 5 September 1998, they explained and demonstrated this technique, one guitar at a time, with Beethoven's "Moonlight" Sonata, another selection on the album.[137] Lams is pleased with listeners' response to the arrangement: "In my experience, *Adagio* is one of the most captivating pieces of music I have ever played for an audience."[138]

A somewhat unexpected string medium for the Barber composition is the mandolin orchestra. As with a symphonic string ensemble, a mandolin

[134]Mac Randall, "Concert Review" (Bottom Line, New York Performance), *Yahoo! Launch* (20 July 1998), www.launch.yahoo.com/read/concert.asp?contentID=158769.

[135]Bert Lams, email (19 August 2004) to the author.

[136]*Ibid.*

[137]California Guitar Trio, interview (5 September 1998) with Daniel Schorr, "California Guitar Trio: NPR," *National Public Radio*, www.npr.org/templates/story/story.php?storyID=1006483.

[138]Bert Lams, email (19 August 2004) to the author. Other guitar groups that have performed an *Adagio* arrangement are Quattro Formaggio and Casting Shadows, both in the Seattle area.

orchestra calls for a range of comparable instruments in the mandolin family: treble mandolins, mandoras, mandocellos. Although there are mandolin equivalents for the bass viol, they are rarely used. Sometimes guitars are added. Mandolin orchestras that have featured an *Adagio* transcription in concert hail from New York City; Providence, Rhode Island; Hillsboro, Oregon; Seoul, South Korea; and Melbourne, Australia. The Oregon Mandolin Orchestra [R] has recorded the work on its album *Live 2000*; Soongsil University Mandolin Orchestra posted its rendition on *YouTube*.[139] No arranger is credited in any of these performances. The musicians, perhaps, simply play from the Schirmer orchestral parts. One must adjust, nonetheless, to the constant but necessary tremolos of this particular ensemble. Unlike a group of marimbas where tremolos may recede into the background, their cumulative effect here inevitably stands out.

Possibly the most exotic string arrangement of *Adagio* that I have encountered is the one by Academy Award-winning composer Ryuichi Sakamoto [R] on his 1990 album *Beauty*. While he accompanies on the piano, Jiang Jian Hua plays the melody on a Chinese instrument, the erhu.[140] As fans of Chinese music know, the instrument is named for its "two-strings," which are bowed on the diagonal with the bow interlocked between the strings and the neck. The sound often resembles the human voice, but in this performance, there is also a hint of the electronic instrument known as the Theremin. This is truly an East-meets-West approach to *Adagio*. The composer met Jiang when he was composing the soundtrack to *The Last Emperor* (1987), for which he won his Oscar®. Wanting to give his score an authentic Chinese sound, he asked her to play the erhu on several tracks. After he prepared his *Adagio* arrangement, it must have entered his subconscious mind when he wrote the music for *Little Buddha* (1993). Some critics compare parts of that score to Barber's composition.

Samuel Barber and the Avant-Garde

One rarely encounters both the name Samuel Barber and the term "avant-garde" in the same sentence; most people consider his music the antithesis of progressive trends in the late twentieth century. Yet two

[139] The video post has since been deleted.

[140] "ADAGIO: Ryuichi Sakamoto," *YouTube* (16 January 2010), posted by yaiga. Unfortunately, *Adagio* is only provided on the Japanese release of the *Beauty* album.

avant-garde works integrate taped performances of *Adagio for Strings* into their approach, and a third starts with it as the basis for an improvisation.

Compiled by David G. Porter in 1987, *First He'll Tell You What Happened While He Was Dead* is a collection of taped pieces that he describes as a "collage of various sounds, musical selections, and excerpts from radio and television."[141] The movements are "different ways of using text-sound within ordered frameworks; each of the borrowed sources is used both referentially (to its source) and as the sound itself."[142] In one movement, "Reagan vs. the Barber *Adagio for Strings,"* Porter took phrases from President Ronald Reagan's "Address to the Nation on the Iran Arms and Contra Aid Controversy" (4 March 1987) and superimposed them on a performance of *Adagio*.[143] The score itself is unchanged; it simply emerges as the soundtrack for a new textual interpretation.

Before the music begins, Reagan assures the American public, "Your trust is what gives a President his powers of leadership and his personal strength." Much of the discourse is a kind of confession with political justifications. Once the music begins, Porter adds other sentences from the speech, sometimes condensed, repeated, or re-ordered. As *Adagio* nears its climax, Reagan confesses, "I did approve [the arms shipments], I just can't say specifically when . . . you take your knocks and then move on, you learn your lesson." When the quiet chords appear, he admits, "by the time you reach my age you've made plenty of mistakes; you pull yourself together, you change, you go forward." During the coda: "I've heard the message from you, the American people. I have a great deal that I want to accomplish with you and for you over the next two years. And the Lord willing, that's exactly what I intend to do." His last words, "Good night, and God bless you," coincide with *Adagio*'s final phrase. This is similar to the "so let it be" juxtaposition of text and music at the Martin Luther King performance mentioned in the previous chapter. Perhaps Porter sensed the same prayerful conclusions at the end of *Adagio,* but gave it an ironic twist.

[141]David G. Porter, notes to the cassette recording (Washington, D.C.: Recorded Sound Reference Center at the Library of Congress, RYB 4282).

[142]*Ibid.*

[143]The text of the speech itself can be found in The Public Papers of President Ronald W. Reagan at The Ronald Reagan Presidential Library (National Archives and Records Administration). See www.reagan.utexas.edu.

Does Porter intend his Reagan-*Adagio* juxtaposition to be serious or a parody? If the President's disclosure is sincere, which at face value may be true, it deserves a serious musical accompaniment. On the other hand, if the confession is viewed strictly as prevarication, a calculated effort to put a "spin" on a potentially volatile political situation, then Barber's plaintive music only reinforces the speech's hollow rhetoric. (Responses probably depend on political affiliation!)

Another avant-garde work incorporating *Adagio for Strings* was a performance without an official title (that I know of). While a tape played the Barber work, the noted improviser Keith Rowe performed segments from Cornelius Cardew's *Treatise* (1963-1967), a work of "free graphics, without a single symbol whose meaning has been agreed in advance."[144] Rowe, a founding member of the British group AMM, is best known for his improvisations on the table-top guitar, an electric guitar laid flat on a table and prepared with various small objects, such as paper clips, springs, and brushes, much like John Cage's prepared piano. In fact, the instrument is sometimes called a "prepared guitar." To this appliance he sometimes adds electronic devices.

In the mid-1960s Rowe became friends with Cardew, an avant-garde composer associated with AMM, who pushed the group more into the "indeterminacy" of the post-Cage generation. Shortly after Cardew was killed in 1981 by a hit and run driver, Rowe and fellow musician Phil Minton devised a memorial to him incorporating an improvisation based on some pages from *Treatise*. The performance took place at the Arnolfini Gallery in Bristol, United Kingdom, known for its experimental and electronic events. But why *Adagio?* To that question Rowe responded, "I think it's because of its American association. . . . I think the Barber was played at Kennedy's death." When asked if Cardew would have appreciated being compared to Kennedy, Rowe replied, "Well, music gets used, whether you like it or not."[145] Of course, Barber also died in 1981. While it may only be a coincidence, is it possible that Rowe's performance was a memorial to both Cardew and Barber? As far as I know, Rowe has never commented on that possibility. I wonder what Barber would have thought of such a use of his music.

[144]Francis Routh, "On Cardew's Scratch Orchestra," *Music Web International* (April 1970); reprinted www.musicweb-international.com/SandH/2002/Jan02/cardew.htm.

[145]Dan Warburton, interview (January 2001) with Keith Rowe; reprinted www.paristranstlantic.com/magazine/interviews/rowe.html).

Bone Dance is a group of four musicians—Janice Porrohman (a.k.a. Janet Pilcher), Jeremy Rustovich (a.k.a. Peter Longfingers), Larry Sturtz (a.k.a. Johnny Bedlam), and Stuart Fingenbaum—who describe themselves as a "music motley," a chamber group with an "explorational approach." Critic J. Edward Tremlett has referred to them as "chamberpunk," a term they do not particularly like.[146] The men play an arrangement of *Adagio for Strings* for flute, violin, and cello, while Porrohman reads excerpts from the last letters of the Rosenbergs, the Jewish-American couple caught up in the intrigues of the Cold War in the 1950s. The group's approach allows pieces to be "reconstructed." Tremlett complained, "Sometimes I could recognize those pieces, however distorted and idiosyncratic their performance. And sometimes I was totally puzzled, wondering if I wasn't hearing two or more pieces stacked atop one another like building blocks."[147] This is likely to be the scenario for the group's take on *Adagio*.

While the scores generated by the Barber work described in this chapter can be properly considered transcriptions or arrangements, the treatments by David G. Porter, Keith Rowe, and Bone Dance probably fit more accurately another designation: transmogrification. This term can account for their distancing themselves so completely from the composer's original concept. Finally, can there be more musical echoes of *Adagio for Strings*? Given the number and variety of pieces discussed above, one might think that all possible combinations of instruments have now been exhausted. But that underestimates the ingenuity of musicians, who never seem to run out of new ideas to adapt Barber's composition for their performing needs.

[146]Edward Tremlett, "Bone Dance, A Musical Motley for *Changeling: The Dreaming* and *Wraith: The Oblivion, Sounds,*" *The Wraith Project* (December 2003); reprinted www.cattail.nu/wraithproject/archives/0404bonedance.html.

[147]*Ibid.*

CHAPTER 5

Adagio and the Performing Arts

While performances of *Adagio for Strings,* the string quartet excerpt, and Agnus Dei provide focused musical experiences all in their own right, a number of choreographers, stage directors, and other entrepreneurs have appropriated one of the versions as a component of their own artistic creations. Most prominent is its service as the accompaniment for ballet and other types of dance. There are currently over one-hundred different dances set to Barber's composition—ranging from the traditional (Kirov) to the experimental (Baryshnikov) and from professional companies to university dance departments.[1] A portion of *Adagio* has also been adopted as underscoring for dramatic productions. Less expected, perhaps, is its introduction as a carefully integrated part of ice-skating routines, outdoor festivals, acrobatic and body-building displays, and other performance media. Under such circumstances the work has reached an even larger audience, notably those who would not normally attend concerts. As a result, it has become an even more prevalent and popular favorite. In this chapter I will deal with some of the more notable (and creative) examples of this phenomenon.

An Invitation to the Dance

> Samuel Barber's *Adagio for Strings* has cried in vain for adequate dance treatment almost from the moment it was written.
>
> —Dean Wallace, "Ballet '64 Shows Big Improvement" (19 April 2004).[2]

In 1964 Richard Gibson answered this cry for a dance treatment with *Adagio for Ten and Two,* staged for the summer season of the San Francisco Ballet. It seems strange that it would take choreographers twenty-five years from the work's inception to realize its dance potential, yet, to the best of my knowledge, Gibson's is the earliest choreographic setting. Since then, professional choreographers from both national and regional companies have selected it—as well as the quartet movement and Agnus Dei—as the musical foundation for many ballet and modern dance exhibitions. The styles of dance have been widely diverse. The

[1]A selected list of such choreographed dances is provided in Appendix 5.

[2]Dean Wallace, quoted in Richard Gibson, "Ballet '64 Shows Big Improvement" [unidentified newspaper clipping sent by Gibson to the author, 19 April 2004]. Wallace is a professional dance critic.

slow tempo is perfect for a *pas de deux,* but it is equally suitable for solo dances as well as stagings for larger ensembles. The music's modest length makes it ideal for a short dance; choreographers of full-length productions have often incorporated it into a longer program with other similar or contrasting selections.

The Traditional Male-Female *Pas de Deux*

A *pas de deux* is often considered the high point of a full-length ballet, the much-anticipated moment when both the prima ballerina and her male partner deliver their most difficult and beautiful movements. A *pas de deux,* moreover, may be conceived as separate and independent, as is the case with the four dances described below. Although they originate in three different countries—the former Soviet Union, Argentina, and the United States—they do not communicate nationalistic views but rather convey universal relationships between men and women as expressed by male and female dancers. The dances do not portray specific characters (*e.g.*, no prince or princess is ever implied), nor do they impart complex and linear story lines. Important psychological meanings may extend beyond a mere abstract concept. Furthermore, they often combine—in varying degrees—gestures and other aspects of both traditional ballet and modern dance.

BARBER'S *ADAGIO*: KIROV BALLET COMPANY

In 1990 Oleg Vinogradov, then director and artistic director of the Kirov Ballet, choreographed a *pas de deux* to *Adagio for Strings* for two of its leading dancers, Yelena Yevteyeva and Eldar Aliev. He devised the work for their guest appearance with the Australian Ballet in November of that year. Shortly thereafter they went to Denmark to shoot the video version, which proved to be a difficult taping session.[3] Aliev recalled:

> We started at 8:00 AM and finished at 9:00 PM. We had to do it twenty-three or twenty-four times. My feet were bleeding because they had a very strange cover for the floor; it wasn't marley (a typical material for dance flooring) because that reflects

[3]The Kirov performance is available on DVD: *Kirov Classics* [formerly called *The Maryinsky Ballet St. Petersburg Mixed Bill*] (Kultur International Films, 1991). It has often been featured on *Classic Arts Showcase*, a Satellite Programming Service used as a filler on local PBS outlets.

> the light. This surface was very sticky, and I was dancing in bare feet. By the end there was no skin on the soles of my feet.[4]

Despite such obstacles the performance looks calm, effortless, and elegant.

The dance exhibits the aesthetic of classical ballet but with some crossover features from modern dance. While it contains typical ballet steps, *e.g., bourée, developé* (various leg extensions), and *port de bras* (traditional arm positions), it also has modern elements. For instance, one movement borrows a *promenade* from ballet, where the male lifts his partner, but her unusual birdlike movement on his shoulders is more like modern dance. Dancer and choreographer Cynthia Pratt noted that the dance is "cooler than the music; the movements are positional rather than emotional. It is about form rather than passion."[5] By this, she implies that the dancers undergo a series of poses, gradually and smoothly moving in and out of one position to another. There is very little "choreographic" movement in the traditional sense—more like slow acrobatics.[6] The pale blue costumes, designed by Vinogradov, may contribute to the coolness. She concluded, "there is more concern about the beauty of the line than any real connection between the dancers."[7] This suggests that the music may be at odds with the choreography. Yet Aliev is convinced that Vinogradov's intention was "not to follow the musical beats but to follow the musical expression. He expressed himself by the way he heard the music—the way he envisioned the illustration of it."[8] Indeed, the choreography is more active as the music approaches the climax, with the dancers collapsing gracefully on the floor in time for the quiet chords. At the end, after the music itself has ended, the two move apart, with the female dancer rolling to the front of the stage, leaving the male dancer standing far upstage.

Is the dance strictly abstract, or is there a hidden, psychological subtext attached to it? Dance critic Jann Parry referred to it in rather

[4]Eldar Aliev, interview (14 June 2004) with the author. According to Aliev, the main challenge was the atmospheric use of fog on stage; they could not make any cuts or edits because the fog would appear in different layers in the finished film. Therefore they had to capture the dance in one complete take. (They must have given up on this approach because I see no evidence of fog in the final production.)

[5]Cynthia Pratt, interview (1 May 2004) with the author.

[6]For actual acrobatic performances accompanied by *Adagio*, see later in this chapter.

[7]Cynthia Pratt, interview (1 May 2004) with the author.

[8]Eldar Aliev, interview (14 June 2004) with the author.

overt sexual tones: "twin souls . . . yearn for freedom from oppression or, possibly, freedom of expression by going through most of the permutations in the Kama Sutra. Agonized expressions indicate that this is art."[9] She also implied that it is "acrobatic porn posing as ballet."[10] Another reviewer thought the two dancers represented Adam and Eve.[11] Frankly, I think that both critics have imposed extraneous meanings onto the work. Compared to the next two examples, this one is the least programmatic, the most abstract.

A year after leaving the Kirov in 1997, Vinogradov became artistic director of the Universal Ballet of Korea, a company created by the Rev. Sun Myung Moon of the Unification Church (whose members are better known as "Moonies"). Dancer Julia Pak was engaged to marry his son, but, when he was killed in a car crash, she married his ghost (!) and took the name Julia H. Moon. She became the company's ballerina-in-chief and general director. Aliev remembered that, when he went to Korea to work with this new company, Vinogradov restaged *Adagio* for him and Moon: "I remember rehearsing with her, but I don't know if she ever performed it."[12] She may not have, but Tatiana Ariskina and Dae-Won Lee danced it when Universal Ballet performed in Chicago, Washington, D.C., Los Angeles, and the Redland's Bowl.

ECOS: BALLET ARGENTINO

Argentinian Mauricio Wainrot also staged a *pas de deux* to *Adagio for Strings,* which became prominent in the repertoire of Julio Bocca's Ballet Argentino: *Ecos.*[13] Wainrot originally choreographed it in 1992 for Eldar Aliev and Leslie Browne (of the movie *Turning Point* fame). They first danced it in Montreal at *Le Jeune de Québec* and a year later at *Les Galas des Etoiles*. Aliev remembered:

> The producer invited Wainrot to devise a piece for Leslie Brown and me. We danced to *Adagio for Strings,* but it was a completely

[9]Jann Parry, "Arts (Dance): Ancient and Modern," *The* [London] *Observer* (18 July 1993), 56.

[10]*Ibid.*

[11]"Redlands Bowl 2001 Season," *Redlands Web*, www.redlandsweb.com/calendar/Bowl2001/july17.htm.

[12]Eldar Aliev, interview (14 June 2004) with the author.

[13]The dance was featured on programs during the company's tours of South America (2001), the United States (2002), and Europe (2003).

different choreography from Vinogradov's. Wainrot's was a completely different concept, a completely different vision of the music.[14]

Bocca confessed, "I always liked Barber's *Adagio* and, when I saw Mauricio's *pas de deux*, I liked it even more."[15] He therefore secured the rights for his company. Pedro Ignazio Calderon conducted the Orquesta Sinfónica Nacional Argentina for a recording designed especially for this new production.

In his choreography Wainrot attempts to tell more of a story than Vinogradov. His program notes sum up the narrative: the dance reflects the intimacy of two lovers who meet in the night, discover each other, fall in love, and "continue together in an imaginary journey."[16] Reviewer Kate Snedeker observed that the dance was

> clearly about mature love, and one could see this relationship expressed in the relaxed, flowing quality of the dancing. With nearly perfect timing in the partnering, one could believe that these were intimate lovers who knew each other's bodies well. The lighting enhanced the feeling of intimacy as it focused on the two dancers, bathing them in a gentle glow, with the darkness around them giving an illusion of a wall through which the audience was getting a glimpse at a private scene.[17]

At the beginning the dancers are presented in silhouette but are gradually illuminated as the dance progresses. As in Vinogradov's choreography, movements are based on ballet steps but in a modern form. Much of the time the male dancer partners the female as he would in classical ballet, but at other times both dancers move on or close to the floor, typical of modern dance. At the climax of the music the male dancer lifts his

[14]Eldar Aliev, interview (14 June 2004) with the author.

[15]Julio Bocca, email (3 April 2004) to the author. [Translation by Linda M. Willem]

[16]Mauricio Wainrot, from the program notes for *Ecos*: "La intimidad de dos amantes es la que refleja esta obra. Es nocturna y en sus movimentos ellos se encuentran, se descubren y se aman, y siguen juntos un camino imaginario." The intimacy of two lovers is reflected in this work. It is night and they encounter each other in their movements, they are discovered and love each other as they continue together in an imaginary journey. [Translation by Jacob Hallman]

[17]Kate Snedeker, "Julio Bocca and Ballet Argentino," *Criticaldance.com Selected Reviews*, www.criticaldance.com/reviews/2002/bocca_ballet-argentina_021108.html.

partner, slowly lowers her, and gives her a brief kiss. As Snedeker described it:

> The connection between the two dancers was captured in one brief moment when the circle formed by their arms, hands clasped, was illuminated from behind and above. It was a powerful image of connection that needed no further illumination of body or face to convey emotion. And hand in hand, the dancers left the stage, to "follow an imaginary Route."[18]

Most critics were impressed. Punch Shaw considered *Ecos* "visually stunning" and "as languid and emotional as Barber's haunting score."[19] R. M. Campbell responded with comparable praise:

> Bocca was all sinewy line. His legato phrases were seamless and perfectly finished. His partner, Cecilia Figaredo, . . . represents a ravishing sense of spirit and style. That they paralleled Barber's *Adagio for Strings*, is an understatement.[20]

Bocca admitted that, while the Barber score is "very beautiful to dance to, it wasn't difficult for us technically. To me it isn't sad, but very romantic. I think that the audience really likes the romanticism it implies, and we are living in an age when people need those feelings."[21] Wainrot's *pas de deux* is, indeed, warmer than Vinogradov's. Its romantic nature is vivid and lingers in the memory long after the dance is over.

YOUTH: HARKNESS BALLET

The Harkness Ballet presented its version of *Adagio for Strings* in New York at the Broadway Theater in November 1967. It was choreographed by Richard Wagner (not the Ring Cycle composer) for Lone Isaksen and

[18] *Ibid.*

[19] Punch Shaw, "Fine Program Suffers from Overdone Audio," [Fort Worth, Tex.] *Star-Telegram* (30 March 2004).

[20] R. M. Campbell, "Terrific Dancers Propel Ballet Argentino," *Seattle Post-Intelligencer* (10 April 2004). Prior to the American tour Bocca's partners were Rosana Pérez and Eleonora Cassiano; others who have danced in this work are Hernán Piquín, Alejandro Parenet, and Silvina Perillo.

[21] Julio Bocca, email (3 April 2004) to the author. [Translation by Linda M. Willem]

Lawrence Rhodes, principal dancer of the company. Reviewer Don McDonagh remarked, "As a choreographer, Wagner obviously doesn't subscribe to the notion that youths have all the fun"; in this moving ballet "a young couple exquisitely missed connections."[22] He noted that Rhodes

> was touched lightly by a vision of a girl who disappeared almost as quickly as it took him to be aware of her. Miss Isaksen, the vision and the reality of his dreams, remained just out of reach, whether she was standing beside him or poignantly taunting his memory.[23]

He described the plot with the cliché, "boy meets girl, boy loses girl," and added that "the alternating moments of elation and despair were clearly projected and that at the end, with the disappearance of his dream woman, the boy was left crouched in the interrogating glare of lights palpably pressing him to the ground."[24] *New York Times* dance critic Clive Barnes was only moderately impressed: the ballet describes "adolescent love, its pain and fervor, the duet is corn, yet corn quite shrewdly sown by Mr. Wagner, and rapturously reaped" by the dancers.[25] Another critic, Doris Hering, thought the company's New York City debut was a "provocative one that holds exciting potential."[26] Isaksen and Rhodes later performed the *pas de deux* with the National Ballet of the Netherlands, which was televised on *Camera Three,* the CBS arts program, on 4 April 1971.[27] Then, in 1982, former Harkness dancer Finis Jhung restaged *Youth* for Juan Gautreux and Sandra Chinn (still with Wagner's choreography) for his new company, Chamber Ballet U.S.A.

[22]Don McDonagh, "Premiere of 'Youth,' Ballet of Lost Love Given by Harkness," *The New York Times* (8 November 1967), 57.

[23]*Ibid.*

[24]*Ibid.*

[25]Clive Barnes, "Dance by Richardson," *The New York Times* (13 November 1967), 64.

[26]Doris Hering, "Presstime News," *Dance Magazine* XXXXI/12 (December 1967), 6.

[27]A copy of this program is available for viewing at the dance division of the New York Public Library, Lincoln Center (MGZIC 9-778 and MGZHB-2670). Rhodes became artistic director for the Harkness Ballet in 1968, but unfortunately that exciting potential was barely realized because the company disbanded two years later.

PER SONJA: WASHASHORE DANCE ENSEMBLE

In August 2001 the WashAshore Dance Ensemble (WADE) presented a program at Cape Cod Community College of several dances, notably *Per Sonja* set to *Adagio for Strings*. An innovative feature of Ivan Cavallari's choreography was the incorporation of graphic arts. The new work was characterized as

> a modernist exploration in wit and emotion. Each dancer, wearing a white leotard, dipped a brush into pots of paint and drew on each other separately and then simultaneously. On a white screen, he outlined her figure, and she his; they removed their clothes and faded into the screen, ending their tandem narratives with a decidedly postmodern twist. The daring piece featured frantic gestures danced with great intensity.[28]

Another critic noted that the work "beautifully and reverently explored the relationships of woman and man, and of humanity to dance and art as [the dancers] painted on a canvas and then dissolve into it."[29] While this is not exactly a multimedia performance, the body painting certainly added a new dimension to the traditional concept of choreography.

The Same-Sex *Pas de Deux*

A choreographer may decide for a variety of reasons to put a different spin on the traditional male-female *pas de deux*—pardon the pun—by featuring a same-sex duo. Such choreography may merely convey a sense of warmth between the partners. With a couple dancing to the romantic strains of Barber's music, it may imply a gay relationship, but it is often a matter of interpretation.

PURPLE BEND #1 & *#2*: MIAMI CITY BALLET AND BALLET GAMONET

Jimmy Gamonet De Los Heros, resident choreographer for Miami City Ballet during the 1990s, created *Purple Bend* to *Adagio* as a *pas de deux*

[28]Gigi Berardi and Jennifer Chipman, "Guests Get Their Feet Wet," *Dance Magazine* (December 2001), 100. The dancers were Bridget Briener and Douglas Lee.

[29]Ellen C. Chahey, "WashAshore Dances Make a Splash at 4Cs," *The Barnstable* [Mass.] *Patriot* (9 August 2001); reprinted www.barnstable-patriot.com/08-09-01-news/arts4.html. Other dances staged as a *pas de deux* include "Adagio for Two" (Miriam Mahdaviani), "Appassionato" (Milena Leben), "Façade" (Jeffrey Tan), and "Lament" (John Meehan). See Appendix 5 for a selected list of *pas de deux* performances.

for two female dancers. In the traditional *pas de deux* the climax of the dance often occurs when the male partner lifts the female. Unless one of the women in the duet is particularly robust, this type of movement is unlikely. In this particular ballet the climactic moment of both the score and the choreography occurs when the dancers draw together in a gentle embrace and hardly move at all.

In 2005 Gamonet revived the work for his own company, Ballet Gamonet Maximum Dance. According to critic Melanie Klesse, "anguish, sorrow and love are all played out as their bodies merge and diverge, en Pointe. Their relationship is ambiguous, but as with any couple, their relationship writhes with an emotional intensity that only love can bring."[30] Another critic, Guillermo Perez, discerned an erotic chemistry between the two, asserting that "you knew these women had shared more than lipstick."[31] It is difficult to tell whether this was a feature of the work originally, was brought out more in this later staging, or was merely a figment of the reviewer's imagination. Yet the capitalization in the title in the program—*PUrple BEnd*—certainly makes one stop and think; the dance is described as "an exploration of a powerful friendship told through an unconventional Pas de Deux."[32]

In 1992 Gamonet re-choreographed the work for two male dancers and re-titled it *Purple Bend 2*. According to critic Alan M. Kriegsman, "the movement owed far more to modern dance conventions—floor work, contractions, acrobatic partnering techniques—than to anything classical, and the music served primarily as an atmospheric backdrop."[33] Appearing in flesh-toned briefs, the men were "aptly feverish as they alternately support and contend with each other in front of an enigmatic red slab. A fit prop, perhaps, for a ballet in itself no small enigma."[34] This description suggests that much of the choreography of *Purple Bend 2* differs from the

[30]Melanie Klesse, "Ballet Gamonet Defies Convention," *Edge* (21 October 2005). The dancers in the Miami Ballet production were Iliana Lopez and Sally Ann Isaacks. In the Maximum Dance production, they were, at first, Britt Juleen and DeAnn Petruschke and, later, Jennifer Carlynn Kronenberg and Myrna Kamara.

[31]Guillermo Perez, "Jimmy Gamonet and Ballet Troupe Fill Audience with Delight," [Fort Lauderdale, Fla.] *Sun-Sentinel* (12 October 2005).

[32]Program notes from Ballet Gamonet (Miami: Gusman Theater, 7 October 2005).

[33]Alan M. Kriegsman, "Dance: The Bright Balanchine Breed," *Washington Post* (25 July 1992), B: 1. The dancers were Yanis Pikieris and Oliver Kovach.

[34]*Ibid.*

first, especially because men would move their bodies differently than women. While the male version was apparently more athletic, the general enigmatic mood may have been similar in both.

When the Gamonet company revived the work in February 2007, Perez observed:

> The male incarnation of coupled support and stresses gave the near-nude Simon Silva and Paul Thrussell a wonderful chance to chisel out eye-catching poses and to unfurl fidgety phrases against a red canvas. Samuel Barber's *Adagio for Strings* spread silky elegance over the brawny activities.[35]

Does the erotic element implied in the female version carry over into this one? Two "aptly feverish" men dancing "near-nude" suggests it, but "brawny activities" could be either straight or gay. Critic George Volsky perceives the two versions differently. In the female version one woman is clearly the "dominatrix;" in the male version the two are equal, "showing off, as it were, sometimes playfully, sometimes dashingly, the beauty of their bodies rather than their emotional involvement, or lack of it."[36]

The nearly complete performances of both dances posted on *YouTube* do not seem to project much of a homoerotic subtext.[37] The female version exhibits warmth. The male version, indeed, contains "fidgety phrases," often at odds with the smooth-flowing music; but, in my opinion, the only hints of gay eroticism occurs at the end when the two men strike a pose reminiscent of photographs from 1950s physique magazines. While the gay nature of both versions of *Purple Bend* may lie in the eye (and mind) of the beholder, Gamonet's own sexual orientation may have filtered through his choreography, even if he did not specifically intend it.[38]

[35]Guillermo Perez, "Ballet Gamonet's Season Closer Invests Measured Strides with Emotive Depths," [Fort Lauderdale, Fla.] *Sun-Sentinel* (16 May 2007).

[36]George Volsky, "Gamonet Saves Best for Last," *Coral Gables* [Fla.] *Gazette* (17 May 2007); reprinted www.cggazette.com/absolutenm/templates/ indextemp.aspx?articleid=2939&zoneid=1. This article contains a color picture of the two dancers.

[37]See "Andres Figueroa & Edgar Anido (Purple Bend)," *YouTube* (4 March 2008), posted by Andresfelipefl/.

[38]About one minute of both Purple Bend I and II were once posted on the Internet; the female version was found on the Gamonet website and the male version on *YouTube*. In these brief excerpts I could not detect any overt sexual implications.

EARTHLY LOVE, HEAVENLY SPIRITS: MORGANSCOTT BALLET

In contrast to the two versions of *Purple Bend*, the gay message of the MorganScott choreography of *Earthy Love, Heavenly Spirits* is unequivocal. In March 1999, six months after gay student Matthew Shepard was tortured and left to die outside of Laramie, Wyoming, MorganScott Ballet presented a program in his honor, *Remembering Matthew Shepard: A Vigil in Dance.* As part of the program, the company's co-founder, Daniel Scott, conceived the idea for a ballet, *Earthly Love, Heavenly Spirits: Dance against Hate,* which his partner Edward Morgan choreographed. In order to select the most appropriate music, they listened to *Adagio for Strings* as well as the Adagietto, Movement IV, from Mahler's Fifth Symphony. They concluded that, while both pieces had the desired transcendent effect, the passion communicated in Barber's work had more warmth. "The tension in Mahler's Adagietto conveys angst, whereas the tension in Barber's *Adagio* conveys yearning."[39] Scott revealed that they had always wanted to create a ballet to *Adagio* but felt obliged to wait for the right concept and the right time. "This composition is special to Edward and me in that it achieves great emotional depth with a deceptively simple, elegant structure and progression. We subscribe to the ballet notion that 'simplicity is beauty,' and *Adagio* exemplifies that notion in music."[40] The choreography reinforces this simplicity with unpretentious, lyrical movements. Lifts and other aspects of "partnering," are used sparingly.

Scott and Morgan staged the *pas de deux* at the Danspace Project of St. Mark's Church-in-the-Bowery "because of the 'religious' people who said 'God hates Fags' and 'Matthew Shepard got what he deserved.'"[41] Scott remembered hearing the newscast about the young man's death: "I saw myself as a student at his age and what could have happened to me. I was horrified and wanted to do something about it."[42] The result was a male *pas de deux*.[43] According to Scott, the dance illustrates

[39]Daniel Scott, email (11 February 2006) to the author.

[40]*Ibid.*

[41]*Ibid.*

[42]Daniel Scott, quoted in Joseph Carman, "Dance Partners–Remembering Matthew Shepard: A Celebration of Love, Dance Concert," *The Advocate* (23 October 2001).

[43]This was first danced by Joseph Alexander and Jean Ledon Louis.

> the spiritual aspect of a gay relationship without denying the physical, sexual aspect. Our bodies determine so much about our earthly existence, yet we are also spiritual beings. Edward and I consider that our sexual orientation is not a flaw that distances us from heaven, but just another wonderful variation in creation as heavenly as any other. The title that came to me as I walked to work one day, *Earthly Love, Heavenly Spirits,* was the distillation of these concepts.[44]

There is no specific storyline. Scott and Morgan contend that "dance and music are best married in abstraction, but we should see the compassion and devotion as well as chemistry" between the dancers, the "abstract expression of romantic relationships that nurture us in this life and that, due to their spiritual nature, endure beyond this earthly realm."[45] For them, the title has true meaning. Critic Jennifer Dunning described the dance as a "gentle paean to love," performed "with an affecting lack of sentimentality."[46] Later, in the summer of 1999, the dance was revived on the beach at Fire Island, but with Edward Morgan himself dancing with Joseph Alexander.

Illustration 5.1. Joseph Alexander and Edward Morgan of the MorganScott Ballet, Performance of *Earthly Love, Heavenly Spirits*, Fire Island, New York, 1999

Courtesy of the MorganScott Ballet

Image by Daniel Scott

[44]Daniel Scott, email (11 February 2006) to the author.

[45]*Ibid.*

[46]Jennifer Dunning, "Dance Review: A Tribute to a Gay Student Who Was Slain," *The New York Times* (3 April 1999), B: 15. A portion of the proceeds went to the New York City Lesbian & Gay Anti-Violence Project.

The Double and Extended *Pas de Deux*

In time the very idea of the ballet duet became a point of departure for various artistic experiments resulting from the addition of another pair of dancers. Three of the dances described below may be considered "double" *pas de deux*. In one, the main male-female pair is mirrored by their "alter egos"; in the second, by their older counterparts; a third combines male-male and female-female couples. Another example might be considered an extended *pas de deux* in which the two principals are clearly separated from but are integrated into a larger *corps de ballet*.

THROUGH THE EDGE: WASHINGTON NATIONAL BALLET

In 1967 Michael Lopuszanski choreographed *Through the Edge* to *Adagio for Strings* for the National Ballet of Washington, D.C. When it was presented in New York City, critic Clive Barnes condemned the music as "very possibly the most sadly flatulent piece of popularly acclaimed music written this century," surely the most vituperative and vitriolic criticism of *Adagio* ever uttered![47]

The ballet portrays a boy and girl and their "unconsciouses" and shows their struggle and the final fulfillment of their suppressed desires.[48] They wear ordinary clothes whereas their alter egos appear in silver body paint. Four chairs figure prominently as stage props. According to Barnes, the dancers "struggle out some relationship together whereby boy gets girl, then unconscious selves are satisfied, and the chairs occupied."[49] Critic Marcia Marks noted that, while the dance comes to a clear resolution, the choreography does not build to a dramatic climax.[50] Barnes was less impressed: "the jump-and-grope-and-grasp style of choreography gave little opportunity to the dancers who always looked bravely as if better steps were just around the corner."[51] They evidently never found them.

[47]Clive Barnes, "Dance: 2 Old, 2 New by National Ballet," *The New York Times* (30 March 1967), 53.

[48]Marcia Marks, "Getting to Know You: A Review of the National Ballet of Washington," *Dance Magazine* XXXXI/5 (May 1967), 64. The word, "unconsciouses" probably occurred in the program notes because both Barnes and Marks refer to it; Marks suggested that "subconsciouses" might be better.

[49]Clive Barnes, "Dance: 2 Old, 2 New," *The New York Times*, 53.

[50]Marcia Marks, "Getting to Know You," *Dance Magazine*, 64.

[51]Clive Barnes, "Dance: 2 Old, 2 New," *The New York Times*, 53.

SUSPENDED BREATH: JAMES SEWELL DANCE COMPANY

In addition to the orchestral *Adagio,* Barber's Agnus Dei has also inspired choreography. James Sewell appropriated it in "Suspended Breath," the fourth part of his full-length ballet *Good Mourning* (ca. 1997). In a double *pas de deux* Stéphane André and Hitomi Yamada portray a young couple while Sally Rousse and Shouze Ma enact older counterparts. The company's executive director, Gary Peterson, described it as "the life reminiscences of a caregiver for a dying spouse."[52] Dance critic Anna Kisselgoff regarded it as an

> unconventional essay on grief that ended with an image of euthanasia: a woman puts a pillow on her dying husband's face and curls up on a chair as his double and spirit rise up to kiss her. Here . . . the viewer was jarred, never informed about where the ballet was going, on either a formal or emotional level. Very few choreographers can hold attention in this way.[53]

Sewell explained how he decided to incorporate Agnus Dei into his dance in the following manner:

> I had listened to the *Adagio* for years. One day, the image of the music and euthanasia came to mind. I had no specific project but it stayed with me, and I did nothing with it because the whole thing felt out of place. Later when choreographing *Suspended Breath,* I listened to the music again in the context of the emerging movement, and discovered that it is very effective, sets a very strong tone and supports [the dance] in several ways. There is a story in *Adagio for Strings,* and it took me years to hear my story, although it is not one I would have expected. It is always tricky to choreograph to a well-known piece of music because people's experience with it will affect their perceptions of the ballet. In *Suspended Breath,* however, I think the choreographic image

[52]Gary Peterson, quoted in "'Good Mourning': New Life and a New Ballet," *James Sewell Ballet's 1997-1998 Newsletter*; reprinted www.jsballet.org/html/meet/how.html.

[53]Anna Kisselgoff, "James Sewell Brings Stunning Surprises amid Deft Moves," *The New York Times* (19 March 2001), E: 5.

> works because it is strong enough to balance whatever other images people may have.[54]

The theme of euthanasia drew an outraged reaction from one of his closest associates: "You can't do that to that beautiful piece of music!" Sewell responded:

> I know that people might react strongly and think I'm taking a position on the issue, but this is the image that emerged from the music for me. . . . Sad music, in a minor key, has always made me feel at peace. We have come to find that if your mourning is good, it brings you to another place of new life.[55]

EARTHLY LOVE, HEAVENLY SPIRITS (REVISED): MORGANSCOTT BALLET

On the third anniversary of Matthew Shepard's death the MorganScott company revived its *Earthly Love, Heavenly Spirits* as a part of another tribute,[56] but for this staging Morgan and Scott transformed the dance into a double *pas de deux* by adding a female couple. Because the 9 / 11 tragedy had occurred, they therefore decided to draw a parallel between the hate crime committed against Shepard and what they considered a similar crime against America: "We wanted to broaden the scope of concern and wanted to express a sense of community because of the touching community response that we witnessed to those tragic events."[57] Scott believes that the revised form of the dance is

> still an expression of the physical and spiritual aspects of romantic relationships, but with the two couples dancing side by side and then joining together at *Adagio*'s crescendo, we were able to express the idea of community coming together. In performance,

[54]James Sewell, email (25 October 2005) to the author.

[55]James Sewell, quoted in "'Good Mourning': New Life and a New Ballet," *James Sewell Ballet's 1997-1998 Newsletter*; reprinted www.jsballet.org/html/meet/how.html. In March 2000 Sewell brought "Suspended Breath" to Dale Warland's "Cathedral Classics" concert, where the singers accompanied the dance with a live performance of Agnus Dei.

[56]*Matthew Shepard: A Celebration of Love* occurred at the LGBT [Lesbian, Gay, Bisexual, and Transgender] Community Center in New York City (7 October 2001).

[57]Daniel Scott, email (11 February 2006) to the author.

> when the four joined hands at the climax—boy-boy, girl-girl—the audience broke into applause.[58]

These two partners hope that whatever music they use in their dances, the audience will hear it in a new way. Scott is convinced that the audience's response to *Earthly Love* proved that they had succeeded, that they "had touched the audience, which was most important to us."[59] Surely this is an important goal of all choreographers.

ADAGIO FOR TEN AND TWO: SAN FRANCISCO BALLET

For his San Francisco Ballet staging of the orchestral *Adagio* Richard Gibson contextualized the basic premise of the *pas de deux* with a small *corps de ballet,* a concept derived from classical choreography. (The main *pas de deux* from *Swan Lake* unfolds with a gaggle of tutued waterfowl in the background.) Critic Dean Wallace deemed the title appropriate: *Adagio for Ten and Two* is, indeed, a synthesis of a *pas de douze* and a *pas de deux.*[60] Gibson deployed his twelve dancers with an "unerring eye for pattern and design; and he sets off the solo couple with some truly original material."[61] Although reviewer Stanley Eichelbaum called it "a sunny and charming abstraction,"[62] others perceived more of a romantic subtext. Doris Hering, for instance, characterized the theme as "deeply subjective, centering around two young people who separate from their peers to come briefly and poignantly together and then are reabsorbed into the group, presumably to continue their search for love."[63] Eichelbaum observed:

> Like Barber's music, the ballet is reflective and romantic. . . . Handsomely choreographed for ten ensemble dancers and two

[58]*Ibid.* The company later took this version to upstate New York for a performance at a seminar entitled "Heroism Knows No Stereotypes," where the audience also broke into applause when the four dancers joined hands.

[59]*Ibid.* In 2007 Morgan and Scott's collaboration ended, and the company became known as The EdwardMorgan Ballet NYC.

[60]Dean Wallace, quoted in Richard Gibson, "Ballet '64 Shows Big Improvement" [unidentified newspaper clipping].

[61]*Ibid.*

[62]Stanley Eichelbaum, "Two Impressive Ballet Premieres," *San Francisco Examiner* (7 July 1964), 27.

[63]Doris Hering, "Clean, Clear Change of Pace," *Dance Magazine* XL (August 1966), 57.

> soloists . . . it was beautifully and efficiently executed. . . . It has style, elegance and an engaging simplicity of pattern and form that is most engaging.[64]

The choreography produced an "almost unbearable tension," as the girl came "crushing forward" over the boy's head," yet the work contained "moments of utter simplicity, as when the separated couple reached briefly toward each other."[65]

Gibson has restaged his dance several times over the last few decades. For the Peninsula Ballet Theatre, with fewer accompanying dancers, he changed the title to *Adagio for Seven and Two.* Perhaps the title has undergone several changes at different times to accommodate varying numbers in the *corps de ballet.* Gibson remains pleased that the ballet has attracted a great deal of attention: "I still hear from people today who were inspired by the collaboration of music and choreography so many years ago."[66] The work entered the repertoire of Chamberdance San Francisco in spring 2002.

For Solo or for Ensemble

In addition to the *pas de deux, Adagio for Strings* has been called into service for ballets featuring a single performer or an unconventional number of dancers. Deprived of group dynamics, a solo dance is often meant to reflect an individual's inner feelings, a choreographic version of a monologue in a drama. Chief of the Canyon Concert Ballet, Robert Sher-Machherndl, choreographed *Scarlet* (1999) to *Adagio* for himself alone: "I just started with the steps. At first I thought of using [the Adagietto from] Mahler's Fifth Symphony, but I came to Barber's music. It fits the solo. It's also very contemporary. It's very nice, gorgeous music."[67] Another modern dance solo set to the same music, *Eighteen Months* (2009), was choreographed and performed by Maria Caruso, the artistic director for the Bodiography Contemporary Ballet. She created it as a result of a

[64]Stanley Eichelbaum, "Two Ballet Premieres," *San Francisco Examiner*, 27. The soloists were David Anderson and Zola Dishong.

[65]Doris Hering, "Peninsula Ballet Theatre," *Dance Magazine*, 57.

[66]Richard Gibson, email (19 April 2004) to the author.

[67]Robert Sher-Machherndl, quoted in Glenn Giffin, "New Year, New Director: Canyon Concert Ballet Also Will Have New Building Soon," *Denver Post* (29 October 1999), E: 20. Note the similar decision between Mahler and Barber by the MorganScott Company.

painful breakup: "The piece seeks to show that emotional wounds can be just as devastating as physical ones."[68] Such a work fits the criteria of a choreographic monologue perfectly.

In March 2000 the Brazilian company Ballet Bahia performed a program in Jerusalem, including *Trinity* as choreographed by Luis Arrieta. While such a title might communicate religious symbolism, it may also carry a double meaning: a dance for three participants. Reviewer Ora Brafman observed that the work "caught some of the intense beauty and passion" of Barber's music.[69]

In 2000 former Royal Ballet soloist Antony Dowson choreographed *Adagio for Strings* for English National Ballet School pupils as part of a tribute "Gala for Dame Beryl Gray," the company's artistic director and former ballerina with the Sadler's Wells Ballet. Six men and one woman moved "slowly, gracefully and mesmerizingly around, above, below and beside a large pole, which was passed among the group, sometimes used like a *barre* and sometimes like a pole-vault."[70] In September 2002 readers of *Ballet* magazine were asked to submit nominations for an end-of-season poll, including Best Production and Best Staging. One reader suggested Dowson's dance for the "eye-opener of the year" because it was "simple yet far more moving" than other more extravagant productions.[71]

Among Other Musical Works

Adagio for Strings, as a single piece of music, provided the impetus for the works cited above, short in duration and concise in impression and meaning. In other situations it functions as only one part of a full-length dance, either as a major movement or as an interlude, a brief diversion from other types of music.

[68]Steve Sucato, "Reviving the Present," *Dance Archives* (18 November 2004).

[69]Ora Brafman, "Dance Review: Brazilian Troupe Disappoints," *Jerusalem Post* (13 March 2000); reprinted www.jpost.com/Editions/2000/03/13/Culture/Arts.3989.html.

[70]Ann Williams, "Dame Beryl Gray Gala," *Ballet* (27 March 2002). The work was later performed at the Chelsea Festival, with Sonia Aguilar again in the lead, and again at the Ballet School's annual year-end performance with Akari Manabe. The men may or may not have been the same as in the March performance. The female dancer was Aguilar.

[71]Letter to the Editor, *Ballet* (September 2002); reprinted www.ballet.co.uk/magazines/yr_02/sp02/pollresults2001_02.htm.

STIGMATA: GREGORY HANCOCK DANCE THEATER

The Gregory Hancock Dance Theater maintains a large repertoire ranging from short works to full-length productions, including *Stigmata* (1989). Approximately thirty-eight minutes in duration, this work pairs music from the movie *Wings of Desire* (1989) with *Adagio for Strings*. Hancock conceived his dance when he visited Medjugorje, Yugoslavia, a town noted for apparitions of the Virgin Mary: "I was sitting on a hill with crosses when I heard *Adagio for Strings* in my head. It seemed the perfect fit for a section of a modern dance piece that would be inspired by the last hours of Jesus' [*sic*] life."[72] The dance concerns the crucifixion of Christ and the women who witness it, among them his mother and Mary Magdalene, "women who gave Jesus water and wiped his face on his way to the crucifixion. Jesus interacts with the women en route to his final destiny."[73] Hancock maintains that the stigmata in his title are not the actual bleeding of palms or ankles, but a psychological state. He recalled the interaction of *Adagio* and the choreography:

> The women are dressed in black and veiled, their movements simply reflect the quality and movement of the strings—spiraling and layering. In the piece I chose to have the dancer portraying Jesus make his own ascent to the cross—constructed as a barricade of lumber—a rather "crown of thorns" looking structure. At the climax of *Adagio* he is on the cross. I listened to many versions of this piece until I found one that was the best tempo for the movement and that also had a very long pause after the climax. After the pause, an angel ascends to the cross and kisses Jesus, who then descends and ends up in the arms of his mother in the traditional "pieta" image with the angel above taking his place on the cross. . . .[74]

Mary Magdalene kisses his feet, and another woman kisses his forehead. "There are extremely beautiful images in this piece that reflect *Adagio* very

[72]Gregory Hancock, emails (20 and 29 March 2005) to the author.

[73]*Ibid.*

[74]*Ibid.*

well."[75] A choreographer must be gratified when the beauty of the music enhances the beauty and vision of his or her dance movements.

After deciding on the Barber for the ending, Hancock had to select music for the opening scenes and eventually settled on tracks from Jürgen Knieper's score for the 1987 motion picture *Wings of Desire* [*Der Himmel über Berlin*]: "Sky over Berlin" for "Angel Variation," "The Cathedral of Books" for "Jesus in Gethsemane," and "The Old Mercedes" for "Jesus and Mary Magdalene." He found the juxtaposition of such diverse pieces of music to be appealing: "I like combining music to form an entire dance piece. For me the selections from *Wings of Desire* also had a nice feel for the piece I was creating and seemed to blend very well with *Adagio*."[76]

WHO'S WHO: EIFMAN BALLET

Russian choreographer Boris Eifman introduced *Adagio for Strings* in one section of his comic ballet *Who's Who* (2003) inspired by one of his favorite American films, *Some Like It Hot* (1959). Part of the ballet is based on his thoughts about that film. His story concerns two Russian ballet dancers Alex and Max, who emigrate in the 1920s from the Soviet Union to the United States. Fleeing the Russian Revolution, they look for a better life and artistic freedom. After several fruitless auditions, they are finally accepted for a nightclub act, but only as showgirls. (Just picture Jack Lemmon and Tony Curtis in tutus.)

Eifman first considered creating a serious ballet, but after the events of 11 September 2001 he decided that "there was too much drama and tragedy around and I needed to bring something beautiful. My previous work was more dramatic. This work is very optimistic, there's a lot of humor and people will laugh."[77] Yet critic Robert Gottlieb was not very amused. He maintained that the dance steps were a "pastiche of pastiche of pastiche," that the dance is a "mishmash of misguided ambition and talentless posturing," that the dancers are "flashy and without substance," and that Eifman's ideas are "derivative and tawdry."[78]

[75]*Ibid.*

[76]*Ibid.*

[77]Boris Eifman, quoted in Vicki Sanders, "Eifman's Ballet Set for Boston," *Boston Herald* (13 March 2003). The dancers were Yuri Smekalov and Constantine Matulevsky.

[78]Robert Gottlieb, "The Inevitable, Awful Eifman Drags Us Back to the 1920s," *New York Observer* (21 April 2003), 19.

The eclectic score exhibits a wide variety of styles, mainly popular music, rags by Joplin, jazz by Duke Ellington and Dave Brubeck, but only a few classical pieces, notably Rachmaninoff. The music for Scene 12, "Nostalgia," is Barber's *Adagio*. Interjecting the compositions of classical composers into a basically jazz-pop score may result in too great a musical contrast. Yet those excerpts are introduced in contrasting "vision" scenes, where Alex nostalgically recalls the days of czarist Russia. In other words, then and there is represented by calm, romantic music; and here and now, by jazz and pop. Reviewer Theodore Bale regarded the music selection as naïve, particularly the "insufferable" classical selections: "Eifman is either lazy or clueless when it comes to choosing scores for his hollow choreography."[79] Bale either failed to realize—or chose to ignore—Eifman's distinction between "then and now." He deemed the work a "dreadful two-act spectacle," in which Eifman had "hit an all-time low," and wryly suggested that the work be re-titled *Why, Why*.[80] In contrast, Roberta E. Zlokower called it a "must-experience artistic adventure,"[81] and Clive Barnes, often severely caustic in his criticisms, considered it a "sweet, funny, wildly imaginative and, yes, charmingly Russian view of America and why we like it hot."[82]

DRACULA: NEW MEXICO BALLET COMPANY

Patricia Dickinson choreographed her full-length ballet *Dracula* (1999) for the New Mexico Ballet Company. The character, of course, is based on the daylight-challenged, black-cloaked character from Bram Stoker's novel (1897). That cloak plays a large part in the ballet: it is forty-by-twenty-four feet and "equipped with wing-like mechanisms allowing Dracula to fly over the stage to make grand entrances and exits."[83]

[79]Theodore Bale, "Dreadful Ballet: 'Who's Who Should Be Called, 'Why, Why,'" *Boston Herald* (15 March 2003).

[80]*Ibid.*

[81]Roberta E. Zlokower, "Eifman Ballet of St. Petersburg: Who's Who, a Ballet in Two Acts," *Explore-Dance* (13 April 2003); reprinted www.exploredance.com/eifmanballet41303.html.

[82]Clive Barnes, "American as Russian Ballet," *New York Post* (7 April 2003). Although Eifman's company toured many cities in 2003, *Who's Who* was danced only in Boston, Washington, D.C., and New York. It was performed in St. Petersburg, Russia, at the end of 2003 and in Jerusalem in June 2004. There is a good picture of the *pas de deux* between Igor Siadzko and Alexei Turko in Annette Grant, "From Russia, With Love," *The New York Times* (30 March 2003), II: 22.

[83]Jennifer Noyer, "Dance Review: Dracula, N.M. Ballet," *Albuquerque* [N.M.] *Journal* (16 October 2006); reprinted www.abqjournal.com/main/2006/10/16/entertainment/dance-review-dracula-n-m-ballet-oct-16.html.

Dickinson chose pieces by fifteen composers, notably the Barber work, which is inserted several times in the story. It first occurs in a *pas de deux* for Prince Vladimir and his wife, later reincarnated as Mina Harker, the protagonist of the gothic novel invoked. In the opinion of reviewer Jennifer Noyer, "both dancers projected an intense and tender connection in their dramatic roles . . . with embraces sweeping into ecstatic lifts," and Barber's music "became the leitmotif for the love story, repeated when Dracula met Mina centuries later."[84] At the end, when the love story has concluded, the Agnus Dei version by the Robert Shaw Festival Singers was heard. This dance has become so popular that it has been revived, in a revised form, around Halloween several times since its première.[85]

Barber's String Quartet: Modern and Post-Modern Dance

Other works such as *HeartBeat:mb* and *Exit* were staged to the Adagio movement from Barber's String Quartet. These two were conceived at different times, under different circumstances, and with totally contrasting concepts and choreographies.

HEARTBEAT: MB: MIKHAIL BARYSHNIKOV

In 1997 Mikhail Baryshnikov devised a solo dance for his White Oak Dance Project entitled *HeartBeat: mb,* which he adapted from an earlier work by Christopher Janney called simply *HeartBeat.* Janney conceived the work at The Center for Advanced Visual Studies of the Massachusetts Institute of Technology (MIT) in 1981; Sara Rudner staged it in 1983 for the Twyla Tharp Dance Company. The dance requires the use of a "bio-engineering device" that monitors the electrical impulses from a person's brain to the heart and the surrounding muscles via wireless telemetry.[86] Because Janney thought of a heartbeat as an inner drum, he regarded it as the track for a dance to which he added tabla rhythms of India, whispered phrases derived from jazz scat singing, and recited passages from medical texts concerning the heart's function.[87]

[84] *Ibid.*

[85] A two-minute excerpt of *Dracula* was posted "Dracula Excerpts," *YouTube* (1 February 2011) by Robin Rupe. It concludes with a part of the Agnus Dei *pas de deux.*

[86] Lynn Heinemann, interview with Christopher Janney, "Janney and Baryshnikov Create Electrocardio-Choreography," *MIT Tech Talk* (13 May 1998); reprinted www.web.mit.edu/newsoffice/tt/1998/may13/artheart.html.

[87] *Ibid.*

When Baryshnikov adapted the work for his own solo performance, he re-titled it *HeartBeat: mb* to signify his personal interpretation: his own heartbeat now set the tempo. Patches on his bare torso and neck send signals to a machine with him on stage. According to critic Laura Shapiro:

> the pace of the thump-thump-thump both elicits his movement and reacts to it, Baryshnikov is practically translucent here: we see the still unsurpassed elegance of his classical technique, but we see it shaping moves that emanate directly from his personality, his very blood and breath.[88]

Baryshnikov added Barber's Adagio movement toward the end of the dance to complement the beat of the heart. "I always thought this music was about memory and mortality, and it's personal to me because I knew Sam Barber quite well. I've danced to his music before, and we kept in touch until his death in 1981."[89]

In performance the movement was played live by four string players of the White Oak Chamber Ensemble: Nicolas Danielson, Margaret Jones, violins; David Bursack, viola; and Wendy Sutter, cello. Jones, also the coordinator for the ensemble, recalled how the music was selected:

> When we were putting the piece together, Mischa called me into his office to talk about ideas for the music. While retaining the heartbeat and several other ideas from the original dance, he still hadn't decided on what music to add. We bandied about a few possibilities including a Bach chorale. We then watched a video that showed him rehearsing in the studio to the heart monitor. At the appropriate time of the dance he put on a CD of the Kronos String Quartet playing *Adagio* and asked me what I thought of it. "Without question," I told him, "don't consider anything else," because it was so perfect.[90]

[88]Laura Shapiro, "Mischa's New Moves: After a Trip Home and with a Solo Tour about to Begin, Mikhail Baryshnikov Is Dancing Past 50," *Newsweek* CXXXI (19 January 1998), 19.

[89]Mikhail Baryshnikov, quoted in Christine Temin, "Baryshnikov Makes Himself Modern," *Boston Globe* (10 May 1998), N: 2.

[90]Margaret Jones, interview (21 May 2004) with the author.

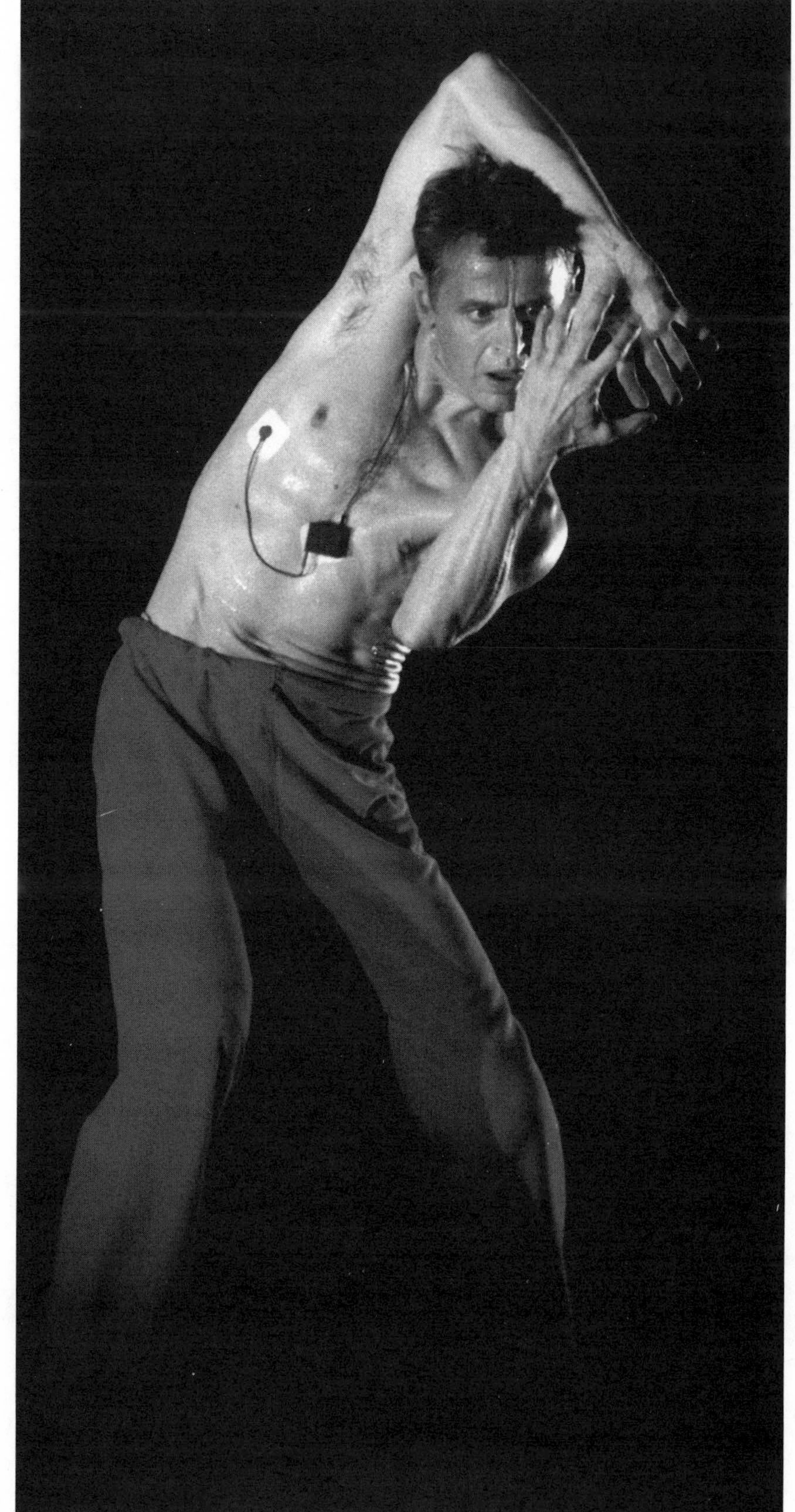

Illustration 5.2. Mikhail Baryshnikov, Performance of *HeartBeat: mb*, City Center, New York City, 1998

Image by Gary Friedman

When the other musicians heard this recording, they agreed that it was the obvious choice. Janney has explained that, while the recitation of medical texts depicts the heart as an "almost cold, anesthetic machine," the Barber work shows the other end of the spectrum, evoking the heart as "the seat of the soul."[91] Baryshnikov ultimately chose this piece for its "continuous line of phrasing that complements the beat of the heart."[92]

The dance is a structured improvisation. Janney is the creator, the choreography is directed by Sara Rudner, but the actual improvisational movement is determined by Baryshnikov, who avowed, "I cannot give myself credit as a choreographer, but there's more of my input than when I usually work with choreographers."[93] The dance begins as he walks onto the stage accompanied by only the sound of his heartbeat. According to Jones, the initial moments were striking:

> He would do a step or two and then the more he danced the more his heartbeat speed increased. He would change the step; he would bend over suddenly and the beat would slow down. His heart would occasionally skip a beat and when that happened he would stop, look around and treat the moment very humorously.[94]

The skipped beat is a result of his heart arrhythmia: "When I get nervous, it speeds up, and I have to adjust the choreography. My heart is a cranky machine."[95]

All this contributes to the unique improvisatory conditions of each performance. Because of the improvisation, the length of sections varies. While the overall structure of the dance is set, Baryshnikov determines how long he wants to take to move from one part to another. Naturally this affects the accompaniment; musicians need to watch him closely for cues. Jones related the problems:

[91]Lynn Heinemann, "Janney and Baryshnikov Create Electrocardio-Choreography," *MIT Tech Talk* (13 May 1998).

[92]Jennifer Dunning, "Dance; At 50, Taking the Stage (and a Risk) Alone," *The New York Times* (18 January 1998), 43.

[93]Mikhail Baryshnikov, quoted in Hilary Ostlere, "Baryshnikov Light and Dark," *Dance Magazine* (May 1998), 47.

[94]Margaret Jones, interview (21 May 2004) with the author.

[95]Mikhail Baryshnikov, quoted in Christine Temin, "Baryshnikov Makes Himself Modern," *Boston Globe* (10 May 1998), N: 2.

While he was still dancing, there would be a rather dramatic light change and he would bend over again to slow down his heartbeat. Then after a visual cue I would count a number of beats and then start *Adagio*. The challenge was that while we were playing it, the heartbeat was still going on very loudly.[96]

Indeed, what made it so challenging was that the musicians did not try to coordinate the adagio pulse to Baryshnikov's heartbeat but had to find and maintain their own appropriate pace. Trying to match the two speeds would result in different tempos of the music at each performance, neither a practical nor aesthetically pleasing prospect. Besides, the contrasting tempos, recalled Jones, made it extremely effective. Janney is convinced that Barber's music bears "tremendous power" and that the sound of the heartbeat and the quartet "work very well together; they don't conflict."[97] One reviewer noted that during Adagio "Baryshnikov worked up to some strenuous leaps and jumps that climaxed just as the music did."[98] When the quartet concluded, Baryshnikov was left on stage with only the sound of his heartbeat, the sound that began the dance.

Baryshnikov first performed *HeartBeat: mb* on a tour of Europe and as part of an American tour the following year. Jones reported that the work was a great success everywhere. "The question on everyone's mind was, 'was that really Baryshnikov's heartbeat that we heard?' They just couldn't believe it. It was really well received. It is a very moving piece."[99] The soloist remembered an Italian performance, attended by people who had undergone open-heart surgery. The reaction was amazing: "they felt it was about them, they were very uneasy, they stopped to check their pulse."[100] Shapiro interpreted all this in positive terms: "that's what dancing should do, of course—make us feel uneasy, check our pulses, discover onstage the workings of our hearts. Baryshnikov couldn't have pulled this off 20 years ago—he didn't have the depth. Today, his depth

[96]Margaret Jones, interview (21 May 2004) with the author.

[97]Christopher Janney, quoted in Sandra L. Giardi, "To the Beat of an Inner Drum," *TheatreBill* (May 1998).

[98]Marcia B. Siegel, "Mysterious Histories: Mikhail Baryshnikov and White Oak Dance On," *Boston Phoenix* (21-28 May 1998); reprinted www.bostonphoenix.com/archive/dance/98/05/21/WHITE_OAK_DANCE_PROJECT.html.

[99]Margaret Jones, interview (21 May 2004) with the author.

[100]Laura Shapiro, "Mischa's New Moves," *Newsweek* (1998), 19.

is what makes him dance."[101] *HeartBeat:mb* is a startling component of a long and brilliant dance career.

EXIT: DEBORAH HAY

Another dance choreographed to Barber's quartet movement is *Exit* by Deborah Hay, a veteran of the Judson Dance Theater, part of a significant post-modern dance tradition that had its heyday in New York in the 1960s. Post-modern dance transcends the notions of modern dance as set forth by Martha Graham, Merce Cunningham, and others. Hay was among several choreographers who pushed the envelope of dance into a realm where some audience members questioned whether it was dance at all. In 1995, long after the demise of the Judson group but still conforming to its post-modern principles, Hay conceived *Exit* as a solo for herself.

The dance began to coalesce firmly in her mind when she attended a workshop at Wesleyan University, where she observed a dance by Christie O'Neal, who had choreographed her work to the string quartet movement. According to Hay, "the music so moved me that each time she performed I became more convinced that my greatest challenge as a choreographer would be to use . . . adagio for my new dance."[102] This decision must have surprised her colleagues and, indeed, Hay herself because she had not used pre-composed music for her dances since 1962. She believed that "the idea of choreographing to music bordered on coercion. I don't like being controlled by rhythm. I don't want any one outside influence to determine the course of the development or performance of my dances."[103] But in the string quartet movement rhythm is not a major factor; its slow tempo and meter changes virtually negate a traditional rhythmic flow. Therefore, she could be free to create without any rhythmic constraint.

When she played the music on her car tape-deck, "It evoked copious tears and loud cries." Once when she was listening to it while driving on a dirt road in Vermont, the surrounding forest yielded to "serene pastures, like a dress sliding from a woman's shoulders. At that moment, on that day, Barber's Adagio came to its attenuated end and . . . 'Exit' was born."[104]

[101]*Ibid.*

[102]Deborah Hay, *My Body, the Buddhist* (Hanover, N.H.: Wesleyan University Press, 2000), 7.

[103]*Ibid.*, 74.

[104]*Ibid.*, 7-8.

Hay explained the title: "as the lights come up, the performer is seen standing to one side of the stage. The impulse to begin moving comes after the music starts."[105] It is an appeal to exit. "In so doing, she notices she is also entering. The two experiences are as inseparable in life as they are occurrences in her body."[106] Then the dancer lifts her arm in the direction she will travel and moves diagonally across the stage:

> The arm leads or follows the body. There are three or four opportunities for the performer to turn back and face in the direction where the dance began and herein acknowledge her past. . . . Each time the dancer turns to look back, she feels an overbearing recall or personal history steeped in heartbreak and loss. When the last turn is made, instead of contemplating the past, the dancer keeps turning, passing through the past back into the present. She disengages from the past but it is not erased. In a moment's absorption the past is recognized and carried forward —past and future, exiting and entering, direct yet without linearity, wound and suspended.[107]

Near the end, the stage lighting fades to purple but with a bright light shining from the corner where the dancer is headed for her exit. The time it takes to cross the stage and to leave it is timed to correspond to the length of the Adagio score.

Hay's description implies that the action here is primarily walking, a movement not normally associated with dance. Other body gestures are also minimal. This style of dance can be considered the equivalent of minimalist art and music, both of which were emerging at the time of the Judson Dance Theater. Critic Lucia Mauro asserted that Hay as well as other Judson choreographers "favored pedestrian movement over the more heroic dance of their time."[108] After the demise of the Judson Dance Theater, Hay continued to employ post-modern aspects of minimalism in her later works, including *Exit*.

[105]*Ibid.*, 74.

[106]*Ibid.*

[107]*Ibid.*, 74-76.

[108]Lucia Mauro, "Dance Review: White Oak Dance Project at the Dance Center of Columbia College," *The Hartford* [Conn.] *Courant* (19 November 2000); reprinted www.courant.com/mmx-9751_lgcy03871746.story.

In 2000 Scott Heron, who had studied and performed with Hay in Austin, Texas, presented his own take on *Exit* at New York's Public School 122 as a prelude to his full-length dance, *The Water*. Critic Deborah Jowitt observed that he began his program with a "mesmerizing" interpretation of *Exit*. To Barber's *Adagio* he slowly crossed the room, "gazing at his destination, turning to stare at where he's come from. The movement is minimal."[109] According to this description, his approach is similar to Hay's, but because the work is largely conceptual, he could easily devise his own version while crediting her with the choreography. Critic Paul Ben-Itzak responded with ample favor: "the brave choice of simplicity—in the choreography, in the dancing—I found infinitely, quietly moving."[110]

Meanwhile, that same year, *Exit* caught the attention of Baryshnikov, who added it to works by other Judson choreographers in a program appropriately titled *PASTForward* for his White Oak Dance Project. He watched some of the dances, both live and on old films; met some of the choreographers, notably Hay; and ultimately organized a program that was meant "to ensure that [JDT's] role in dance history is not overlooked."[111]

The minimalist walking style of choreography allows and, perhaps, encourages non-dancers to participate in a performance. Accordingly, in his staging Baryshnikov changed it from a solo work to an ensemble performance, calling it a "community piece . . . wonderful for people to participate in."[112] The ensemble version of *Exit* seems to be just as effective as the solo version. Critic Suzanne Weiss described it as "a journey from darkness into light, death to eternity, the unknown to safety, simply with a large number of people walking slowly across the stage, sometimes turning, sometimes stopping, occasionally raising a hand."[113] One performer, Asimina Chremos, fondly remembered how much she loved performing *Exit*:

[109]Deborah Jowitt, "Vision-Shifts," *The Village Voice* (11 April 2000); reprinted www.villagevoice.com /2000-04-11/dance/vision-shifts/.

[110]Paul Ben-Itzak, "Flash Review: The Kitchen Sink Heron Straddles 'Water' at P.S. 122," *Dance Insider* (7 April 2000). A photograph of Heron in *Exit* is published in Deborah Hay, *My Body*, 8.

[111]Cheryl Tobey, "White Oak at Dance Center of Columbia College, November 18, 2001," part two of "Bodies of History and Historical Bodies: Baryshnikov and the Judson Legacy," *PAJ: A Journal of Performance and Art* XXIII/3 (September 2001), 20.

[112]Gabrielle Barnett, "An Interview with Mikhail Baryshnikov, Artistic Director, White Oak Dance Project," *Critical Dance* (October 2000); reprinted www.criticaldance.com/interviews/2001/ mbaryshnikov010401.html.

[113]Suzanne Weiss, "White Oak Dance Project: Past Forward," *Culture Vulture* (1 November 2000); reprinted www.culturevulture.net/Dance/WhiteOak.htm.

> It's about walking towards the future and stopping to look back at your past, progressing along a diagonal from downstage right to upstage left, all to the highly emotional Barber String Quartet . . . the silent moment . . . reinforces that idea that looking into the future is like falling into a void.[114]

After the White Oak staging, even Hay seems to prefer the ensemble version of *Exit*. In October 2001, when she restaged it at Arizona State University, she also embraced non-dancers (not literally), primarily students from several, diverse performing organizations in the area, allowing "exciting and interpersonal exchanges between individuals whose lives may not intersect."[115] Hay has showcased community members in *Exit* ever since. Concerning a performance in 2005 at the Performing Dance Company of the University of Utah, she commented:

> When I looked at non-dancers on stage, I was fascinated by the beauty of movement that could be performed by ordinary people. After that experience, I never stepped foot in a dance studio again. I tried instead to unlearn dance patterning, to undo my behavioral and social patterning.[116]

One critic observed, "Hay's choice to use performers without formal training results in the presentation of raw, human emotion."[117]

Despite modifications of choreography, *Adagio* has remained intact through all the performances. Hay obviously believes that it is ideal for the mood and intention of her pedestrian choreographic concept. The slow tempo, moreover, may be even more conducive to walking than to elaborate dance steps.

[114]Asimina Chremos, "White Oak Diary: Past Forward to the Future," *The Dance Insider* (21 November 2000); reprinted www.danceinsider.com/1121_1.html.

[115]"AZ: Arizona State University," *Dance USA, Programs and Publications*, www.danceusa.org/programs_publications/choreography_app.htm. The groups were D.A.R.T. (Dance Arizona Repertory Theatre, ASU's student repertory company) and the Silvestre Herrera Elementary School in Nuestro Barrio, a high poverty neighborhood in south Phoenix.

[116]Lindsay Drury, "Modern Dance: Shaken, Not Stirred," *Daily* [Salt Lake City] *Utah Chronicle* (26 October 2005); reprinted www.dailyutahchronicle.com/?p=30454.

[117]Alexandra Gregory, "Reaching New Depths: Modern Dancers Submerge the Senses, Explore New Territory," *Daily Utah Chronicle* (3 November 2005), A&E; reprinted www.dailyutahchronicle.com/?p=34370.

Performing Arts on Ice

Whether ice dancing is an art or a sport is debatable, but those who watch skating competitions are usually aware of the artistic nature of the performances. Former skater and television commentator Dick Button avers that the technical aspect of a performance is important, "but it is the music and the beauty of skating that takes it out of the realm of being just pure sport."[118] Because many such exhibitions are choreographed to classical music, it should not be surprising to find *Adagio for Strings* among the accompaniments chosen.

SKATING DUOS

The duo Judy Blumberg and Michael Seibert skated to *Adagio* in the late 1980s. Reviewing one of their presentations, critic Anna Kisselgoff observed the "affinity between ice skating and theatrical dancing."[119] In fact, these skaters had worked with members of the American Ballet Theater in order to infuse dance elements into their routine. While both contributed, Seibert created most of the choreography. Because of time constraints, only a portion of the music could be used. They began with the cello statement and proceeded through the climax, when Michael held Judy in an upside-down lift; the audience enthusiastically applauded. When *Adagio* cut to the last phrases of the coda, she climbed onto his back in a kind of "piggy-back" hold. Kisselgoff described much of their routine as a "continuously changing, beautiful embrace."[120]

In 1987, when Blumberg and Seibert skated to the same music at the Professional World Cup Championships, one commentator remarked, "they have that very classy, unhurried look of true champions";[121] another

[118]Dick Button, *State Farm US Figure Skating Championship,* held in St. Louis, Missouri on ESPN2 (12 January 2006).

[119]Anna Kisselgoff, "Dance: Focusing on Ice Skating's Choreographic Aspect," *The New York Times* (22 May 1988), 49.

[120]*Ibid.*

[121]Quoted in *YouTube* (2 July 2006), posted by mkfanforever. This performance was taped on 21 December 1987 and telecast on ESPN on Christmas Eve, 24 December 1987. In 1991 the duo revived their *Adagio* on the tour Skating II with Katarina Witt and Brian Boitano. Prior to this, in November 1989 in Denver, these ice skaters had expanded their duet into a trio, with superstar Robin Cousins as a part of his program, *Elegance on Ice*. Lois Yuen's photographs of this performance can be found by contacting her at lois.yuen@aol.com; additional pictures are available at Google Images.

stated, "everything is part of the overall impression: the hands, the fingers, the facial expressions."[122]

Through much of 2005 ice-dancing champions Naomi Lang and Peter Tchernyshev skated to Barber's *Adagio,* this time enhanced by a narrative, possibly by Tchernyshev himself. During the opening thoughts of isolation—"we sail through the universe of life, chasing our hopes and dreams. . . . Strangers passing, vanishing into the unknown as we stay our course"—the skaters are aloof from each other and remain far apart on the rink. When the narrative reaches "and then it happens . . . another soul wraps itself around our own," they finally begin to move together. During the rise to the musical climax, the narrative disappears, as if no words were necessary to convey the passion. For a while the skaters lie motionless on the ice. During the final phrases of the coda, the reader continues: "as we continue our journey alone, looking into the sky, waiting for another miracle. . . . Hope, love, moment, that is what life is about." Such a perspective contributes another layer to an already emotional piece of music.[123]

In 2008 Pacific Coast Sectional Champions, ice dancers Chelsi Guillen and Danny Curzon also skated to *Adagio for Strings.* Curzon explained, "This is such an imposing and haunting piece of music that it sucks you in. We really wanted to go for a really mature and elegant look this season, so we picked this piece knowing that we would grow into it by the end of the season."[124] Commenting on their performance at the 2008 United States Figure Skating Championship, reviewer Elvin Walker emphasized their sensitivity to the music: "What really separated the team from the rest of the field was their attention to interpreting the music. They shared it with each other and, in turn, invited the audience to watch."[125]

[122]Anna Kisselgoff, "Dance," *The New York Times* (22 May 1988).

[123]This performance was given at the Michael Weiss Foundation fundraiser (17 September 2005), at "Alexei Yagudin and Friends" in St. Petersburg (2 October 2005), and at the year-end Oberstdorf Gala (30 December 2005). Photographs by EMJO from the Yagudin special are online at www.absolute skating.com/photogallery/2005alexeiandfriends-2.html.

[124]Danny Curzon, quoted in Elvin Walker, "2008 U.S. Figure Skating Champions," *Golden Skate* (25 January 2008); reprinted www.goldenskate.com/articles/2007/us_5.shtml.

[125]Elvin Walker, "2008 U.S. Figure Skating Champions," *Golden Skate* (25 January 2008); reprinted www.goldenskate.com/articles/2007/us_5.shtml.

SAVOIR FAIRE OF MATT SAVOIE

Several young men have skated to the Barber *Adagio for Strings* in solo exhibitions, notably Matt Savoie, who featured it throughout 2005 and early 2006. To one reviewer his performance at the 2005 United States Figure Skating Championships "tugged at the heartstrings of the audience in a way only this haunting music can."[126] Savoie confided, "This was a different type of short program for me; I find this music very beautiful and subtle. Usually my short programs have been more flashy, but this one has a whole different mood."[127] He liked working with his choreographer Tom Dickson "because he doesn't seem to want to impose a character on me, but rather, to find characters, music, and movements that accentuate positive aspects of my personality and skating."[128] Indeed, when Savoie skated, he often felt that his program was representational: "[It] is not necessarily a person, but more like an idea. In my short program, in which I skate to Adagio for Strings, there is an aspect of mourning but also an aspect of anticipation—a sort of appreciation for something bigger than oneself."[129] These ideas were suggested in his performance.

Television viewers have had the opportunity to watch Savoie skate to *Adagio* on several occasions. He was at his best at the 2005 Nationals (ESPN2). Dick Button noted how well the choreography matched the Barber excerpt: "every step follows the sense of the idea, of the mood, the sensitivity of the music."[130] At the Figure Skating Championship in St. Louis in January 2006 he reiterated the music's importance: "to me, watching him is all about listening to the music and watching the flow of the edges."[131] When Savoie later skated at the Olympic Games, commentators often chose the words "beautiful" and "gorgeous" to characterize his performance. Former skater Sandra Bezic remarked,

[126]Elvin Walker, "2005 US Figure Skating Championship–Men's Short," *Golden Skate* (14 January 2005); reprinted www.goldenskate.com/articles/2004/011405b.shtml.

[127]Matt Savoie, quoted in Marge Reynolds, "Peoria Skater 4th in Short Program," [Portland, Ore.] *Journal Star* (14 January 2005).

[128]*Ibid.*

[129]Nancy Ridgeway, "Ice Dreams: A Bradley Spin on the Olympics," *Bradley Hilltopics* XII/2 (Spring 2006); www.lydia.bradley.edu/hilltopics/06spring/olympics/.

[130]Dick Button, quoted at 1:47 mark in "Matt Savoie 2005 U.S. Nationals Short Program," *YouTube* (14 July 2010), posted by Zuranthium.

[131]Dick Button, *Figure Skating Championships* (12 January 2006), ESPN2 telecast.

"everything about this program is fluid; perfect music selection for him, Barber's *Adagio for Strings*," later adding, "he brings something very special to figure skating with his sophistication [and] his introspective approach."[132] At the World Figure Skating International Showcase in April 2006, Olympic champion Peggy Fleming called him "a wonderful stylist."[133] Such comments emphasize his artistry over his technique. To me, his performances are beautiful but not spectacular; yet there is no question that his smooth, confident, balletic lines reinforce the calm, serene flow of *Adagio for Strings*.[134] Matt, indeed, has *savoir faire*.

OTHER SKATERS

Some solo skaters have juxtaposed parts of *Adagio for Strings* with other pieces of music in their routines. Fedor Andreev, born in Russia but skating for Canada, combined a portion of Ferry Corsten's trance *Adagio* with Yves Deruyter's "Feel Free" for the 2000 competition of Skate Canada. Because Deruyter's song is trance, Corsten's trance mix provided a good companion, with one piece logically flowing into the other. Andreev, moreover, likes trance music and admires both Corsten and Tiësto.[135] (Trance mixes are discussed in Chapter 7.) When Australian Bradley Santer skated to *Adagio* during the 2003-2004 season, the music for his routine combined two excerpts from the film score *Matrix Reloaded:* "Furious Angels" by Rob Dougan, and "Tea House" by Juno Reactor, with William Ørbit's transcription of *Adagio*.[136] At the 2003 Midwestern Sectional Championships, Sam Dafoe skated to a routine that linked a Barber excerpt with Vivaldi's "Winter" from the *Four Seasons*.

Barber Treads the Boards

Over the years several stage directors have appropriated a portion of *Adagio for Strings* as background music for dramatic productions, which

[132] Sandra Bezic, *Olympic Games: Men's Short Program* (13 February 2006), NBC telecast.

[133] Peggy Fleming, *World Figure Skating International Showcase* (15 April 2006), ABC telecast.

[134] Matt Savoie placed ninth with his *Adagio* program at the 2006 World Figure Skating Championships at Calgary, Alberta in March.

[135] "Profile," *Fedor Andreev, the Site*, www.theskateblade.com/fedor/profile.htm. Andreev also performed this routine later in November at the Cup of Russia competition in St. Petersburg. See "Fedor Andreev," *YouTube* (14 February 2009), posted by siberia82.

[136] Photographs of Santer from the 2000 Four Continents competition are provided by J. Barry Mittan, "Picture of the Week," *International Figure Skating* (15 March 2005), www.ifsmagazine.com/weekpics-auto/6-6-2004.php.

vary a great deal according to type, time period, and style. The way this music is presented in these productions, moreover, varies significantly, depending on the theatrical context.

BARBER AND SHAKESPEARE

A twentieth-century work such as Barber's *Adagio for Strings* may seem out of place in a Shakespeare play, but in the following productions the directors update the time period and / or change the locale. The time frame may move from one century to another with the music shifting from one period or country to another. As a result, *Adagio* often has acquired distinctive and intriguing musical companions.

In 1980 Yukio Ninagawa directed the Toho Company of Japan in Masane Tsukayama's adaptation of Shakespeare's *Macbeth*. Because he transferred the setting to the sixteenth-century Japanese civil wars, the production borrowed features from Kabuki theater—gestures, poses, entrances through the audience, traditional Japanese sliding screens, and falling cherry blossoms. The music consisted of a mixture of both traditional Buddhist chants and contrasting Western classical music by Brahms and Fauré as well as Barber's *Adagio*. The production certainly represented an East-meets-West concept. Author Simon Williams has suggested that the music's serenity implies "reconciliation beyond the violence of the action."[137] Two or three times "the rage of the battle was suspended and all that could be heard was the peace of Fauré's and Barber's music, as if Macbeth would be part of a universe in which even his violence would be assuaged."[138] When *Adagio* underscored Macduff's killing of Macbeth, critic Michael Billington was convinced that the music contributed a "sense of melancholy."[139]

An *Adagio* excerpt appeared near the end of the English Shakespeare Company's production of *Richard III*. In 1989 the company's founders, Michael Bogdanov and Michael Pennington, concatenated parts of several Shakespearean histories into a twenty-two-hour series tracing the rise and fall of the Lancastrian dynasty, *Wars of the Roses*. The dramatization mixed modern elements with traditional Elizabethan conventions, with

[137]Simon Williams, "The Tragic Actor and Shakespeare," *The Cambridge Companion to Shakespeare on Stage*, ed. Stanley Wells and Sarah Stanton (Cambridge: Cambridge University Press, 2002), 135.

[138]*Ibid.*

[139]Michael Billington, "Samurai Macbeth," *Manchester Guardian Weekly* (8 September 1985), 20. In August of 1985 the Toho Company brought this production to the Edinburgh Festival.

musical anachronisms bridging various centuries. By the time the plot reached *Richard III,* the setting was the 1980s, with appropriate staging and costumes.

The cycle was taped for BBC television; for such a production, however, many music cues in the stage production were deemed too expensive. As producer John Paul Chapple remembered, "had we re-licensed the music precisely, we would have ended up with an astronomical bill."[140] Therefore, composer Mark Fishlock was employed to rescore and / or re-record some of the cues. But Chapple realized that others, such as *Adagio,* "were so integral a part of the scenes in which they were featured, that they simply could not be replaced or a whole part of the scenes' meaning would be lost."[141]

The segment with *Adagio* may well prove his point. Here, after King Richard yells from off-stage his famous line, "My horse, my horse, my kingdom for a horse," he and his rival, Henry, Earl of Richmond, confront each other on Bosworth Field. The first two minutes of the composition accompany these helmeted figures in medieval armor, the Apollonian Richmond in gold (Charles Dale) and the King (Andrew Jarvis), looking like Nosferatu in villainous black. They "fought a graceful, highly stylized battle" exuding "a weariness that epitomized the long sequence of battles and squabbles."[142] At first, Richard has the upper hand, as he knocks off Richmond's helmet and causes him to drop his sword, but eventually Richmond prevails, killing the King by slitting his throat and stabbing him in the neck. This is fight manager Malcolm Ransom's interpretation of Shakespeare's simple stage direction: "they fight. Richard is slain." Barber's music fades into the background as Richmond pronounces over the King's dead body:

> God and your arms be praised, victorious friends,
> The day is ours, the bloody dog is dead.

According to author David Fuller, the musical passage in this scene

[140]John Paul Chapple, quoted in Michael Bogdanov and Michael Pennington, *The English Shakespeare Company: The Story of the Wars of the Roses, 1986-1989* (London: Nick Hern Books, 1990), 232. The videotaped production is available from Films for the Humanities and Sciences. *Richard III* is FFH 2776.

[141]*Ibid.*

[142]Alan C. Dessen, *Rescripting Shakespeare: The Text, the Director, and Modern Productions* (Cambridge: Cambridge University Press, 2002), 125.

> adds a melancholy tone of valediction: against the overall antiroyalist drift of the production this music suggests that, either in the death of Richard as an individual, or in the demise of the world he represents, something of value will be lost in the brave new world of efficient technology, lip service idealism, and bland image-making represented (in this production) by Richmond.[143]

This "bland image-making" clearly manifests itself in the final scene, as Richmond, now dressed in suit and tie, enters a television studio for a Scottish "State of the Union" address to the nation. *Adagio* first makes a crescendo, functioning as a sound-bridge between the scenes, then fades out as Richmond is seated at a desk; a stagehand touches up Richmond's makeup and combs his hair. This modern element directly contrasts with the more traditional, albeit stylized, Elizabethan sword fight that preceded it. Barber's music is the link between them. Often influenced by movies and pop culture, Bogdanov confessed, "it was a trick picked up from the film, *Platoon*."[144] A trick, maybe, but an effective one.

For The Falstaff Project at the University of British Columbia Errol Durbach wrote a similar consolidation of Shakespeare's histories but this time emphasizing the role of Sir John Falstaff, as "excavated" from *Henry IV* (Parts One and Two), *Richard II*, and *Henry V*. Yet, instead of piecing several scenes together, he has formulated his own story, leaping from one time period to another. For instance, Hotspur's rebellion is shown on a television newscast, and some characters arrive on motorcycles. Music for the production is similarly eclectic. Director John Wright explained:

> We used *Adagio* along with visuals from centuries of bloody war at the height of the great battle scene (equivalent to *Henry IV*, Part I, Act V, scene 4.) In our anachronistic version Hal staggers on upstage, exhausted, while the faces of wounded soldiers are projected on a scrim in front of him. When *Adagio* ends, the scrim is lifted and Hotspur appears. He challenges Hal, rushes toward him with sword raised and Hal simply shoots him with his revolver.[145]

[143]David Fuller, "The Bogdanov Version: The English Shakespeare Company 'Wars of the Roses,'" *Literature/Film Quarterly* XXXIII/2 (2005), 141.

[144]Michael Bogdanov and Michael Pennington, *The English Shakespeare Company*, 109.

[145]John Wright, email (31 January 2006) to the author.

Did Wright crib from *Raiders of the Lost Ark* where Indiana Jones pulls out his gun and shoots the man with the whip? He remembered seeing that scene but did not recall whether he saw it before or after he made his decision. Yet he is convinced that "the effect on the audience was all you could wish for—a touch of comic shock and a profound sorrow."[146] *Adagio* was an important contribution to this effect.

THE DIARY OF ANNE FRANK

In November and December 2001 *Adagio for Strings* could be found in a production of *The Diary of Anne Frank* in Seekonk, Massachusetts. Director Vern Slater described how it was employed:

> Originally, I had not planned to use any music in the production, but I was dissuaded of this notion, for which I'm extremely grateful. We never would have been able to obtain the level of emotion we attained had we not utilized Barber's lovely *Adagio for Strings* to serve as counterpoint to the climactic scene where the Franks await in fear for the arrival of the inevitable—their discovery by the Nazis.[147]

In a 1991 production of the same play at Northwestern College in St. Paul, Minnesota, director Patsy Miller was about to cut the final scene because she felt it was anti-climactic but promised she would reconsider if the right kind of music could be found to accompany it. When a cast member brought in a recording of the Barber work, everyone knew that this was what the scene needed. (Note the similarity to Baryshnikov and Jones mentioned earlier.) Minister, actor, and writer Troy Cady, who played Anne's father Otto, recalled:

> After the pronouncement of the play's final line, "She puts me to shame," Otto Frank closed the diary and, as he painfully bowed his head, the lights faded softly. With that the music began to swell, truly taking over everything. If volition is seated in the

[146] John Wright, email (13 April 2006) to the author.

[147] Vern Slater, "The Diary of Anne Frank," *Bird Soup and Hummus* (November-December 2001), www.geocities.com/vernslater/annefrank.html.

human soul, *Adagio* seemed to participate in living humanity that night. It literally moved us to fresh depths of sense and action.[148]

For the curtain calls the actors did not take traditional bows but stood with their faces to the backdrop, away from the audience. Projected against the clouds of the surreal set were photographs of Holocaust victims. At the end of most plays, members of the audience gradually get up and leave, but this time they seemed stunned into immobility. Cady remembered that they "just sat there, quiet and still for an unusual amount of time. At each performance, the actors stood in wonder at this phenomenon."[149]

One night, when members of the local Jewish community attended, a man who had survived incarceration at the Bergen-Belsen concentration camp

> rose quietly from his seat to pay his respects to those whose lives had been taken. No one else in the auditorium stood up that night, but he had been touched so deeply, it didn't matter to him that he was the only person standing. He stood still there in his place, until the time came for everyone to leave. We were honored that it touched him in that way.[150]

The play combined with *Adagio* may touch viewers in many ways. They can provide a more powerful experience together.[151]

BARBER'S *ADAGIO*: ALWAYS GOOD FOR A LAUGH!

In the late twentieth and early twenty-first centuries *Adagio for Strings* took on a new but slightly disturbing role. In plays, films, and television shows it began to underscore scenes that poke fun at its placement in serious drama. The introduction of *Adagio* in comedic situations reveals, moreover, how the work has changed in perception in recent years. The following are a few cases where the music functions as a form of theatrical parody.[152]

[148]Troy Cady, email (17 June 2005) to author.

[149]*Ibid.*

[150]*Ibid.*

[151]Consult a list of other dramatic productions featuring *Adagio* in Appendix 5.

[152]Similar instances in film and television will be discussed in Chapter 8.

Only the group known as The Trap (Jeremy Limb, Paul Litchfield, and Dan Mersh) would have the nerve to entitle its production *Bad Play,* which they performed at the Edinburgh Festival Fringe in 2002. But the title is meant as a spoof of an inadequate and inept theatrical production, perhaps a warped depiction of the destruction of the World Trade Center. After two of the actors entered and did some warm-up exercises, a third arrived from the back of the auditorium, and the technical manager brought up *Adagio for Strings* to begin the show. The threadbare quality became apparent when models of the twin towers were projected on a backdrop while pebbles were thrown at them until they collapsed. The performers resurrected *Adagio*, the signature tune of the 9 / 11 tragedy, in connection with their own deliberately poor taste depiction of the event.

For the Circle X Theatre Company in Los Angeles Alice Dodd and Jillian Armenante composed a lampoon of typical Gothic novels titled *In Flagrante Gothicto* (2000), satirizing "the more constipated aspects of just about everything ever conceived by the Bronte sisters."[153] This production boasted narrative voice-overs along with a musical accompaniment of a perverse nature. The Ninth Symphony of Beethoven, for example, melded into the "emotive lava flow of Samuel Barber's *Adagio for Strings,* all juxtaposed against a lunatic dramatic resolution."[154]

Shelley Berc and Andrei Belgrader adapted Molière's comedy *Les Fourberies de Scapin* (shortened to *Scapin*) for a Seattle production in September 2002. While adhering to the spirit of seventeenth-century French comedy, its creative team also "winks at modernity: Rusty Magi's bouncy musical score inserts sedate lute flourishes, doo-wop ditties, Samuel Barber's *Adagio for Strings,* and lusty outbursts of gospel and blues. And as the spirit moves them, the actors banter with patrons and toss off slangy one-liners."[155]

For the off-off-Broadway production of *The Transparency of Val* (2003) by Stephen Belber, director Sam Helfrich juxtaposed contrasting kinds of music in the underscore, including a "wicked use" of *Adagio for Strings* for a battle scene, "a gag that, one assumes, would not amuse

[153]Steven Leigh Morris, "Happy Times Are Here Again," *LA Weekly* (6-12 October 2000).

[154]*Ibid.*

[155]Misha Berson, "'Scapin' Soars, Slips as Musical Comedy," *Seattle Times* (20 September 2002), E: 3.

Oliver Stone."[156] Reviewer David Barbour concluded that "you have to sympathize with Val. His mother is growing younger by the minute. His girlfriend is turning into a hermaphrodite and his beloved teacher turns out to be a pedophile."[157] The play is a "wild, *Candide*-like attack on every value society holds dear."[158]

In Theater, Poetry, Dance, Multimedia, and Mime

Barber's *Adagio* has been introduced into other theatrical ventures, not limited to ordinary dramas. *Figurations* is a stage presentation (as opposed to a literal "play") consisting of eighteen linked vignettes written by poet Ted Richer. They can be understood as "playlets probing and recording the poet's rites of passage and other seminal experiences. The poet frequently interrogates the action, then withdraws to react, reabsorb and rewrite thereby transforming meaning and action."[159] Critic David Selby described the vignettes as "miniature Beckettian monologues and dialogues, each lasting only a minute or two."[160] (Indeed, Samuel Beckett immediately came to mind when I read *Figurations*.) In the final part, "Adagio," two characters listen and dance to the Barber work. Embedded in the poetic dialogue are the following lines:

> We listen.
> What is that?
> The sound, slow, wrenching.
> "Adagio for Strings, Samuel Barber."

They consider it as funeral music, Whose is it: Yours? Mine? Ours?

> "It's in dancing, too."
> "Ah . . ."

[156]"Seen Off of Broadway," *Lighting Dimensions* (2 August 2002); reprinted www.lightingdimensions.com/newsarticle.asp. Photographs from the productions are supplied on the director's website: www.samhelfrich.com/TRANSPARENCYMOV.swf.

[157]*Ibid.*

[158]*Ibid.*

[159]Ted Richer, *The Writer in the Story and Other Figurations* (Guildford, Surrey, UK: Apocalypse Books, 2004), jacket summary.

[160]David Selby, [London] *Sunday Telegraph* (7 October 2001). The two characters were played by Todd Hearon and Kim Crocker in the production directed by Maggie Dietz at Boston's Bridge Theatre Company in 2001.

"A pas de deux, in ballet . . ."
"Oh . . ."
". . . balancing, lifting, spinning . . ."
"Ah . . ."
". . . and turning."

And toward the end:

"I wonder . . . could we dance . . ."
"Maybe . . ."
". . . to funeral music?"
We listen.
"Why not . . . it's our funeral."[161]

Selby called the lines "inner voices made audible."[162] Their spacing on the page implies a great deal of silence in the speaking: an avant-garde John Cage concept thrust upon a conservative Barber aesthetic. Reviewer Larry Stark identified this particular figuration as a "perfect metaphor for the entire production."[163] In order to comprehend the importance of *Adagio* in Richer's life, one only has to consider his statement: "Barber's work lives in my being—it is the sound of me and I can't get away from it."[164]

At London's Barbican Center in 2004 Tel Aviv-based choreographer Ohad Naharin staged *Naharin's Virus* for his Batsheva Dance Company. The dance, exploring explicit criticisms of the Israeli foreign policy in the Middle East, is accompanied by both Arab and Israeli music. A portion of Barber's *Adagio* is played during a solo female dance with a recitation, "my mother, she wanted a boy." Naharin confessed, "I like the mixture of things. The coherency has to come out of the composition, not out of the ability to say . . . this is music, this is ethnic, or this is dance. It's about the

[161]Ted Richer, email (13 June 2012) to the author. A complete version of the *Adagio* "figuration" is provided in the author's subsequent publication Ted Richer, *The Writer in the Story*, 83-86.

[162]David Selby, *Sunday Telegraph* (7 October 2001).

[163]Larry Stark, "What Happened in Boston, Willie," *The Theater Mirror* (2001); reprinted www.theatermirror.com/fbtcbcals.htm

[164]Ted Richer, email (13 June 2012) to the author.

mix between sacred and ritual."[165] In addition, a dancer reads excerpts from Peter Hanke's anti-play, *Offending the Audience,* written in 1966 at the height of the absurdist, avant-garde theatrical movement. He tells the audience, "We don't represent anything. There is no plot. God is an invention, like pizza."[166] The narrator eventually gets around to offending the audience with "a monologue of wide-ranging, scurrilous-ironic abuse of us sitting targets—tiresome more than offensive." [167] Critic David Dougill complained that by this time he was propping his eyes open.[168]

15 Head, a professional, nonprofit, experimental theater lab, was a resident company at the Red Eye Theater in Minneapolis. Many of its productions were collaborations derived from rehearsals, such as *Sacred Space* (2003), a show based on visual imagery rather than text. Artistic director Joe Stanley compiled a portfolio of twenty-six paintings, notably works by René Magritte, Edward Hopper, and Salvador Dalí, and charged the company to help him create an evening of theater based on responses to the artworks. Projections of the painting were accompanied by such diverse music as doo-wop from The Bobs and traditional Bulgarian songs; Barber's Agnus Dei, sung offstage, began in total darkness. The painting associated with this particular piece has yet to be identified, probably John Singer Sargeant's "Fumée d'ambre gris." "Deeply felt, highly personal moments are at once unique and universal. It's a lesson well worth learning, lovingly taught in a beautiful and giddily elegant production," according to Dominic P. Papatola.[169] Gordon Royce was more skeptical: "it doesn't always succeed. Moments of text don't add much, and as in any theater, when the performers appear effortless, the scene soars. When they labor, it's because the image isn't transparent."[170] The company disbanded a few years later.

[165]Ohad Naharin, quoted in Maggie Foyer, "Ohad Naharin Interview," *Dance Europe* (June 2004).

[166]David Dougill, "Not All Black and White," *The* [London] *Times* (9 May 2004), 33. This portion was incorporated into *Deca Dance,* performed at the Spoleto USA Festival, May 2007, but *Adagio* was not used. An archival tape of *Naharin's Virus*, with the *Adagio* portion, is available for viewing (with permission) at the Dance Division of the New York Public Library, Lincoln Center.

[167]*Ibid.*

[168]*Ibid.*

[169]Dominic P. Papatola, "'Sacred Spaces' Fills the Senses," *St. Paul* [Minn.] *Pioneer Press* (3 November 2003), B: 4. Reviews of the production fail to mention which art works were associated with specific pieces of music.

[170]Gordon Royce, "15 HEAD Taps the Senses in a New Work," [Minneapolis, Minn.] *Star Tribune* (1 November 2003), B: 4.

Adagio for Strings was, in addition, featured in a performance by the Leningrad theater company, Terra Mobile, created in 1983 by artistic director Vadim Miheenko. The theatrical form is close to mime but combining with it break-dance aesthetics, street theater, clowning, and acrobatic movement.[171] A good illustration of the concept is *Gogol's Coat* (1991), an avant-garde elaboration of Nikolai Vasilievich Gogol's short story *The Overcoat* (1842), portraying the "frigidity, sterility, artificiality, hypocrisy, and shallowness of life and society."[172] It may seem strange that a decidedly Russian ensemble enacting such a quintessential Russian story would incorporate an American composition such as Barber's. Yet those in charge of the production must have been convinced that this particular music was important in setting the desired tone.

Greasepaint and Halos is a skit / clowning troupe from Greensboro College (N.C.), whose purpose is to teach and share their Christian faith through the arts. On 5 April 2001 the troupe presented *The Passion Mime,* staged to *Adagio for Strings.* As with historic passion plays, it told the story of the last days in the life of Jesus, with actors assuming the identities of several characters.

For Drum and Bugle Corps and Marching Band

Those who have difficulty imagining *Adagio for Strings* in a drum and bugle corps performance may be still thinking of the old corps, with only valve-less bugles incapable of playing much more than triadic melodies and fanfares. Today's new, more sophisticated corps boast modern instruments, including almost any brass instrument, and can perform virtually any type of music, dependent only on the creativity of the show's designer.

The way *Adagio* is presented—and how much of it occurs in a performance—varies from one organization to another. A typical show is usually long enough to accommodate a full work if desired, but most bands want much of their routines to be more energetic, especially at the beginning and / or end. Therefore, a short excerpt is likely to function as the contrasting "ballad" portion in the midst of other faster pieces, as is the case with the Santa Clara (Calif.) Vanguard. In another instance, for an exhibition by the Zydeco Color Guard (Dayton, Ohio), almost all of *Adagio*

[171]"Terra Mobile, Mime-Dance Theater Group," [Moscow] *Teatralnaya Zhizn* VI (March 1991); reprinted www.afronord.tripod.com/rat/listing.html.

[172]*Ibid.*

is programmed (although in three different guises), but such a constantly slow tempo for an entire program is unusual. It was, however, appropriate for this group's memorial to 9 / 11. With other ensembles, such as the Center Grove Marching Band (Greenwood, Ind.) and the Mighty Marching Chargers (Fairfax County, Va.), portions of *Adagio* are interspersed with and layered into passages of other pieces—a true integration of materials.

According to *The Drum Corps Data Base*, the Sacramento (Calif.) Mandarins were in their 1993 routine the first drum corps to play *Adagio for Strings*. Since then, other corps groups and bands have performed it.[173] Yet it was ultimately the Santa Clara Vanguard that impressed everyone with its presentation of the Barber work in its *Age of Reverence* show. Many consider it to be the standard against which all subsequent corps performances with *Adagio* are to be judged.

SANTA CLARA VANGUARD: *THE AGE OF REVERENCE*

CD Track 10

It was the 2000 Drum Corps International (DCI) world championship finals at the University of Maryland where the Santa Clara Vanguard presented *The Age of Reverence*. Arranged by Dean Westman and Jim Casella, it linked together a part of Barber's *Prayers of Kierkegaard,* two Bartók excerpts, plus a bit of Barber's *Adagio* called by its choral title Agnus Dei.[174] Casella and the group's choreographer Myron Rosander described the concept in the following manner:

> Often introspective and serene, as well as clashing and angry, "The Age of Reverence" explored the many facets of faith and hope, searching and questioning, adoration and inner growth. SCV mesmerized all with unexpected, sensitive music that collectively sought a higher purpose in life.[175]

Adagio's inclusion in such a "higher purpose" justifies the religious, choral title. The whole concept is a far cry from the old drum and bugle corps, traipsing around the field playing "When the Saint's Go Marching In!"

[173]See Appendix 5 for examples.

[174]The audio performance appears on the ensemble's compact discs *State of the Art II 2000* and *Symphonic Celebrations,* Vol. 4. The full routine is given on the DVD, *DCI 2000 World Championships,* which shows multiple views of the routine: multi-camera, high camera, views of only the percussion or the color guard.

[175]Liner notes to *DCI 2000 World Championships* DVD.

The Barber portion (ca. 2 1/2 minutes) began with the opening phrase but immediately jumped to the climactic phrase, spiced up with tam-tams and drum rolls. One color guard member tossed his (mock) rifle in the air for an incredible number of turns and caught it at just the right moment. The band held out the two chords at the end of the climax well beyond the expectation of the audience, which then broke out into enthusiastic applause. Linda Garbarino, SCV Booster Club President, claimed that it "raised the hair on your neck."[176] Brian Phillips, quad line section leader of the Seattle Cascades declared, "I really liked the last chord—loud things are way cooler than not loud things."[177] The final phrase of the coda then followed, with a diminuendo that visual effects judge Marie Czapinski described as "a whisper."[178] According to Garbarino, "Again we proved that Vanguard is the one to explore new territory in drum corps by ending our show on a single soft, diminishing note."[179]

The group formations during *Adagio* are less formal than in the other sections of *The Age of Reverence*. Because this is the ballad part of the routine, the band avoids straight lines and creates curvilinear forms. As Czapinski put it, "After all that organization, the free form is a good contrast."[180] Toward the end, most color guard members abandon their rifles and become dancers.

Barber's music was not a part of the original sequence but according to Rosander was substituted for a John Adams piece that proved to be "scary and challenging."[181] Besides, Casella and Rosander were "kinda dying to do" *Adagio* sometime anyway. Rosander realized that

> When you take a piece of music with this emotional caliber, you really have to be very cautious that you do it justice. This is a once in a lifetime opportunity to do Barber's *Adagio*. In the color guard approach we had to go kind of over the top, a feel

[176]Linda Garbarino, quoted in Linda Garbarino and Jerry Marshall, "Message from the President," *Vanguardian* XXXIII/3 (September, 2000), 1; reprinted www.scvanguard.org.

[177]Brian Phillips, "Seattle Cascades Quad Line Section Leader" [interview], *Aria: The DCI.org Interview* (23 June 2005), www.dci.org/news/.

[178]Marie Czapinski, *DCI 2000 World Championships*, Track 5.

[179]Linda Garbarino, "Message from the President," *Vanguardian*, 1-2.

[180]Marie Czapinski, *DCI 2000 World Championships*, Track 5.

[181]Myron Rosander, *DCI 2000 World Championships*, Track 3 [paraphrase].

of coming apart at the seams in terms of an emotional aggressive approach to the music so that the audience can fully understand what you are feeling at the time—what the performers were trying to convey, which is a complete sense of anguish, a high degree of anger, intensity and emotion.[182]

This music has become so inextricably associated with the Vanguard that the group now uses a short variant for one of its warm-up exercises. Designated as either "powerchord #7" or "horn line warm-up #3," it starts with a buildup of a single chord (perhaps to get everyone in tune), after which some of the opening chords and melodic fragments of *Adagio* slowly emerge. When members of the horn line warm up in the lot outside their performance area, they often attract a large crowd. Toward the end of the warm-up period, usually after other musical exercises, they play the *Adagio* variant. Although Vanguard has not played their main *Adagio* arrangement for several years, this short reminder is often enough to excite fans.[183]

A TRIPLE WHAMMY BY THE ZYDECO COLOR GUARD

Sometimes—usually indoors during the off-season—only the color guard of a drum corps performs a routine. In 2008 one such group, the Zydeco Color Guard, based in Dayton, Ohio, performed a memorial to Flight 93, the hijacked plane that crashed in western Pennsylvania on the day of the terrorist attacks in 2001. When indoor performances cannot accommodate a live band, recordings are sometimes used. In this case the choreographer(s) juxtaposed three different versions of *Adagio for Strings*. The routine began with a recording of the vocalise version, proceeding up through the cadence (rehearsal [2]), at which point the string quartet took over, playing up through the climax. The color guard activity increased, starting with only one member swirling a white flag (others had rifles); one by one the other members exchanged their rifles for white flags leading to a precision tossing of them at the final chord of the climax. At the quiet chords the soundtrack switched to the Agnus Dei transcription. For the ending the guards again performed with a single

[182]*Ibid.*

[183]Video and audio clips can be located at *Santa Clara Vanguard*, www.scvanguard.org/on_the_road/. The video clip shows the group in 2004, led by Gino Cipriani, during their semi-finals warm-up at the DCI World Championships in Denver, Colorado. See "SCV–Adagio for Strings," *YouTube* (10 September 2006), posted by andy9ajc9.

white flag while the choir sang the opening and closing phrases of the coda. This presentation is a clever use of Barber's music, well coordinated with the routine and culminating in a suitable memorial.[184]

INTEGRATING *ADAGIO*: CENTER GROVE MARCHING BAND AND THE MIGHTY MARCHING CHARGERS

While the Vanguard, as well as other groups, has juxtaposed a segment of *Adagio for Strings* with several other pieces of music for their routines, at least two bands have actually integrated the work with other music in their presentations. For its 1998 show, *A Study in Contrast,* the Center Grove Marching Band interspersed parts of Barber's *Adagio* with the composer's *Medea's Dance of Vengeance* (1956), sometimes alternating, sometimes layered upon each other.[185] Director Kevin Schuessler confided that he likes "taking left turns" and "as soon as you get hooked into my thought process I will go in another direction that automatically feeds into the opposite. The good thing about *Adagio* and *Medea* is that they are such polar opposites."[186] The result is indeed a study in contrast.

In the first movement a group of dancers performs to the beginning of *Adagio* played by winds and a string quartet in arc formation. Another group enters playing music from *Medea,* layering it on top of *Adagio,* but in triple tempo. At first Schuessler thought this could be achieved casually, without a fixed ratio of tempos, but he later decided that the transition needed a stricter relationship. Finally the *Medea* music overtakes *Adagio,* which then disappears. Schuessler confessed, "We tried not to lose the feeling of freeness of *Adagio* while were we doing *Medea.*"[187] The second movement, logically called "Collage," interweaves fragments of both works. From Schuessler's viewpoint, "the great thing about *Adagio* is its simplicity; the harmonic tension and resolution that it creates. Our shows are based on tension and release."[188] The finale features mainly *Medea's Dance of Vengeance*, reaching a musical and dramatic climax, but when

[184]See "Zydeco Colorguard 2008," *YouTube* (9 July 2008), posted by julymeg90. This file suffers from poor video and audio quality, however. There were apparently brief narratives at the beginning and the end of the routine, which are undecipherable.

[185]This music was originally part of Barber's full-length *Medea* ballet of 1946.

[186]Kevin Schuessler, interview (31 May 2004) with the author.

[187]*Ibid.*

[188]*Ibid.*

the sound subsides, the low brass bring in the quiet chords of *Adagio*. Nearly the whole coda of *Adagio* is presented, ending with the subdued sound of the string quartet. Both audience and participants liked the show. For the participants it was a long and difficult learning process. Schuessler reflected, "I think everybody had some emotional attachment to it. It was a very demanding show; it kicked their tails."[189]

In 2001 the theme of the Virginia Showcase of Bands was "The Cold War." The contribution of the Mighty Marching Chargers from Chantilly High School of Fairfax was *Two Worlds*: a confrontation of twentieth-century music from the United States and from the former Soviet Union, juxtaposing music of Barber and Dmitri Shostakovich. The leaders, Keith Taylor and Alan Johnson, asserted that "the intertwining of musical ideas represent the struggle and tensions between the two great superpowers of the 20th Century."[190] Movement III begins with part of the final movement of Shostakovich's Fifth Symphony, but after a minute or so it transforms into *Adagio for Strings*. Periodically short motives from the Shostakovich work are layered in.[191]

OTHERS

In November 2001 the Tarpon Springs High School Marching Band of Apopka, Florida, directed by Kevin Ford, performed *Life Is a Journey,* which included *Adagio for Strings* plus John Adams's *Short Ride in a Fast Machine* (1986) and music from the movie *The Perfect Storm* (2000). The music was enhanced by a display of large pictures with diverse images meant to illustrate the themes of the different pieces of music: Albert Einstein; Tiananmen Square; John F. Kennedy, Jr.; and the Columbine school shootings. (I have no information indicating which picture was associated with *Adagio*. My hunch is JFK, Jr., and / or Columbine.)

The Portage [Mich.] Northern High School Band presented a program in 2004 called *Metamorphosis*. Beginning with a brief excerpt from Hindemith's Symphony in B-flat for Band (1951), the group segued into

[189]*A Study in Contrasts* is on a DVD of the 23rd Annual Grand National Championships of Bands of America (12-14 November 1998) at the RCA Dome, Indianapolis, Ind. It contains both the broadcast view, with many angles and close-ups, plus one complete overhead view. The routine is described at "CGTB's 1998 Program," *Center Grove Trojan Band*, www.geocities.com/Vienna/Strasse/6689/98/html.

[190]Keith Taylor and Alan Johnson, *Herndon High School*, www.herndonband.org/showcase2001lineup.htm.

[191]An excerpt on the band's website reveals how the Shostakovich merging into the first phrase of *Adagio*. See "Two Worlds," *Mighty Marching Chargers* (2001), www.dcfree.net/chantillybandmusic/Marching.html.

Barber's *Medea's Dance of Vengeance* and then into *Adagio for Strings*. Near the end of latter segment the horn line "morphed" into the Hindemith March from his *Symphonic Metamorphosis* (1943).

Introducing at least a portion of *Adagio* into a band or drum corps routine has recently become somewhat of a fad, although the excerpt is sometimes barely recognizable. Many such groups are listed in Appendix 5. In addition to these, at least two ensembles in the United Kingdom have also presented *Adagio:* the Encore Drum and Bugle Corps from Sandy, Bedfordshire (in a routine called *Field of Dreams*) and The Senators from Eastleigh, Hampshire.

BEYOND THE CORPS: STAR OF INDIANA

Bill Cook and Jim Mason founded Star of Indiana in Bloomington, Indiana in 1984 to "bring together leading professional music instructors, choreographers and arrangers to provide advanced musical education to some of the nation's most talented student musicians."[192] The group won first place in the Drum Corps International World Championship in 1991. In 1993 the ensemble added excerpts from Barber's *Medea* to its program, but it never performed a version of *Adagio* until the Canadian Brass invited it to become a part of *Brass Theater,* a touring program with costumes and art montages, plus precision flag, rifle, and sword drills. Interestingly, for this performance the Canadian Brass asked Star of Indiana to replace its bugles with more standard concert brass instruments because "the bugle is really a second-class instrument. It's tuned in a really bad key (E-flat) and is not compatible with the normal B-flat instruments."[193] John Tatgenhorst arranged *Adagio for Strings* for these two combined forces. The difference between his arrangement and McNeff's original one for the Canadian Brass is apparent from the start: whereas McNeff assigns the opening melody to the horn, Tatgenhorst uses a trumpet. He occasionally adds a few passing tones to the bass line and a fairly long pedal point in the climactic passage. The Canadian Brass begins the piece, one per part, gradually adding Star of Indiana until a full sound is achieved. The original, smaller configuration then returns in the coda. In this performance the Canadian Brass borrowed staging and lighting effects from its own presentation. At the conclusion

[192]Bill Cook, "Star of Indiana History," www.cookgroup.com/star/history.html.

[193]Gene Watts, quoted in Bob Portzman, "Brass Chuckles," *St. Paul* [Minn.] *Pioneer Press* (31 July 1995).

four members of the group turn their backs to the audience, leaving only the French horn player facing forward for his final solo phrase.[194]

In 2001 Star of Indiana adapted some of its routines for *Blast,* a long-running stage show in London and on Broadway, followed in 2003 by a sequel, *Blast II: Shockwave,* an even more spectacular show. Amid the energetic numbers were two classical pieces, excerpts from Orff's *Carmina Burana* and Barber's *Adagio for Strings.* Mason stated, "I just pick music I like, that touched me or moved me when I was younger or pieces that I always wanted to do. The key is to . . . take the audience on a journey."[195] More woodwinds were added, turning the group into more of a concert band. Some performers, however, were physically quite active, doing back bends, splits, rolling and jumping. Reviewing the show, Matt Briddell described the action:

> The musicians stand beneath the pit structure and are largely unseen. One of Jim Moore's best features, he and another girl dance on, around, and climb through two cage structures. As the music builds to its climax, what appears to be a rescue scene develops as the girl climbs up the inside of one of the cages while Jim is atop the other with an outstretched arm. The way they present it, it doesn't look like she's going to make it. Saxes started off the song, but give way to the brass. They reappear as the full ensemble crescendos to the peak of the song. . . . The sound they produced was chilling, to say the least.[196]

Reviewer Chip Chandler thought the two structures were "an oblique commemoration" of the Twin Towers.[197]

Because drum corps units are constantly trying out new routines with new music, it is doubtful that any of the above shows with *Adagio* will ever be revived, at least in competition. Yet other ensembles, mainly marching bands, have also begun to program an excerpt from this composition. It

[194]"Brass Theatre," *YouTube* (23 September 2006), posted by RaquelRod. The show enjoyed an eight-week sixteen-city tour.

[195]Chip Chandler, "Musicians Become Athletes," *Amarillo* [Tex.] *Globe-News* (26 January 2003); reprinted www.amarillo.com/stories/012603/ent_blast2.shtml.

[196]Matt Briddell, "Shockwave: On Stage in Bloomington, IN," *DrumCorpPlanet* (5 January 2003).

[197]Chip Chandler, "Blast II: Incredible Show of Raw Power, Energy," *Amarillo Globe-News* (30 January 2003); reprinted www.amarillonet.com. In late 2002 and early 2003 *Shockwave* toured the country, and a shorter version eliminating *Adagio* was presented at the EPCOT Center in Florida.

seems to have obtained a relatively permanent place in this particular musical world.[198]

Al fresco: Music for Outdoor Spectacles

Because *Adagio for Strings* is written for a string orchestra, its usual venue is appropriately indoors, taking advantage of concert hall acoustics and ambiance. Yet some productions take it outdoors (often by recordings) to enhance their presentations.

SON ET LUMIÈRE

Adagio for Strings was given a prominent part in a spectacular sound and light show at Plymouth, England in June 2005, a celebration of the 200th anniversary of Lord Nelson's victory at Trafalgar (the actual event occurred in October 1805). Seventeen ships from five nations re-enacted the battle with tons of gunpowder, state of the art pyrotechnics, and a replica of an eighteenth-century frigate standing in for Nelson's ship, *The Victory*. About 250,000 spectators watched the event from shore, while members of the royal family viewed it from ships in the harbor. The re-enactment, lasting a little over forty minutes, was narrated by actor Robert Hardy of *All Creatures Great and Small* fame and was directed by Simon Garret, with Alex Naylor as Nelson.

Adagio entered as the battle got under way; at first it was difficult to hear it amid gunfire and narrative. The musical climax occurred just as Nelson is wounded, after a lead musket ball fired from a French ship struck him in the shoulder. Hardy vividly described it: "it cuts through his thorax, fractures two of his ribs, punctures his lungs, severs an artery, breaks his spine and lodges in the muscles of his back." Witnessing the event was his captain, Thomas Masterman Hardy (a coincidence of names, or an ancestor of the narrator?). As the music reached the end of the climax, Nelson told him, "They've done for me at last, Hardy. My backbone is shot through." The music then jumped to the final phrase of the coda as the narrator exclaimed, "he could die now if he chose to let go . . . but the end of the battle is still uncertain; men and ships are still fighting and still in danger. He will stay with them for three more terrible hours." A huge

[198]See Appendix 5 for a list of marching ensembles to program *Adagio* in their shows.

battle ensued, after which Nelson died to the music of "In paradisum" from Fauré's Requiem.[199]

FOUNTAINS AND FIREWORKS

In 2008 a portion of *Adagio for Strings* was quoted in an arrangement played at the Magic Fountain at the top of Barcelona's Montjuïc. During the excerpt the fountain, illuminated by colored lights, sprayed water high in the air. The website for the fountain calls it a "spectacular display of colour, light, motion, music and water acrobatics"; mixed altogether, the result is "pure magic!"[200] There seems not to be, however, any attempt to coordinate the rise and fall of the water with the highs and lows of the music. Unfortunately, the Barber portion only lasted about a minute. A full performance with constantly changing lights and water acrobatics could be a thoroughly entertaining magical experience.

A performance of *Adagio for Strings* may seem inappropriate for a fireworks display, yet it was adopted for such circumstances at the final outdoor concert of the 2007 Edinburgh International Festival. It was part of an all-American program by the Scottish Chamber Orchestra, conducted by Clark Rundell, along with Bernstein's *Candide* Overture and Copland's "Buckaroo Holiday." Wilf Scott and Keith Webb of Pyrovision supervised the pyrotechnic display taking place above Edinburgh Castle. Indeed, a spectacular bombardment of fireworks is highly suitable for the Bernstein and Copland works, but, according to Scott, for *Adagio* it was "a question of creating a mood with a piece like that, trying to get fireworks to do, in a way, what lighting could do."[201] Webb compared it to painting: "it's just that you have the biggest palate in the world, you've got the sky with

[199]BBC coverage of this event was available through much of July 2005 at www.news.bbc.co.uk/2/hi/uk_news/4632949.stm#. *Adagio for Strings* was also part of an "audio-visual spectacle," designed by lighting director Sergio Rossi, in Athens at the Odeon of Herodes Atticus on 21 September 2001. It was performed by the Athens State Symphony Orchestra and conducted by Nikos Tsouchlos.

[200]The fountain is located near the Museu National d'Art Catalunya. As of December 2012 there were four files of the *Adagio* performance on *YouTube*: "Barcelona Montjuic Fountains: Samuel Barber–Adagio for Strings," *YouTube* (10 September 2008), posted by Dorin Moise; "Barcelona–The Magic Fountain 2 (Adagio For Strings)," *YouTube* (15 October 2008), posted by curaheee; "Fontaña Mágica–Barcelona (Samuel Barber–Adagio for Strings)," *YouTube* (4 October 2009), posted by pamisiu194; "Adagio For Strings in Plaça d'Espanya Barcelona's with Fountain Show," *YouTube* (7 March 2010), posted by mtsirik. While the music is the same, each video was taken on a different night displaying different colors and water effects.

[201]Wilf Scott, quoted in Liam Rudden, "US Theme Brings Festival to Rousing Finale," [Edinburgh] *The Scotsman* (31 August 2007); reprinted www.scotsman.com/news/us-theme-brings-festival-to-rousing-finale-1-1330348.

which to play."[202] A *BBC News* reporter concluded that the fireworks enhanced the tone of the Barber piece: "Silent flashes of colour flared from the castle battlements, echoing 'the emotional pull' of the piece."[203] In addition, the castle itself was given a green glow by roman candles. Columnist Keith Bruce noted the passing of a few trains added some "aural competition," but he commended the fireworks as being "bravely sparse and made the most of the silhouette of the castle."[204] Nevertheless, *Adagio*'s rise to the climax could be made even more exciting with a sky full of light.

Later in November 2007 *Adagio* accompanied a fireworks display on the other side of Hadrian's Wall in Carlisle, United Kingdom. Columnist Julie Armstrong witnessed the show: "As Rossini's William Tell Overture gave way to Barber's heartbreaking Adagio for Strings, wide-eyed children, hoisted onto their parents' shoulders gazed upward, mesmerized by the sparkling fountains of purple and silver."[205] About 35,000 people attended the event, held as a fundraiser for the local Rotary Club.

If the orchestral *Adagio* is forced to compete with the noise generated by fireworks, a trance dance version might stand a better chance to be heard. Ferry Corsten's remix (see Chapter 7) was part of the July 2008 L'International des Feux Loto in Québec in a show by Howard and Sons, the Australian pyrotechnics team. Their presentation "Evolve" showcased various pieces of music that "evolved" by means of covers, arrangements, remixes, and re-recordings.[206] Corsten's remix clearly fit the bill.

A ROLLING SCENARIO: REVENGE OF IVARR THE BONELESS

In May 2004 Vikings of Middle England presented a re-enactment from Dark Ages British history about the Danish King Ragnar Lothbrog and his vengeance-seeking sons, including Ivarr the Boneless. (Did he suffer

[202]Keith Webb, quoted in Liam Rudden, "US Theme Brings Festival to Rousing Finale," [Edinburgh] *The Scotsman* (31 August 2007).

[203]"How Do You Choreograph Fireworks to Live Music?" *BBC News* (3 September 2007); reprinted www.news.bbc.co.uk/2/hi/uk_news/magazine/6976248.stm

[204]"Explosive Festival Finale Stirs Up a Riot of Vegas Colors," [Glasgow] *Herald* (4 September 2007), 16.

[205]Julie Armstrong, "Park's Pinnacle of Pyrotechnics," [Carlisle, Cumbria] *Cumberland News* (9 September 2007); reprinted www.cumberlandnews.co.uk/news/park-s-pinnacle-of-pyrotechnics-1.351047?referrerPath=2.1825/news.

[206]"Montréal International Fireworks Competition Report," *La Ronde* (18 July 2008), www.montreal-fireworks.com/cgi-bin/rep.cgi?head2008,australia2008,tail2008.

from osteogenesis imperfecta?) The drama unfolds by means of a "rolling scenario," in which scenes are played out in different locations, while the audience moves about (in an orderly fashion) to watch them. For this production, staged on the grounds of Tutbury Castle in Staffordshire, many scenes were enhanced by music piped in on loudspeakers. *Adagio* underscored the scene in which Ivarr confronts his archenemy Osberht in battle. Osberht is victorious, giving Ivarr's Viking force a temporary setback.

> As the triumphant Osberht gives thanks to God for victory and Ivarr and his brothers retreat to lick their wounds within the city of York, the poignant strains of Barber's *Adagio for Strings* floats over the blood-soaked battlefield, now bestrewn with the bodies of the dead and dying. Mournful cries of bereaved wives and the heart wrenching sobbing of newly fatherless children make the scene particularly moving.[207]

While this could be construed as a parody of battle scenes in *Platoon* (see Chapter 8), the intent seems serious and, as the above writer remarked, "moving." It is one of many connections with war that the Barber score has acquired since that film was first released.

THE MAGIC OF *ADAGIO* OR AGNUS DEI SUBMERGED

One of the more unusual associations of Barber's Agnus Dei occurred in May 2006 on an ABC television special: it served as the background for magician David Blaine's escape act, "Drowned Alive." Because of the circumstances, his demonstration loosely qualifies as an *al fresco* event. Prominently displayed in the plaza of New York's Lincoln Center, he spent a week immersed in a small water-filled plexiglass sphere. As the *pièce de résistance* he undertook the stunt of holding his breath for nine minutes while attempting a Houdini-esque escape from handcuffs. Barber's choral music started to play shortly after he began this final trick. Because the recordings of this piece tend to last about nine minutes, Blaine presumably planned to emerge from the tank just as the music reached the end of the climax.

[207]Damian Brooke, "Revenge of Ivarr the Boneless," *Vikings of Middle England*, www.vikingsofmiddle england.co.uk/scene_revenge.html.

Both his act and the music, however, proved to be anticlimactic. At about 6:50 the announcer interjected into his running commentary, "there is a problem; he is fighting," and at 7:08 medical attendants pulled Blaine from the tank in a weakened condition and gave him oxygen. Because no one stopped the music, it continued through this process with the musical climax now ironically coinciding with Blaine's rescue. Cynics could surmise that this life-or-death moment was calculated to produce a much more sensational effect than had he succeeded with the original escape. Yet the crowd watching him in the plaza may not have heard the music, which was probably directed only to the television audience. Blaine justified his attempt to break the old mark (eight minutes, fifty-five seconds) by claiming "Magic brings people together who might not [otherwise] come together."[208] As television reviewer Ginia Bellafante put it, "well, so does an airport."[209]

ADAGIO GOES TO THE CIRCUS

Circus, he wrote? Surely not one of the world's most serene orchestral pieces as background for exotic animals, clowns, lion tamers, and trapeze artists! Well, not quite. Cirque Éloize is part of the "new circus" concept, an animal-free, "post-modern version of a multi-century-old tradition."[210] Most people would recognize the type through Cirque du Soleil. In 2000 Cirque Éloize, a similar but smaller group, programmed *Adagio for Strings* for its *Cirque Orchestra*. Jeannot Painchaud, the group's artistic director, explained, "we offer a multidisciplinary form; it's circus all right, but it's also theater, dance and music."[211] He explained that the term "éloize," Acadian French for "heat lightning" (*éclais de chaleur* in Metropolitan French), was selected for the name of the troupe to "symbolize electric, youthful energy."[212] Choreographer for the group, Johanne Madore, described the intent:

[208]David Blaine, quoted in Dion Semeniuk, "David Blaine Bringing People Together," *Press Article*, www.pressarticle.com/entertainment/406/david-blaine-bringing-people-together.

[209]Ginia Bellafante, "Thinking Up, and Overthinking, Stunts," *The New York Times* (9 May 2006), B: 4. The escape attempt later appeared on *YouTube* but has since been deleted.

[210]Stephane Baillargeon, "An American Fairy Tale: Cirque Éloize," *Le Devoir* (24 February 2002).

[211]Jeannot Painchaud, quoted in *ibid.*

[212]Jeannot Painchaud, quoted in Zan Dubin, "At Cirque Eloize, 'the Special Effects Are the Artists,'" *Los Angeles Times* (20 April 1995); reprinted www.articles.latimes.com/1995-04-20/news/ol-56584_1_special-effects.

> The idea is to fuse dance with arts of the circus. Dancing isn't just a question of combining steps. You can incorporate the spirit of dance into anything. . . . It's not just a technical thing. It's a consciousness, a poetic feeling. It's a way of thinking.[213]

As the company traveled around the country, local orchestras, such as the Pacific Symphony in Los Angeles, the San Diego Symphony, and the San Antonio Symphony, performed the music live. At New York City Center, where the performance was entitled "A Winter's Night of Fancy," it was accompanied by the Orchestra of St. Luke's.

Near the beginning of the program *Adagio* underscored Jano Chiasson in motion high in the air carried aloft by two broad bands of hanging white silk. For much of the performance he wraps either his arms or torso in the white cloths, while four men pull on a rope attached to a high, unseen pully to make him ascend.[214] Most of his movements are graceful and slow, but during the silence after the climax he spins rapidly. According to critic Matthew Gurewitsch, Chiasson "soars in a spiral and plummets like a stone."[215] He continued his description with dance terminology:

> As the danseur in the adagio of a classical *pas de deux* discreetly extends the leaps of the ballerina, the silk supports him, counteracting the pull of the earth. Mr. Chiasson's arrow-sharp arabesques and panther-soft turning jumps reinforce the resemblance.[216]

Chiasson himself contributed to the analogy: "I can't describe exactly how I see the fabric, but I see it as alive, not just fabric, but like my partner, actually. Like a woman, most of the time. And then, the sails are my wings, helping me to fly, bringing me up in the air."[217]

[213]Johanne Madore, quoted in Matthew Gurewitsch, "Inspired by Dance, A Circus Is Writing the Poetry of Flight," *The New York Times* (17 February 2002), A: 8.

[214]A nearly complete videotape of a performance was uploaded: "Jano Chiasson Fabric Act," *YouTube* (4 August 2010), posted by stellydansa. The orchestra and conductor, clearly visible throughout the performance, are not identified.

[215]Matthew Gurewitsch, "Inspired by Dance," *The New York Times* (17 February 2002), A: 9.

[216]*Ibid.*

[217]Jano Chiasson, quoted in *ibid.*

Critics have compared Chiasson's flight to various mythical winged creatures: to an angel "suspended by the white webbing straps whose trains look like large wings,"[218] to Pegasus "floating in the wind,"[219] and to a second Icarus "on the cusp between lyric and heroic."[220] *Cirque Orchestra* was first presented at the Festival International de Lanaudière, at the Trois-Rivières's Parc Portuaire in Montreal, and afterwards on an international tour of Europe, the United States, and the Far East. A one-hour version was telecast on Hong Kong-based TVB Pearl in December 2003 and in the United Kingdom with the Performance Channel in October 2004. So far, it has not been broadcast on television in the United States.[221]

If the performance by Cirque Éloize can be discussed under the rubric "*Adagio* Goes to the Circus," then the following two presentations might be better described as "The Circus Comes to *Adagio*." The Australian duo Equilibrio (Simonne Smiles and Chris Mayhew) performed in 2007 an acrobatic program to *Adagio for Strings* onstage with the Wollongong Symphony Orchestra from New South Wales.[222] They repeated the routine elsewhere, notably on a cruise ship in the Arctic "with icebergs floating by."[223] They contend that their work was inspired by the Kirov Ballet *pas de deux* with Yelena Yevteyeva and Eldar Aliev (discussed earlier in this chapter). Keeping in mind choreographer Cynthia Pratt's description of that dance as being "positional," it is a logical step to move toward the general posing aspect of an acrobatic display. Minimal choreographic elements in the ballet transfer well to the graceful movements of the Equilibrio performance. Many movements are nearly the same in both forms, illustrating that dance and acrobatics have much in common.

Similarly at a September 2008 concert by the California Symphony Orchestra, two acrobats performed a slow body sculpture routine to the same music. Iouri Safranov (formerly of the Ringling Brothers Circus)

[218]Stephane Baillargeon, "An American Fairy Tale," *Le Devoir* [Montréal] (24 February 2002).

[219]Jean Paul Sylvain, "The Gracefulness of Superb Bodies in Motion," *Le Journal de Montréal* (25 February 2002).

[220]Matthew Gurewitsch, "Inspired by Dance," *The New York Times* (17 February 2002), A: 9.

[221]Several good photographs of Chiasson's performance are available at "Cirque Orchestra," *Cirque Éloize*, www.cirque-eloize.com/en/photo-gallery. This act is similar to one performed by Alexander Streltsov in Cirque Ingenieux a few years earlier, but not to *Adagio for Strings*.

[222]"Equilibrio Barber's Adagio," *YouTube* (6 July 2008), posted by casmayhew.

[223]"About Me," *Chris Mayhew*, www.myspace.com/artdancer/music.

and Nikolai Melnikov (formerly of Cirque du Soleil) teamed up for a slow, graceful display that one critic called "jaw-droppingly impressive."[224] Barry Jekowsky, the orchestra director, characterized their presentation in rather glowing terms: "Though breathtaking by itself, when *Adagio for Strings* is performed with Iouri and Nikolai, it becomes a spectacular collaboration of music and body sculpture. What they do visually with music is extraordinary."[225] Yet reviewer Sue Gilmore argued that Barber's music "lent more to the acrobatics than the acrobatics lent to the music."[226] Both acrobatic pairs remind me of athletes once known as contortionists, whose bodies slowly twist through precisely controlled handstands, balancing positions, and other feats of physical strength. Both are, indeed, an unusual amalgamation of circus and classical music.

ADAGIO AND THE BODY BEAUTIFUL OR MUSIC TO FLEX MUSCLES BY

When one spends a great deal of effort pumping iron and achieves a desired muscular physique, one way to show off the results is to enter body-building competitions. To impress the judges, each contestant must devise a routine with standard poses but with a sense of imagination. Background music is an important component of this endeavor. One contestant who entered a competition in Wenatchee, Washington on 14 September 2002 selected *Adagio for Strings*. How did his choice come about? After the contestant, well into his sixties, had taken part in a Senior Bodybuilding program, he asked his trainer Harry Hayfield to help develop a posing routine. Not satisfied with the music that contestants had chosen for previous competitions, they wanted something more uplifting. Meanwhile, Hayfield had seen a BBC program about the World Trade Center tragedies, noting its effective use of Barber's *Adagio* to accompany some of the scenes. When he later heard William Ørbit's synthesizer version, he suggested to the contestant that it might be even more suitable for his routine. Because the contest was only a few days after the first anniversary of 9 / 11, the contestant followed his trainer's

224Quoted without attribution in "California Symphony to Present Adagio for Strings Accompanied by Former Cirque de Soleil Acrobats" [press release] (18 September 2008); reprinted www.foggiapr.com/downloads/new/CaliforniaSymp.

225Barry Jekowsky, quoted in *ibid.*

226Sue Gilmore, "Review: California Symphony Opens Season with Acrobats," [San Jose, Calif.] *Mercury News* (13 October 2008).

advice, which reinforced his theme of "breaking free from the chains of terrorism." The judges were so impressed that they awarded him a medal for best overall posing routine and a trophy for the master overall class.[227]

Conclusion

A body sculpture program is one more example of the positional movement mentioned by choreographer Cynthia Pratt. From the Kirov Ballet through the elegant motions of Equilibrio and extending to the posing routine of a dedicated body-builder, Barber's *Adagio for Strings* is ideal music to enhance the slow exhibition of bodily movements. The examples described in this survey illustrate that performances of *Adagio for Strings* reach well beyond the concert hall and recording studio into some highly unusual territories.

[227]Harry Hayfield, email (14 April 2004) to the author.

> Barber's *Adagio* was playing on CBC FM at the time I was nearing the completion of *Autumn Pattern*. A remarkable piece. Undoubtedly the painting was affected by the music.
>
> —Canadian Painter Robert Genn (13 October 2006).[1]

One provocative means of judging the significance of a work of art is to consider its impact on those individuals who express their creativity through other media. It is one kind of achievement for a master painter to influence a colleague or for a seasoned poet to help another find his or her voice. And yet, for a novelist to influence a composer or for a sculptor to influence a dancer suggests an accomplishment of a different order. In this chapter I document a well-known fact: Barber's *Adagio for Strings* has inspired an array of non-musicians—artists and authors—in their creation of new art. Their explanations for this phenomenon are, of course, varied as well as personal. Some embrace this music as they work for its power to define mood or to elicit a bittersweet yearning. Others take explicit advantage of its connotations to enrich their own points of view. Still others announce the connection and borrow Barber's title. If a certain degree of greatness can be ascribed to those works that cross over the boundaries of one art to find influence in the realm of another, the case for this particular composition is strong indeed.

"My Soul and My Heart's Inspiration"[2]

After the Calgary Symphony Orchestra commissioned Robert Genn to paint a central piece for one of its fund-raisers, he had yet to begin the work when the auctioneer asked for a title. Genn confessed, "I pulled a title out of the atmosphere: 'Autumn Pattern' (2 November 2001)."[3] He painted the canvas while listening to classical music:

[1]Robert Genn, email (13 October 2006) to the author.

[2]With due apologies to the Righteous Brothers.

[3]Robert Genn, email (13 October 2006) to the author. Despite the prolific output of this painter, I could find only a few titles with specific musical references: three with the title "In the Halls of the Mountain King," one "L'apres midi, st. Pol Brittany," and two with composer's names, "Derelict with Chopin and Decaying Light" and "Gulf Patterns with J. S. Bach."

> I often include the name of a piece of music in the title of my paintings. There is no question that music has an effect on the painting process—permitting the painter to be "lost" for periods of time when a more subconscious rhythm takes over and the nether-parts of the brain are activated. Barber's *Adagio* is open to a lot of interpretation—but I would characterize it as ennui and a sensitive reflection of things passed—with a glimmer of rebirth and optimism.[4]

Presumably, Genn attempted to infuse some of these attributes into his *Autumn Pattern.*

In 2004 Welsh artist Shelley Hocknell completed two abstract paintings with the simple generic names *Untitled 1* and *2,* but she has acknowledged that they were inspired, in part, by *Adagio for Strings.*

> I was trying to paint with no conscious objectivity; I wanted to allow the emotive feelings of the music dictate the marks, colours and movement of the painting. I find *Adagio* by turns sad and rapturous. For me it conjures feelings of flight or moving through water. I see diagonals and elevating forms. It also suits the physical painting process—the building crescendos, opulent harmonies and minor keys stimulate certain kinds of mark-making which are hard to describe in words, and impossible to construct independently of the sounds. The music guides and dismisses the objective world, opening up to a dreamlike passivity.[5]

Both paintings are oil on panel, the same size (92 x 136 centimeters), and similar in style, probably intended to be displayed together as a pair. One is a study in shades of red with a dark red area near the bottom right while the other has a predominance of different shades of blue.[6]

Glass sculptor Milon Townsend comes from a musical family (his father was a music teacher), and *Adagio for Strings* was one of the pieces he heard repeatedly while he was growing up. He is convinced that the music invokes

[4] *Ibid.*

[5] Shelley Hocknell, email (26 August 2004) to the author.

[6] Both works can be seen at *Shelley Zentner,* www.shelleyhocknell.com/red.html.

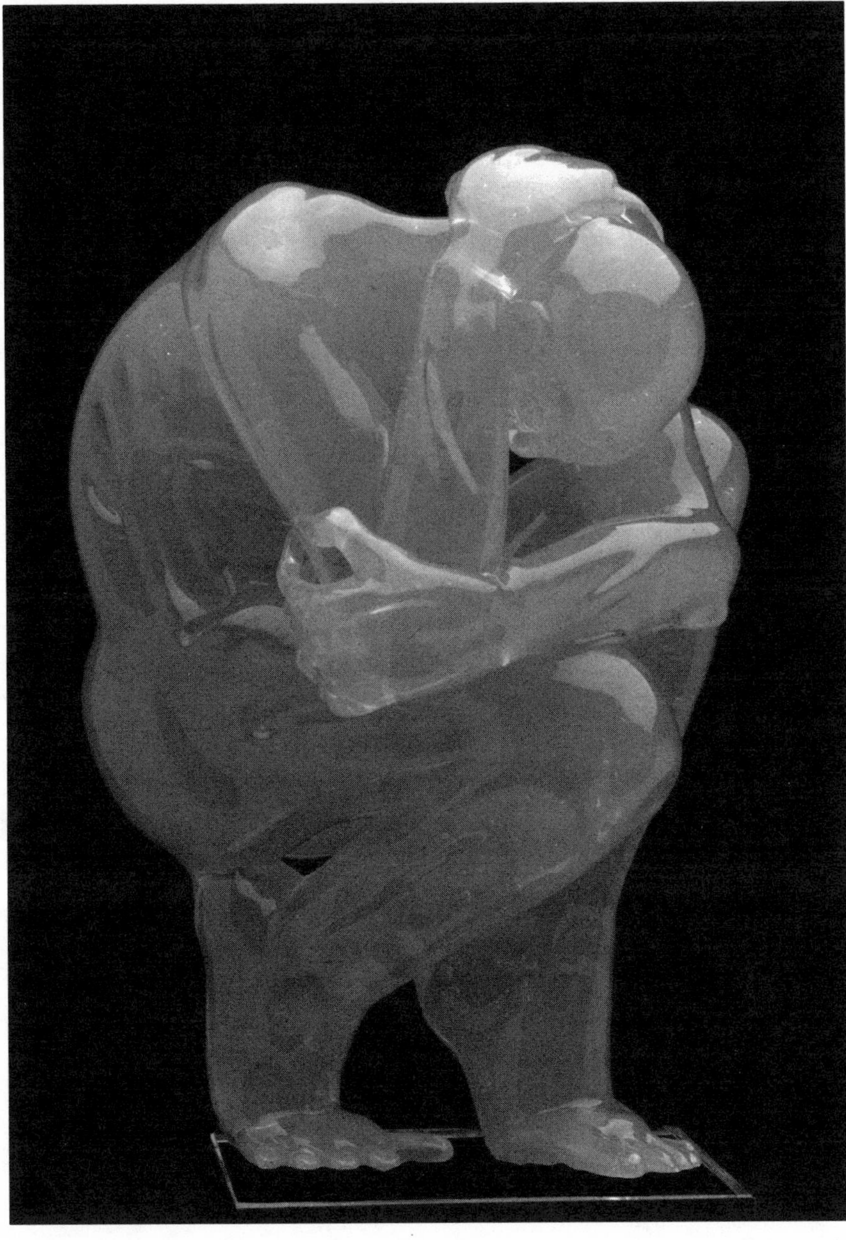

Illustration 6.1. *Mourn* by Milon Townsend, 2001

Courtesy of Townsend Glass

> sweeping melancholy, profound, visceral inexpressible emotions. For me, that mood typified the events of Sept. 11, and after I saw the planes crash into the towers, I had to do something. The first piece that I did was *Mourn*, in black, and then I did a similar one, later, in peach.[7]

He listened to this piece as he worked on *Mourn*:

[7]Milon Townsend, email (14 December 2005) to the author.

> Something about music like that takes me out of who 'I' am. Music is an interesting blend of intellect and emotion. It engages part of our mind and psyche that needs to abstract, weigh, measure, and think of the invisible, leading fairly directly to the emotions, by way of logic. *Adagio* always moves me.[8]

The sculpture is a relatively small, crouching figure, pulled inward on itself, with one arm curved over its head. "I have always found myself drawn to the introspective figure, the contained, constrained form."[9] He told Debbie Tarsitano, another artist who works with glass, that the title evoked the sadness of 11 September. The figure is "retreating, yet remains unbeaten and powerful."[10]

Do artists retain the musical relationship to sculptures and paintings after they are completed? Robert Genn believes that it is often true: "A lot of artists report that they are able to remember specific pieces of music they were listening to when they view their previous paintings—even after several years. For a while I thought I was unique in this ability—but it is quite common—a sort of audio imprint."[11] Undoubtedly for him, and probably other artists as well, *Adagio for Strings* has been imprinted in their own minds as an integral part of their artistic creations.

Like several of these visual artists, authors sometimes listen to music to get themselves into the right mood, to get their creative juices flowing, and occasionally to overcome writer's block. When working on her novel *Gods Old and Dark* (2004), Holly Lisle experienced difficulty writing a particular scene:

> Today I had a tough scene to write. . . . I put on *Adagio for Strings* from the *Platoon* soundtrack, and looped it with *Acoustic #3* by the Goo Goo Dolls, and with my external darkness pretty much

[8] *Ibid.*

[9] *Ibid.*

[10] Debbie Tarsitano, "Patriot Dreams: Interview with Milon Townsend," *Art Magazine* (January 2002); reprinted at www.tarsitanopaperweights.com. The figure in peach can be seen at www.crystal-fox.com/index.cfm/Body_Language_Series.htm.

[11] Robert Genn, email (13 October 2006) to the author.

> hardwired by sound, dove into one of the hardest character scenes I've had to write in quite some time.[12]

Frankly, I would be interested in hearing an *Adagio*-Goo Goo Dolls loop.

As far as I know, *Adagio for Strings* does not figure specifically in Mara Purl's "Milford-Haven" novels. Yet when she was asked which music most inspired her to write or what she liked to listen to while writing, she mentioned the Barber work.[13] Likewise, Alan Furst, writer of spy novels such as *Night Soldiers* (1988), uses music for inspiration and finds that it helps "mask out the noise of the world"; he listens to *Adagio* when he is writing "elegiac scenes" and when a character in his novel *The World at Night* (1996) listens to it on his radio.[14] Roméo Dallaire, former force commander of the United Nations' Assistance Mission in Rwanda, listened to *Adagio* when he wrote Chapter 11, "To Go or To Stay?" of *Shake Hands with the Devil: The Failure of Humanity in Rwanda* (2004),[15] his account of that country's genocide. It undoubtedly provided the right frame of mind to describe such atrocities.

Tom Bissell's story, "Animals in Our Lives" (2005), concerns Franklin, a young man who returns to the United States after an extended trip to Kyrgyzstan only to find that his relationship with his fiancée Elizabeth has suffered from their time apart. Bissell concluded that "all of Barber's stuff is great" but listened to *Adagio* "incessantly" while writing this story to help him capture some of the sadness of Franklin's return.

> I first discovered it long ago, on some mail-order compilation of classical love songs my mother had lying around. I think Victoria's Secret put out the CD in question as some promotional gimmick. The mind boggles. At any rate, the song is so damned

[12]Holly Lisle, "*Darkness*: Soundtracks," *Holly Lisle: Official Author Homepage*, www.hollylisle.com/category/books/soundtracks/page/2/.

[13]Mara Purl, quoted in "Amazon.com Talks to Mara Purl," www.amazon.com/exec/obidos/show-interview/p-m-urlara/102-5595833-9487359.

[14]Richard Dyer, "Cloak and Typewriter Spy Master Alan Furst Explores Moral Choice in His Period Novels," *Boston Globe* (27 March 2001), E: 1.

[15]Roméo Dallaire and Brent Beardsley, *Shake Hands with the Devil: The Failure of Humanity in Rwanda* (New York: Carroll & Graf, 2004), 263-327. For a re-enactment of this process with *Adagio* as actual background music, see Chapter 11.

> sorrowful I don't know what the musicologists at Victoria's Secret were thinking. Love song? It's a death song.[16]

In his story *Adagio* is not associated with an actual death, but the death of a relationship. One might easily picture Bissell listening to this music as he writes Franklin's last thoughts in the story:

> As his hand lifts, he knows nothing but the solace he will take from the sad, lovely girl who comes to him, sometimes, behind his eyes, and tells him how much she loves him. And he will live, for a little while, on that imagined bit of love, until he no longer needs it, or her, or the girl whose face she wears.[17]

Likewise, readers might have this same music in mind as they read those words.

Some authors do not want any kind of music playing when they write. In an interview Barbara Kyle, author of many Tudor Era novels, disclosed, "I can hardly bear to hear a radio playing [even] in the next room. I find music too potent."[18] After finishing a particularly difficult passage in which Ralph, a "beloved character" was burned at the stake, she "innocently" put on a compact disc of Barber's *Adagio*. "I broke down weeping for Ralph. I'm just a terrible sucker for potent music."[19] Music may inspire some authors but frustrate others.

While *Adagio for Strings* was clearly on the mind of several poets when they transferred their thoughts and feelings about it into verse form, they need not have listened to it while they were putting words to paper (or computer). For instance, John Matthias admitted that it is a piece that he likes a great deal, "but I didn't need to play it as I wrote as it's pretty much in my head."[20] The remainder of this chapter reveals the results of

[16]Tom Bissell, "The Lighthearted Boy," megagamerz.com. The recording was indeed *Victoria's Secret Classics by Request*, Vol. 4, with *Adagio* performed by the London Symphony Orchestra.

[17]Tom Bissell, "Animals in Our Lives," *Lives in St. Petersburg: and Other Stories* (New York: Pantheon Books, 2005), 210.

[18]Barbara Kyle, quoted in "The Hot Author Report" (7 September 2011), www.thehotauthorreport.com/interview-with-barbara-kyle-author-of-the-queen's-gamble.

[19]*Ibid.*

[20]John Matthias, email (16 December 2007) to the author.

Adagio's inspiration—the paintings, sculptures, poems, novels, and short stories that owe their existence, at least in part, to Barber's work.

In a Painting

Sometimes *Adagio* has inspired artists to the extent that they consider their art a visual reflection of the music. In fact, several have titled their works *Adagio for Strings,* including New Zealand painter Austin Davies. Although his construction is made of one continuous flat panel, about 41 by 17 inches long, it folds into many sections, giving it the characteristic look of a three-dimensional object. It must stand on its own; it cannot be displayed on a wall. Four folds on the left side and one on the right are found, with the central fold being the largest. Although it is asymmetrical, it looks balanced. Many of his creations are constructed in this folded manner, yet no two are alike. It is basically abstract, for unlike some of his other depictions, some of which incorporate Vermeer paintings, no recognizable figures are portrayed. The acrylic colors might be called "fall colors": shades of brown that blend into one another, a great deal of reddish orange, plus a small area of yellow.[21]

Art professor Thompson Lehnert exhibited his painting *Adagio for Strings* in September 2004 at the Summit Art Space in Akron, Ohio. While he describes the painting as a "colorful, non-representational oil-paint composition,"[22] its blue colors are reminiscent of either a seascape or an underwater view. The blues progress from light to dark, from the top to the bottom of the canvas. How the paintings of both Davies and Lehnert relate to their titles is not immediately apparent, but they must surely reflect some aspect of this piece and constitute a visual interpretation of its nature.

Illustration 6.2.
Adagio for Strings
by Austin Davies

Courtesy of Belinda Davies

[21] *Austin Davies,* www.austindavies.co.nz/sub1.htm.

[22] Thompson Lehnert, *Welcome to Summit Artspace,* www.summitartspace.org/exhibitions.html.

Two artists as students also attempted to transform this piece into paintings. As a senior at Sam Houston State University, Oscar Barraza exhibited several paintings at the Lowman Student Center Art Gallery in Huntsville, Texas. One titled *Adagio* presents a "crouching figure with black and dark red paint dripping down the canvas."[23] He painted it while listening to the Barber composition, which he considers "the saddest song. I use painting as therapy because I'm not very vocal. I am more introverted, and these paintings are about getting things out."[24] Fiona Taylor also produced an *Adagio for Strings,* which was displayed at a South Australia art show in 2002. It is a portrait of an unidentified man, fashioned in paint, printing ink, wood, jute, sand, and glue. According to her description:

> This portrait is based on a theme of contrasting elements. The repetition of the lines and their predictable pattern create stability, and the loose shapes suggest chaos. The man's expression, along with the dramatic angles and strength, communicates immense tension.[25]

Immediately noticeable is the idea of a "painting within a painting," in this case one surrounded by the "chaotic" loose shapes. It is already framed and is set at a slight angle to a larger frame. These paintings titled *Adagio for Strings* clearly vary a great deal, depending on the imagination of the artist.

As Integral Component of an Artwork

In addition to listening for inspiration or creating an artwork that is intended to reflect the mood of the music, some artists actually incorporate Barber's music into the art itself. These days art may extend beyond the painted canvas or freestanding sculpture to feature sound as an integral part of an artistic creation. Such expression encompasses video art, which contains both a visual and audio component; electronic painting, where the artist not only creates an artwork through computer graphics but adds

[23]Oscar Barraza, quoted in Emily Peacock, "Graduating Senior's Art on Display," *The Houstonian* (6 December 2005).

[24]*Ibid.*

[25]Fiona Taylor, quoted in *Senior Secondary Assessment Board of South Australia*, www.ssabsa.sa.edu/arts /2002art/2002show/2d/pages/2PIC0009_jpg.htm.

a musical soundtrack; and photochoreography, a unique form of visual and musical cooperation, where slides are projected behind an orchestra performing specific pieces of music.

VIDEO ART

Sam Taylor-Wood has exhibited her video and photographic art at galleries since 1991. Her installations "depict human dramas and isolated emotional instances . . . people in solitary, awkward or vulnerable moments."[26] Fitting this description is *Brontosaurus* (1995), a video of a nude man (full frontal) dancing ecstatically to *Adagio for Strings*. In the corner of the screen is a small, red stegosaurus, which is misnamed in the title. She described how this piece originated:

> First I filmed a man who was dancing naked in his bedroom, to the rhythm of very fast techno-jungle music. Then I took away the music and projected the film in slow motion. While I was filming, his movements became almost alien, they made no sense, he went through all these motions and they ended up seeming clumsy. In slow motion they became very beautiful, but totally ungainly.[27]

She then searched for a piece of music to fit the new slow-motion format of her video. She wanted music that

> highlighted the classicism of those movements, but at the same time the jarring, weird, ludicrousness of what he was doing. I watched it with loads of different pieces of music; everything from The Rolling Stones to the Beastie Boys to Wagner. As soon as I saw the film together with [*Adagio*] it came slap-bang together and became something completely different to what it had started out as. It became a eulogy, a death dance, and at the same time a dance of life.[28]

[26]"Moving Pictures: Highlights," *Guggenheim Museum–Moving Pictures*, www.pastexhibitions.guggenheim.org/moving_pictures/highlights_9a.html.

[27]"Notes for Teachers" [Brochure for Tate Gallery Exhibition *Real Life: Film and Video Art* (26 October 2002-26 January 2003)], *Tate St. Ives*, 2002-2003.

[28]"Notes for Students," [Hayward Gallery Exhibition (25 April-21 June 2002)]; reprinted www.haywardeducation.org.uk/assets/teachpacks/HG-taylorwoodpdf.pdf.

In 2003 she exhibited the video in a room at London's Tate Gallery. Watching the work there, critic Philip Hensher noticed that because of the high volume, the music leaked into the other artistic displays:

> Sam Taylor-Wood's famous video, in which a man with an amazing bounding willy is accompanied by the high kitsch of Samuel Barber's *Adagio for Strings*, seemed to have its volume turned up far too high. You could still hear its plangent string sounds rooms away, and, looking at Francis Bacon, the naff soundtrack to the emotions was still insisting that you find everything incredibly poignant. . . . Bacon has his own emotional implications; Barber has his; and one of them is going to lose, and one of them does.[29]

He identifies one of the inevitable hazards of employing sound as part of a visual art display. Critic Richard Dormant was not convinced that this music is the appropriate soundtrack in this context: "I suppose Barber's music is meant to suggest that beneath ebullient gaiety lies the avoidance of death's inevitability, but since, for me, the Adagio is pure kitsch and the man's dancing risible, I find it curiously uninvolving."[30] These critics' attitudes may be influenced by their pre-conceived views of the piece. If they consider it to be "high" or "pure" kitsch, then that attitude will also color their evaluation of the video.

In response to the exposition of Taylor-Wood's video at the Montreal Museum of Contemporary Art (11 October 2002 to 2 February 2003) reviewer Marilou Lemmens commented:

> The man's slim body, with a long, thin penis swinging in circles, reveals a strange beauty, his movements charged with the solemn, lyrical character of the music. This unexpected alliance, truly disconcerting at first, proves to be fascinating and triggers the mind. In my opinion, this is one of her most successful works.

[29]Philip Hensher, quoted in David Cohen, "Noises Off in the Sacred Grove" *Tate* (1 June 2001); reprinted www.artcritical.com/ noisesoff.htm.

[30]Richard Dorment, "What Lies Beneath," [London] *Telegraph* (1 May 2002); reprinted www.telegraph.co.uk/culture/art/3576685/What-lies-beneath.html.

> It possesses rich, semantic and evocative power that is at times missing in her other works.[31]

Brontosaurus has also been exhibited in the Netherlands, Ireland, and the United States. After its show at the Museum of Modern Art, the museum kept a copy and archives it among several video works under the title "New Video from Great Britain." The question then arises, if the video can be viewed in a screening room, does it still qualify as art or is it just a movie?

In 2002 Chicago's Donald Young Gallery exhibited Hirsch Perlman's video projections, *Two Affect Studies*. The first, showing the "billowing rise of cigarette smoke," complemented the œuvre "so perfectly that the burning out of the cigarette is as poetic as it is definitive."[32] Shot in black and white with a stationary camera, this work resembles an offspring of an early Andy Warhol "minimalist" underground movie. Art critic Bernard Cooper first thought that it might seem incongruous for this music to accompany "so mundane an image":

> Perlman's DVD makes the correlation so apt that within a minute, you'd swear Barber's score is a requiem for tobacco. Trails of cigarette smoke swoon to the violins. A lengthening ash finally falls as the orchestra strikes a climactic chord. Now and then the entire image sputters with static in sync with the music.[33]

In general, he is convinced that Perlman's artistic output is

> charged with a surprising pathos; his disposable materials and purposely amateurish execution (never have murky lighting and

[31]Marilou Lemmens, "Refined Beauty and British Deportment: Sam Taylor-Wood's Retrospective at the Montreal Museum of Contemporary Art," Lumen-Photography Foundation, 2002. See Marilou Lemmens, "review: MONTREAL," *ajánló Budapestlból:*, www.photolumen.hu/english/review_montreal.html. A brief clip from this video—naked man, tiny stegosaurus and all—appears in the midst of Taylor-Wood's documentary, including her own commentary about her works, at "Sam Taylor-Wood Documentary | Sam Taylor-Wood-Factual TV," www.factualtv.com/documentary/Sam-Taylor-wood. One can see a still photograph from the video at Milada Slizinska, "Gallery 2 12.12.- 18.02.2001," *SAM TAYLOR-WOOD*, www.csw.art.pl/new/2000/samtaylor_e.html.

[32]Rebecca Epstein or Emily Letorneau, "Hirsch Perlman at Donald Young Gallery," www.donald young.com/perlman/perlman_pr.html.

[33]Bernard Cooper, "Speak, Memory: Hirsch Perlman and Francesca Gabbiani Search for the Ethereal," *Los Angeles Magazine* (November 2002), 140.

> blizzards of static been more expressive) suggest that the world he observes, and the art he makes from these observations, are fallible.[34]

Will video art endure in this and the following centuries? Only future generations of art lovers will determine its fate.[35]

ADAGIO AND ELECTRONIC PAINTING

In the even newer art form of electronic painting the artist uses the computer to create images, which can either be permanently set or become a part of an artistic animation. One artist created a short video, "Terragen-Abiathar Adagio"[36] (1′22″) using the Terragen 640 x 344, a "scenery generator" capable of "photorealistic results for professional landscape visualization."[37] It shows a flowing river with snow-capped mountains in the background. The first two phrases of *Adagio*—from an uncredited electronic version, probably William Ørbit's (see Chapter 7)—are heard, fading out during the third.

While the above example shows a finished product, other videos reveal a painting in progress. A fine example, on *YouTube*, is "Cold Bed Time Lapse Digital Painting Workshop," where a painting emerges before the viewer's eyes, with Barber's *Adagio for Strings* accompanying the process. Its videographer, Rory Lane Lutter, describes the scenario: "an old man sobs shivering in bed. His wife has recently died and he is cold and alone."[38] The time lapse shows the evolution from sketches to a more or less finished outcome. It presents a painting within a painting, a wedding portrait of the man and his wife. Wearing a veil, she holds flowers and looks happy. The moonlight, entering through the window, shines directly on her, leaving his part of the portrait in shadow. Midway through, the videographer changes the man's arm position from a casual extension outward to arms folded around himself. This represents another case of

[34] *Ibid.*

[35] A still photograph from this video can be seen at "Hirsch Perlman" *About This Artwork* | *The Art Institute of Chicago*, www.artic.edu/aic/collections/artwork/184207, 2007. Simply seeing a photograph of two cigarettes in an ashtray, however, loses a great deal from Perlman's original video presentation.

[36] "Terragen-Abiathar Adagio," *Google Video* (30 November 2004), posted by Dan Parnham.

[37] "Planetside Software," *Home*, www.planetside.co.uk.

[38] "Cold Bed Time Lapse Digital Painting Workshop," *YouTube* (5 February 2007), posted by PimpOfPixels. [Timelapse Digital Painting, 120x original speed, ca. 2007]

Barber's music ending after the climax, rather than proceeding to the coda. At least the videographer admits that it is an excerpt.

A similar process is revealed in "Scarlett Johansson–Speed Painting by Nico Di Mattia," in which a trance mix of *Adagio* accompanies a portrait of the actress as the presentation slowly emerges from sketch to full color rendering. Viewers can watch the step-by-step process as the artist, using a digital tablet from Photoshop, gradually adds flesh tones and shadows to produce an almost photo-realistic painting. In the video itself the process takes about six minutes, but it undoubtedly took many hours of painstaking work to produce the final result. On the other hand, speed is what computer painting is all about.[39]

While not exactly video painting, another posting on *YouTube* shows the progress of a sketch from the first beginning lines to finished product. As the first few minutes of William Ørbit's synthesizer version of *Adagio for Strings* unfolds, the artist slowly reveals his hand-drawn re-creation of the poster to the movie *3:10 to Yuma* (2007), with Russell Crowe in the upper portion and Christian Bale in the lower. The artist probably uses a "stop-motion" technique rather than any complex computer animation.[40]

ADAGIO AND PHOTOCHOREOGRAPHY

Photochoreography is a term coined by James Westwater for the coordination of projected slides of his own photographs with live orchestra performances. He defines the concept as "an innovative art form that is simultaneously expanding the boundaries of creative expression and helping today's orchestras bring the joy of classical music to larger, more diverse audiences."[41] One such presentation, *Reflections of the Spirit* (1994), is coordinated with *Adagio for Strings* and is intended as homage to the ancient Anasazi Indians, who lived in the Four Corners area of the Southwest United States. Westwater took most of his photographs at Mesa Verde, Chaco Canyon, and Canyon de Chelly.[42] During the performance he manipulates a number of slide projectors, originally six but now, thanks

[39]"Scarlett Johansson–Speed Painting by Nico Di Mattia," *YouTube* (4 March 2007), posted by macpuletta.

[40]"The 3:10 to Yuma: Russell Crowe and Christian Bale Drawing," *YouTube* (22 November 2007), posted by thekingofdefford.

[41]James Westwater, "Background," *The Photochoreography of James Westwater*, www.home.earthlink.net/~westwater/images/background.html.

[42]These photographs can be seen at "Reflections of the Spirit," *Westwater Arts Photochoreography*, www.westwaterarts.com/ros.html.

to advancements in technology, three "advanced whisper-quiet digital projectors." Upon three screens, he sometimes projects three individual scenes but at other times provides a single three-panel panorama (as shown in Illustration 6.3):

> I project my photography, precisely choreographed to the music, onto the giant screens that are suspended above and in front of the orchestra. . . . I personally direct the performance of my photography to each specific live performance of the music. The conductor and musicians devote full energies to the musical performance. I concentrate on the precise integration of music and photography.[43]

How did he decide on Barber's *Adagio* for this presentation? For some time he was searching for music to accompany his photographs of Native America.

> As I was flying over Monument Valley on my way to a concert engagement on the west coast, I was listening to an audio tape of some of my favorite pieces of music when *Adagio* began playing. The coming together of interest, concern, intent, place and music all happened at 30,000 feet above Monument Valley. A light went on in my mind and I saw images related to Native America in my mind as I listened to *Adagio*. I knew then that, for me, it was the right piece for that subject. I chose it also because it evokes in me qualities I associate with Native America: including melancholy, strength, spirituality, dignity, solemnity, beauty, depth, reflection, harmony and balance.[44]

One critic reported that the serenity of the Barber composition "matches the serenity of the landscape with its lights and shadows as the sun completes a full day's circuit."[45]

[43]James Westwater, "Background," *Photochoreography*, www.home.earthlink.net/~westwater/images /background.html.

[44]James Westwater, email (24 January 2005) to the author.

[45]"Wedding the Arts," *The* [Durham, N.C.] *Independent*; reprinted in *The Photochoreography of James Westwater*, www.home.earthlink.net/~westwater/images/wedding.html.

Illustration 6.3. *Adagio for Strings* with *Reflections of the Spirit* by James Westwater

Westwater also appended an optional introduction to the presentation, an invocation to the Great Spirit, spoken in English, Navajo, and American Indian sign language, to honor Indian culture and help educate audiences about Native American life and wisdom.[46] Betty "Red Ant" LaFontaine, a full-blooded Navajo educator, was the first to present this invocation. Westwater suggests that each orchestra invite a Native American to recite this invocation, but, in lieu of that, "anyone the orchestra chooses that hopefully will bring the appropriate qualities to the delivery."[47] *Reflections of the Spirit* is one of sixteen shows that he has performed with various orchestras throughout the United States over the past twenty-five years.

Pictures at an Exhibition

In addition to becoming an integral part of another artwork, *Adagio* has been used to provide the sonic atmosphere for displays of paintings and sculptures. Sean Landers borrows subjects and entire styles from twentieth-century artists and puts his own creative spin on them. In May 2001 he presented a show at New York City's Andrea Rosen Gallery consisting of his take on paintings by Pablo Picasso. With tongue in cheek (I hope) his voice resounds through a loud speaker while, as the ubiquitous *Adagio* plays in the background, he recites a "loony letter to Picasso . . . mimicking the bombastic cadences of a bad commencement address"; he then asks, "Who will this century's Picasso be?" and replies, "Ladies and Gentlemen, it is I."[48] Because Picasso himself put his own interpretation

[46]"Red Ant," *The Photochoreography of James Westwater*, www.home.earthlink.net/~westwater/images/redant.html.

[47]James Westwater, email (24 January 2005) to the author.

[48]Mia Fineman, "I, Picasso," *The Village Voice* (8 May 2001).

on paintings of earlier artists, he might have approved of Landers's endeavors.

In October 1996 the Baltimore Museum of Art presented an exhibit of paintings by American artist Andrew Wyeth. Critic Henry Allen asserted, "Here are 50 more brown pictures by Andrew Wyeth. Brown, brown, brown . . . they aren't as good as his earlier pictures, but they're just as brown."[49] For this particular exhibit Wyeth's wife produced a film with childhood photographs of the artist and brown hawks soaring to *Adagio for Strings.* Allen further observed, "Andrew, in brown, walks around a brown winter landscape his fans have come to think of as their own. If he's not America's Painter, he's certainly America's Hermit."[50] What can brown do for you?

For the following example, *Adagio for Strings* was not literally present for the display of a photograph but existed only in the photographer's imagination. Graham Nash, best known as a member of the 1970s rock group Crosby, Stills, Nash (and sometimes Young), has been interested in photography for as long as he has been interested in music. He confided, "images and music—to me it's all the same energy."[51] He began taking photographs by age five and has admitted that there is not much separating his musical self from his photographic persona. In 2006 the Museum of Photographic Arts in San Diego presented *Eye to Eye,* displaying many of his photographs, both those that he had collected and those that he had taken himself. It contains one of Neil Young driving down a country road, which Nash describes as being "very misty, very moody, very gray and I can almost hear Samuel Barber's 'Adagio for Strings' when I look at that image."[52] He once told his son Will that *Adagio* should be part of his record collection because it is "heart-lifting and beautifully sad."[53] These must be his feelings when he contemplates his portrait of Young.

[49]Henry Allen, "Tans for the Memory: In Baltimore Andrew Wyeth's Browning of America," *Washington Post* (2 October 1996), B: 1.

[50]*Ibid.*

[51]Graham Nash, quoted in Christopher Reynolds, "His Music as Images: 'Eye to Eye' Is Graham Nash's First Major Museum Photo Exhibit," *Los Angeles Times* (2 February 2006).

[52]*Ibid.*

[53]Graham Nash, quoted in Jonathan Craven, "Dear Old Dad's Advice: Lonely Heart's Club to Ex Convict's Tale," [Pembroke, Ont.] *Daily Observer* (13 June 2005).

In Poetry

Several poets and authors have referred to this famous composition in their literary works. Placing it in such a context may allow the music to be perceived in a new light, either an author's interpretation of ideas by a straightforward narrator or a more biased view of a dramatic character. In poetry sometimes it is the main focus, often indicated by the title; at other times, especially in novels, it is simply mentioned as a part of a larger scene or dramatic situation.

In some of his poems John Matthias treats music "as esthetics and history," articulating "biography as texture . . . as well as the historical context in which the music is written and performed."[54] Both *Adagio for Strings* and its composer form the basis of his poem "A Note on Barber's Adagio" (2000), which narrates the composer's journey through the Midwest on the day of John F. Kennedy's assassination.

> . . . Back in Autumn 1963
> Samuel Barber was alone and driving through
> November rain in Iowa or Kansas.
> When he turned on his radio he heard
> them playing his *Adagio for Strings.*
> Sick to death of his most famous composition,
> he turned the dial through the static
> until once again, and clearly—
> the *Adagio for Strings.* When a third station, too,
> and then a fourth, were playing it, he thought
> he must be going mad. He turned off the radio
> and stopped the car and got out by a fence
> staring at the endless open space in front of him
> where someone on a tractor plowed
> on slowly in the rain . . .
>
> The president had been assassinated
> earlier that day, but Barber didn't know it yet.
> He only knew that every station in America was playing
> his *Adagio for Strings.*
> He only knew he didn't know

[54]Michael Barrett, review of *Pages: New Poems and Cuttings* by John Matthias (Athens, Ohio: Swallow, 2000), *Samizdat* V (Spring 2000); reprinted www.samizdateditions.com/issue5/review-matthias.html.

why he should be responsible for such an ecstasy of grief.[55]

According to reviewer Anthony Walton, the image of a man plowing his field becomes a symbol of the composer's achievement and failure:

> By examining the way in which Barber's great composition came to overshadow the rest of his career, marking him forever as the composer Americans turn to when they wish to signify profound sorrow, Matthias manages to "make strange" this now-remote yet signal event. Barber, at once an individual and a choral reflection of ourselves, stands bewildered at this change in his life.[56]

Matthias is uncertain whether the attitude he attributes to the composer in his poem is real or a result of his creative imagination. He remembers hearing *Adagio* at the time of the Kennedy assassination and sometimes considers it "an ecstasy of grief" but is dubious about the origins of his narrative:

> Long before I wrote the poem I am sure that I heard this story somewhere. But I didn't start checking until after it was finished; then I couldn't find it in any of the obvious studies of Barber's music. So I may have made it up. I don't, however, think it matters to the poem if the whole thing is apocryphal.[57]

Some people, including critics, believe the tale to be true, while others do not. Indeed, as a piece of creative writing, it matters very little. Barber was occasionally bored by his most famous piece and wished others had achieved its popularity (see Chapter 12); he was somewhat dismayed that it took on such a "funereal" tone. Ironically, the piece was written at a time described by Menotti as the kind of summer where "you have to stop in the middle of the day to say to yourself: 'This is too wonderful.'"[58]

[55]John Matthias, "A Note on Barber's Adagio," *Pages: New Poems and Cuttings* (Athens, Ohio: Swallow, 2000), 29. Reprint Permission Courtesy of © John Matthias.

[56]Anthony Walton, "The Poetry of John Matthias," *Electronic Book Review* (10 September 2002), www.electronicbookreview.com/thread/electropoetics/appreciative.

[57]John Matthias, email (16 December 2007) to the author.

[58]Gian Carlo Menotti, letter (September 1936) to Orlando Cole, Collection of Orlando Cole, Curtis Institute of Music.

At that time Barber probably thought he was writing music that simply expressed ecstasy, not an "ecstasy of grief." Barber's attitude is consistent with the thoughts Matthias ascribed to him. The poet reports that this poem has become quite popular, both as a text and at poetry readings.[59]

In Frank R. Chappell's poem "A Note on Values" (2004) Barber's *Adagio* forms the imaginary soundtrack for images that the narrator sees on the ceiling of the bus on which he is traveling. The piece figures prominently in the first stanza:

> I stared at the shadows
> Passing on the ceiling of the bus
> Dancing back and forth
> And creating a private black and white
> Film for me
> And I was the only one who noticed
> Who seemed intrigued
> And Samuel Barber's
> *Adagio for Strings* carried me through
> The city streets
> With the shadows on the ceiling[60]

Although Barber's name recurs in the second stanza, neither he nor his composition is mentioned in the remainder of the poem.

Other poems relate the effect of Barber's *Adagio* on the narrator, which may or may not reflect the attitude of the poet. After all, poet and narrator are not necessarily the same person. Mark Jarman has published several poems, including *Adagio for Strings* (2001), in which poet and narrator are one. The following excerpts illustrate how this music affected his early married life, where he lived, and memories of his neighbors:

> A piece by Samuel Barber finds its way
> To me and brings with it those painful years
> In Evansville, early in our marriage.
>
> . . .
>
> It does return more fully than I'd like,

[59]*Ibid.*

[60]Frank R. Chappell, "A Note on Values," *An Atheist Who Prays: Paradoxical Poetry* (Lincoln, Neb.: iUniverse, 2004), 27.

Listening to Barber, but so do Bill and Edna,
Who dwelled below us in a basement room,
Dank as the earth banked to its half-blind windows.

Near the conclusion of the poem he confides:

Yet I seem to be consoled by their sad lives
Just as the saddest music I've ever heard,
This piece by Barber, in a way consoles me.
We don't have to go back. We made it through.[61]

The poem is autobiographical; Jarman and his wife indeed lived in Evansville in the early years of their marriage, although Bill and Edna are composites of neighbors. Jarman first heard Barber's "saddest music" in David Lynch's film *The Elephant Man* (1980) and ever since has associated it with the pathos of John Merrick's condition and innocence (see Chapter 8). He explains the relationship in the following manner: "Innocence or the memory of innocence is, to me, always poignant but also consoling. Though always lost, it has always existed. The existence and inevitable loss of innocence both seem to be celebrated by *Adagio for Strings.*"[62]

Barber's music also brings back memories to Neil Shepard in his partly autobiographical poem, "Listening to Samuel Barber's Adagio for Strings" (1998), illustrating differences of interest between him and his lover. The following are the first and third strophes, plus a couplet:

My eyes are older now, easily distracted
by the light that slips from the edge
of a cloud. The woman spread-eagled
above me barely blocks my view.
The music I've loaned her—Samuel Barber's
Adagio for Strings blares from her
boom-box, and I hear the first words
dictated from empty space:
The gods have gone away.

. . . .

[61]Mark Jarman, "Adagio for Strings," *Quarterly West* LIII (2001), 18-19.

[62]Mark Jarman, email (14 December 2007) to the author. The poet is a member of the faculty of Vanderbilt University.

and we sat and talked of Blaise Pascal,
Samuel Barber, *and the boys,* as she
would say. She said *music without words*
is *like scat-singing to someone*
who can't speak jive. Do you love me?
she said. *Name five things you love.*
We made two lists, his and hers.
The recordings of Glenn Gould. U2.
Nietzche's *Beyond Good and Evil.* Superman comics.
The outtakes of Charlie Parker's "Embraceable You." U2.
The Minoan goddess in the Met exactly eight inches tall
in hammered gold. Catwoman comics.
Samuel Barber's *Adagio for Strings.* U.

You never mentioned me, she said.
I mentioned U.[63]

Shepard has loved *Adagio for Strings* ever since a colleague introduced it to him. Thinking that his girlfriend might like it, too, he loaned her a recording that he had indeed played during their lovemaking episodes. But she, nonetheless, found it to be "depressing." Not a good omen. Their list of "favorite things," moreover, easily reveals that her "decidedly popular tastes" clash with his more intellectual pursuits. Their relationship was fated not to last, as is apparent from the beginning of the final stanza:

My eyes are older now when Barber's strings
Greet me. She's just walked out.[64]

With a sense of relief Shepard pleasantly confessed, "*Adagio* was playing on my stereo when she later walked out of the house (and out of the relationship). I'm very happy that happened, and I have Samuel Barber to thank for making it happen."[65]

Even though Shepard's relationship did not turn out well, he clearly still loves the Barber composition, but that does not seem to be the case

[63]Neil Shepard, "Listening to Samuel Barber's *Adagio for Strings,*" *Quarterly West* XLVII (1998), 14-15.

[64]*Ibid.*, 15.

[65]Neil Shepard, email (18 December 2007) to the author.

for John Brian Perkins, as he relates in his poem, "A Little Annoying Night Music." Remembering *Adagio* from more pleasant times in the past—a Proustian outlook—has changed his attitude toward the music now that his lover is no longer present. The poem begins:

> I used to listen to Barber's "Adagio for Strings"
> At night while we lay sleeping
> And the swells of the music
> Would cast my mind into dreaming
> where I became Olivier
> And the smoky dunes of sleep
> Would take me far and deep

And ends with the following:

> Now, I awake alone
> In morning's drowsy corner
> Wrapped in sheets like head dress
> Where wind sounds like wind
> And sand tastes like snow dying
> And Barber's strings
> Are now terribly annoying.[66]

Time and circumstance can alter one's perception of a seemingly unchangeable work of art.[67]

In Prose

Adagio for Strings has also entered the world of the novel and short story. In the following examples—diverse in style, content, and scope—the authors refer to this piece to conjure up the right musical atmosphere for the scenes they attempt to depict. All the primary versions have been referenced: *e.g.*, the string quartet in Emer Martin's *More Bread or I'll Appear* (1999); the orchestral version in Julius Lester's *Autobiography of God* (2004) and others; the organ arrangement in Jean Shields's *Air Burial*

[66]John Brian Perkins, "A Little Annoying Night Music," *The Fruit of Falling Down* (Bloomington, Ind.: Xlibris, 2003), 47.

[67]See Appendix 6 for a list of other poems in which *Adagio for Strings* is referenced.

(2002); and the Agnus Dei in Karin Bundesen Baltzell and Georgianne Nienaber's *Horse Sense* (2006).[68]

ADAGIO AS CATALYST

While *Adagio for Strings* plays a minor role in the structure of most novels, in at least one case it literally sets into motion the machinations of the whole plot, as might be discerned by its title: *The Adagio—A Mystery* (2007). In this mystery novel by Alan K. Austin, Robert Thompson catches Jack Duncan having sex with his wife Louise. Rather than automatically retaliating, he instead invites Jack to dinner! During the course of the evening he plays a recording of the Barber composition for Jack, who immediately becomes enthralled with it. He first notices how the strings "softly, gradually, hypnotically, were circling upward, three notes at a time pausing and retreating and rising again."[69] But, as the music climbs to the climax, it gives him an ominous feeling of foreboding:

> Barber's music was winding a chrysalis around me. The cellos were a Greek Chorus sounding a mournful warning that something terrible lay ahead. The violins and violas continued their slow progression upward, continued spinning their threads, until at last the cellos, left far behind, fell silent. Freed from their mothering restraint, the violins seized on a shrill chord of ecstasy—or madness. But the note was too brilliant, too white hot, to hold, and the music melted into another chord momentarily more beautiful than the one before. That chord in turn melted into another so dense there seemed no room to breathe. The music, desperately seeking harmony or relief, had created an excruciating, heartbreaking wail that went on and on. As the orchestra finished the piece with quiet, comforting chords, I was still hearing that wail.[70]

[68]Emer Martin, *More Bread or I'll Appear* (Boston: Houghton Mifflin, 1999); Julius Lester, *The Autobiography of God* (New York: St. Martin's, 2004); Jean Shields, *Air Burial* (New York: Carroll & Graf, 2002); and Karin Bundesen Baltzell and Georgianne Nienaber, *Horse Sense* (New York: Authors Choice Press, 2006).

[69]Alan K. Austin, *The Adagio: A Mystery* (Bloomington, Ind.: iUniverse, 2007), 5.

[70]*Ibid.*, 5-6.

It is, indeed, the wail—rather than any other part of the music itself—that haunts Jack from this point on. Without revealing his motivation Thompson loaned Jack the recording to take home with him. When Jack played the record, that mournful warning of something terrible made itself manifest. He was just about to fall asleep when the work reached its climax. He was in "some hazy state between sleep and waking" when he heard a woman's scream—"someone in big trouble." Fully awake, he played the music again, but the scream was not present. Later he listened to it again, and this time, Jack compared the music's climb to the climax to Sisyphus pushing a stone up the mountain. *Adagio* again finally arrived at

> the brilliant, shrill high chord. Heaven? Redemption? But finding there instead a greater agony. A piercing shriek of music. There it was again! My eyes flew open. *Not* just strings. A woman *screaming!*[71]

After playing the recording for friends, none of them ever heard the scream. At times he even began to doubt that he ever heard it himself. Austin describes that Jack is haunted by the scream "because of the incongruity and horror of its interference in a piece of sublime music."[72] Later, when Louise and Robert are murdered, Jack becomes a suspect. Using the screaming woman's voice as his main clue, he attempts to trace it and try to solve the mystery.

In describing his own view of Barber's *Adagio,* Austin acknowledges that "It has been a favorite of mine for years and finally wrenched this bit of imagination out of me."[73] The music finally reaches a series of chords that are so dense that "the music is almost overpowering in its beauty and intensity. And that's where the scream goes . . . if there ever was a scream."[74] When he first listened to the work, the climactic chord was jarring to him. "It really sounded like a scream to me. When I first heard it, in the back of my head I thought, 'This could be a good mystery.'"[75]

[71]*Ibid.*, 7-8.

[72]Alan K. Austin, quoted in Tyler R. Tichelaar, "Interview with Alan K. Austin, Author of *The Adagio: A Mystery*," www.readerviews.com/InterviewAustinAlan.html.

[73]*Ibid.*

[74]*Ibid.*

[75]Alan K. Austin, quoted in Foss Farrar, "Retired Journalist Releases New Book," *Ark City Traveler* (18 April 2008).

The author also professed, "I've always detected something musical in great writing and hoped that, without trying to, my own would have bits of that quality."[76]

LITERARY FUNERALS AND MEMORIAL SERVICES

Because *Adagio for Strings* has appeared frequently in connection with deaths, funerals, and memorial services, it is logical that some authors invoke it in their fictional accounts as well. In Forrest Johnson's short story collection *A Parson's Tales* (2000) Ed Bryant, who is dying of AIDS complications, has chosen it to be played at his memorial service "as the song for the congregation."[77] He is lying in a bed in the living room of the house that he shared with his companion Lou when Logan, his pastor, comes to finalize the contents of his service.

> Ed's mother was beside the bed holding his hand. Lou sat in a corner of the room. A nurse stood next to him. Ed was breathing heavily. There was low music in the background. Logan recognized the Barber piece, *Adagio for Strings*.[78]

At that moment Ed's dog started howling; Ed was dead. Not only did he request *Adagio* for his service, but he had actually died while listening to it. The remainder of the short story deals with the service itself. While *Adagio* is not specifically referenced again, the reader presumes that the service proceeded according to Ed's wishes and that Barber's music was played and moved the congregation.

Adagio for Strings also figures in "The Laying On of Hands" (2002), Alan Bennett's amusing, often hilarious short story concerning the funeral of Clive Dunlop (a.k.a. Max, Philip, and Bunny), aged 34 ("but some thought him younger"), who was a masseur ("he had the touch") and black ("though palely so").[79] He may or may not have died of AIDS. The service was presided over by Father Geoffrey Jolliffe, Clive's friend and occasional sexual partner who was "Anglican but with Romish inclinations that were

[76]Alan K. Austin, quoted in Tyler R. Tichelaar, "Interview with Alan K. Austin."

[77]*Ibid.*

[78]Forrest Johnson, *A Parson's Tales* (Bloomington, Ind.: Xlibris, 2000).

[79]Alan Bennett, "The Laying On of Hands," *The Laying On of Hands: Stories* (New York: Picador, 2002), 16-17.

not so much doctrinal as ceremonial and certainly sartorial. . . . He looked well in his cloak . . . a priest with a bit of a swish to him."[80] Immediately before the ceremony began:

> The organist was meanwhile playing an arrangement of Samuel Barber's *Adagio for Strings,* which many in the congregation were enjoying, having been made familiar with the tune from its frequent airing on Classic FM. Seeing no conclusion in the offing Father Jolliffe pressed a button behind a pillar to alert the organist that they were ready to begin. The Barber now came to a sharp and unceremonious close but since random terminations were not unusual on Classic FM, nobody noticed.[81]

Funeral rites may not always be confined to human beings. Lorrie Moore's short story, "Four Calling Birds, Three French Hens" (1998), concerns Aileen's reaction to the death of her pet cat, Bert. As a kind of impromptu memorial service she put a few somber pieces of music on her record player, including *Adagio,* much to the chagrin of her husband Jack. The narrator relates that the cat's ashes were "packed into a cheesy pink-posied tin" and placed on the mantel. The house seemed lonely, and Aileen began to drink. After telling Jack that Bert was "verbal as a dog," Jack scowled.

> "Get a grip," said Jack, eyeing her glass of blended malt. Puccini's "Humming Chorus," the Brahms "Alto Rhapsody," and Samuel Barber's "Adagio for Strings" all murmured in succession from the stereo. He flicked it off. "You've got a daughter. There are holidays ahead. That cat wouldn't have shed one tear over you."[82]

Even the most ardent cat lovers have to admit that Jack might be right. Is a memorial to a pet limited to an author's fantasy? Check out Chapter 10 later in this book.

[80]*Ibid.*

[81]*Ibid.*, 25-26.

[82]Lorrie Moore, "Four Calling Birds, Three French Hens," *Birds of America* (New York: Picador, 1998), 111-12 [originally published as "If Only Bert Were Here"]; reprinted in the anthology *In Our Nature: Stories of Wildness* (Athens: University of Georgia Press, 2002), 184-98.

TO STIR THE EMOTIONS OR CONJURE UP MEMORIES

Authors have sometimes relied on a performance of *Adagio for Strings* to portray emotional feelings in their characters or to induce them into remembering past events, either pleasant or unsettling. In a few instances characters attend a concert in which the Barber work is being performed and it is often the specific performance, the interpretation of the conductor, that moves them.

The following two characters react quite differently when they hear a performance of it. In Valerie Christie's mystery novel *The Mysterious Affair at Redfield* (2002) her sleuth, Thérèse McNab, attends a concert conducted by Ian MacIver. She "loved to watch him wield his baton gracefully, emphatically and dramatically."[83] When he conducted *Adagio,* one of her favorite pieces, "the music welled up in a constant motion that caused Thérèse's emotions to well up, too. Tears began to spill from her eyes.[84] In contrast, Jan, a character in Fredericka Heller's novel, *Out of the Shadow,* has quite a different reaction when she hears the work in concert. After the orchestra played Dvořák's Seventh Symphony, she "happily escaped" into Barber's *Adagio for Strings.* "I was feeling elated when it suddenly came to an end, all too soon."[85] These two contrasting emotional responses to this composition may, indeed, be a key to its popularity and success.

Young Charles (Chigger) Dingilliam in *Bouncing Off the Moon* (2001), David Gerrold's science fiction novel, has a much more personal response to *Adagio for Strings.* Lying in a hospital bed, Chigger recalls the first time he heard his father conduct the composition many years earlier:

> He was lost in the music. And his hands were like living creatures—he didn't use a baton; he just stroked the air and the music poured forth. He coaxed Adagio into life and let it fill the auditorium. I don't think I took a breath for the entire ten minutes. I'd never heard anything like that before in my life. I had never known such sounds were possible. And afterward, I kept playing it over and over again, always trying to recapture

[83]Valerie Christie, *The Mysterious Affair at Redfield* (Bloomington, Ind.: Xlibris, 2002), 85.

[84]*Ibid.*

[85]Fredericka Heller, *Out of the Shadow* (Bloomington, Ind.: Authorhouse, 2002), 14-15.

> that same initial *wundersturm*. I wished I could tell him how much I loved his music.[86]

Later, his father also recalls this incident: "You were listening to the music as deeply as anyone I've ever seen. I was so happy for you that day—because you'd discovered something all on your own."[87]

Chigger's account must surely reflect the author's view of the work. When I suggested this relationship to Gerrold, he replied, "Yes, you are right. Chigger was speaking for me."[88] The author describes music as "passion you can hear," adding:

> I almost always have music playing when I'm writing, and from time to time a piece of music will suddenly step forward in my consciousness to evoke powerful emotions and feelings. I came to Barber's Adagio fairly late, but it is one of those pieces that whispers to me instead of shouting. Whenever I hear Adagio, it is an invitation to surrender to its thoughtful heart.[89]

No wonder Chigger loves his father's performance so much.

Sometimes authors use either the chance broadcast of this piece on the radio or the deliberate playing of a recording to bring their characters to the point of memory or nostalgia. For instance, this music happens to be playing on a car radio in George Parker's *The Atomic Kid: Adventures in the Antiworld* (2004). Hunter, an enigmatic secret agent, is cruising the Leitz Academy of Educational Excellence, where he plans to meet his brother Steve. As he is waiting, the radio plays Barber's "wonderfully melancholic" *Adagio*:

> The music was too good to leave; the soaring strings were dredging up memories he hadn't visited in decades. . . . The

[86]David Gerrold, *Bouncing off the Moon* (New York: Tom Doherty Associates, 2001), 242.

[87]*Ibid*, 243.

[88]David Gerrold, email (9 June 2012) to the author.

[89]David Gerrold, email (17 December 2007) to the author.

music was intoxicating, in it he saw faces from the past, and felt the pang of lost loves.[90]

Leaning back in his seat, he closed his eyes; "the music was playing magical games with his imagination. He wasn't really sure he had ever known what meditation was, but he had to admit as this moment in time expanded, he was pretty damn close to it."[91] Parker gave the following further explication:

> It is one of those truly ecstatic moments that builds out of complete despair into a comprehensive understanding of exactly where one is at this very moment in time. One would call it enlightenment if it lasted for eternity, but it doesn't, it never will, it is purely an elevation to another plateau of understanding. Hunter comes away from the moment with a more profound knowledge of where he fits in this jigsaw puzzle called his life, and he knows with certainty that there is a force at work he has never encountered before.[92]

Such a profound interpretation of this music on the part of a fictional character implies that the work produces a similar effect on the author. Has George Parker projected his own feelings about *Adagio* onto Hunter? When I suggested this, he replied, "Every character in a book is a facet of an author's character."[93] Although he never paraphrased David Gerrold's exact words, he might have said, "Hunter was speaking for me."

Parker likes classical music such as pieces by Górecki, Haydn, "and a whole host of music that I hear from time to time but don't know the name of. This, in fact, was how *Adagio for Strings* came into my life."[94] Like Hunter, Parker has felt that it has "tugged long forgotten memories from my heart and my mind; it enveloped me in a cocoon of self reflection, and it

[90]George Parker, *The Atomic Kid: Adventures in the Antiworld* (New York: Bookman Publishing, 2004), 141.

[91]*Ibid.*

[92]George Parker, email (20 December 2005) to the author.

[93]*Ibid.*

[94]George Parker, email (27 January 2006) to the author.

lifted me from one imagined plateau of existence up to another."[95] Sometimes authors and characters share a common aesthetic.

While Hunter's encounter with *Adagio* was mere chance, Randy Waterhouse, a character in Neal Stephenson's novel *Cryptonomicon* (2000), plays it deliberately. He has returned to his hometown for a nostalgia trip:

> Randy has that moving-through-syrup feeling he gets when enacting some emotionally huge transition in his life. He puts Samuel Barber's *Adagio for Strings* on the Acura's stereo and drives very slowly down the main street of the town, looking all around at the remains of the coffeehouses, bars, pizza places, and Thai restaurants where, for many years, he prosecuted his social life.[96]

Playing this particular piece in the background apparently works because "the evening's tour is still a flurry of odd, emotionally charged images in his memory, but he's beginning to sort it out a little, to run the numbers, as it were."[97]

Putting a compact disc of *Adagio for Strings* on the stereo may have worked for Randy Waterhouse, but for Barbara Harris, the main and reflective (perhaps even neurotic) character in Mary Rakow's *The Memory Room* (2002), it takes a much greater effort. She needs to play the music several times in succession for it to achieve its effect. She has coped with life by means of her hobbies of music and gardening. Inside the chapter, "Musica," she intermixes aspects of both hobbies with her ambivalent feelings toward her father and listens to *Adagio* to come to terms with her painful past. Throughout the novel Rakow intersperses Barbara's thoughts with lines from the works of Romanian poet Paul Celan.

In the following passage the lines in italics are taken from Celan's acceptance speech when he won the Bremen Prize for literature in 1958. The rather poetic typography is the author's original.

[95] *Ibid.*

[96] Neal Stephenson, *Cryptonomicon* (New York: HarperCollins, 2000), 584.

[97] *Ibid.*

I play Samuel Barber's "Adagio for Strings," turning the volume up, play it a second time. There is a piece of this memory,

Reachable, near and not lost.

I start it again. Listen a third time. There is some thing that I need to find. Some shred.

there remained amid the losses
this one thing

Finally I listen outside, dig my hands into the dirt. I play it once more. Then I find this: That my father's voice, waking me, bringing me back, became, for me, the root of all music. There in his weeping, in his calling out my name. I gave this weeping sound not to him, but to music itself.

I turn the volume up so the music fills my garden, reaches out through the hedge. . . .

Telling me that under all this, there was something good. Inside my loop we play the "Adagio for Strings." Hear how the music goes into the darkness, making light rise up? Do you hear it?[98]

The Celan passages form a recurring leitmotif throughout the novel. The meaning of the phrase, "this one thing," is not identified here, but it was the first time it appeared: "this one thing: language."[99] Rakow either presumes that the reader will remember the final word or deliberately omits it to shade the meaning. Perhaps she has transferred the meaning to a "musical language." Inspired by her thoughts of *Adagio* and Celan's words, Barbara constructs her own poem:

Music, strings adagioed and fair,
Angels with continents at their polished feet.
Invisible one who waited all these years, who came
with capes of tasselled gold, not bound

[98]Mary Rakow, *The Memory Room* (Emeryville, Calif.: Shoemaker and Hoard, 2002), 355-57.

[99]*Ibid.*

by parent, rope or limb.[100]

Rakow's mixture of prose, poetry, memory, and philosophy fulfills the publisher's description of the work as a "poetic novel in verse." The cited passage, taken out of context, may not seem to make sense. It must be read and appreciated within the complex fabric of this entire book.

AND I FIND *ADAGIO* "SPINNING 'ROUND IN MY BRAIN"[101]

There need not be an actual (diegetic) presentation of *Adagio* in a scene for its effects to be significant. Sometimes a character knows the work so well that it starts playing in his or her head. For instance, in Kim Stanley Robinson's science-fiction novel *Icehenge* (1998), Barber's music resounds through the mind of archeologist Hjalmar Nederland as he contemplates the Martian landscape. While he explores the area, he expresses his thoughts on the panorama before him:

> Out on the rim on a cloudy day: chocolate thunderheads scudded north, and thick bolts of lightening alternated with shafts of buttery sunlight. . . . Below me my team worked in the dead city. Strolling the rim edge I examined its texture as if I could see the world beneath the rock. Samuel Barber's "Adagio for Strings" floated through my mind.[102]

In M. R. M. Parrott's short story "On the Page" (2002) an elderly gentleman remembers when, being a waiter in his youth, he served the poet Robert Frost. He thought of lines from Frost's poem *Birches:*

> *When I see birches bend to left and right*
> *Across the lines of straighter darker trees,*
> *I like to think some boy's been swinging them.*

> After he had finished his duties that night, the gentleman stepped outside, into the cool dark of the evening, while, in his head, he began to hear Barber's Adagio for strings [*sic*]. He walked up a

[100]*Ibid.*

[101]Borrowed from the lyrics of the Coots and Gillespie song, "You Go to My Head" (1938).

[102]Kim Stanley Robinson, *Icehenge* (New York: Orb Edition, 1998), 121.

small hill and looked at the edge of the wood as the wind blew through the trees, bending them slightly, and as the strings wove through themselves into a sonic climax. He remembered his moment with Frost, and those lines of his poem.

"I wonder if this is what Robert Frost was thinking," he thought to himself as the wind blew through the leaves of the trees, and the strings played on.

> *You may see their trunks arching in the woods*
> *Years afterwards, trailing their leaves on the ground.*

"Was it just like this; did it feel like this?," he recited to himself as he looked out at the trees, up at the night sky and onward to the canopy of stars.[103]

Parrott combines several ideas in this passage: a general prose narrative of the old man's recollection of Frost, literal quotations from a Frost poem, and the musical reference to Barber's composition as possible reflection of that poem. Parrott related how this story came about:

> The short story is actually a true one. I was at a book signing when a gentleman went on about writing and how he had heard the Adagio and Frost in his mind. It saddened me because I knew the music, and as he recited the poem, I was hearing how much more painful it is to want to write and be unable to get it out. The despair of the creative angst set against Barber as a soundtrack was very palpable. I still wonder what it must have took for him to tell me that story, and I wanted to honour him by writing about it.[104]

As revealed in this passage, truth, fiction, music, and poetry can become a powerful united force in storytelling.

ADAGIO SETS THE MOOD (SOMETIMES RIGHT, SOMETIMES WRONG)

Rather than invoking a sense of nostalgia, some authors simply bring in *Adagio* as background music for work, study, or other activities. At the

[103]M. R. M. Parrott, "On the Page," *A Bartered Tide* (Columbia, S.C.: Rimric, 2002), 31-32.

[104]M. R. M. Parrott, email (13 December 2007) to the author.

beginning of Homer H. Hickam, Jr.'s *Back to the Moon* (2001), a cross between science fiction and a thriller, Jack Medaris is part of a team assembling a giant robot:

> The doleful strains of Barber's *Adagio for Strings* accompanied the technicians as they moved slowly and reverently around the machine's oddly shaped pyramid of spheres, rods, and cables. Antennae protruded from each level of the machine. Its "arms" were two extendible and jointed booms. At the end of one of the booms was a digger, a rakelike device. The other arm had a groping claw.[105]

The music, provided by a compact disc player outside the clean room of the hangar, is being piped in through speakers in the four corners of the bay.

How did this particular piece of music end up here? Hickam has admired the composition for many years, hearing it at the time of the Kennedy assassination and in *Platoon*. He later realized that it was suitable music for this scene:

> I wanted to put the reader into the same mood as the technicians and to do that I decided that I would have music in the background that would change during the different stages of their work. As the chapter begins, the technicians are listening to *Adagio for Strings*. This is because I perceive the music to be somber, serious, and wonderfully complex while also being focused, intent, and determined.[106]

It is, indeed, the type of music that would keep the workers focused, intent, and determined; faster music might be distracting, causing careless work habits. When the device is tested, the music changes to Orff's *Carmina Burana*, and after the test is successful, the technicians celebrate to Elvis Presley's "Jailhouse Rock." Hickam's editor doubted that readers would "pick up" on these musical references and suggested omitting them, but he left them in anyway. "I trust my readers to be intelligent. I figured even

[105]Homer H. Hickam, Jr., *Back to the Moon* (New York: Dell Publishers, 2001), 3.

[106]Homer H. Hickam, Jr., email (13 March 2005) to the author.

if they didn't know it, they'd go listen to the music and that would even more thoroughly snap them into the scene."[107]

Hickam brought his own expertise to the novel. At one time he had worked for the National Aeronautical and Space Administration (NASA), where he directed and trained payload specialist teams for extravehicular activities (EVAs) to repair the Hubble Space Telescope. In fact, when he was watching technicians prepare a test for a deep space probe at NASA's Jet Propulsion Laboratory in Pasadena, he first got the idea to use *Adagio:* it was playing from speakers in the clean room. "This allowed me with great confidence to write the opening scene of *Back to the Moon* with my fictional technicians listening to those mournful, stirring notes."[108] It is possible that someday a movie will be made of Hickam's novel and that he will either be a scriptwriter or a consultant on the project. If so, I hope that *Adagio* will make it into that scene.

It does not take a rocket scientist, like Hickam, to realize that brain surgery is an arduous, life-or-death operation. It does not take a brain surgeon, either! In his novel *Saturday* (2005) Ian McEwan relates how surgeon Henry Perowne operates on the brain of a young man. Henry likes to listen to music during surgery, playing Bach's *Goldberg Variations* through much of the main part of the operation. But after he sews the skin of the scalp with 2-o Vicryl and punches in the skin staples, McEwan asks his assistant to put on *Adagio for Strings*, even though "it's been played to death on the radio these past years. This languorous, meditative music suggests a long labour coming to an end at last."[109]

Can listening to *Adagio* aid the study process? In William Venator's *Wither This Land* (2003), a student known only as Flood is alone in his dorm room trying to read an assignment, but a fellow student on the floor below has turned on his radio resulting in "a low humming and drumming sound." To counteract this noise, Flood turns on his own radio, first to a rock station and then to a classical station.

> Barber's Adagio had just commenced. Good, he thought, this is perfect for reading to. The Adagio softened the thumping from below and allowed Flood to return to his reading. Then his

[107]*Ibid.*

[108]*Ibid.*

[109]Ian McEwan, *Saturday* (New York: Random House, 2005), 264.

> neighbor turned the music up slightly; this time the low bass had been replaced by a fast, drilling, monotonic bass beat. . . . His floor shook. Shit, he thought, I can't concentrate . . . he banged twice on the ceiling, his room shook, the tea in the cup rippled, a book fell off the shelf. "This is a bloody joke," he said, getting up. He went down the stairs and banged on the door.[110]

All to no avail; the student in that room suggested that Flood do his reading in the school library. At first the provocateur turned the music up even louder, but his girlfriend persuaded him to turn it down. Nevertheless, back in his room Flood could still hear it as he attempted to read his assignment.

In some cases *Adagio* is simply too solemn or sad for the occasion; it could inadvertently induce a depression. Hannah Ives is Marcia Talley's sleuth in several mystery novels. In a part of *In Death's Shadow* (2004), she was bored, restless, "and a little bit glum."[111] As she puttered around the kitchen, she turned on the radio to classical station WBJC but had to confess, "it's hard to sing along to Bach, and the Barber 'Adagio for Strings' made me feel like jumping off the Bay Bridge, so I switched to WINX Shore Country radio. Stompin' songs from Jimmy Buffet, Alabama, and the Soggy Bottom Boys can perk me up every time."[112] Unfortunately, it didn't work this time. She sat down at her kitchen table and "started to bawl."[113]

But what if a depressing mood is just what a person wants? In her memoir *Project Girl* (2000)—so titled because it begins with her life in a black housing project in Brooklyn—Janet McDonald recalls such a time when she was a student at Vassar and, on a misguided impulse, decided to commit suicide. After taking several pills, she played a recording of Beethoven's Moonlight Sonata, lay down on the bed and "waited for drowsiness and death" to envelope her.[114] A half hour passed.

> Nothing was happening. I put on another record for ambiance, Samuel Barber's "Adagio for Strings." I continued to wait to be

[110]William Venator, *Wither This Land* (London: WritersPrintShop, 2003), 87.

[111]Marcia Talley, *In Death's Shadow* (New York: HarperCollins, 2004), 262.

[112]*Ibid.*

[113]*Ibid.*

[114]Janet McDonald, *Project Girl* (Berkeley: University of California Press, 2000), 74.

> whisked away to the happy heaven of young poets and rock stars. After an hour without even the slightest yawn, I realized I had been duped. Placebos! I thought, angrily. . . . I was also relieved, as much as I didn't want to admit it. No one was happier to have lived to tell the tale than I was.[115]

The book continues through the next several years of academic and professional success (she eventually became a lawyer) but also through incidents of drug abuse and jail. It is ultimately the story of one woman who struggles to triumph over adversity and to realize her dreams. Janet McDonald died of cancer in April 2007 at the age of 53.

ADAGIO IN HEAVEN AND PURGATORY

In two different stories *Adagio for Strings* breaks out of its worldly confines of the concert hall, radio, and compact disc players and in one case ascends to Heaven and in the other descends (if that is the right direction) to Purgatory. When Alice Sebold's novel *The Lovely Bones* (2002) begins, the narrator Susie Salmon finds herself in Heaven, having been raped and murdered when she was fourteen years old. From this vantage point she observes members of her family on Earth, who are trying to cope with her death. In one scene she unexpectedly encounters her grandfather and dances with him as she did when they were both alive:

> We danced so slowly to a song that on Earth had always made my grandfather cry.
>
> "Do you remember?" he asked.
>
> "Barber!"
>
> "Adagio for Strings," he said.
>
> But as we danced and spun—none of the herky-jerky awkwardness of Earth—what I remembered was how I'd found him crying to this music and asked him why.

[115]*Ibid.*, 74-75.

> "Sometimes you cry, Susie, even when someone you love has been gone a long time." He had held me against him then, just briefly, and then I had to run outside to play again with Lindsey [her sister] in what seemed like my grandfather's huge backyard.
>
> We didn't speak any more that night, but we danced for hours in that timeless blue light.[116]

Sebold combines two emotions in this scene: a girl's nostalgia for her childhood and a grandfather's sadness for the loss of a loved one, probably his wife. Thus nostalgia blends with sadness as they do, in the opinion of many, in *Adagio for Strings* itself. In her review of the novel Lisa Allardice asserted:

> With its overwhelming affirmation of Christian values, the family and community, it is not hard to understand why *The Lovely Bones* has been such a success in the US. There are candlelight vigils around the murder site, and Sebold seems to invoke a sense of national mourning, so it is no surprise to hear a celestial rendition of Barber's Adagio for Strings."[117]

Because the book is somewhat autobiographical (Sebold was also raped when she was a teenager), she may have a personal connection to this piece of music. Did it help her come to terms with her own tragedy? Did her own grandfather, or other older relative, play the music when she was a child?

On a much lighter note, Michael Fedo's short story (or brief character sketch) "The Musicians' Corner in Purgatory" (2004) concerns musicians consigned to that place of expiation, where they "sit around and talk shop. Many of them still gather in the mists after centuries of residency and expand their musical horizons."[118] They are not, however, allowed

[116]Alice Sebold, *The Lovely Bones* (New York: Little, Brown, 2002), 260-61. In late 2009 the film version, directed by Peter Jackson, was released, but the scene of Susie dancing with her grandfather to *Adagio* does not appear. I was disappointed. Yet in the credits Bruce Phillips, the grandfather, is listed despite the fact that he is never seen. Perhaps this scene was filmed but ended on the cutting room floor.

[117]Lisa Allardice, "Novel of the Week: The Lovely Bones," *New Statesman* CXXXI/4601 (19 August 2002); reprinted www.newstatesman.com/node/143639.

[118]Michael Fedo, "The Musicians' Corner in Purgatory," *Whistling Shade: A Twin Cities Literary Journal* IV/1 (Spring 2004); reprinted www.whistlingshade.com/0401/purgatory.html.

to extol the merits of their own music or else they will be punished by being "subjected to repeated readings from 'The Bridges of Madison County' and selected poems of Edgar Guest."[119] (That sounds more like Hell than Purgatory to me!) Because many of the musicians flourished in different centuries, their aesthetic differences make their conversations border on the bizarre. In one episode Mozart converses with Elvis Presley and Frank Sinatra, who at one point inquires about his fellow Rat Pack members:

> "Anybody seen Sammy or Dean?"
>
> "Sammy?" said Mozart, and he hummed a few bars of "Adagio for Strings." "Herr Barber is here but keeps to the shadows. He's let Ludwig intimidate him, I'm afraid."
>
> Sinatra briefly studied Mozart, then faced Elvis. "Who are these cretins? Don't they know who I'm talking about?
>
> "Ol' Wolfie's kind of a tease, Frank."[120]

This is like Steve Allen's old television show, *Meeting of the Minds,* musician's style.

SORRY, WRONG NUMBER

Yet with so many literary *Adagio* references, someone is bound to get things wrong. In her novel *A Summer in the Country* (2002) Marcia Willett relates a conversation between two female chums, Frummie and Louise. Frummie is convinced that it is often the music in a film that "really rouses the emotions." Louise then ponders what some of her favorite films would be like without their classical soundtracks: *Death in Venice* (1971) without Mahler, *The Deer Hunter* (1978) without Samuel Barber. Barber's music in *The Deer Hunter?* Either Louise confused two different Vietnam War films, or Willett did.[121]

[119]*Ibid.*

[120]*Ibid.*

[121]Marcia Willett, *A Summer in the Country* (New York: St. Martin's Press, 2002), 158. This is not the only time this has happened. Norman Lebrecht in *The Companion to 20th-Century Music* (New York: Simon and Schuster, 1992), 18, also asserts that *Adagio* was used in the *Deer Hunter*. Finally, *Adagio*

Although the following example is not exactly wrong, it does suggest a curious orientation to *Adagio*. In Deborah Smith's *Charming Grace* (2004) Grace Vance is lying atop a long table in the greenhouse behind the mansion. As she lay there, the Barber work "moaned from a CD player, surely the most heartbreaking baroque music in the universe."[122] Baroque music? Did she (or Smith) mistake the time period, or did she mean the word without the capital B, as in "bizarre"? If so, that would be an unusual, even unique description of the work. Or has Smith, like several others, confused Barber's *Adagio* with Albinoni's Adagio in G Minor? (See Chapter 11.)

Clearly, when artists, poets, and prose writers refer to *Adagio for Strings* in their works, they depend on the public's recognition of it to achieve the desired effect. If it were not such a familiar piece of music, any reference to it would be enigmatic; its effectiveness would be lost. Luckily, this is not the case. Many art lovers, poetry aficionados, and novel readers know this music, recognize its sound, and above all realize its emotional impact. Therefore they should be able to respond to the creative references and understand how a piece of music can enhance an artist's work.

supposedly appeared in the Vietnam War film *Apocalypse Now* (1979); see S. James Wegg, "Multi-Discipline Program Yields Mixed Results," *JWR Articles: Live Event–Mendelssohn Choir of Pittsburgh (Conductor: Robert Page)* (13 October 2004), www.jamesweggreview.org/Articles.aspx?ID=421.

[122]Deborah Smith, *Charming Grace* (New York: Little Brown, 2004), 133.

> This is 1999, we're all chucking genres in the pot. It's not meant to be offensive, it's not meant to be hectoring. It just is. And I'm not going to worry about it.
>
> —William Ørbit, *dancesite* (March 2000).[1]

This postmodern comment by William Ørbit, whose synthesizer version of *Adagio for Strings* was enthusiastically embraced throughout England in 1999, illustrates one of the most unexpected and amazing details surrounding the piece: its infiltration into the worlds of popular music and jazz. It is unexpected because a classical composition rarely makes its way into these realms and amazing because this particular work became so recognizable and beloved by so many people. A pop treatment of *Adagio* may take many forms: an arrangement for different instruments (*e.g.*, for marimbas), an introduction to a song (*e.g.*, by Puff Daddy), a phrase or two extracted for trance dancing (*e.g.*, by Tiësto), or a rendition given a jazz flavor (*e.g.*, by Larry McDonough). In most cases the *Adagio* portion contrasts greatly with the artist's established musical style.[2] The translation of Barber's *Adagio for Strings* into commercial idioms is a complicated but fascinating tale.[3]

As Introduction

Several pop musicians have preceded their rock ballads with musical preparation by Barber's *Adagio*. Billy Joel and Jon Lord of Deep Purple evidently believed that its mood was appropriate for and compatible with specific songs of their own creation. The group Bastille adopted a similar approach for an album of covers. In addition, Robert Smith of The Cure clearly found a connection between *Adagio* and one of his group's most favored songs. Indeed, this British band began a series of rock concerts with the opening of the recorded orchestral performance from the film *Platoon*. In a slightly different context Diddy must have adopted the

[1]William Ørbit, quoted in "William Orbit on Squatting, Madonna, and Margaret Thatcher: Interview–(part 1)," *dancesite* (March 2000), www.dancesite.com/news3.shtml.

[2]For details concerning the performances and recordings referenced in this chapter, please consult Appendix 7.

[3]This chapter is inspired, in part, by a paper presented by Luke Howard at the First International Samuel Barber Symposium in Richmond, Va.: "Whose Adagio? The Pop-Culture Repercussions of Barber's *Adagio for Strings*." He later published an updated edition as "The Popular Reception of Samuel Barber's *Adagio for Strings*," *American Music* XXV/1 (Spring 2007), 50-80.

Agnus Dei to reinforce his own emotional and public response to the death of a friend.

BILLY JOEL

Billy Joel, who took piano lessons as a kid, has always expressed an interest in classical music and initially sought to write music like the composers he admired. In a 1996 question-and-answer session with a collegiate audience he discussed his first encounter with the Barber work.[4] One night in 1980 Joel was traveling on a highway, was frustrated because of the traffic and the weather, and was listening to his car radio. "I was driving along, it's raining, the sky is cloudy and really gloomy, and I heard this piece of music."[5] He could not identify it; he knew he had heard it before but had never actually "tuned into it." Just as the music reached its climax, Joel recalled, "The sun shoots out of the clouds, it stops raining, the traffic clears up. I had to pull over! I burst out crying!"[6] He asked himself half-humorously, "What's happening to me? I've lost control!"[7] At that point he phoned his friend Bill Zampino to discover the name and composer of that music. Zampino remembered the incident:

> He hummed and sang it over the receiver as I searched my record collection, until I realized it was Samuel Barber's *Adagio for Strings,* one of the most emotional pieces in classical music. . . . And after that night on the highway, it probably [became] Billy's favorite piece of music in the world.[8]

Joel later declared: "this is what I love about music. It is what I want to write—to create music like that."[9]

[4]Billy Joel, "New Billy Joel Question and Answer" (C. W. Post College of the University of Long Island, 1 February 1996) [video], www.billyjoel.com/news.

[5]*Ibid.*

[6]*Ibid.* Coincidentally, Laura Burhenn, a member of the duo Georgie-James, had a similar experience: "The most moved I've ever been by a piece of music was chancing upon Samuel Barber's 'Adagio for Strings' on the car radio on a cold rainy night. That song worked its way under my skin, down into my bones—powerful, indeed, a whole story told without words." Laura Burhenn, quoted in Alex Lee Thomson, "Georgie James Interview with Alex Lee Thomson," *Rockfeedback* (January 2008); reprinted www.rockfeedback. com.

[7]*Ibid.*

[8]Bill Zampino, quoted in Timothy White, "A Portrait of the Artist," *Billboard* (3 December 1994), 16.

[9]Billy Joel, "New Billy Joel Question and Answer," www.billyjoel.com/news.

Illustration 7.1
Billy Joel,
Performance of
"An Innocent Man,"
Burswood Dome,
Perth, Australia,
7 November 2006

Image by *Wikipedia*
User Deedar70

The rock star incorporated a portion of the Barber work into one of his concerts. He was about to perform a show in Miami on 16 April 1994 when, as the prelude to his song "Shades of Grey," he played *Adagio* on his synthesizer string setting. Zampino claimed that he was distraught over the breakup with his wife. Yet Joel asserted that adding *Adagio* to the performance that night was not a consequence of his divorce but the result of his losing regular contact with his daughter. Both the song's lyrics and *Adagio*'s somber tone reflected Joel's distress:

> The more I find out the less that I know
> Black and white is how it should be

But shades of grey are the colors I see.[10]

Zampino was moved by Joel's impromptu rendition of Barber's music on that occasion: "I looked at the pain on his face, and it was a heart-rending moment. But that's one of Billy's greatest talents: He finds ways to preserve and keep alive things that he loves."[11] As far as I know, no recording exists of this performance, nor did Joel ever record *Adagio* as an introduction to this or any other song. He did, however, improvise a portion of it as part of the 1996 question / answer session referenced earlier. The video gives the listener an idea of what the audience heard that night in Florida.

DEEP PURPLE

In 1996, when the British rock band Deep Purple performed concerts in various European cities, keyboardist Jon Lord introduced its early song "When a Blind Man Cries" with an improvisation based on *Adagio for Strings*. This juxtaposition of rock and classical music was not new to Deep Purple. Because many of the group's songs incorporate quotations from classical masters such as Bach, Beethoven, and Grieg, it was not surprising for Lord to borrow from Barber.[12]

At some point Lord must have noticed that the two pieces might work together. Using the "strings" selection on the synthesizer, Lord played the *Adagio* phrases basically unchanged, sometimes only the first one (as in Paris at the Olympia on 17 June 1996) or the first two (as in Karlshamn, Sweden); he moved on to a free improvisation over a few chords from the work. At other shows he either strayed further from the Barber theme or created entirely independent improvisations. For several performances, notably one telecast in Stuttgart in October 2000, the band hired the Romanian Philharmonic Orchestra, conducted by Paul Mann, to perform the beginning two phrases of *Adagio* as an "intro to the intro," which then linked to a guitar improvisation backed by chords on the keyboard. The

[10]Lyrics submitted by ronstillman@cableone.net, "Shades of Grey Lyrics: Billy Joel," *Sing365.com Save Your Time*, www.sing365.com.

[11]Bill Zampino, quoted in Timothy White, "A Portrait of the Artist," 16; and in Hank Bordowitz, *Billy Joel: The Life and Times of an Angry Young Man* (New York: Billboard Books, 2006), 189.

[12]For a list of borrowings, see Janell Duxbury, "Deep Purple Classical Quotes," *The Highway Star*, www.thehighwaystar.com/rosas/misc/classic.htm.

orchestra provided a lush string accompaniment during the song itself, but, in spite of a few opportunities, it never again quoted the Barber piece.[13]

Any borrowing should reflect the mood of the music and the meaning of the lyrics of the song it introduces, as was the case with Billy Joel. In a similar way, the words of "When a Blind Man Cries" are compatible with the perceived melancholy of *Adagio*. A line from the first verse—"Hear me grieving, I'm lying on the floor"—or the refrain—"I'm a blind man, I'm a blind man and my world is pale / when a blind man cries, Lord, you know there ain't no sadder tale" provide ample evidence of this connection.[14] Deep Purple featured the song with its *Adagio* introduction on its travels—during the Royal Albert Tour in 2000 and during the tour of the United Kingdom the following September. Is it possible that Jon Lord had heard about Billy Joel's use of *Adagio*? Although Joel and Deep Purple stem from two different popular music traditions, *Adagio* works equally well as a musical and psychological preparation for both "Shades of Grey" and "When a Blind Man Cries."

BASTILLE

The four-man, London-based group Bastille released *Other People's Heartache* (2012), a collection of songs that deal with the anguish of love. The qualification "other people's" is appropriate here because each track represents a cover of another artist's hit. The very first on the recording is identified by the title "Adagio for Strings," which is slightly misleading because the Barber work functions only as the introduction to the song "What Is Love?" (Oddly, the title "What Is Love?" is not found on the album itself.) The introduction begins with helicopter noises and a few distant spoken phrases (perhaps derived directly from the film *Platoon*) and leads into a performance of *Adagio*'s first two phrases, sung (probably) by the four band members. Because they resort to the nonsense syllables ("pah-pah-pah"), it is, roughly speaking, a vocalise. The second phrase goes a little too low for the main singer and is almost inaudible.

[13]Listen to the Stuttgart performance on "When a Blind Man Cries," *YouTube* (6 November 2008), posted by Conneyfogle.

[14]The song is credited to the whole group as it existed in 1971, often referred to as Mark II (Ritchie Blackmore, Ian Gillan, Roger Glover, Lord, and Ian Paice). This version of "When a Blind Man Cries," is Track 3 on the second disc of *Live at the Olympia '96* (1997). The audio version of this performance with a photograph slideshow of the ensemble was also posted "Deep Purple–When a Blind Man Cries–Live at Hans Martin Schleyer Halle, Stuttgart Germany 2000," *YouTube* (4 February 2012) by texblues85. A video from a 1995 performance in Mumbai, India, with Jon Lord playing a comparable opening on keyboard can be found at "Deep Purple–When a Blind Man Cries HD 1995 (Live in India)," *YouTube* (20 July 2009), posted by oiesoudou; one from Karlshamn, Sweden (one of the best illustrations) was likewise uploaded "Deep Purple–When a Blind Man Cries–Live 1996," *YouTube* (16 September 2009), posted by stargazer2080.

The song itself was originally recorded to much acclaim in 1993 by the Trinidad-German Eurodance artist Haddaway (Nestor Alexander) and has known many reincarnations since then—other covers, remixes, and samplings. Dan Smith, front man for Bastille, sings the main melody with details from Haddaway's original song mixed in: the main beat, a motivic accompanimental figure, and a secondary female vocal counterpoint. Toward the end, it incorporates, almost like a coda, a bit of Rihanna's "We Found Love" (2011). As such, the track generally fits the definition of a mixtape or even a mash-up.[15]

THE CURE

In 2000 the venerable band The Cure went on the road with its Dream Tour and began each program with a tape of *Adagio for Strings*. Robert Smith, lead singer and a founder of the British group, acknowledged that he wanted an introduction "that would get both us and the audience in the same right mood at the start of every show and I thought Barber's Adagio would do this . . . (and I love it!)."[16] He has loved it for years. In 1996 he was among those pop musicians polled by *Billboard* concerning listening preferences. Six of his ten picks were classical pieces, including this work by Barber.[17] He later avowed, "sometimes I play very melancholic music when I'm in a melancholic mood . . . like the beautiful Adagio by Samuel Barber, that I only play at night."[18]

On The Cure's Dream Tour *Adagio* (from the *Platoon* soundtrack), resounded for a few minutes before slowly merging into the song "Out of This World." The music was coordinated with a screen at the back of the stage filled with a blue sky and stars, appropriate to the "otherworldliness" of the song, which begins:

> When we look back at it all as I know we will
> You and me, wide eyed; I wonder . . .
> Will we really remember how it feels to be this alive?

[15]A mashup is a recording created by digitally combining and synchronizing instrumental tracks with vocal tracks from two or more different songs. A mixtape, in this case, is a previously released song used by another musician to show that he or she can rap or sing better than the original artist.

[16]Robert Smith, quoted in Craig Parker, "Chain of Flowers Interview with Robert Smith" (14 July 2001), www.ourworld/compu serve.com/homepages/ChainofFLowers/robertint.html.

[17]"What They're Listening To," *Billboard,* reprinted *Atlanta Journal and Constitution* (5 September 1996), 4: C.

[18]Serge Simonart, "The Bats in the Head of Robert 'The Cure' Smith Are OK," *HUMO Belgian Magazine* (23 February 2000).

The links among the song, the starry sky, and Barber's music made a great impact on audiences.[19]

This introduction does not precede "Out of this World" on the group's commercial release, but it does so on two later albums: *Bloodflowers* (2000) and *Rarities*, Vol. 2 (2003).[20] In 2002, when The Cure performed at the Tempodrom in Berlin, "Out of this World" began the *Bloodflowers* set but without *Adagio*. Its use as prelude may depend on the circumstances. In June 2008 it introduced The Cure's concerts at the Toyota Center in Houston, at the Shrine Auditorium in Los Angeles, and at New York's Radio City Music Hall, but not the one at Madison Square Garden.[21]

SEAN COMBS: "PUFF DADDY," "PUFFY," "THE PUFFMEISTER," "P. DIDDY," "HIS DIDDYNESS," OR JUST PLAIN "DIDDY"

Puff Daddy (Sean Combs) prefaced the song "I'll Be Missing You" on his *No Way Out* release (1997) with the first twenty measures of Barber's Agnus Dei, sampled from a recording attributed to a Concordia College Choir.[22] The song is a memorial to his friend and colleague: the rapper Notorious B.I.G. (Christopher Wallace, also known as Biggie Smalls), who had been murdered earlier that year. The choir sings the introduction as Puff Daddy delivers the following "eulogy":

> Every day I wake up, I hope I'm dreamin'. I can't believe this shit. I can't believe you ain't here. Sometimes it's just hard for me to wake up; it's just hard to just keep going. It's like I feel empty inside without you being here. I would do anything to

[19]The length of the *Adagio* segment varied from one performance to another. One night in Brisbane, Australia, when the performers were late coming to the stage, *Adagio* had to be repeated.

[20]*Adagio* does precede "Out of this World" on the bootleg compact disc *Live in München* (2000) from amidst crowd noises: listen to the album or download it at www.mp3adrenalin.com/live-in=munchen-04-09-2000-bootleg-?alb72691/. Recently the Belgian tribute band Curiosity played *Adagio* as the introduction not only to "Out of This World" but also to two other songs by The Cure.

[21]The group's Houston performance of this song in June 2008 can be found at "Out of this World–The Cure," *YouTube* (13 June 2008), posted by abrashTX. The *Adagio* portion of the introduction was substantial; the posted excerpt consisted of the cello statement up through the end of the piece. Cheering of the crowd makes it difficult to hear. This upload, however, may not be complete; the taped section may have started after *Adagio* had already begun, and it is possible that the entire piece was used.

[22]The author of the liner notes mistakenly connects this passage to the introduction of the whole album, which actually quotes the beginning of Tchaikovsky's "Cherubim Hymn" from Liturgy of St. John Chrysostom. The error is compounded by the Hal Leonard piano-vocal score, where the Tchaikovsky passage is called an "adaptation of 'Agnus Dei' from Adagio for Strings" by Barber. A note states "this arrangement Copyright 1998 by G. Schirmer, Inc." Does Schirmer think it is an Adagio arrangement? Does Schirmer now have a copyright on a bit of Tchaikovsky? Rene Clausen, director of the famed Concordia College Choir in Moorhead, Minnesota, assures me that it was not this group that gave the performance.

Illustration 7.2. Puff Daddy, Performance of "Coming Home," Fort Hood, Texas, 11 December 2010

Image by Alexander Vaughn

> bring you back. I'd give all this shit up—shit don't mean nothin'. I saw your son today—he looked just like you. You was the greatest. You'll always be the greatest. I'll miss you BIG. Can't wait 'til that day when I see your face again. I can't wait 'til that day when I see your face again.[23]

The passage is spoken freely, not in rhyming rap mode like the remainder of the song. Musicologist Robert Fink called it a "maudlin Barry White-style confession of loss."[24] As for the music, reviewer Dan Cairns came to

[23]Diddy, taken from the recording. The version is slightly reworded in "SAAM," *Survey of African American Music*, www.facstaff.uww.edu/allsenjm/SAAM/TEXTS/IBMU.htm.

[24]Robert Fink, "Elvis Everywhere: Musicology and Popular Music Studies at the Twilight of the Canon," *American Music* XVI/2 (Summer 1998), 152; reprinted *Rock Over the Edge,* ed. Roger Beebe, Denise Fulbrook, and Ben Saunders (Durham, N.C.: Duke University Press, 2002), 60.

the conclusion that Puffy "clubbed the choral adaptation [of *Adagio*] to death."[25] Yet overkill is seldom a liability in such situations.

The song itself is based on "Every Breath You Take" (1983), which Sting wrote for the Police. Its text was replaced with "Every step I take." Diddy remembered seeing this Police video on MTV a few weeks after B.I.G.'s murder: "When I heard the song, I felt that Biggie was talking to me. . . . So I wanted to talk back to him through that song in my way."[26]

Fink maintained that he "swallows the song whole."[27] For Puff Daddy to insist, however, that "I did it my way" is a bit misleading. The new lyrics were actually ghost-written by rapper Sauce Money (Todd Gaither), who received a Grammy for this song in 1997.[28] So, whose ideas are expressed in the new text? Diddy's, Sauce's, or even Faith Evans's (B.I.G.'s widow)? When P. Diddy gets an idea, he frequently delegates the working out of details to others. In this instance he probably devised the general concept and, perhaps, the new title and then invited Sauce to fit new words to the rest of the tune. Sauce confirmed this course of events:

> Writing for Puff is easy, he gives you the blueprint, the direction. He tells you "I wanna say this. . . ." For "I'll Be Missing You," we sat down and he told me what he wanted. And being as that my mother had just passed not long before, I just added sprinkles in there."[29]

Yet Puffy, with the added sprinkles of Sauce, completely reinterprets—or misinterprets—the mood of the song and the meaning of the words. The sentiment of his title, "I'll Be Missing You," is far removed from Sting's original line, "I'll be watching you," an ominous threat by an obsessive stalker. Sting maintains that his song addresses issues of "surveillance and control,"[30] whereas Diddy's concerns loss and grief. Whatever the collaboration may have been in the construction of the song itself, there is little doubt that His Diddyness alone concocted the eulogy spoken during the Agnus Dei introduction.

[25]Dan Cairns "Barber Strop," *Sunday Times* (25 June 2000).

[26]Diddy, quoted in Margena A. Christian, "Sean 'Puffy' Combs," *Jet* (12 January 1998), 35.

[27]Robert Fink, "Elvis Everywhere," *American Music*, 152.

[28]Described in "I'll Be Missing You," *Wikipedia*, www.en.wikipedia.org/wiki/I'll _Be_Missing_You.

[29]Sauce Money, quoted in Apana D. Boyd, "Lyrics to Go," *Vibe* VI/8 (October 1998), 62.

[30]Sting, quoted in VH1's "Storytellers," *Song Facts*, www.songfacts.com/detail.php?id=548.

The song was a tremendous hit: #1 on the *Billboard* "Hot 100" and "R&B / Hip-Hop Songs" lists for over six months beginning in June 1997 and the winner of the MTV "Best R&B Video" award. In September 1997 the Puffmeister performed an elaborate version of it on the MTV Music Video Awards show with Faith Evans, who did most of the singing, and with Sting himself, who sang his original lyrics. The result, therefore, was an amalgamation of the original and transformed songs, sending, if one paid close attention, a truly mixed message. For this occasion the Agnus Dei introduction was shortened to only the first two phrases while Puff Daddy spoke a pared down eulogy (just the first five lines). A gospel choir appeared on stage throughout the song, but I am not convinced that they sang the Barber introduction; its members may have been lip-synching to the original pre-recorded soundtrack. Because of the recent death of Princess Diana, Puffy added her name to his tribute: "clap your hands for B.I.G., clap your hands for Princess Diana."[31]

Author Garth Alper, discussing this song in terms of postmodernism, contended that the Barber-Combs juxtaposition illustrates both the "fading distinction between 'high art' and popular culture" and a certain aspect of multiculturalism in the display of "historically anomalous styles" within an individual work.[32] *Adagio* is, of course, an American expression framed in a European classical aesthetic; rap music stems from an urban, African-American aesthetic:

> That Combs would choose to merge rap with Barber speaks to how the linking of previously uncombined genres has now become much more commonplace. . . . Samuel Barber can now be heard in Lincoln Center, in the movie *Platoon,* and on the booming car stereos of millions of young adults.[33]

According to Alper, Combs's incorporation of classical music into the popular music tradition is essentially a reversal of the normal crossover tendency in recent music:

> A large portion of twentieth-century popular music performed and listened to by whites has been based on African-American

[31]He recycled the song for two other recordings: *Tribute to the Notorious B.I.G* (1997) and a commemorative album for Princess Diana's Memorial Fund, *Diana Princess of Wales Tribute* (1997).

[32]Garth Alper, "Making Sense out of Postmodern Music?" *Popular Music and Society* XXIV/4 (Winter 2000), 2.

[33]*Ibid.*, 9.

musical invention. By composing rap music that uses samples of music from the white classical tradition, Combs has turned this tendency upside down. . . . The process demonstrates one way in which irony can be produced from postmodern genre blending.[34]

What did the rap crowd think of Barber's Agnus Dei as a prelude? Some Internet bloggers were curious enough to ask each other about it. Yet those who did not buy the original compact disc may not have been aware of it because it was not part of the video version on the MTV rotation schedule. After the MTV awards show the Barber introduction grew progressively shorter until it totally disappeared. For instance, when Diddy toured the country with a show featuring this song, he shortened both the Barber excerpt and the eulogy. Then, for performances in 2006 and 2007 Diddy replaced Agnus Dei with an entirely new introduction. Did he have second thoughts about the Barber? Did he consider it too far removed from the general rap style of the rest of the song? Or were there possible copyright problems?[35]

There is apparently no prior association between Combs and Barber before the conception of this song. Whose idea was it to add Agnus Dei in this manner? Did Combs know and like it? Was he aware that Billy Joel and Deep Purple had adopted the instrumental version in a similar manner? Was its selection intended to transfer the Sacrificial Lamb of Christ to the recently martyred figure of Biggie Smalls? While this may be a plausible association on an intellectual level, how many of Diddy's listeners would have made this connection?

As Pop Arrangement

In the spirit of an introduction Barber's *Adagio* has been embraced in its various identities: as live keyboard improvisation (Joel, Lord), as pre-recorded orchestral prelude (The Cure), as choral background (Diddy), and as vocalise (Bastille). While these examples show how musicians introduce their songs with *Adagio,* the following illustrate the way other musicians arrange and transform the work into new pop pieces. The

[34]*Ibid.*

[35]Watching Sting's song followed by Diddy's makes for a good comparison-contrast. See the live performances of "Sting: Every Breath You Take. Live in Berlin 2010 (14/15)," *YouTube* (23 December 2010), posted by popkantor and "Puff Daddy ft. Sting I'll Be Missing You," *YouTube* (25 June 2009), posted by deltamima. Several performances have also been posted on *YouTube* including the MTV performance with Sting, plus others with the shorter Barber introduction and the original Sting song.

individual who, unwittingly, started the whole movement was William Mark Wainwright, better known as William Ørbit.

ADAGIO IN A SYNTH

Ørbit received his nickname (without the affected slash) because his friends thought he seemed to be in an orbit of his own. After producing albums for other musicians, such as Madonnna and Bono, he produced his own *Pieces in a Modern Style* (2000) with synthesizer interpretations of classical pieces, *Adagio for Strings* among them. This album was initially released in 1995 but remained available for only two days because the Estonian composer Arvo Pärt denied permission to appropriate one of his works. A few years later Ørbit decided to scrap the Pärt component and proceeded to issue the recording without it.

His *Adagio* is more of a transcription than an arrangement. As critic Michael Hubbard speculated, "it is as if Ørbit has recognised that these pieces are beautiful as they are, and any large scale tampering would only be detrimental."[36] Ørbit's respect for the work may be one reason he did not toy much with it. The extent of the changes he made, in general, depended on the piece itself:

> It's all about what feels right at the time, rather than, "I better start manipulating and changing things because I have to, because that's the agenda." Say for instance "Adagio for Strings." It's very simple. It's hardly changed at all. It's the original arrangement with a timbral shift. Basically, it's the same thing.[37]

Ørbit did make a few minor modifications. He made, for example, a diminuendo on the final chord of the climax rather than sustaining the dynamic level, much like the Curtis String Quartet performance described earlier (see Chapter 2). He then turned the quiet chord passage into an exact sequence by altering the melody into falling fifths (see Example 7.1). Moreover, at the very end, the A in the final F-major chord fades out slightly ahead of the other notes, leaving a rather "medieval" open fifth as the last sound of the piece.

[36]Michael Hubbard, "William Orbit–Pieces in a Modern Style," *musicOMH* (17 January 2000), www.musicomh.com/albums/william-orbit.htm.

[37]William Ørbit, quoted in Mark Seymour, "Orbit Discusses Madonna, New Album, Helicopters," *William Orbit News* (31 March 2000), www.warnermusic.com.au/artists/news.asp?action=read&newsid=276&artistid=937.

Example 7.1. Ørbit Modifications to the Quiet Chords Passage

When asked "what is it about this piece that is so compelling," he replied, "It's really one of the greatest pieces of musical construction. . . . My interpretation is simply shining the spotlight on it for people who maybe haven't experienced it."[38] He later told columnist Nick Coleman:

> I must admit it does upset me a bit that it's become popularised in the way it has, but that doesn't stop Adagio from being a great piece of music. . . . It gets me every time; it hits a big melancholy spot in me. I think it's the way it's so long-measured and never seems to end. It climbs in three big arcs and then gradually subsides, burrowing deeper into the emotions as it goes. . . . Adagio is beautiful.[39]

Critics have registered mixed reviews of his transcription. Ian Grey considered it to be "notoriously lachrymose" and an "ersatz Vangelis-ism."[40] (Ouch!) Patrick Bryant compared it to the "incidental music from a porn flick."[41] Mike Pattenden argued that the transcription "reveals the album's major weakness—synths cannot compete with the real thing. Even the most expensive units sound cheap, twee and weedy when placed next to an orchestra."[42] Michael Hubbard maintained a similar view: "it's as if the musical emotion has been prised away by some ghastly robot, intent on homogenising the world into a one-size-fits-all feeling."[43] DAC Cromwell, an ambient electro-acoustic composer, expressed one of the most scathing criticisms:

[38] *Ibid.*

[39] William Ørbit, quoted in Nick Coleman and William Ørbit, "Record Producer and Musician William Ørbit on Samuel Barber's Adagio for Strings," *The Independent* (3 March 1995), 26.

[40] Ian Grey, "Review | Pieces in a Modern Style by William Orbit," *bluecoupe* (March 2000), www.bluecoupe.com/reviews/orbit_pieces.html.

[41] Patrick Bryant, "William Ørbit: Pieces in a Modern Style," *Boston Phoenix CD Reviews* (6 March 2000), www.weeklywire.com/ww/03-06-00/boston-music-clips.html.

[42] Mike Pattenden, "The Big Album," *The* [London] *Times* (15 January 2000).

[43] Michael Hubbard, "William Orbit–Pieces in a Modern Style," *musicOMH.*

> A few weeks ago, while driving across the Illinois prairie, this crippled and damaged version of Samuel Barber's *Adagio for Strings* came tumbling out of the stereo like some hideous musical fart. This was not mere remixing at work here, but what appeared to be the result of some deranged and incompetent drivelmeister jamming poor Maestro Barber's work into some deranged MC-303-driven Cuisinart and hitting the "wreck" button. I was horrified to find that this was . . . the product of one William Orbit. . . . Yee, gods.[44]

Yet other critics admired Ørbit's effort. While David Kirby admitted that it is difficult to play this music well without the strings it was written for, he perceived a warmth in the synthesized sound that others have missed: "for those who say the machine has no soul, they should listen to Ørbit's rendition of this piece. If they don't hear soul in there, they're not listening."[45] Chris Charles, BBC entertainment reviewer, called Ørbit's interpretation "simply sublime. Nine minutes of soothing, soaring strings that could reduce a rabid dog to man's best friend in seconds."[46] One posting on *YouTube* emphasizing this soothing quality billed it as "9 minutes and 31 seconds of beautiful Electronica sadness."[47] The video's images, comprised of still photographs and computerized graphics in slow motion, enhance this state of mind.

In the United States snippets of Ørbit's "Samuel Barber's *Adagio for Strings*" (its more or less official title) have been heard on radio and television shows. It made it into the rarefied atmosphere of NPR's *All Things Considered* on 16 March 2000, when it followed the reading of letters from listeners concerning the price of gasoline, the lawsuit against Unocal, and the buzzards' annual return to Hinkley, Ohio. It was just a sound bite without specific justification. Later that year, brief video clips were heard in a more logical context on two episodes of CNN's

[44]DAC Cromwell, "The Cranky Guy Sez Come Up with Yer Own Damn Ideas!!!" *Creative Synth* (18 October 2000), www.creativesynth.com/columns/001_Crankyguy_113.html. Cromwell derived the DAC of his name from his initials, much like golfer "Fuzzy" Zoeller (Frank Urban Zoeller, Jr.).

[45]David Kirby, "William Orbit: Piece in a Modern Style," *Choler Magazine* (21 March 2000), www.choler.com/ reviews/orbit_pieces.shtml.

[46]Chris Charles, "CD Review: William Orbit," *BBC Entertainment Section* (16 January 2000), www.news.bbc.co.uk/2/hi/entertainment/602236.stm.

[47]Considering the popularity of Ørbit's transcription, it is surprising how few video versions appear on *YouTube*. Many that cite his name are more often Corsten's or Tiësto's version, discussed next.

WorldBeat, both of which accompanied a brief commentary by Ørbit about technology and the importance of presenting "good tunes."[48]

In October 2001 Ørbit closed Karlheinz Stockhausen's Electronic Festival at London's Barbican Centre with a modification of his own *Adagio* with additional woodwinds and brass, while the choral group, The Sixteen, sang the Agnus Dei text. When the enthralled audience demanded more, Ørbit repeated the whole musical selection as an encore. The Barbican performance seems closer in style and tempo to Ferry Corsten's remix, which had just started to find favor in dance clubs (see the next section). Ørbit seems to have accepted Corsten's concept as his own and now prefers it—or something like it—to his earlier, more conventional version.

What did Ørbit think of his unexpected success? "I get disoriented by it all sometimes, and my answer is to go and do music. It answers all the questions in life for me."[49] Little did he realize at that time that his synthesized *Adagio* would give birth to so many offspring. Soon the most prominent and most unforeseen transformations of his transcription would be heard in Belgian and Dutch dance clubs as part of the techno and trance dance trends of the late 1990s.

ADAGIO, "I'D LIKE TO PUT YOU IN A TRANCE"[50]

New pop transformations of *Adagio* seem to be creeping out of the woodwork every day. A favorite form is trance, a type of dance music derived from techno that has attracted many fans, especially in Europe, since the 1990s. In this style layers of sound weave in and out, "tweaking the effects to create ever-more hypnotic, propulsive combinations."[51] According to Tony McGuinness, a member of the British trance trio Above and Beyond, the first time Barber's *Adagio for Strings* was heard in a trance context was instigated by Paul Oakenfold. "Once he'd done it, classical music in a club made sense."[52]

[48]Serena Yang, "Today's D.J.s Taking Center Stage," *CNN* (aired 7 May 2000), www.transcripts.cnn.com/TRANSCRIPTS/0005/07/wbt.00.html.

[49]William Ørbit, quoted in Donna Freydkin, "Entertainment from Madonna to Maurice Ravel, This William Is in Orbit," *CNN* (9 February 2000), www.articles.cnn.com/2000-02-09/entertainment/orbit_1_madonnas-classical-music-charts?_s=PM:SHOWBIZ.

[50]A brazen theft of a line from Madonna's song, "Erotica," *Erotica* (Maverick, 9 18782-2, 1992).

[51]"Trance Music," *Wikipedia*, www.wikipedia.org/wik/Trance_music.

[52]Tony McGuinness, quoted in "Is Paul Oakenfold the Greatest DJ of All Time" [interview], *Mixmag* (10 November 2010); reprinted www.mixmag.net/words/news/is-paul-oakenfold-the-greatest-dj-of-all-time.

Oakenfold ("Oakey" or "Oakie"), a true pioneer in the field, was one of the most important deejays of 1990s dance music. After he heard the trance sound in the 1980s on the Mediterranean island of Ibiza (off the coast of Spain), he brought it back to London. Around the same time he became intrigued with *Adagio for Strings* and programmed the recording by the Vancouver Symphony Orchestra (from the *Platoon* soundtrack) on a few of his radio sets in England. He then combined these diverse musical interests by appropriating a small portion of this recording for his dance album *fluoro* (1996).[53] For this endeavor he added punctuating effects on the synthesizer to the original string sound. Because his presentation is so brief (47 seconds), it is probably intended merely as a slow transition between two fast tracks on the album, "New Kicks" and "Kabalah." This quiet bridge may also be *Adagio*'s first use as a "chillout" on the dance-floor. This fleeting, almost incidental reference just might have been the "new kick" that spawned an obsession for this piece among trance afficionados for the next seventeen years.[54]

Ferry Corsten is the prominent Belgian deejay whose trance remix of Ørbit's *Adagio* actually made the piece take off. A typical remix begins with the track of a fairly slow original song that is then transformed into an upbeat dance track for clubs. The Ørbit transcription came to Corsten through middleman Tony McGuinness (of Above and Beyond), who worked at Warner Studios in 1995, the time of the first aborted release of *Pieces in a Modern Style*. McGuinness became especially fond of the *Adagio* track: "I'd come home from clubbing and stick it on, and thought it might make a good trance record. My brother and I started mucking about with it in my studio."[55] He then talked with Ørbit about turning it into a dance mix. "He was very keen. . . . I sent the midi files to Ferry Corsten, and he did the mix to my brief. . . . He did a great job."[56]

[53]There is much confusion over the title and label of this recording. Because the album cover has *fluoro* in large yellow print, I have come to the conclusion that that is the official title. Beneath this word is Perfecto Fluoro: Oakenfold, which I take to be the record label and mixer-producer. Some people refer to the album itself as *Perfecto Fluoro*, and Amazon gives Atlantic UK as the label, but that may be just the distributor. *Adagio* is on the second compact disc in each set.

[54]Oakenfold must still like Barber's original *Adagio for Strings* because he included a portion of Bernstein's recording with the New York Philharmonic on his double-compact-disc set, *The Goa Mix 2011* (2010). The Barber work was not a part of *The Goa Mix* (OTCD01, 1994), which had been broadcast earlier on the BBC in 1994.

[55]Tony McGuinness, "Interview with 'Above and Beyond' Part II," *Trance.Nu V3.51*; reprinted www.trance.nu/v3/interview_show.php?id=129&SIU=.

[56]*Ibid.*

Corsten was pleased with the opportunity to work with Barber's music. On more than one occasion he has acknowledged that he is proud of his remix, calling it his favorite. "First of all, I loved the original piece of music";[57] it is "just a piece of art and it was a dream of mine to work with something as beautiful as that."[58] Yet he later confessed, "it was such a challenge to make something like that into a trance mix without losing the value of the song."[59] (One may debate whether he succeeded.)

Not only was Ørbit "keen" on Corsten's potential mixing project, he, too, was equally satisfied with the final result. He proclaimed that Corsten fabricated a "fantastic mix"[60] and expressed genuine appreciation:

> The guy completely "gets it." I was excited from the moment I heard it. . . . He altered it but kept its fundamental essence. Ferry must have some classical understanding or sympathy or something, he's certainly very talented. I think he's marvelous."[61]

He confessed, "I reckon it was Ferry's mix that set the whole thing rolling. He's got everybody's ears pricked up."[62] Ørbit believes that his own version and Corsten's make a good combination: his own is "kinda quiet," but Corsten's "is anything but quiet, blastin' away."[63]

Corsten's remix exhibits what I consider to be a five-part structure shown in Table 7.1: Prelude, *Adagio* 1, *Adagio* 2, *Adagio* 3, and Coda (on the next page). The two-minute prelude, with its constantly building rhythmic patterns, leads directly to the typical trance breakdown, in this case consisting of original Barber phrases in Ørbit's synthesizer setting. They now serve as the theme for a kind of variation set, in which the Barber phrases are constantly repeated with added rhythms and thicker textures. The coda, returning to material from the introduction, brings the piece to a logical conclusion. Whatever purists may think of Corsten's

[57]"Ferry Corsten Interview, Trance Republic," *YouTube* (3 January 2006), posted by janeway 259.

[58]Ferry Corsten, quoted in Glittergirl, "Interview: Ferry Corsten," *Groovanauts* (21 December 2003); reprinted www.groovanauts.com/board/articles.php?article_id=80.

[59]Ferry Corsten, quoted in Mr. Spencer, "The Ferry Corsten Interview," *Mr. Spencer* (17 June 2002); reprinted www.mrspencer.co.za/modules.php?name=News&file=article&sid=593.

[60]William Ørbit, quoted in Nic Harcourt, "Morning Becomes Eclectic," radio show from KCREW [Santa Monica, Calif.] (19 January 2000).

[61]William Ørbit, quoted in "William Orbit on Squatting," *dancesite*, www.dancesite.com/news3.shtml.

[62]William Ørbit, quoted in Nic Harcourt, "Morning Becomes Eclectic," radio show from KCREW.

[63]*Ibid.*

trance transformation—some are appalled—they might be compelled to concede that its structure is coherent, rational, and ultimately satisfying. Even the loudest, most climactic section of the piece logically occurs shortly after four minutes, around the golden section. Although Corsten probably did not have that concept in mind, it, nevertheless, matches the climactic phi point of Barber's original.[64]

Table 7.1. Form of Ferry Corsten's Remix

0:00	0:30	1:30	2:15
PRELUDE			ADAGIO 1
rhythmic patterns	more complex pattern	4-note descending motive	phrases 1 & 2 breakdown

3:15	4:00	5:30
ADAGIO 2	ADAGIO 3	CODA
added rhythms	more rhythms, thicker texture	much like the prelude

When the remix was released, Corsten along with several other deejays played it in clubs in many different countries and spread his fame quickly. After a while, his *Adagio* became more popular than Ørbit's, to the extent that when individuals refer to Ørbit's effort, it is often Corsten's remix that they truly mean. Indeed, many postings on *YouTube* with the title "William Orbit-Barber's Adagio for Strings" (or a variant) are, in fact, Corsten's but do not mention his name. He won "Best Remixing Award" at Dance Star 2000—the World Online Worldwide Dance Music Awards. In a poll taken in 2001 at DI Forums Board the largest number of those responding assessed Corsten's remix as "simply amazing!" (See Table 7.2.)

Corsten's remix was borrowed—again, without referencing his name—for the soundtrack of a music video disseminated in 2000 on MTV and the television station Bravo! Canada and can now be found on Ørbit's website, MTV Overdrive, and other postings on *YouTube*. It begins with a framed picture of a tree in a flat landscape; as the camera slowly zooms in, the untranced Ørbit phrase begins at what had been the breakdown portion

[64]Corsten also made a shorter version (ca. 3:43) for radio air play, "Radio Edit." Its prelude is half as long, taking less time to build up the rhythmic complex before *Adagio* enters.

of the remix.[65] As the energetic beat intensifies, the tree remains the same, but the background changes from static landscape to a busy, fast-motion scene: buildings going up, people racing by, etc. The music fades out after about three and a half minutes as the camera zooms out to reveal the tree in its original context. The tree, the single stable element surviving all the changes going on around it, could be considered a visual metaphor for *Adagio* itself. Whatever happens to it—synthesization, adulteration, and more—it remains constant; it never loses its integrity.

Table 7.2. Poll of Remarks Concerning Corsten's Remix (2001)[66]

COMMENT	VOTES	PERCENTAGE
Simply amazing	553	87.36%
Very good	33	5.21%
Decent	12	1.90%
Pretty bad	8	1.26%
No thanks, not my style!	27	4.27%

Tiësto (Tijs Verwest), Corsten's deejay colleague and former partner,[67] also produced a remix of Ørbit's *Adagio for Strings*. It was originally presented in May 2003 at the Gelredome Stadium in Arnhem, Netherlands as the introduction to his first live solo event, *Tiësto in Concert* (2003).[68] Why *Adagio*? He explained, "I wanted to have a grand opening with a track people already know, but still in a different mode."[69] He recalled, "It was the opening tune in front of 25,000 people, so I guess that's why it became a very special track. . . . I really like classical music, and *Adagio*

[65]With time, however, the online community has taken notice of this attribution error. As of June 2012 there were at least eleven postings of this video on *YouTube* with only one of them not giving credit to Corsten.

[66]"View Poll Results: William Orbit–Adagio for Strings (Ferry Corsten Remix)," *DI Forums Board*, www.forums.di.fm/showthread.php?t=619.

[67]Tiësto, quoted in DeepJ Max, "Interview 55," *Welkom bij Tiëstoworld.nl–The Official Tiëstoworld Website* (11 June 2004), www.tiestoworld.nl/interview55.htm. Regarding his nickname Tiësto has stated, "Everybody had to have a DJ name in the beginning of the 90's and I just gave it an Italian sound. . . . Everybody in the world can say 'Tiësto,' but nobody can say 'Tijs Verwest.'"

[68]A variant of the same performance with distant shots interspersed with amateur video clip is also supplied on disc two of the DVD set *Tiësto in Concert* (2003). This clip is titled "Fan of Tiësto."

[69]Tiësto, quoted in DeepJ Max, "Interview 55," *Welkom bij Tiëstoworld.nl.*

was always one of my favorite pieces."[70] After an introduction, he began his remix. At the same time tubes of blue lights radiated out from his circular deejay booth and simulated the turning of a giant LP record, an appropriate image because live mixing at concerts even today requires the spinning of old-fashioned vinyl recordings. In addition, spotlights, laser beams, and columns of fireworks blasted high into the air. The cheering crowd danced as large video monitors displayed his name and image. This particularly splashy opening is probably the most flamboyant visual accompaniment *Adagio* has ever received.

Tiësto has played his *Adagio* remix on most concerts as he toured the world. Because it has become the piece that fans most want to hear, he usually places it strategically either at or near the end of his concerts. He fondly remembers one occasion in Athens in September 2003:

> It was near the waterfall in a venue with about 4000 people.
> It was 7 in the morning and the sunrise was on its way.
> An incredible moment I will never forget, 4000 screaming
> Greeks with hands in the air, sunrise and Adagio playing.
> I had goosebumps all over! Moments like that remind me
> of the reason why I want to be a deejay.[71]

Tiësto is amazed at *Adagio*'s popularity. His fans eagerly awaited its availability on compact disc, but he was at first reluctant to release it. "I just made it for myself to play out because it's one of my favourite songs."[72] After receiving many requests, however, he decided to share it on his *Just Be* album (2004) that he launched at Amsterdam's Heineken Music Hall. Although the venue is different, the show looks similar on video clips to the one at the Gelredome; his booth is surrounded by red rather than blue light, and *Adagio* is shorter.

Meanwhile, after his program in Greece, Tiësto was approached by a member of the Athens Organizing Committee for the Olympic Games, someone who had seen the *Tiësto in Concert* DVD, and was asked to play music at the opening ceremony of the 2004 games. He welcomed the opportunity: "there are no words to describe what an enormous honor it

[70]Tiësto, quoted in Sean O'Neal, "One Moment in Time," *Philadelphia City Paper* (23 September 2004), www.philadelphiacitypaper.net/articles/2004-09-23/music.shtml.

[71]Tiësto, "Petite Déclaration de Tiësto," *Tranceaddict* (16 September 2003), www.tranceaddict.com/forums/showthread/t-129204.html.

[72]Tiësto, "In the Spotlight," *In the Mix* (September 2003), www.inthemix.com.au/p/np/viewnews.php?id=11546.

is to be asked to play at the opening ceremonies. It is the highlight of my career so far."[73] From his platform at the Olympic Stadium, he spun his records for about ninety minutes while athletes from 202 nations paraded in. His *Adagio* remix was the culmination of the session, played when the delegations from Turkmenistan, Tunisia, Yemen, the Philippines, and Finland entered. Some of his American fans, however, were disappointed that television commentators never acknowledged him or ever showed a close-up of him. They particularly singled out NBC's announcers for incessant, inane chatter, to the point that they could hardly hear the music at all. Even more frustrating, the network broke for commercials in the middle of *Adagio*! When the telecast resumed, it was still playing as representatives from Fiji, Chile, and Hong Kong entered. Yet viewers of European, Canadian, and South American networks may have heard Tiësto's music more clearly and without interruption. Some reported that not only did their stations acknowledge him, but at least one (*i.e.*, the CBC) provided a short segment about him.[74] Tiësto later recalled:

> That was very groundbreaking for everybody, to put a DJ right there and let him play for two hours while the parade of the athletes was going on. That was a really big thing. I was playing right under the Olympic flame. That was very memorable. At the moment I was super nervous 'cause, you know, 4.7 billion [*sic*] people are watching on the television. It is funny you think right now in Africa, somewhere in a small village, people are watching television and hear my music. That was really amazing.[75]

For that performance he remixed *Adagio* slightly to accommodate the vast venue of the stadium. "I used nice, distorted sounds to make it very

[73]Tiësto, quoted in Sean O'Neal, "One Moment in Time," *Philadelphia City Paper*. The day before the 2004 Olympic opening ceremonies, he was interviewed on National Public Radio, where a sound bite from his *Adagio* remix was played. Tiësto, featured in Neal Conan, "Olympics Preview," *Talk of the Nation* (11 August 2011), rebroadcast www.npr.org/templates/story/story.php?storyId=3846371.

[74]Although there was no verbal introduction of Tiësto, the live feed of the parade (without commentary) briefly showed him at his audio booth, with his name displayed on the screen for a few seconds during the entrance of the Angolan athletes. Various videos of sections of the athlete entrance ceremony have been posted on *YouTube*; although Tiësto's music may still be heard, however, videos showing him have since been removed.

[75]Tiësto, quoted in Bron, "Interviews Deel 9–On the Download," *Tiestoworld.nl* (6 March 2009), www.tiestoworld.nl/interviewsdeel9.html. The month after the Olympics he released a compact disc called *Parade of the Athletes* (2004), consisting of the main tracks that he played for the ceremony. On the album *Adagio* is somewhat shorter (5:57) than the version he played that night. The longer first version, however, is available on *Parade of the Athletes Unmixed* (2004).

dramatic, so I made the strings sound huge and the bass lines very large. I was thinking in big terms."[76] On that evening more people around the world—possibly close to four billion—heard at least the first phrase of *Adagio for Strings* at the same time than at any other time in its history.[77]

Tiësto still offers his remix in his many public appearances around the world because audiences expect it. He told *New York Times* reporter Johanna Keller:

> The reaction is phenomenal. When I play the Adagio, and they hear the bass line and the high sounds, people start screaming. Then at the first break of the track, people scream again. The reactions are the same, all around the world.[78]

Barber would probably be astounded—and possibly abashed—that any part of his *Adagio* would elicit screams.

The structure of Tiësto's remix differs from Corsten's but is equally logical in its balanced form: a rhythmic introduction, Part 1 (the first appearance of the *Adagio* melody), a typical breakdown, Part 2, and a coda. Table 7.3 presents an approximation of the form. The breakdown occurs almost exactly halfway through the piece, when the buildup of melodic and rhythmic patterns of Part 1 suddenly disappears. It is the only time that Ørbit's synthesized, untranced treatment of the phrase comes in; otherwise, the main phrase is constantly repeated with changes or added rhythmic tracks. The result is a kind of theme and variations similar to Corsten's or even to a Baroque chaconne. An interesting aspect is a high B-flat near the end of the introduction (ca. 1:00) that blends into the first note of the Barber melody; later at the coda that same pitch recurs (ca. 7:00) and lends a sense of unity to both sections and to the piece as a whole.[79]

[76]Tiësto, quoted in Johanna Keller, "An Adagio for Strings, and for the Ages," *The New York Times* (5 March 2010); reprinted www.nytimes.com/2010/03/07/arts/music/07barber.html.

[77]When NBC telecast the ceremony, it took a commercial break in the middle of *Adagio*, which, fortunately, was still playing when the telecast resumed. In February 2010 Olympic audiences in many parts of the world were able to hear another version of the work as part of that year's opening ceremony. This time when NBC took a commerical break, it missed the entire *Adagio* presentation! American audiences never even knew it was there.

[78]Tiësto, quoted in Johanna Keller, "Adagio for Strings" *The New York Times.*

[79]This description is of the CD and DVD versions. When Tiësto mixes *Adagio* in live performances, the length and order of events may change. For instance, in a performance on 11 August 2005 at Polaventa Hall, Bucharest, Romania, he slowed down the main *Adagio* phrase and gradually speeded it up, as might happen in an eastern European dance. See "Tiesto–Adagio for Strings+Olympic Flame," *Google*

Table 7.3. Approximate Form of Tiësto's Remix

0:00	1:25	3:40	4:20	6:40	7:30
INTRO	PART 1	BREAK-DOWN	PART 2	CODA	
high B-flat—> various rhythms	first notes of *Adagio*, short-long rhythm phrase 1 only	buildup stops, "pure" Ørbit	almost a repeat of Part 1	high B-flat—> rhythm only	fades

Both the Corsten and Tiësto remixes are typical trance dances with a driving beat and a breakdown followed by a resumption of the beat. The main difference is the approach to Barber's original phrases. Corsten borrows the first two phrases whereas Tiësto borrows only the first, making the two remixes easy to tell apart. By concentrating only on the beginning phrase, Tiësto creates a more "minimalistic" impression—more repetitions are required to fill out the time. Repeating just the first phrase, however, presents a slightly jarring harmonic effect. The two-phrase loop-in with Corsten's remix ends on the final chord from phrase 2. Because the third phrase in Barber and Ørbit begins exactly like the first, it may take a few seconds to realize that the music has not continued into this phrase but has actually returned to phrase 1; the transition is smooth. On the other hand, the final chord of phrase 1 in Tiësto's version does not logically lead back to the first chord, making the return more abrupt, even jolting. Yet the more this loop is heard—and there are plenty of opportunities—the more reasonable it seems. Corsten, however, remains somewhat critical of Tiësto's reliance on such a short fragment:

> To me, it's a cool record, but it misses the whole point of the original or what my remix was trying to prove. *Pieces in a Modern Style* was about classical music made with modern-day synthesizers with total respect to the original. I was asked to make a version for the dancefloor but with much respect to the original. In my piece, you hear a longer piece of the original classical version, whereas in Tiësto's version, he only loops the

Video Website (8 July 2006), posted by TrArCeFeR. Things do not always go well during an *Adagio* performance. At one performance, an embarrassed Tiësto tried to adjust controls knobs after the sounds simply stop. See "Tiesto–Fatal Error in Adagio," *YouTube* (19 May 2008), posted by rafaelironmaiden.

> first, most recognizable piece. You just can't compare it to the original classical piece because it is such a little loop.[80]

One could, of course, quibble over whether the presence of one or two phrases from a string quartet movement of sixty-nine measures makes much difference.

A critical comparison of the two remixes is inevitable with opinions divided as to which is better. According to reviewer Scott Richardson, Tiësto's

> is nothing like the grand Ferry Corsten remix which is your typical uplifting trance. Rather it's a more driving and experimental remix of the classic. The main melody is driven by a synth that I can only describe as totally amazing. . . . It has so much power that it really makes this track. The familiar long strings section is retained, and when that powerful synth drops in for the main melody, the track totally blows you away.[81]

Stuart Barrie asserted, "It's been done before but not with this power and intensity. This foot to the floor version kicks ass. A simply awesome record that's destined to become an all-time classic."[82]

Although listeners seem to prefer Corsten's remix (see Table 7.4), Tiësto's is far more ubiquitous, perhaps because he plays it in public more frequently. This is borne out by the large number of Tiësto video clips posted on *YouTube*, far more than Corsten's. In fact, over half of all *Adagio for Strings* postings on that site are excerpts from his various concerts all over the world (they can hardly be called performances). Some are full-length, others are absurdly short (15 seconds); most are flawed by horrible sound quality and intended primarily as personal reminders for die-hard trance fans of their night at the club or arena.[83]

[80]Ferry Corsten, quoted in Justin Kleinfeld, "Unguarded Moments: Battle of the Re-mixes," *Remix* (1 September 2006), www.remixmag.com/artists/remix_unguarded_moments/.

[81]Scott Richardson, "Review: Tiësto–Just Be," *Trancetribe* (27 April 2004), www.transtribe.com/pages/other_reviews.php?id=8.

[82]Stuart Barrie, "The Razz: Clubbing Nation–Just Be a Tiësto Fan," *Scottish Daily Record* (21 May 2004).

[83]For the use of Tiësto's *Adagio* as soundtrack for amateur music videos, see Chapter 9. Other deejays playing his mix include the following: Minimalistix (Steve Sidewinder [Andy Vandierendonck], Brian Koner, and Joey Morton), K-Complex (Nu Energy), and Stu Allan (Hardcore EP6), Dave Pearce, Eddie Halliwell (@Tantra), Judge Jules, Armin van Buuren, DJ Sammy. When these clips appear on *YouTube*, the deejay is seldom, if ever, seen.

OTHER REMIXES

When Ørbit re-released *Pieces in a Modern Style* with the limited edition EP, he programmed not only his own transcription of *Adagio* on the main disc but also included bonus tracks of Corsten's remix and one by André "ATB" Tanneberger on the second disc. Tanneberger's, like Corsten's, begins with a prelude and a section of trance rhythms. A pause leads into *Adagio,* but after only the first phrase it is transformed into an entirely new piece. That is, it is not the same kind of "*Adagio* variation set" as Corsten's and Tiësto's. In early 2005 Tiësto produced an all-*Adagio* album with the time-honored title *Adagio for Strings,* featuring not only his full-length original but also a shorter "radio edit." He also asked other remixers on the trance scene to contribute their own: the Belgian Fred Baker (Frédéric Backer); the Dutch deejay partners Danjo (Raijer) and Rob Styles (Robbert Vroegindeweij); and the Dutch prodigy Phynn (Finne Jager). On several concerts during his tours in 2005 Tiësto played either the Baker or Danjo-Styles remix rather than his own. Later in 2005 Scottish deejay John Fernie added his own to the pool.

Table 7.4. Comparison of Different Trance Versions in a Non-scientific Poll from Tranceaddict Forums (2012)[84]

MUSIC	VOTES	PERCENTAGE
Ferry Corsten Remix	77	50.33%
Tiësto Remix	35	22.88%
Original by Barber	21	13.73%
Danjo and Styles Remix	8	5.23%
Phynn Remix	5	3.27%
William Ørbit	2	1.31%
Silver and Burt Remix	2	1.31%
Fred Baker Remix	1	0.65%
ATB Remix	1	0.65%
Fernie Remix	1	0.65%

In an unscientific poll from *Tranceaddict Forums,* listeners were invited to compare versions. The results of this poll varied from time to time (those shown in Table 7.4 are taken from September 2012), and yet

[84]"Adagio for Strings [Best]," *Tranceaddict* (25 May 2005), www.tranceaddict.com/forums/showthread.php?s=ca3fc4d676b9230193de24212ba90330&threadid=253530&highlight=%22adagio+for+strings%22&forumid=29.

Corsten's always maintained a commanding lead, with Tiësto's placing at a distant second. Yet it is gratifying that Barber's original ranks third. The newer remixes received very few votes. In recent years Tiësto's version has become extremely popular. The latest polls, nonetheless, suggest that Corsten's mix remains the favorite among hard-core trance listeners.

Do these remixes contribute anything new? Trance fans may like the shifting around of elements with slight changes to the beat or melody, but frankly they all sound pretty much the same. Sometimes a remix of a remix is a rehash.[85] Yet a few, especially those on the *DanceIndustries* website, add some distinctive features.[86] Mark van Biljouw's mix is similar to others, but in the middle he manipulates the first two notes of *Adagio* (B-flat to A), alternating back and forth as a kind of "development section." In Moldano's a voice announces "Adagio for Strings" immediately before the tune enters.[87]

CD Track 11

Spanish deejay MillàN (Antonio Millán) and Scottish producer Iced (Martin Newstead) also concocted novel twists for their remixes. After a lengthy introduction MilláN in his "Adagio remix" superimposed a reading of a passage from the Book of Genesis by the American astronaut Frank Borman in lunar orbit on Christmas Eve 1968. At the phrase "let there be light" *Adagio* emerges as a musical light of the world, similar to but subtler than Franz Joseph Haydn's monumental C-major chord in *The Creation* (1798). MilláN explained this mixture of astronomy and music:

> I've always felt a special interest in astronomy, the space race, the conquest of outer space, and every time I heard Adagio for Strings and closed my eyes, I would imagine new worlds to explore. I would think about the origins of the universe and its creation. I decided to insert that fragment by Frank Borman in order to work into the theme all of those thoughts and sensations that Samuel Barber's song produced in me. It is one of the most marvelous melodies in the history of music and, as you well say, represents the light of the world.[88]

[85]The Danjo-Styles, Phynn, and Baker remixes also can be found on *Just Be: Remixed* (2006). Tiësto's original mix is included in his *Tiësto in Concert* DVD from Arnhem, the Netherlands.

[86]Danceindustries.com is an online music, commercial digital distribution network and publishing company.

[87]This announcement was deleted from "Silver Sanctuary vs. Whirlwing Remix," *YouTube* (20 May 2010), posted by Iceferno R. M. X. No one seems to know or at least be willing to reveal the real name of the elusive and enigmatic Moldano.

MilláN has constructed a well-balanced, well-framed form, shown in Table 7.5. A fairly subdued rhythmic pattern begins the work, and a similar pattern of nearly the same length ends it. After about three minutes into the piece, after the Borman quotation, MilláN first presents a plain melodic version of *Adagio*'s first two phrases followed by a straightforward harmonization of them (like Corsten) and later about three minutes from the end provides a simple harmonized version. Between are the principal dance transformations of his thematic material. Although he may not have planned it precisely, the loudest, most energetic statements of the *Adagio* phrases occur near the phi point of the structure. This is another similarity to Corsten's mix, but probably not derived from it.

Table 7.5. Organization of MilláN's Remix

0:00	2:50	3:15	3:40	5:15
subdued rhythm	Borman reading	*Adagio* melody	*Adagio* + harmony	loudest sound
ca. 6:20	7:00	7:45	8:30	10:30
phi point	loudest sound	*Adagio* + harmony	subdued rhythm	end

Another contributor to this specialized repertory, Iced imposed a quieter concept on *Adagio* in his remix: "I wanted to take a laid back approach as a lot of the mixes I had heard were all sort of in-your-face tracks; I wanted a more chilled-out track rather than a full-on pumping tune."[89] One distinctive feature of his track is a three-note motive first heard in the bass-line of the introduction, which underscores then the entire mix and functions as a modern-day ground bass.

In addition, both Moldano and Iced alter Barber's first phrase. The former altered the D-flats in the first phrase to D-naturals, inexplicably shifting the mode of the melody from minor to major. Ironically, this restores the mode in Barber's original sketch (see Chapter 3), although

[88]Antonio MilláN, email (15 August 2005) to the author. "Siempre he sentido un especial interés por la astronomía, la carrera espacial, la conquista del espacio; Y cada vez que escuchaba el Adagio for Strings y cerraba los ojos me imaginaba nuevos mundos por explorar. Pensaba en los orígenes del universo y en su creación. Decidí meter ese fragmento de Frank Borman para plasmar en el tema todos esos pensamientos y sensaciones que me produjeron la canción de Samuel Barber. Es una de las melodías más maravillosas de la historia de la música y como tu bien dices representa la luz del mundo." [Translation by Linda M. Willem]

[89]Martin Newstead (Iced), email (23 March 2006) to the author.

Moldano was likely unaware of it. Iced omitted a few notes, maintaining that he shortened it slightly to be different from all the other remixes so that his would be "unique."[90] Example 7.2 shows how Moldano's and Iced's melodies compare to the Barber's theme. Such alterations will come as quite a surprise to the listener who knows the original.

Example 7.2. Alterations to Barber's Melody

Yet another retooling of the work combines Tiësto's *Adagio* with the song "Satellite" by Oceanlab. Stephen Kimble, producer of the remix, must have heard the resemblance between one particular instrumental phrase in the song and the main phrase in Tiësto's mix. This combination consists of an instrumental introduction, followed by a passage of the song that ends with "you pray to me, your lucky star, your singing satellite." It then proceeds into a portion of Tiësto's mix, which starts with the slow Ørbit phrase, moves on to some trance phrases, returns for more of the song, and finishes with additional Tiësto and a brief instrumental coda.[91] The resulting structure is diagrammed in Table 7.6. This song can be used to illustrate *Adagio's* dramatic journey in popular culture: from [1] the original string quartet movement to [2] orchestral *Adagio* to [3] Ørbit's transcription to [4] Tiësto's remix to [5] the Oceanlab song. Would Barber even recognize it?

[90]Martin Newstead (Iced), email (25 March 2006) to the author.

[91]See "Tiesto Vs Oceanlab–Adagio For Satellite 2005 (7th Sin)," *YouTube* (18 August 2008), posted by Kavaliwtis1. This is merely the original soundtrack with a still placard of the title. For videos of the original Oceanlab song, see "OceanLab–Satellite (Official Music Video)," *YouTube* (5 November 2007), posted by armadamusic.

Table 7.6. Approximate Form of Kimble's Remix with "Satellite"

0:00	1:00	2:20	4:00	5:10	6:00-7:49
Intro	Song	Tiësto's *Adagio*	More Song	More Tiësto	Coda

THE SKIP RAIDERS: "ANOTHER DAY"

All the remixes discussed to this point trace their origins to Ørbit's seminal synthesizer transcription, but others can claim a different creative genealogy. Phrases from another synthesized *Adagio for Strings* are heard in the song "Another Day," produced by Tim Ericson and Sandy Nuttgens, the duo known as The Skip Raiders. Nuttgens decided on the name after he overheard a pub conversation about the raiding of "skips," trash bins that people rummage through looking for salvageable computer parts.[92] The term is appropriate not only for this particular partnership but for all musicians, producers, or deejays who raid their material from existing sources, recycling it into newly transformed compositions. It was Ericson who hatched the idea of writing a song with references to Barber's music:

> One night I had the idea of putting the music from *Platoon* [note his cinematic orientation toward *Adagio*] into a kicking dance track. After having a couple of large ones, I was overwhelmed by the power and emotion of the music. I'd never particularly been into classical music and always associated it with being boring and not for me but was struck by the thought that if I could deliver this piece straight onto a dance floor somehow I'd be on to a winner. Soon after this I met Sandy Nuttgens who was instantly sold on the idea and we started . . . working on various versions of the track which became "Another Day."[93]

In June 1999, when Paul Oakenfold heard "Another Day" on the British Green Party election program on BBC radio, he consequently asked the Skip Raiders for permission to add it to an album for his own label. The timing, however, was rather poor because Ørbit's version had just been issued. One reviewer commented:

[92]It is roughly the British equivalent of the American phrase "dumpster diving." Looking up the term "skip raiders" on the Internet might result in references to actual skip raiding.

[93]Tim Ericson, *Skip Raiders,* www.skipraiders.com. Notice the similarity of inspiration with Tony McGuinness for the Ferry Corsten remix, mentioned earlier.

> The Skip Raiders must have been sick when William Ørbit released his *Adagio for Strings* as their version of the classic has been around since last year. The Skip's version is a much tougher beast than Ørbit's though. . . . The Radio Edit is the top mix, it boasts a punchy drum track, there's some excellent quirky 'n' dirty little synth sounds peppered about and Jada does some inspired wailing.[94]

Luke Howard, a scholar who often addresses issues in pop culture, observed that the "Skip Raiders juxtapose the *Adagio* with an intentionally uninflected pop voice singing an intentionally generic text, completely devoid of explicit emotion."[95] Jada (Julie Anne Tully) is the singer who sings the song's banal, periodic, and repetitive lyrics: "It's just another day. Like any other day. Are you going my way?" Diddy had deliberately juxtaposed Agnus Dei with his eulogy for Notorious B.I.G. to produce an emotional effect; this text, fused with *Adagio,* seems to avoid it altogether.

The number of spin-offs of this piece is truly mind-boggling, and I still do not know if I have them all sorted out. But here goes. The original song title is "Skip Raiders Feat. [featuring] Jada Another Day." In 1999 Perfecto Records issued a "demo" LP containing: "Radio Mix" (3:28), "Perfecto Remix" (7:37), "Perfecto Remix Edit" (4:03), "Perfecto Dub" (7:37), and "Perfecto Trance Mix" (11:36). It is logical that the shortest would be the radio mix because stations thrive on short pieces and that the longest would be the trance mix, the one that people can dance to in clubs well into the night. The following year Perfecto produced a compact disc of the album, removing "Perfecto Dub" but adding "Brainbug Remix" (Alberto Bertapelle) (6:13), "Moonchild Remix" (6:41), and "Radio Mix AD 2000" (6:04). Other related projects include "Strings" and "Club Sky Mix."

In 2005 the first minute each of "Radio Mix AD 2000," "Perfecto Remix Edit," and "Brainbug Remix" were audio tracks on the Skip Raiders website. Comparing these excerpts is a good way to understand the concepts and techniques of mixing. Three elements are common to all: (1) Barber's *Adagio,* (2) the text sung by Jada, and (3) some sort of dance beat. The way they are presented, developed, and juxtaposed is different each time, as is evident in Table 7.7. Each mix begins differently; moreover,

[94] *Ibid.*

[95] Luke Howard, "The Popular Reception of *Adagio for Strings,*" *American Music,* 71. Jada was also known as Scarlet when she sang with the Swedish techno-country band, rednex. A brief video clip of her singing her "Just another day" lyrics can be found at "Skip Raiders feat. Jada 'Just Another Day' in Ibiza!," *YouTube* (28 December 2007), posted by klubbeatz.

Table 7.7. Comparisons of the First Minute of Each of the Mixes Posted on the Skip Raiders Website (2005)

Seconds:	:05	:10	:15	:20	:25	:30	:35	:40	:45	:50	:55
RADIO MIX 2000											
Intro Piano	bell-like sound	*Adagio*	"it's just another day"	fadeout of "its just another day"	"it's just another day" returns		"like any other day"	"are you going my way?"			
PERFECTO REMIX EDIT											
Adagio	"it's just" another day" with beat		"it's just another day" fades back in	"like any other day"		"are you going my way" beat begins	(*Adagio*)	much of *Adagio* is reinforced by notes on synthesizer *Adagio* in rhythm			
BRAINBUG REMIX											
beat begins		added ostinato "swooshing sound"	another ostinato "maracas-like"					"it's just another day" *Adagio*			

Jada's first line, the *Adagio* quotation, and the techno beat all are heard at different places in each piece. This can all be realized thanks to today's innovative mixing technology becoming continuously more sophisticated.

"Strings," the simplest of all, may be the original synthesizer track the Skip Raiders produced before they added Jada and the trance beat. Because only an unmixed *Adagio* is present, neither the terms "mix" or "remix" are appropriate. This short version (2:15) presents repetitions of *Adagio*'s first two phrases of Barber, but with interesting twists. In this case, the first chord starts quietly and swells to a full sound, lasting an incredible fifteen seconds all by itself. It ends surprisingly with an extra B-flat minor chord. I noted in Chapter 3 that the second phrase of *Adagio* ends on an F-major chord, the dominant of B-flat minor. This approach supplies the missing tonic chord, the only time that I know of where the insertion of a V - I resolution attempts to solve the "tonality problem."

"Strings" is located on the third compact disc of the Perfecto set *The After Hours*, a time in dance clubs when things slow down and cool off a bit. It is appropriately placed here among other mellow pieces suitable for a "chillout." What is found on Oakenfold's album *Great Wall* (ca. 2:00) consists of a one-minute synthesizer presentation of the first two phrases of *Adagio* followed by another minute with Jada's opening line, "It's just another day," occasionally superimposed on it. Without a trance beat, it may be considered midway between the chillout "Strings" and the fuller dance club versions.[96] The Skip Raiders remained together until 2002, when they decided to go their separate ways.

OTHERS

In 2004 Delerium (Rhyss Fulber and Bill Leeb) issued the album *Chimera*. For the instrumental song "Eternal Odyssey," the two men superimposed on their main track the first two phrases of Agnus Dei, sampled from the recording by the Winchester Cathedral Choir. The phrases first enter about one-third of the way through the song and again about two-thirds of the way, the second time a little louder with a synth sound doubling the melody. Because the jungle-like beat of the song

[96]Oakenfold was so taken with the Skip Raiders original version that he included it twice on his radio program *Urban Soundtracks,* which ran for several years on the Galaxy FM network in Great Britain. Each episode featured a condensed version of a novel, either classic or modern, read by a famous actor, with Oakenfold providing a musical sound track. "Another Day" appeared on episodes #8, Nick Hornby's *Hi Fidelity* (28 August 1999) and #11, Roald Dahl's *Charlie and the Chocolate Factory* (27 November 1999). For a discussion of "Another Day" in the movie *Kevin and Perry Go Large,* see Chapter 8.

does not coincide with the tempo of the choral sample, the two elements coexist in constant flux, creating cross-rhythms, yet seldom interfering with each other. All the parts fall into place, producing a unified whole.

In recent years two electric string quartets, comprised of extremely photogenic young women, have emerged from Great Britain: bond (the name sometimes capitalized, sometimes not) and Escala. Both ensembles champion a similar "electric" sound, and yet their respective approaches to *Adagio for Strings* are greatly different.

The members of bond are classically trained. Their music, despite such a background, is more of a crossover into the dance sounds of the club scene. Their take on *Adagio for Strings* is found on *Classified* (2004), but judging by the sound, one would hardly know that bond was a string quartet: they are totally engulfed by the Royal Philharmonic Orchestra and layers of techno beats. Arranged by the four musicians themselves, plus Martin "Youth" Glover and R. Kerr, their version begins with a synthesized drum track, adds the orchestral *Adagio,* then layers in the beats. As in the remix by Corsten, only the first two phrases of *Adagio* are treated, but unlike most trance versions, there is never a breakdown section in which the Barber portion is presented quietly. The beat just rolls on. Eos Chater, one of bond's violinists, describes the arrangement in the following way:

> William Orbit did a version that is all electronic, this one has live strings so it's a larger sound, and the beat is quite tribal. It's such a powerful piece in its pure form, I think the arrangement works really well. It's like a churning engine. The string parts are very fast, so the piece has real momentum.[97]

Some critics approve of what bond has done to Barber's music, but others are not persuaded. A reviewer for the Dealtime website complained, "During *Adagio for Strings,* I found myself wondering who that idiot was who kept pounding on garbage cans while the musicians were trying to play."[98] Bradley Bambarger considered bond's arrangements a "new set of advertising jingles masquerading as music."[99] In particular, he disputed its

[97]Claire Hill, "Classical Music Star Steals the Attention with 'Museum Piece,'" [Cardiff, Wales] *Western Mail* (11 September 2004), www.icwales.icnetwork.co.uk. The other members of the quartet are Haylie Ecker, violin; Tania Davis, viola; and Gay-Yee Westeroff, cello.

[98]Tesseract, "Bond Find a New Sound–More Fusion, Less Confusion," *DealTime* (16 November 2004), www.dealtime.com/xPR-Classified_Bond_Pop-RD-161936936580.

[99]Bradley Bambarger, "Cultivating the Classical Crossover," [Newark, N.J.] *Star-Ledger* (1 November 2004).

version of *Adagio:* "the pre-eminent music of American mourning overlaid with a jungle-kitsch rhythm track?"[100] And yet bond's *Adagio* is not far removed from other pop versions.

Escala, referred to by one reviewer as "an infinitely more musically talented Spice Girls," performs an *Adagio* that represents an extreme contrast to bond's on its eponymously named album (2009).[101] The arrangement by Chris Elliot is much closer to the original, consisting entirely of Barber's phrases in his designated adagio tempo. The length is only a little over four minutes because the second half of the viola statement is omitted and the performance ends surprisingly after the quiet chords. Is this better or worse than ending on the final F-flat major chord of the climax? If the theory that the work is cast in an F-Phrygian mode (see Chapter 3) is taken seriously, then the F-major chord at the close of the passage is just as logical as the same one at the very end. Yet some listeners who know the original must surely have a feeling of unfinished business.

Unlike bond's vigorous trance-like rendition, Escala's is much closer to the model: quiet and understated. The only intrusion is an unexpected and superfluous drum beat during the climax. Whereas bond's string sound is completely swallowed up by the orchestra, Escala's strings usually stand out in a soloistic manner from an accompaniment supplied by either a live orchestra or electronically enhanced lines by other members of the quartet. For instance, at the beginning a solo violin plays the melody, with the lower parts being delivered by the orchestra. Later, when the cello carries the melody, it is played as a solo, while the orchestra plays the upper parts. Most significant, however, is the viola statement (first two phrases only) that now stands out as a true melody, one of the few times in any performance or recording that it does not recede into the overall texture.

IL DIVO'S "DOV'È L'AMORE"

All of the pop arrangements of *Adagio for Strings* described up to this point either incorporate portions of the Barber "tune" as an instrumental feature or borrow phrases from the Agnus Dei as a choral trope. No one —except the composer himself—has actually added words to *Adagio*'s

[100]*Ibid.*

[101]Jane Gordon, "Escala Exclusive: The Bow Belles Electrify America," *Mail Online* (19 May 2009), www.dailymail.co.uk. The author's comparison is based on the view by the group's tour manager Paul Higgins. The members of Escala are Victoria Lyon and Izzy Johnston, violins; Chantal Leverton, viola; and Tasya Hodges, cello. The group's debut album, closing with "Adagio," is simply called *Escala* (2009).

melodic phrases, that is, not until recently. The lack of a vocal version of *Adagio* was rather unusual, given the fact that two other famous adagios, the so-called Albinoni Adagio and the slow movement from Joaquin Rodrigo's guitar *Concierto de Aranjuez* (1939), have both been given lyrics (in various languages) and, in the process, have been transformed into popular songs. Now, it was Barber's turn.

Il Divo is an operatic pop ("popera") vocal group, specializing in what might be considered crossover song arrangements. The unit is truly international in its make-up: Spanish baritone Carlos Marin, Swiss tenor Urs Bühler, American tenor David Miller, and French singer Sébastien Izambard. For their album *Wicked Game* (2011), songwriters and arrangers Marco Marinangeli and Savan Kotecha created a passionate Italian love song, "Dov'è l'amore," out of passages from Barber's *Adagio for Strings.*[102] Marinangeli considered it probably his most interesting adaptation for the album; he professes to be "a big fan" of Barber.[103] The new words capture two of *Adagio*'s rather conflicting moods: love and loss. The first line sets up the lamentation: "where is love, where is the passion?" Before the album was issued, the group premièred the song at the UK Artist of the Decade award show. Critiques of that performance were generally favorable, as were reviews of the recording released later.

The song is organized in two distinct sections, separated by a clear orchestral phrase borrowed from Barber. Yet the form is not quite the same as the original. Barber's piece takes a single long time-span to arrive at the climax, whereas the Il Divo song reaches its climax twice, each time arriving at the same high pitch. Yet there are similarities. The song begins much the same way as *Adagio,* with the first vocal phrases coinciding rather closely with Barber's opening musical lines. But then the music veers off into totally new but compatible territory for the song's most climactic phrases: "you spoke to me in song, now I speak in tears" [*mi parlavi col canto, ora parlo col pianto*]. More importantly, however, the arrangement matches Barber's original Fibonacci design. For the main climax of the string quartet movement (and *Adagio*), Barber had stretched his classical phi point to a more extended 72%, which coincides exactly with the climactic point reached in the second half of the song. Both pieces conclude, moreover, with the same calm Mahleresque coda.

[102]This song is not to be confused with one with the same Italian title made famous a decade earlier by Cher nor with the quartet's earlier "Adagio," a vocal version of the Albinoni-Giazotto composition.

[103]Marco Marinangeli, quoted in Simone Sello, "Marco Marinangeli: Grammy-nominated Italian Composer," *Ganzo* (18 October 2011), www.ganzomag.com/marco-marinangeli-italian-composer-usa.html.

During this passage the initial question, "Where is love?" is quietly reiterated. In its serene resignation the text is nearly as appropriate as the hypothetical "amen" that I suggested earlier (see Chapter 3).

ADDENDUM: PAUL MCCARTNEY—A PIANO STAB AT *ADAGIO*?

"The Beatles were a mess in 1968 and early 1969, working together in a shaky truce," contended *Rolling Stone* columnist David Fricke.[104] On 3 January 1969, at the start of the "Get Back" sessions at Twickenham Studios, Paul McCartney was playing the piano while waiting for the others to arrive. Beatles authorities, Doug Sulpy and Ray Scheighardt, have claimed that he was attempting to improvise on Barber's *Adagio for Strings*.[105] Fricke agrees that the first thing McCartney played was a "solo piano stab" at *Adagio*.[106]

The three takes of Paul's improvisations, recorded on the 3rd, 8th and 10th of the month, are often referred to as "Paul's Piano Intro," "Paul's Piano Theme," or "Paul's Piano Piece," respectively. Frankly, I think that they only superficially resemble *Adagio*. The one on *Let it Be. . . Naked* (2003), the first on the "Fly on the Wall" bonus disc, sounds "classical" and displays a few harmonies reminiscent of Barber's opening phrase and a melody that winds around diatonically, but it could just be an unrelated, free improvisation. Luke Howard concurs: "the tracks in question bear little compelling similarity to Barber's *Adagio*."[107] Besides, is it likely that McCartney, especially as early as 1969, would have been familiar with this American composer's music? It was confined mainly to recordings and concert hall performances and had yet to surface in movies or in pop arrangements. Despite these misgivings, the Barber attribution persists. Maybe we should come together. Such speculation could take us down a long and winding road. Perhaps we can get back to this at another time; so for the moment we probably should just let it be.[108]

[104]David Fricke, "Buried Treasure: The Full Story behind the Beatles Album That Never Was," *Rolling Stone* CMXVI (20 February 2003).

[105]Doug Sulpy and Ray Scheighardt, *Get Back: The Unauthorized Chronicle of the Beatles' "Let It Be" Disaster* (New York: St. Martin, 1994), 26.

[106]David Fricke, "Buried Treasure," *Rolling Stone* CMXVI.

[107]Luke Howard, "The Popular Reception of *Adagio for Strings*," *American Music*, 65.

[108]The documentary *Let It Be* (1970) opens with Paul's first improvisation. A bearded Paul plays the piano while a bearded Ringo listens. A beardless George joins them. Because this film has not been officially available since the 1980s, only bootleg versions occasionally appear on *YouTube*.

All That Jazz

While the preceding Barber borrowings are clearly grounded in a pop music tradition, others are closer to jazz, although these days it is harder to make such a distinction. Several jazz musicians—especially guitarists—have arranged *Adagio for Strings* but have seldom added any obvious jazz-like features, such as a hot rhythm or blues harmonies. Their re-creations, usually intended as a respite from other more traditional jazz pieces in a recorded set, range from relatively straightforward performances to barely recognizable improvisations on the tune or the opening chords.

GUITAR SOLOS AND VARIOUS DUOS

In 1995 Glenn Alexander, jazz guitarist and teacher at Wichita State University, issued an album *Oria,* named for his daughter and meaning "golden" and "dawning." *Jazz Times* contributor Bill Milkowski called the collection his "most heartfelt expression to date," containing an "astonishing rendition" of *Adagio for Strings* and considers *Oria* a change from Alexander's earlier "slash-burn" days when he was a "solid body Strat strangler who went for the fretboard burn in a firebreathing fusion context."[109] Compared to that, his treatment of the Barber work is bound to be a total contrast.

Alexander became first acquainted with *Adagio* when a musician friend "turned him on" to the Ormandy recording with the Philadelphia Orchestra. He also heard it in a documentary about the JFK assassination and, of course, in *Platoon*. In his opinion, "the piece is so incredible to me and simply moves me, sometimes to tears, with its extraordinary beauty. It is one of the most beautiful pieces of music I've ever heard in my life."[110] He then decided to adapt the piece for guitar:

> When I was recording *Oria,* I wanted to do a solo piece in the classical idiom but A: felt Nylon had been recorded so much and is not my forte and B: I have this pretty unique thing of playing with electric guitar with a long reverb and a volume pedal so there is no attack on the notes and they just ooze out. So I thought that it would be pretty darned unique and different to record [*Adagio*] that way.[111]

[109]Bill Milkowski, "Departure Point: Glenn Alexander," *Jazz Times* (August 1996), 25.

[110]Glenn Alexander, email (28 June 2004) to the author.

[111]*Ibid.*

Alexander fashioned his version directly from the string quartet and recorded it "live" on solo electric guitar with no additional synthesizer sounds or overdubbing, a fact many listeners might not realize. He admits that when "most people hear it they think it's a guitar synth or layered, overdubbed guitars."[112] To contribute to the effect, he had to tune the low E string down to C in order to cover the range. "In sustained parts I blew on the strings, causing them to vibrate and, coupled with the reverb, it gives it the illusion of bowed strings."[113] *Adagio*'s position in the middle of the album is quite a contrast to the jazz sound of all the other pieces in the collection. Alexander confessed, "It was probably the hardest thing I've ever recorded. I only hope that Samuel isn't rolling over in his grave."[114] If the trance versions of *Adagio* did not cause rumblings in the composer's grave, I doubt that this relaxed one would cause even a minor tremor.[115]

Although much of Larry Coryell's recording *American Odyssey* (1990) consists of Ryuta Suzuki's solo guitar arrangements of classical favorites, her instrumentation of *Adagio for Strings* is scored for saxophone solo and acoustic guitar accompaniment. For the most part, jazz icon Wayne Shorter plays the melody on soprano sax, but when the top part rests or when it does not present the main melody, Coryell plays it on guitar. In order to intensify the climax, he resorts to a few tremolos. The quiet chord passage after the climax is particularly effective here because the sax drops out, leaving only Coryell's smooth, mellow guitar sound. This also allows Shorter time to switch from soprano to tenor sax for the coda, a pleasant contrast to the sound dominating the rest of the piece. The tenor sax seems able to convey an even more melancholy mood than the soprano. Coryell conceded that this recording session was one of the most challenging he ever did; in fact, Shorter was initially reluctant to do it.[116] Nevertheless, their collaboration resulted in a seemingly effortless and poignant presentation of *Adagio*.

According to reviewer Darren Scott, Steve Trovato transformed *Adagio for Strings* into a "guitar symphony" on *About Time* (2002), "overall a very

[112]*Ibid.*

[113]*Ibid.*

[114]*Ibid.*

[115]For a photograph of the actual tombstone see Chapter 10, page 441. It looks quite secure.

[116]Larry Coryell, conversation (31 January 2005) with the author.

powerful recording."[117] The critic characterized Trovato as "the great Chameleon" for his ability to mold his style to each piece of music he performs. Some commentators acknowledged that, if they did not know better, they might think a different guitarist was performing each piece. Trovato likes the challenge of adapting to different types of music:

> So many people draw a big thick line between country, rock, blues, classical, jazz, or whatever. I think music is music. Music is an expression of a personality and a feeling. Once you get to the place where, hopefully, you can inspire people to feel something—smile, laugh, cry, or whatever—then styles don't matter any more.[118]

Hearing *Adagio for Strings* in *Platoon* gave him goosebumps: "it was so moving and sad."[119] Trovato made his first trial recording of Barber's piece with the EBow®, a hand-held electronic bow for the guitar used by many rock musicians since the mid-1970s.[120] It produces an energy field that vibrates and sustains the guitar strings, allowing them to mimic Barber's orchestral sound.

To begin with, Trovato recorded each track with the device (on his Roland GR-30 Guitar Synth), but the result was unsatisfactory:

> I played it back and it sounded like a gigantic kazoo orchestra. It sounded terrible. So I borrowed a guitar synth to replace some of the E-bow parts. I had to EQ the violin and cello patches to sound authentic. I had to add the vibrato because the synth doesn't automatically do that. . . . Then I started recording the whole song from top down. If the melody was on the violin, I'd record that part first then add five violas, cellos and double basses. The second or third time through, the melody appears on the cello, so I recorded that first and added the violas and double

[117]Darren Scott, "Steve Trovato, the Great Chameleon," *Tune-up Magazine* (February 2002), www.stevetrovato.com/reviews.htm.

[118]Steve Trovato, quoted in Jim Walk, "Steve Trovato Interview–Part 2" *AFG Sound Hole* 15 (Fall 2002), www.social.rr.com/felten michelle/trovato2.htm. AFG is the acronym for the Association of Fingerstyle Guitarists.

[119]*Ibid.*

[120]Thanks to Frank Felice for supplying me information about the Ebow.

> basses underneath. It took me about three months to record that thing.[121]

The result is truly distinctive. Most listeners would have no idea which instruments (or synthesizers) are playing the piece. One unusual aspect of the performance is Trovato's phrasing. On most phrases he unexpectedly pauses (*à la* Mahler) before the final chord, *e.g.,* before the A-flat chord in the fourth measure. The climb to the climax is gentle rather than dramatic, but as with other performers he ends on the F-flat chord, leaving the listener up in the air, not only for this piece but, because it is the final track, for the entire album.

Trovato is pleased with the critical acclaim the album has received: "I'm so proud of it. It came out well. I listen to it sometimes and say, 'Wow, is that me?'"[122] John Heidt, critic for *Vintage Guitar Magazine* registered praise in an unequivocal manner: "Yikes! Talk about your chops, Steve Trovato's got 'em."[123]

IMPROVISING ON *ADAGIO*

Adagio for Strings is one of several "classical" pieces that Danney Alkana subjects to a modern interpretation with an improvisation for synthesizer and electric guitar on *Rock the Bach* (1999).[124] He grew up listening to both classical and popular music, but after the Beatles came along he "got lost in pop music"; nevertheless, he never totally forgot classical music: "It's just something that's part of me."[125] On this album he fused these two musical interests:

> My intentions are to promote the Masters to a listener who may never have been exposed to classical music otherwise. For the rocker, my greatest desire and hope is that you wear out the CD, experience many hours of enjoyment, and want to hear more. If so, I will be there."[126]

[121]Steve Trovato, quoted in Jim Walk, "Steve Trovato Interview," *AFG Sound Hole* 15 (Fall 2002).

[122]*Ibid.*

[123]John Heidt, "Review: Steve Trovato's About Time," *Vintage Guitar Magazine* (January 2002), www.cdbaby.com/cd/trovato.

[124]Despite the title, only one Bach piece is found on the album.

[125]Danney Alkana, quoted in Steve Robles, *San Bernadino Sun* (2004); reprinted www.fourwinds-music.com/html/danney.htm.

Phrases from Barber's original, played on a synthesizer, hover in the background, often obscured by "nature sounds" probably also produced on a synthesizer. On top of this Alkana improvises on his guitar and either reinforces phrases from *Adagio* or adds short jazz-style riffs, imparting an otherworldly quality to the mixture.

On his album *sh* (1999) Steve Hahn improvises on *Adagio for Strings* on an instrument known as the Chapman Stick®, a kind of amalgamation of a double bass and a guitar invented by Emmett Chapman in 1969. The large number of strings (ten to twelve) may be tuned in different ways, but the bass side is usually ordered in fifths and the guitar side, in fourths. The performer does not pluck or strum the strings but merely taps them allowing both hands to produce various sounds—melody, harmony, and bass line all at the same time. Many bassists or guitarists have become proficient on the new instrument. Hahn started playing it in 1989 and studied with Chapman in 1991 and 1992. Since then he has become known as one of the instrument's foremost practitioners.

Hahn begins his "Adagio" with the final segment of Barber's coda but then improvises entirely on the opening E-flat minor seventh chord. Some of the phrases reference Barber's melody while others go far astray. The harmony desperately wants to resolve to F-major but never does, not even at the end. The final track on the disc, "sh," however, could be considered its resolution. Phrases within that particular track often resemble those in *Adagio,* especially the four-note Mahleresque cadence. Chapman himself commented that the album "has a live improvised flow, one idea seems to spawn the next."[127] Quite possibly, "Adagio" transforms into "sh." Yet even this piece—and indeed the entire album—ends with a sense of suspension. Fellow Stick-player Ray Ashley described this improvisation as "moving" and "elegiac."[128]

Jazz flutist Holly Hofmann and pianist Mike Wofford, her husband, often perform together as a jazz duo. For *Live at Athenaeum Jazz, Vol. 2* (2007) Hofmann treated the fragment from *Adagio for Strings* shown in Example 7.3 as a "springboard" for "Free Day (for Samuel Barber)."[129] The gesture is basically the ending of the first phrase minus two notes (those

[126]*Ibid.*, and Randy Krbechek, "Weekly Reviews of CDs and New Albums," *CD Shakedown* (1999), www.cdshakedown.com/Indie_Reviews/rockthebach.htm.

[127]Emmett Chapman, *Sticknews Digest* 20 (October 1998); reprinted www.deepchocolate.com/crits.htm.

[128]Ray Ashley, "Hey Stickwire Folks," *Stickwire* (July 1998); reprinted www.deepchocolate.com/reviews.htm. There is a representative picture of Hahn holding his Stick in the liner notes.

[129]This was performed at the Athenaeum Music and Arts Library in La Jolla, Calif.

with the bracket). The flute introduces this unaccompanied theme. Once the piano joins in, the two musicians improvise on the fragment, at times changing intervals, but usually preserving the tune's "winding around" profile. In the middle of the piece and in the spirit of a jazz development section the piano gradually adds a pulse, and the flute improvisations become more elaborate. Near the end both instruments return to a more recognizable form of the melody. Hofmann avers that she and Wofford have always admired Barber and dedicated the piece to him, as is apparent from the full title. Hofmann explained that their duet was inspired by *Adagio* but is not an arrangement:

> My little piece was based on my deep respect for the way Barber weaves a motif throughout an entire composition. *Free Day* was an experiment in taking a small Barber melodic fragment and developing it without assigning a traditional song form. Some of Barber's writing is improvisatory in nature, and my piece is a free improvisation based on my feeling when listening to his music.[130]

The result is a Barber-inspired but independently designed jazz creation.

Example 7.3. Comparison of Hofmann's Melodic Fragment to Barber's

TWO BANDS AND A COOL COMBO

Adagio for Strings has also been scored for jazz band or jazz combo. The Liberation Music Orchestra, a large jazz ensemble known for the leftist political orientation of its members and initially led by bass player Charlie Haden, has occasionally played Carla Bley's arrangement, which was disseminated on its *Not in Our Name* album (2005). Bley, the group's pianist and current leader, conceived the notion to arrange the Barber piece when she recalled seeing the dead bodies in the film *Platoon* and hearing a list of names read on television of soldiers who had died in Iraq.

[130]Holly Hofmann, email (14 May 2012) to the author.

For her, the work "represents the sadness of people dying for political reasons."[131] In fact, critic John Henry thought that her arrangement "seems like a funeral dirge for all those who have died in Iraq—and not just our soldiers."[132] Haden confessed: "I was a little bit afraid of the Adagio because Samuel Barber's composition with string orchestra is so delicate that you really have to play it precisely and in tune. But everybody did great. And the arrangement is so great. . . ."[133]

The performance is fairly "straight," without Bley's usual lush piano chords, Matt Wilson's drums, or any jazz improvisations. The main hint of jazz is Haden's pizzicato punctuation heard periodically (quite often unexpectedly) throughout the piece. Various instruments take the melody: trumpets at the beginning, followed by horn, trombone, and tenor sax. In the coda the melody is doubled by trumpet and horn.

Critical reviews have been generally favorable but with reservations. For instance, Andrew Gilbert described it as "lush and compelling, but in this context it seems manipulative, more agitprop than art, though the piece's undeniable impact speaks to [Bley's] uncommon gift."[134] John Henry observed that "occasionally Bley's voicings for the band make it sound like a little revolutionary marching band in some South American country, and I'm sure that is quite intentional.[135] Another critic referred to it as a "close enough for jazz" performance, making it "all the more moving" in its roughness.[136] Frankly, in the context of the other pieces on the album, I think the *Adagio* performance is shaky, just barely holding together. The group seems out of its element here.

Jazz musician Gary Urwin recently formed an all-star jazz orchestra. For *Living in the Moment* (2003) he incorporated passages from *Adagio for Strings* into his arrangement of Billy Strayhorn's incredibly gorgeous classic popular song, "Lush Life" (1933-1938). The combination of jazz and classical idioms shows his desire to push boundaries: "I was looking

[131]Dan Ouellette, "Maybe We Should Take Machine Guns Out and Shoot Everyone in the Audience: Charlie Haden and Carla Bley Take the Offensive with the Liberation Music Orchestra,'" *Downbeat* LXXIII/1 (January 2006), 42-45.

[132]John Henry, "Charlie Haden Liberation Orchestra–Not In Our Name–Verve," *Audiophile Audition* (18 December 2005), www.audaud.com/2005/12/charlie-haden-liberation-music-orchestra-not-in-our-name-verve/.

[133]Charlie Haden, "Biography," *The Verve Music Group*, www.vervemusicgroup.com/charliehaden/bio/.

[134]Andrew Gilbert, "A Jazz Orchestra Meant to Liberate," *San Francisco Chronicle* (4 December 2005).

[135]John Henry, "Charlie Haden Liberation Orchestra," *Audiophile Audition.*

[136]"CD Listing Post / Brief Reviews of Select Releases," *Buffalo News* (21 August 2005), G: 3.

for depth, substance and fun. I also wanted to take chances, sometimes writing as close to the edge as makes musical sense."[137]

Table 7.8 reveals the pattern of integration of Barber's music into the Strayhorn song. The introduction consists of passages from the final phrases of "Lush Life," followed by the first *Adagio* insertion (Adagio 1). The song's verse then occurs, up to the point where a vocal rendition would deliver the phrase, "I thought for a while that your poignant smile was tinged with the sadness of a great love for me." This is a perfect place for Adagio 2 to interrupt the verse. Although lyrics are not sung in this arrangement, those who know the song should remember the words and make an appropriate emotional connection with the Barber quotation. After the verse, the chorus of the song comes in, repeated with jazz improvisations and cadenzas for flute and saxophone. For the song's final phrase (to the text "of those whose lives are lonely, too"), the tempo is somewhat relaxed and leads into Adagio 3 (end of the coda), summing up and coalescing the sadness of both pieces. (Urwin's arrangement of "Lush Life" exhibits a seemingly cheerful up-tempo, and yet its inherent sadness is still communicated.) Urwin considers both "Lush Life" and *Adagio* to be classics "from very different modes of music, but in a more fundamental way I felt that they have similar emotional content. I tried to integrate them in a way that works with this instrumentation and within this idiom."[138] Listeners who love the song or the Barber composition, or both, are likely to be intrigued and moved by this ingenious amalgamation.

CD Track 12

Larry McDonough, a jazz musician (and law school professor) in the Minneapolis-St. Paul area, has arranged *Adagio for Strings* for his small jazz combo Off Beat. "I always loved it, even before it became more widely known in *Platoon* and *Elephant Man.*"[139] While his piano style has a hint of Dave Brubeck, his *Adagio* arrangement reminds many listeners of the cool jazz of the Modern Jazz Quartet:

> I started playing a solo piano version a few years ago, playing it fairly straight. When I started to improvise over it, my ideas were similar to John Lewis, so I decided to try it out for the group, which

[137]Gary Urwin, liner notes to *Living for the Moment*, perf. Gary Urwin Jazz Orchestra (Sea Breeze, 2123, 2003).

[138]*Ibid.*

[139]Larry McDonough, email (8 November 2004) to the author.

already had a MJQ sound. The harmonies have a jazz quality to them, similar to Miles Davis and Bill Evans.[140]

At the beginning, trumpet and saxophone play the melody, while block chords on the piano, a bowed bass, and drums with brushes provide the accompaniment. Throughout the rest of the piece, the piano provides the harmonies while the trumpet, saxophone, bass (pizzicato), and piano take turns improvising on the melody. A recording of this arrangement was made into a compact disc demo *Larry McDonough and Off Beat: Live, Cooking at the Dakota* (2002). Because it was live, the performance was, in McDonough's words, "a little rough"; the product was never commercially released. Yet audiences have responded well to his performances, and he hopes one day to do a studio recording. In the meantime, he still experiments with the Barber work.

Table 7.8. Urwin's Synthesis of *Adagio for Strings* and Strayhorn's "Lush Life"

0:00	ca. 0:45	1:10	ca. 2:15	2:45	4:00
Intro	Adagio 1 mm. 1-8	Lush Life most of verse	Adagio 2 mm. 8-19	Lush Life last phrase of verse plus chorus	chorus improv

5:10	6:05	8:00	8:30	9:00
flute cadenza	verse most of chorus	saxophone cadenza	end of chorus	Adagio 3 (coda) mm. 67-69

For a New Age

If a number of these appropriations of *Adagio for Strings* seem close to the New Age concept, such an assessment may not be far off the mark. Some albums with this piece are marketed to promote the music's ethereal or spiritual aspect rather than its intense sadness or tragic ambiance. One packaging ploy places a traditional orchestral performance of *Adagio*, without any changes, in a collection with other quiet pieces. For instance, *Shadows and Light: Ambient Music from Another Time* (1995) features Bernstein's performance of Barber with the Los Angeles Philharmonic,

[140]*Ibid.*

along with Beethoven, Mahler, and Elgar. The concept and compilation is credited to R. Peter Munves. In the liner notes John Dilberto rhapsodizes, "with [*Adagio*'s] rising chord progression and shimmering strings, I could see it as dawn breaking off the Atlantic, the slow motion flight of a hawk or a deep inward journey towards revelation."[141] He has clearly—and blatantly—put a New Age spin on *Adagio*.

Another approach is to ask arrangers to turn *Adagio* into an essentially new work, often with different instruments, making cuts where they deem appropriate and, perhaps, adding ambient sounds at strategic places. For his album *Number Our Days* (1999) Chris Snidow produced several original electronic pieces but also contributed an interpretation of *Adagio for Strings*. He had been "deeply enchanted" with it ever since he first heard it in *Platoon:* "I have always found it one of the most moving, evocative, and beautiful pieces written."[142] Calling his music "Biblical Sound Pictures," he hopes to "connect people in some more abstract way to the Bible. It is designed for meditation, prayer and relaxation."[143] While the album may not be exclusively aimed at New Age listeners, that audience seems a likely target. Philosophy, religion, meditation, and music converge in this New Age. His interpretation begins with an amorphous, synthesized sound from which the opening B-flat of *Adagio*'s first phrase gradually emerges. Changes from the original are minimal: a different bass pitch, a change of harmony (which may startle fans of the orchestral version), and a new countermelody. His arrangement stops abruptly after the climax. Despite the controversial ending, his synthesizer sound, to me, seems richer, fuller, and warmer than William Ørbit's.

Serenata (1999), one of three releases in the compact disc set *The Quantic Nature Collection*, is billed as "a relaxing, harmonious union of classical music and the gentle sounds of nature." In fact "water music" permeates the entire album, sounding variously like a flowing stream, a waterfall, and ocean waves. Composer-pianist Alain Lemay played *Adagio for Strings* on a "sample library,"[144] producing a tasteful rendition with "little tampering of sound or texture."[145] He related, "I worked hard to

[141]John Dilberto, liner notes to *Shadows and Light: Ambient Music from Another Time* (Deutsche Grammophon, G2-45922, 1995).

[142]Chris Snidow, email (2 November 2004) to the author.

[143]*Ibid.*

[144]This concept is well explained under "Sample library," *Wikipedia*, www.en.wikipedia.org/wiki /Sample_library.

[145]Alain Lemay, email (10 July 2012) to the author. Lemay is the director of Quantic Éditions.

give the illusion of a real orchestra."[146] Waterfall sounds appear through the whole piece, temporarily reduced to a trickle during the "cello" statement. The only major change occurs during the climactic section; because this is a "relaxing" album the music gets quieter as the melodic line rises, and as a result, the quiet chord passage is actually slightly louder than the climatic phrase! After the coda about a minute of water music and bird chirping function as a transition into the next piece. Relating his own view of the Barber work, Lemay added, "*Adagio* has a special, powerful energy hidden within the music."[147] He undoubtedly sought to reveal some of that hidden energy in his performance.

Windham Hill, the quintessential practitioner and virtual founder of New Age music, has produced the album *Adagio: A Windham Hill Collection* (2003) devoted to slow movements by classical masters such as J. S. Bach, Charles Gounod, and Edvard Grieg, but now transformed into New Age clones. Philip Aaberg arranged Barber's *Adagio for Strings* for acoustic piano and synthesizer. In the liner notes radio commentator John Schaefer observed that "Aaberg's solo piano reading of the piece avoids the melodrama of the big orchestral version, and looks back to the intimacy and the quiet emotion of the original string quartet version."[148] Aaberg clearly has great respect for the original:

> I've always heard a certain innocence and naïveté in Barber's music that is greatly appealing. I've read far too many reviews that call *Adagio* "maudlin." To me, it is one of the rare pieces of "authentic," or "inspired" music. It's also extremely well crafted; it is so well written that it really plays itself.[149]

In his album notes he further commented, "I love it because it is simple and emotionally direct, while complex enough to be enduring. . . . My own love of the under-used sustaining qualities of the piano gave me the courage to try it."[150]

[146]*Ibid.*

[147]*Ibid.*

[148]John A. Schaefer, liner notes to *Adagio: A Windham Hill Collection* (Windham Hill Records, 11648, 2003).

[149]Philip Aaberg, email (7 June 2004) to the author.

[150]*Ibid.*

Aaberg's arrangement begins with a piano solo, but by the second phrase he adds synthesized sounds, which continue through the climax. There they are necessary to sustain the sound; the piano chords simply decay too quickly. The performance lasts only six minutes, not due to any cuts, but because he moves the piece along briskly. As part of his piano style, he uses a great deal of pedaling and extensive rubato in his phrasing. The atmosphere suggests a Chopin nocturne. He, however, prefers to think of it as an elegy. He confided, "The difficulty in performing the piece is avoiding a too-emotional involvement while playing."[151] Indeed, he demonstrates admirable restraint by avoiding a rhythm section or other New Age bells and whistles so prevalent in his colleagues' derivatives on the remainder of the album (*e.g.*, David Benoit's jazz improvisation in the middle of a Brahms *Intermezzo*). According to the album notes: "with performances of some of the most beautiful melodies by some of Windham Hill's finest musicians, *Adagio* is the perfect lifestyle album. Whether setting the mood for relaxing, dining or a quiet moment, *Adagio* is the ultimate soundtrack to free the mind."[152] Such a statement makes it clear that the music on the recording is aimed at the New Age listener.

The Taliesin Orchestra (named for the eleventh-century Celtic poet, not Frank Lloyd Wright's home in Spring Green, Wisconsin) was created by Trammell Starks, who arranged the music, played the keyboard, and produced the album. Therapist Shari Sorbo asserted that the group's *Sacred* (2002) communicates

> respect for the greatness of time honored songs, yet involving an upbeat tone that embraces all ages of listeners. Each track invites the listener to journey deeper into his or her own soul. Bringing together flavorful combinations of music, chanting, strings, and piano. *Adagio for Strings* is included in this eclectic mix of celestial songs. *Sacred* is a whole body, mind and soul experience.[153]

The principal sound is that of synthesized strings with a breathy "ooh-ooh" chorus singing the melody, which may be the overdubbed voice of one of the producers, Felicia Starks. Entitled the "main theme from *Adagio for*

[151]*Ibid.*

[152]John A. Schaefer, liner notes to *Adagio: A Windham Hill Collection* (2003).

[153]Shari Sorbo, "Media Reviews: Sacred," *Science of Mind* (October 2002), www.scienceofmind.com/archive_review_links/media_october02.html.

Strings," the arrangement consists of only the initial two phrases plus the coda. The whole piece lasts only three minutes, but the first phrase alone takes over a minute, rivaling the slow tempo of Bernstein's recordings. This condensation also avoids the all too jarring climactic section, which would interfere with the transcendental state intended for the New Age listener. As the last chord fades away, some unexpected and "extraneous sounds" are added.[154] In a poll taken by Sky.fm in 2005, an Internet radio network, listeners rated the arrangement highly:

Table 7.9. Sky.fm Poll of Listener Opinions of *Adagio for Strings* (2005)[155]

COMMENT	VOTES	PERCENTAGE
Simply amazing	50	83.33%
Very good	6	10.00%
Decent	1	1.66%
Pretty bad	1	1.66%
No thanks, not my style!	2	3.33%

The Brave (German-born Claus or Klaus Zundel) produced the quasi-liturgical *Classical Spirit* (2003) that combines an arrangement of *Adagio for Strings* with a sampling of sacred Russian choral music. Juxtaposing two such diverse musical sources is the basis of much of his composing. He explained, "I go shopping around the world for the finest musical ingredients from the most exciting musical centers. Then I bring them home to create the best fusion of sound."[156] The album, defined as "chill-out music," implicitly belongs in the New Age category confirmed by the record company's mission statement: "we believe there is a place within us all . . . of vision and clarity where the rhythm of life moves in harmony with a higher consciousness, the purpose of our music is to take you there."[157] As album annotator Anthony Head reflected, "Barber's *Adagio*

154 "Main Theme from Adagio for Strings," *YouTube* (25 April 2009), posted by Rivka92.

155 www.forums.sky.fm/showthread.php?t=8422. An amateur videographer has used the Taliesin arrangement as background for the final scenes of the Schwarzenegger movie, *Terminator 2*. See "Taliesin Orchestra-Adagio for Strings," *YouTube* (11 March 2007), posted by drybeverage.

156 Claus Zundel, quoted in Anthony Head, liner notes to *Classical Spirit* (Higher Octave Music, 13138, 2003).

157 Neil Horner, "Classical Spirit–The Brave [NH]: Classical CD Reviews–June 2003 MusicWeb (UK)," *Music Web International* (July 2003), www.musicwebinternational.com/classRev/2003/July03/Classical_Spirit.htm.

becomes haunting and beautiful at the same time, with cathedral organ and muted synths in celestial conversation."[158] This is a rhapsodic but apt description of the effect, but was not this music always "haunting and beautiful"?

The five-minute piece is cast in A B A B′ form, with the two A sections consisting of the first two phrases of *Adagio* either played on a pipe organ or a convincing synthesized facsimile. The B sections are taken from an unidentified Russian choral composition.[159] The Brave's artful concoction illustrates his "fusion of sound" because the first four notes of the choral piece are identical to the beginning four notes of the Barber melody. One reviewer, however, was perturbed that a few "cheesy electronic beeps and clicks" intrude, sounding like "R2D2 chirping away."[160] As the last chords of the Russian anthem come to a close, the breathy voice of Susann Caroll, reading from her own poetry, intones: "Leave me to myselfs [*sic*] I'll sit and fade away / 'til I'm nothing but a spirit and I lose this form of clay." The Brave justified his approach: "If these artists lived now, they would want a fresh sound; they would want their music to speak to all cultures with a contemporary appeal."[161] While some may doubt this, his arrangement is likely to appeal to contemporary listeners.[162]

Where Does It Belong?

My survey provides ample evidence that Barber's music has been manipulated by a host of dedicated secondary agents for their own gratification and, in the process, ideas first heard in his string quartet movement of 1936 have been disseminated to millions of music lovers who might have remained untouched by his work unless they were avid fans of the cinema. To end this discussion, I call attention to a French musician known as Direct to Dreams (Bruno Meunier). He has "doubled-down" on the well-traveled approach by incorporating excerpts from both *Adagio for Strings* and Agnus Dei into an arrangement called "Adagio for Strings Barber Remix" (2009). In this four-minute work he presents the first two phrases (about one minute each) basically in alternation in the order: (A) Agnus Dei; (A) Agnus Dei; (B) *Adagio for Strings*; (A)

[158]Anthony Head, liner notes to *Classical Spirit* (2003).

[159]Unfortunately, in his liner notes, The Brave does not list any titles of his borrowed Russian samples.

[160]"Interesting But Leaves Something to be Desired," *Amazon.com* (16 April 2004), posted by xpogi.

[161]Claus Zundel, quoted in Anthony Head, liner notes to *Classical Spirit* (2003).

[162]Other recordings with a New Age orientation containing *Adagio* are identified in Appendix 7.

Agnus Dei. Into these excerpts he blends a rhythmic pulse too mild to be considered trance or techno, but more than a "chill-out" or a simple rhythmic accompaniment. In some respects, it sounds like a combination of a watered-down trance and an unobtrusive New Age sound. His creation conforms reasonably well to the description of ambient music as proposed by Brian Eno, the musician credited with inventing the term: "Ambient music must be able to accommodate many levels of listening attention without enforcing one in particular; it must be as ignorable as it is interesting."[163] This Barber arrangement, as well as many of those described in this chapter, might be considered interesting but could easily be ignored.

Before its acceptance in popular music and jazz *Adagio for Strings* was familiar primarily to concert-goers and record collectors. All these pop culture appropriations have dramatically widened its circle of friends. But if these fans only recognize the work by means of such transformations, one may wonder if they truly know it at all. Can those be believed when they say they love the work if their only exposure is a single phrase in Tiësto's trance remix? Yet, for some, a pop version may become a portal, a musical doorway to the "real" *Adagio*. They may purchase—or these days download to their iPods—Barber's orchestral *Adagio*, thereby embracing it as one of the few classical compositions (maybe the only) in their listening library. In that case one might well trust Internet bloggers who claim it is their favorite "song."

[163]Brian Eno, liner notes to *Ambient 1: Music for Airports*, perf. Brian Eno, synthesizer and electric piano, *et al.* (Polydor, PVC 7908 (AMB 001), 1978).

CHAPTER 8

Adagio in Motion Pictures and Television

> Classical music has been more abused than any other kind in movies, ever since *Brief Encounter* sniveled along to Rachmaninoff and with the demise of the great film score composers . . . the abuse is getting worse. Composers are regularly hijacked to prettify a picture and give the audience a hot flush of culture. Think of poor Samuel Barber, press-ganged into *Platoon*.
>
> —Anthony Lane, *Nobody's Perfect* (2003).[1]

Introduction

While critic Anthony Lane's attitude toward the use of *Adagio for Strings* in *Platoon* is less than enthusiastic, others believe that this music enhances the production by adding pathos to scenes that might not have made as dramatic an impact otherwise.[2] Yet *Platoon* was not the first to employ Barber's music for this purpose. Ever since Christopher Larkin introduced a brief excerpt in *A Very Natural Thing* (1974), it has been heard in many different films over the last forty years. The orchestral format is the standard choice, but the Agnus Dei, the organ transcription, and even trance versions can also be found. The only option overlooked so far is the original string quartet movement. Because in this chapter I do not discuss the movies in chronological sequence, Table 8.1 (on the following page) is provided to report the order in which they were released and to identify the genre of the film (drama, comedy, or documentary) and the country of origin. (A similar chart of *Adagio* in television series is provided later in this chapter in Table 8.12 along with discussion.)

Some meaningful generalizations can be made. Most of the films under consideration are domestic although a few originate in foreign countries (with three from France and one from Spain). Most are dramas, but several comedies and documentaries also feature the Barber piece. Its inclusion in drama vis-à-vis comedy shows a clear trend: starting entirely with dramas, moving through a comedic phase, and, in more recent times, returning to drama. For instance, in movies dating from the 1970s through the 1990s, such as *The Elephant Man, Lorenzo's Oil,* and, of course,

[1]Anthony Lane, *Nobody's Perfect: Writings from The New Yorker* (New York: Alfred A. Knopf, 2003), 9.

[2]Spoiler Alert! In the following chapter I disclose important clues and endings of various films and television shows.

Platoon, the composition underscores dramatic events, reinforces sincere emotions of the characters, and effectively evokes a solemn mood or reaction from the audience. But in the first few years of the twenty-first century all that began to change; Barber's score became a device of parody intended to elicit a smile or a laugh in such diverse movies as *Amélie, S1mØne,* and *Kevin and Perry Go Large*. What brought on this about-face? When any dramatic device is overused, it becomes a cliché, vulnerable to satiric treatment. Such was the fate of *Adagio* during those years when its serious dramatic capability was undermined by its overuse, a path that resulted in its being re-channeled into humor.

Table 8.1. Film Soundtracks

YEAR	FILM TITLE	COUNTRY	GENRE
1974	*A Very Natural Thing*	US	Drama
1980	*The Elephant Man*	US	Drama
1983	*El Norte* [The North]	US / UK	Drama
1986	*Platoon*	US	Action / Drama
1992	*Lorenzo's Oil*	US	Drama
1994	*Les Roseaux sauvages* [Wild Reeds]	France	Drama
1995	*The Scarlet Letter*	US	Drama
1996	*The Crime of the Century*	US	Drama
1997	*The Garden of Redemption*	US	Drama
1997	*Tour of the Inferno: Revisiting Platoon*	US	Documentary
1999	*Rocky Marciano*	US	Drama
2000	*Kevin and Perry Go Large*	UK	Comedy
2001	*Amélie*	France	Comedy
2002	*S1mØne*	US	Comedy
2003	*Reconstruction*	Denmark	Drama
2003	*Swimming Upstream*	US	Drama
2004	*ma mère* [My Mother]	France	Drama
2004	*Shake Hands with the Devil*	US	Documentary
2004	*Peace One Day*	US	Documentary
2006	*Tenacious D in the Pick of Destiny*	US	Comedy
2006	*Ficción* [Fiction]	Spain	Drama
2007	*Sicko*	US	Documentary

But just when it seemed that *Adagio* has been ruined forever as a means of sincere expression, a few movies restored its earlier dramatic integrity. In 2004 the drama *ma mère* and the documentaries *Shake Hands with the Devil* and *Peace One Day* called attention again to its impact in a serious cinematic context. Yet Barber's ordeal with comedy has not completely abated, as can be seen with its presence in *Tenacious D in the Pick of Destiny*. A role for *Adagio* has been clearly established in many film genres, and its appeal in this regard is likely to continue. What is fascinating is how differently this music functions in each movie, ranging from a single cue in one significant moment to several references in multiple scene complexes.

One Brief Shining Moment: A Single Dramatic Gesture or Comic Jest

Table 8.2. Dramas

YEAR	FILM TITLE PERFORMING ARTISTS	FILM DIRECTOR MEDIUM
1974	*A Very Natural Thing* Uncredited	Christopher Larkin Orchestra
1980	*The Elephant Man* London Symphony Orchestra (Previn)	David Lynch Orchestra
1996	*The Crime of the Century* Uncredited	Mark Rydell Orchestra
2003	*Swimming Upstream* Capella Istropolitana	Russell Mulcahy Orchestra
2006	*Ficción* Royal Scottish National Orchestra (Alsop)	Cesc Gay Orchestra

Table 8.3. Comedies

YEAR	FILM TITLE PERFORMING ARTISTS	FILM DIRECTOR MEDIUM
2001	*Amélie* Capella Istropolitana	Jean-Pierre Jeunet Orchestra
2006	*Tenacious D in the Pick of Destiny* St. John's Episcopal Cathedral Choir	Liam Lynch Chorus

A VERY NATURAL THING

Most film buffs believe that the history of *Adagio for Strings* in movies began with David Lynch's *The Elephant Man*. They are unaware that it was heard probably for the first time in a minor classic of gay cinema, *A Very Natural Thing*. While the film itself is a landmark, portraying pre-AIDS relationships from a realistic and sympathetic viewpoint, the short musical excerpt is quite incidental—almost an afterthought—effortlessly accompanying a near soft-porn scene without much dramatic significance. Even so, it is well co-ordinated with the action. Two naked men writhe sensually during *Adagio*'s climactic phrase, performed here with as much restraint as the sex itself. Neither climax is exaggerated. If ever a listener projected a sexual climax onto the musical one, this scene reinforces it. The quiet chord passage then forms a transition to the "morning after" episode.

Unless they were classical music fans, those who first attended this film may never have heard this music before. To those old enough to remember it from the funereal context of Roosevelt (unlikely) or Kennedy (possibly), such associations probably never entered their minds. Luke Howard reached a telling conclusion: "in 1974 the associations of this music with death had apparently not been established sufficiently to rule out other plausible associations for the audience."[3] *Adagio*'s connections to cinematic death were several years away.

Yet, what about today's viewers who see that movie after the many subsequent death-related films of recent years? Do they bring a different perspective? Do they impose a sense of doom on the two lovers, who, later in the film, split up? I doubt it. I never watched this film until recently, but I had no difficulty in accepting the scene with its *Adagio* accompaniment strictly in erotic terms, without the foreshadowing of a failed relationship.

THE ELEPHANT MAN

Near the conclusion of David Lynch's *The Elephant Man, Adagio for Strings* begins its long association with death when the title character, John Merrick (John Hurt), "allows himself to die." After enjoying one of the best days of his life and, perhaps, thinking that his life could get no better, he goes to bed. He has always had to sleep with his head elevated to avoid

[3]Luke Howard, "The Popular Reception of Samuel Barber's *Adagio for Strings*," *American Music* XXV/1 (Spring 2007), 56. Howard's brief discussion of this movie is the only one that I am aware of.

suffocation, but this night he decides to sleep "like a normal person."[4] *Adagio* is so integral to the scene that Lynch's biographer, Michel Chion, was convinced that the director had the idea from the beginning: "That the piece works without seeming to be added on suggests that Lynch filmed the scene on the basis of the grave liturgical rhythms of the music."[5] Yet *Adagio* was brought to the scene almost as an afterthought. With his project nearly completed, the director recalled:

> It was a Sunday afternoon and I was lying on my couch. I heard this adagio for strings. It washed over me. It was just so unbelievably beautiful and so perfect for the ending of the film. And I called [the film's producer] Jonathan Sanger and I said, "we gotta get this adagio for strings." He went out and bought nine different versions, 'cause I didn't know which version I had heard. I listened to all of them and none of them were doing it for me. Finally he found Andre Previn's version. . . . The same notes, the same orchestration, but completely different feeling.[6]

In Lynch's view "it was perfect and beautiful"; Previn just "knocked it out of the park"; it "fell in perfectly" with everything that happened in that scene and "supported it in the most beautiful way."[7]

As a result of this encounter, Lynch adopted *Adagio* as a "temp track"[8] for the scene and wanted to retain it for the final cut but was "worried about getting to use it."[9] John Morris, who had been contracted as composer for the film, had already written music for this scene. The

[4]Noah Adams, "Profile: Composer Samuel Barber's 'Adagio for Strings,'" *All Things Considered* [National Public Radio] (13 March 2000), 2. This is cinematic fabrication; Merrick died a natural death in the middle of the day.

[5]Michel Chion, *David Lynch,* trans. Robert Julian (London: British Film Institute, 1995), 52.

[6]Marie Pohl, "David Lynch on Meditation," *Süddeutsche Zeitung* (13 May 2006); reprinted www.businessportal24.com/de/a/30092.

[7]David Lynch, quoted in Noah Adams, "Profile: Composer Samuel Barber," *All Things Considered* (13 March 2000), 2. It is indeed Previn's recording that is heard in the movie and is included on the soundtrack album.

[8]A "temp score" or "temp track" is a temporary use of music for editing purposes. The director has no intention of adopting it in the final cut. Yet sometimes the director becomes so enthralled with his temp track that he insists on carrying it over into the final cut of the film, often much to the dismay of the composer hired to provide original music. Such an incident occurs with Oliver Stone and *Platoon.*

[9]David Lynch, quoted in David Lynch and Chris Rodley, *Lynch on Lynch*, 2nd ed. (New York: Farrar, Straus, and Giroux, 2005), 104.

director acknowledged that "John did a great job, but I just had to have this piece of music."[10] Moreover, he not only needed to persuade Morris to approve the addition of Barber's music but also had to "sell" the idea to executive producer Mel Brooks.[11] As a result, a double screening of the scene—first with *Adagio* and second with Morris's newly composed music—was set up for Brooks, Morris, and others. Lynch remembered:

> Afterwards there was silence, and so I thought everybody was going to vote. But after the silence Mel turned to John Morris and said very kindly, "John, I gotta tell you I like the *Adagio for Strings*. It works better for the picture." And John said, "fine. But it's not like I'm winning. It's like winning for the film."[12]

Of course, Lynch prevailed. But years later, in 1997, Morris anticipated *Adagio*'s eventual overuse:

> I told him he was making a big mistake. . . . *Adagio for Strings* is so pretty that it would work anywhere for anything. I told Lynch this piece is going to be used over and over again in the future. And every time it's used in a movie it's going to diminish the effect of the scene. Now when people see *The Elephant Man* they go . . . ahhh, that's the music from *Platoon*. Right away the effect is cut off and the audience is distracted. You should wed it to the original score and leave it alone. He said "no" and I told him he would regret it.[13]

One reason that Barber's music seems so appropriate here is due to the nature of much of Morris's main score, often as uplifting and almost as classical sounding, particularly the music called "Merrick and the Psalm" on the soundtrack album. Therefore the actual classical track of *Adagio* is not at odds with Morris's general musical tone.

[10]*Ibid.*

[11]Yes, zany Mel was the executive producer of this ultra-serious movie but insisted that his name be eliminated from the credits, lest viewers think that the film was a comedy or satire.

[12]David Lynch, quoted in David Lynch and Chris Rodley, *Lynch on Lynch*, 104.

[13]John Morris, quoted in "Lost Issue Wednesday: John Morris Interview (1997), Part One," *Film Score Monthly* (22 August 2001); reprinted www.filmscoremonthly.com/articles/2001/22_/Aug—Lost_Issue _John_Morris_ Interview_Part_One.asp.

Prior to the final scene Merrick has attended a ballet dedicated to him by society matron, Mrs. Kendal (Anne Bancroft). Afterwards, back in his room, he bids farewell to his mentor, Frederick Treves (Anthony Hopkins), who does not realize that this will be their last meeting. After Treves leaves, the opening phrase of *Adagio for Strings* unfolds as Merrick looks at the model cathedral he has been constructing. He utters a short, sobbing cry and moves toward his bed. After removing the pillows that had propped him up through all previous nights, he smoothes his sheets and gets into bed. When he lies down flat, a brief moment of choking is heard. The viewer never sees him again but knows that he is about to die. The camera pans across the room to a Bible and two small photographs, one of his mother and one of Mrs. Kendal. The camera returns to the model cathedral in front of an open window, and while the curtains gently sway in the breeze, the camera focuses on the stars through the window. An image of his mother recites lines from a poem by Alfred Lord Tennyson, "Nothing Will Die" from *Juvenilia* (1830):

> Never, oh! never, nothing will die;
> The stream flows,
> The wind blows,
> The heart beats.

Adagio then cuts to the final phrase of the coda as she repeats, "Nothing will die."

While this ending produces an emotional impact, what is the purpose of the image of Merrick's mother and these few lines of poetry? This is what film critics sometimes refer to as an unmotivated scene, a situation where an earlier scene could have provided a logical link but for some reason was left out. In the original script this ending is motivated by a previous exchange in which Merrick and Treves read a longer excerpt from the Tennyson poem. The book of his poetry was a valued part of Merrick's small library of literary classics; it may have originally belonged to his mother. He probably heard her recite this particular poem when he was a child. After reading a passage from the poem, Merrick asks Treves whether he can be cured. Treves's response is unequivocal: "I can care for you but I can't cure you." The poetry-reading portion of that scene unfortunately ended up on the cutting room floor, thereby severing a valuable dramatic connection. Omitting these details saved less than a minute of screen time, a minor consideration, but without them viewers have no idea why Merrick's mother utters these words at the end, who wrote them, or what is the nature of their significance. The poem and Merrick's hopelessness were linked together in the first scene and later form the basis of the final scene.[14] What if the earlier scene had been retained? Would the dramatic connection have been enhanced by a musical parallel with *Adagio* in both scenes? Unlikely. Lynch viewed Barber's music as an emotional accompaniment strictly to the ending and probably would not have wanted to preview the music earlier in the movie. A musical parallel could have been achieved, however, if Morris had been allowed to use his own music for both scenes, probably "Recapitulation," the final cut on the soundtrack album.

Critics disagree on the effectiveness of *Adagio* in the movie. Mark Zimmer considered the decision a "misstep," claiming that *Adagio,* "the most heart-rending music ever written," was already "incredibly moving."[15] It achieved musical "overkill" and for the first time "makes the viewer feel manipulated rather than genuinely moved."[16] Yet John Hurt, who is so convincing in the title role, believes that the audience is likely to be moved emotionally by this scene: "if you can manage to get to the end of *The Elephant Man* without being moved, I don't think you'd be someone I'd want to know."[17] Film critic Michael O'Sullivan expressed his personal view: "To this day, I can't listen to Samuel Barber's Adagio for Strings without getting teary at the memory of the final scene in 'The Elephant Man.'"[18] Few audience members emerge from this cinematic experience unscathed.

[14]For the complete script, see Ashley Montagu, "Based on THE ELEPHANT MAN (A Study in Human Dignity)," (11 June 2004), www.awesomefilm.com/script/elephantman.txt. Reviewer P. D. Clemens recalled seeing the full scene in a preview screening at the 20th Century Fox Studios prior to its release to the public. Although deleted scenes from other Lynch movies are provided on his multi-CD set, this one is not. This brief scene could have been significant for the understanding of the film's ending. Unless Lynch or someone else discovers it, one must presume that it was indeed left on the cutting room floor.

[15]Mark Zimmer, "dOc DVD Review: The Elephant Man (1980)," *digitallyOBSESSED!com* (10 December 2001), www.digitallyobsessed.com/displaylegacy.php?ID=2769.

[16]*Ibid.*

[17]John Hurt, quoted in "Introspective Cast and Crew Interviews" a special feature on the DVD issue of the film.

[18]Michael O'Sullivan, "Amenabar's Meaning Lost at 'Sea,'" *Washington Post* (17 December 2004), WE: 41.

THE CRIME OF THE CENTURY

Possibly the most dramatic, even melodramatic, cinematic use of *Adagio for Strings* occurs near the end of Mark Rydell's *The Crime of the Century* (HBO), which tells the story of Bruno Richard Hauptmann's arrest and trial for the kidnapping and murder of Charles and Anne Lindbergh's baby. Composer John Frizzell, perhaps taking his cue from John Morris and George Delerue (composer for *Platoon*), created his own score to be compatible with Barber's music. He borrows the main rising third motive, moving up in sequence, resulting in his own "Adagio" for strings. This passage, somewhat obscured within his main theme, is introduced during the opening credits and is recapitulated a few times later: briefly when Hauptmann's wife Anna (Isabella Rossellini) visits him in the prison but primarily during the announcement of the verdict inside the courtroom. In doing so, Frizzell imprints this music in the subconscious mind of the viewer, preparing the audience psychologically for the single appearance of the actual Barber *Adagio,* which, by the time it arrives, is totally logical. As Luke Howard puts it, "the transition into the *Adagio* at the climax seems not only dramatically appropriate but inevitable."[19]

This transition begins when Hauptmann (Richard Rea) is prepared for execution at the prison in Trenton, New Jersey. The chaplain reads a passage from the Bible (John 14: 2) relevant to those facing death: "In my Father's house are many mansions. . . . I go to prepare a place for you." The scene then switches to the Hauptmann home, where Anna quietly sings the opening phrases of Brahms's Lullaby to their own child, while *Adagio* continues along with it. Tension is created because the two pieces of music never quite fit together.

Adagio begins the climb to the climax as Hauptmann is led out of his cell toward the execution chamber. After he is strapped into the electric chair and is blindfolded, the electrocution noisily begins, with his body going through convulsions just as the music reaches the climatic chords. (High melodrama, indeed!) Even the silence, the pause that is so welcome just after the climax, is interrupted by the loud ringing of the governor's telephone, with news informing him of the execution. He had worked to save Hauptmann's life, but New Jersey law did not permit him to commute the sentence. During the quiet chords Anna is given the fatal news: "It's over. No confession." She screams. Ironically, unlike a performance of *Adagio for Strings* in a concert hall, neither the silence nor the quiet chords

[19]Luke Howard, "The Popular Reception of *Adagio for Strings*," *American Music*, 59.

are able to release the tension from the climax. The music now cuts to the final two phrases of the coda as statements appear on the screen relating the futures of several of the movie's characters, notably Anna, who proclaimed her husband's innocence until her death in 1994. Remaining on the screen are Hauptmann's own words:

> I'm glad that my life in a world which has not understood me has ended. Soon I will be at home with my Lord. As I love my Lord, so I am dying an innocent man. They think when I die, the case will die. They think it will be like a book I close. But the book, it will never close.

As the credits roll, the music returns to Frizzell's "sound-alike" score, re-emphasizing its close resemblance to the Barber composition.

SWIMMING UPSTREAM

Adagio's appearance in *Swimming Upstream* is far less melodramatic. The movie dramatizes the true story of Tony Fingleton (Jesse Spencer), who became a champion swimmer despite the indifference of his father Harold (Geoffrey Rush). Near the beginning of the film Tony speaks in a voice-over: "I was always a little afraid of my father. From my earliest memory there was nothing I could do to please him. I just never connected with him." Near the end, after Tony succeeds many times in his swimming endeavors, still without Harold's approval or encouragement, the two of them are walking along the wharves where his father works. He asks his father if he remembers the first time he took him to the pool and put him in the water. *Adagio for Strings* enters as background music, continuing throughout the remainder of the scene. Tony confesses to his father: "I remember being terrified of drowning. You had me there and just let me go. I didn't go under—I floated, and then I swam away from you, across to the other side." Harold, indeed, remembers, but before becoming too sentimental, he decides that he has other things to do. Extending a quivering hand to Tony, he says, "you've got guts," and as they gently shake hands, he continues, "Don't give up on me, son." After they part, Tony addresses the audience, again in a voice-over: "It's funny how the stumbling blocks of life can help make us better people. I never had the support of my father, but in the end, that's what gave me the strength to seek something more than I could have ever imagined."

Adagio, while not inappropriate to the scene, does not have the impact it does in other dramatic movies; any slow, sustained music would have sufficed. One reviewer, convinced that the presence of the Barber excerpt trivialized the music, addressed his comments to director Russell Mulcahy:

> If you're going to use Samuel Barber's immortal *Adagio for Strings,* you'd better make damn sure that it's accompanying some life-or-death type of images. . . . Juxtaposed against a facile father-son heart-to-heart, it proves to be a fatal miscalculation of the audience's investment in the characters of the story, and fails to live up to the legacy of the music's previous usage (much less to its own harrowing intensity).[20]

Yet must this music be linked only to highly dramatic situations for it to be effective? Must it always convey "a harrowing intensity"? More than just a "facile father-son heart-to-heart," this scene is the culmination of their relationship and, on its own level, as important as the deaths of the Elephant Man and *Platoon*'s Elias and the near death of Lorenzo in *Lorenzo's Oil.* Although *Adagio* resounds quietly and briefly during a tentative handshake, trying to compensate for a lifetime of indifference, it may still produce an emotional impact. This scene must be seen and understood on its own terms and within the context of the entire movie.

FICCIÓN

Whereas *Adagio for Strings* is not overly dramatic in *Swimming Upsteam,* at least it underscores a significant scene in the storyline. Yet its single occurrence in the Spanish film *Ficción* is even less dramatic and occurs quite early in the narrative, before much of the plot (such as it is) has gotten underway. Alex (Eduard Fernández) has gone to a small house in the countryside in order to complete a screenplay, but he is suffering from writer's block. One morning he turns on the radio, changes the dial from a pop station to a classical one on which a Chopin piano piece is just concluding. It does not interest him much, but when the next piece, Barber's *Adagio,* begins, he pays closer attention and twice turns up the volume so that he can better appreciate it. The music is clearly diegetic, that is, music that the character actually hears, not just background. As it plays, Alex fidgets and has a look of melancholy on his face. *Adagio* either means something specific to him, or he is simply struck by that fact that it

[20]Todd Gilchrist, "Swimming Upstream: A Pretty Good Drama That Ultimately Gets Too Caught Up in Its Own Current," *Filmforce* (7 February 2005).

matches his own mood. His sad state may be due to the lack of progress in his writing, or he may feel that life is passing him by. It is probably a combination of both. Shortly afterwards he looks nostalgically at old photographs of himself and a friend in younger days.

As simple as it seems, the technique of the music's presentation, however, is complex. When the Chopin piece ends, *Adagio* starts not at the beginning but with the third phrase. It is continuous until Alex steps from the house onto the lawn, at which point the music skips ahead to the coda. A radio station is unlikely to play such an abridged version. On the other hand, *Adagio* logically becomes quieter at this moment, just as it should if the musical source is located inside the house. Yet, inexplicably, as Alex moves closer to the camera, the music makes a crescendo and jumps ahead to the last phase of the coda.

How can this be explained? Has diegetic music been transformed into background music? Or, once he has exited the house, has the music switched from an external radio source to an internal one inside his brain? *Adagio* may have affected him so much that, even when he is outdoors and can no longer hear it, it still lingers in his mind. (This "music spinning 'round in my brain" syndrome happens to most people at one point or another.) If so, it has become "meta-diegetic" or "subjective diegetic," narratological terms referring to an experience that takes place strictly in a character's mind. *Adagio* is on the verge of reaching the final cadence when Alex suddenly sees a cow grazing in the yard, a sight that jolts him back to reality and one that stops the music before its reaches its final cadence. The only logical explanation is that the music begins diegetically and then discreetly transforms into either a non-diegetic or meta-diegetic presentation.[21] While occurring occasionally in movies, such ambivalence is not the norm.[22] *Adagio* never returns—it was never a vital musical element to begin with. It only functions to convey the character's mood, perhaps the simplest use of this particular music in any film or television program discussed in this chapter.

[21]In two scenes shortly after this, Debussy's "Claire de lune" and a movement from Mahler's Third Symphony are referenced. It is difficult to tell if Alex is listening to these pieces as he works or if director Cesc Gay is simply reinforcing the character's melancholy mood with background music.

[22]Ambivalence is not as rare in films as one might think. Gay's colleague, the Spanish film director Carlos Saura, occasionally makes his audience wonder whether the music is diegetic or not. "Diegesis," *Wikipedia*, www.en.wikipedia.org/wiki/Diegesis, provides a list of several examples, along with good explanations.

AMÉLIE

An early comic or ironic use of *Adagio for Strings* in film—perhaps the earliest—occurs in Jean-Pierre Jeunet's French comedy-fantasy *Amélie*. At the beginning of the movie the title character is leading a fairly carefree existence, but on 30 August 1997 an event changes her life forever: Lady Diana, Princess of Wales, dies in a car crash. From that moment on, Amélie resolves to play an influential part in other people's lives, to be "a good deed doer."[23] Mother Teresa, moreover, had also died, and the media coverage of her death may have lingered in the protagonist's memory. At first Amélie stays in the background, quietly observing the results of her philanthropy, but at one point she seems to regret her anonymity and longs, subconsciously, for recognition. While watching television one evening, she encounters a black-and-white newsreel of her own funeral, complete with shaky hand-held camera angles and narration. *Adagio* is logically presented as a dirge, but this time as a backdrop for a parody news report.

In the typical style of parody every aspect of the pseudo-newsreel is exaggerated. As if he were talking about Princess Diana and Mother Teresa, the narrator refers to Amélie as the "Godmother of Outcasts" and the "Madonna of the Unloved." He continues: "in the streets of Paris, countless throngs of mourners lined her funeral route in silence with the measureless grief of newly orphaned children." Her modest good deeds have been magnified into great humanitarian works. An intertitle reads: "UNE GRANDE ŒUVRE MONDIALE DE SECOURS HUMAIN."[24] She is transformed into the image of Mother Teresa, when, outside the Basilica of Sacré-Coeur in Montmartre, she washes a blind man's feet, a prominent ritual of Mother Teresa's ministry. The opening passage of the *Adagio* accompanies the whole scene, with its super-seriousness now contributing to the parody effect. Because the movie itself is a fantasy, this scene is an "imagined fantasy" within the film. Luke Howard asserted that "using the *Adagio* in this more abstracted context recognizes its role as a symbol of grieving without actually attempting to elicit a genuine sympathetic response from the viewer who, with carefully calculated irony, knows

[23]This characterization was spoken to Dorothy in *The Wizard of Oz* by the humbug wizard.

[24]Translation: A grand work of global human assistance.

that the (fictional) 'real' Amélie has not actually died."[25] After this, her adventures continue; all resolves happily. Barber's music was appropriate strictly for this one incident; there is no justification for its return.

This scene is one of four described in this chapter in which the treatment of *Adagio* is rather ambiguous.[26] If the newsreel is considered a separate entity, then *Adagio* is simply appropriate background music, similar to the actual documentaries discussed later. On this level, it is non-diegetic. Yet Amélie is depicted watching this newsreel on television. She sees the images and hears Barber's music accompanying them. Because it is real to her, it should be considered diegetic. But audience members, who see the images and hear the soundtrack with her, quickly realize that the newsreel itself is a product of her imagination. Unlike *Adagio*'s role in *Ficción* where the music starts as an audible performance (a fact that the viewers clearly understand) and then becomes meta-diegetic, its use in *Amélie* must be considered totally meta-diegetic. Both directors are essentially toying with their audience.

TENACIOUS D IN THE PICK OF DESTINY

A brief passage from Barber's Agnus Dei is heard in the rock music comedy *Tenacious D in the Pick of Destiny.* In this outrageous R-rated farce, JB (Jack Black), an aspiring rock singer, encounters KG (Kyle Gass), whom he has idolized for years as a rock-and-roll legend. But eventually JB becomes disillusioned with him, realizing that KG is neither the role model nor mentor he had presumed. The situation comes to a head when KG reveals that he spent the last of their rent money. After JB vents his anger, KG admits that he used that money to buy a brand new guitar for JB. As the glorious sound of the St. John's Episcopal Cathedral Choir singing Barber's Agnus Dei soars in the background, the camera pans upward on the body and neck of the instrument revealing its impressive design and sheen. According to film scholar Julie McQuinn, the music is intended to "sanctify" this new guitar, "creating a sonic halo of ethereal voices around

[25]Luke Howard, "The Popular Reception of *Adagio for Strings*," *American Music*, 62. The decision to use *Adagio* may have been made by either the director Jean-Pierre Jeunet or the composer of the main soundtrack, Yann Tiersen.

[26]The first, in *Ficción*, was discussed above. Another occurs in the dream sequence in the French movie *Les Roseaux sauvages*. In addition, characters dance to a trance version of *Adagio* in *Kevin and Perry Go Large*, and two women converse in a nightclub while another trance version is being played in the British drama series, *At Home with the Braithwaites*. All three are discussed in this text.

it, marking an ironically divine moment devoid of any sadness."[27] The music reaches the climactic phrase (*dona nobis pacem*) just as the camera reaches the top of the instrument. JB is almost in tears as he realizes what KG has done. This results in a rapprochement: their stormy relationship has been granted peace. Then, as the soundtrack plays a quiet chord passage similar to and in the same mood as Barber's, JB tells KG: "stop packin'; dude, we're gonna pay the rent, with our rock."[28] This sets the stage for the main plot of the movie, the search for "the pick of destiny" to bring sound to this magnificent instrument. They next arrive at their band name: Tenacious D. How this happens must be seen to be believed. No clues here!

Twin (Dramatic) Peaks: Two Parallel Scenes

Table 8.4. Complementary Scenes

YEAR	FILM TITLE PERFORMING ARTISTS	FILM DIRECTOR MEDIUM
1983	*El Norte* Uncredited	Gregory Nava Orchestra
1995	*The Scarlet Letter* Robert Shaw Festival Singers	Roland Joffé Chorus
1997	*The Garden of Redemption* Uncredited	Thomas Michael Donnelly Chorus
1997	*S1mØne* Dale Warland Singers	Andrew Niccol Chorus

EL NORTE

Whereas *Adagio for Strings* is heard only once in each of the preceding productions, it—or more often Agnus Dei—accompanies two closely related scenes in several others. The first is *El Norte*, a film concerning Enrique and Rosa Xuncax (David Villalpando and Zaide Silvia Gutiérrez),

[27]Julie McQuinn, "Listening Again to Barber's *Adagio for Strings* as Film Music," *American Music* XXVII/4 (Winter 2009), 464.

[28]"Tenacious D The Pick of Destiny (Full Movie)," *YouTube* (16 June 2007), posted by InsaneSPEC. The scene described above begins at minute 24:40. The idea for using Barber's Agnus Dei might have come from score composers Andrew Gross and John King or even from Black and Gass themselves. No one seems to own up to it.

a brother and sister who live in Guatemala but long for a better life "in the North" [*en el norte*]. After their father is killed and their mother taken away, Enrique decides to embark on the journey to the United States. During the scene when Rosa tells him that she wants to join him, *Adagio* underscores their hopes for a better life (those lines that will recur later in the film are underlined):

Rosa: I'm so afraid.

Enrique: But the money, we don't have enough. (Rosa shows him the money that their aunt has given her.) And your sweetheart?

Rosa: The past is gone forever, Enrique. I've lost my father and my mother (she touches his face) and when I thought you were gone I never felt so alone. I won't let you leave me. We have to stay together whether we live or die. You're my whole family now.

Enrique: Yes, you are right, Rosita. We have to stay together. But we are not going to die. We're going to live! And in the north—we won't be treated this way. We'll make a lot of money. We'll have everything we want. And we'll return one day. We'll have good luck now—I'm sure of it![29]

Adagio reaches its climax at the end of this dialogue as they hug each other.

Director Gregory Nava identified this scene as "the heart of the film"; one reason the film succeeded, in his estimation, was "the beauty of this particular sequence."[30] Clearly contributing to this beauty is *Adagio*. Its placement was his own idea: "I wanted to have an American piece of music that would reflect the bittersweet nature of the North and what it would mean"; it became a "very beautiful counterpoint to the dialogue of that scene."[31] This underscoring represents a complete contrast to the indigenous Guatemalan music heard during the first half-hour of the movie. That music was used primarily diegetically for local color: villagers

[29]These passages and English translations of dialogue in other foreign movies come directly from the subtitles.

[30]Gregory Nava, "Director's Commentary," *El Norte* (Janus Films: The Criterion Collection, 2009).

[31]*Ibid.*

playing instruments, people singing at a funeral. *Adagio for Strings*, of course, is distinctly non-diegetic, appropriated strictly for dramatic and emotional purposes. In my view, it is also uplifting music that supports hopes and dreams of the Guatemalan siblings.

After the long, arduous journey northward, they arrive in Los Angeles, where they find jobs and make their first efforts at a better life. Toward the end of the movie Rosa contracts an illness and is taken to a hospital. Enrique's visit to her there is a variation of the earlier scene, described above, but now they both are disillusioned with the life they had sought. Enrique, nonetheless, repeats many of the same words of encouragement he had uttered before, but now merely to comfort Rosa; he realizes that their dreams will never come true. *Adagio* returns to emphasize the dialogue, solidifying the parallels between the two scenes. One addition is the sound of the clock in Rosa's hospital room: time is ticking away for her.

Enrique: Are you feeling better Rosa?

Rosa: Yes, in my dreams, I felt afraid. I felt like that day in San Pedro [the site of the earlier scene] when I thought you would never come back. But when I woke up, you were here, with me.

Enrique: Of course. You're the only family I have. We have to stay together.

Rosa: Life here is very hard, Enrique. We're not free. Isn't it true that we're not free?

Enrique: Yes, life is difficult here. You have to work very hard.

Rosa: In our own land we have no home. They want to kill us. There's no home for us there. In Mexico there is only poverty—we can't make a home there either. And here in the north we aren't accepted. When will we find a home, Enrique? Maybe when we die we'll find a home.

Enrique: Don't say that, Rosita. It's hard but we're going to have luck . . . and we'll get everything we want. We'll make a lot of money and we'll return to our village. And when we walk down the streets—people will look at us with envy. (He smiles.) Things are changing. Yes, we'll have a lot of luck now. I'm sure of it. (Rosa closes her eyes.) The only thing is to not lose faith. That's it—

the important thing is not to lose faith. (She dies.)
Rosita! Rosa! Rosa! Rosa, no!

When Rosa dies, the music swells to the climax and drowns out the ticking clock; her time has run out.

It is easy to see the relationship between these two scenes when their respective dialogues are read back to back, but the scenes are over an hour and a half apart with many others in between—some serious, some comic. Nava redeploys the Barber excerpt for the later scene to reinforce what he calls the "circular structure" of the film.[32] This return of dialogue and music functions much the same way it does in an opera (*e.g.*, Massenet's *Manon* and Puccini's *La Bohème*), when a character, approaching death, repeats lines of dialogue to music first heard during scenes of happier days—but with heightened emotion.[33] Comparing the two segments, Nava observed: "Even as [the characters] came together in the earlier scene, they come apart in this one."[34] Some consider *Adagio* uplifting while others perceive it as tragic. Both attributes are emphasized here: the audience shares the characters' hope in the first and their despair in the second. Barber's music remains equally effective in both.

THE SCARLET LETTER

In the following films it is Barber's Agnus Dei that is inserted in two related scenes. The sacred text is appropriate both in *The Scarlet Letter,* where it first accompanies worship in a New England church, and in *The Garden of Redemption*, where it first occurs during action in a public square across from the local cathedral. No sermon or sacred building appears in *S1mØne,* but there Agnus Dei serves a different purpose.

In *The Scarlet Letter* the choral version is attached to two scenes: the first, to accompany the minister's sermon and, later, to call attention to the same character's violation of his own moral teachings. Unlike *The Elephant Man* and *Platoon,* where the directors foisted *Adagio* onto their composers, this time the film's composer, John Barry, selected it. He

[32]*Ibid.*

[33]Manon repeats a few phrases from the first act near the end of the opera; likewise Mimì restates her phrase "Mi chiamano Mimì," and even Rudolfo's line, "Che gelida manina" at the end of *La Bohème* as she nears death. Pushing the comparison a bit further, Cervantes (as Don Quixote) reprises part of "The Impossible Dream" near his death in *The Man of La Mancha.*

[34]Gregory Nava, "Director's Commentary," *El Norte.*

recalled hearing the recording of Agnus Dei by the Dale Warland Singers: "It was just gorgeous. I thought that would be so wonderful over the long sermon and a few other places, so I said, 'If you can buy that, it would be a big help.'"[35] In fact, it does first appear when Arthur Dimmesdale (Gary Oldman) preaches an evangelical sermon, for which Barry contends it "works beautifully."[36] The sermon hints at later events in the preacher's life: he pontificates that each human being should strive to be a model of perfection, "an example for all the world to marvel at." He cautions, however, that the quest often ends in failure "because we covet, we lust after what is not ours."[37] Little does he realize then that he, personally, will ultimately fail this test.

The Barber theme recurs near the end of the film when Dimmesdale declares his love for Hester Prynne (Demi Moore), the married woman he has lusted after, a woman who was never meant to be his. Not only has he violated the tenth commandment, but she has violated the seventh: "Thou shalt not commit adultery." The music continues as he prays with her and their illegitimate daughter for God to protect his family. In fact, the cleric justifies his love for Hester rather than feeling shame on account of it, thus contradicting his previous sermon. Agnus Dei is logical at both moments. In this film Dimmesdale's justification is totally at odds with the emotions and motivations of the character in Nathaniel Hawthorne's original novel. Only Barber's music can, perhaps, make sense of the situation.[38]

Barry also wanted the same music to accompany Hester's bathing scene early in the movie. "I spotted the scene that way but they didn't like it."[39] He explained:

> They didn't think it worked as well as it did in the preacher scene. I said, "I think you're wrong. I think it really brings her thoughts of the preacher to the front line, and it also gives a nude scene a

[35]John Barry, quoted in Michael Schelle, *The Score: Interviews with Film Composers* (Los Angeles: Silman-James Press, 1999), 36.

[36]*Ibid.*

[37]*Ibid.*

[38]Note that Agnus Dei does not underscore the love scene, as stated by Luke Howard, "The Popular Reception of *Adagio for Strings*," *American Music*, 63.

[39]John Barry, quoted in Michael Schelle, *The Score*, 38. Spotting occurs before the final cut of a film is made—when the composer, the director, the music editor, and possibly others decide on the ultimate placement and function of the music.

touch of class, keeping it on a higher level." They didn't go for it, so they repeated my main love theme in the bath scene, which I thought was totally wrong. Even if I had had time to write a new theme there, it wouldn't have sounded anything like that. It's just one of those areas where you disagree and, in retrospect, I still think I was absolutely right. It was a scene that the critics took a real stab at, but I believe the Barber would have helped.[40]

I think "they" were right this time. The love theme was established at their first meeting, when Pastor Dimmesdale tried to dislodge Hester's buggy from the mud. She had previously seen him swimming in the nude but did not yet realize he was the local preacher. In the bath scene, occurring shortly after his sermon, she sensually caresses herself while thinking of the naked body of Dimmesdale. In addition, scenes of him are intercut to show that he is also thinking of her. Because their sensuality relates more to their first encounter than to his sermon, the use of the love theme is logical; Agnus Dei would seem to me to be a miscalculation.

Critics universally panned this adaptation of *The Scarlet Letter*. Peter Travers called it "a loser: wrongheaded, overwrought, anachronistic, laughably acted and screechingly dull."[41] Jonathan Broxton concluded that the film's only saving grace was the "utterly gorgeous score by John Barry," including Barber's "magical, almost spiritual" Agnus Dei, and that "the quality of the music bears no relation to the quality of the film it was written for."[42] (While Barber may not be spinning in his grave, Hawthorne probably is.)

THE GARDEN OF REDEMPTION

The Garden of Redemption takes place during the last years of World War II, when Nazi soldiers controlled the village of Viano and other parts of northern Italy. The invaders have tortured Aldo (Jorge Sanz) to death for being an American sympathizer and have strung his body up on a pillar in the plaza facing the local cathedral. When his lover Adriana (Embeth Davidtz) clutches at his legs and weeps, Don Paulo Montale (Anthony LaPaglia), a priest who has latent romantic feelings for her, cuts down the

[40]*Ibid.*

[41]Peter Travers, "The Scarlet Letter," *Rolling Stone* DCCXXI (16 November 1995), 117.

[42]Jonathan Broxton, *Soundtrack Review* [University of Sheffield] (1998); reprinted www.shef.ac.uk/-cm1jwb/scarlecd.htm.

body. At the beginning of this scene a four-minute passage from Barber's Agnus Dei begins and bridges into the next scene. No dialogue is heard, only the quiet sobs of Adriana's grief. Does the music represent Aldo's death, Adriana's love for him, or the priest's feelings for her? Such questions do not have clear answers in this scene but may be resolved when the music returns near the end of the film.

After Adriana is arrested as a conspirator, Don Paulo is sentenced to death for abetting her escape. Agnus Dei returns as the members of a firing squad take aim to execute him, but the riflemen pause when they hear the sound of American airplanes in the distance. In the meantime soldiers recapture Adriana, who rushes into the priest's arms. The firing squad repositions and shoots at the couple, but Don Paulo shields Adriana as both fall into a recently dug grave. The American liberators later find the couple in a death embrace, but, although Don Paulo is dead, Adriana is still alive. His redemptive sacrifice has succeeded.

How does this reiteration of Barber's music relate to the first? Both are associated with death, one with Aldo and the other with Paulo, both of whom loved Adriana, but this is probably not the main connection. In the first scene Don Paulo is vaguely aware of his feelings for Adriana but dares not express them; he merely cuts down Aldo's body as a sympathetic gesture. While she truly loves Aldo, she has simultaneously developed subconscious feelings for the priest. By the end of the movie they both fully realize their mutual love. Therefore the music becomes a *Liebestod,* a Wagnerian redemption—first an implicit, then an explicit love revealed in the pathos of death.

S1MØNE AND THE BURDEN OF DREAMS

The overuse of *Adagio* in films may make it seem trite, but in *S1mØne* trite music appropriately underscores an equally trite scene. While the orchestral version might have been sufficient to convey the required sense of banality, the director has chosen the more emotional, texted version of Barber's Agnus Dei to communicate an even more exaggerated triteness. But which director: Niccol, the director of the film itself, or the director of an incredibly inept film-within-a-film *Sunrise, Sunset,* Viktor Taransky (Al Pacino)?

Taransky has experienced difficulty with his leading lady, Nicola Anders (Winona Ryder), whose prima donna attitude has forced him to consider firing her even though the film is nearly complete. Early in the plot of *S1mØne* he and a group of film moguls view rushes of the day's shooting of *Sunrise, Sunset.* As the title suggests, it is one long cliché, validated by a death scene that the moguls (and the viewers) are forced to watch. Reinforcing the heavy-handedness, Barber's Agnus Dei is already on the soundtrack, despite the fact that background music is seldom added this early to an incomplete movie, not even a temp track. The passage beginning with the quiet chords accompanies the dialogue when Valerie questions from her deathbed: "Jack? Jack? Are you there?" One of the viewers wryly observes, "She's good. You can hardly tell she's reading off the TelePrompter®." Jack replies: "I'm right beside you." Enrapt in his own performance, Hal Sinclair (Jay Mohr), the actor who plays this character, watches with a pleased expression. He is clueless! At the end of the scene the projector is turned off, causing the film to flip and the music to die unnaturally rather than fade out. Thus, a cheesy film is accompanied by the quintessential cinematic death music: the choral version of *Adagio for Strings.*

Later that same deathbed scene is presented to a preview audience, but in the meantime Taransky has re-shot it, replacing Anders with a computer-generated image (CGI) named Simone. Although this is how his new "star" is billed, her name is often spelled in "computerese": S1mØne (short for SimulationOne). The scene again portrays the heroine's death, and Agnus Dei again arrives at the quiet chord passage with dialogue—although it might seem impossible—even worse than before:

Valerie:	Jack, are you there?
Jack:	Something like this can happen. What is it for?
Valerie:	Why are we here? Is that what you're asking, Jack? Why are we here? No why! Just here! Just here! [She dies.]

The members of the preview audience love it! One viewer even weeps. Unlike *Adagio*'s appearances in *El Norte,* where the two presentations differ in emotional intent, or in *The Scarlet Letter,* where the first idea is contradicted in the second, here Barber's music simply accompanies an even worse version of the same scene.

Sunrise, Sunset is ultimately a triumph for Taransky, who must keep Simone's computerized identity a secret. He then "casts" her in *Eternity Forever,* his next film with a title implying an even cheesier movie, which seems to be verified by the brief clip shown. This excerpt is underscored by a passage from Fauré's Requiem, another "weepy" cliché. Because Agnus Dei was inextricably tied to *Sunrise, Sunset,* it is never repeated—except for a brief moment. Simone has been nominated for an Oscar for both movies. (What were the members of the Academy thinking?!) As the titles are announced at the ceremony, appropriate music is played: a few seconds of Barber blend seamlessly into a few seconds of Fauré. Just as the two movies resemble each other, so do their respective musical themes. Resorting to Agnus Dei in this film represents another instance of music determined by the director, perhaps against the wishes of the film composer. Carter Burwell, who composed most of the score, had little to say about it—except that he was not involved in the decision.[43]

Does Niccol believe that computer images could replace actors? In an interview he replied, "As long as you are moved by a performance, it doesn't matter," but then avowed, "I think that the problem is that it's hard to get a genuine performance from pixels. It's easy to fool the eye but it's hard to fool the heart."[44] Frankly, I view any computer image in a movie as a glorified cartoon, no matter how skillfully it has been created or how cleverly integrated into the scene. Just think of Jar Jar Binks!

In the Wagnerian Spirit: Cinematic Leitmotif

Table 8.5. As a Leitmotif

YEAR	FILM TITLE PERFORMING ARTISTS	FILM DIRECTOR MEDIUM
1986	*Platoon* Vancouver Symphony Orchestra (Delerue)	Oliver Stone Orchestra
1994	*Les Roseaux sauvages* I Musici	André Téchiné Orchestra
2003	*Reconstruction* Academy of St. Martin in the Fields (Mariner)	Christoffer Boe Orchestra
2004	*ma mère* New College, Oxford (Higginbottom)	Christophe Honoré Chorus

PLATOON

In addition to enhancing a single scene—for sex, death, or humor—or to setting up dramatic parallels, *Adagio for Strings* is sometimes heard several times within a movie. As a result, the application of Barber's music

[43]Carter Burwell, email (17 October 2006) to the author.

[44]Andrew Niccol, quoted in Rebecca Murray, "Andrew Niccol Talks about 'Simone,'" *About.com,* www.movies.about.com/library /weekly/aa081402b.htm.

often approaches the function of a Wagnerian leitmotif. This is its role in Oliver Stone's *Platoon*.

Like David Lynch, Stone encountered *Adagio* in a roundabout way. He recalled, "For the opening of the film, we wanted a noble theme, a solemn theme, an austere one."[45] While the movie was undergoing the editing process, one of his producers suggested the Barber piece as a temp track. Liking the music intensely, the director then asked his composer, George Delerue, to "follow this style."[46] (Note the parallel situation with Lynch and Morris.) Delerue remembered Stone telling him, "'I do not ask much of you, but. . . .' Right away I thought, here's a big problem."[47] He then composed a great deal of string music, trying to emulate *Adagio*'s mood. Stone confessed that Delerue "worked very hard, very long hours to match the majesty of Barber, but it was impossible . . . this opening theme can not be matched."[48] He added, "I fell in love with it and it was such a strong counterpoint to the brutality and savagery of the [film's] imagery."[49] "The brutality was so strong . . . there was more power to me in the dark strings of Samuel Barber's *Adagio*."[50] Delerue noted that Stone, having listened to this music over and over again, had become completely obsessed with it:

> But after the final mixing process, only about 25 minutes of my music remained and the Adagio appeared several times. It did not offend me, I well understood it but said I did not want to see my name in the credits because, to be entirely honest, I thought it would be annoying to hear Barber's music but see "original music by Georges Delerue" on the screen.[51]

[45]Oliver Stone, "Director's Commentary," *Platoon* [DVD] (Live / Artisan, 1997).

[46]*Ibid.*

[47]George Delerue, quoted in Frédéric Gimello-Mesplomb, *Georges Delerue: une vie* (Hélette: Jean Curutchet, 1998), 155. "Je ne vous demande pas de faire ça, mais. . . . J'ai tout de suite pensé qu'il allait y avoir un gros problème." (Translation by Larry Riggs and the author.)

[48]Oliver Stone, "Commentary," *Platoon.*

[49]Noah Adams, "Samuel Barber," *All Things Considered*, 1.

[50]*The Oliver Stone Connection* (Universal Music Special Markets, UMD 80530, 1998). The compact disc set includes a discussion of how music is used in many of his movies.

[51]Georges Delerue, quoted in Frédéric Gimello-Mesplomb, *Georges Delerue*, 155. "Donc, à la fin du mixage, il y a à peu près 25 minutes qui restent à moi et l'emploi plusieurs fois de l'Adagio. Je n'étais pas fâché, je comprenais très bien, simplement j'ai dit que je ne voulais pas avoir mon nom sur le générique de début parce que je trouvais ça embêtant, tout à fait honnêtement, d'entendre la

Yet despite negotiations between director Stone and Delerue's agent to compromise with the phrase "additional music by George Delerue," the phrase "original music" was retained in the final credits. Presumably audience members realize that this designation refers to music other than *Adagio* or to the pop tunes treated diegetically throughout. For the soundtrack Delerue conducted the Vancouver Symphony Orchestra in Barber's score and what remained of his own.

Stone claimed that he became aware of Lynch's use of *Adagio* in *The Elephant Man* only as he was preparing the final cut of his own film. "If David had used it to the degree of being identified wholly with that picture, I would have hesitated for sure."[52] Lynch, however, was not pleased at hearing the same music in *Platoon:*

> I'm sorry, I really respect Oliver Stone, but . . . it just killed me to see the music there, and I didn't feel it worked as good. . . . I'm seeing *The Elephant Man* on the screen and *Platoon* at the same time. So, you know, people should be able to put music in the films they believe in. So it just, personally, wasn't sitting right with me. But . . . that piece of music is so beautiful, I'm surprised it's not in almost every film.[53]

Adagio (mm. 1-19) first occurs during the opening credits, bridging into the initial action where Chris Taylor (Charlie Sheen) lands in Vietnam and sees the unloading of body bags. Stone believes that the tension of this scene is "indescribable and you sense idealism and it drives you—it chills you."[54] The music is nearly drowned out by helicopter and airplane noises, with the result that both music and sound effects complement one another. From then on, *Adagio* is usually associated with Chris—from this initiation into the war through his final helicopter ride out of the combat zone. For the next fifteen minutes there is no music whatsoever, only noises and the sounds of nature. Later, as Chris narrates (as a voice-over) a letter to his grandmother, one of several throughout the movie, a quiet

musique de Samuel Barber et de voir "Musique originale de George Delerue. . . ." [Translation by Larry Riggs and the author]

[52]Oliver Stone, "Commentary," *Platoon.*

[53]David Lynch, quoted in Noah Adams, "Samuel Barber," *All Things Considered,* 2.

[54]Oliver Stone, quoted in Noah Adams, "Samuel Barber," *All Things Considered,* 1.

string sound is heard that at first implies a recurrence of *Adagio,* but it is Delerue's original music, almost a variation on Barber's theme. Both begin with a sustained pitch, followed by a step-wise wandering passage. Barbara Heyman astutely observed, "there were only a few measures of original music integrated into the film track, but they so resembled the *Adagio* in character, it was hard to differentiate them from Barber's music."[55] Indeed, Delerue tried to "match the majesty" of *Adagio.* His *Adagio*-style music, however, only occurs once more, in a later scene in which Chris Taylor returns, by jeep, to the soldier camp.[56]

Barber's music next underscores the action when the platoon torches a Vietnamese village. Calm music matches the calm, deliberate manner in which the village is destroyed. If Stone considered its first appearance "chilling," this is even more so, stopping abruptly at the climactic point, as Chris prevents the platoon members from gang-raping a twelve year-old girl. As the director later observed, "this scene had a lot of impact on people, especially [when] the Barber comes in."[57] Harsh reality halts the impressionistic view of the blazing village. Julie McQuinn described the tension between sound and sight:

> The music is beautiful, and even the flaming village is visually beautiful, but the entire sequence is not. The excesses and contrast are tools here, not intended to portray the soldiers as heroes, but to intensify the violence and cruelty that came just before, to make the audience uncomfortable.[58]

Adagio links this scene to the next by continuing almost where it left off. The soldiers are leading off women and children, while others "look back at their village in ruins, homes burning, livestock dead or scattered,

[55]Barbara B. Heyman, *Samuel Barber: The Composer and His Music* (New York: Oxford University Press, 1992), 174, footnote.

[56]Delerue contributed another style of music to the movie, which occurs five different times, often in short doses. It is a Bartók-ian "night music" sound, appropriate to scenes in the Vietnamese jungle, with imitations of birds and insects. It is particularly reminiscent of the second movement of *Music for Strings, Percussion and Celesta* (1937). Perhaps Stone again told Delerue to "follow this style," but now referring to Bartók.

[57]Oliver Stone, "Commentary," *Platoon.*

[58]Julie McQuinn, "Filmic Counterpoint: Barber's *Adagio for Strings* as a Voice in a Time of War" [unpublished manuscript], *International Samuel Barber Symposium* (23 March 2001), 3. Thanks to Dr. McQuinn for supplying me a copy of her work.

belongings thrown and broken in the dirt."[59] If sadness is inherent in the music, it is certainly evoked and emphasized in this scene. Stone uses the first two phrases of the coda, the second of which is the altered version discussed in Chapter 3. Please recall that Deryck Cooke referred to its melodic contour as "despair connected with death" and argued that it "clearly expresses a powerful assertion of fundamental unhappiness"[60]: protest plus anguish, a perfect description of this scene. It is the only time in the movie where this anguished version of the theme appears; as such, it significantly marks the film's dramatic and musical midpoint. From the beginning of the movie to this point, the form of *Adagio* is basically encapsulated: [1] The opening phrases give way to [2] the climactic phrases, which in turn resolve into [3] the coda.[61]

It also marks the halfway point in the movie, both dramatically and musically. Everything then backtracks to a less emotional level. The action calms down for *Adagio*'s next appearance, accompanying another of Chris's letters to his grandmother, beginning: "I struggle to maintain not only my strength but my sanity. It's all a blur. I don't know what's right and what's wrong anymore." It is the only time in the movie that the authentic Barber theme accompanies one of these letters. Initially it was one of Delerue's sound-alike passages; at other times there is no music at all. Having reached the coda in the earlier village scene, the music now returns to its opening phrases. In a sense, both action and music start all over again. The third phrase continues shortly thereafter in a scene that is literally "the calm before the storm." When gunfire signals an ambush, the music suddenly stops, reinforcing the abrupt change in the drama.

The music again builds to its climax for *Platoon*'s most memorable scene: a rescue mission during which Elias (Willem Dafoe) dramatically dies:

> The death of Elias is long and heart-wrenching, and the *Adagio* is as prominent as the visual images. Stone isolates this as a significant moment, forcing us to watch and listen as Elias falls and rises again and again, running, then crawling from the enemy.

[59]Oliver Stone, Screenplay, 55; reprinted "Platoon (1986)," *Screenplays for You*, www.sfy.ru/sfy.html?script=platoon. This and further quotations from the script are taken from this source.

[60]Deryck Cooke, *The Language of Music* (London: Oxford University Press, 1959), 162-63.

[61]Oddly, neither here nor at any place in the film do the quiet chords occur. One would have thought that they might have played a suitable role somewhere in the movie.

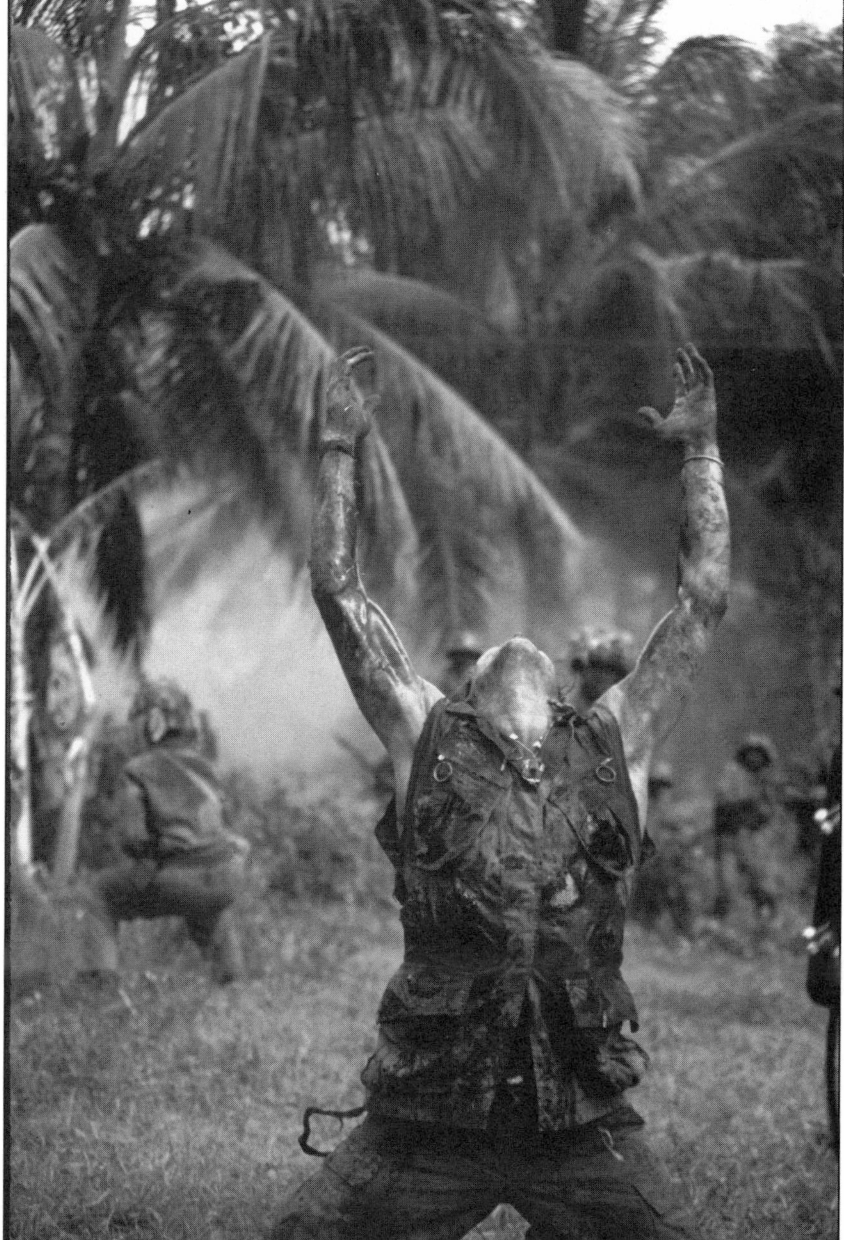

Illustration 8.1. The Death of Sergeant Elias (Willem Dafoe) from *Platoon*

Courtesy of MGM Media Licensing

> The music moves toward its climax just as Elias raises his arms as if crucified and falls for the last time.[62]

Film critic Thor J. Haga described the scene as a prominent moment of symbolism in which two systems joined in an unorthodox combination of "visual / musical dissonance":

[62]Julie McQuinn, "Filmic Counterpoint: Barber's *Adagio for Strings*," 3.

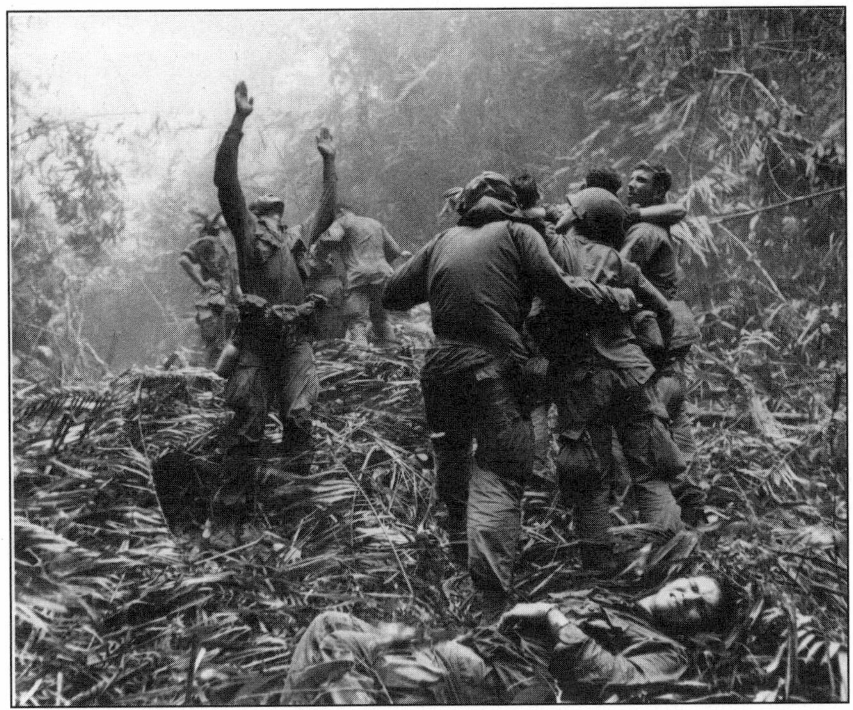

Illustration 8.2. Photograph of a Battle Scene by Art Greenspon, A Company, 101st Airborne Division, Ashau Valley (near Hue), Vietnam, 30 April 1968

Courtesy of © The Associated Press

> The scene in itself is violent and unambiguous, but receives an extra ironic-symbolic dimension through the inclusion of . . . "Adagio for Strings." The piece, which has strong religious connotations, makes Elias appear as a Christ figure; through his suffering, he sacrifices himself "for humanity" even if everything seems pointless.[63]

The script contains the following instructions: "he falls to his knees, still stretching upwards for life" and "Elias crucified." The religious allegory is absolutely explicit, not a figment of critics' imaginations. David Parsons has suggested that Elias's upraised arms might have been inspired by the photograph (No. 13) of a real paratrooper in Vietnam taken by Art Greenspon in 1968.[64]

For this scene, Stone uses the dramatic climb to the climax of Barber's *Adagio,* which to a certain extent repeats the impact of the torching of the village scene over an hour earlier. Yet the performance is slightly different this time. For that first presentation Delerue, conductor of the score as well as partial composer, had the orchestra rise to the climax gently,

[63]Thor J. Haga, "Film Music Ex Narratio," *Film Score Monthly* (21 August 2002).

[64]David Parsons, "American Soldiers as Victims in Vietnam," *Picturing American History,* www.picturinghistory.gc.cuny.edu/item.php?item_id=214.

restraining the intensity. Now, for the crucifixion scene, the orchestra rises to its fullest unrestrained, climactic sound. In other words, the first "gentle" climax marks the secondary high point of the film, whereas the "full" climax marks the principal one. This apex is only slightly later than the phi point of the entire movie, which theoretically should have occurred only a scant seven minutes earlier. Over a period of two hours, many movie viewers would sense that the phi point of both drama and music occur at approximately the same time.

About a half hour later, the opening of *Adagio* returns during another rescue mission. Finally, "the wounded Chris is literally lifted up out of the morass. . . . When a helicopter bears him homeward, the action evokes a strong sense of transcendence,"[65] fully realized when this music is supplied for the last time, almost complete, as accompaniment for his final reflective monologue. Stone comments, "there's Samuel Barber—sort of sums it up —elegy."[66] The script indicates: "Now the chopper is moving fast over the devastation. The jungle forever locked in his memory, Chris looks back as copious, quiet tears flow from his eyes" and offers this assessment:

> I think now, looking back, we did not fight the enemy, we fought ourselves—and the enemy was in us. [pause] The war is over for me now, but it will always be there—the rest of my days. As I am sure Elias will be fighting with Barnes for what Rhah called possession of my soul. [pause] There are times since, I have felt like a child, born of those two fathers. [pause] But be that as it may, those of us who did make it have an obligation to build again, to teach to others what we know and to try with what's left of our lives, to find a goodness and meaning to this life. . . .

This final monologue meets the criterion for what is known as "narrative enveloping," in which the end of the film echoes the beginning.

According to author Thomas Prasch, this enveloping takes place with both the music and the air transport. The movie opens as Taylor is flown into Vietnam to Barber's *Adagio* and ends as he is flown out to the same

[65]Judy Lee Kinney, "Gardens of Stone, *Platoon* and Hamburger Hill: Ritual and Remembrance," *Inventing Vietnam: The War in Film and Television,* ed. Michael Anderegg (Philadelphia: Temple University Press, 1991), 161.

[66]Oliver Stone, "Commentary," *Platoon.*

music.[67] The fact that nearly the entire piece is recapitulated, not just an excerpt, also lends a note of finality to the whole drama. According to the script, "the music surges now to its full strength as we replay bits of film with each actor's name listed."

Table 8.6. Placement of *Adagio for Strings* as a Leitmotif in *Platoon*

	[1]	[2]	[3]
	opening phrases	"gentle" climax	coda
mm.	1-19	35-50	57-64
hr.: min.: sec.	0:00:00	53:00:00	55:30:00
action	Chris arrives	torching village	leaving village

	[4]	[5]	[6]
	opening phrases	continuation	"full" climax
mm.	1-8	8-13	37-53
hr.: min.: sec.	1:00:20	1:02:00	1:16:00
action	letter to grandma	calm before storm	Elias crucified

	[7]	[8]
	opening phrases	nearly full presentation
mm.	1-7	1-50
hr.: min.: sec.	1:47:00	1:49:00-1:54:40
action	Chris carried out on stretcher	Chris's monologue —> credits

Yet it is disappointing that the credits finish before the music, which fades out right before the climax. Of course, most of the audience has gone home by then, but it is frustrating for loyal credit-watchers who wish the music would continue to the end, yet even more so for those watching the film on television. Premium cable channels may play the full credits (e.g., Encore Action Channel in March 2008), but other networks are so eager to publicize other shows that the music is interrupted by promotional announcements. A British viewer of BBC 3 complained to the network that *Adagio* was "muted and the credits hidden, whilst a ghastly advert for *Sex Warts and All* [a documentary about sexually transmitted diseases]

[67]Thomas Prasch, "*Platoon* and the Mythology of Realism," *Search and Clear: Critical Responses to Selected Literature and Films of the Vietnam War,* ed. William J. Searle (Bowling Green: Bowling Green State University Press, 1988), 200-01.

intruded in"; the Programme Complaints Unit replied that, as a practical consideration, channels "have to operate in an increasingly competitive broadcasting environment."[68] This is even truer in the United States. In February 2007, at the end of a *Platoon* telecast on the non-premium cable channel American Movie Classics (AMC), the music prevailed through the pictures of the cast, but the remainder of the credits were squeezed to the bottom third of the screen (unreadable!), a promo was inserted above it (annoying!), and Samuel Barber's composition was totally obliterated (infuriating!).

In general, critics believed that *Adagio* lent an elegiac quality to the film, setting it apart from previous war movies. Judy Lee Kinney argued that *Platoon* combines "combat stories with a tone so elegiac and full of grief that [it reflects] something quite different from the celebratory heroics of traditional action-oriented American combat films like *The Sands of Iwo Jima* (1949)."[69] On the other hand, Pauline Kael thought that Barber's theme, "in its soupy orchestration by George Delerue," along with the opening epigraph from Ecclesiastes, "Rejoice O young man, in thy youth," made the movie "grandiloquent before it even gets rolling."[70] In similar language John Simon also referred to Delerue's "soupier orchestration," used for "just about everything from rushing into battle to achieving existential epiphanies in the mud. This already stale piece of Barber's now joins the so-called Albinoni Adagio and Pachelbel Canon as one of the cloacas of classical music."[71] Considering Simon's proclivity for lexical obfuscation, I had to look up "cloaca" in the dictionary. It means a "receptacle of filth." Poor *Adagio!* Poor Barber! Contrary to the views of both Kael and Simon and despite the credits that state that *Adagio* was "arranged" by George Delerue, there is no indication that he ever "souped up" Barber's orchestration.

While most critics thought the use of voice-overs was a good idea, Gregory P. Dorr disagreed: "Sheen's narration is superfluous, burdening indescribably stirring images with second-rate prose"[72] or, in Simon's

[68]*Programme Complaints Unit*, www.logofree.org/?mode=interruption_log.

[69]Judy Lee Kinney, "Gardens of Stone, *Platoon* and Hamburger Hill," 153.

[70]Pauline Kael, "Little Shocks, Big Shocks," *The New Yorker* LXII/47 (12 January 1987), 95.

[71]John Simon, "Platoon–Movie Reviews," *National Review* (13 March 1987).

[72]Gregory P. Dorr, "Review: Platoon: Special Edition," *DVD Journal* (2001); reprinted www.dvdjournal.com/reviews/p/platoon_se.shtml.

words, "tie-dye prose."[73] Especially in the young man's letter to his grandmother, Dorr claimed that it

> shows a desperation to reveal too much. Maybe, just maybe, Chris Taylor's grandma is strong enough to grapple with sentiments like, "Hell is the impossibility of reason," but such threatens to turn an otherwise moving portrait of war into intellectual masturbation.[74]

Critic Stanley Kauffmann told author Bert Cardullo in an interview that, in spite of the fact that *Adagio* has been criticized for being "arty and obtrusive," it ironically carried forward the film's epigraph; it sounds an elegiac note," which continues throughout the movie "in a context that is far from rejoicing."[75]

Marin Alsop, who has conducted the Barber score with several major orchestras and has recorded it as well, served as a member of the studio orchestra that performed some of the soundtrack for *Platoon*. As she watched the screen showing the film to be synchronized with the music, her first thought was "ugh, this doesn't fit at all. But, of course, now I think it fits to perfection, because I've been conditioned by the power of those visuals to associate *Adagio* with traumatic events."[76]

Does *Adagio* pull the viewer into the story or put the viewer off? Author Frank Beaver argued that "Depending on one's critical preferences, the application of elevated music in *Platoon* either had added a tragic tone to the presentation of men at war or had in its artsiness distanced the viewer from the immediacy of war's fury."[77] While Andrew Grossman agreed that sentimental music accompanying horrific scenes of violence seems like a "grand idea," in *Platoon* it is "unwise and ill-judged" and turns the movie into "a celluloid Vietnam Memorial by draping it in the

[73]John Simon, "Platoon–Movie Reviews," *National Review* (13 March 1987).

[74]Gregory P. Dorr, "Platoon: Special Edition," *DVD Journal* (2001); reprinted www.dvdjournal.com/reviews/p/platoon_se.shtml.

[75]Stanley Kauffmann, quoted in Bert Cardullo, "The Film Generation and After: A Conversation with Stanley Kauffmann," *Conversations with Stanley Kauffmann,* ed. Bert Cardullo (Jackson: University Press of Mississippi, 2003), 187.

[76]Marin Alsop, quoted in Johanna Keller, "An Adagio for Strings, and for the Ages," *The New York Times* (5 March 2010); reprinted www.nytimes.com/2010/03/07/arts/music/07barber.html.

[77]Frank Beaver, *Oliver Stone: Wakeup Cinema* (New York: Twayne Publishers, 1994), 95.

borrowed, exhausted, yet still-resounding cries of Barber's *Adagio for Strings*."[78] Audience members must decide for themselves whether they are being moved or manipulated.

What were Barber's views about the placement of his music in films? Neither his reaction to Lynch's borrowing for *The Elephant Man* nor his approval of Stone's usage were documented. Menotti confided to Barbara Heyman that he thought the composer would "not have been amused by its success in this film and might not have allowed the *Adagio* to be used."[79] Composer John Corigliano, reportedly, was visiting Barber when he learned about it:

> Nobody bothered to tell Schirmer or Sam that they were doing this. Sam was very ill with cancer at the time; one of his few delights came from calling Schirmer and saying "Go get 'em!" They didn't ask for permission, they just used the music, as if it were in public domain, and it wasn't. So they had to cough up some money, I think.[80]

Stone confessed that, when he attended the film school at New York University, "we were always ripping off the public domain. We would always use pre-existing music."[81] That may be expedient for a film student, but *Adagio for Strings* is not a property in the public domain; a professional director must be more accountable. Stone claims that Menotti told him that he wished Barber had lived to see how well recordings of the work sold after the movie was issued. Taking a certain amount of credit for himself, Stone boasted, "I'm glad the movie helped bring attention to it—worldwide."[82]

Before *Platoon* was released, the film's music consultant Bud Carr tried to interest several record companies in a soundtrack album. At first he had

[78]Andrew Grossman, "How to Murder John Williams," *Bright Lights Film Journal* (November 2004); reprinted www.brightlightsfilm.com/46/music.htm.

[79]Gian Carlo Menotti, quoted in Barbara B. Heyman, *Samuel Barber* (1992), 174.

[80]John Corigliano, quoted in Michael Begg, interview, *Twentieth-Century Ltd.* [radio program], CJSF Radio (Vancouver, B.C.: Simon Fraser University); reprinted www2.sfu.ca/twentieth-centuryltd/corigliano2.html.

[81]Oliver Stone, quoted in *Oliver Stone Collection* (Universal Music Special Markets, UMD 80530, 1998), Track 1.

[82]*Ibid.*

little luck because no one wanted to issue a recording of music associated with the Vietnam War; their representatives asked, "Who wants an album of music about the Vietnam war?" One executive told him, "no one is going to . . . come out of that film humming a song."[83] The downbeat war subject was thought too depressing for a successful album, but that was before the movie achieved popularity and before anyone realized how crucial *Adagio* was going to be for its success. By the time *Platoon* won the Oscar® for best picture, record company executives realized that an album was not only feasible but a potential best seller. Therefore one was rushed out as quickly as possible.[84] *Adagio* is performed twice on the recording.[85] The short first track (ca. 1:44) presents music from the coda with the sounds of gunfire and explosions, and the second is augmented by helicopter noises as well as Sheen's monologue. While such sound effects and dialogue remind listeners of the cinematic context, it could become rather distracting with repeated listenings. It might have been better had the second track presented only an unencumbered performance. Most people interested in soundtrack albums buy them for the music selections and expect them to be distanced from the original dramatic situations; they would otherwise buy a DVD of the movie.[86] Barber's music is also provided on the more generic compact disc *Essential War Film Themes*,[87] but inexplicably it takes the form of the choral Agnus Dei. Could not the record producers obtain the rights to the orchestral version?

A BRIEF DIGRESSION: PERFORMING *ADAGIO* IN VIETNAM

Early in November 1998 the Orpheus Chamber Orchestra, headed by Julian Fifer, performed a concert in the restored Hanoi Opera House as a celebration of the end of the Cold War. It was the first American orchestra to perform there since the Vietnam War. The concert featured *Adagio for Strings* because Fifer thought that the repertoire needed an "accessible"

[83]Bud Carr, quoted in Robert Hilburn, "Record Labels Scrambling for 'Platoon' Sound Track," *Los Angeles Times* (18 April 1987); reprinted www.articles.latimes.com/1987-04-18/entertainment/ca-910_1_film.

[84]Robert Hilburn, "Army of Record Labels Cashing in on Platoon," *Toronto Star* (19 April 1987), G: 4.

[85]*Platoon: Original Motion Picture Soundtrack and Songs from the Era*, perf. various artists (Atlantic Records, 81742-2, 1987).

[86]*The Oliver Stone Connection*. This compact disc set also presents the performance conducted by Delerue, preceded by Oliver Stone's comments on the use of *Adagio* in the film. Other compact discs containing classical music in film scores never use the Delerue performance.

[87]*Essential War Film Themes Soundtrack CD*, perf. various artists (Union Square Music, 630, 2008).

American work, and it "fit the bill."[88] Yet even the members of audiences in Vietnam associated it with *Platoon*. "We thought we'd be able to get away with it here, without the overtones, but we had no idea of the size of the Vietnamese bootleg videotape market, or that the public recognition for that film is well over ninety percent."[89] Later that month this event was reported on NPR's *Weekend Saturday*. The introduction by host Scott Simon and a brief sound bite of *Adagio* were followed by comments and interviews by Jonathan Birchall. He recalled "the rich mournful tones" of this composition "sounded out before a packed audience in the ornate auditorium. . . . It seemed an appropriate choice for a concert which had a special significance for many of the members of the Orpheus group."[90]

A few years later, on 13 September 2001, James MacDonald led the Ho Chi Minh City Orchestra in a performance of *Adagio* at the HCMC Conservatory of Music. The concert, which was meant to coincide with "an introduction of American music to the conservatory students and music lovers," had been planned and programmed before the attacks on the World Trade Center in New York City.[91]

A BRIEF DIGRESSION: WHO'S ON FIRST, WHAT'S ON SECOND?

Many individuals, especially classical music lovers, probably first knew *Adagio for Strings* from concert hall performances and recordings and only later became aware of its presence in *Platoon* and other films. But what about those who had never heard it before it entered movie theaters, especially the young crowd? In 2002 the staff of *The Guardian,* a British newspaper, collared a cross-section of young adults in London and played them various pieces of classical music, including *Adagio*. Some of their reactions were the following:

> I know that, that's from a war film, *Platoon*.

[88]Julian Fifer, quoted in "What's an Orchestra without a Conductor Doing in Vietnam," *PR Newswire* (5 November 1998), 15.

[89]Ken Smith, "Orpheus Goes to Vietnam," *American Record Guide* LXII/3 (May 1999), 15.

[90]Jonathan Birchall, "ASEAN Wrap-Up," *National Public Radio* (16 November 1998); www.npr.org/templates/story/story.php?storyId=1023800.

[91]"Concerts," *Saigon Times Daily* (12 September 2001). Ho Chi Minh City was formerly known as Saigon.

I know this. Andagio [*sic*] in G minor, from *Platoon*. William Orbit covered it. The composer begins with an "s."

It sounds like Holst's *The Planets*. Was it used in the *Matrix*?

I've got a remix of this . . . trance version . . . that was in *Platoon*.

Reminds me of something but I couldn't say.[92]

None of those asked—at least those represented in the final report—could associate this particular music with Barber or even knew his name. To many, this music is indelibly associated with movie soundtracks. Alf Clausen, composer of soundtracks for many television shows (e.g., *The Simpsons, Fame, Wizards and Warriors*), elaborated on this predicament:

> If you talk to anybody in their 20's and play a copy of Samuel Barber's *Adagio for Strings* and say "have you heard that before?" they'll say, "Yes, we've heard that before and we really like it." And you say "where is it from?" And they'll say "oh, *Platoon*," because they had never been exposed to that until *Platoon* came out. Whereas, back a ways in time it would have been possible to hear a piece like that with more frequency, actually in a school music program, and to realize that there was a composer by the name of Samuel Barber who actually wrote that before *Platoon*.[93]

Clausen himself contributed to the web of *Adagio-Platoon* associations by incorporating a phrase or two in several episodes of *The Simpsons* (see below).

Critic Herbert Glass once called the piece "the chart-topping 'Theme from Platoon,' as the world now refers to *Adagio for Strings*—a melody millions can hum but probably few can ascribe."[94] Conductor Leonard Slatkin once admonished a Boston Pops audience not to think of the music as the "Theme from 'Platoon,'" but static from his microphone reminded

[92]Johnny Sharp, "Roll Over Beethoven," *The* [Manchester] *Guardian* (14 September 2002); reprinted www.guardian.co.uk/music/2002/sep/14/classicalmusicandopera.artsfeatures.

[93]Doug Adams, "The Simpsons' Secret Weapon," *Film Score Monthly* (March 1997); reprinted www.filmscoremonthly.com/features/clausen.asp.

[94]Herbert Glass, "It's Time to Bring Back Samuel Barber," *Los Angeles Times* (14 July 1991), 53.

the audience of gunfire, and everyone laughed.[95] Decades after the film was first released, *Platoon* and *Adagio* are still inextricably linked. All this may be true, but how many older radio listeners first knew Rossini's *William Tell Overture* (1829) by listening to the *Lone Ranger* (radio, 1933-1954; television, 1949-1957)? As a child, I first heard Wagner's overture to *The Flying Dutchman* (1843) as the theme for the television space opera *Captain Video* (1949-1955). And how many people have gone into record stores asking for Mozart's "Elvira Madigan" Piano Concerto (1785)?

What about those who already know *Adagio* as a piece of serious concert music, unencumbered by the dramatic trappings of movie plots? Its inclusion in such scenes could actually undermine the director's intentions. The audience could lose the proposed close connection with the narrative and lament, "Oh, there's *Adagio for Strings,"* or even worse, "Oh, no, there's *Adagio for Strings,* again!" There is always a danger of inserting familiar music into a newly composed film score. If music is meant as background, such usage calls attention to itself and paradoxically distances viewers from the scene at the very moment when the director wants to pull them in. When British actor Anthony Stewart Head (known primarily as "Rippen" Giles in the television series *Buffy the Vampire Slayer*) was asked to name his favorite piece of music, he gave the following reply:

> it's always been *Adagio for Strings* by Samuel Barber—except when bloody Oliver Stone used it for *Platoon*. He just, excuse the expression, f***ed it for everybody. Whenever any of those pieces of music becomes a classic, they just get used for commercials and things, and suddenly, it changes its status.[96]

Did Oliver Stone ruin this piece forever, or did he add further pathos to the work by its treatment in his movie?

Ultimately Stone was pleased with the way *Adagio* was integrated into *Platoon:* "I think it is a special piece. . . . [It] worked beautifully as the theme of the movie."[97] He added,

[95]Richard Dyer, "Leonard Slatkin Brings Fresh Approach to the Pops," *Boston Globe* (23 May 1990), 49.

[96]Anthony Stewart Head, quoted in Kenneth Plume, "10 Questions: Anthony Stewart Head," *FilmForce* (12 January 2002), www.tv.ign.com/articles/317/317440p1.html.

[97]Oliver Stone, *Oliver Stone Connection,* Track 19.

> Nobody has used *Adagio* as the theme for an entire movie. It has been used in . . . one scene in *The Elephant Man,* one scene [actually two] in *El Norte*. So I committed to it fully, and used it as my theme of youth, and nobody has used it like that. Now I don't think anybody will after *Platoon.*[98]

His 1990 prediction was naively premature and was soon proved wrong. *Adagio*'s film career had barely begun.

LES ROSEAUX SAUVAGES [WILD REEDS]

André Téchiné used several popular songs diegetically in *Les Roseaux sauvages,* but he borrowed *Adagio for Strings* only as background music for special scenes. He realized that it had appeared extensively in *Platoon*, but he had not seen that movie before deciding to add it in his own.[99] The theme of war is the common link between these two films. In *Platoon* the horrors of the Vietnam War are vividly portrayed, whereas here the war of Algerian independence is never seen, only the effects it has on Henri (Frédéric Gorny), an Algerian boy whose father has died from a bombing attack.

When *Adagio* is appropriated in most movies, it is usually only its "main theme," the most recognizable phrase or phrases. Although this is the primary part of *Adagio* heard in *Roseaux,* the quiet chord passage also appears, but to a lesser extent. The main theme is introduced four times, first when the two lead characters, Serge and François (Stéphane Rideau and Gaël Morel), are seen riding a motorbike in the countryside; François lovingly rests his head on Serge's back. The music enters as the noise of the bike suddenly stops, and François, seemingly in a voice-over, relates the events of that day: "He'd never been in a big city. He stared at everything. He was funny. At the nightclub he couldn't dance, so he drank. He wouldn't leave. We left at closing time. He was dead drunk." Such a narration is unexpected because it is inconsistent with the film's general narrative technique. After the scene changes, however, the audience realizes that it is not a true voice-over: François is telling this story to his and Serge's mutual "girlfriend" Maïté (Élodie Bouchez). In other words, the music functions as a "sound bridge" between the

[98]Fred Karlin and Rayburn Wright, *On the Track: A Guide to Contemporary Film Scores* (New York: Schirmer, 2004), 467.

[99]André Téchiné, quoted in Julie McQuinn, email (9 January 2003) to the author.

two scenes. This treatment implies that it is a "love theme" for the two boys. Julie McQuinn believes that it "represents feelings of François, the sonorous strings clearly corresponding to the intensity of emotion surging through him."[100] Yet this theme's later appearances blur this interpretation.

The main *Adagio* theme is next found in a surreal "double scene." Maïte's schoolteacher mother, Madame Alvarez (Michéle Moretti), has been confined to a mental hospital because she feels partly responsible that Serge's brother, Pierre, died in the war.[101] As the scene begins, a dutiful nurse tells her "it is time to eat your vegetables," and so they go (presumably) to the cafeteria. When the nurse turns on the radio, the Barber work happens to be playing. Taken at face value, the music seems to be diegetic, an integral part of the scene, and triggers Madame Alvarez's visions of Pierre. According to McQuinn:

> We are then drawn into her memory as she relives the dance that they shared together at his wedding. As the music reaches its climax, Mme. Alvarez and Pierre are slowly and happily spinning. Again, *Adagio* has effected a move through time and a shift from the outer world to the inner world of experience.[102]

When she suddenly wakes up in bed, the first part of the scene is replayed with exactly the same dialogue. The audience now surmises that she has dreamed this experience. As a result, the situation is comparable to the imagined newsreel in *Amélie*, in which the music is part of a meta-diegetic scene. Yes, she hears *Adagio* in her dreams and brings to the surface her own memories, but it only seems diegetic to members of the film audience who hear this music in a different way than she does. While the music plays, there is no reason to suspect that it is not real. It only becomes apparent when the audience realizes, when the early part of the scene is replayed a few moments later, that the music was only a part of her dream-state. While the pseudo-diegetic moment in *Amélie* is played for laughs, this serious scene presents one of the most complex uses of *Adagio*—in terms of meaning and interpretation—in any film.

[100]Julie McQuinn, "Filmic Counterpoint: Barber's *Adagio for Strings*," 6-7.

[101]Luke Howard, "The Popular Reception of *Adagio for Strings*," *American Music*, 60. Note that Mme. Alvarez is not the "grieving" widow as Howard describes her.

[102]Julie McQuinn, "Filmic Counterpoint: Barber's *Adagio for Strings*," 7.

It is an odd coincidence that, in the many and varied uses of *Adagio* in the movies discussed in this chapter, no scene actually presents a true, or at least unambiguous, diegetic performance. One would think that a character in some movie would know and like it well enough to sit back and listen to a recording of it. This stands in contrast to the many such incidences in poems, novels, and stories as illustrated in Chapter 6.

Later, the Barber theme is recapitulated when Mme. Alvarez meets the Algerian wife of her substitute teacher Monsieur Morelli (Fatia Maite and Jacques Nolot, respectively). The music has now reverted to its clear non-diegetic function, and the transformed second phrase from the coda once again expresses, in Deryck Cooke's words cited earlier, "a powerful assertion of a fundamental unhappiness."[103] She cannot escape the consequences of her failure to help her former student.

Near the end of the movie Serge, François, Maïté, and Henri decide to go for a swim. Yet only Serge and François actually swim, leaving the other two to consummate their love—or, perhaps, only to relieve their sexual attraction. After Henri leaves, Maïté flings herself at François, probably a guilt reaction. As Serge looks on, a snippet of *Adagio*'s main phrase is heard. What does his face reveal? Are his feelings beginning to change toward François? The movie ends as the three of them walk away.

When *Adagio*'s quiet chord passage sounds, it is not nearly as obvious as the main theme and is so short (3 to 10 seconds) that it may go by unnoticed. It is associated mainly with Henri and his preoccupation with the Algerian war. The passage is first heard when he, François, and Serge are in their beds in the school dormitory. François asks Henri, "Why did you come to bother us?" to which he replies, "I swear I didn't intend to. With his brother dead, [Serge] understands war, like me." The other reference is even shorter: Maïté has sheltered Henri in her apartment where he sees a poster about the war. This brief passage demonstrates that a quick glance at a poster is enough to remind him of the pain of the war.

It is difficult to relate all these *Adagio* occurrences. Sometimes it symbolizes the affection of the two boys: overtly for François and covertly for Serge. At other times it is associated with Madame Alvarez and her guilty reactions for not protecting Pierre. In her scenes the viewer seems to peer into her subconscious mind. McQuinn concludes, "She has finally come face to face with the moral ambiguities of war."[104] The quiet chord

[103]Deryck Cooke, *The Language of Music*, 156. See this and other Cooke comments in Chapter 3.

[104]Julie McQuinn, "Filmic Counterpoint: Barber's *Adagio for Strings*," 8.

passage underscores Henri's understanding of the war, or at least his emotional response to it. Amid diegetic pop songs throughout the film, *Adagio* stands out as the only non-diegetic piece, and it is during these passages that audience members gain access into the characters' minds, trying to penetrate their inner thoughts and emotions.

RECONSTRUCTION

Peering into the minds of characters is a far more difficult task in Christoffer Boe's *Reconstruction,* a film that critic Bill Stamets called a "sophisticated romantic and reflexive farce."[105] The enigmatic movie causes viewers to question what is actually happening, a confusion reinforced by *Adagio*'s equally enigmatic appearances, all of which are open to various interpretations. The first occurs early in the story. Alex (Nikolaj Lie Kaas) and Simone (Marie Bonnevie), who are having an affair, are dining at a restaurant with Alex's father when Alex abruptly leaves. As his father asks Simone whether Alex loves her, the music begins and triggers in her mind a memory, one that is communicated to viewers in a flashback:

Simone: Do you love me?
Alex: Yes.
Simone: Why don't you ever say so?
Alex: I do say so!
Simone: Only when I ask. Never by yourself.
Alex: I love you.

When the restaurant scene resumes, Simone answers "yes" to the father's question, and he says, "goodbye, Simone; it was nice while it lasted," probably referring to the evening at the restaurant. But the farewell may foreshadow the end of the lovers' relationship. In fact, the flashback indicates that he may not love her as much as she loves him. *Adagio* bridges into the next episode, in which Alex encounters Aimée (played by the same actress) in a subway station, where they exchange furtive glances. She is the wife of August (Krister Henriksson), who is writing a story about her. When Simone rushes in, they all board the train, and the music fades out. From then on, Alex and Aimée play a romantic cat-and-mouse game, coming to a *denouement* in a surrealistic scene accompanied by a nearly

[105]Bill Stamets, "Find Out 'What Jackie Knew' at Film Festival," *Chicago Sun-Times* (10 October 2003).

complete performance of the work. Aimée thinks that Alex has stood her up, and when he encounters her on the street, he attempts to apologize. This scene is relatively straightforward so far. The surrealistic aspect intrudes when the setting suddenly shifts to August working on his story, writing the very scene being presented! He reads from his manuscript:

> Alex has wavered at the decisive moment. He's losing Aimée. The last one. The only one, can their love survive? What will it take? A test [pause] for him and for her [pause] of his love for her. Stupid perhaps? If he turns around [pause] if he doubts [pause] she will disappear.

This is a literary allusion to the familiar Greek legend in which Orpheus looks back at Euridice as he leads her up from Hades; his doubt sends her back. As *Adagio* reaches the climax, this myth is reenacted: Alex turns around, Aimée vanishes, and the music stops. Later, near the end of the movie, the final phrase of *Adagio* sounds during a near replay of one of their earlier scenes. That incident started their complex relationship; this one now ends it. Did August change his mind and rewrite the story?

What relates the three *Adagio* presentations to each other? I think that the music signifies and reinforces a sense of loss. In the first scene Simone is about to lose Alex, possibly because he is bored with her, and the encounter with Aimée at the subway precipitates the end. The second time he literally loses Aimée, during the Orpheus re-enactment. As August narrates, it is a test of their love, and perhaps they both lose. At the end Aimée loses Alex, as he walks away from her bed without waking her. The use of Barber's music is subtle, not as clearly delineated as in other movies. At least it is not associated with death (*Elephant Man, Platoon, El Norte*), near death (*Lorenzo's Oil*), or parody (*S1mØne*). Boe downplays the tragic tone that many people hear in the music and emphasizes the sense of melancholy, a feeling appropriate to an impending loss. Because the effect created by the *Adagio* scenes seems one of sadness rather than tragedy, I am not tempted to cry. They are sad but not tragic. In fact, all lives seem to get back on track.

Boe may have had Barber's music in mind even while writing his screenplay. When he considered Kaas for the role, he sent him a copy of the script and a compact disc with a music track for each scene.

According to Kaas, "when you'd read a page of a scene, it fit with the length of the song, so you got a rush, a sense of the way it had been conceived. That's his way of filming and thinking and working."[106] Kaas does not divulge which pieces were provided on the disc or if any of them ended up in the final cut, but, due to the fact that *Adagio* plays such a crucial part in the story, it is likely that it accompanied at least one of the scenes, probably the one with the re-enactment of the Greek myth.

Critics were mixed concerning the treatment of *Adagio* in the film. John Hartl was convinced that it gives the movie "a surprisingly sombre tone,"[107] but N. P. Thompson concluded, "Boe cues copious reprises of Barber's well-flogged war-horse Adagio for Strings—a dead giveaway that what the director knows about classical music would fit snugly in the confines of a very small sock."[108] On the other hand, Grant Wilkinson favorably compared the impact of *Adagio* in this film to that in *Platoon,* even arguing that it produces a "greater and subtler effect."[109] Obviously Boe considered *Adagio* an important element of the film, and its suitability should not depend on whether it was "well-flogged" or not.

MA MÈRE

Any production that presents Barber's Agnus Dei is bound to impart a religious subtext, which is true for *ma mère,* the movie based on Georges Bataille's sensational post-World War II novel about a mother and her sheltered teenage son. In this graphic coming-of-age story Hélène (Isabelle Huppert) introduces her son Pierre (Louis Garrel), who has been brought up strictly in a Catholic boarding school, to her overindulgent, overt sexual lifestyle. Agnus Dei occurs several times throughout the movie, first in two brief scenes on the beach when Pierre is alone with his thoughts, reflecting apparently on his religious values. The opening "Agnus Dei" phrase is used for the first; its continuation "*qui tollis peccata mundi,*" is used for the second. A longer version is referenced later in a nightclub scene in a particularly fascinating way. Here the form of the entire Agnus Dei is

[106]Nikolaj Lie Kaas, *Reconstruction* (New York: Palm Pictures, 2005). Kaas is quoted in the interview for the DVD edition of this film.

[107]John Hartl, "In 'Reconstruction,' a One-Night Stand, a World of Trouble," *Seattle Times* (24 May 2004), E: 4.

[108]N. P. Thompson, "Ciphers When We Meet," *Movies into Film* (6 March 2004), www.nptonline.wordpress.com/2004/03/06/ciphers-when-we-meet-reconstruction/.

[109]Grant Wilkinson, "Review: Reconstruction" (December 2003), www.purpletommy.co.uk/voices/REVIEW-20Reconstruction.htm.

capsulated: [1] the opening four phrases, [2] phrases three and four of the cello statement, [3] buildup to and inclusion of the climax, and [4] the first two phrases of the coda. It is as if Pierre's religious life is playing out in his mind, but speeding by in fast-forward motion. Meanwhile the dance music in the nightclub is superimposed upon Barber's music. Because the beat of the nightclub music, sometime resembling a heartbeat, does not correspond exactly to the pulse of Agnus Dei, the mixture communicates Pierre's inner confusion. What better way could there be than to represent the conflict between his religious, moral upbringing and the lure of sexual freedom than to subject Barber's choral score to a trance beat?

In the final beach scene Pierre is convinced he has come to terms with his religious past and has reconciled his love for God with his increasing awareness of his love (or lust) for a girl named Hansi. Juxtaposed on the background of the longest continuous segment of Agnus Dei (the first 31 measures) he conveys his thoughts and feelings in a letter to his mother, which the audience hears as a voice-over:

> Sometimes I can admit if I love Hansi's ass so much, then it's because I want God to curse it. I now associate joy, that faraway joy in God that I know. I admit they're both equally holy. Her ass makes me realize I never really loved God. I was reciting catechism, that's all. God is something other than my old prayers. He's my way of losing my senses. By loving Hansi, I hope to slowly lose my senses. . . . It doesn't always make me feel happy. I don't think I lose my senses more with Hansi than with God.

This statement helps explain why the music was not placed in a previous beach scene, in which Pierre is seen reciting catechism. By this time he had begun to lose his moral commitment to religion, and the words had become meaningless to him, mere mindless patter. Therefore for that behavior the religious tone of Agnus Dei was inappropriate, only silence. But now lust has replaced his earlier devotion to God, and Barber's music returns in a newer blasphemous context. Pierre is yet another Sacrificial Lamb, subjected, this time, to his mother's sexual depravity.

This movie is not for all tastes. Does the clever and uplifting use of Barber's music raise its level of quality? After all, it nearly worked for *The Scarlet Letter.* In this case it is possible, but for many *ma mère* remains glorified, pretentious soft-core pornography.

"There's More Than One Way to Make You Cry":[110] A Multiplicity of *Adagios*

Table 8.7. Films Featuring Different Versions

YEAR	FILM TITLE PERFORMING ARTISTS	FILM DIRECTOR MEDIUM
1992	*Lorenzo's Oil*	George Miller
	City of London Sinfonia	Orchestra
	Corydon Singers	Chorus
1999	*Rocky Marciano*	Charles Winkler
	Uncredited	Orchestra
	Uncredited	Chorus
	Uncredited	Organ
2000	*Kevin and Perry Go Large*	Ed Bye
	Philip Page	Synthesizer
	Skip Raiders ("Another Day")	Trance Band

Even multiple presentations of *Adagio for Strings* or Agnus Dei may not be enough to fulfill a director's desire for the musical enhancement of dramatic scenes. In a few cases more than one version of *Adagio* can be found in the same movie, signifying different contexts and points of view.

LORENZO'S OIL: ADAGIO FOR STRINGS AND AGNUS DEI

Lorenzo's Oil is based on the true story of how Lorenzo Odone (Zack O'Malley Greenburg) and his parents, Augusto (Nick Nolte) and Michaela (Susan Sarandon), come to terms with and attempt to find a cure for his degenerative condition, adrenoleukodystrophy (ALD). Music supervisor Christine Woodruff, probably in consultation with director George Miller, assembled an unusual concoction of music for the soundtrack, ranging from African songs to Russian church music (why for a presumably Roman Catholic family?) to both *Adagio for Strings* and Agnus Dei. The two latter works are juxtaposed near the beginning of the film after a doctor tells Lorenzo's parents about their son's disease. In the succeeding scene the first two phrases of choral score accompany the parents as they find

[110]From the Marilyn Manson (a.k.a. Brian Hugh Warner) song "Pretty as a Swastika," *The High End of Low* (Interscope, B0013016-02, 2009). This borrowing is not meant to imply, however, that the song's title or any other of its controversial lyrics are applicable in this situation.

Lorenzo in the hospital corridor. He makes a perfectly normal request from a perfectly normal child: "When we get home, can we read a story?" But he is only temporarily lucid. Miller related the importance of sound effects and music to this scene in this fashion:

> The parents, having learned of the terrible diagnosis and prognosis of their son, have to make the long walk out of the doctor's office. We enhanced their demeanor, their mood, their anguish, by the exaggerated sound of their footsteps, by the laughter of the little girl [a passerby], and with the music. They are hiding their emotions because they don't want their son to know how they are feeling, and yet the music is telling us how they feel.[111]

It is through the power of music in such a situation that the underlying emotional aspects of characters can be conveyed beyond the spoken word. Author Marilyn Chandler McEntyre suggested that the music here "adumbrates the cycles of hope and defeat to come."[112] When the setting switches to a library, where Augusto is looking up the condition in medical dictionaries, the music switches to the orchestra version.[113] Although a short pause occurs between the two pieces, the juxtaposition is so close that they almost seem to blend into one continuous musical composition.

Adagio then disappears for a long period of time. In the meantime Lorenzo's health deteriorates to such an extent that his parents lose whatever hope they had. At their deepest desperation the music returns in various segments, but unlike the sequences in *Platoon* and of the Agnus Dei excerpts in *ma mère*, they are presented out of original order. For a moment during the quiet chords, Michaela vows, "We're not going to expose ourselves to doubt and despair," which happens despite her determination. It is not unreasonable to associate the quiet chord passage with hope and courage. When the boy is suffering at his worst, *Adagio*—and only that music—returns several times within the span of about twenty minutes. The music unfolds during the following event: Lorenzo can hardly breathe and almost chokes on his own saliva; Michaela's sister

[111]"Episode 3: Once upon a Time," *How Art Made the World* [BBC Series] (17 July 2006). Telecast in the United States on most PBS stations.

[112]Marilyn Chandler McEntyre, "Institutional Impediments: Medical Bureaucracies in the Movies," *In Cultural Sutures: Medicine and Media* (Durham, N.C.: Duke University Press, 2004), 182.

[113]See "Lorenzo's Oil–Nick Nolte's Agony," *YouTube* (30 July 2007), posted by HisWestiness.

shows Augusto photos in a family album (life as it used to be); she and her sister quarrel, precipitating a quarrel between Michaela and Augusto; and the doctor expresses his frustration: "I don't know what else to do." When the doctor utters the warning, "I don't think he'll have to endure it much longer," *Adagio* reaches its climactic phrase. The music loses a degree of effectiveness, however, by the manipulation of the volume level in order to accommodate the dialogue, and the swell on the last chord is overdone. Yet it is appropriate that the most emotional part of the music coincides with the most dramatic and emotional moment in the film. It occurs even closer to the phi point of the movie than Elias's crucifixion scene in *Platoon*. Events coordinated with *Adagio* can be diagrammed as follows:

Table 8.8. Instrumental Development in *Lorenzo's Oil*

[1]	[2]	[3]	[4]
opening phrases	quiet chords	coda	climax
mm. 1-11	53-56	57-66	35-63
hr. min. 1:12	1:15	1:15:30	1:19:40
Augusto marks chart 1	"Doubt and despair"	Augusto marks chart 2; family album	Sister leaves, Lorenzo chokes, doctor despairs

Throughout this segment of the movie, only the orchestral *Adagio* is used. Why not Agnus Dei? That is difficult to answer, but its placement near the beginning may underscore only the potential deterioration of Lorenzo's health, a more uplifting version of the music while the parents are still optimistic. Once Lorenzo succumbs to the disease, only the orchestral version is appropriate because it had been associated with his likely death.

Shortly afterward, a note of optimism returns. Thanks to Augusto's investigation of chemical procedures, a formula is developed to produce a medicine (the titular Lorenzo's oil) that allows the boy's health and mental abilities to improve slightly. During this hopeful period—the rest of the movie—*Adagio* completely disappears. Apparently the director and music advisor want the viewers to associate the emotional quality of this music with hopelessness, in a word, a "despair" leitmotif. McEntyre contends that the movie "provides a rich repertoire of both visual and musical cues that link the arts to medicine in their common concern with the fundamental human experiences of suffering and death."[114] Recent studies have shown that the oil can stall the effects of the disease. Augusto Odone is convinced that "the new research gives me the vindication I've long sought. Lorenzo's oil may not be a miracle for everyone with the disease, but for many, it works."[115] During his last years Lorenzo could not see, hear, speak, or move on his own. He died a day after his thirtieth birthday in May 2008.

ROCKY MARCIANO

The way *Adagio for Strings* is presented in *Rocky Marciano* is unique. While *Lorenzo's Oil* juxtaposes *Adagio* with Agnus Dei, this movie goes a step further: here *Adagio* is first transformed into Agnus Dei, which in turn segues into the organ transcription [R]. This sequence occurs only in the climactic fight scene between Marciano (Jon Favreau) and Joe Louis (Duane Davis). The fight is interspersed with flash-forward scenes of Marciano visiting Louis in the locker room immediately after the fight and also years later at the mental institution where Joe has been confined. Table 8.9 shows the process. The music, moreover, backtracks on itself when there is a change of instrumentation; yet it tends to sound like one continuous piece from beginning to end. The number of measures adds to about eighty-five, only slightly longer than if the orchestral movement had been played out in its entirety.

Table 8.9. Instrumentational Development in *Rocky Marciano*

Orchestra	Chorus	Organ
Adagio for Strings —>	Agnus Dei —>	Organ Arrangement
mm. 1-26	mm. 8-35	mm. 29-69

The fight begins without music, only the sounds of the cheering crowd and boxing gloves hitting their targets. At first it is an even match, but by Round 3 the ringside announcer proclaims: "Marciano seems to be getting stronger." *Adagio* begins as an accompaniment for a brief flash-forward scene of Rocky's visit to Joe in the mental hospital. When the bout returns,

[114]Marilyn Chandler McEntyre, "Institutional Impediments: Medical Bureaucracies," 182.

[115]Alex Raksin, "Lorenzo's Oil Shows Promise in Treating Genetic Illness," *Los Angeles Times* (12 July 2005); reprinted www.articles.latimes.com/2005/jul/12/science/sci-lorenzo12.

the announcer's comments, the crowd noises, and the sounds of boxing punches are all added to *Adagio*. It is interesting but rather disconcerting to hear Barber's smooth-flowing music punctuated by jarring jabs, often unrealistically amplified to enhance the dramatic effect. After Marciano connects with a climactic punch, the music switches to Agnus Dei, with the fight, often in slow motion, taking on an almost religious sensibility. Has Louis now become the Sacrificial Lamb? Marciano knocks down his opponent with such brutal force that they both realize the fight is over. When the scene suddenly shifts to the locker room after the fight, the choral arrangement gives way to the organ version, playing quietly at first. Quick cuts back and forth from the locker room to the mental ward are so cleverly juxtaposed that it seems like one continuous conversation, all fused together by organ music. Eventually the musical climax coincides with the climax of the dialogue when Rocky tells Joe, "They say you're crazy," to which Joe replies, "I ain't crazy; I just got nothin' left." The coda commences when Rocky encounters the hospital administrator in the hall and shoves some money into his hand for Joe's care. Obviously he feels somewhat responsible for Louis's condition, which probably began much earlier and was simply exacerbated by the fight. Louis never boxed again, however.

The three versions may have been selected—by music supervisor Richard S. Kaufman probably—strictly for the sake of variety. (It is, after all, a long sequence.) The specific use of the orchestral *Adagio* for the main part of the fight, the choral arrangement for the knockout and its aftermath, and the organ transcription for Joe's later hospital confinement, nonetheless, all coordinate well together. Each scene conveys a specific emotion, and the three formats reinforce them.[116]

KEVIN AND PERRY GO LARGE

This movie features characters that British comedian Harry Enfield originally created for his popular television series: Kevin, a horny teenager played by Enfield, even though he was in his thirties at the time of the film, and Perry, his male companion played by actress Kathy Burke, also from his series. The production, a send-up of teenage gross-out films (*e.g.*, *National Lampoon's Animal House*, *American Pie)*, was characterized by one critic as a "spotty faced safari in the hormonal jungle with ridiculously

[116]The entire movie was posted in short segments on *YouTube*. See "Rocky Marciano Movie Part 9," *YouTube* (23 August 2010), posted by iliaBox. This sequence, including the fight, the locker room, and hospital, is split between Parts 9 and 10. The *Adagio* portion begins at 3:40 on Part 9.

juvenile sex fantasies and much Pythonesque grotesquery . . . nothing less than a Geek tragedy."[117]

This movie seems an unlikely place to find Barber's solemn *Adagio for Strings*, and yet here it is put to good effect. Throughout the film the two sexually inexperienced teenagers try to correct this situation. In an early scene Kevin inadvertently spends the night in the same bed with a girl after a drunken party, and as he leaves, he claims to have "shagged" her (which he did not). When she later confronts him on the street with the truth and taunts him by calling him a virgin (which he is), the surrounding crowd joins her in the name-calling. It is during this scene of humiliation and debasement that *Adagio* is introduced.[118] Should the audience feel sorry for Kevin, or is the scene too stylized, too satirical to summon sympathy? (His embarrassed blush is accomplished with exaggerated facial makeup.) *Adagio* has elicited various responses over the years—from emotional uplift to grief and sadness. Seldom has it caused a giggle, but that is likely to happen here.

Later in the film the boys spend a holiday on the island of Ibiza, a trendy destination for partygoers and trance dance fanatics. They have finally succeeded in escorting two girls to Amnesia, the hottest local dance club, where everything is going right for a change. Both couples are dancing to the Skip Raiders' take on *Adagio*, "Another Day."[119] When two revellers on a balcony vomit on (just) Kevin and Perry, the trance remix cleverly morphs into the traditional orchestral version, and the dancing stops. Humiliated, the boys quietly bid goodnight to their dates. Although they are not responsible for such a disgusting predicament, they could hardly continue dancing. When the dancing resumes, however, the orchestral *Adagio* merges back into the trance version. As the boys walk down the street, the orchestral *Adagio* reemerges from the trance version. Like the earlier scene, the orchestral version is associated with humiliation. The whole scene, lasting only a few minutes, is one of the most clever juxtapositions of two totally different versions of Barber's *Adagio* in any film. Diegetic and non-diegetic music quickly and logically alternate.

[117]Ian Shutter, "Kevin and Perry Go Large," *VideoVista* (November 2000); reprinted "Dowse Goes to the Movies, New Century of Cinema," www.dowse.com/kevinandperrygolarge.html.

[118]Although this music sounds like the authentic orchestral version, it is actually a convincing synthesized facsimile credited to Philip Page.

[119]Only a small portion of "Another Day" is heard in the movie and never does Jada sing the lyrics. The track on the soundtrack album (Virgin, VTDCDX 298, 2000), listed as "Perfecto Dub Mix," is the complete six-and-a-half-minute Skip Raiders version.

How should the members of the audience respond? By now viewers are likely to regard the boys as sympathetic characters and want them to succeed in both their musical and romantic ventures. In any event, all ends happily: no more humiliation—no more *Adagio*.[120]

Table 8.10. Instrumentational Development in *Kevin and Perry Go Large*

Trance	Orchestra	Trance	Orchestra
Adagio —>	*Adagio* —>	*Adagio* —>	*Adagio*
dancing and revelry	vomiting sequence; boys leave the club	dancing continues with the others	walking sadly down the street

Documentaries

Table 8.11. Documentary Features

YEAR	FILM TITLE PERFORMING ARTISTS	FILM DIRECTOR MEDIUM
1990	*Soldiers of Music*	Susan Froemke *et al.*
	National Symphony Orchestra (Rostropovich)	Orchestra
1997	*Tour of the Inferno: Revisiting Platoon*	Oliver Stone
	Vancouver Symphony Orchestra (Delerue)	Orchestra
2004	*Shake Hands with the Devil*	Peter Raymont
	Studio Orchestra (Mark Korven)	Orchestra
2004	*Peace One Day*	Jeremy Gilley
	Royal Liverpool Philharmonic (Libor Pesek)	Orchestra
2007	*Sicko*	Michael Moore
	Brno Philharmonic Orchestra	Orchestra

The narrative of feature films is a logical placement for *Adagio for Strings*, and yet documentaries may also benefit from it. In the following five examples *Adagio* typically enhances one main scene and reinforces the director's intended emotional purpose.

[120]The boys, however, barely escape additional humiliation when a videotape exposing sexual activity of Perry's parents is shown another night at Amnesia. Although the parents are disgraced, Kevin and Perry are praised for their videotape. When shame turns to triumph, there is no further need for *Adagio*.

SOLDIERS OF MUSIC: ROSTROPOVICH RETURNS TO RUSSIA (PBS)

In *Soldiers of Music, Adagio* is saved for the final scene and the credits. In February 1990 the musical celebrities Mstislav Rostropovich and his wife Galina Vishnevskaya, along with their daughter Olga, traveled to Moscow with the National Symphony Orchestra (NSO) as part of a cultural exchange program between the United States and the Soviet Union. They returned to their homeland after a sixteen-year period of self-exile and official accusations of "activities damaging to the prestige of the Soviet Union." Their citizenships had been revoked, moreover, for harboring author and political dissident Aleksandr Solzhenitsyn. The return, both a celebration and a memorial, was filmed for a documentary. Its title is borrowed from a phrase of their friend and colleague Dmitri Shostakovich, who once proclaimed, "we are all soldiers of music . . . stand firm, play to the end." Rostropovich echoed those words when he avowed, "these past sixteen years that we were in the West . . . we have been true soldiers of our Russian art, Russian Music."[121] During his visit he conducted the NSO at Moscow Conservatory's Great Hall. Poet Yevgeny Yevtushenko, who attended the concert, later remarked:

> He is one of our greatest musicians and we were deprived of him for these many years. The joy of our people at Slava's return can barely be explained and probably not understood by a foreigner. He is Russian, and he is ours. He makes us proud.[122]

The selections were "full of sad messages": the *Pathétique* Symphony of Tchaikovsky, the Fifth Symphony of Shostakovich, and the "elegiac" *Adagio for Strings*.[123] Critic Craig R. Whitney reported that the Barber work "spoke in profound and instantly intelligible terms to the Russian audience."[124] Rostropovich's intense emotion was communicated

[121]Michael Parks, "A 'True Soldier of Russian Art' Picks Up Where He Left Off," *Los Angeles Times* (14 February 1990), F: 1. The documentary by Susan Froemke, Peter Gelb, Albert Maysles, and Bob Eisenhardt, presented in English and Russian with English subtitles, was later marketed on videotape by Cami Video, with the cooperation of ZDF, Channel 4, Nos, Orf, PBS, and Sony Classical. It was first shown on most PBS stations on 1 January 1991.

[122]*Ibid.*

[123]Otto Friedrich, "Tears and Triumph," *Time* (26 February 1990), 70. The program was shown live over Soviet television.

[124]Craig R. Whitney, "Rostropovich Is Home at Last With Just a Touch of America," *The New York Times* (14 February 1990), C: 13.

throughout the performance, especially during the climax; the audience responded with applause and cheers.[125]

The documentary begins as the Rostropovich family is greeted by a huge crowd of fans at the Moscow airport. They are later honored at a testimonial dinner and then visit the grave of their friend Andrei Sakharov. Excerpts show the maestro practicing his cello as well as rehearsing the orchestra in several pieces, but not *Adagio.* A four-minute passage of that work, however, occurs at the end where it accompanies daughter and father on their ride to the airport for their return flight to the United States. (Galina went to the airport separately.) Slava says, "We're off. Good." As the camera scans the Russian landscape of birches in the snow, they grasp each other's hands. Olga smiles and reflects on the visit: "Can you imagine that we were here only for a week? Only seven days, imagine." Her father replies, "It seemed like a year." She adds, "like sixteen years! In one week, we lived the entire sixteen years." These lines lead into the final credits as *Adagio* continues up through the climactic section. The first two chords of the quiet chord passage are omitted, and the music and the documentary end with the final three chords of that passage. The homecoming had been a triumph but also an emotional and physical ordeal. Barber's music underscores their emotional catharsis, a sense of accomplishment that their visit was successful but also a sense of relief that it was over.

TOUR OF THE INFERNO: REVISITING PLATOON

In 1997 Oliver Stone devised a documentary about the filming of *Platoon* that provides descriptions of the many hardships faced by the cast and crew. In its background score is music by Ralph Vaughan Williams, Edward Elgar, and Gustav Mahler, pieces that do not occur in the movie itself. *Adagio for Strings* logically is heard when Willem Dafoe discusses the death of his character, one of the scenes where it was so effective. Near the end, the music is repeated as several of the participating actors discuss the significance of the film: Willem Dafoe ("I look back on it as very gratifying experience"); Charlie Sheen ("I knew we were making a very important film"); Johnny Depp ("I'm really proud to have been involved in that film"); and Tom Beringer ("I have the feeling that this is going to be one of the great movies"). *Adagio* continues as Vietnam

[125]See "Mstislav Rostropovich-Barber-Adagio for Strings Op.11," *YouTube* (27 April 2011), posted by i13012003m.

veterans from Stone's actual platoon discuss their reactions to the film, such as "this movie has a lot to do with [the fact that] I can finally say that I'm very proud to be a Vietnam veteran."[126] In some respects, the presence of *Adagio* in this documentary is just as moving as in *Platoon* itself.

SHAKE HANDS WITH THE DEVIL: THE JOURNEY OF ROMÉO DALLAIRE

Peter Raymont's documentary, *Shake Hands with the Devil: The Journey of Roméo Dallaire,* is based partly on Dallaire's book[127] about his tour of duty as head of United Nation forces in Rwanda in late 1993 but also includes footage of his return there ten years later. The film opens as *Adagio for Strings* accompanies the flight over Lake Victoria into Rwanda. Raymont explained: "Roméo Dallaire used to listen to this piece of music when he was writing his book. . . . He felt it captured the sorrow of the Rwanda genocide, so we thought it was appropriate to start the film with [it]."[128] Yet only a small snippet of the music actually is provided; film score composer Mark Korven merely incorporates a few recognizable fragments into his own fantasia for strings. One reviewer noticed that, "even before a single word is spoken, it is readily apparent in his eyes that [Dallaire] is carrying demons with him that no one ought to have to bear—and they will likely haunt him for the rest of his life."[129] Another reviewer is convinced, however, that Barber's "hackneyed" *Adagio* "over-dramatizes Dallaire's agony."[130] Yet how can his agony be over-dramatized? It has taken him over a decade to come to terms with the genocide, even to the point of attempting suicide on more than one occasion. As he and his wife were flying into the country, he remembers telling her: "I wish I could turn back now . . . to me it seemed like going back into hell." This is heard by

[126]The documentary, originally released in 1997, is now included with the *Platoon* DVD set. In 2002 the cable channel AMC produced a similar half-hour documentary on *Platoon* for its *Backstory* series, designed to follow a run of the movie. Brief passages of *Adagio* appeared here but only because they were already a part of the film clips being presented.

[127]Roméo Dallaire and Brent Beardsley, *Shake Hands with the Devil: The Failure of Humanity in Rwanda* (New York: Carroll & Graf, 2004). This documentary should not be confused with the dramatization of Dallaire's life in Rwanda, simply titled *Shake Hands with the Devil,* directed by Roger Spottiswoode (Seville Pictures, 2007). Raymont's documentary was officially released by the Canadian Broadcasting Corporation (Canada) and California Newsreel (US) in 2004 and 2005.

[128]"Director's Commentary," *Shake Hands with the Devil* (White Pine Pictures, CBC and Société Radio Canada, 2004).

[129]Nate Meyers, "'Review' for Microfilms, Inc.," *digitallyObsessed!,* www.digitallyobsessed.com/show review.php3?=7095.

[130]Elbert Ventura, "The Power of Nightmares," *Reverse Shot Online,* www.reverseshot.com/legacy/dog days05/shake.html.

the viewers as a voice-over. While later musical passages have a mood similar to *Adagio,* Korven never quotes it again.

PEACE ONE DAY

Peace One Day is the documentation of actor (now director) Jeremy Gilley's five-year crusade to persuade the United Nations to devote one day a year to a "global cease-fire day," on which all the world's conflicts might briefly be set aside. Most of the film shows him soliciting support from diplomats, ambassadors, and heads of state; it culminates in a meeting with Secretary-General Kofi Annan, who endorses his idea. Although the United Nations had already established an International Day of Peace in 1981, it was never seriously observed. On 7 September 2001 Gilley's resolution, "Peace One Day"—the name of his organization as well as the film's title—was presented to the General Assembly. In the documentary he introduces the scene with *Adagio*'s first two phrases as solemn background.[131] After a view of the empty assembly room, he whispers into the camera: "the session of the General Assembly has just started, and I'm here in a booth waiting for the United Kingdom to establish the first ever global cease-fire day. Fingers crossed." The music unfolds as Sir Jeremy Greenstock, the United Kingdom representative, presents the resolution, but it stops when he proposes 21 September as United Nations International Day of Peace. The bill was co-sponsored by Costa Rica; when its ambassador, Maria Elena Chassoul, concluded her remarks, "we hope this resolution will be adopted and strongly supported by all the member states," *Adagio*'s climactic passage occurs. The music ends when the Assembly president, concluding that all are in favor, bangs his gavel.

Annan was scheduled to ring the "peace bell" at the United Nations to announce the new Day of Peace on 11 September 2001. Ironically, on that exact date the World Trade Center's twin towers were attacked, and the announcement had to be postponed. Nevertheless, starting in 2002 and each year since, the Day of Peace has been observed with rallies and concerts on 21 September.[132]

[131]"Adagio for Strings," *Classic FM at the Movies*, perf. Royal Liverpool Philharmonic, cond. Libor Pesek (Classic FM, B000FJGR62, 2006).

[132]Other films are reported to use *Adagio* in telling their stories, but I have not seen them to confirm this assertion: the documentary *Fermeture de l'usine Renault à Vilvoode* [Closing Down of a Renault Factory at Vilvoode] (Belgium, 1998), directed by Jan Bucquoy; and a crime thriller, *Jägarna* (1996), directed by Kjell Sundvall, about deer poaching in Sweden. Other possibilities are *Lise et Andre* (France, 2000), *Meine Liebe Rose* (UK / Germany, 1990), and *Falling for You* (US, 1995), a television movie.

WHAT DO WE DO WITH *SICKO*?

Is *Sicko*, Michael Moore's tirade against the American health care system, a serious documentary or a comedy? While he certainly plays some scenes for laughs (often at the expense of the poor victims), he is otherwise deadly serious. In one such scene Barber's *Adagio for Strings* accompanies the testimony before Congress of former claims-examiner Linda Peeno, in which she reveals how her bosses treated their clients. As the music plays, she supplies the following confession:

> In the spring of 1987, as a physician, I denied a man a necessary operation that would have saved his life, and thus caused his death. No person and no group has held me accountable for this, because in fact what I did was save a company half a million dollars. . . . I had one primary duty, and that was to use my medical expertise for the benefit of the organization for which I worked. I was told repeatedly that I was not denying care, I was simply denying payment.

In general, reviewers thought Moore overstepped the boundary of taste by underscoring this scene with Barber's music. Scott Renshaw suggested that the director did not consider the testimony itself dramatic enough and therefore required *Adagio* "to amp up the pathos." (The movie itself he called "almost laughably shameless.")[133] Eunice Wong reminded viewers, "No violins were playing when Peeno made her testimony. The music, ostensibly used to enhance the gravity of the situation, only prevents the audience from realizing the full, unadorned weight of reality."[134] Aaron Mesh went even further:

> Is the use of *Adagio* a joke, a clever parody of the manipulative power of propaganda? No, it's just very bad propaganda. And it reveals a man [Moore] who, even when he's restraining himself,

[133]Scott Renshaw, "Health in a Handbasket," *Salt Lake City Weekly* (28 June 2007); reprinted www.cityweekly.net/utah/article-7-5759-health-in-a-handbasket.html

[134]Eunice Wong, "Movie Reviews: Michael Moore's 'Sicko,'" *Truthdig* (29 June 2007); www.truthdig.com/report/item/20070629_movie_review_michael_moore_sicko/.

thinks so little of his admirers that he feeds them the most transparent sentimental appeals.[135]

I attended the movie with a full audience in its first week of release. Although the audience booed President Bush at his first appearance and laughed at what Moore undoubtedly intended as the "right places," it was ominously silent during the *Adagio*-Peeno scene. My own reaction was a verbal, "oh, no!" (My apologies to those sitting near me.) Of all the applications of *Adagio* in movies and television this is surely the most brazen and calculating. Mark Zimmer's comment about its treatment in *The Elephant Man,* quoted earlier, is even more appropriate here: "it makes the viewer feel manipulated rather than genuinely moved."[136] I do not like being manipulated, or even worse, being told how I am "supposed" to feel. I agree with composer John Cage's position, "I don't mind being moved, but I don't like to be pushed."[137] My reaction was the direct opposite of what the filmmaker intended.

Movie Trailers

If a director knows well in advance that he or she wants *Adagio for Strings* in a film score, a brief excerpt might be introduced in the trailer, the preview of coming attractions, as in those for *Platoon, Roseaux sauvages,* and *Reconstruction.*[138] Stone, Téchiné, and Boe, convinced that Barber's composition would play a vital role in their films, determined that a short presentation in the trailers would intensify their views. Because it is not necessarily the director who decides on the nature of a trailer, it cannot be assumed, however, that these directors controlled the musical content. Yet it would be understandable if *Adagio* were already selected for a movie that time limitations (ca. two minutes) would not permit inclusion (*Rocky Marciano, Lorenzo's Oil, ma mère*). If it plays only a minor part in the

[135]Aaron Mesh, "Physician, Heal Thyself: A Kinder, Gentler Michael Moore Still Stings a Little," *Williamette Week Online* (27 June 2007); reprinted www.wweek.com/portland/article-7206physician _heal_thyself.html.

[136]Mark Zimmer, "Review," *DVD Movie Guide,* 10.

[137]John Cage, quoted in Richard Kostelanetz, "The Aesthetics of John Cage: A Composite Interview," *The Kenyon Review* IX/4 (Autumn 1987), 125.

[138]Trailers are often included in the DVD package for the films. Another source on the Internet is *Reelz Channel*, www.reelzchannel.com. Note some items that are called trailers on *YouTube* are sometimes devised by videographers as tributes.

movie, placing it in the trailer would lend it too great an importance (*Amélie, Sicko*).

In the *Platoon* trailer this music functions as a "book-end" effect. At the beginning it accompanies the narrator's comments about Stone's real-life Vietnam experiences. A pop music tune underscores most of the excerpted scenes, but *Adagio* returns at the end for the pronouncement, "the first real casualty of war is innocence.[139] The first real movie about the war in Vietnam is *Platoon*." This trailer encapsulates the treatment of music in the movie itself: Barber's composition for contemplative moments and diegetic pop music for scenes of army life. Barber's piece is heard throughout the preview for *Roseaux,* reinforcing Téchiné's concept that it is central to his story. In the *Reconstruction* trailer it is inserted during scenes when the lovers exchange glances and when Alex expresses fundamental frustration and during the final minute, as praise from critical reviews and lists of awards are displayed.

In a strange reversal of practice *Adagio* is found in the previews of two other films, *The Messenger* (1999) and *Crash* (2005), but not in the movies themselves. Why? Because a trailer is usually compiled and distributed long before the movie itself, the editing may not be completed and the soundtrack may not have been finalized. Part of Barber's score might have been a temp-track in these films and all that was available. In the one for *The Messenger,* directed by Luc Besson, the music underscores Jeanne (Joan of Arc, the titular Messenger of God) as she explains her visions to the Dauphin. In the full-length feature Eric Serra's newly composed music accompanies the scene. If the director asked him to compose music similar to Barber's, he did not comply. His music is quite different, more mysterious, and more suitable for the hallucinogenic visions that Jeanne describes. In the trailer for Paul Haggis's *Crash,* a hard-edged movie about race relations in Los Angeles, *Adagio* underscores snippets of dialogue that appear in several different places in the final cut of the movie: "In any real city you walk, you know, you brush past people—people bump into you. In LA nobody touches you; you're always behind this metal and glass."[140] In the movie Mark Isham presents his own meditative music for the scenes that contain these lines, now spread out

[139]This is a spin on a phrase attributed to Aeschylus, "in war, truth is the first casualty."

[140]The original trailer was available in mid-2007 on www.apple.com trailers/lions_gate/crash/large.html. Several videos on *YouTube* appear to be the *Crash* trailer but are either the studio's re-editing or a blogger's own invention. They do not contain Barber's *Adagio.*

over several different segments. But unlike Serra's music, his resembles Barber's sound and mood and, to me, is much less intrusive and distracting than *Adagio* itself. I do not know if movie-goers were disappointed that the work did not find its way into the final cut of *The Messenger,* but several Internet bloggers expressed such a view about *Crash.* When they heard it in the trailer, they believed and hoped that it would also be placed in the movie. Were these trailers misleading? Columnist Chris Hewitt contends, "the previews you see when you go to the movies are called trailers, but trai-liars might be closer to the mark."[141] In their defense such advertisements need to convey in two minutes the gist of a story that will eventually take two hours. Their sole purpose is to lure in customers, not provide them with truthful information.

A FINAL DIGRESSION: *ADAGIO* FOR A METHOD ACTOR

Even when *Adagio for Strings* is not part of a soundtrack, it may still be an influential force as a motivational tool in an actor's methodology. Matt Damon and Will Smith are two actors who actually listen to it to acquire the right frame of mind before filming specific scenes. I have not encountered comments by Damon enumerating which scenes he prepared by listening to *Adagio;* on the other hand, Smith reported how Damon encouraged him to try this strategy:

> A big thing I learned from Matt Damon is music. Two hours before a scene he already has his headphones on. He finds something in pieces that take him to the places he needs to be for a scene. He gave me about six or seven pieces of fantastic music. There's the theme from *Platoon,* "Adagio for Strings." I used that for the bathroom scene in the *The Pursuit of Happyness,* and in *I Am Legend* for the post-choking dog scene. I used it in the final scene in *Seven Pounds.* . . . Anything that can carry you to the space you want. After awhile, you learn what things can take you to where you need to be.[142]

[141]Chris Hewitt, "Rule of Thumb: Don't Trust Movie Trailers," *Indianapolis Star* (7 January 2006), E: 9.

[142]Will Smith, quoted in Jeff Niesel, "Suicidal Tendencies," *Scene Magazine* (17 December 2008); reprinted www.clevescene.com/cleveland/suicidal-tendencies/Content?oid=1534451.

The three scenes cited by Smith are all highly charged, tense episodes. Because they contain little or no dialogue, he must convey his emotions strictly through body language and facial expressions. His expression during the choking dog scene is particularly effective. Re-watching these scenes, with the understanding that Smith may have been inspired by *Adagio*, puts them in a new light. The actor may have kept the sound of that music in his mind when the filming took place. Barber's composition, indeed, took him to the emotional places he "needed to be." Of course, this music is not heard in the soundtracks. Yet the scene from *Seven Pounds* (2008) is accompanied by a formidable choral background suggesting the climax in Agnus Dei; likewise the bathroom scene in *The Pursuit of Happyness* (2006) unfolds to quiet music with an *Adagio*-like sound. It is doubtful, however, that the film composers deliberately copied Barber. (For deliberate *Adagio* sound-alikes, see Chapter 11.) After all these scene preparations, nonetheless, Smith may need to find new music. He realized that he has built up so many associations to past films with *Adagio* that it became a problem in helping him on his latest movie.[143]

Television

Adagio for Strings has surfaced in numerous television series in several countries, primarily the United States and Great Britain. In general, it provides emotional background for dramas, ironic accompaniment for comedies, and appropriate support in documentaries. Because television shows are shorter than movies, usually only a half-hour or an hour at the most, *Adagio* excerpts tend to appear in short segments, and usually only once, to enhance a specific scene. Among the following shows, only the sitcom *Seinfeld* and the cartoon *American Dad* present it twice in a single episode, setting up the kind of parallel situation illustrated in the movies discussed previously. Table 8.12 offers a chronological listing of relevant television series, along with their country of origin and genre. This chart reveals similarities to the lists of movies presented earlier (see Table 8.5 and 8.7).

[143]Andy Gray, "Will Smith Is Ready for Risks," [Cleveland] *Tribune Chronicle* (18 December 2008); reprinted www.tribtoday.com/page/content.detail/id/515177/Will-Smith-is-Ready-for-Risks.html.

Table 8.12. Television Series Features

YEAR	FILM TITLE	COUNTRY	GENRE
1973	*The Ascent of Man*	UK / US	Documentary
1991	**Celeste* [Heavenly]	Argentina	Drama
1991	*Soldiers of Music*	US	Documentary
1992	*One Life to Live*	US	Drama (soap opera)
1995	*The Oprah Winfrey Show*	US	Talk Show
1996	*Seinfeld*	US	Comedy (sit-com)
1996	*The Fast Show*	UK	Comedy
1998	*Daria*	US	Comedy (cartoon)
1999	*Red Dwarf*	UK	Comedy
2000	*At Home with the Braithwaites*	UK	Drama-comedy
2001	*Spaced*	UK	Comedy
2002	**Esperança* [Hope]	Brazil	Drama
2003	*ER*	US	Drama
2003	*The Simpsons*	US	Comedy (cartoon)
2004	*Filthy Homes from Hell*	UK	Comedy (reality)
2004	*South Park*	US	Comedy (cartoon)
2006	*Soccer AM*	UK	Comedy (sports)
2007	*Boondocks*	US	Comedy (cartoon)
2009	*American Dad*	US	Comedy (cartoon)
2009	*Big Love*	US	Drama
2010	*Big Brother 11*	UK	Comedy (reality)
2010	*Misfits*	UK	Drama
2010	*That Mitchell and Webb Look*	UK	Comedy
2010	*The Nostalgia Critic*	US	Satire (parody)

Found in all three genres represented, *Adagio* was far more often placed in comedies, notably five American cartoon series. Its return to serious drama, so evident in the movies, is rare on television; in recent years it was used in that capacity in only two programs from the United States and one from the United Kingdom. In addition to the series listed, *Adagio* was heard in two shows from South America (marked by an asterisk). They are not discussed in the following text because neither has been broadcast on American television nor has been issued on videotape or DVD.

Dramas on American and British Television

Table 8.13. Television Dramas

YEAR	SERIES TITLE	NETWORK
1992	*One Life to Live*	ABC
2001	*At Home with the Braithwaites*	BBC / BBC America
2003	*ER*	NBC
2009	*Big Love*	HBO
2010	*Misfits*	British e4

ONE LIFE TO LIVE

Adagio appeared in two episodes of the soap opera *One Life to Live,* both in 1992, when Linda Gottlieb was executive producer and Michael Malone was head writer. In both cases, composer-director Jamie Howarth suggested this music.[144] The first occurred in February during the sequence leading to the death of Megan (Jessica Tuck). Although not played as the character dies, the complete Barber score was adopted for a significant scene preceding it, one where her friend and priest, Andrew (Wortham Krimmer), visits her in her hospital room. He secretly loves her, but she is in love with Jake, yet has some feelings for Andrew, and perhaps subconsciously realizes his love for her. Such are the complexities of soap opera love triangles. *Adagio* begins as Andrew enters the room. Megan, who knows she is dying, tells him that she wants no "solemn dull moods" at her funeral. "I don't want the guests more unhappy than the person in the coffin. . . . No dirges, no formal black clothes. I just want everyone to wear funky bright colors. I want them to dance, and I want music so loud that the cops come."[145] As the music begins its upward climactic phrase, she tells Andrew, "This is hard for me to ask. . . . I need you to promise me that you'll take care of Jake." When the quiet chords enter, Andrew promises: "Listen, I don't have a choice. I am always going to love Jake, always, because he meant so much to you." As the coda begins, she asks him if he remembers the day they met:

[144]Jamie Howarth, email (12 May 2012) to the author. The show featured Howarth's favorite recording: the Saint Louis Symphony Orchestra conducted by Leonard Slatkin in 1981.

[145]"From February 7, 1992" [script], *One Life to Live* (17 November 2002), www.geocities.com /historypg/tr920207.html.

Megan:	I asked you if you believed that people came back from the dead.
Andrew:	And I said something of a person survives.
Megan:	Well, if you're right, I will be seeing you.
Andrew:	I hope so.
Megan:	And if you're wrong—you're out of a job.
Andrew:	We will see each other again.[146]

When he begins to cry, she kisses him on the cheek; he kisses her on the lips and hand. As he leaves, the music reaches its final phrase. This complete performance of *Adagio* accompanies a full eight-minute scene, uninterrupted by commercials, a musico-dramatic sequence never found on soaps these days.[147]

A nearly complete *Adagio* returned later that August. Earlier in the year the writers had introduced the topic of homophobia. To bring this particular story line to a dramatic end, Gottlieb conceived the idea of featuring the AIDS quilt. "The quilt is a strong . . . image. It's visual; it's powerful; it's easily dramatized. It's an abstraction against hatred."[148] The quilt scene is primarily a monologue for Sloane Carpenter (Roy Thinnes) as he talks to his son Andrew, who functioned as a sounding board to Megan in the scene just discussed and now to his father in this one. Malone, the head writer, was fond of this character: "my memory of Andrew is, first of all, his love for Megan and his noble setting-aside of his own pained and unrequited feelings . . . next of course, he was the heart and soul of one of our most controversial (and honored) stories . . . the quilt story."[149]

Sloane Carpenter has had a great deal of difficulty accepting his other son William's homosexuality and his death from AIDS. This scene brings the whole storyline to a climax. On the lawn in front of the quilt Sloane and Andrew unfold William's "patch" with an image of a kite. As *Adagio* begins, the father recalls for Andrew an incident from William's youth when he tried to instruct his son in kite flying:

[146]*Ibid.*

[147]Note that *Adagio for Strings,* not Agnus Dei, underscores this farewell scene, not Megan's actual death.

[148]Connie Passalacqua, "Strong Dose of Reality for ABC's One Life to Live," *Los Angeles Times* (28 August 1992); reprinted www.articles.latimes.com/1992-08-28/entertainment/ca-6184_1_names-project.

[149]Michael Malone, "11/13 Letter," *Letters to Malone* (3 October 2002), www.letterstomalone.tripod.com/index5.html.

> The weather was grey and raw. William had the sniffles. But there was a wind up and I was determined he was gonna fly that kite. Over your mother's protests I marched him down to the tidewater park. I was so fascinated by the prospect of seeing my son master the wind on his way to mastering the world. I didn't pay attention to him; when it was suddenly too cold and he didn't want to do it. "Stop, boy, stop whining, be a man, run, William, run." When he did, he fell down crying. The kite ended up in the branches, a total wreck. I looked at the shredded wreck and I looked at my son and I said, "Is this a Carpenter? It's a disgrace." I raised my hand and I slapped him and I called him a sissy. I dragged him off and slapped him again.[150]

Adagio's climactic section begins as Sloane recounts: "Ah, I knew I was wrong. I wouldn't apologize; too proud, and I pretended like it didn't happen. But you couldn't pretend, could you Will?"[151] At this point the writers have made two subtle but significant changes: one from narrative to direct address—the father now speaks directly to his dead son; second, he uses the more personal "Will" rather than the formal "William." He continues to mix direct and indirect address as he tells Andrew: "He just looked at me with those grey eyes, and I saw a veil come over them. Over the years it became a shield, then a wall. I lost you."[152] As Sloane runs his hand over the quilt patch, he confesses, "I lost you because I couldn't tell you 'I'm sorry, I'm sorry, sorry.'"[153] At this emotional outburst *Adagio* reaches the end of its climactic phrase. He cries as he utters, "Ah, my beautiful boy, my precious son. I miss him so."[154] The music skips to *Adagio*'s final phrase as he walks away. Sensing how difficult it was for his father to make this confession, Andrew follows him.

Notice that in both scenes the dialogue and music build to their respective points simultaneously, suggesting that *Adagio* could not have been arbitrarily added as background. For years I suspected that Gottlieb, Malone, and Howarth knew all along that they wanted *Adagio* to support

[150]"From July 1992" [script], *One Life to Live*, www.oocities.org/historypg/tr9209x2.html.

[151]*Ibid.*

[152]*Ibid.*

[153]*Ibid.*

[154]*Ibid.*

these scenes and therefore constructed the drama and dialogue to coordinate with them. Howarth corroborated that concept:

> We cut the montage sequence to match the Barber Adagio. We played the music to the actors in rehearsal so they knew the mood. It is actually uncanny sometimes how dialogue rhythms seem to magically speak in the same cadence as the music.[155]

I believe, however, that the coordination is more than just uncanny magic; all those involved have shown a clear understanding of the relationship between word and music. Using an early form of Protools, Howarth added the music during post-production, a technique that was new for soap operas in those days. He admitted that he would occationally "slide the music around a bit to fit. Because each phrase ends with a femata and with lots of 6 / 4 bars, it is easy to snip here and there and never give it away."[156] He also recalled that Gottlieb was "real good on music. We spent a fortune during her era."[157]

I think both episodes illustrate effective treatment of this music in a dramatic situation, comparable to any movie. It is no wonder that some soap opera fans look back with nostalgia to the early 1990s episodes of *One Life to Live* as a "golden age": the "Gottlieb-Howarth Era." Marg Harris, compiler of the *OLTL Music History*, concludes:

> In retrospect, those were the years when OLTL was at its peak, dramatically and musically. Perhaps it was a rare time. Currently [late 1997], OLTL is being written to emphasize dialogue rather than music and action. The characteristic quality of the music is still there in the background but it does not seem to be given the priority it once had, not so long ago.[158]

[155]Jamie Howarth, email (12 May 2012) to the author. Thanks to his forward-looking skills, Howarth won three daytime Emmys® and two Directors Guild of America awards.

[156]*Ibid.*

[157]*Ibid.*

[158]Marg Harris, *OLTL Music History* (1997; updated 1998); www.geocities.com/Hollywood/Academy/6053/marg.html. Both scenes are available at the Paley Center, New York City.

Times have changed. It is unlikely that Barber's *Adagio*, either complete or in part, could ever appear on any of today's remaining soap operas.[159]

AT HOME WITH THE BRAITHWAITES

This dramatic-comedy series concerns members of the dysfunctional Braithwaite family and their antics in coping with winning a large sum of money in the lottery. In the third episode of series two (2001) a scene takes place at a nightclub. There Virginia Braithwaite (Sarah Smart), a lesbian, encounters her neighbor Megan Hartnoll (Julie Graham), with whom she is infatuated. While they have a drink, Ferry Corsten's remix of Ørbit's "Samuel Barber's Adagio for Strings" is playing. At first it seems to be merely a suitable diegetic dance beat to provide the proper clubbing atmosphere, but whoever selected it clearly had a dramatic intention. During Corsten's opening "prelude," which is fairly generic, the women's conversation about love is fairly general but, when the recognizable slow part of *Adagio* emerges, the dialogue becomes more personal:

> Virginia: It must be very easy, being normal.
>
> Megan: Well, if it is any consolation, it isn't. Look at me and Mike [her husband]. . . . Why do we do it? God knows. Because it's easier to stick together and pretend, and even when it isn't, people stick together because they're frightened [the slow part of *Adagio* emerges] or weak or mad or because they have to or because they're still in love with each other, in a stupid kind of way, even when they hate each other.
>
> Virginia: I'm still in love with you.
>
> Megan: (with understanding compassion) I know.

As the trance beat is added to Barber's phrases, the two kiss purposefully —not just a friendly peck on the lips but a deeply felt display of both affection and passion. Viewers are probably surprised at their tenderness because neither usually come across as sympathetic characters. For once, their sincere feelings are vividly conveyed as *Adagio* increases in intensity.

[159]After the show's cancellation and after much negotiation, new episodes of *One Life to Live* became available online in 2013.

ER: "THE LOST"

Barber's Agnus Dei occurs near the end of "The Lost," episode two of the tenth season (2003) of NBC's popular medical drama, *ER*. Dr. John Carter (Noah Wyle) flies to the Congo to escort home the body of Luka Kovac (Goran Visnjic), his medical colleague and friend. The two men had worked together in that region during the previous season; Carter had learned of Kovac's murder in the 2003 season opener. The story unfolds on two levels. In the present Carter, his colleague Jillian, and a Red Cross worker search for Kovac in the Congo. Interspersed with these scenes is the story of Kovac told in flashbacks. In one crucial scene he aids a young Congolese girl, whose mother is so grateful that she places a crucifix around his neck and proclaims him a man of God. At this stage neither he nor the viewers realize the significance of her gesture.

Near the end of that episode several people, including Kovac, the woman, and her daughter, have been captured by one of the Congolese rebel factions. Prisoners are taken away one by one and shot; Kovac believes he will be next. At this point Agnus Dei begins. The captors now notice the crucifix, and the woman shouts, "You cannot kill a man of God!" The captors, believing he is a priest, spare his life. Meanwhile both stories merge when Carter finds Kovac still alive. As the choral music continues, they all leave in the back of a truck. The music fades out as Kovac is taken aboard a plane for his return to America.

In this series Barber's music is still associated with death, but only as a fear of an impending experience. Because Kovac's rescue through a misunderstanding creates a kind of religious apotheosis, the choral version, with its sacred text, is a more appropriate accompaniment than the orchestral version. Kovac was nearly a Sacrificial Lamb, spared like the Biblical Isaac at the final moment.[160]

BIG LOVE: "OUTER DARKNESS" AND "FREE AT LAST"

Barber's Agnus Dei was heard twice on the Home Box Office (HBO) series *Big Love*: in episode nine of the third season (15 March 2009) and episode one of the fourth season (10 January 2010). This program depicts the lives of families who belong to the Church of Jesus Christ of Latter Day Saints, more frequently known as the Mormon Church. Stories deal with the conflicts between the church's religious dogma and personal views of

[160]Closing credits do not list the recording, but it is probably the Cambridge University Chamber Choir. The decision here may have been made by Martin Davich, who is credited with the music; but it could also be Sharyn Tylk-Gersh, music editor, or Ann Kline, music supervisor.

faith and belief. Along the way the writers mix in aspects of ethics, family relationships, and sex. The title of the first episode comes from a comment by Bill Hendrickson (Bill Paxton), the male lead who warns his wife Barb (Jean Tripplehorn) that "we will all be cast into the outer darkness," which in Latter-day Saint parlance means a kind of spiritual world for sinners.[161] They have been married for several years, but Bill has now added two more wives to his family (with Barb's approval). While polygamy was initially part of church doctrine, it is no longer condoned. One of the religious officials describes it as "an abomination, a shameful practice that has no place in the modern church." In this episode, after Barb is forced to confess that she is "living in a polygamist relationship," she is informed that she is to be questioned by the church council. To restore her to more active participation in the church, she undergoes an "endowment" ceremony, for which the beginning of Agnus Dei serves as background.

As the ceremony begins, a "temple worker" acting as "the Lord" in charge of the ceremony, asks Barb a series of questions. She cannot answer all of them, but she pledges, "I have come to converse with the Lord through the veil" (which hides the worker, only his arm stretches out to her). He offers the answer: "health in the navel, marrow in the bones, strength in the loins and in the sinews; power in the priesthood be upon me and upon my posterity through all generations of time and throughout all eternity." After repeating this vow she is permitted to walk through the veil and enter the "Celestial Room" containing several people, including her mother and sister, who welcome her with embraces. Agnus Dei continues as Barb's mother (Ellen Burstyn) declares, "this is just a little foretaste of what eternity will look like. This is what binds us to each other." After the music concludes, Barb begins to cry, and her mother asks what is wrong; despite her participation in a ritual to bring her closer to the church, she must still submit to a "disciplinary hearing" the next day.

During this hearing—more like an inquisition—Barb is asked to repent living in this polygamist relationship but refuses to do so. She replies, "I can't forsake my family," which includes not only her own children, but also the other two wives and their children. The council ex-communicates her: "henceforth your name shall be removed from the records." No matter what one's views may be as to the merits of the church's actions, the writers clearly want the audience to empathize with Barb. In her mind, concern for family takes precedence over church dogma.

[161]Alma 40:13. This quotation is an important tenet of *The Book of Mormon.*

This episode created a major controversy even before it was first aired. The Mormons are reluctant to reveal details of their religious ceremonies. This fictional but accurate depiction of a small part of one was considered an invasion of and a violation of the church's private affairs. Yet the text of this ceremony is easily available online. If the content of this ritual is intended as a secret, it is a badly kept one.

Why Agnus Dei? Earlier in the episode a strange character, Hollis Greene (Luke Askew), calls himself a "lamb of God," an epithet that may carry into the ceremony, but the significance is tenuous. The church may provide the endowment ceremony as a means of atoning for sin, representing the Paschal Lamb, but Barb may not quite see it that way. Yet why turn to Barber's setting when one by any composer would have sufficed? The composer for this episode, Anton Sanko, or music supervisors Deva Anderson and Delphine Robertson may know the reason. Following Barber's music, the familiar hymn, "Nearer my God to Thee" (sung to Lowell Mason's BETHANY), offers a somewhat ironic juxtaposition. While Barb may personally feel nearer to God, she has been forced farther from the church.

A portion of the Agnus Dei returns in the episode "Free at Last." After discovering the corpse of the "villainous giant" Roman Grant,[162] Bill Hendrickson hauls the body away in his van and at one opportunity stops to close Roman's still-staring eyes. This is normally a sign of respect, but not in this case due to much animosity between the two characters; here it can be interpreted only as a true "closure" of their turbulent relationship. The first phrase of Agnus Dei makes a suitable accompaniment for this gesture. Later, as an aftermath to this action, Bill and his wives join hands to share a new beginning: "A ghost that has haunted us all through these years is past." Thus the episode's title is justified.

MISFITS

Adagio for Strings can be found—again in its death-accompanying role—in a British sci-fi series, a drama with humorous undertones that features a group of five young "delinquents" who gain supernatural power during a freak thunderstorm. Episode five from season two (2010) of *Misfits* centers on Bruno (Richard Riddell), a gorilla (!) transformed

[162]Cowriter Mark V. Olsen characterized Grant as a "villainous giant" in the "Inside the Episode" feature in *Big Love: The Complete Fourth Season* [DVD] (Playtone, Home Box Office, 2012). My thanks to Linda M. Willem for spotting this Barber excerpt.

into human form during the same storm; his participation is limited to this single installment.

When he attends a fancy dress party, he ironically masquerades as a gorilla. He removes his gorilla head temporarily to ease conversation, especially with Kelly (Lauren Socha), one of the five central characters. (He now looks like a gorilla with a human head.) Having developed romantic feelings for her, he nearly discloses his true identity. Then the police break in to arrest him for a previous crime. Replacing his gorilla head, he abducts Kelly; a stock police chase ensues. With Kelly in his arms, he climbs a tall building. (Just think of another movie in which an ape kidnaps a fair maiden and climbs a skyscraper!) When the police shoot him, he falls, and when his gorilla head is removed, his gorilla face is revealed. Kelly and her friend Nathan (Robert Sheehan), another leading character, now see his real form. About a minute of *Adagio* accompanies his last words: "Do you understand now? I just wanted to be human. It was all worth it, to be with you." Both the scene itself and the music are played seriously, not as parody. This mood, however, is aborted when Nathan asks, "Why is a gorilla wearing a gorilla costume?" This is typical of his off-hand remarks. In the subsequent scene Kelly and Nathan discuss what has transpired. She reflects on Bruno's pleasing demeanor and on the deceptive nature of appearances: "Me, a guy I really liked—he's a fuckin' monkey." After a brief pause, Nathan replies, "Well, technically he was a gorilla, but let's not go there." Again, typical!

Comedies: Live Action (More or Less)

Table 8.14. Television Comedies

Date	Series Title	Network
1996	*Seinfeld*	NBC
1996	*The Fast Show*	BBC
1999	*Red Dwarf*	BBC2
2001	*Spaced*	LWT
2004	*Filthy Homes from Hell*	ITV
2006	*Soccer AM*	Sky
2010	*That Mitchell and Webb Look*	BBC
2010	*Nostalgia Critic*	Channel Awesome

As in movies, the introduction of *Adagio for Strings* on television in serious situations eventually yielded to the role of parody, satire, or a gag. Such humorous incidents do not fit easily into clear-cut categories. *Seinfeld* is accepted as a sit-com, but the genre of *Spaced* is less clearly defined. *Red Dwarf* is a sci-fi comedy; *Fast Show* and *That Mitchell and Webb Look* are sketch comedies. The *Filthy Homes* and *Soccer AM* shows are even more challenging to pigeonhole, the first one being a comedic reality series and the second, a sports comedy anthology. Two poke fun at serious movies while *Nostalgia Critic* acts as a parody film review show. The most difficult of all to define is the unique television series devoted to movie commentaries, *Mystery Science Theater 3000* (see Chapter 11).

SEINFELD: "THE FATIGUES"

A segment of *Adagio for Strings* is heard on *Seinfeld* in "The Fatigues," episode six of season eight (31 October 1996).[163] As usual, this installment has several interlocking plots, one of which concerns the futile efforts of Elaine (Julia Louis-Dreyfus) to fire an employee (the one wearing fatigues). Later, Frank Costanza (Jerry Stiller) has a flashback about his days as a cook in Korea, "slinging hash for the Fighting 103rd." He tells Kramer (Michael Richards) that he regrets preparing prime Texas steer that was past its due date: "I went too far. I over-seasoned it. Men were keeling over all around me." While Frank tells the story, *Adagio* underscores a flashback: "I can still hear the retching, the screaming. I sent sixteen of my own men to the latrines that night. They were just boys." Kramer consoles him: "Frank, you were a boy, too. And it was war. It was a crazy time for everyone." Yes, war can be hell, even in the mess. Even though the setting is Korea rather than Vietnam, the scene clearly lampoons *Platoon*. War is war (as well as hell).

The writers then set up a parallel situation uniting the Elaine and Frank stories. Near the end of the episode, Frank has been persuaded, against his better judgment, to prepare a dinner for a large crowd; Elaine's employee chokes on it. As a result, Frank has another flashback to Korea, prompting a brief reference to *Adagio* while he runs amok and knocks over tables. Like the parallel symbolism of the work in serious films (hope and despair in *El Norte*, potential and expressed love in *Garden of Redemption*), this double-presentation illustrates how a situation in the distant past can

[163]All dialogue quotations are taken from Gregg Kavet and Andy Robin, "The Fatigues," *Seinfeld Scripts*, www.seinfeldscripts.com/TheFatigues.html.

rear its ugly head in the present and cause unexpected chaos. A parody depends inextricably on the audience's familiarity with earlier serious usage. By this time *Adagio* had been borrowed for several film scores, but it is still most clearly associated in viewers' minds with *Platoon*.

THE FAST SHOW

Just as Americans were giggling over *Adagio for Strings* in absurd situations, the British also recognized its satiric potential. Within the span of a decade, *Adagio* was introduced into three British comedies: *The Fast Show, Red Dwarf,* and *Spaced*.

In the mid 1990s *Adagio for Strings* surfaced on the appropriately named, rapid-paced sketch-comedy series, *The Fast Show*. In one recurring segment two off-roaders, Lyndsay Mottram (Paul Whitehouse) and Simon Bush (Charlie Higson) attempt to impress others by having a friend videotape their ill-conceived adventures in the English countryside, where they indulge in sundry activities, such as mountaineering and whitewater rafting. As the promotional paragraph on the BBC website explains: "No amount of bravado could disguise the fact that, when push comes to shove, they are crap." In episode nine from season two (1 March 1996) they are involved in a paintball competition, and they emerge from their tent firing their guns and shouting "paintball!!!" to the strains of *Adagio*. At first it resembles a rather bizarre combination of the paintball scene from *Daria* and the slow-motion shoot-out scene from *Spaced* (both are discussed later on), but this scene antedates them both! Yet there is another connection. As they fire their guns, the action slows down, the picture turns from color to sepia, and the production ends with a freeze frame, a blatant reference to the ending of *Butch Cassidy and the Sundance Kid* (1969).[164] *Adagio* even continues through the beginning part of the final credits.

RED DWARF: "ONLY THE GOOD"

Red Dwarf, a popular sci-fi comedy series originating in the United Kingdom, developed an almost "trekkie" cult following in the United States. (Fans call themselves "dwarfers.") In episode fifty-two (5 April

[164]When the series was introduced in the United States on the USA cable network, it was titled *Brilliant!*, a catchphrase from the show. This very brief clip was posted on *YouTube* as a part of a compilation from the show on 28 April 2007 by wliethof; unfortunately, this video no longer exists there. My thanks to Steve Asunto for not only calling my attention to this clip but also telling me about the *Butch Cassidy* connection.

1999), the final one of the series, Arthur Rimmer (Chris Barrie)—formerly a resident hologram but now restored by nanobots to human form—has entered an anti-universe to find an antidote to combat an alien life form. He has written on an "extremely long" piece of paper the name of this cure, cesiumfrancolithicmyxialobidiumrixydixydoxidexidroxhide,[165] but when he returns to the real universe, it transforms into the viral formula (a sort of anti-antidote), which causes it to burn up spontaneously in his hand. He collapses and, as he lies on the floor, he utters the show's most famous catchword, "Smeg!"[166] This near-lethal disappointment is accompanied by a brief passage from the ubiquitous *Adagio*. When the Grim Reaper (portrayed by director Ed Bye) enters, the viewers assume that it must be Rimmer's swansong:

Grim Reaper:	Arnold Judas Rimmer, your life is over. Come with me. You will travel to the River Styx, where you will place a coin and. . . .
Rimmer:	Not today, Matey. (knees him in the groin) Remember, only the good die young.
Grim Reaper:	(laboured) That has never happened before. . . .

This ending was the third one recorded. Producer and writer Doug Naylor needed to end not only the episode itself and to conclude the last show of the season but indeed to wrap-up the whole eight-season sequence. The first version ended rather cheerfully as the main characters danced a conga line. The second ended far more seriously with the burning formula on the floor, an ending that Naylor finally determined "truly didn't work." At the last minute he decided to insert the Grim Reaper. Chris Barrie remarked later that any of the three endings was satisfactory to him, but he thought the third one with the "punchier ending" was the most fitting. "The whole concept of kicking death in the goobies is well worth having as an ending; it's just so funny."[167] *Adagio for Strings* would not be suitable for the first, upbeat ending, but it had already been added in the second. For the

[165]The name of this formula proves that the show's writers did not suffer from the fear of long words, *i.e.*, hippopotomonstrosesquippedaliophobia. This word is defined in *Dictionary.com*, *Wiktionary.org*, and other sources (sometimes with variant spellings).

[166]While this word is purported to be only a mild expletive, it still would not be wise to say this to a little old British lady during your next trip to England.

[167]Chris Barrie, quoted in *The Tank*, a documentary on the making of season eight featuring interviews with members of the cast and crew. These conversations as well as all three endings are provided on disc

participation of the Grim Reaper, the music simply needed to be extended a few more phrases, ending appropriately and abruptly at the knee to the groin. In both cases, it was the last music heard in the series, apart from the show's traditional theme-song for the credits. Before the credits roll, comes "The End," a sign soon followed by the impudent retort, "the smeg it is!" This paves the way for either a new series or a feature film. So far, Naylor has not been able to obtain funding for the film, but in 2009, ten years after the show ended, UK Channel Dave aired a new three-part episode, "Back to Earth." Ratings were high, but audience reaction was lukewarm at best. For some, it was a smegging disappointment!

SPACED: "GONE"

Spaced, a surreal sit-com from Great Britain, often incorporates satiric references to movies, television shows, and commercials. It is written by Simon Pegg and Jessica Stevenson, who also play the lead characters, Tim Bisley and Daisy Steiner. According to critic Mike Mclaughlin, the show presents "startlingly funny moments of harrowing hyper-reality."[168] In the second season *Adagio for Strings* is inserted in "Gone" (2001), purported to be the cast's favorite episode. The music occurs during a gun-less shoot-out, one of the most surrealistic moments in this (or any other) series, the consequence of the following seemingly unrelated incidents:

1. Daisy uses oregano to make "one of the all-time great chicken stews." As she sniffs it, she says, "oh, mama!"
2. Tim and his friend Mike Watt, who has a military obsession, have a playful, childish confrontation shooting each other with finger pistols, while making appropriate battle noises. They stop when Daisy walks in on them.
3. When Tim and Daisy go pub-crawling, they encounter a young punk who mistakenly believes that Tim has marijuana for sale.
4. Outside the pub, the punk and his gang of scallies accost Tim and Daisy. When she hands him a baggy, he sniffs it and says, "oh, mama!" (Can you guess what is in the baggy?)

three of the DVD set, *Red Dwarf VIII* (BBC Video, 1999). The entire episode is found on disc two. See "Red Dwarf–Last Episode–Only The Good," *YouTube* (6 May 2009), posted by alltimejust. The *Adagio* portion begins at 7:40.

[168]Mike Mclaughlin, "Mike Mclaughlin's Top 5 Region 2 for 2002," *DVD Reviewer* (21 January 2003), www.dvd.reviewer.co.uk/news/article.asp?Index=7010.

Now for the scene that brings all this together. Once the gang realizes that they have been smoking oregano rather than grass (no surprise here), they again confront Tim and Daisy. When he asks her what they should do, they panic and in a moment of desperation go into the fake "finger pistol" shoot-out routine—and it works! As bodies fall, the action converts to slow motion while a segment of *Adagio for Strings* is played. With all lying motionless on the ground, *Adagio* reaches the final chord of the climax, which quickly aborts. Tim and Daisy simply get up and leave.

A writer at the BBC compared the scene to the slow, graceful balletic gunfights in John Woo movies, but the music brings it closer to *Platoon*.[169] Mclaughlin called it a moment of "indulgent silliness," yet it "somehow seems utterly perfect."[170] If taken out of context, this scene does seem silly. Only those who have followed the previous episodes would realize how well such a moment fits into the show's overall concepts.

THE NOSTALGIA CRITIC: "FERNGULLY 2" AND "LOST WORLD JURASSIC PARK 2"

In addition to traditional movies and television, a new form of programming has emerged in the last two decades: digital, online web television. "Programs" are professionally produced strictly for Internet browsers, bypassing the standard media altogether. One such series is *The Nostalgia Critic*, an outrageously pretentious and largely unfunny send-up of film review format—a combination of *Siskel and Ebert* with *Mystery Science Theater 3000* (but compared to the latter, not nearly as inspired). The pseudo-critic, Chicago comedian Doug Walker, retells movie plots, which are disguised as reviews, reduced to about a half-hour, and accompanied by clips from other sources and the critic's own screamingly loud commentary. There were brief excerpts from *Adagio* introduced in two episodes, both from season four (2010).[171] Of course, neither film under consideration contains references to the Barber piece in its soundtrack.

[169]Nonentity, "Battles," *'Spaced'–the TV Series* (13 December 2004), www.news.bbc.co.uk/dna/place-lancashire/plain/A3342539.

[170]Mike Mclaughlin, "Top 5 Region 2 for 2002," *DVD Reviewer*. The DVD edition comes complete with an "Homage-O-Meter," a subtitle track that "points out each show's relentless stream of in-jokes and pop-cultural intertexts."

[171]Episodes are available at several websites, including *YouTube*. Complete scripts of the shows—not the movies themselves—can be found at *Channel Awesome*, www.thatguywiththeglasses.wikia.com.

In a scene from the animated feature *Ferngully 2*, a mother kangaroo amidst a fiery forest cries out, "my baby!" while she raises her arms in the air like Willem Dafoe in *Platoon* and like Sandi in "The Daria Hunter" (see page 384). The critic remarks, "Wow, that was, like, the kangaroo version of *Platoon*." At that moment the scene is presented in slow motion, *Adagio* is added to the soundtrack, and the image of Dafoe is superimposed on the image of the imploring kangaroo mother. Cute.

Adagio recurs in "Lost World: Jurassic Park" in a somewhat similar context concerning the death of an animal. This time villains have killed a dinosaur, a parasaurolophus, but after one of them tries to pronounce the name, he can only refer to its "big red horn and a pompadour—Elvis." The audience sees "our heroes," including Jeff Goldblum, Julianne Moore, and "a doughy guy," staring at the dead creature in disbelief and horror, "and they let it all sink in." Such somber looks call for the sad strains of *Adagio* (about twenty seconds' worth). The critic pompously declares, "What have we become?" and then proclaims, "Truly WE are the savage animal." Clearly MAN is the villain in both movies. In the first, the use of *Adagio* was rather clever, capitalizing on two pre-existing models, but in the second, its presence merely seems like suitable but clichéd death music.

FILTHY HOMES FROM HELL

At first notice, the presence of *Adagio* in a reality show seems odd, that is, until one realizes from the title, *Filthy Homes from Hell*, that reality is going to be played for laughs. The series, described as an "unrelenting exposé of extreme domestic decay," sends a witty cleaning crew into unbelievably dirty residences to eliminate the filth and spruce things up a bit. In a 2004 episode the crew visited Mrs. Kramer, whose refrigerator "produced toxic spores that hospitalized her daughter. An event so traumatic that the programme makers have seen fit to play . . . Barber's *Adagio* . . . over the top of it."[172] Tragedy indeed takes many turns.

[172]Michael Holden, "Like All Such Shows, the Subtext Here Is 'Is the Filthy Person Mad?'," *The Guardian* (24 July 2004); reprinted www.guardian.co.uk/culture/2004/jul/24/screenburn.features16.

Illustration 8.3.
The Abandonment of Sandi Griffin (Janie Mertz) at the Paintball Zone from *Daria*

Illustration 8.4.
The Loss of the Kangaroo's Baby from *Ferngully 2: The Magical Rescue*

SOCCER AM

Soccer AM, a long-running Saturday morning program on British cable, features an eclectic mix of sports, comedy, and entertainment. Viewers in the United States have seen football players reacting to referee decisions with fits of bad temper; comparable theatrical displays happen in British football (soccer) as well. One recurring segment of the show presents clips of such temper tantrums, as players fly in slow motion through the air—"grimacing after receiving a 'vicious' tackle"—to the sound of *Adagio for Strings* enhanced by an air raid siren. "Many of the players look as though they have been shot—a notable element of [*Platoon*] that resulted in the ironic comparison."[173]

BIG BROTHER UK 2010

The long-running British reality show Big Brother UK is part of a large television franchise originating in the Netherlands produced occasionally in the United States. Its premise involves spying on the lives of several "housemates" (with their permission) in a George Orwellian sense, but not as menacing. Nearly the entire *Adagio for Strings* graced the final episode of the 2010 season in a mock funeral service to commemorate the show's demise. Because the Barber work is frequently associated with death, it seems inevitable that it would eventually function as a parody in such circumstances. (In the film *Amélie*, *Adagio* did not accompany an actual funeral, only a post-funeral pseudo-documentary.) A suitably garbed faux-priest presides over the ceremony and intoning "Blessed are they that mourn Big Brother, as they have enjoyed laughter, heartbreak and silly tasks." Attending the ritual, the current housemates, formally attired in black but wearing sunglasses, present eulogies. One reads his original poetry and concludes with a hope: "before the tears have dried / you will be reincarnated on the other side."[174] After the male participants lower the coffin into the ground, the priest offers his benediction: "Big Brother, you were really a big and funny program. We will miss you." Confetti streams from the sky just as *Adagio* reaches (inevitably and not surprisingly) its climax. As might be expected, there were neither quiet chords nor coda.

[173]"AM Soccer," *Wikipedia*, www.en.wikipedia.org/wiki/Soccer_AM. Three such segments were posted on "Soccer AM–Platoon," *YouTube* (February 2006), posted by phillipmufc. They range in length from 0:43 to 1:17. One of the players is "everyone's favourite Chelsea player," Didier Drogba.

[174]See "Big Brother UK 2010," *YouTube* (10 September 2010), posted by dirtymonkey151. The poet may yet get his wish. There have been several attempts to revive the series on this side of the pond (in the United States).

American Cartoon Series

Table 8.15. Television Cartoons

YEAR	SERIES TITLE	NETWORK
1998	*Daria*	MTV
2003	*The Simpsons*	Fox
2004	*South Park*	Comedy Central
2007	*Boondocks*	Cartoon Network
2007	*The Simpsons*	Fox

One of the most surprising television contexts for *Adagio for Strings* is, perhaps, American animated cartoons. While these series listed in Table 8.15 are essentially designed as comic entertainment, they often have serious moments. In comparable situations resorting to Barber's music seems less like "indulgent silliness" and retains at least some of its earnest nature. Note that in many of these cartoons *Adagio for Strings* is introduced when a character begins to regret his or her actions and shows some remorse. Therefore, even in a comic situation, *Adagio* is frequently invoked in more serious moments.

DARIA: "THE DARIA HUNTER"

A brief snippet of *Adagio for Strings* is found in season two, episode fifteen, "The Daria Hunter," from the *Daria* series. The episode begins with the high school history teacher informing his students that they are to embark on a field trip to Jim's Paintballing Jungle to study "how warfare affects all aspects of culture." This becomes a pretext for the writers to toss in all kinds of references to war movies, particularly those about Vietnam: the title is a variant of *The Deer Hunter* (1978); there are visual references to *Full Metal Jacket* (1987), dialogue from *Apocalypse Now,* and *Platoon* is quoted. Near the end of the episode, one student, Sandi, gets left behind as the school buses drive away. When she tries to catch up, she falls in a mud puddle and raises her arms in the air like Willem Dafoe near the end of *Platoon* as the camera pans upward and away from her. Anticipated by

Platoon-like helicopter sounds (no helicopter is on the field trip), *Adagio* emerges for about thirty seconds. P. S. "Those paintball thingy's hurt!"[175]

A TRIFECTA ON *THE SIMPSONS*: "STRONG ARMS OF THE MA," "MARGE GAMER," AND "LITTLE ORPHAN MILLIE"

Short excerpts from *Adagio for Strings* are called into service three times in *The Simpsons*: episode nine of season fourteen, "Strong Arms of the Ma" (2003); episode seventeen of season eighteen, "Marge Gamer" (2007); and episode six of season nineteen, "Little Orphan Millie" (2007). In "Strong Arms," as a result of being mugged, Marge, the matriarch of the Simpson family, starts lifting weights, which leads to steroid abuse, turning her into a bully. Her newly developed strength takes her to Moe's Bar, where she starts a brawl that ends with nearly everyone littered on the floor, an image similar to the bodies strewn about in *Platoon*. One body is caught on a revolving ceiling fan, simulating helicopter blades. A bit of *Adagio* reinforces these *Platoon* references. Just as she is about to hurl another body to the floor, her husband Homer enters. She turns around to face him, still holding the body above her head. He gently reminds her that "somewhere in that sea of bull hormones is the sweet wonderful girl I married who instead of swatting a fly would give it a bath and send it on its way. I would sure like to go home and have Jiffy Pop with her." During these lines Alf Clausen, the show's composer and music coordinator, seems to toy with the *Adagio*'s quiet chords. In a moment of realization, Marge replies: "Oh, my gosh! You're right." Nevertheless she still tosses the guy to the floor. "Steroids have turned me into everything I hate. Let's go home, sweetie." As they leave she tells the survivors, "Club soda will get that blood out."[176]

In "Marge Gamer," young daughter Lisa is watching a DVD about hooliganism in soccer games. The narrator relates: "last year in Brazil an on-field scuffle became so violent that locals say a statue of the Virgin Mary came alive . . . and beat the holy snot out of everyone." As this fracas unfolds, the opening phrase of Barber's *Adagio* is played in the background. Because Mary somewhat resembles Marge (or even Homer in drag), the beating up of the players looks almost like a re-enactment of her barroom brawl several years earlier.

[175]"Season 1: #202 The Daria Hunter" *Absolute Daria Files: TRANSCRIPTS* (2 October 1999), www.angelfire.com/wa/adf/202.html.

[176]Lines of dialogue are taken from a telecast of the episode.

In "Little Orphan Millie" it is found a third time. Millhouse, a friend of the Simpson son Bart, comes to stay with the family when his parents remarry and go on a cruise for their second honeymoon. When they fall overboard and are abandoned in the ocean, two crew members of Festive Cruise Line come to the Simpson house to deliver the bad news. As they drive into Springfield, a few seconds of *Adagio for Strings* accompanies them, but then it stops when they arrive at the door. When one tells Millhouse, "your parents have been lost at sea," the resulting action becomes a parody of the scene in *Saving Private Ryan* (1998) when Mrs. Ryan is told of the death of her sons. Therefore an audio reference to one war movie (*Platoon*) is followed by a visual reference to another (*Private Ryan*).

In my opinion, the *Adagio* references get weaker as they go along. The one in "Strong Arms" is clever, the one in "Gamer" is reasonable, but the one in "Orphan" is simply bland. Are the writers (or Alf Clausen) finally running out of new ideas?

SOUTH PARK GIBES THE PERFORMANCE-ENHANCING DRUGS CULTURE: "UP THE DOWN STEROID"

South Park explores a territory similar to *the Simpsons* episode, "Strong Arms of the Ma" in "Up the Down Steroid" (2004), episode two of season eight, in which Jimmy Valmer competes in the Special Olympics. He is persuaded to intensify his performance by taking steroids, which not only transform his athletic abilities but also make him abusive to friends and family. Midway through the story he is lifting weights in his room when his girlfriend Nancy comes to visit. She tells him that she is leaving him because he has changed: he is no longer "the boy I fell in love with last week during Free Period." The following dialogue takes place with *Adagio for Strings* as accompaniment. (Jimmy's stutter is apparent in the spelling.)

Jimmy: You're not leaving me! You try to leave me and I'll kill you, bitch!

Nancy: You can't treat people like this!

Jimmy: (gets up and walks over to Nancy, then begins beating her with his crutches. She wails.) [This is about where *Adagio for Strings* begins.] I said, shut your mouth, bitch! Why do you make me do it, huh? (He grabs her by the throat and throws her head against the floor, then whacks her on the side of the head a few times.) You're not leavin' anybody!! You just keep your G-goddamned mouth shut and do what you're t-t-told! (He resumes beating her. His mom opens the door to see what's the matter.)

Mom: What the? (tries to stop the beating) Jimmy, oh my God!

Jimmy: (throws his mother off and heads for the door.) Stay away from me you stupid b-b-bitches! (walks down the hall, hits the wall with his right crutch, and breaks down.) No! God! (collapses on his back and bawls.)

In both "Strong Arms of the Ma" and "Up the Down Steroid" the characters do not exhibit their normal behavior; drugs have transformed them into abnormally belligerent people who, as a result, have alienated those closest to them. Jimmy realizes his error when a friend enters the Special Olympics under false pretenses. Only after accusing him of unethical intentions does he realize that he is equally guilty. Marge realizes her mistake only after Homer pleads with her to return home. Her violence in the barroom may be comic, but Jimmy's behavior, with his abusive language and violence against women, is disturbing. In both cases *Adagio* accompanies a false sense of tragedy. The irony may cause some viewers to smile, perhaps in spite of themselves. Could the *South Park* episode be a parody of *The Simpsons* parody? Luke Howard suggests that possibility: one series may have made fun of the other.[177]

A CLEVER JUXTAPOSITION ON *BOONDOCKS*: "HOME ALONE"

In a similar mode, a character in episode ten of season two from *Boondocks*, "Home Alone" (2007), begins to question his actions and motivations. Granddad, fed up with his two constantly quarrelling grandsons, Huey and Riley, decides to take a vacation and leaves them in the care of Uncle Ruckus. The boys do the devastating "home alone" routine and drive him away. Huey, the older of the two, takes advantage of the situation and essentially holds his little brother prisoner, but the effort takes too much out of him. He laments, "I rarely slept. I soon forgot which one of us was the prisoner." At this moment *Adagio* enters, and Huey's perpetual "mean look" (his threatening arched eyebrows) begins to soften. What is interesting sequentially is how this music is presented. Scenes of the two boys quickly alternate with scenes of Granddad NOT having a good time on vacation. The situation is bad for all of them. Brief

[177]Luke Howard, "The Popular Reception of *Adagio for Strings*," 62. *South Park* released episode seven from season six cleverly entitled "Simpsons Already Did It."

moments of the boys, with a few seconds of *Adagio,* are quickly inter-cut with brief moments of Granddad and a few seconds of upbeat "vacation" music. I know of no other dramatic situation where Barber's score is so effectively juxtaposed with other contrasting music (except, maybe the nightclub scene in *Kevin and Perry*). It may be the concept of music coordinator Laif Taylor or music consultant Dean "DC" Charles.

A DOUBLE TAKE ON *AMERICAN DAD*: "IN COUNTRY . . . CLUB"

So far the only cartoon that presents *Adagio for Strings* in two different parts of the same episode is *American Dad,* a series that focuses on yet another dysfunctional family, the Smiths. In the first episode from season five, "In Country . . . Club," in part a parody of the Bruce Willis movie, *In Country* (1989), son Steve has been given the opportunity to sing the National Anthem at a local Veterans Day ceremony. But his father Stan, not satisfied with his son's rehearsals, thinks that he would benefit from participating in the country club's re-enactment of battles from the Vietnam War on the golf course. This is a golden opportunity for the show's writers to insert a passage from *Adagio* at some appropriate moment, but their reference to it is more than just casual. Excerpts come in two related scenes for both humorous and serious effects. Stan himself, also taking part in this war re-enactment, is captured and is about to be tortured by being forced to listen to his captors read the movie script from *Sex and the City* (2008). But Steve, to the strains of *Adagio for Strings,* rescues his father, who tells him, "You saved me, I'm so proud of you," a rare tender moment between father and son.

Meanwhile Steve is adversely affected by this war re-enactment and begins to suffer from post-traumatic stress disorder (PTSD)—or, as the nurse more correctly calls it in this context, PTWRSD (post-traumatic war re-enactment stress disorder)—and barricades himself in the golf cart building, where his father was held captive. It is now Stan's turn to rescue his son, admitting to him, "I pushed you too hard . . . you're doing great on your own." This prompts a return of *Adagio*, appropriate not only as a reversal of the previous rescue but also as another tender (but temporary) moment between father and son. Again, this piece is associated with a character who feels remorse. Stan at last realizes that he has badgered his son and apologizes for it. At the end, Steve's singing of the National Anthem still does not please his father (or many of the viewers either), who tells the man standing next to him that the boy is his neighbor's son. This "twin peaks" presentation of *Adagio* combines the dramatic effectiveness of two scenes with a twist (*El Norte* or *S1mØne*) with the comedic aspect of a war trauma (*Seinfeld*) plus a brief moment of father-son tenderness (*Swimming Upstream*).

Television Documentaries

Table 8.16. Television Documentaries

YEAR	SERIES TITLE	NETWORK
1973	*The Ascent of Man*	BBC / PBS
1995	*The Oprah Winfrey Show*	Syndicated
2002	*In Memoriam: New York City*	HBO
2002	*Frontline: "Faith and Doubt at Ground Zero"*	PBS
2005	*Doctor Who Confidential*	BBC
2007	*The Conspiracy Files*	BBC

Adagio for Strings has also been featured on several documentaries on American and British television as well as the talk show *Oprah*. Another, an episode from *The Ascent of Man*, originated on the BBC and crossed the pond for a presentation on PBS.[178]

THE ASCENT OF MAN: "LOWER THAN THE ANGELS"

One of the earliest television appearances of *Adagio for Strings*—the earliest, perhaps—occurred in the British cultural series, *The Ascent of Man,* written and hosted by Polish polymath Jacob Bronowski. In the first episode he compares a baby's behavior with an adult athlete. While a baby crawls in slow motion to the accompaniment of phrases from the Barber score, Bronowski informs viewers that its brain

> will form a whole repertoire of subtle, complex movements and make them second nature to him. Now the cerebellum is in control. All that the conscious mind has to do is to issue a command. And by fourteen months the command is "Stand!"

[178]Because of their connection with the attack on the World Trade Center, a discussion of the documentaries *In Memoriam: New York City* and "Faith and Doubt at Ground Zero," an episode from the long-running PBS series *Frontline*, will be postponed until the next chapter.

The baby rises as the music reaches the end of the phrase, but, when he falls down, he immediately morphs into an adult athlete ready to start a race. The music temporarily switches from Barber to another piece of music while the athlete's movements are compared to that of a gazelle. When the runner transforms into a pole-vaulter, the climactic phrase of *Adagio* returns to accompany several slow motion views of his actions. Bronowski comments, "the athlete's mind is fixed ahead of him, building up his skill and he vaults into the future." Both the baby and athlete need energy to "build up their skills," one to stand, the other to vault. Thus the musical phrase that "builds up" to the climax is appropriate for both actions. Bronowski, moreover, had stated earlier that "what the athlete experiences in such a moment is not fear but exaltation." On a lesser scale, a baby might feel something similar in its achievement of standing (certainly its parents would). Bronowski, perhaps advised by his music consultants, must have been convinced that *Adagio*'s climactic phrase does not cry out in anguish but in joy, proving that one need not associate this music only with sadness and death.[179]

THE OPRAH WINFREY SHOW: "CRYING SHAME"

On 5 June 1995 Oprah Winfrey devoted an episode of her talk show to youth violence with victims of such crimes, a district attorney, and several perpetrators as her guests. Closing the show is a collage of stills and short film clips of various people discussing such violence with a part of *Adagio for Strings* in the background, at first quiet and then insistent. An announcer proclaims, "Little kids, not even in middle school, are already becoming violent criminals." A photograph shows two boys handcuffed together, with a voice saying, "Yeah, those kids, they shoot at you. They don't even think about it." There is a view of a touch-tone phone with a screaming voice, presumably a 911 call. A newspaper clipping reads "5-year-old fires gun at school" followed by a photograph of the child being arrested. Writer Kathleen Dixon observed, "the modernist attempt at conclusion seems to invite an expression of grief over the loss of a generation of children and perhaps the loss of the kind of civil, communal society that would protect them (and us) from senseless violence and early

[179]Jacob Bronowski, "Lower Than the Angels" (Episode 1), *The Ascent of Man* (BBC with Time-Life Films). This was telecast in the UK May through July 1973 and in the US in 1975. See the auxiliary text: Jacob Bronowski, *The Ascent of Man* (New York: Little, Brown, 1973), 30-36.

death."[180] According to her view, *Adagio*, combined with slow-motion photography, imparted an elegiac quality, much like its impact in *Platoon* and other movies. She even referred to it as a kind of "film ending."[181]

An unfortunate juxtaposition, however, occurred during the last moments of this sequence as the credits began to roll. Networks love to cram a lot of information into a small block of time, especially "promos" of other shows. While stark and serious images were being projected, a voice-over reminded viewers that "two hours of laughs come your way tonight, starting with *Boy Meets World,* followed by *Ellen*! Then is Gloria having an affair with Hope's ex-husband? Find out on *Hope and Gloria.*" The result is a "funeral collage . . . experienced in dialogue with the voice of commerce, the network's peppy self advertisement," in Dixon's opinion. She concluded:

> The tensions that result in this dialogic interchange are complex. They are the relations between "high art" and "low," the tragic and the comic, the desire for wholeness or depth and . . . the expression of anger and sorrow and the expression of hyperbolic cheerfulness. Very likely the viewer will laugh.[182]

Because the voice-over does not totally blot out *Adagio,* poignant music, startling images, and a cheerful promo all communicate at the same time. In this instance, the combination of high and low art is simultaneous rather than successive, making the film clip inadvertently ironic precisely when the intent is to send a direct, serious, and unencumbered message. This is a situation where humanitarian interests are compromised by the demands of commercialism.

DOCTOR WHO CONFIDENTIAL: "A TIME AND A PLACE"

After many years of absence on British television, the popular sci-fi series *Doctor Who* was resurrected by the BBC in 2005. During its first run each episode was followed by a half-hour behind-the-scenes documentary, *Doctor Who Confidential,* essentially a "making of" the *Doctor Who* series.

[180]Kathleen Dixon, "The Dialogic Genres of Oprah Winfrey's 'Crying Shame,'" *Journal of Popular Culture* XXXV/2 (September 1998), 189. My thanks to Kathleen Dixon for sending me a tape of the show.

[181]Kathleen Dixon, interview (15 October 2004) with the author.

[182]Kathleen Dixon, "The Dialogic Genres," *Journal of Popular Culture*, 189.

After the episode, "Father's Day," concerning the doctor's companion Rose and her bonding with her father, was the *Confidential* episode, "A Time and a Place." *Adagio for Strings* is quoted during the final part, with the musical climax occurring as Rose (Billie Piper) witnesses the death of her father (Shaun Dingwall). This music does not recur during the same scene in the "Father's Day" episode itself. As with movie trailers, this documentary may have been edited before original music was added to the actual episode.[183] Yet there was probably no deliberate attempt to match *Adagio* with the scene from the show. In addition to showing brief clips, the documentary also includes comments by those involved with the production, such as the producer, head writer, and also Piper and Dingwall themselves. That is, the original scenes are placed in an entirely new documentary-style context as illustrations of the interpretation of the episode. Barber's music, running throughout the whole sequence, provides continuity.

THE CONSPIRACY FILES: "9 / 11"

The BBC series *The Conspiracy Files* brought *Adagio for Strings* into one scene in "9 / 11," an episode obviously related to the attacks on the World Trade Center and the Pentagon. The series attempts to sort out the information (and misinformation) that governments and media may have deliberately suppressed about this incident. Any conspiracy theory, including several about 9 / 11, tends to polarize the population: those who believe in the conspiracy are convinced that the program's producers did not go far enough to inform the public and those who do not believe in it are convinced that the producers were biased in its favor. A member of this latter group called the program a "jokeumentary," and a reviewer for *Prison Planet* argued that the program was tainted by "gross factual inaccuracies, yellow journalism, and manipulative and biased editing."[184]

One such manipulation is the sound of *Adagio* during one segment of the show, featuring an interview with U.S. Senator Bob Graham, co-chair of the Congressional Inquiry into 9 / 11. He states that "there are too many secrets, that is, information that has not been made available to the public

[183]The BBC made a fifteen-minute version that retained the *Adagio* segment. See www.bbc.co.uk /doctorwho/confidential. Neither the Sci-fi Channel in 2006 nor BBC America (2007) included the *Confidential* postludes.

[184]Paul Joseph Watson, "BBC Hit Piece and Tissue of Lies, Bias and Emotional Manipulation," *Prison Planet* (19 February 2007); reprinted www.prisonplanet.com/articles/february2007/190207/tissueoflies. htm.

. . . eroding public confidence." The show's producers insert Barber's music here as background to make this all appear to be more credible and potentially more persuasive, much the way Michael Moore did in *Sicko*. One blogger who picked up on *Adagio*'s manipulative impact believes it to be "a very apt piece of music for such a mockery of journalism, for it crystallizes the sad state of journalism at the BBC and also the sad state of the human race."[185] *Adagio*'s latest disturbing role? Propaganda.

OTHERS (BRIEFLY)

In March 1994 the Public Broadcasting Service (PBS) series *Frontline* presented "Sarajevo: The Living and the Dead." Filmmaker Radovan Tadic followed several Sarajevans for six months after the attack on the city's Holiday Inn. Roaming through the streets, he recorded the thoughts of a variety of people: a boy who fetches water for his family, a newlywed couple, and a psychiatrist in a mental hospital. *Adagio* accompanies some of these scenes.

In 1999 Music Television (MTV) produced a half-hour documentary, "To the Holocaust: BIOrhythm," devoted to "the menace of hate" and concerning Bert Strauss, a German Holocaust survivor. The program's unusual format—without narration in MTV music-video style—juxtaposes fast cuts of old photographs with Strauss's own coming-of-age images. The documentary "winds down on a note of excruciating sadness," with *Adagio* underscoring slow-motion footage of a "skeletal corpse being dragged along the ground, its feet making shallow grooves in the dirt, followed by other bodies being flung into a ditch."[186] Critic Howard Rosenberg reported that the result "purposely assaulted" the viewer but was "stunningly effective. What's amazing about this series is how much it is able to say, so powerfully, with such brevity."[187]

Television Promos

The promo functions for a television show the way a trailer does for a movie: to bring in additional viewers and, more importantly, to assure

[185]"BBC's Suck-up to the Official 9/11 Conspiracy," *The Truth Serum Blog*, www.thetruthserumblog.blogspot.com. The three-minute *Adagio* segment was once available on *YouTube* (20 August 2008), posted by carrierwavx2. The video no longer exists.

[186]Howard Rosenberg, "Truth, Anguish and Jump-Cuts," *Los Angeles Times*, Home Edition (30 April 2000), 5; reprinted www.articles.latimes.com/2000/apr/30/entertainment/ca-24883.

[187]*Ibid.* The program aired on 17 November 1999.

higher ratings. In 2002 Great Britain's Nine network used William Ørbit's transcription of *Adagio for Strings* as background music for promos of the World Cup Soccer tournament, running for two months prior to the games. In the fall of 2005 BBC Northern Ireland presented "The Harrowing," the fourth installment of its series, *Messiah,* starring detective chief inspector Red Metcalfe (Ken Stott), expert at tracking down serial killers. Barber's Agnus Dei (Accentus Chamber Choir) graced the promo, but in the series itself two other sacred choral works filled in: passages from both Mozart's and Fauré's Requiems. When the series came to BBC America in April 2006, there was evidently not enough time to squeeze the Barber clip into the two newly edited thirty-second advertisements.

Meanwhile in the United States PBS quoted a passage from Agnus Dei to promote *Auschwitz: Inside the Nazi State.* With photographs of concentration camps on the screen, a voice-over asks, "How could such evil exist? In order to understand the Nazi mind, you have to go inside the Nazi state." As in the case of *Messiah,* Barber's music is heard in the promo but not in the actual program.

Final Credits

Tracking down and documenting the many borrowings of Barber's *Adagio for Strings* in the realms of movies and television have been challenging adventures. I fear they are never-ending tasks. *Adagio* continues to pop up in places both expected and unexpected. Such instances have slowed down in recent years, however. A saturation point may have been reached where yet another association would no longer enhance the dramatic situation, but—as in the case of *Sicko*—would actually be detrimental to it. (See the "A 'Trite' Work or a Cliché?" section in Chapter 12). But the creative powers of writers, producers, and directors of the entertainment industry should not be underestimated. If *Adagio for Strings* has worked before, it can work again!

> I'm responsible for putting Sam [Harris] through that and so wish we could edit and make it better. Never did we expect a million+ views out of something so . . . uhmm . . . moving.
>
> —Publicity Spokesman Michael Agostino (24 October 2012).[1]

Introduction

One of the most popular destinations on the Internet is *YouTube*, the universal hosting site where amateur videographers can upload their own work for public dissemination.[2] Some postings look quite professional while others are self-indulgent, amateurish junk. In this chapter I am concerned with such videos involving some version of Barber's *Adagio for Strings*; I almost entirely refer to items that were uploaded between the years 2006 and 2010. But *YouTube* videos are a tricky and ephemeral business. Unlike the relative permanency of books, articles, and even videodiscs, amateur videos may, in the words of Ira Gershwin, "just be passing fancies and in time may go." The number of items changes daily: new ones are added; others disappear. Those who contribute their own efforts have the right to remove them at any time, and *YouTube* censors may delete an entry if it appears to violate copyright laws or public decency. By the time this book goes to press, many interesting ones will be gone.[3] But at the moment (July 2013) entering "adagio for strings" into the search slot will yield over 213,000 entries! It is rather remarkable that approximately one-fifth are Tiësto "performances"—some complete, others lasting only a few seconds.[4]

Some postings may be missed, nonetheless, if the video is only identified by the keyword "adagio." Simplifying a search to that single word may yield additional hits, but it will also lead to the so-called Albinoni Adagio[5] (see Chapter 11), the slow movement from Joaquin

[1]Michael Agostino, email (24 October 2012) to the author. Agostino is referring to the Sam Harris parody of Soulja Boy Tell'em's "Crank That." See my discussion of this posting on pages 410-11.

[2]*YouTube* was founded in California in 2005 by former Paypal employees Chad Hurley, Steve Chen, and Jawed Karim. Sold to Google Inc. for $1.65 billion in 2006, it is the most successful video hosting site to date, available in over fifty languages.

[3]Such postings already removed from *YouTube* are identified in the text by an asterisk (*).

[4]See, for example, "Tiësto–Adagio for Strings," *YouTube* (18 March 2008), posted by officialtiesto.

[5]"Adagio in G Minor (Albinoni)," *YouTube* (6 March 2007), posted by eddieexplorer.

Rodrigo's *Concierto de Aranjuez* (1939),[6] or other such movements. Searching the name "Samuel Barber" may also provide a few results that did not match the others. In addition, some performances originating outside the United States are labeled with a translation of the title, such as the Spanish *Adagio para cuerdas,*[7] the Italian *Adagio per archi,*[8] and the French *Adagio pour cordes.*[9] Without this information one might miss the gorgeous performance of "Adagio per archi" with Simon Rattle conducting the Berlin Philharmonic, a clip submitted by an organization that identified the music in Italian.[10]

In general, *Adagio* videos on *YouTube* tend to fall into three broad categories: 1) simple "uploads" of the work's performance, often by non-professional groups, unchanged in any way; 2) original footage combined with a recording of *Adagio* as an audio track; and 3) totally "borrowed" material, where a commercial recording of *Adagio* becomes the track for video stock taken from other sources, such as television shows, films, and computer games, but now reordered, shortened, or otherwise reworked to produce a new creation. In my survey I have organized relevant postings on *YouTube* into categories that are not necessarily exclusive. It would be possible to place a number of videos meaningfully in more than one. A sports video can also be interpreted as a tribute, or a memorial to 9 / 11 can be considered a video vignette. Aware of the issues of overlapping, I have placed examples where they make the most sense to me.

Simple Uploads

Most of the simple uploads, such as the skating exhibitions by Matt Savoie[11] and the Last of the Proms performance led by Leonard Slatkin,[12] are taken directly from television programming (see Chapter 10). Others

[6]"Concierto de Aranjuez by Joaquín Rodrigo II–Adagio," *YouTube* (31 May 2007), posted by Efraín Amaya.

[7]"Adagio para Cuerdas–Samuel Barber," *YouTube* (17 April 2008), posted by CamerataExtrema.

[8]"ADAGIO per ARCHI," *YouTube* (24 April 2007), posted by idyllium.

[9]"Rosée de Diamant Musique Samuel Barber Adagio pour Cordes," *YouTube* (20 May 2009), posted by frederick292.

[10]"Samuel Barber: Adagio for Strings (S. Rattle, cond.)," *YouTube* (27 October 2012), posted by firefox142857.

[11]"Matt Savoie 2005 Four Continents SP," *YouTube* (24 December 2007), posted by jedellis.

[12]"Proms 2001–Adagio for String 9-11 Tribute," *YouTube* (28 May 2007), posted by RupertJones.

capture untouched scenes from movies where the music is already placed, such as *ma mère*[13] and *Reconstruction.*[14] Many of these are discussed in other chapters of this book (see Chapter 8). Some videos are simple uploads of audio performances of *Adagio* or Agnus Dei taken from commercial recordings as a kind of mp3 source just for listening purposes; nothing new is added to them on the screen. Two such examples are Raymond Leppard's concert performance of *Adagio* with the Indianapolis Symphony Orchestra, with only a visual identification of the performers,[15] and Agnus Dei by the Choir of Trinity College, Cambridge, with a portrait of Barber as the single visual component.[16]

Other contributors have created a musical reminder rather than a marketable item by recording their own local or amateur performances, always from a single camera—often shaky and sometimes out of focus—stationed somewhere in the audience. It is a matter of "see how good we were when we played *Adagio*!" Among such performances are an *Adagio for Strings* by the San Diego School of Creative and Performing Arts (SDSCPA) High School orchestra[17] and Agnus Dei by the Azusa Pacific University Choir.[18] Some amateur musicians, usually soloists without the benefit of an audience, have taped a version of *Adagio* directly for a *YouTube* posting: more a practice session than an actual performance. Such entertainments, especially those on the piano or synthesizer, vary considerably in quality. One of the most professional sounding is a feature of student Gen Hirano performing his own arrangement.[19] Among versions for other instruments are student Juan Manuel playing the *Adagio* melody on saxophone[20] and "Adagio for Strings . . . Electric Guitar," basically an

[13]"Ma mere (clip)," *YouTube* (23 January 2010), posted by Kinoteatr3z. *Adagio* may be heard accompanying the film at the 3:10 and 6:40 marks.

[14]"Реконструкция (Reconstruction)–Adagio for Strings," *YouTube* (9 March 2010), posted by labrussca.

[15]"Adagio for Strings–Raymond Leppard," *YouTube* (24 March 2007), posted by PatriciaHDaly.

[16]"Samuel Barber: Agnus Dei (Adagio for Strings)," *YouTube* (1 November 2007), posted by lee32uk.

[17]"Adagio for Strings," *YouTube* (8 June 2007), posted by katroscar.

[18]"Agnus Dei," *YouTube* (28 February 2007), posted by sc0tlas.

[19]"Gen Hirano Performing Samuel Barber's Adagio for Strings," *YouTube* (30 May 2010), posted by komrade666.

[20]"Juan Manuel–Samuel Barber: Adagio for Strings," *YouTube* (23 November 2006), posted by hmariod.

improvisation on electric guitar in which melody and harmony do not always coincide.[21]

Amateur Trance Mixes

Ørbit's synthesizer transcription of *Adagio* and the trance remixes by Tiësto and Corsten have inspired amateurs to create their own renditions. Because remix technology is readily available on computer software programs, some individuals take a pre-existent *Adagio* recording, even Corsten's or Tiësto's, and refashion it into a personal music statement. Sometimes a video component is added, but often it is just the soundtrack that is important. Some are quite crude; others are rather skillful and are intended for commercial distribution. Many mixes were constructed using a DAW (Digital Audio Workstation), usually Fruity Loops, now known as FL Studio, which the company describes on its homepage as "a fully featured, open-architecture music creation and production environment."[22] The workstation itself may be the video component of the finalized audio presentation, such as "Adagio for Strings donk FL Studio."[23] In the professional-looking "DJ Tiësto–Adagio for Strings (NELLOXX Remix)," fragments of the Tiësto version are occasionally recognizable whereas other sounds are new.* Nelloxx sometimes speeds up the melody and at other times repeats a small portion as an ostinato. That is, he does some true, sophisticated remixing. He explains his inspiration for the remix:

> DJ Electro started a little Remix Contest and now you are listening to my Contribution. I am not familiar with Tiesto's Work, neither I dig this Style of Hardtrance, but I must admit he uses pretty good and pumping Beats for his Tracks. This was the Point where I choosed [*sic*] to make this Remix, which is not the first of its Kind.[24]

Others add a visual element to their *Adagio* clips, often only a single frame, either the announcement of title of the remix (and / or remixer) or

[21]"Adagio For Strings op.11–Samuel Barber–Electric Guitar," *YouTube* (21 August 2009), posted by Kevin Toine.

[22]"Download FL Studio 10.0.9.c," *Fiberdownload*, www.fiberdownload.com/Download/20493/ FL-Studio-XXL.

[23]"Adagio for Strings Donk FL Studios," *YouTube* (26 October 2007), posted by 02curwda.

[24]Nelloxx, "DJ Tiesto–Adagio for Strings (NELLOXX Remix)," *Flixya-Share Everything*, www.static.flixya.com/video/204967/DJ-Tiesto-Adagio-for-Strings-NELLOXX-Remix.

a single photograph. In "Adagio for Strings 2009 . . . [R.A.F. Zone remix]" the video component consists of photographs of mountain scenery.[25] Inventive visual effects, such as kaleidoscopic images that constantly transform throughout the presentation, may also be created on a computer to accompany the music.

In addition, there are "how to" demonstrations of the creation of an electronic-trance *Adagio,* starting with a few trial sounds, one or two harmonies, or a rhythm track.[26] A keyboard design on the side of the screen often shows the remixer selecting the pitches for his or her *Adagio* melody. After a few minutes these musical elements eventually coalesce into a trance *Adagio* mix. In another video the keys on a synthesizer light up for every note being played.[27]

Scenic Landscapes

The heart of this chapter is devoted to the creative re-use of *Adagio for Strings* in audio-video combinations, usually those derived from highly contrasting sources. Such a post-modern combination can be technically called a "bricolage," defined as the "construction or creation of a work from a diverse range of things that happen to be available."[28] The term, however, rarely appears on *YouTube.* But does mixing *Adagio* with ordinary photographs and television stills constitute a meeting of "high" and "low" culture? Perhaps, but I doubt that many *YouTube* users consider this Barber work to be particularly "high." It has become such a vital part of American culture in general that most individuals do not elevate it to a lofty pedestal. The music is as accessible as the images it accompanies, and in most instances sight and sound coexist comfortably together, without a jarring cultural effect.

The juxtaposition of *Adagio* with images may originate in two ways: 1) the producer may decide to start with a full performance of *Adagio* and then coordinate it with images thought compatible with the mood of the music; or 2) images may be planned as a miniature drama or collection

[25]"Adagio for Strings 2009 / I Feel Love [R.A.F. Zone Remix] nlx78," *YouTube* (22 October 2009), posted by N LX.

[26]One such example is "Adagio for Strings–Tiësto (Fruity Loops 7)–Juaco," *YouTube* (14 May 2008), posted by oscarva. Another has the informative title, "How to Create From Scratch, Tiësto–Adagio for Strings on FL Studio (Arron Murray)," *YouTube* (17 May 2007), posted by Arron Murray.

[27]"How To Play Adagio for Strings–Samuel Barber on Piano / Keyboard," *YouTube* (26 March 2009), posted by Jordan D.

[28]"Bricolage," *Wikipedia*, www.en.wikipedia.org/wiki/Bricolage.

of scenes, and the videographer later decides that *Adagio*, or a portion of it, is appropriate musical enhancement. It is not always apparent which course of action has been taken. Yet, if the length of the video exactly matches the length of a complete Barber performance, then it is likely that the music was chosen first and images were arranged in accord with it.[29]

Perhaps the simplest kind of video is a montage of film clips or photographs of beautiful scenery, with neither agenda nor narrative. A certain amount of editing is necessary whether the sources are still images or video clips. The most straightforward strategy for still images is a variant of the slide-show, just one photograph after another. Other techniques can add more dash to the presentation. For example, an image can fade in or out; it can materialize or de-materialize from generated pixels; or it may be slowly zoomed, in or out. Such approaches are sometimes called the "Ken Burns effect" because the award-winning producer / director relied on them to create his many documentary series out of still photographs.[30] While video clips already have motion, they also can be enhanced with Burns-like effects. These techniques can be observed in the "beautiful landscape" concept, found in many creations, with Barber's *Adagio for Strings* frequently defining the mood. Instead of exhibiting a somber tone, the work in this context more often conveys a sense of calm and serenity or awe and wonder. For instance, in one video the music accompanies views of the Grand Canyon as a small plane flies over it.* In another, Agnus Dei enhances views, taken from power paragliders, of the Glamis Sand Dunes in southern California.[31] For a video about Wellington, New Zealand, the orchestral version is played for the shoreline by day ("the lonely and isolated side") whereas Tiësto's remix fits the mood for nightlife in the city ("the vibrant and colourful side").[32] In a rather minimalistic format is "Sunset Adagio for Strings," which shows a complete ten-minute setting of the sun into the ocean (not really).[33] The videographer admitted

[29]This was the case for the *Adagio* scenes in *One Life to Live*, discussed in Chapter 8, page 367-71.

[30]"The Ken Burns Effect," *Wikipedia*, www.en.wikipedia.org/wiki/Ken_Burns_effect. The expression was used by Apple in 2003 for a feature in its iMovie 3 software. Although this type of photographic manipulation existed before Burns came along, the term has now become a common expression.

[31]"PPG for Morons: BOOTCAMP Day 4," *YouTube* (1 March 2008), posted by Paul Anthem. Agnus Dei begins at 1:45.

[32]"5-Minute Short Film on Wellington (New Zealand)," *YouTube* (15 January 2007), posted by mondo34.

[33]"Sunset Adagio for Strings," *YouTube* (27 November 2008), posted by Coco Esteves.

that he was depressed; the "sun setting and the music resonated with my mood really well."

If earthly landscapes are inadequate, why not blast off the planet for outer space? Agnus Dei accompanies several postings with photographs of celestial bodies and galaxies. They may have been inspired by the computer game *Homeworld,* where Barber's music is associated with astronomical vistas (see Chapter 11).[34] Several videos contain footage of lunar eclipses;[35] other examples transport viewers farther from Earth with NASA photographs of the Orion Nebula, Cat's Eye Nebula, and the formation of planets.[36]

Historical Documentaries: War, 9 / 11, and Disasters

Another staple of the *YouTube* repertory might be called "mini-documentaries," usually addressing serious subjects. For many, Barber's *Adagio for Strings* or Agnus Dei is deemed appropriate background. A popular type is a memorial to war victims, probably inspired by the appropriation of the orchestral version in *Platoon*. One example presents the entire orchestral *Adagio* along with newsreel footage taken during World War I, showing soldiers marching, men digging trenches, and cannons firing, and photographs of many soldiers lying dead on the battlefield.[37] Another is a tribute to the thousands of soldiers who died in the battle of Ypres in the spring of 1915.* It begins with Lieutenant Colonel John McCrae's famous poem, "In Flanders Fields" (1915), printed on the screen. Black-and-white photographs of bodies strewn on battlefields and in trenches are shown as the music builds to its climax, enhanced by one final color photograph of red poppies blowing in a field. In other words, the short video is a visual interpretation of the poem.

World War II is a common theme. One photo essay calls attention to soldiers in the European campaign. It shows the battlefields at Normandy and Juno Beach, including cemeteries, especially the one with rows of white crosses (and a star of David) at Omaha Beach.* Another concludes telling the story of a visit to Caen in Normandy where a French woman thanked the American tourists for the sacrifices of their deceased relatives

34"Paul Ruskay–Homeworld," *YouTube* (25 July 2011), posted by ketinadrealista.

35"Lunar Eclipse 2008," *YouTube* (4 March 2009), posted by endlessdream94.

36"Barber's Adagio for Strings, Op. 11," *YouTube* (22 February 2007), posted by Lyecoatha.

37"World War I Deaths–In Memory of the Slain," *YouTube* (18 August 2006), posted by jagorev.

on D-Day.[38] Yet another concerns the June 1944 Medal of Honor Allied Assault (Mohaa) at Omaha Beach.* During the presentation Agnus Dei is occasionally obscured by sounds of gunfire and yelling. "Adagio German WWII Fallen Memorial" ensures that the German soldiers (and civilians) who died during World War II are not forgotten.[39] Barber's music underscores photographs of soldiers, corpses, and gravestones. Sad faces appear on the screen as the music reaches its climax. At the quiet chord passage two intertitles read: "5.8 million military dead; 1.6 million German civilians dead." Much of the coda is joined with a series of military identification documents, with names, personal information, and photographs: a kind of military passport. Near the end, death dates of these specific soldiers are superimposed on the screen. This sequence puts a human face on war. During the music's final phrase are shown two newspaper headlines: "War Over" and "Peace."

Other memorable *Adagio* videos are reminders of Nazi concentration camps.[40] "Auschwitz" is a video montage.[41] The entire score is heard showing sepia photographs *à la* Ken Burns from a Spanish tourist's trip to the concentration camp. Equally distressing is a video created by two students for a class project, "Joseph Mengele The Angel of Death."* As *Adagio* fades in and out as background music, the video shows scenes from documentaries, such as Leonard Nimoy's *In Search of* (1976-1982) and a heart-breaking interview with a survivor who was forced to kill her own baby. But most gruesome of all is "Hitler and the Nazi Germany: 3. Jew: Extermination Camps," set to a part of the Adagio movement from the String Quartet with films documenting the atrocities at various camps (e.g., Nordhausen, Orhdruf, and Buchenwald).* Shown are emaciated bodies, both dead and alive. For as long as this music has been equated with tragedy, this particular video must surely present the consummate but most nauseating association.

While no current videos with *Adagio* honor fighting forces in the Korean War, the Vietnam War is represented by a video with film clips

[38]"Normandy 2012–D Day Landings 06/06/1944," *YouTube* (19 September 2012), posted by lukebuckley1.

[39]"Adagio for Strings German War Memorial WWII Deutsche Zweiten Welt Krieg Kriegerdenkmal," *YouTube* (3 September 2009), posted by BadgemanDFW.

[40]A representative example of these memorial videos is "The Holocaust–Pictures and Videos Part 1," *YouTube* (15 May 2008), posted by Arsenal341.

[41]"Auschwitz," *YouTube* (2 November 2006), posted by Guillermo Gallego Lora.

of the 1968 Tet offensive.[42] Views of burning villages look just like scenes from *Platoon,* only this is the real thing. Moving forward in history, one particular video contains a list of twenty-five soldiers who lost their lives in the Iraq War during December 2007.[43] Accompanying the names, some with photographs, is the cello statement of *Adagio.*

Several videos address war in general. "Adagio Slideshow" begins with paintings depicting battles during the colonial period, moves on to photographs from the Civil War, and works its way through both World Wars up through the War on Terror.[44] "War Is Always War" was made in memory of all war victims.* The first part of *Adagio* appears with photographs juxtaposing the tragedy of 9 / 11 and the ensuing war in Iraq, with many pictures of wounded children in Baghdad. In "Barber–Agnus Dei" part of the composer's choral transcription seems apt for gruesome photographs from various wars.* At the end the question, "do we need it?" is answered by "why not try peace for a while? If we find war is better, it would not be difficult to fight again." This might be considered a reply to the plea, *dona nobis pacem*.

The historical event of 9 / 11 is the subject of numerous videos. One presents Agnus Dei as background for a compilation of photographs beginning with majestic shots of the World Trade Center before the attack, followed by clips of the attacking planes and agonizing pictures of firemen alongside soot-coated survivors.[45] In another example the producer first presents his own dramatic music for the attacks themselves and then part of Ørbit's transcription to enhance the visual documentation of fragments of the buildings and firemen helping people out of the rubble. The last image is one of the American flag flying amidst the debris.[46] In several all too graphic videos *Adagio* is the track for people leaping from the towers, rather than burning to death,[47] an idea that may have been derived from the *In Memoriam: New York City* (2002) television documentary, which is described in the next chapter.

[42]"Vietnam War–Adagio for Strings," *YouTube* (6 February 2010), posted by kmcgeachin.

[43]"Faces of the Fallen–December 2007," *YouTube* (21 March 2008), posted by AsianPolitics.

[44]"Adagio Slideshow," *YouTube* (19 April 2007), posted by cellopatrick.

[45]"Agnus Dei," *YouTube* (11 September 2006), posted by PeregrineJohn.

[46]"9/11: Remembering the Jumpers [Edit 1]," *YouTube* (11 September 2007), posted by mind0vermood.

[47]The preceding video has been reposted by multiple users including the jumper scenes.

Other videos with clips from news documentaries were made as part of a fifth anniversary observance in 2006. One shows a pre-attack view of the twin towers at night, which is followed immediately by the two blue-light columns that were projected at Ground Zero during one of the memorial ceremonies.* Another shows the 9 / 11 NYC Memorial Flag Park in Inwood, New York, a historically Irish (now Dominican) borough in upper Manhattan.* Accompanied by the Adagio movement from the String Quartet, it begins with the following words printed on the screen: "5 years after the day the towers fell, we remember." Each American flag is modified to include the title "Flags of Heroes" and the names of all the victims printed on the stripes.

The aftermath of natural disasters, such as Hurricane Katrina and the Minneapolis 35W Bridge collapse, are likewise addressed on *YouTube*.[48] One begins with news footage, including dialogue, from CNN on the day of the Twin Towers attack and continues with Agnus Dei accompanying photographs of the Hurricane Katrina disaster.* Another one strictly addressing the hurricane shows children, refugees, corpses in the water, and a parent holding a child.* As the videographer puts it, "God forbid we ever forget and neglect the innocent kids who lived through Katrina and will be forever affected by it." Only a few days after the collapse of the bridge in Minnesota, someone posted a memorial tribute "to those lost, missing and injured and to the loved ones that grieve."[49] *Adagio* is added to a news report a few days after the event, and as it continues, news commentaries are imposed on it. During the music's final phrase the 23rd Psalm is printed on the screen.

SANDY HOOK

The impossibility of comprehending the wanton death of innocent children takes to new heights in the wake of school violence. Several videographers have posted moving tributes to the victims of the shooting at Sandy Hook Elementary School in Newtown, Connecticut in December 2012, some set to a complete performance of *Adagio for Strings*. One video begins and ends with people holding signs, opening with "I am love.

[48]See "Hurricane Katrina: Return to New Orleans," *YouTube* (2 September 2007), posted by ZouiGJ and "St. Bernard Parish–One Year After the Federal Flood," *YouTube* (13 September 2007), posted by scoutp.

[49]"Video Memorial–35W Bridge Collapse, Minneapolis Minnesota," *YouTube* (5 August 2007), posted by drakkar91.

I am Newtown" and concluding with "our hearts are broken."[50] Between the signs, the main content consists simply of photographs of the victims, the seven adults and all but one of the students (no photograph available), followed by their names and ages. Particularly heartbreaking is the sight of smiling faces of optimistic human beings, not knowing, of course, of the fate that awaited them. They all had so much more life to live. Because the video does not attempt to tell a story of the massacre, the images do not become more dramatic or tragic as the music approaches the climax. But this is partly due to the choice of the recording. Andrew Schenk's performance of *Adagio* with the New Zealand Symphony Orchestra does not exaggerate the climactic moment; he keeps it within the general dynamic range that Barber intended.

On the other hand "A Tribute to the Victims of Sandy Hook" does allow the form of *Adagio* to influence its content.[51] During the main part of the music simple portraits of the victims are shown, but as *Adagio* reaches the climax, the illustrations switch to horror-stricken individuals, shocked at hearing the news of the tragedy. At the quiet chord passage attention turns to those mourning the event, heads often bowed in prayer or meditation. During the last phrase of the coda all the names of the victims are displayed. This well constructed video is somewhat marred, however, by a preachy statement of anti-violence after the music has ended.

"Newtown and Sandy Hook Memorial" emphasizes the mourning period after the tragedy, showing photographs of make-shift shrines with hundreds of bouquets of flowers and dozens of stuffed animal toys, interspersed with commemorative mottos such as "never forget" and "forever in our hearts."[52] Because the tragedy occurred so close to Christmas, the climax shows decorated trees with a fire engine in the background. The quiet chord passage is enhanced by a huge American flag. Only at the coda are photographs displayed of some of the children and adults. The video ends with the image of a candle and a statue of a weeping angel.

"Sandy Hook Elementary School 12/14/2012–RIP 26 New Souls in Heaven" begins as a quick-paced photo-montage of the victims, set to a

[50]"Sandy Hook Tribute (Adagio for Strings)," *YouTube* (18 December 2012), posted by MrAugustusfinch.

[51]"A Tribute to the Victims of Sandy Hook," *YouTube* (21 December 2012), posted by WellnessNowNetwork.

[52]"Newtown and Sandy Hook Memorial" *YouTube* (20 December 2012), posted by Jerry Angelica.

faster-tempo *Adagio*, but it switches midway through to many photographs of grieving families and individuals, including President Obama.[53] At the climax appears the sign: "Symbols of Grief, Despair and, Yet Hope." The coda ends with "rest in peace those 26 new angels." "We Remember Sandy Hook Elementary School Victims" shows likenesses of victims superimposed on a candle-lighting ceremony.[54] It ends at the *Adagio* climax with the message, "May They Rest in Peace." Finally, a simple tribute accompanied by a complete *Adagio* performance consists entirely of a flickering candle illuminating a single yellow rose.[55] As usual, in situations of death and tragedy, *Adagio* serves well in these poignant memorials to the senseless loss of young life.

Documentaries with an Agenda

Instead of focusing on a single historical event, some videographers have assembled a miniature documentary to advance a cause that they believe needs further support, some accompanied by *Adagio*. In "A Commercial for Compassion" it serves as the underscore for photographs, many from the Children at Risk Foundation (CARF), of homeless and poor street children around the world.[56] Intertitles quote Buddha ("Have compassion for all beings"), Muhammad ("Allah is compassionate and loves compassion in all things"), and the Bible ("And Jesus, moved with compassion, reached out his hand").

Other postings endorse political messages. The beginning of *Adagio* underscores a public service message urging people to get out and vote.[57] The Democratic Party is not specifically endorsed, but support for it is unambiguously implied by the presence of newspaper headlines criticizing George W. Bush: "Our Patriots fought tyranny and secured the rights of Americans. Today, those rights are under attack in the 2006 elections." Its visual component emphasizes American patriotism, such as a painting of George Washington crossing the Delaware and a portrait of the Founding Fathers holding important historical documents. In 2008 excerpts from

[53]"Sandy Hook Elementary School 12/14/2012–RIP 26 New Souls in Heaven," *YouTube* (18 December 2012), posted by John Smith.

[54]"We Remember Sandy Hook Elementary School Victims," *YouTube* (21 December 2012), posted by RedKnightTV.

[55]"For the Children," *YouTube* (15 December 2012), posted by tieemiami.

[56]"A Commercial for Compassion," *YouTube* (13 November 2007), posted by Gaiamuse.

[57]"It Was 1776 All Over Again," *YouTube* (13 August 2006), posted by 1776Again.

Illustration 9.1. *YouTube* Posting, President Obama's Speech on Race, National Constitution Center, Philadelphia, Pennsylvania

Courtesy of Mark Hartley

Adagio accompanied campaign messages from Barack Obama (notably, his speech on race)[58] and Hillary Clinton (an explanation of her visit to Bosnia).*

Some videos with *Adagio* advocate environmental causes. Global Warming is the subject of a collage of weather disasters with comments from television documentaries, such as "global warming is real" and "of the twenty one hottest years on record, twenty have occurred since 1980."[59] Presenting the case for recycling is a video consisting of a brief slide show showing paper cups, plastic bottles, and other debris left on the ground at various sites.[60] At the end an intertitle reads: "Don't Pollute; Recycle." One advocating social change through peace shows film clips and photographs of peace advocates such as Mahatma Gandhi, Martin Luther King, Jr., and Nelson Mandela.[61]

With Agnus Dei in the background a video on Animal Rights begins not coincidentally with a photograph of a small lamb.[62] Other scenes document the inhumane treatment of animals, culminating in scenes

[58]"Barack Obama's Speech on Race, Set to Adagio for Strings," *YouTube* (19 March 2008), posted by markus1379.

[59]"Adagio for the Earth (or Global Warming 101)," *YouTube* (30 July 2006), posted by VaginalMcGruder.

[60]"Adagio for Recycling," *YouTube* (9 September 2006), posted by sgtjonson.

[61]"Social Change Through The Power of Peace Adagio for Strings," *YouTube* (6 June 2006), posted by sellaseat.

[62]"Agnus Dei–Liberation," *YouTube* (20 December 2007), posted by RyanRoboto.

of white rabbits being slaughtered at a factory followed by quotations supporting the animal rights cause.[63] It also contains scenes of animal rights activists themselves, treated in a less than dignified manner by the police. (See also the "vegetable rights" video later in this chapter.) Another video explains the cruelty involved in calf roping in rodeos, intensified by slow motion video clips.[64]

A documentary simply called "Martin Luther" might at first imply a general biography of the pioneering church reformer, but it is instead a revealing, unsettling study of his defamation of the Jews.* With *Adagio* as background the video juxtaposes extreme anti-Semitic statements from his treatise, *Von den Juden und Ihren Lügen* [On the Jews and Their Lies] (1543), with the eventual fulfillment of these views in the Nazi Germany of the 1930s. For instance, Bernhard Rust, Hitler's Education Minister, declared: "I think the time is past when one may not say the names of Hitler and Luther in the same breath. They belong together; they are of the same old stamp."[65] This video is quite a revelation because many people have never been made aware of Luther's dark side.

Personal Tributes and Memorials

Popular among *YouTube* enthusiasts is the tribute to public figures, including actors and athletes. Two of the actors lionized in this manner are presumed to have committed suicide. In "Marilyn Monroe on Samuel Barber" *Adagio* becomes the soundtrack for some of the actresses' scenes from Henry Hattaway's film *Niagara* (1953), usually in slow motion.[66] Views of her distraught face ironically mirror the true, sad events of her life off-screen. In another example, Agnus Dei is the backdrop for a montage of photographs and film clips of the late actor Jonathan Brandis, best known from the sci-fi television series, *seaQuest*.* The musical climax occurs as the screen reveals announcements of his death at age twenty-seven: "teen heartthrob takes his life." During the coda a quotation from

[63]"All God's Creatures–*Warning, Graphic Images*," *YouTube* (29 May 2008), posted by raggatt. Pierre Troubetzkoy: Why should man expect his prayer for mercy to be heard by what is above him when he shows no mercy to what is under him? Thomas Edison: Non-violence leads to the highest ethics, which is the goal of all evolution. Until we stop harming all other living beings we are still savages.

[64]"Calf Roping," *YouTube* (24 December 2007), posted by standingatthedoor.

[65]Bernhard Rust, quoted in *The Holy Reich: Nazi Conceptions of Christianity, 1919-1945* (Cambridge: Cambridge University Press, 2004), 136-37.

[66]"Marilyn Monroe on Samuel Barber," *YouTube* (15 April 2007), posted by durcetcurval.

Edgar Allen Poe appears on the screen: "All that we see or seem is but a dream within a dream." This could apply to both Jonathan and Marilyn.

Among living actors honored in a similar manner are Amanda Tapping and Alan Rickman. The Tapping tribute contains scenes of her portrayal of Lt. Col. Samantha Carter on the television series *Stargate SG-1*, often with male co-stars, especially Richard Dean Anderson.[67] In "Adagio for Alan Rickman" black-and-white photographs reveal how different the versatile actor can look in diverse roles—with or without beard; dark, blond, or greying hair.[68] The Tiësto remix is borrowed here; at the slow part of *Adagio* the photographs rather dramatically switch to color.

Sports figures have also received this form of hero-worship. One with a complete orchestral *Adagio* shows the Swiss tennis champion, Roger Federer, in spectacular action on the court; emphasized, often in slow motion, are the beauty of his moves as well as his skill.* With a portion of Tiësto's remix another is devoted to photographs of boxer Mike Tyson along with film-clips from his matches.[69] "Nigel Mansell: The F1 Years," a compilation of clips of the British race car driver in several Formula One races, culminates with his victories in 1992 when he was declared World Champion.* It is set to a portion of the Corsten remix. There is also homage to Ayrton Senna, the Brazilian racecar driver who died after his car crashed during a 1994 race.[70] The buildup to the climax of the music begins as the video shows slow motion films of him immediately before the beginning of the race; the actual musical climax is coordinated with the crash itself.

Not all videos devoted to public figures are truly respectful of their subjects; some, in fact, are downright insulting. For instance, one insult video about Senna reveals the videographer as a disgruntled racing fan, one who thinks that the driver is overrated.[71] He juxtaposes photographs of the racer with images of Jim Carrey mugging for the camera and other grotesque shots. *YouTube* allows and encourages viewer comments,

[67]"SG1's Amanda Tapping 'Thank You' to William Orbit's Adagio," *YouTube* (2 April 2007), posted by muckypups1.

[68]"Adagio for Alan Rickman," *YouTube* (25 October 2006), posted by Rickmanlover.

[69]See "Mike Tyson Training Highlight Reel from www.mike-tyson.info," *YouTube* (8 June 2007), posted by Steven R74; and "Mike Tyson Ferry Corsten–Adagio for Strings," *YouTube* (3 April 2010), posted by Ir0niClconic.

[70]See "A Senna Tribute," *YouTube* (19 January 2008), posted by sennanumber1fan; and "Tributo a Fernando Alonso y Ayrton Senna–de Todo Sobre la Formula Uno," *YouTube* (16 March 2012), posted by Jesus gonzalez Martinez.

[71]"My Loving Tribute to Ayrton Senna," *YouTube* (15 February 2010), posted by ayrtonLOSERsenna.

indicated by a "thumbs up" or "thumbs down" symbol. Most Senna fans were appalled by this video, giving it the "down" ratio of 70 to 8. Many of the accompanying comments, however, were just as abusive as this videographer's. Internet bloggers often "vent their spleen" under the cover of anonymity.

Dramatic and Comic Video Vignettes

Creativity on *YouTube* is clearly evident in the great number of projects shot by videographers themselves, who then edit the clips into a (usually) coherent story and coordinate them with a suitable musical soundtrack, such as *Adagio for Strings*. These miniature dramas, which I have called "video vignettes," range from serious to comic plus a few ambiguous items that are hard to pin down.

Barber's composition, not surprisingly, is the background for several serious dramas. "Adagio for Love" shows a young man (Josh Casaubon), mourning the loss of his girlfriend (or wife).[72] Much of the (non-)action takes place in his bedroom as he pensively looks at her photograph and tries to fall asleep. When this fails, he leaves his apartment building to ride the subway where, coinciding with the music's climax, he breaks down in tears. During the quiet chord passage, he is seen at a cemetery, the first indication that this is not a romantic breakup but a separation by death. During the coda he places a ring on her tombstone. On the other hand, a romantic breakup rather than death is the subject of "The Letter."[73] As *Adagio* plays, a woman slips a farewell letter under the door to a man's apartment. She also places in the envelope a heart-shaped necklace that he has presumably given her. The video concludes with a well-known maxim: "All good things come to an end."

In a side-splittingly funny lampoon singer-actor Sam Harris recites —with mock seriousness—the lyrics of the rap song, "Crank That," by Soulja Boy Tell'em (yes, that is DeAndre Cortez Way's rap name), as if it were the eloquent musings of a T. S. Eliot.[74] During the recitation he sits in a comfortable chair *à la* Alastair Cooke on PBS's *Masterpiece Theatre* (first aired in 1971). The video is even introduced by that show's theme,

[72]"Adagio for Love," *YouTube* (25 October 2006), posted by heyfreedom.

[73]"The Letter," *YouTube* (12 September 2006), posted by SurgicalSteel.

[74]"Sam Harris Recites CRANK THAT Song Lyrics by Soulja Boy Tell'em," *YouTube* (18 September 2007), posted by SamHarrisCOM. To get the most out of this lampoon, it might be a good idea to hear Soulja Boy's original song; there are several postings on *YouTube*. See "Soulja Boy Tell'em–Crank That (Soulja Boy)," *YouTube* (22 November 2009), posted by SouljaBoyTellemVEVO.

Illustration 9.2. *YouTube* Posting with User Comment, Parody of "Crank That" by Sam Harris

Courtesy of Michael Agostino

"Rondeau" from *Suite de Symphonies* (1729) by Jean-Joseph Mouret. But it is poor *Adagio for Strings* that gets stuck accompanying Harris's dramatic recitation, which includes the following expressions: "Watch me crank dat Soulja Boy," "Then super man dat ho," and "I'm jocking on yo bitch ass." As a conscientious musicologist, I should probably try to elucidate the subtleties of the rap lingo, but that would be like explaining a one-liner delivered by a Borscht Belt comedian. It would spoil the fun.[75] Extending the parody, a sentence on the site reads, "he chose a piece of lyric poetry that spoke to his heart."[76] At the end Harris thanks the viewers and cries. This dramatic recitation is given in the spirit of comedian Steve Allen, who often gave comparable readings of rock and roll lyrics in the 1950s, before R-rated words became so commonplace.

What would Barber think of this rap language recitation in connection with his beloved *Adagio*? There is no question that he was a highly sexual being, but he usually kept his sexual and his musical outputs separate from each other. It is hard to keep a straight face, nevertheless, when hearing rap lyrics being recited by a quintessential white boy who could start a whole new career as Phat Sammy S Master Soul.[77]

[75]Instead I refer the reader to: www.rapgenius.com/Soulja-boy-crank-that-lyrics where each phrase is "translated." Most of it has to do with male masturbation, especially ejaculation. Like cockney rhyme-slang, it contains a whole world of meaning typically hidden from all but the in-crowd.

[76]"Sam Harris Recites CRANK THAT," *YouTube* (18 September 2007), posted by SamHarrisCOM. Lyrics by DeAndre Cortez Way.

[77]This is a suggestion for Harris's rap name at the website: www.myrapname.com. My rap name could be Ruler Wayne W Tone; it may come in handy some day. Remember Beaver's mother Barbara Billingsly speaking jive in the movie, *Airplane* (1980)?

Just as *Adagio for Strings* has appeared as an element of parody in movies and television shows, it also turns up in a humorous context in amateur videos. With comedy often in the mind of the beholder, it may not be possible to determine why or even if the following examples are funny. "Bus Uncle," one of the most popular *YouTube* clips during the summer of 2006, was videotaped on a Hong Kong bus and shows an elderly Japanese man, later identified as Roger Chan, but often referred to as "uncle," a respectful way of addressing an older man.[78] He was talking rather loudly on his cell-phone when a young man (Elvis Ho) asked him to lower his voice. Chan then berated him for six minutes, including the phrase that became a worldwide motto, "I've got pressure, you've got pressure!" Jon Fong caught this moment on tape. It became so popular that television commentator Jane Wells featured it in a segment on CNBC on 8 June 2006, not only publicizing its content but the *YouTube* site as well. By the fall of that year there were over 400 re-postings of the clip, including parodies and one using a portion of *Adagio*. Before the tirade begins, the screen reads: "All he wanted to do was talk on his phone and relax from his stress . . . but someone HAD to tap him on his back."*

"Coffee Noir," filmed as an interview in *cinema verité* style, tells the story with black-and-white flashbacks of a man's "tragic struggle against a serious coffee addiction."[79] Lemon Boy confesses how his addiction started, lies about how many cups he has drunk, and breaks down in tears, all to repetitions of the first two phrases of Ørbit's transcription. In "Ultimate Sugar Relapse / Freakout," Jon resolves to give up sugar, but after eating one Oreo all his will power disappears leading him to the refrigerator where he takes out a squeeze bottle of chocolate syrup and squirts it all over his face and chest.[80] After running outside screaming, he reenacts the famed Elias scene from *Platoon,* accompanied by the obligatory ten seconds of *Adagio for Strings.* The videographer adds, "chocolate lovers and fetishes, this video is for you." Keeping to the food and drink motif is "Roast Beef," in which "a young man has a dream of making the perfect sandwich."[81] During the song, "Our Day Will Come," he enthusiastically gathers all the necessary ingredients. The question

[78]"巴士阿叔–Bus Uncle (雙語字幕–Bilingual Subtitle)," *YouTube* (11 May 2006), posted by beautyjeonjihyun.

[79]"Coffee Noir," *YouTube* (6 August 2006), posted by timbo808.

[80]"Ultimate Sugar Relapse / Freakout," *YouTube* (6 July 2012), posted by InfamousPlay.

[81]"Roast Beef," *YouTube* (6 October 2006), posted by Justin Adams.

"Does he succeed?" may be answered during the second half, when the screen shows a room full of ingredients scattered on the floor to the cello statement of *Adagio*. At the end he whispers, "roast beef." What does it mean? Does he die from this experience, or is he just exhausted?

Crossing a comedy with a documentary results in a "mockumentary," often a satire of an otherwise worthy cause, as in videographer Jon Calvo's "Plant Cruelty."[82] While acknowledging that the prevention of cruelty to animals is a true cause, he takes the extreme position of trying to arouse sympathy for plants with the same intense commitment. He begins with film clips of plows riding roughshod over small plants while the quiet chord passage and the beginning of the coda play in the background. Later footage shows modern industrial agriculture alternating with printed messages such as "Every year billions of helpless plants are mercilessly slaughtered." Calvo's solution to this "worldwide epidemic" is to contact local representatives, eat more meat, and send him lots of money.

Sometimes videos seem to send both serious and comic messages; either that, or the producer's comedic perception has escaped my old-fashioned sense of humor. In "Adagio for Humanity" the creator leaves it up to the viewer: it is either "powerful tragedy or farcical comedy. . . . You decide."[83] Presented in jerky, super-slow motion, a man stumbles and collapses on a hillside to a brief passage from *Adagio*. Is it a tragedy? Well, he is smiling at the end. In "The Interrogation" a miniature drama seems to be playing out in a serious manner.[84] A young couple have an argument (strictly pantomime, no dialogue); the girl leaves with a suitcase; another man picks her up in his car, while the first one returns to his apartment, dejected. This scenario may be serious, but the "overly dramatic music," the orchestral *Adagio*, has been added "for humorous effect." Thus the overall intent appears to be parody. The histrionic is fairly convincing, and the music confirms it.

Less obvious in their comic nature are "Retrete" and "BFM Cheat." "Retrete" [Toilet], a claymation video described by its creator as "La historia de un plastimono con pez" [The history of a claymation figure with fish], features a lonely man who notices that the water in his goldfish

[82]"Plant Cruelty (What Animal Lovers Fail to Mention)," *You Tube* (27 March 2007), posted by Calvolini.

[83]"AdagioforHumanity," *You Tube* (20 June 2006), posted by annoyingidiot.

[84]"The Interrogation," *You Tube* (20 April 2006), posted by Sefiros.

bowl has evaporated.[85] His pet fish lies at the bottom, presumably dead. He turns on his radio for suitably sad music and encounters Barber's infamous tearjerker. It is so affecting that it, indeed, brings tears to his eyes. As he cries into the goldfish bowl, his tears add sufficient water to revive his pet. "BFM Cheat" depicts a poker game that "turns bad."[86] Odd characters play the game until someone is caught cheating. When the shooting begins, so does *Adagio for Strings*. Is this funny?

Glorification of Athletes

Videos of sports might at first seem to be an unlikely venue for *Adagio for Strings*. Because many athletic contests are high-energy encounters between extremely competitive teams, the music's slow tempo might tend to counteract such activity. In those cases, one of the trance versions would seem more fitting.

Some form of *Adagio* is associated with clips from European soccer matches. Again Tiësto's energetic remix serves as a good soundtrack for action on the field. While some videos showcase entire teams in action (*e.g.*, Manchester United,* Real Madrid),[87] others concentrate on specific athletes (*e.g.*, Liverpool's Steven Gerrard).[88] Two videos feature the famed Brazilian striker Ronaldo Luís Nazário de Lima, commonly known as Ronaldo.* One is devoted to the principal forward of Real Madrid, superstar Cristiano Ronaldo dos Santos Aveiro,* while the other shows another Brazilian soccer sensation, Ronaldo Assis Moreira, nicknamed Ronaldinho [Little Ronaldo], who plays for Brazilian club Atlético Mineiro as of this publication.* One soccer fan features an epic showdown between Cristiano Ronaldo and Ronaldinho.[89] Another incorporates the sport into a miniature drama. "Live the Chelsea Dream," with Corsten's remix, shows not only clips from British football but coordinates them with views of a young boy, sitting alone at the edge of a field, walking around, and contemplating a future career.* Scenes of the Chelsea Football Club swirl around in his head (depicted for the viewer on screen) as he dreams of being a famous player. While trance versions of *Adagio* accompany

[85]"Retrete," *YouTube* (7 September 2006), posted by chibizumi.

[86]"BFM Cheat," *YouTube* (22 March 2007), posted by BandageFaceMan.

[87]"Adagio for Strings ft. Real Madrid," *YouTube* (8 June 2011), posted by JayDean74.

[88]"Gerrard the Legend," *YouTube* (18 June 2008), posted by Damian Emanuel. The *Adagio* portion begins at 1:40.

[89]"Cristiano Ronaldo vs. Ronaldinho," *YouTube* (24 January 2009), posted by CR7Ronaldo07.

most soccer videos, the orchestral version seems right for a match between Cardiff City and Barnsley.* The complete Bernstein recording underscores the semifinals of the (FIFA) World Cup of 1982 between France and West Germany.*

Two martial arts videos use Tiësto's *Adagio* for background. "Beijing Wushu Team 2005 Tour" looks like gymnastics with a Chinese sword.[90] "Russian Style" shows the martial arts technique developed by Alexsey Alekseyevich Kadochnikov, Systema Kadochnikov; principles of physics, mechanics, and psychology are applied to hand-to-hand combat.[91] In both of these the remix is handled rather cleverly: slow motion footage of the fighter during the slow *Adagio* section contrasts with fast floor action for the trance dance beat. In the latter video vigorous action is presented in a jerky "fast forward" style that synchronizes with the music. A third video illustrating a class in the Korean martial arts form, Tae Kwon Do, features the creator's own *Adagio* remix, quite different from Tiësto's.[92] The sounds of kicking and splitting square boards and of the participant's verbal grunts add suitable percussive punctuation throughout. A fourth example has Corsten's *Adagio* remix set to several rounds of a kickboxing match at the 1997 world championships in Natthapong, Thailand.[93] While other music is played during the boxers' entrance and the fighting of round one, Corsten's music sounds through the rest of the fight. It somehow works; the animated soundtrack is particularly effective at the end for the winner's victory celebration.

In other sports Tiësto's remix provides accompaniment for hockey action in clips from games by the Pittsburgh Penguins.[94] The posting is also a tribute to two of the team's most prominent players, Sidney Crosby and Marc-André Fleary. Although no videographer, so far, has chosen to accompany baseball footage with *Adagio*, one began his "moving tribute" to former Yankee Stadium with a brief passage from Barber's Agnus Dei.[95]

[90]"Beijing Wushu Team 2005 Tour," *YouTube* (20 June 2006), posted by wushubabe92. "Wushu" is considered the "correct" term for Chinese martial arts rather than the more familiar "kung fu."

[91]"Russian Style 1 (Original Russian Style)," *YouTube* (2 December 2006), posted by RedBerkut.

[92]"Tae Kwon Do–Gurtprüfung AHS 07," *YouTube* (31 March 2008), posted by carbonmusic.

[93]"Natthapong Thaibox–Weltmeister 1997," *YouTube* (10 July 2008), posted by MrHuman. The *Adagio* portion begins at 1:33.

[94]"Sidney Crosby & Marc-Andre Fleury Tribute," *YouTube* (8 February 2009), posted by floorballgirl33.

[95]"MOVING TRIBUTE TO YANKEE STADIUM," *YouTube* (22 September 2008), posted by SureShotDC.

Images in this segment are devoted to vintage photographs of not only the stadium itself but of legends Babe Ruth, Roger Maris, and Mickey Mantle. After thirty-five seconds of Agnus Dei, however, the true nature of this videographer's intent becomes clear. The shock of Alex Rodriguez lying on the diamond in obvious pain morphs into a bawdy clip of a young Red Sox aficionado flashing opposing fans. The Yankees insult video mirrors the boorish exhibition mentioned earlier against Ayrton Senna, this time continuing with depictions of the Boston skyline, scenes from the team's World Series victory in 2004, and, of course, a burning New York Yankees baseball cap. By then, Barber's transcription had been befittingly replaced by music from Celtic punk band, the Pogues.

Is wrestling a sport or an entertainment, or both—or neither? Adding music such as *Adagio* does not help clarify the situation but probably shifts it more toward the entertainment side. One video has slow-motion clips from a wrestling match between Stone Cold Steve Austin and Bret Hart coordinated with the orchestral *Adagio*.[96] The opening passage is suitably grand for the wrestlers as they swagger into the arena. When the music builds to the climax, the action becomes more gruesome, culminating in Hart emerging victorious over a bloodied Stone Cold, who lies helpless on the mat. Another video follows the antics of white-faced Sting of World Championship Wrestling (WCW) in the general mayhem of the ring.[97] (This is not the policeman.) This time Phynn's trance remix bolsters the action.

One of the cleverest applications of an excerpt from the orchestral *Adagio* occurs during the last few minutes of the 2006 Western Conference playoffs (game four) of the NBA (National Basketball Association) between the Los Angeles Lakers and the Phoenix Suns. Initially, the idea of using this music in clips from a basketball game, as on *ABC Sports* on 20 April 2006, seems incongruous: slow music to vigorous activity across the court. And yet the videographer formulated a cunning plan. The Suns were leading until the last twelve seconds on the clock, when the Lakers tied the game and forced overtime. Near the end of overtime the Suns were again in the lead, but by only a single point. As *Adagio* approaches its climax, Kobe Bryant gains possession of the ball. During the silence after the climactic chord he sinks a long-distance shot—barely beating the buzzer—and enables the Lakers to win. This crucial shot occurs not only during the

[96]"Emotional Wrestling Montage," *YouTube* (18 November 2007), posted by Maverick2212.

[97]"Adagio for Sting," *YouTube* (26 June 2007), posted by THEBIGSEXC.

musical silence but also with the elimination of the crowd noise that had always overlapped with the music throughout the earlier part of the video. This silence, plus a slow motion view of the ball going through the hoop, creates an intense special effect, quite different from the game itself.* The crowd noise then returns with the quiet chords, repeated several times. Jack Nicholson, whose attendance at Lakers games is legendary, is shown with a pleased expression.[98] The sad sound of the quiet chords probably indicates a disappointment for the videographer, who, I suspect, is a Suns fan.

In another video the serene sounds of an unaccredited recording of Agnus Dei accompany high diver Dana Kunze as he prepares for his 1984 world record dive of 172 feet.[99] (That is a distance taller than the Statue of Liberty, base to torch.) The music, beginning with the cello entry, builds to the climax as tension mounts for his dive, a reverse triple somersault, which the videographer coordinates with the pause between the loud F-flat major chord and the following quiet chord passage. The audio technique is similar to that used for Bryant's basketball shot in the previous example. Kunze's record was topped by Randy Dickison (174′8″) in 1985 and Oliver Favre (177′) in 1987.

Energetic trance remixes of *Adagio* have become commonplace for soundtracks of music videos about cars, planes, and other fast-moving vehicles. Tiësto's remix supports several, including short clips of the Ferrari-F360 speeding down a country road and the Nissan Skyline R34 GTR racing around a track.[100] His or Corsten's remix co-ordinates well with speed in videos with a motorcycle, Russian tanks, and an intercept fighter airplane.[101] "Suzuki Hayabusa Tribute" consists of scenes of the Japanese motorcycle speeding down the road.* A dashboard-mounted camera delivers the driver's perspective: the instrument panel and a view of the road ahead. Another video shows the SU30 long-range Russian intercept fighter in spectacular maneuvers.* Both power and speed are a part of "The Royal Navy," in which planes and helicopters take off from and land on an aircraft carrier, rockets are launched, and submarines

[98]"Top 10 Celebrity Lakers Fans," *NBA.com*, www.nba.com/features/lakers_celebs_070309.html. Jack Nicholson is the most closely associated celebrity fan with the Los Angeles Lakers.

[99]"Dana Kunze World Record Dive with Barber's Agnus Dei," *YouTube* (5 September 2009), posted by Sloppyorrus.

[100]"Ferrari-F360 & DjTiesto–Adagio for Strings," *YouTube* (3 August 2006), posted by taruMutlu.

[101]"Yamaha YDH–Details & Tips," *YouTube* (22 October 2008), posted by SasedaReal.

emerge from under water.[102] Army tanks are normally associated more with power rather than speed, but in "Russian Tank Mix is the Best" the T-80, T-80U and Black Eagle move quickly.[103]

Scenes from Movies and Television Shows

Many videographers reassemble scenes from movies into coherent videos, many with *Adagio for Strings*. A logical source is *Platoon* (as if that movie did not already contain enough of the work.) In "Platoon Music Video" *Adagio* appears with several such clips, notably Elias's famous "crucifixion" scene, placed just before the climax of the music.[104] Then, in a reversal, scenes from the beginning of the movie (opening epigraph, body bags, etc.) are shown during the coda. Other videos present stills derived from the movie, with each of the main platoon members given a brief character study and shown in typical situations.* Two other videos transport *Adagio* into scenes from *Saving Private Ryan* (1998), replacing John Williams's *Adagio*-like music, perhaps convincing viewers that Barber's music would have worked just as well.[105] A third replaces Williams's music with the Direct to Dreams remix, mentioned in Chapter 7.[106] It also replaces Nick Glennie-Smith's soundtrack in the Mel Gibson war movie, *We Were Soldiers* (2002).* For many, *Adagio* is inextricably linked with war with these creations reinforcing this connection.

Some videographers reach back to silent movies for footage. One presents a scene from British film pioneer James Williamson's depiction of Hans Christian Andersen's story, *The Little Match Seller* (1902).[107] Part of Barber's Agnus Dei is suitably solemn for the last moments of the little girl's life as she strikes her last matches and envisions the warmth of a home, a Christmas tree, and a roast goose dinner. At the end an angel lifts her soul to heaven. Interspersed between the scenes are appropriate quotations such as "freedom would be meaningless without security in

[102]"The Royal Navy," *YouTube* (11 January 2007), posted by ieuz123.

[103]"Russian Tank Mix is the Best," *YouTube* (6 December 2010), posted by mariobrosik.

[104]"Platoon Music Video," *YouTube* (10 June 2006), posted by Zicod.

[105]"Saving Private Ryan / Band of Brothers Mix!," *YouTube* (5 December 2006), posted by ponchoyo. For a few actual Williams *Adagio* look-alikes, see Chapter 11.

[106]"Platoon–Adagio for Strings Barber Remix–Music by Direct to Dreams," *YouTube* (21 September 2009), posted by Direct2Dreams.

[107]"Re: What's Your Favourite Quotes?," *YouTube* (13 April 2007), posted by kawthari.

the home and in the streets" (Nelson Mandela) and "If you can't feed a hundred people, then just feed one" (Mother Teresa). Barber's music perfectly enhances the poignancy of this scene.

Juan Barragan and Justin Hawk, a two-man team, used a portion of Tiësto's trance version of *Adagio* in 2009 to accompany the famed robot transformation scene in Fritz Lang's landmark silent film *Metropolis* (1927).[108] In this scene the mad scientist Rotwang (Rudolf Klein-Rogge) transforms the human Maria (Brigitte Helm) into his gynoid, Futura.[109] This is the earliest android depiction on film and one of the most elaborate transformation scenes ever devised for the cinema.[110] These men have added sound effects and some generic musical sounds to the first minute of the episode. Then as Rotwang prepares to throw the switch to begin the full operation, he lowers his head and closes his eyes. No intertitle is inserted at that moment in the original film, but the videographers have added his possible thought: "This is the final moment," a reasonable interpretation of the scientist's gesture. At this "final moment" the music score subtly merges into the Tiësto introduction. The electronic beat corresponds almost exactly to the neon-like light circles rising and falling around the gynoid's metallic form. Just when Maria's human face is transferred to the robot, the main *Adagio* phrase enters. The robot has become "'humanized" in much the same manner that Tiësto's electronic, "robotic" trance beat has become the more "human" sound of Samuel Barber's melody. The whole soundtrack is so successful in enhancing the scene that one might imagine it was composed specifically for the movie.

Several videos introduce an *Adagio* trance remix as the soundtrack for violent movie fight scenes. *Green Street Hooligans* (2005), known as *Green Street* in the United Kingdom, is the source of a music video in which two opposing factions, fans of rival British football teams, slug it out after the game, often shown in slow motion.[111] "Jet Li: Tiësto," borrows scenes from *Unleashed* (2005), a.k.a. *Danny the Dog*.* Danny (Jet Li) has been brought up as a dog and trained to fight like a gladiator by his owner, Bart (Bob Hoskins). *Adagio*'s trance beat supports kicks and head bashings during martial arts scenes. Tiësto's remix is also the basis for a collection

[108]"Metropolis Laboratory Scene Re-dub," *YouTube* (3 June 2009), posted by JTHawk30.

[109]Futura is her name in the original novel (1922) by Thea von Harbou.

[110]See "Maschinenmensch," *Wikipedia,* www.en.wikipedia.org/wiki/Maschinenmensch for speculation on how the laboratory scene was filmed. It took so long to complete that Helm fainted during the shooting.

[111]"Football Factory 'n' Green Street Fights," *YouTube* (4 August 2008), posted by liamoh7.

of scenes from *The Matrix* (1999), with much hand-to-hand and weapon-to-weapon combat between Neo (Keanu Reeves) and his adversaries.[112] Also present is the infamous scene of a creature crawling into his navel. (Remember: "the matrix has you!") Corsten's remix is found in "Narnia Battle Scene."* Excerpts from *The Chronicles of Narnia: The Lion, The Witch and the Wardrobe* (2005) fit the music: the slow *Adagio* portion for the participants as they position themselves for battle, then the faster trance part during the battle itself.

Videographers often assemble scenes from television series to *Adagio* accompaniment, as in a video with clips from the USA mini-series, *Attila* with incredibly pumped Gerard Butler in the title role battling the forces of Caesar Valentian (Reg Rogers).* The music is coordinated with important actions in the film. Other music videos borrow clips from British television or movie dramatizations of nineteenth-century novels. *Adagio* is used for scenes from the BBC serialization of Elizabeth Gaskell's *North and South*.* Because all clips feature actor John Thornton (playing Richard Armitage), the video might also be considered homage to him. It is well planned out; a rigorous fight scene goes along with the climax of the music, with an intimate scene during the quiet chord passage.

Charlotte Brontë's novel *Jane Eyre* has been dramatized many times in both feature films and television mini-series. "Three Faces of Jane Eyre" juxtaposes scenes from the Franco Zeffirelli film (1996) with Charlotte Gainsbourg as Jane and William Hurt as Rochester and from two television serializations, one from A&E with Samantha Morton and Ciarán Hinds (1997) and the other from BBC (shown in the US on *Masterpiece Theatre*) with Ruth Wilson and Toby Stephens (2006).* Clips from all three sources are cleverly interspersed throughout a playing of Barber's *Adagio*. It is interesting to watch the characters evolve through the story, from Jane's childhood through the happy ending, as the actors keep changing. Great care has been taken in the way the different versions are combined. The disastrous near-wedding of Jane and Rochester and the struggle with the mysterious tower resident all happen during the music's climactic phrases; the couple's romantic encounter transpires during the last phrases of the coda. And they lived happily ever after.

Adagio is also a frequent selection for videos derived from science fiction or fantasy television shows. There is often a narrow distinction between the two genres, both of which may contain supernatural or bizarre events. Such videos borrow footage from sci-fi shows such as

112"Matrix Revolutions–Battle for Zion," *YouTube* (11 August 2007), posted by LostAngel88.

Supernatural,[113] *Battlestar Galactica,*[114] *Farscape,** and *Smallville.*[115] Film clips or stills from the series *Lost* are featured in several videos. Tiësto's *Adagio* remix is the score to "LOST.Adagio For Strings," where clips are well coordinated with the music; some scenes flash on the screen to the beat of the music, nighttime images occur during the slow section, and video action increases along with the musical buildup.[116] Set to the orchestral *Adagio,* other videos present more poignant scenes, such as those concerning Kate's pregnancy, which forces her to leave the island.[117]

Just as videographers pay tribute to deceased actors, others do the same to fictional characters, both in television series and films. To honor such characters may seem odd, but they have often been portrayed so realistically that, to an audience, they take on a life of their own and appear to be real people. Many have died during the run of a television show or during a sequence of movies. *Lost* was a particularly lethal television series; over the long run of the show, over twenty characters have been sacrificed. One posting presents a photographic sequence of many of them, including at the *Adagio* climax Charlie Pace (Dominic Monaghan), a particular favorite among viewers. Starting off as a past drug addict and failed rock star, at the end he became somewhat of a hero. In an interview Monaghan said of his character, "that he saved people's lives is something that allowed him to die with dignity."[118] At the quiet chord passage a clever intertitle pun reads: "Rest in Pace." Another video focuses on Mr. Eko (Adewale Akinnuoye), whose death by a mysterious "black cloud" is depicted at the climax of the music. John Locke (Terry O'Quinn), who discovers him, closes Eko's eyes during the quiet chord passage. At the end, the screen reads, "R.I.P. Mr. Eko."[119] One movie admirer has devised a video honoring characters that have died in the various *Harry Potter* movies ("the good guys, of course"). He uses *Adagio*

[113]"Swan Song | Supernatural 5x22 | Adagio for Strings," *YouTube* (3 May 2011), posted by NorweganWood.

[114]"Starbuck's Death," *YouTube* (23 April 2007), posted by jsgould.

[115]"Smallville–Lionel Luthor's Funeral," *YouTube* (18 April 2008), posted by japa28.

[116]"LOST.Adagio for Strings (A Nalom Production)," *YouTube* (14 August 2006), posted by Markyz8.

[117]"Adagio for Strings Jate / Skate AU," *YouTube* (18 March 2008), posted by NikkiMonique.

[118]Dominic Monaghan, quoted in Shawna Malcom, "Sorry, Charlie: *Lost* Star Wanted to 'Die' a Hero," *TV Guide* (24 May 2007).

[119]Other videos include scenes from the NBC series, *Heroes* (using the Tiësto remix), and the Fox series, *Prison Break* (with the orchestral *Adagio*).

because it was "the saddest music I could think of." One fan of the *Horatio Hornblower* mini-series (based on the C. S. Forester character, originating on British ITV in March 2008 and coming to American A&E in 2009) assembled scenes set to this music that specifically honored his favorite character, Archie Kennedy (Jamie Bamber).

In Chapter 8 *Adagio for Strings* was cited in connection with the soap opera, *One Life to Live*. Now a soap fan has used Barber's Agnus Dei to accompany scenes from *General Hospital,* when Connor Bishop (Tyler Christopher) raped Emily Quartermaine (Natalia Livingston).[120] The video honors the show itself, the character Emily, and the actress who portrayed her. The video begins with the rape itself and then moves to the scene where she later shot him. Much of it depicts her emotional reaction to these events with bits of dialogue superimposed on the music. Near the end she tells Lucky Spencer (Greg Vaughan), lying comatose in his hospital bed:

> I wish that I could erase what happened, but I can't, so I'm going to do the next best thing, I'm never going to speak of it to anyone . . . someday it will be as if it never happened at all; as if Connor never attacked me and raped me. Someday it will be just a memory that fades and fades, and then is gone.[121]

At the musical climax, as she prays by Lucky's bed, he comes out of his coma. The video is a miniature soap opera in itself, set to a single piece of music, but at the same time it is a tribute to Livingston, whose superb acting is revealed by means of these clips.

AMV and Video Games

A prominent fad in music videos is the borrowing of scenes from Japanese comic strips (manga) or television and movie cartoons (anime) and setting them to a piece of music, resulting in an anime music video (AMV). A popular musical choice is a version of *Adagio for Strings,* usually Tiësto's remix.

The series *Naruto* is a source of several *Adagio* AMVs. While some, such as "The Relationship"[122] and "Naruto AMV–Adagio for Strings,"* are

[120] "Emily-Agnus Dei," *YouTube* (17 September 2006), posted by NLdotcom.

[121] *Ibid.* The scene occurs at the 4:13 mark in the video.

[122] "The Relationship," *YouTube* (24 August 2006), posted by 0kashii.

straightforward, "Just One of Those Days" is controversial.* It includes a portion of the orchestral *Adagio* in the midst of the song, "Break Stuff" from the album *Significant Other* (1999) by the rap / nu metal / punk band, Limp Bizkit. The music is background for clips of Uzmaki Naruto's confrontation with Uchihe Sasuke. It appears as Naruto lies defeated on the ground; a portion of the Limp Bizkit song returns, but there is no music for the ending, only dialogue from the original anime. This may be the most bizarre *Adagio* pairing with a mainstream tune, ever.[123] Another character from the series, Sabaku no Gaara [Gaara of the Desert] is the focus of several video tributes, using part of the orchestral *Adagio*.* Gaara's creator, Masahi Kishimoto, considers the character almost "a mirror image" of Naruto: opposite, yet similar. Gaara, "universally rejected and ignored," is easily recognizable by his facial tattoo and his raccoon-like eyes, based on the Japanese folk animal, Tanuki. The use of *Adagio* as background music may be intended to elicit sympathy for the character.

Creating an AMV out of still panels of a simple manga is more challenging. Whereas anime images are already in motion, manga cels are a series of "freeze frames" requiring a technique to give the illusion of constant movement. The creator of "Godchild–Kaori Yuki"* achieves this sense of animation with the "Ken Burns effect" mentioned earlier. It uses most of *Adagio*. Likewise the original manga of *Naruto* is the source of "SasoDei–Adagio for Strings."* The word, "Sasodei" is derived from the names of two prominent members of Akastsuki, a fictional crime organization: Akasun Sasori, who once was human but became a puppet (revealing the complexity of manga/anime stories!), and his companion, Deidara. Despite Diedara's feminine appearance, the character is male, sometimes creating gender confusion for new fans. The video, set to Agnus Dei, depicts them at various ages, from children to young adults.*

Another video source is computer games, such as those from the Metal Gear Solid series, begun in the 1990s. *Adagio* is the score for the video, "Metal Gear Solid 3–Horrors of War,"* based primarily on the final scene from "Snake Eater," the third game in the series. In this video, President Lyndon Johnson (the action takes place in the 1960s), hands Naked Snake a Distinguished Service Cross and confers upon him the title of Big Boss, followed by flashbacks to events leading up to this

[123]"Limp Bizkit–Break Stuff," *YouTube* (5 October 2009), posted by LimpBizkitVEVO. Although the original Naruto vs. Sasuke / *Adagio* / Break Stuff combination has been removed, one can imagine such a juxtaposition by listening to the Limp Bizkit music video.

ceremony. The fourth installment of the series, "Guns of the Patriots," is a stealth-based game in which mercenaries fight proxy battles for PMCs (private military companies). It features Solid Snake (a.k.a. Old Snake) working to assassinate Liquid in the Middle East. He also, thanks to Dr. Naomi Hunter, discovers his impending death has been accelerated due to the programming of his engineered genes from the time he was cloned. The quiet chords end just as Solid Snake and Liquid have their final showdown on top of Outer Heaven, a nation-state located just 200 kilometers north of Galzburg, South Africa.[124] Yet another scene is set to Barber's Agnus Dei. The producer comments, "I believe the song perfectly fits this video and the situation it's in."[125] A final video for "Metal Gear Platoon," features the Corsten remix.[126] Apparently for the uploader, the DJ's non-role in the film is trivial; however, users comments were not as welcoming.

Other "First person shooter" (FPS) games, such as the *Halo* series, provide material for other videos, some of which were devised even prior to the game's release. A one-minute television commercial for *Halo 3* was first presented at a Microsoft press conference and then to the general public on ESPN *Monday Night Football* on 4 December 2006. It has inspired many music videos with different pieces of music, including *Adagio*, substituted for the original soundtrack, which consisted mainly of combat noises. The commercial begins with dialogue between two kids lying on the ground and looking up into the sky. One asks, "Ever wonder what's up there?" Following this is a dramatic combat scene, where "covenant plasma projectiles bombard the area." The video, "Halo 3 Remix" starts with a passage from Barber's Agnus Dei, underscoring the dialogue then moves on to Grieg's "Hall of the Mountain King" for the dramatic combat.[127] The final phrase of Agnus Dei appears at the very end.

While these videos all use pre-existing games, another requires greater creativity. "My 1st Mugen Video" contains characters from M.U.G.E.N., not a game in itself, but a "game engine" which, according to *Wikipedia*, allows creation of "characters, background stages and other game objects

[124]"Metal Gear Solid 4: Adagio for Strings," *YouTube* (4 July 2008), posted by John Scott. Galzburg is a fictitious location.

[125]"Metal Gear Adagio: Song for the Patriots," *YouTube* (7 July 2007), posted by BigBrotherWii.

[126]"Metal Gear Platoon," *YouTube* (5 August 2006), posted by OxoRee.

[127]"Halo 3 Remix," *YouTube* (19 January 2007), posted by DannoHung.

through interpreted text files, graphics, and sound compilations."[128] There are several "rounds" of combat, including one accompanied by part of Tiësto's remix.

Recycled Music Videos: Replacement, Juxtaposition, and Superposition

While some videographers have taken scenes from movies and television games, others have created new works out of previously existing music videos. In this process, all or part of the video track is retained, but the audio portion is often changed according to one of three basic techniques: 1) completely replacing the original music with new music (such as *Adagio for Strings*), 2) juxtaposing both old and new music sources (original plus *Adagio*), and 3) simultaneously combining both old and new music sources in counterpoint. Several videographers have employed one or more of these three techniques in their recycling of Michael Jackson videos.

"Adagio Stranger In Moscow"[129] uses the first portion of Jackson's video, "Stranger In Moscow"[130] but with the opening of *Adagio for Strings* (William Ørbit's arrangement) replacing Jackson's vocal version. Because the King of Pop's voice is no longer on the soundtrack, the video has been re-edited to exclude all views of him, which would show him lip-syncing the words of the original song. The new video focuses on the Muscovites themselves and the raindrops replenishing the Russian capital.

A good juxtaposition of the Barber score with an original soundtrack also focuses on the pop star. "Michael Jackson: Child's heart and Adagio" begins with his song "A Child's Heart," accompanying clips of his early less complicated days (with the Jackson Five) plus "innocent" scenes of his playing with children (pre-trial days) and a tour of Neverland Ranch with Oprah Winfrey.* When the music switches to Corsten's remix, there are clips of the older, post-trial Jackson; one scene shows an image of him on the ground, his body decaying to dust. The video might be considered a "mini-biography" showing the change from the youthful singer with his early successes to a more somber beleaguered man. The two pieces of music reinforce this evolution.

[128]"MvC EoH Combos / Bugs," *YouTube* (20 July 2008), posted by BlueDrumV.

[129]"Adagio Stranger in Moscow," *YouTube* (9 December 2006), posted by angelgijon.

[130]"Michael Jackson–Stranger in Moscow," *YouTube* (2 October 2009), posted by MichaelJacksonVEVO.

Another Jackson song is featured in "michael jackson, chistina aguillar [*sic*], adagio for strings," a good example of the superposition of musical soundtracks.* It contains the orchestral *Adagio for Strings* with two song melodies layered upon it: first Jackson's "They Don't Care about Us," and then Christina Aguilera's "Beautiful." They accompany various images, primarily a man on a bike and sketches of angels. While the decisive beat of Jackson's song successfully coordinates with the tempo of *Adagio* in the first half of the video, less successful is the second half where Aguilera's song, in a different key and with a slightly different beat, clashes with Barber's music.

After Jackson's untimely death, several *YouTube* videographers devised tributes to him, several with a version of *Adagio*. One version, "Adagio for Michael Jackson," uses the complete orchestral work;[131] another, "Michael Jackson–They Broke You," has a brief excerpt;[132] while a third, "The Day Michael Jackson Died and the World Mourned," uses the complete Agnus Dei.* The first presents various photographs of the mature Michael, both in black and white and in color, plus others that are enhanced artistically, approaching the effect of video art. There is no attempt to tell a story. The others show photographs of Michael basically in chronological order from youth to shortly before his death, somewhat like the mini-biographies mentioned earlier, but now with a sense of closure. The one that includes "they broke you" in the title shows photographs of him, usually with a sad countenance, implicating society for being complicit in his troubles and, ultimately, his death. In "The Day Michael Jackson Died"* more upbeat images appear until the music soars to the climax, at which point the pictures switch to the grief-stricken faces of fans as they receive news of his death and views of those who mourned after his funeral. At the very end of the coda, when the choir sings *dona nobis pacem*, the photographs return to a calmer, more relaxed Michael, the image that most fans prefer to remember. Perhaps he has been granted peace at last.

It is apparent from such examples that *Adagio for Strings* is a viable track for many different kinds of music videos. While it seems sensible from the start in scenes from war movies and romantic dramas, it is unusual and sometimes totally unexpected in highlight reels and rap parodies. Yet many of these videos, produced by ordinary people with extraordinary imaginations, show a great deal of creativity.

[131]"Adagio for Michael Jackson," *YouTube* (30 November 2009), posted by mjalbatros.

[132]"Michael Jackson–They Broke You," *YouTube* (27 October 2009), posted by TheRaGiTe.

> Somewhat to the composer's dismay, the Adagio for Strings has acquired a funereal tinge.
>
> —Nathan Broder, *Samuel Barber* (1956).[1]

Introduction

In 1994, long after the composer's death, Paul Wittke, Barber's editor at G. Schirmer, reported that "it surprised and often disturbed Barber that this deeply felt work was so often performed at solemn occasions. To him it was 'just music' (a typical Barber evasion)."[2] *Adagio for Strings* has been heard, nevertheless, at funeral services and memorial concerts all over the world for the last seven decades.[3] One of the earliest uses—if not the earliest—occurred at the funeral of Barber's good friend, violinist and writer Gama Gilbert, who actually died in Barber's apartment in New York City when the composer was away.[4] During his service at the Universalist Funeral Chapel in September 1940 the Primrose String Quartet played the Adagio movement from Barber's String Quartet.[5] Gilbert had been a member of the Curtis String Quartet, which had championed the work in the 1930s. Therefore the selection was more than just appropriate funereal music: it represented a direct personal connection. Later, in November of the same year, Joseph Levine conducted the New Center of Music Chamber Orchestra in the full orchestral *Adagio* at New York's Town Hall in Gilbert's honor.[6]

Perhaps the earliest performance of *Adagio* at a memorial event for war victims was held at the Duluth (Minn.) Armory on 18 March 1945 to honor those lost in World War II. In addition to the invocation, prayer,

[1]Nathan Broder, *Samuel Barber* (New York: G. Schirmer, 1956), 74.

[2]Paul Wittke, *Samuel Barber: An Improvisatory Portrait* (New York: G. Schirmer, 1994), 13.

[3]See Appendix 10 for a calendar of memorial services that featured *Adagio*. A number of these are discussed in this chapter.

[4]Barber disclosed this information to fellow composer Mario Castelnuovo Tedesco in a letter (16 January 1941), held in the Castelnuovo Collection at the Library of Congress. See Wayne C. Wentzel, *Samuel Barber: A Research and Information Guide*, 2nd ed. (New York: Routledge, 2010), 358-59 [Cast-Ted 1].

[5]William Primrose was the violist in the ensemble.

[6]Barbara B. Heyman, *Samuel Barber: The Composer and His Music* (New York: Oxford University Press, 1992), 166. Heyman maintains that it was Gama Gilbert who suggested to Barber that he orchestrate the string quartet movement for Toscanini.

address, and benediction, Tauno Hannikainen conducted the Duluth Symphony Orchestra in Barber's *Adagio*. In keeping with the dignity of the circumstances, the program notes delivered a request: "Please do not applaud during or after this service." These occasions set the standard for *Adagio*'s role in commemorations for decades to come.

For Heads of State and Other Dignitaries

SETTING THE RECORD STRAIGHT: PRESIDENTS FRANKLIN D. ROOSEVELT AND JOHN F. KENNEDY

Despite oral and written reports to the contrary, there is no verifiable evidence that *Adagio for Strings* was played at the funeral of either Franklin Delano Roosevelt or John Fitzgerald Kennedy. True, it was heard on the radio after the announcements of their deaths, but the accounts of the services, well documented in newspapers, do not indicate that a string orchestra was on hand to play any kind of concert music.

Adagio was broadcast on the radio from New York City a few minutes after the notification of Roosevelt's passing on 12 April 1945. Networks canceled their regular schedules to devote time to the reading of tributes and to the playing of music in his memory, initiating the funereal tone that people have associated with *Adagio* ever since. Also played were both Charles Gounod's and Franz Schubert's "Ave Maria," some music of Tchaikovsky, and "Home on the Range," one of the President's favorite songs.

Adagio was part of the British Broadcasting Company (BBC) radio's Roosevelt tribute two days later. The announcer first proclaimed: "We in Britain, who now pay this act of homage to Franklin Delano Roosevelt, are remembering his achievement . . . Roosevelt, the man, whose warm human voice sustained hopes of his fellow man in every continent of the world."[7] Then he read a passage from Roosevelt's Second Inaugural Address, "I See One-Third of a Nation Ill-Housed," with *Adagio* following immediately. Neither the name of the orchestra nor the conductor was mentioned; the BBC Orchestra probably played the work live. When it concluded, the announcer quoted excerpts from another speech, "The Light of Democracy" from 15 March 1941, in which Roosevelt expressed his feelings about Great Britain. The orchestra then offered "Nimrod" from Elgar's "Enigma" Variations (1899), which has become the mourning music

[7] Library of Congress tape LWO 9324 Reel 9, A: 1.

for Britain as *Adagio* has for the United States. Thus, as early as 1945, these pieces have linked the two countries in grief.

There were two funeral rites for the President: one at the White House on Saturday and one for his interment in Hyde Park the next day. The main music for these were his favorite hymn tunes, such as ST. CATHERINE ("Faith of Our Fathers"), and Chopin's ubiquitous dirge (1837) from his Sonata in B-Flat Minor for piano (1839). Neither a string quartet nor a string orchestra was present on either occasion.

Indeed, *Adagio* continues to be associated with FDR. In 2003 Decca issued a four-disc set, *Threads of Glory: 200 Years of America in Words and Music,* containing speeches by famous Americans accompanied by music by native composers.[8] Lorne Greene (of Bonanza fame) reads passages from Roosevelt's "Four Freedoms" speech, his discourse to Congress on 6 January 1941, with *Adagio* providing the background. Ronnie Aldrich led the London Festival Orchestra. In addition, the Pittsburgh Symphony devoted portions of several programs during the 2003-2005 seasons to "Commemorating the End of World War II," with works inspired by or associated with that War. In February 2005 guest conductor Peter Oundjian presented *Adagio* on a program broadcast for FDR's death.

While many sources state unequivocally that *Adagio for Strings* was performed at the funeral service of President Kennedy, there is no concrete evidence of it.[9] Musicologist Irving Lowens warned, "every momentous event breeds legends, and already the legend about the music that accompanied the dead march proliferates. Some are entirely wrong."[10] He gave an hour-by-hour description of all the music at ceremonies associated with Kennedy's funeral rites on 25 November 1963, from 10:48 A.M., when the casket was placed in Capitol Plaza, to the closing ceremony at Arlington National Cemetery that afternoon. While much music was played at different times and places throughout the day, the Barber work is nowhere in sight. People may remember hearing it on the radio between the assassination and the funeral. In fact, an embarrassing incident occurred on CBS radio momentarily after JFK's assassination had

[8](Decca, 028947520023, 2003).

[9]Luke Howard, "The Popular Reception of Samuel Barber's *Adagio for Strings*," *American Music* XXV/1 (Spring 2007), 54.

[10]Irving Lowens, "Accurate Listing of Funeral Music [for Kennedy]," *Washington Star* (1 December 1963).

been confirmed. A news broadcaster solemnly proclaimed in stentorian tones: "It has just been announced that President Kennedy is dead." Then someone started to play a recording of *Adagio* but at the wrong speed![11] The careless disk jockey forgot to change the turntable to 33 1/3 RPM from the "pop music" speed of 45 RPM. The mistake was caught, and the music faded out after about ten seconds.[12]

Howard Mitchell conducted the National Symphony Orchestra in a memorial to the President on the evening after the burial. Author Elise K. Kirk recorded the event in the following manner:

> One of the most hauntingly moving was the National Symphony's post-midnight performances to a completely empty Constitution Hall, a few blocks from the White House.[13] The orchestra . . . played Debussy's La Mer in memory of the president's love of the ocean and his valor as a naval officer; [and] the Adagio for Strings by the American composer Samuel Barber, the last distinguished representative of the arts to be invited to the White House before the president's death.[14]

Mitchell referred to Kennedy as a "neighbor" of the orchestra and an "ardent supporter of the symphony"; according to one member of the ensemble, the concert was the orchestra's way of "paying respect to the President in the manner we know best—by playing music."[15]

[11]"JFK'S ASSASSINATION (WCCO-RADIO)(PART 1) [5 HOURS OF NEW AUDIO ADDED]," *YouTube* (31 August 2012), posted by DavidVonPein1. The turntable gaffe occurs at 36:42.

[12]Luke Howard, "The Popular Reception of *Adagio for Strings*," *American Music*, 55. Luke Howard contended that it was Neil Strawser; my sources indicate the announcer was Alan Jackson (not the singer).

[13]Why an empty house? The orchestra played for a videotaping by NBC for a later telecast. I am not certain that this program was ever broadcast. A perusal through issues of *TV Guide* during November and December of 1963 shows no listing for it. If it were televised live, the announcement of such an impromptu performance may not have met the publication deadline of television listings.

[14]Elise K. Kirk, *Music at the White House: A History of the American Spirit* (Chicago: University of Chicago Press, 1986), 301-02.

[15]Howard Mitchell, quoted in "National Symphony Gives Concert for 'Neighbor,'" *The New York Times* (27 November 1963), 22.

SERVICES FOR PRINCESS GRACE AND PRINCE RAINIER OF MONACO

The obsequies for Princess Grace of Monaco on 18 September 1982 at the Monte Carlo Cathedral featured several classical creations, notably, one of her favorites—*Adagio for Strings*. In January 1959 she and the Prince had heard it when they attended the inaugural concert of the Orchestra of the Principality of Monaco, conducted by Charles Munch, and found it to be extremely moving. They, of course, may have known and appreciated the work long before. During its performance in the Cathedral Prince Albert "covered his face in his black-gloved hands. Princess Caroline, who wept, turned toward her father, who sat next to her by the altar, but the Prince, partly slumped, eyes half closed, did not raise his head."[16] Princess Stephanie, who had survived the car crash that killed her mother, was still in the hospital but watched part of the ceremony on television with her husband. When she began to "sob uncontrollably," he had to switch the set off.[17]

At the Kennedy Center the following March, Mstislav Rostropovich directed the National Symphony Orchestra in a musical tribute, "Princess Grace Remembered." During the performance of *Adagio for Strings* photographs of her at various stages of her life were projected onto a screen. Watching from a box of honor were President Ronald Reagan, Prince Albert, and Princess Caroline.[18] (First Lady Nancy Reagan was a participant in the proceedings.)

Twenty-three years later, on 15 April 2005, *Adagio for Strings* returned to the Monaco Cathedral under similar circumstances after the death of Prince Rainier. Princess Caroline, president of the Monaco orchestra society, selected the music; she undoubtedly remembered how effective *Adagio* had been at her mother's service and wanted the same musical memorial for her father. Prince Albert, heir to the principality, sat with his sisters at the right of the altar. Immediately after the choir sang the communion chant, the Monte Carlo Philharmonic Orchestra began *Adagio* for the communion ritual. The royal family "blinked back tears" as the music "mournfully echoed" through the church; Princess Stephanie sat

[16]John Vincour, "For Princess's Family, The Parting Is Forlorn," *The New York Times* (19 September 1982), 16.

[17]Valentina Artsrunik, *Monaco's Wild Child: Princess Stephanie Biography* (London: Artnik, 2004), 48.

[18]The program was telecast on the PBS *Great Performances* series the following September near the first anniversary of the Princess's death.

"slumped in grief, clutching a handkerchief in her hands."[19] One observer noticed three fundamental aspects of the ceremony: the deep sadness of the Prince and Princesses, the presence of Rainier's dog Odin, and the choral and instrumental music, particularly the "touching" and "tranquil" *Adagio*. In his or her opinion it was

> at the same time both enchanting and nostalgic, as was the life of Rainier, a prince whose life contained moments of genuine happiness (like those only known in fairy tales), and of profound pain, with sudden tragedies that he could or could not face but which he always bore with great dignity. The music brought to mind the life of Rainer, as if a list of images were passing through our memory to the sound of this masterpiece.[20]

Later performances of *Adagio for Strings* in Monaco will probably remind the remaining members of the Grimaldi family of the touching and tranquil presentations at their parents' funerals. They may always have to blink back tears.

MEMORIAL CONCERTS FOR MARTIN LUTHER KING, JR.

Although *Adagio for Strings* was not played at either of Martin Luther King's two funerals on 9 April 1968, several orchestras have presented it at memorial concerts on or near his birthday, as for instance the Atlanta Symphony Orchestra under the leadership of Robert Spano on "A King Celebration 2003." Thomas Wilkins directed the work with the Cleveland Orchestra on 14 January 2001 in connection with the "Martin Luther King, Jr., Celebration Concert" and with the Philadelphia Orchestra beginning in 2004. These latter performances are particularly memorable because they featured storyteller Charlotte Blake Alston reading passages from King's "I Have a Dream" speech, which Wilkins selected and coordinated with *Adagio*. He perceives a resemblance between Barber's musical approach and qualities of rhetorical speech:

[19]Jocelyn Gecker, "Grief for Prince Chills Sun-splashed Monaco," *Chicago Tribune* (16 April 2005), 3.

[20]Posted on the Prince Rainier Grimaldi website, rainiergrimaldi.blogspot.com; "entre ensoñadora y nostálgica a la vez, y es que asi fué [*sic*] la vida de Rainiero, un príncipe por cuya vida pasaron etapas de auténtica felicidad (parecidas a las que solamente se conocen en los cuentos de hadas) y de profundo dolor, con tragedias súbitas que pudo o no pudo afrontar pero que siempre sobrellevó con gran dignidad. La musica recordaba la vida de Rainiero, como si fuese una lista de imágenes pasando por nuestro recuerdo al son de esta obra maestra." [Translation by Linda M. Willem]

> The music seemed to be perfect because of the way the musical material is presented. The idea of the execution of a phrase followed by a pause [the manner in which *Adagio* begins] seems to match the way speeches are delivered. Once a thought is presented, the listener must have a moment (even if ever so brief) to ponder what has just been said.[21]

Alston was pleased with the prospect: "the opportunity to participate in presenting the 'marriage' of the Adagio and selected excerpts from King's speeches was incredibly powerful."[22] Yet when she was told that she would be narrating to the Barber work, her initial response was disbelief: "You want me to talk over the Adagio?" She feared that she would be chastised as "the woman who ruined Barber's Adagio for Strings" but happily reports that it "turned out to be quite the opposite."[23]

> As I rehearsed speaking over the music that often brought tears to my eyes, I actually had to concentrate on not getting emotional myself as I spoke. Before I went out on stage I kept praying, "Let me get through this without breaking down." The text and music blended together quite successfully, producing an artistic and emotional journey that led to the "Free at last . . ." climax spoken in the silence after the big musical crescendo. Maestro Wilkins had originally timed the text so those words would be spoken right at the crescendo but decided in rehearsal that he wanted it in the silence.[24]

Wilkins compares the effect of this musical-textual crescendo to that of "a good southern Baptist sermon."

> The music indeed gets to a fevered pitch the likes of which the soul can hardly bear . . . and then there's silence . . . exactly what is needed. The music that follows to the end for me is an

[21]Thomas Wilkins, email (25 January 2006) to the author.

[22]Charlotte Blake Alston, email (8 August 2005) to the author.

[23]*Ibid.*

[24]Charlotte Blake Alston, email (13 October 3005) to the author.

opportunity for the body and mind and indeed the spirit to affirm the truth it just witnessed.[25]

Alston agrees: "The text continued with words of hope and a charge for all of us to become the active, cooperative participants in creating the future we wish to see."[26]

The first time this enhanced *Adagio* was scheduled, it was played just before intermission, and Alston remembered that several orchestra members left the stage and embraced her. She recalled, "One said she'd listened to those words many times, but this was the first time she really heard them, listened with her heart, and understood."[27] Clearly the whole was greater than the sum of the parts. When Wilkins first conceived of this narrated version for Cleveland, he used a male former opera singer as the narrator. "From now on I will only use Charlotte. She has a great sense of timing of the music (which makes my job a lot easier) and more importantly . . . she is a true wordsmith."[28] Wilkins and Alston have repeated their collaboration for several years.[29]

Martin Luther King's words were also associated with *Adagio for Strings* at the "African American Showcase Concert" with Chelsea Tipton II conducting the Savannah Symphony Orchestra. Designed as a kickoff for Black History Month on 5 February 2000, the program featured works not only by Black composers but also pieces by Shostakovich and Barber. *Adagio* was immediately followed by a recitation from King's "Letter from Birmingham Jail."[30] As in the Wilkins-Alston performance, the words were probably deliberately connected to the music.

[25]Thomas Wilkins, email (25 January 2005) to the author.

[26]Charlotte Blake Alston, email (13 October 2005) to the author.

[27]*Ibid.*

[28]Thomas Wilkins, email (25 January 2005) to the author.

[29]Was King fond of Barber's *Adagio?* While nothing seems to be written about such a predilection, he did have an interest in classical music. His mother played the piano and encouraged her children to take lessons. He was a member of the glee club as a student at Morehouse College. His regard for classical music may have been spurred on by his wife Coretta Scott, who studied voice at the New England Conservatory. On one of their first dates they attended a concert of the Boston Symphony Orchestra. He once wrote that Donizetti's *Lucia di Lammermoor* (1839) was one of his favorite operas, implying that he liked several others. It may not prove that he liked *Adagio*, but it leaves open the possibility.

[30]Written during his incarceration, this open letter was written on 16 April 1963. It was excerpted in various publications; the full text was published by King in *Why We Can't Wait* (Denver: Mentor Books by The New American Library, 1964).

Another type of juxtaposition took place at a King memorial concert by Paul Freeman's Chicago Sinfonietta in January 2008. The Deeply Rooted Dance Theater presented its own choreographic interpretation of *Adagio* as a tribute to King but not necessarily as an attempt to depict any aspect of his life or work. According to critic Bryant Manning, "Replete with dexterous lifts and twirls, the nine dancers masterfully brought out the balletic character that is so deeply embedded in this heartfelt music"; the orchestra's rendering "quieted the hall for 10 thoroughly absorbing minutes."[31] The Sinfonietta performance constituted a heartfelt and hopeful homage to a man who espoused non-violence.

OTHERS

Details surrounding the role of *Adagio* in tributes to other politicians and celebrities during the 1950s have proved challenging to document. Both Broder and Heyman reported that on 11 September 1950 *Adagio for Strings* was broadcast in South Africa on the death of Jan Christiaan Smuts, the country's prime minister.[32] That does not necessarily mean "at his funeral." They also maintained that it was performed "in memory of Senator Robert A. Taft" after his death on 31 July 1953.[33] While Broder wrote only that it was performed as an act of mourning, Heyman asserted that it was broadcast as well. In addition, people seem to have a faulty memory of how or when *Adagio* was played after Albert Einstein's death in April 1955. Heyman contended that it was part of his funeral,[34] but this cannot be the case because his will clearly stipulated that there be no funeral. Only family and friends attended his cremation, before which a friend read a passage from the works of Goethe. It is highly unlikely that an orchestra was present or could even be squeezed into the confined space. If the Barber piece should be correctly associated with his death, it must have been played at some sort of remembrance service.

In more recent times it is notable that the Barber work has transcended cultural boundaries and has been accepted as an expression of sadness and loss in the Middle East. In November 1995, after the assassination

[31]Bryant Manning, "Chicago Sinfonietta Takes King Tribute to Lofty New Heights," *Chicago Sun-Times* (23 January 2008).

[32]Nathan Broder, *Samuel Barber* (New York: G. Schirmer, 1954), 74; and Barbara B. Heyman, *Samuel Barber* (1992), 173.

[33]*Ibid.*

[34]Barbara B. Heyman, *Samuel Barber* (1992), 173. She gives no source.

of Israeli Prime Minister Yitzhak Rabin, the Israel Sinfonietta Beersheba performed *Adagio* in his memory. Then on 4 December, the day marking the end of sheloshim, the Jewish mourning period, Yoel Levi conducted it on a memorial program with the Israel Philharmonic. He hoped that it would serve not only as a tribute to a great man but also provide "healing through music in a symbolic way."[35] On 14 February 2005, after a bomb exploded near former prime minister of Lebanon Rafic Hariri's motorcade killing him and his bodyguards, radio stations "switched from upbeat pop hits" to Barber's *Adagio*. Faculty and students at the American University of Beirut gathered in the cafeteria to watch television coverage. "When they announced he was dead, the university went quiet, completely."[36]

The Requiem Mass for Pope John Paul II on 2 April 2005 did not contain any orchestral music, only choral settings of the appropriate liturgical texts. During the next week, however, at least two radio programs scheduled Barber's Agnus Dei as a part of retrospectives of the Pope's life. One on CBC's *Tapestry*, "Upon This Rock: Portrait of a Pope," provided commentary by the Pope's biographer, George Wiegel, and Rosemary Ganley, assistant editor of *Catholic News Times*. A week later the Australian radio program, *The Rhythm Divine*, featured Agnus Dei in "Rites of Mourning." According to its host Geoff Wood, the Pope's death had "focused the world's attention on the Latin mass and the rituals of mourning."[37] Because much of the Agnus Dei text is similar to that in the Requiem Mass, he played the choral version.[38]

Adagio was also chosen for concerts given in the Pope's memory. A week after the funeral Charles Ansbacher included it on a concert with the Belarussian State Symphony. The following month the Fondazione Pro Musica e Arte Sacra presented it in Rome in the Papal Basilica of St. Mary Major at an event originally planned to celebrate the Pope's 85th birthday but altered to become a memorial. Angelo Comastri, General

[35]Scott Wilson, "In Israel, Levi Will Conduct Rabin Tribute," *The Atlanta Constitution* (4 December 1995), B: 2.

[36]Anthony Letayf, quoted in Annia Ciezadlo, "Cedar or Sapling," *The Nation* (28 March 2005); reprinted www.thenation.com/article/cedar-or-sapling#.

[37]Geoff Wood, "Rites of Mourning," *The Rhythm Divine* (13 April 2005); reprinted www.abc.net.au/rn /rhythmdivine/stories/2005/1343613.htm. The Trinity College Choir recording was played on *Tapestry*; the Westminster Cathedral Choir recording, on *The Rhythm Divine*.

[38]The text Barber set is taken from the Ordinary of the Mass; the text of the Requiem Mass is somewhat different.

Vicar of Vatican City, first gave a tribute to the Holy Father, after which Rudolf Piehlmayer conducted the Augsburg Philharmonic Orchestra in *Adagio* "as a last farewell to a great man."[39] In March of the following year The Canticum Novum Singers gave recitals in Connecticut and New York in the Pope's memory with Palestrina's Pope Marcellus Mass and Barber's Agnus Dei.[40]

For Composers, Conductors, and Other Musicians

SAMUEL BARBER AND GIAN CARLO MENOTTI

Surprisingly, but also significantly, *Adagio for Strings* was not a part of Barber's own funeral service in January 1981 at the First Presbyterian Church in his hometown of West Chester, Pennsylvania. Donald Collup, who sang *Dover Beach* on that occasion, related that, not only had Barber told him he did not want *Adagio* at his funeral, but the composer's mother had made the same request.[41] Barber must have recognized its overuse in such circumstances because he once said to Paul Wittke, "It is too banal a thing to do."[42] He undoubtedly mentioned this request to Menotti, who commented, "He did mind that it was always played at funerals! [laughs] As a matter of fact, I was very careful not to have it played at his funeral . . . . He liked the piece but thought he had written much better music than that."[43] In his will he specified music for this service, mainly Bach chorale preludes but also his own choral piece, "Let Down the Bars, O Death" (1936). This and several other Barber works—but not *Adagio*—were part of a memorial service on 9 February 1981 at St. Bartholomew's Church in New York City.

As with the deaths of FDR and JFK, radio stations throughout the country played *Adagio* following the announcement of Barber's death. Critic James R. Oestreich remembered such an occasion in New York:

[39]info-soci@aiams.it, Associazione Internazionale Amici della Musica Sacra.

[40]Performances occurred on 25 March 2006 at St. Mary's Roman Catholic Church in Ridgefield, Connecticut and on 2 April 2006 in New York City at Holy Trinity Roman Catholic Church.

[41]Donald Collup, "all my yesterdays," *amy.html*, www.collup.com/amy.html.

[42]Paul Wittke, "Samuel Barber: A Personal Note" [Introduction], *Samuel Barber: Complete Piano Music* (New York: G. Schirmer, 1986).

[43]Gian Carlo Menotti, quoted in Peter Dickinson, *Samuel Barber Remembered: A Centenary Tribute* (Rochester, N.Y.: University of Rochester Press, 2010), 68. Dickinson's interview with Menotti is dated 6 April 1981.

On the evening of Jan. 23, 1981, a listener aware of Samuel Barber's serious illness turned on a classical New York radio station to find the composer's Adagio for Strings immediately followed by Knoxville: Summer of 1915. At a time when classical stations programmed conservatively yet far more meaningfully than today, such a concentrated dose of a contemporary American composer not named Copland or Bernstein could signify only one thing: Barber had died.[44]

Only a week before Barber died, conductor and composer Lukas Foss had added *Adagio* to his program with the Brooklyn Philharmonia "as a tribute to the composer, who is gravely ill with cancer."[45] Little did he realize how ill Barber was and how little time he had left. Less than a week after Barber's death, Leonard Bernstein added *Adagio* to his concert with the New York Philharmonic Orchestra. Critic Donal Henahan considered it "an ideal tribute to the composer, and even the applause of part of the audience at its conclusion did not quite destroy the spell."[46] Head of the symphonic division at G. Schirmer Hans Heinsheimer was pleased with Bernstein's gesture but noted that Barber's music "needs no special occasion to be played. Much of it will remain alive, to be heard and enjoyed as a permanent memorial."[47]

Barber's own last experience with the work occurred a few weeks earlier, when several musicians came to New York City's University Hospital to play for him.[48] Among those attending were friends and colleagues, such as Menotti, composer / violinist Charles Turner, pianist

[44]James R. Oestreich, "For a Change, 2 Barber Pieces on a Program," *The New York Times* (28 September 1990), C: 28.

[45]Peter G. Davis, "Concert: Brooklyn Philharmonia in Ives, Sessions and Beethoven," *The New York Times* (16 January 1981), 3, 19.

[46]Donal Henahan, "Music: Bernstein Leads 3 Works by Copland," *The New York Times* (30 January 1981), C: 11.

[47]Hans Heinsheimer, "Adagio for Sam," *Opera News* (14 March 1981), 31. Bernstein himself was honored shortly after his death (16 October 1990) when David Zinman opened his Philadelphia Orchestra concert with *Adagio*.

[48]There are discrepancies concerning the date of this hospital performance. Heyman, in *Samuel Barber* (1992), 508, stated that it was New Year's Eve 1980, but White, in Peter Dickinson, *Samuel Barber Remembered*, 144, contended that it occurred on 11 January 1981. Turner mentioned in the same Dickinson volume, 77, that it took place a week before Barber's death, which would move it closer to 16 January 1981. In her study, 508, Heyman reported that Barber was discharged from the hospital on 18 January. The performance, therefore, had to have happened before that date.

John Browning, and tenor Robert White.[49] Students from the Juilliard School of Music played the Adagio movement of the String Quartet. Menotti considered their performance "very moving. . . . I don't know how much [Barber] took in, but he listened and at the end said, 'thank you: beautiful.'"[50] White concurred that it was "very beautiful, very moving and done with a lot of love";[51] he was reminded that whatever Barber felt when he wrote the Adagio movement still "lurked" in his "heart of hearts."[52] Listening to *Adagio* under these circumstances was an emotional experience for everyone there. Browning recalled that when the movement finished, "everybody in the room broke up—we could hardly hang on to ourselves."[53] Turner confessed, "This was a very difficult scene for me because it was like being at Sam's funeral while he was still alive."[54]

Although *Adagio for Strings* was given no part in Barber's funeral, the original string quartet movement was played at the funeral of his (nearly) lifelong companion, Gian Carlo Menotti, in the Cathedrale de Monaco on 10 February 2007 by Quatuor Dell'Arte, the principal string players of the Monte Carlo Philharmonic Orchestra.[55] Then, the following May, *Adagio* concluded a concert honoring Menotti at the Spoleto Festival USA, which he had founded in Charleston, South Carolina thirty years earlier. "Tribute: Gian Carlo Menotti" also presented two of Menotti's own works as well as eulogies by Joseph Flummerfelt, the festival's Artistic Director for Choral Activities, and Charleston mayor Joseph P. Riley. The festival's artistic associate John Kennedy conducted the young string players of the Ginn

[49]Others in attendance were William Schuman and his wife Frances, philanthropist Alice Tully, flutist Ransom Wilson, and composer John Corigliano.

[50]Gian Carlo Menotti, quoted in Peter Dickinson, *Samuel Barber Remembered*, 20.

[51]Robert White, quoted in Peter Dickinson, *Samuel Barber Remembered*, 144. Arthur Johnson's interview with White is dated February 1981.

[52]*Ibid.*, 147.

[53]John Browning, quoted in Peter Dickinson, *Samuel Barber Remembered*, 140. Dickinson's interview with Browning is dated 13 May 1981.

[54]Charles Turner, quoted in Peter Dickinson, *Samuel Barber Remembered*, 77. Dickinson's interview with Turner is dated 13 May 1981.

[55]David Lefèvre, Marius Mocanu, François Mereaux, and Jacques Perrone.

Resorts Spoleto Festival USA Orchestra[56] in the performance of *Adagio*, during which slides of Menotti, showing him surrounded by colleagues and patrons of the Festival over the years, were projected on a screen. Candid photographs portrayed him in various moods, from smiling to pensive. Kennedy believes that *Adagio* "seemed obvious as the choice of a non-Menotti work."[57]

In his review of the concert Joshua Rosenblum confided, "I've never especially liked this piece, but as soon as the orchestra played the opening two chords, I started sobbing like a baby."[58] I attended this event but did not cry (although I got a little misty) because, to me, the performance was moving but not sentimental. In particular, the rise to the climax was not overwrought. This restraint is consistent with Kennedy's approach to *Adagio*:

> It is not a sad or morose piece and I have a real aversion to extremely slow and maudlin interpretations of it. To me it is an optimistic work about love and hope. I told the orchestra that they should achieve a quality of sound that says "I will love you forever" with utter conviction and confidence. Its tenderness and optimism communicate a universal kind of love and the fullness of an overflowing heart. It sounds a love of assurance, and one can hear love of music, love of child, love of life. That is to me what the Adagio says in music. In the circumstances of having the honorific role of leading it at Menotti's memorial in Charleston, where the emotions are very complicated, it felt completely cathartic and beautiful to "let go" of Gian Carlo and express our gratitude through this amazingly generous music.[59]

It was a fitting farewell to Menotti, who was living with Samuel Barber at St. Wolfgang when the Adagio movement of the quartet came to life.

[56]According to the program booklet for the 2007 Festival (page 120), this orchestra, "formed anew each year through nationwide auditions," comprises "young professionals and advanced students of many nationalities." Later that summer the audio of Kennedy's performance was posted on the Internet: Patrick Sharbaugh, "The Spoleto Buzz," *Charleston* [S.C.] *City Paper* (1 June 2007), www.spoletobuzz.ccpblogs.com/category/special-events/.

[57]John Kennedy, email (18 June 2007) to the author.

[58]Joshua Rosenblum, "A Deeply Moving Tribute," *Charleston* [S.C.] *Post and Courier* (2 June 2007).

[59]John Kennedy, email (18 June 2007) to the author.

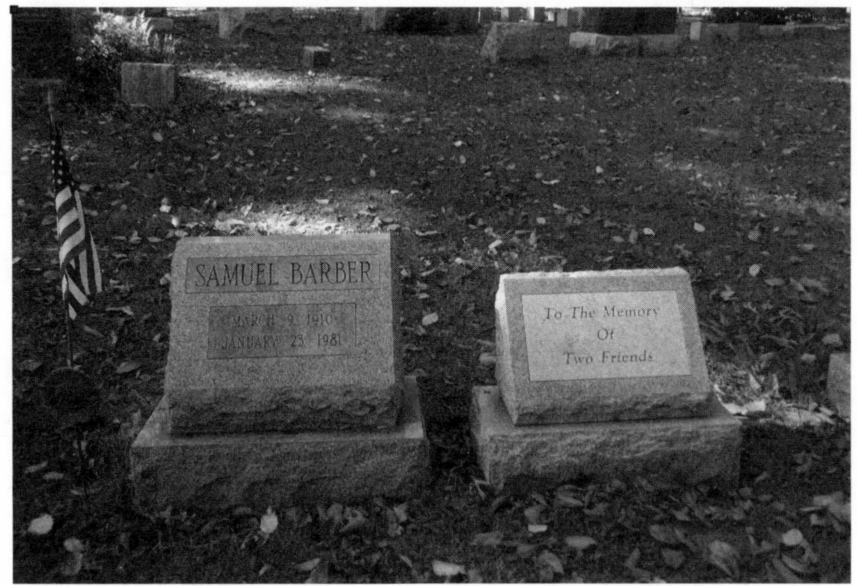

Illustration 10.1. Barber's Grave with His Tribute to Gian Carlo Menotti, Oaklands Cemetery, West Chester, Pennsylvania, October 2012

Courtesy of the Board of Managers Oaklands Cemetery

Image by Jim Kwambold

Barber was buried in Oaklands Cemetery outside of West Chester. The modest headstone merely gives his name and the dates of his birth and death. His will stipulated that a grave was to be reserved next to his for Menotti, if he chose to be buried there. Menotti was well aware of this and a few years after Barber's death seemed willing to comply:

> I would like to have my body sent to West Chester to be buried next to Sam Barber. A plot awaits me there, and in Sam's will he instructed that, if I am buried elsewhere, a marker should be put on that empty plot that reads, "to the memory of a great friendship." But I fully expect to be with him.[60]

It was not to be. Menotti was laid to rest near Yester House, his estate in Scotland for the last years of his life. He either changed his mind, or his adopted son, Francis ("Chip") Phelan, may have made the decision against his will. There is, however, a headstone on the empty grave next to Barber's with an inscription similar to the one quoted by Menotti: "To the Memory of Two Friends." Nonetheless, the two composers, separated in life, are now also separated in death.

[60]Gian Carlo Menotti, quoted in John Ardoin, *Stages of Menotti* (Garden City, N.Y.: Doubleday, 1985), 234 ["Dialogue IV"].

OTHER MUSICIANS

In 1993 James Sedares succeeded Andrew Schenck after his untimely death when conductor of the New Zealand Symphony Orchestra. One of Sedares's first recordings was devoted to the orchestral music of Norman Dello Joio, but *Adagio for Strings* was performed in Schenck's memory at the conclusion of the endeavor. In liner notes Michael Fine, the album's producer, identified the intention:

> Though Andrew's early death prevented his career from attaining the heights his talents deserved, all of us who worked with him knew him for a consummate musician, a good friend, and an extraordinary human being. . . . New Zealand and especially the New Zealand Symphony Orchestra held a special place in Andrew's affections. I couldn't imagine a more fitting tribute than to ask his friend and colleague James Sedares and the New Zealand Symphony to record Barber's Adagio in his memory.[61]

In 1995 a performance of *Adagio for Strings* concluded a memorial concert at Indiana University following the death of Josef Gingold, long-time violin teacher and artist-in-residence.[62] An ensemble was constituted of members of the string faculty as well as current and former students, including Joshua Bell, one of Gingold's most prominent and successful disciples. Another pupil, Paul Biss, conducted the work and delivered introductory remarks, ending with the confession: "we adored him and we will forever cherish his memory."[63] The circumstances produced a truly heart-felt performance, as lovely as could be heard anywhere.

At a 1998 memorial for Vincent de Frank, the founding conductor of the Memphis Symphony Orchestra, a unique musical incident took place. Just as a string octet was completing *Adagio*, the bells in a nearby tower unexpectedly chimed in. "The Adagio ends with four notes that sound like a sort of question," reflected Marsha Evans, one of the mourners who had worked with de Frank for several years. "At the end of this performance,

[61]Michael Fine, liner notes to *Norman Dello Joio*, perf. New Zealand Symphony Orchestra, cond. James Sedares (Koch International Classics, 7243, 1995).

[62]Gingold's acquaintance with *Adagio* went back several decades. He was one of the violinists in the Primrose String Quartet when it played the Adagio movement from Barber's String Quartet at the funeral service for Gama Gilbert back in 1940.

[63]A videotape of the concert with comments by Gingold's associates is held in the Cook Music Library at Indiana University.

the bells played what seemed like the same four notes in the same key at almost exactly the same time. It was kind of mystical."[64] Apparently carilloneur Paul Hicks decided to contribute his own measure of respect to the maestro.

In February 1999 the Cleveland Orchestra remembered Robert Shaw, its former associate conductor and choral director, by performing *Adagio for Strings*. Shaw was highly praised for his recording of the Agnus Dei transcription. A month later the Houston Symphony, with guest conductor Hugh Wolff, also paid homage to Shaw with a program on which *Adagio* led directly into the orchestra's chorus singing of Mozart's "Ave verum corpus." Because *Adagio* "carries much somber emotional weight," it thus became "unexpectedly appropriate" as an introduction to the brief Mozart piece.[65]

"Celebrating Harry: Orchestral Favorites Honoring the Late Harry Ellis Dickson" was the name given a pair of concerts of the Boston Classical Orchestra on 21 and 23 November 2003, dedicated to Dickson, its former musical director and a former Boston Symphony Orchestra member who had died the previous March. His successor, Steven Lipsitt, conducted the orchestra in several works that Dickson had particularly favored, notably *Adagio for Strings*.

Adagio's appearances are not confined to memorial tributes for only classical musicians. Mary Travers, the female third of folk revival trio Peter, Paul and Mary, died in September 2009 after a battle with leukemia. She specifically requested that the Barber work be played at the service in her memory, held two months later at New York City's Riverside Church on what would have been her seventy-third birthday. The Ethel String Quartet performed it near the end of the proceedings. Furthermore, the orchestral version by the Czech National Symphony Orchestra concludes *The Prague Sessions*, the trio's most recent "posthumous" album, recorded just before Travers's death and issued shortly after it.[66]

[64]Whitney Smith, "Bells of Idlewild Presbyterian Church Unique in Memphis," *The* [Memphis, Tenn.] *Commercial Appeal* (26 November 1998), F: 1.

[65]Charles Ward, "Wolff Guides Symphony through Somber Effort," *The Houston Chronicle* (30 March 1999), 4.

[66]*The Prague Sessions*, perf. Peter, Paul and Mary (Rhino, 523477, 2010).

For Victims and Unsung Heroes

The cited performances of *Adagio for Strings* have honored prominent individuals, but the work has been invoked many times for those, often anonymous, who have died as a result of criminal shootings, fires, natural disasters, or mass genocide. These performances became opportunities for survivors to grieve and to pay respects to those lost.

UNIVERSITY STUDENTS

Always numbing are the inexplicable murders of young people on college campuses. On 8 May 1970, four days after the National Guard killed several students at Kent State University, Leopold Stokowski led the American Symphony Orchestra in a memorial concert at Carnegie Hall. When the orchestra finished playing *Adagio for Strings,* he spoke to the audience about his feelings concerning the shootings and also let members of the orchestra express their thoughts.

Emil Sanielevici, a student at the University of Pittsburgh, was one of five casualties of a shooting spree in Wilkinsburg, Pennsylvania. At a service held for him on 7 March 2000 in Heinz Chapel on the Pitt campus his classmates, instructors, and the university provost all spoke, and an organist played Barber's *Adagio* and other classical selections chosen by the young man's family. In April 2007 a disgruntled student shot to death thirty-two students at Virginia Tech (Polytechnic) Institute. In the memorial concert with the Roanoke Symphony Orchestra, director David Wiley prefaced his "hushed and reverent" performance of *Adagio* by a moment of silence in memory of the victims.[67] A few days later during a service at the University of Iowa, "the solemn notes" of Barber's *Adagio,* played by the university band, "hung in the gray afternoon air as students and administrators stood in front of the Old Capitol to pay their respects to the victims."[68] This university community was particularly sympathetic because a similar incident had occurred on its campus in 1991.

THE HOLOCAUST AND OTHER GENOCIDES

During the last few years orchestras have turned to Barber's *Adagio* to pay homage to the victims of the Holocaust and other genocides. In

[67]Beth Williamson, "Hall Augments Gorgeous Orchestra Performance," *Roanoke* [Va.] *Times* (23 April 2007).

[68]Colin Burke, "UI Community Pauses to Reflect," *The Daily Iowan* [Iowa City, Iowa] (24 April 2007). A brief video clip of this service appeared on newspaper's website, www.dailyiowan.com.

March 2001 the Texas Master Chorale from the Houston area presented "Forever Remembered." While Holocaust Cantata (1999) by Donald McCullough was the main attraction, the group also performed Agnus Dei. In 2005, the sixtieth anniversary of the liberation of Nazi concentration camps, Richard Fleischman led the South Florida Renaissance Orchestra in "Remember! A Concert in Memory of the Holocaust," in Fort Lauderdale and Palm Beach Gardens, both of which featured *Adagio for Strings*.

In March 2004 a forum, "Tolerance, Then and Now," was held in Long Beach, California, to honor genocide victims from many times and places. It opened with a concert by the Long Beach Poly High String Orchestra playing *Adagio for Strings*, with "heart-wrenching" pictures of genocide victims projected onto a large screen.[69] Following this were testimonials by Buddy Tanaka, who as a teenager had been relocated to an internment camp for Japanese-Americans in Wyoming; Renee Firestone, a Czechoslovakian Holocaust survivor; Jonathan Dok, a survivor of the "killing fields" of Cambodia; and Houri Berberian, whose family members were victims of the Armenian genocide.

One could debate whether the World War II bombings of Hiroshima and Nagasaki constitute genocide; nevertheless, thousands of innocent people were killed. In August 2007, the sixty-second anniversary of the bombing, a ceremony took place at Nagasaki Peace Park, the center of the blast. Japanese Prime Minister Shinzō Abe and members of the opposition party headed the event, attended by about 5,500 people. With Barber's *Adagio* playing over loudspeakers, atomic bomb survivors and relatives burnt incense and offered prayers. Many expressed concerns about the survivors, now elderly and suffering from radiation-related illnesses.[70]

THE VICTIMS OF NATURAL DISASTERS

Other concerts featuring *Adagio for Strings* have honored the victims of devastating earthquakes, life-threatening hurricanes, and deadly tidal waves. In January 2001 a major earthquake hit the Gujarat region of India, killing 20,000 people and injuring 200,000 more. Robert Rÿker conducted the Japan Philharmonic Chamber Orchestra the following April to aid the victims; the Tokyo concert opened with *Adagio*:

[69] Kristopher Hanson, "Survivors Teach a Lesson Against Hatred," *Long Beach Press-Telegram* (4 March 2004); reprinted www.presstelegram.com.

[70] Eric Johnston, "Nagasaki Mayor Slams Nuclear Talk, Tests," *The Japan Times* (19 August 2007).

> I wanted the program to reflect two aspects of the disaster—tragedy and hope. For the first half of the concert . . . Shostakovich's agonized Symphony for Strings seemed to express the torment of that terrible tragedy. For the second half, Schubert's optimistic Death and the Maiden offered welcome relief from the troubled tension. And to capture the mixed emotions at the opening of the program, what better than Barber's melancholy Adagio for Strings?[71]

On 26 December 2004 a tsunami killed over 150,000 people in Thailand and Indonesia and left many more homeless. Orchestras the world over performed for fundraisers, the proceeds going to charitable organizations such as The American Red Cross, the Tidal Wave Relief Fund, and United Way South Asia Response Fund. Many orchestras in the United States, Canada, and the United Kingdom programmed Barber's *Adagio for Strings* for these events.[72]

Because of the horrors of Hurricane Katrina in the fall of 2005 some Gulf Coast area orchestras were obligated to forego their regular subscription series, but others carried on despite obstacles. For example, the benefit concerts of the Plano Symphony Orchestra, directed by Hector Guzman, and the Baton Rouge Symphony Orchestra, directed by Timothy Muffitt, both featured *Adagio*. The ensemble hardest hit by the Katrina tragedy was the Louisiana Philharmonic Orchestra, whose members were forced to relocate to other parts of the country. Yet about two-thirds of them managed to reassemble in California in February 2006 to perform with the San Luis Obispo Symphony. *Adagio* was heard on "The Heart and Soul Benefit Concert," with proceeds going to displaced musicians. The Sacramento Metropolitan Orchestra programmed *Adagio* for a benefit the following September. Orchestras at American universities also participated in similar efforts for the hurricane refugees, with *Adagio* serving as the centerpiece of several events: the University of Southern Mississippi's Symphony Orchestra on 4 October 2005 and a group of musicians in the music department at the University of Texas at Arlington on 15 October 2005.

[71]Robert Rÿker, "Style in Conducting, Part VI: At the Workdesk," *Midwest Clinic on Conducting* (3 December 2002), www.midwestclinic.com/clincianmaterials/2002/ryker.pdf.

[72]For a partial list, see Appendix 10.

FIREFIGHTERS

Over the years many firefighters have lost their lives trying to save others. A terrible disaster killed six firemen in December 1999 at the Worcester Cold Storage and Warehouse Company building in Worcester, Massachusetts. Nearly a year afterward, in November 2000, President Bill Clinton, Vice President Al Gore, and other dignitaries joined 13,000 firefighters and 2,000 family members and friends in a memorial service organized by the International Association of Fire Fighters. Doug Weeks conducted an orchestra in several works, including *Adagio for Strings*. He reflected, "I hope that the music . . . helped provide some catharsis for the families and community."[73]

On Memorial Day 2002 Tysons Corner Center, in McLean, Virginia, sponsored a ceremony for the firefighters and rescue departments of Fairfax County and of the cities of Fairfax and Falls Church. Kathy Hannon, the center's general manager, asserted that "firefighters put their lives on the line each day to protect us. Through this tribute ceremony, we hope to express our gratitude to these brave men and women for their selfless dedication to the community."[74] Part of the ceremony was devoted to the George Mason University String Orchestra's performance of Barber's *Adagio*.

A moving tribute took place at the opening of the Fire Department Instruction Conference (FDIC) in Indianapolis on 13 April 2005. Richard Auldon Clark led a small string ensemble of Butler University students in a performance of *Adagio for Strings* followed by an arrangement of Edward MacDowell's "To a Wild Rose." Clark considers both quintessentially American. He picked *Adagio* "not for its somber quality but for its beauty and reverence" and regards it as "the pinnacle of American string writing of the 20th century—and beyond. No other string piece comes close to it. It has a spiritual quality to it, almost a prayer, but not an elegy. Instead it is uplifting."[75] As the music unfolded, the names of 107 firefighters who had died in the line of duty during the previous year were read as an honor roll. Several thousand comrades and the victims' relatives and spouses watched large television screens showing a map of the United States. As a

[73]Doug Weeks, "Worcester Still Mourning its Everyday Heroes," *The Wire* XIII/2 (November 2000); reprinted www.wpi.edu/News/Wire/Nov00/heros.html.

[74]Kathy Hannon, "Tysons Corner Center Hosts Firefighter Tribute Event" [Tysons Corner Center Press Release], www.shoptysons.com/about/pressreleases21.cfm.

[75]Richard Auldon Clark, interview (3 May 2005) with the author.

loved one's name was read, each relative in the audience lit an electronic candle, and a flame appeared on the map appropriate to the city of each firefighter. Tim Brimmer, the music coordinator of the event, observed that "it was a beautiful and powerful performance of Adagio. It was very well received and moved the audience to tears."[76]

OTHERS

Adagio for Strings has by now been associated with worthy causes that approach the spectrum of human misery. Some are surrounded with controversy. In April 1988 the Binghamton (N.Y.) String Quartet performed Barber's String Quartet at an "Earth Fest" concert to support the Children of Chernobyl Relief Fund. This organization aids an orphanage near Kiev with over 200 children suffering from chronic illnesses and birth defects in the wake of radiation exposure from the Chernobyl nuclear plant. Other performances have honored those suffering political-ethnic crimes. In June 1998 Gisele Becker conducted the Agnus Dei by the Cantate Chamber Singers for "Music for Unsung Heroes" at the Bradley Hills Presbyterian Church of Bethesda, Maryland. In January 2003 in Manchester, New Hampshire, an angry crowd called for the resignation of the local bishop, John B. McCormack. More than 200 protesters demonstrated to show solidarity with the victims of alleged sexual abuse, not by the bishop himself, but by priests under his jurisdiction. The Barber piece set the mood for the demonstration: it was played on loudspeakers throughout a recitation of the names of eighty-three possible victims. "Then there was a silent march around the cathedral and finally a series of angry speeches from regional and national leaders of the movement to hold church officials accountable for the abuse crisis."[77] As critics pointed out, however, "The music played perfectly for the numerous television cameras recording the event, reminding many that the march was media-driven."[78] The latter is a fine example of *Adagio for Strings* as an agent of propaganda.

Depending on one's political orientation, the Metro bombings that took place in Moscow on 29 March 2010 could be considered an ethnic

[76]Tim Brimmer, interview (3 May 2005) with the author.

[77]Douglas Belkin, "Protesters Aim to Force N. H. Bishop to Step Down," *Boston Globe* (27 January 2003), A: 1.

[78]Thomas Farragher and Matt Carroll, "Bishop Often Sided with Priests in Abuse Cases," *Boston Globe* (26 January 2003).

crime, a terrorist attack, or a valiant manifestation of a Chechen separatist movement. Whatever its characterization, it resulted in the deaths of at least thirty-nine and the injuring of over sixty Russian citizens. Although several memorial commemorations undoubtedly occurred during the ensuing weeks, one with Barber's *Adagio* was presented a week later on 4 April at the beginning of a soccer match between two prominent Russian teams: Dinamo and Lokomotiv, at the latter team's stadium. John Baines, correspondent for *A Different League*, aptly described the atmosphere during this performance:

> As the ground fell silent, the poignant and emotive sound of Barber's Adagio for Strings rang hauntingly around the Lokomotiv Stadium. In that moment, the game, the money, the result and the sport, all paled into insignificance when compared to the cost of human life.[79]

That Russians would choose an American composition for its memorial has little to do with East-West détente or any change in global tensions; rather it reveals how much Barber's *Adagio* has entered the public perception of sadness and remembrance.

For the Victims of 9 / 11

With the tragedy that took place on 11 September 2001, another date "that will live in infamy," the "funereal tinge" of *Adagio* resonated in full force. Probably more people heard some version of it in this context than ever before. The Barber piece has, indeed, become our national music for mourning.

MEMORIAL CONCERTS

For concerts already scheduled for the days immediately following the attacks, conductors and managers had to decide whether to postpone the events or carry on despite the emotional turmoil that they themselves were all undoubtedly feeling. Orchestras that forged ahead often changed their concert's title, turning it into either a remembrance or a patriotic

[79]John Baines, "Red Review: CSKA Cannot Mask Russia's Shortfalls," *A Different League* (9 April 2010), www.adifferentleague.co.uk/p6_0_2343_red-review-cska-cannot-mask-russia%E2%80%99s-shortfalls.html#.URDFVkojiCw.

American program.[80] Some extended the title to give the audience a sense of hope and comfort, while others became programs of reflection or meditation.[81] Many doubled as fund-raisers for the American Red Cross or other charitable organizations, such as the United Way of America's September 11th Disaster Fund, and The Twin Towers Emergency Fund.

The repertoires of these programs were also altered, often with *Adagio for Strings* being added at the last minute, as in the concert later that same evening by the Colorado Springs Symphony, with Leighton Smith on the podium, and Esa-Pekka Salonen's concert with the Los Angeles Chamber Orchestra at the Hollywood Bowl on 13 September. Because the attacks occurred early in September, some concerts were the first of the season, originally designed to be joyous and celebratory. Therefore, instead of simply being added, *Adagio* sometimes replaced previously announced, more flamboyant pieces, such as Berlioz's *Roman Carnival Overture* for The Savannah Symphony Orchestra and The Waukesha Symphony or Ravel's *Boléro* for The Syracuse Symphony. Other deletions were works by contemporary composers. Royston Nash, conductor of the Cape (Cod) Symphony Orchestra put Barber's *Adagio* in the place of Kauko Kahila's "Brass Ride Fanfare," a joyous opening gesture for a new season, one not suitable for the mood of the audience so soon after the attacks. In a similar fashion, at a concert of the Knoxville Symphony Orchestra, *Adagio* was substituted for Dan Welcher's overture *Spumante*, which opens with a "pop and a burst of bubbles," clearly inappropriate in this context.[82]

At many concerts *Adagio* was paired with the "Star Spangled Banner." Those originally scheduled as season openers may have already planned it: playing the anthem is a traditional way to begin a new season. But in the days after the attacks, the National Anthem took on a more meaningful role, especially when coupled with *Adagio*. At the concert of the Florida Orchestra, "there was something profound about gathering in a concert hall after Sept 11, to sing a teary Star-Spangled Banner, [and] counter the

[80]Consider, for example, the North Carolina Symphony's "A Concert in Memoriam"; the Cincinnati Orchestra's "To the Honor and Memory"; Iowa State University Orchestra's "Music for America"; and the Nashville Symphony Orchestra's "Spirit of America."

[81]Atlanta Symphony's "Music of Recovery, Music of Healing, Music of Hope"; University of Michigan Orchestra's "Music of Meditation"; and the combined orchestras of Minnesota and St. Paul's "Elegy."

[82]"Works," *Dan Welcher: Composer and Conductor*, www.danwelcher.com.

anxiety and grief of those days with Samuel Barber's keening Adagio."[83] For Paavo Järvi, adding *Adagio* to the Cincinnati Orchestra program after the anthem was an emotional experience. Not only was it the first concert of the season, but also his debut as music director. When he was asked why he conducted *Adagio* without a baton, he admitted that he had picked it up but realized that his hands were shaking so much from nervousness that he had to put it back down.[84] No wonder he described the work as "one of the most touching and deeply felt pieces of music by an American composer."[85] In a later interview he expanded on these thoughts: "It's amazing just how powerful that piece actually is . . . . It's about inner strength. It has a sense of mourning in it, something universal."[86] Such feelings were undoubtedly intensified by the emotional nature of the occasion.

Sometimes the conductor directly addressed the audience about music's healing power and the merits of sharing *Adagio* as a community. At the Chicago Symphony Daniel Barenboim told the audience: "music is not something to be enjoyed only in good times. In fact culture is even more important in difficult times when there is sadness and tragedy all around us. It can give you solace."[87] Before the Madison Symphony Orchestra concert began, conductor John DeMain declared:

> This attack on all of the civilized world has left us shocked, bereaved, confused and uncertain. . . . Tonight we honor those victims of these terrible acts. We do so with a program filled with beauty and love. We begin this evening's concert by asking all of you to light a candle of remembrance in your hearts as we play American composer Samuel Barber's Adagio for Strings.[88]

[83]John Fleming, "Stage 2001: Performance Kept Spirits Strong," *St. Petersburg* [Fla.] *Times* (23 December 2001). The two pieces were also juxtaposed at concerts of the Madison Symphony Orchestra, the Topeka Symphony Orchestra, and the Fresno Philharmonic Orchestra.

[84]Paavo Järvi, "Pittsburghers! Circle This Date!" *The Paavo Project* (3 April 2005), www.paavoproject.blogspot.com/2005_04_01_paavoproject_archive.html.

[85]Paavo Järvi, "Don't Let Them Win," *Cincinnati Post* (13 September 2001).

[86]Paavo Järvi, quoted in Alan Scheidt, "Remembrance of Things Past: The CSO's First DVD Commemorates Paavo's Historical Debut," [Cincinatti] *CityBeat* (21 November 2006); reprinted *The Paavo Project* (23 November 2006), www. paavoproject.blogspot.fr/2006/11/cso-dvd-remembrance-of-things-past.html.

[87]Glendy Mattalia, "CSO, Lyric Opera Stage Galas," *Chicago Tribune* (27 September 2001), 7.

[88]Jess Anderson, "MSO: Eroica Trio," *Madison* [Wis.] *Music Review* (September 2001).

Critics noted that *Adagio* moved audiences in a profound manner. After the Syracuse Symphony Orchestra program John Johnson claimed, "never have I heard Barber's ode to beauty . . . played more wonderfully. The breathtaking quality of the work left the audience appropriately breathless."[89] In Cincinnati Rich Copley watched handkerchiefs come out all around Music Hall and recalled a similar occasion a week later when the Lexington Philharmonic played *Adagio*.[90] At the performance in Madison, Wisconsin, Jacob Stockinger professed that, "all distance between performers and listeners evaporated. You simply had to be there, and weep in solidarity."[91]

Conductors often asked the audience to refrain from applause in order to maintain the solemn atmosphere of a meditation or elegy. At the Seattle Symphony Orchestra concert, critic Melinda Bargreen observed that, in fact, silence was a "rare commodity in a concert hall, where the extended absence of sound knocks you back on your heels."[92] After hearing the performance by the Knoxville Symphony Orchestra, critic Harold Duckett reflected that

> in the long moment when two thousand people . . . sat in sustained silence . . . it was as though the profound sadness of Samuel Barber's Adagio for Strings had not died away but had been transformed into a voiceless language. [It] is among the most painful music ever written [and] was presented with deeply soulful expression.[93]

Under the direction of Chelsea Tipton II, the Savannah Symphony Orchestra performed a "moving memorial" outdoors at the Skidaway Institute of Oceanography. In this venue the dark, somber quality of

[89]John Johnson, "A Cathartic Evening of Music, SSO and Guest Play Well in Works by Barber, Beethoven, Korngold," [Syracuse, N.Y.] *Post-Standard* (22 September 2001), E: 4.

[90]Richard Copley "Sustaining Tones," *Lexington* [Ky.] *Herald-Leader* (11 September 2005).

[91]Jacob Stockinger, "At Time of Sorrow, Music Reaches the Sublime," *Wisconsin State Journal* (27 September 2001), 20.

[92]Melinda Bargreen, "Symphony Delivers an Emotional Opener," *Seattle Times* (22 September 2001), E: 3.

[93]Harold Duckett, "Knoxville Symphony's Concert Brilliant but Sad," *Knoxville* [Tenn.] *News Sentinel* (15 September 2001), B: 6.

Adagio ironically contrasted with the sunny day on which the concert was performed:

> Barber's Adagio for Strings . . . remains a piercing expression of human sorrow. In the gorgeous setting—a sunlit afternoon, the wind gusting through the Spanish moss on Skidaway's oaks—the moment of silence following the music was sharply poignant, the radiant scene reminding us of the thousands of people who'll never again savor a glorious afternoon.[94]

LEONARD SLATKIN, THE BBC ORCHESTRA, AND THE NATIONAL SYMPHONY ORCHESTRA

The words and actions of maestro Leonard Slatkin, as they relate to timely concerts in the British capital and the American capital, can be perceived as emblematic—or even symbolic—of the emotional state of affairs that surrounded performances of Barber's *Adagio for Strings* after the September terrorist attacks. On that day he was preparing the BBC Orchestra for the Last Night of the Proms series in London's Royal Albert Hall. On 14 September, as a preview of this annual festivity, the British newscast *Newsnight* featured an excerpt from Barber's score as the accompaniment for film clips of the remains of the World Trade Center and scenes of people struggling to get away from the smoky debris, some being led, others being carried out.[95]

The next night Slatkin added *Adagio* to the Proms program to meet the more solemn requirements of the event. Sir Nicholas Kenyon, director of the occasion, elaborated: "everybody feels that the rumbustious jollity associated with it simply is not appropriate as this dreadful story unfolds. We feel it is vital to respond to people's mood at this sombre and difficult time."[96] Slatkin agreed: "I couldn't have done a traditional Last Night. I wasn't in a party mood."[97] In his own words, "The music, the intensive

[94]"The Scene," *Savannah* [Ga.] *Morning News* (15 September 2001); reprinted www.savannahnow.com/diversions/stories/092101/EVTscene.shtml.

[95]"Samuel Barber's Adagio for Strings," *BBC Newsnight | Newsnight | Attack on America* (14 September 2001), www.news.bbc.co.uk/2/hi/events/newsnight/1613971.stm.

[96]Andrew Clements, "Arts: A Night to Forget," *The* [Manchester] *Guardian* (15 September 2001), 4.

[97]Norman Lebrecht, "Leonard Slatkin–Last Night of the Proms," *La Scena Musicale* (11 September 2001), www.scena.org/columns/lebrecht/020911-NL-slatkind.html.

Illustration 10.2. Publicity Still of Conductor Leonard Slatkin

Courtesy © Columbia Artists Management LLC

Image by Donald Dietz

emotion of [*Adagio*] has come to mean something very special, not just for Americans but, I think, for everyone. It is our music for grief."[98] Before conducting the piece Slatkin asked the audience to observe a moment of silence.

The number of individuals who witnessed this performance was staggering to say nothing of its prominence at the top of the list of most watched *Adagio* performances on *YouTube*.[99] A throng of those unable to be seated in Albert Hall gathered in nearby Hyde Park to watch a giant television screen. Critic Sue Carroll observed, "Forty thousand people stayed silent for three minutes before the orchestra drifted into Barber's *Adagio for Strings*. Words can convey all manner of emotions. But only music has the power to reduce 40,000 people to tears."[100] During the work

> cameras moved slowly between shots of the conductor, sections of the orchestra, and static views of the whole Albert Hall. All the while the pictures remained secondary to the music, taking their

[98]"Sombre Proms Reflect Public Grief," *BBC News* (15 September 2001), www.news.bbc.co.uk/2/hi/entertainment/1546547.stm.

[99]"Samuel Barber–Adagio for Strings, Op. 11," *YouTube* (1 December 2006), posted by AUVIEX.

[100]Sue Carroll, "Silence at the Proms in the Park," *The* [London] *Daily Mirror* (19 September 2001), 19.

cue from sounds, and underscoring the power of the evocative melodies and harmonies with restraint and dignity.[101]

In addition, the program was broadcast live in Great Britain on BBC Radio 3, BBC Television, and BBC Online as well as in the United States on National Public Radio stations. According to Dan DeVany, vice president and general manager of WETA, "bringing this broadcast to Washington connects listeners in our nation's capital with our friends in England who have known the tragedy of attacks on their native soil. Through music, we can affirm our shared humanity."[102] Slatkin confessed that this task was the single most difficult nine minutes or so of his career because he was in tears the whole time: "All the images that I only knew from television and talking to people on the phone had just come into full focus."[103]

Critics were mixed in their assessment of both the concert in general and the performance of *Adagio* in particular. Philip Hensher was also close to tears but wondered at the "mysterious transformations wrought by circumstances. Normally, I rather dislike [*Adagio*] and its shamelessly low-rent imitation of the finale of Mahler's Ninth Symphony; on Saturday night, it worked with terrible directness."[104] Andrew Clements was rather convinced that the presentation was a "strangely unsatisfactory occasion, certainly not the mindless jamboree of tradition but then not a fully fledged memorial concert either."[105] On the other hand, Stephen Pollard hoped that such innovations would continue in subsequent years:

It is probably too much to hope that the new-look Last Night will be anything other than nausea interrupta, but there could not

[101]Ian Jones, "The Last Night of the Proms," *Off the Telly* (15 September 2001), www.offthetelly.co.uk/reviews/2001/lastnightproms.htm.

[102]"WETA 90.9 FM to Broadcast Revised Program of the British Proms," *Inside WETA* (14 September 2001); reprinted www.weta.org/inside/press/index.php?n=0024. The second half of the program was telecast on *BBC America* and music from the program was featured on 17 September on *Performance Today* (National Public Radio). The BBC *Adagio* performance interspersed newsreel footage of the tragedy with the grief-stricken faces of those who witnessed the event.

[103]Jacki Lyden, "Leonard Slatkin Discusses the Tribute Concert to be Held at the Kennedy Center in Washington," *All Things Considered* [National Public Radio] (22 September 2001).

[104]Phil Hensher, "We're in No Mood for an Ode to Joy," *The* [London] *Independent* (17 September 2001), www.independent.co.uk/voices/commentators/philip-hensher/philip-hensher--were-in-no-mood-for-an-ode-to-joy-669546.html.

[105]Andrew Clements, "Classical Proms: Slatkin Ends Proms on a Sombre Note," *The Guardian* (17 September 2001), 21.

> have been a better choice than Barber's Adagio for Strings . . . to represent what Leonard Slatkin . . . called "unity through music" . . . to help underscore the long healing process that must take place.[106]

Slatkin had only a few days before returning home to prepare for the opening night of the National Symphony Orchestra season at the Kennedy Center on 19 September. As with the Proms series, he decided to change the program to reflect the emotions of the time, programming *Adagio* after the "Star Spangled Banner." *Washington Post* art and architecture critic Philip Kennicott felt that the Barber "works, perhaps, because it captures one thing that is very specific about grief, and it captures it like no other piece in the repertoire: Grief is exhausting."[107] His reflection on the power of this music and its function in these circumstances as prayer is striking:

> Performances of Barber's Adagio get slower and slower, especially when it's played to mark the occasion of tragedy; the NSO kept it moving, through its upper-register catharsis, through the despairing return to the opening material. The strings played beautifully. Slatkin asked that the audience not applaud, offering the piece more as a prayer than a performance; the audience obliged with silence. When thousands of people remain silent at the request of a musician, one senses an absolute submission to the power of the work.[108]

Later that month the NSO scheduled *Adagio* for another special program, "A Concert for America: A Tribute." In preparation, Slatkin told the audience:

> Most of what we are about to play is sober and reflective . . . something in our music that has touched souls in ways that were unimaginable . . . that is the power of music: the emotions that take us through; the feeling of comfort, solace, everything we can feel condensed into those incredible notes and melodies . . . . If

[106]Stephen Pollard, "Moved to Tears," *New Statesman* (24 September 2001), www.newstatesman.com /node/141232.

[107]Philip Kennicott, "Sounding the Right Notes," *The Washington Post* (21 September 2001), C: 7.

[108]*Ibid.*

one piece of music is said to reflect our feelings during this time, it's the piece we are about play, Samuel Barber's Adagio for Strings.[109]

Critic Teresa Wiltz recorded the reaction of the audience in the following description: "through the melancholy whisperings of Barber's *Adagio for Strings*, one could hear, ever so softly, the sound of a man in the audience weeping, his girlfriend softly patting his arm. The whispers of bows slid on strings, softer and softer still until the sound wafted away."[110]

THE STRING QUARTET IN MEMORIAM

In addition to orchestras, string quartets adjusted their programs in light of the terrorist attacks to present a performance of either the entire String Quartet or just the Adagio movement. The Emerson String Quartet performed a concert on 16 September titled "Music and Reflection" at Lincoln Center's Avery Fisher Hall with the Barber movement plus string quartets by Beethoven and Bartók. Beverly Sills, chair of Lincoln Center, introduced the event: "We hope our afternoon together with these great artists, and with this timeless music, will help us to begin the difficult journey of healing."[111] Bruce Fagin, a member of the Lower Manhattan Cultural Council, was moved even as the members of the quartet entered the stage. He confessed, "when they first came out, tears were falling from [violinist Eugene Drucker's] cheeks, and that's when I started crying. Some people started to sob around me."[112] Critic Alex Ross noticed that the group, "still shaken by the event, sounded vulnerable, not quite in control, and thus came closer to the heart of the music than they have on their usual brilliant nights."[113] They played

[109]Leonard Slatkin, quoted in Philip Kennicott, "Sounding the Right Notes: National Symphony Opens Season with an Altered Program," *Washington Post* (20 September 2001), C: 1.

[110]Teresa Wiltz, "The Strains of a Nation's Grief," *Washington Post* (25 September 2001), C: 1. The performance was projected on large screens in the foyer for those unable to be seated in the hall. It was broadcast live over Washington D.C. radio station WETA-FM and later telecast on the 28 September 2001 by PBS.

[111]Elena Park, "Lincoln Center and Emerson Quartet Pay Tribute to the Missing and Deceased in World Trade Center and Pentagon Attacks," *Andante* (17 September 2001).

[112]*Ibid.*

[113]Alex Ross, "Requiems: New Yorkers Take Refuge in Patriotic Hymns and Brahms," *The New Yorker* (8 October 2001), 78.

> Barber's panoramic Adagio, which brought people to tears, and Bartok's desolate Second Quartet, which made them squirm. Bartok's dissonances had a too familiar ring, like a flashback to Tuesday. In recent days I've found that my musical appetites are more limited than usual, and the dark, disturbing component of the twentieth-century repertory has been hard to take.[114]

Other groups followed suit by adding the Adagio movement to their scheduled programs. The critics were impressed. Herman Trotter thought that the Ying Quartet's rendition on 13 September at the University of Buffalo "struck a singularly appropriate spiritual tone."[115] Clarke Bustard wrote that the "uninhibited passion" that the Shanghai group brought to the movement on 19 September at the University of Richmond "proved to be the spirit that governed the whole evening."[116] Dale T. Knobel, the president of Denison University in Granville, Ohio, invited the campus community to attend a "Service of Remembrance and Healing" on 20 September for an evening of music, readings, and dance. Following the "Adagio" by the Denison String Quartet, Professor of English David Baker read a poem entitled "A Walk" by Katha Pollitt, frequent contributor to *The Nation*. Ilse Zadrozny admitted that the Miami String Quartet's "eloquent and touching performance" of the Adagio movement in Montreal on 23 September brought tears to her eyes: "The music is filled with great sadness, but its affecting melodic beauty also offers consolation in times of bereavement."[117]

In a comparable spirit, the complete Barber quartet was performed by The Miró String Quartet on the Dumbarton Oaks Concert Series in Washington D.C. on 13 October and by The Corigliano Quartet at Dickinson College in Carlisle, Pennsylvania on 6 November. The Miró concert was dedicated to longtime volunteer Bryan Jack, who perished on the airliner that crashed into the Pentagon. Philip Kennicott observed, "The quartet played [Adagio] 'straight,' neither downplaying the unsettled textures of the first movement nor inflating the lyricism of the second;

[114]*Ibid.*, 80.

[115]Herman Trotter, "The Ying Quartet Opens the Slee Cycle with Barber's Adagio," *Buffalo* [N.Y.] *News* (14 September 2001), G: 15.

[116]Clarke Bustard, "Music Speaks What Words Can Only Mumble," *Richmond* [Va.] *Times Dispatch* (20 September 2001), D: 15.

[117]Ilse Zadrozny, "Beauty in Time of Grief," *The* [Montreal] *Gazette* (24 September 2001), B: 5.

the quartet played it as Barber wrote it, rather than warp the sentiments to fit the occasion.[118] The Corigliano performance was part of a benefit to support firefighters and police officers who helped during the 9 / 11 crisis and to set up a scholarship program.

SERVICES OF REMEMBRANCE

After the 9 / 11 tragedies churches and other organizations held religious services, often non-denominational or multi-denominational, to honor the victims. The focus for many of them was *Adagio for Strings*. On the evening of 11 September students and faculty of Scripps College and the members of the Claremont, California community gathered for a "poignant and touching" event. As a recording of Barber's *Adagio* was played, "the names of the victims were projected on the auditorium walls." At the conclusion members of the community "silently recessed, took up votive lights, and formed a candlelight procession through the campus. . . . They placed their candles on the cement steps, held hands and embraced, and quietly left."[119]

The terrorists killed not only Americans but also individuals of many other nationalities representing approximately twelve percent of the casualties. Cantor Fitzgerald, a British firm with offices on the 101st to 105th floor of the North Tower, lost 658 employees. On the following Friday a memorial service in connection with the American community in the United Kingdom was held in London at St. Paul's Cathedral to honor those employees and others who died. For the prelude Mark Williams, assistant sub-organist of the Cathedral, played various solemn pieces, including R. Naylor's arrangement of *Adagio for Strings*. The Queen, the Prince of Wales, and the Duke of Edinburgh attended. The Duchess of York, scheduled to visit the Cantor Fitzgerald office on the day of the attack, professed, "We are in deep remembrance from everyone who fell victim to the attack and now we must fight onwards."[120]

On 28 October thousands of family members gathered at Ground Zero, the remains of the World Trade Center, to mourn the victims.

[118]Philip Kennicott, "Miro: The Art of the Quartet; Dumbarton Series Opens with a Formidable Foursome," *Washington Post* (15 October 2001), CO: 5.

[119]"Scripps Remembers September 11," *Scripps College Bulletin Online* (Fall 2002), www.scrippscol.edu /~dept/pr/bulletin/Fall02/news.html.

[120]Jenny McCartney, "City Turns Out to Mourn and Show Defiance," *The* [London] *Telegraph* (7 October 2001).

During the service, remarks were given by a Roman Catholic archbishop, a rabbi, a Protestant minister, and a Muslim imam. In addition to other selections, St. Luke's Orchestra played *Adagio for Strings* as the television cameras showed people in the crowd waving flags, "weeping, or unable to weep, or defiantly holding photographs to the sky—and when as well they showed completely, for the first time, the real look at that colossal ruin, it became just too much, and one had to leave the room."[121] Christoph Eschenbach, who conducted the orchestra, recalled the smoldering site: "it was still smoking. They were spraying it with water but the water was so noisy they had to stop and after a while we almost fainted."[122] It was likewise a moving memorial for those watching it live on television.

ADAGIO, 9 / 11 ON THE RADIO AND TELEVISION

Radio stations across the country reacted to the attacks by playing appropriate music, including *Adagio for Strings*. WFCC in the Cape Cod, Massachusetts area played it shortly after the attacks and also later in the day. Assistant program director Paul Bachmann was convinced that, after airing eight hours of news on the attacks, the station turned to "more contemplative music . . . pieces that are quiet and introspective."[123] Other stations did the same.

The tragedy was the subject of radio programs for several weeks. On *The Connection* on Boston's WBUR, an interview show with listener call-ins, the episode "Moving On" on 24 September addressed callers' personal reactions to the tragedy and their attempts to "move on" with their lives. Philip Kennicott talked about the recent NSO performance of Beethoven's Ninth Symphony and Richard McNally, psychology professor at Harvard University, discussed post-traumatic stress disorder. A short sound bite of *Adagio* was played following the discussion as a transition into the next segment.

On 2 October NPR's *Talk of the Nation* presented "Analysis: How People Are Coping with the Terrorist Attacks of September 11th." In a call-in segment listeners talked about the music they had listened to since the attacks. Some considered music to be a "balm for sadness."

[121]Daniel Henninger, "Now We See Why Killing a Person Forfeits One's Life," *Wall Street Journal* (2 November 2001), A: 14.

[122]Mary Blume, "Eschenbach's United Effort behind 'Ring,'" [New York] *International Herald Tribune* (13 October 2005).

[123]Bill O'Neill, "Crisis Pares Radio's Song Lists," *Cape Cod* [Mass.] *Times* (20 September 2001).

Host Neal Conan then played an audio clip of *Adagio for Strings*. Fred Child, host of *Performance Today*, acknowledged that "music for grieving was in the first couple of days," that *Adagio* had been requested "over and over again."[124] On 12 October 2001 this particular program was discussed at the University of California-Los Angeles as part of "Musical Perspectives: A Roundtable on Music, Community, Politics, and Violence." One guest, Lebanese scholar and musician Ali Jihad Racy, who addressed the topic "Music Humanizing Our Visions: Reflections on September 11," made a poignant declaration: "I know well how sadness affects people and how music and poetry enable human beings to cope and come to terms with their fragile existence."[125] As an illustration, he cited the callers to the *Talk of the Nation* program and emphasized how music choices, like *Adagio* "fit their state of mourning."[126] He contended that one result of repeated listening to music of this type is "psychological transformation," which addresses three emotional issues: 1) mourning, or the exteriorization of the painful sense of loss; 2) the need to be uplifted emotionally; and 3) a sense of reassurance, recovery, and strength.[127] Even if Samuel Barber did not intend all this—although emotional uplift was probably among his purposes—listeners often experience these emotions when they listen to this particular composition.

The Barber Agnus Dei, in the form of the Dale Warland recorded performance, was broadcast on the Associated Press radio program *First Person* on 15 February 2002, alongside interviews and topical discussions of current interest. In a segment titled "The Problem of Evil" host Christa Tippet spoke with victims and descendants of victims of Nazi terror concerning the concepts of good and evil, which were, in the last part of the program, extended to the more recent tragedies. While interviewing Robert Pollack, biologist and director of Columbia University's Center for Science and Religion, she commented on President Bush's idea that the terrorists were part of an "axis of evil."[128] Pollack steered the discussion

[124]Fred Child, interview with Neal Conan, *Talk of the Nation* [NPR]; reprinted www.npr.org/programs/pt/features/911_totn.html.

[125]Ali Jihad Racy, "Musical Perspectives on Sept. 11: A Roundtable on Music, Community, Politics, and Violence," *ECHO: A Music-Centered Journal* III/2 (Fall 2001), www.echo.ucla.edu.

[126]*Ibid.*

[127]*Ibid.*

[128]George W. Bush, "State of the Union Address," (29 January 2002); reprinted www.johnstonsarchive.net/policy/bushstun2002.html.

to the concept of free will. While Agnus Dei played in the background, Pollack expounded: "The terrorists knew they were going to die and made the free will act to kill strangers, and the people on that forced plane (Flight 93) knew they were going to die and made the free will act to save strangers."[129] Accompanying these words with that music was appropriate on two levels. First, the orchestral *Adagio* had been associated with the victims of the attacks throughout the mourning period and was still valid several months later. But the decision to use the Agnus Dei version may have had a subtler justification. The Lamb of God can be associated with the selfless sacrifice of the lives of the passengers aboard that flight. Some theologians may debate whether Christ's sacrifice was of his own free will or God's destiny, but the passengers' self-sacrifice was comprehensible, real, and ultimately commendable.[130]

Television documentaries focusing on interviews with survivors and explorations of the causes were produced in response to the tragedies. Two such shows made effective use of *Adagio for Strings* to set mood and enhance ideas and concepts: *In Memoriam: New York City, 9/11/01* by HBO and "Faith and Doubt at Ground Zero" by PBS's *Frontline*.[131]

In Memoriam: New York City, broadcast first on 26 May 2002, follows New York City mayor Rudy Giuliani through the day of 11 September 2001. The result is a "gripping, sorrowful" film that communicates through images and sounds "too terrible to be seen or heard eight months ago."[132] Leonard Slatkin, who recorded the soundtrack with the New York Philharmonic especially for the film, admitted that he was touched to be asked to participate in this project: "They said they felt an American presence as a conductor for this project was very important. And I am truly honored to be involved."[133] The soundtrack was devoted to pre-existing compositions by Americans: Aaron Copland, John Corigliano,

[129]Robert Pollack, "The Problem of Evil," *Speaking of Faith* (15 February 2002), www.speakingoffaith.publicradio.org/programs/2002/02/15_evil.

[130]*Ibid.*

[131]Both films are disseminated commercially on DVD and may also be viewed on various websites on the Internet.

[132]Caryn James, "TV Weekend; A Chronicle of Horror, and Hope," *The New York Times* (24 May 2002); reprinted www.nytimes.com/2002/05/24/movies/tv-weekend-a-chronicle-of-horror-and-hope.html.

[133]Leonard Slatkin, quoted in *HBO Documentaries*, www.hbo.com/docs/911/music.html.

Ellen Taaffe Zwilich, William Schuman, and Samuel Barber. Three works by Barber, including *Adagio for Strings*, were invoked. Slatkin accepted the pieces selected as "examples of Americans speaking in their most lyric, most heartfelt way."[134]

Adagio is heard twice during the film. First it fades in as Richard Sheirer, director of Emergency Management, recalls seeing people jump from the windows of the towers rather than being burned to death: "Think about people so desperate, that they would choose that way to die. They had to know they were going to die. There's no way of surviving it, and that image will never leave."[135] The music accompanies a series of photographs by Richard Drew and Bolivar Arellano, shots of the falling bodies and the faces of the horror-stricken onlookers.[136] When *Adagio* recurs later, it accompanies excerpts from speeches given at the Ground Zero service previously mentioned, held on 28 October 2001. First Rabbi Joseph Potasnik eloquently expressed the grief: "We come here today to hold those who hurt so much, to help those who need so much, and to hear those who cry so much."[137] People held up pictures of loved ones as Cardinal Edward Egan told them, "We've lost parents, brothers and sisters, sons and daughters, husbands and wives, beloved relatives and friends. They were innocent, and they were brutally, viciously, unjustly taken from us."[138] The same *Adagio* passage underscores these remarks as in the earlier scene. Critic Anna Quindlen noted that, although *Adagio* was "breathtaking," the real soundtrack is the "disembodied voices of people repeating these words: 'O, my God.' Sometimes blasphemy becomes a prayer."[139] Naturally this is a difficult show to watch, but as reviewer Frazier Moore put it, "as tough as it is, 'In Memoriam' may make you stronger, leading you to greater clarity through your tears."[140]

[134]*Ibid.*

[135]Richard Sheirer, quoted in *In Memoriam: New York City, 9/11/01* [DVD], prod. Brad Grey, Dyllan McGee, Jessica Malter, John Hoffman, and Jon Lieberman (Brad Grey Picture for Home Box Office [HBO], 2002).

[136]One of Drew's photographs was published in Tom Junod's article in *Esquire* and represents the point of departure for one movement in Richard Blackford's cantata, *Not in Our Time*, both of which were cited later in this chapter.

[137]Joseph Potasnik, quoted in *In Memoriam: New York City* [DVD], (2002).

[138]Edward Egan, quoted in *In Memoriam: New York City* [DVD], (2002).

[139]Anna Quindlen, "Look at What They've Done," *Newsweek* (3 June 2002), 68.

[140]Frazier Moore, "HBO Documentary Revisits 9-11," *Firehouse Daily News* (24 May 2002).

On 2 September 2002 PBS aired "Faith and Doubt at Ground Zero" on its series *Frontline*. Helen Whitney, compiler of the program, interviewed 850 people in its preparation, not only those who had lost family and those who were caught in the towers, but also firemen's widows, CEOs, and security guards. She also talked to a Catholic priest, a Jewish rabbi, a Lutheran minister, and a professor of Islamic law, some of whom found their own faith shaken by the events.

Music is used effectively throughout the production. While a few pieces, such as slow movements from Beethoven's String Quartet, Op. 131, and Schubert's "Death and the Maiden" Quartet are returned more than once, *Adagio for Strings* is reserved for a single moment near the end in a segment titled "Act 5: Ground Zero" and for presenting reactions from relatives who lost loved ones. Some recall their feelings as they sat through the service at Ground Zero on 28 October 2001. Attorney Terry McGovern considered the music to be "extremely comforting."[141] She reflected on its positive impact: "It took us out of the very horrifying reality and transported me to this place of hope that we could aspire for something better, and that perhaps something better does exist, and that whatever was left of my incredibly fabulous mother in that—in that mess was not the end of her spirit."[142]

Adagio continues through the epilogue, where people comment on those who leaped from the towers rather than being burned in the building (similar to *In Memoriam: New York City*). While some admired the power and courage of those decisions, Ian McEwan protested that interpretation: "it spoke to me of sheer panic. . . . I found no hope in that at all. If there is a God, he's a very indifferent one."[143] The comments are coordinated with *Adagio* and various images. During hopeful comments the public sees the "blue towers," the projected light show from the first anniversary commemoration, but during McEwan's pessimistic views, the smoldering towers are shown. The effectiveness of *Adagio*, however, is compromised near the end of the film by questionable editing. Someone decided to omit a few measures of the coda in order to insert a short passage from the slow movement of String Quintet in C Major by Schubert. While the Barber / Schubert juxtaposition was a potentially effective idea, the music editors

[141]Terry McGovern, quoted in *Faith and Doubt at Ground Zero* [DVD], prod. Helen Whitney (PBS Video, 2003).

[142]*Ibid.*

[143]Ian McEwan, quoted in *Faith and Doubt at Ground Zero* [DVD], (2003).

could have allowed *Adagio* to run its course and then capped it off with just a phrase or two from Schubert![144]

FIRST ANNIVERSARY CONCERTS AND MEMORIALS

Instead of making last-minute additions to an already fixed program as they did the previous year, managers and conductors could plan for memorial concerts in 2002. As a result, *Adagio* was chosen even more frequently. A few days before the first anniversary Dagang Chen led the Woodlands (Houston) Symphony Orchestra in a program that featured it. On the eve of the anniversary the Johnstown (Penn.) Symphony Orchestra performed at Seven Springs resort, near the crash site of Flight 93. Alice Hogan, the mother of a man on that plane (Mark Bingham), recalled that, when the orchestra played *Adagio* and a screen "showed the faces of our 40 loved ones, . . . the feeling was just palpable. It was a lovely experience."[145]

In order to coincide with the timing of the previous year's attacks, the memorial service at Ground Zero started early in the morning. The Adagio of Barber's String Quartet was one of several works performed while people from different ethnic backgrounds read the 2,801 names of those who died, from Gordon Aamoth, Jr., to Igor Zukelman. Various ensembles provided "elegant accompaniment to the painful cadence of the names."[146] The Juilliard String Quartet was playing the Barber movement when the names arrived at "W." People released balloons, which drifted by a sign reading, "We Will Never Forget."[147] A reporter for *The New York Times* commented that, as this occurred, "now and then, the wind would blow so hard that it would rumble like thunder through the microphones; now and then, brown billows would rise from the pit to anoint listeners with dust."[148] A year later the names were again read at Ground Zero, but

[144]Helen Whitney and Ron Rosenbaum, "Transcript," *Transcripts | Faith and Doubt at Ground Zero | FRONTLINE | PBS*, www.pbs.org/wgbh/pages/frontline/shows/faith/etc/script.html.

[145]Alice Hogan, interview with Carol Lin, *CNN* (11 September 2002), www.cnnstudentnews.com/TRANSCRIPTS/02/09/11se.44.html.

[146]"Solemn Commemoration on Anniversary of 9-11," *LowerManhattan.info–Information to Build On* (11 September 2002), www.lowermanhattan.info/news/solemn_commemoration_on_anniversary_99376.asp. Although 2,801 names were read during the service, the official death tally from the 9 / 11 attacks rests at 2,996 (2,977 victims and 19 hijackers) along with a bomb-sniffing dog named Sirius.

[147]The Paley Center in New York City has a tape of the ABC coverage showing the reading of names shortly after the start of the Barber quartet: "ABC News Special: Live: Ground Zero" (T: 73906).

[148]Dan Barry, "A Day of Tributes, Tears and the Litany of the Lost," *The New York Times* (12 September 2002), B: 23.

the Adagio from Barber's String Quartet was not played, nor was it played in the next few years.

Choral organizations programmed Barber's Agnus Dei for memorials in cities around the world. For instance, the Russian Chamber Choir sang it on a program given in cooperation with the Embassy in Moscow on 10 September 2002. Ambassador Alexander Vershbow emphasized the international origins of the victims: "The victims weren't only Americans, but citizens of 90 countries, men, women, people like ourselves. We Americans were very touched by the expressions of support we received from Russia."[149]

The following day American conductor Gilbert Levine directed the Münchener Bach-Chor in a performance of Agnus Dei at the Church of St. Peter and St. Paul in Cracow, Poland. He maintained that, "since that day, one year ago, Barber's *Adagio for Strings* has become a kind of musical symbol of the American spirit. . . . This prayer is direct, the sacrifice clear. The music is climactic and evocative, and quintessentially American."[150] He added, "This evening's music is the best this musician can do to try to express our sorrow, our solidarity and our determination for a better tomorrow."[151]

A year after the crash of Flight 93, the Pittsburgh Symphony performed "A Concert for Heroes" as a fund-raiser for the Somerset County Flight 93 Memorial Fund. Directed by Robert Page, the Mendelssohn Choir of Pittsburgh performed Agnus Dei. In connection with this work, Robin Walsh read from "Remembering Flight 93."[152] County Executive Jim Roddey declared, "This evening was a further demonstration that the musicians of the Pittsburgh Symphony are not only some of our finest ambassadors, but also some of our finest citizens."[153]

[149]Alexander Vershbow, "Hundreds Attend Sept. 11 Commemoration Concert in Moscow," *Associated Press Worldstream* (10 September 2002).

[150]"Music for Respect and Tolerance," *Europamusicale–Music Connects*, www.europamusicale.de/10gedenk/eng/index.html. The program was telecast on Polish television, on PBS in the United States, and on NPR (the audio portion). The program, with interviews, appears as a webcast at the above site. An interview with an American singer from the choir begins with the group rehearsing Agnus Dei.

[151]*Ibid.*

[152]Marisol Bello, "A Day of Reflection," [Pittsburgh, Penn.] *Tribune-Review* (12 September 2002); reprinted www.triblive.com/x/pittsburghtrib/news/regional/s_91038.html#axzz2Ih9phFa1.

[153]Jim Roddey, quoted in *ibid.* The program was broadcast live over WQED-FM. Later Cary Choral Artists included Agnus Dei on a program, "From Darkness to Light" at Meredith College [Raleigh, N.C.] (29 September 2002).

FIRST ANNIVERSARY MEMORIALS ON RADIO AND TELEVISION

To observe the first anniversary of the attacks, many classical radio stations broadcast *Adagio for Strings* at various times throughout the day. In Chicago WFMT aired a live performance of the original second movement by the Avila String Quartet. Billed as a "daily two-hour music soundscape," eclectic music program *Echoes* (Public Radio International), brings together a wide array of styles: acoustic, electronic, jazz, space music, avant-garde, and rock. Although *Adagio for Strings* does not seem to fit any of these categories, it was squeezed into the playlist on at least two occasions.[154] It began "A Requiem Soundscape" on 11 September 2002 with Bernstein's recording with the Los Angeles Philharmonic. In opening notes the host, John Dilberto, described *Adagio* as "a piece that is always becoming, as if it's always been playing and even after its last chord fades away, the music could just keep going."[155] Philip Aaberg's new-age, piano-synthesizer arrangement began a 2003 memorial program, "An Echoes Requiem" (see Chapter 7). Because *Echoes* listeners are more accustomed to a soothing but not truly classical approach, this particular performance matched the context. *Adagio* was the only "classical" piece selected both years.

WCET, Cincinnati's PBS station, telecast *Adagio* in "To the Honor and Memory," Paavo Järvi's inaugural concert with the Cincinnati Symphony Orchestra was taped the previous year (see previous section, Memorial Concerts). In 2003 PBS telecast a shorter version in which the *Adagio* performance was omitted. Performing rights might also have prevented its inclusion. The omission here is misleading because there is no acknowledgment that the Barber piece was part of the original program. Viewers, therefore, get the false impression that they are witnessing the whole concert.[156]

[154]"A Requiem Soundscape," *Echoes Playlist* (11 September 2002), www.echoes.org/playlists/wk37-02.html.

[155]John Dilberto, liner notes to *Shadow and Light*, perf. Los Angeles Philharmonic, cond. Leonard Bernstein (Deutsche Grammophon, G2-45922, 1995).

[156]See Mary Ellyn Hutton, "Music in Cincinnati: Järvi Inaugural Shone in Shadow of 9-11," *Brandenburg Productions* (9 November 2006), www.brandenburgproductions.com/sept_2008v2_057.htm. In 2006 the CSO Bravo Shop issued a DVD of the entire concert, restoring *Adagio* but placing it at the end as a special tribute. While it is not a bad idea to isolate the work, separating it from the National Anthem loses the effective juxtaposition.

ANNIVERSARY PERFORMANCES OF *ADAGIO*

Perhaps due to the saturation during the months following the attacks and during first anniversary events, *Adagio for Strings* was not heard as frequently in subsequent years. In 2006, however, as part of a fifth year commemoration, *Adagio* was again performed at the Ground Zero ceremony and on other occasions. One memorable performance of the full String Quartet was given by the Shanghai Quartet on Bargemusic, a converted barge afloat on the East River near the Brooklyn Bridge. During the performance one could see lower Manhattan through the window behind them, the blue shafts of light emanating from the former site of the World Trade Center.

Journalist Robert Bridge reported the happenings surrounding a fifth anniversary commemoration held on the grounds of the United States Embassy in Moscow. Members of the diplomatic corps gathered around the American flag as Ambassador William Burns gave a short speech, and a representative of the embassy staff read a poem by Emily Dickinson. Then, following a moment of silence, two members of the Marine guards lowered the flag to half-staff. *Adagio for Strings* began to play (probably a recording, but possibly a Marine Band, Bridge does not specify), and it "slowly conquered the silence."[157] Unfortunately, the bottom of the flag got tangled around the pole. As the piece continued with its "almost violent crescendo," the flag seemed to gain strength, and "just as the music hits its peak the wind pushes it straight out like a sail on the sea"; Bridge confided, "Even at half-staff, I have never seen the American flag look so good."[158]

In 2010 New Muse (New Music Everywhere) staged *Adagio*—for the ensemble's first performance anywhere—on the steps of the Capitol building in Madison, Wisconsin. Prior to the event its members had invited other string players to join them, resulting in what can be called a "flashmob" performance. New Muse, of course, had no idea how many musicians would show up. A huge downpour of rain came shortly before this spontaneous rendition but cleared up exactly when the piece was set to start: 8:45 A.M., the time when the first plane struck the North Tower of the World Trade Center. Approximately sixty musicians—not only string players but also several singers performing the Agnus Dei transcription—plus several dancers delivered a true multi-media presentation. Conductor

[157]Robert Bridge, "Poetic Justice," *Moscow News* (15 September 2006), 15.

[158]*Ibid.*

of the group Jerry Hui commented, "For a brief eight minutes, we were all brought together by the music and movement."[159]

Because it was the tenth anniversary of the tragedy, more than the typical number of memorial concerts took place in 2011, many of which featured a performance of Barber's *Adagio*. The work had various musical companions, some of which were traditional, such as Copland's *Fanfare for the Common Man*, and various Requiem movements, from Mozart to Fauré. On other concerts were more recent compositions, written since the tragedy and relating aspects of the event. One of the most effective of these was a new six-movement cantata by British composer Richard Blackford, titled *Not in Our Time*, commissioned and performed by the Bournemouth Symphony Orchestra and Chorus. In addition to other texts, this work incorporated passages (in Movement IV) from an article by American journalist Tom Junod, which contains a photograph taken by Associated Press photographer Richard Drew of a man leaping from the towers rather than being burned alive in the conflagration. The text for this movement, appropriately titled "The Falling Man," begins with Junod's opening sentences: "He departs this earth like an arrow. If he were not falling, he might well be flying."[160] This quotation was also spoken as a part of the narration preceding the *Adagio* performance, thus linking the two works. Two British actors spoke the narration, both before *Adagio* and during Blackford's work: Simon Callow at Cheltenham on 11 September and Charles Dance at Poole on 13 September.

For Veterans on Holiday Observances

MEMORIAL DAY

Since Memorial Day in 1990 until his death in 2009, conductor Erich Kunzel led the National Symphony Orchestra in an annual holiday gala on the West Lawn of the Nation's Capitol, with thousands of people attending and millions watching on PBS television stations. *Adagio for Strings* has been given prominence several times, usually in connection

[159]"New Music Everywhere," *The College Music Society*, live.music.org. The performance, somewhat awkwardly edited, is available at "NEW MUSE–9/11/2010 Flashmob Performance," *YouTube* (29 September 2010), posted by jonathankuuskoski.

[160]Tom Junod, "The Falling Man," *Esquire* CXL/3 (September 2003), 177. The text for the entire cantata was posted at www.scribd.com/doc/116399891/NI-6161. "The Falling Man" text is on page 13. In addition to being a part of the *Esquire* article, this photograph is also available at several online sites and is one of three by Drew featured as a part of *In Memoriam: New York City*, a documentary discussed earlier in this chapter.

with poetry or drama readings. In 1996 the orchestra's interpretation underscored the narration of actor Charles Durning, with a passage written by a disabled veteran.

One of the most touching concerts was the one in 1990, featuring music associated with several American wars, from "Yankee Doodle" (Revolutionary War) through *Adagio* (Vietnam). Reviewer Joseph McLellan singled out the circumstances of the latter's performance as "perhaps the most moving moment" of the program.[161] As the music played actress Colleen Dewhurst read a letter left at the Vietnam Veterans Memorial by Margaret Stock, the mother of a soldier who had died in the war. He had volunteered to fly his helicopter for an extra trip the day he fell. As the camera showed his name at the wall, Dewhurst read the mother's message:

> I came to this black wall again to see and touch your name. . . . I used to wonder how scared and homesick you must have been in that strange country, . . . I would rather have had you for 21 years, and all the pain that goes with losing you, than never to have had you at all. Mom.[162]

David Field reported that during her reading "even the strong wept."[163] In each of the three programs *Adagio* was associated with the Vietnam War, undoubtedly due to Oliver Stone's use of it in *Platoon*. Once that association was made, it has become rather difficult to separate the music from that war.

On Memorial Day 2004 *Adagio* surfaced near the end of CBS's *60 Minutes*. Andy Rooney, who usually gave rather acerbic comments on trivial matters, altered his satirical outlook on this occasion to present a photomontage of more than 800 American soldiers slain in Iraq since the beginning of the war. With *Adagio for Strings* in the background, he showed about eleven minutes of photographs; no names were read, no running commentary. Whether the use of *Adagio* was Rooney's decision or others at CBS, it was probably selected because of its association with the Vietnam War, now shifted to a contemporary conflict. At the end

[161]Joseph McLellan, "NSO at the Capitol, Honoring the Fallen," *Washington Post* (28 May 1990), B: 1.

[162]Margaret Stock, quoted in *ibid.*

[163]David Field, "NSO, Vietnam Readings Leave No Dry Eye," *Washington Times* (29 May 1990), E: 3.

Rooney expressed his own sentiments: "On this Memorial Day, we should certainly honor those who have died at war, but we should dedicate this day, not so much to their memory, but to the search for a way to end the idiocy of the wars that killed them."[164] With such a statement Rooney could hardly be less acerbic or trivial.

INDEPENDENCE DAY

In most years the Fourth of July is a day of high spirits, a celebration of the nation's independence, but after the 9 / 11 attacks that day became tempered by sadness. Amidst the festivities, music such as *Adagio for Strings* lends a note of solemnity. For many years the Boston Pops has celebrated America's birthday with a concert at the Hatch Shell on the Charles River Esplanade. Conductor Keith Lockhart explained that, because of the attacks, the 2002 celebration would be different: Barber's *Adagio* was part of the program that honored the heroes of 9 / 11 but also remembered "those who have died in defense of the very principles we celebrate each and every Fourth of July."[165] Five years later Lockhart again programmed *Adagio* on his July 4th concert as a tribute to fallen servicemen and women.

Two days before Independence Day 2006 the Riverside County Philharmonic held a "Concert for Heroes" at the Riverside (Calif.) National Cemetery. Conductor Patrick Flynn and Michael Goldware, the founder and chief fund-raiser for the event, chose Barber's *Adagio* to be played to honor prisoners of war and those missing in action. Goldware explained, "I feel obliged to do it, to honor the men and women interred in Riverside Cemetery."[166]

VETERANS DAY

In 1996 Donald Kendrick selected Barber's *Adagio for Strings* for the Sacramento Festival Orchestra's "Veterans Day Salute," a tradition that

[164]Andy Rooney, quoted in Rebecca Leung, "Rooney: Memorial Day," *CBS 60 Minutes* (5 December 2007), www.cbsnews.com/stories/2004/05/25/60minutes/rooney/main619533.shtml.

[165]Richard Dyer, "Manilow, McGovern Top Pop's July 4th," *Boston Globe* (7 June 2002). On 30 June at Boston's Symphony Hall, the Pops also included *Adagio* in "An American Salute," a warm-up for the Esplanade concert. Broadcast live locally over WCVB-TV and nationally on the A&E Network, the concert was entitled "POPS Goes the Fourth! 2002."

[166]Pat O'Brien, "Patriotic Concert Salutes Members of the Armed Services," *The Press Enterprise* (28 June 2006), www.pe.com. The Madison Wisconsin Chamber Orchestra also held a pre-Fourth of July concert on 3 July 2002 entitled "America Remembers." The concert included *Adagio* with narration by Tom Treece, a decorated Vietnam veteran.

Michael Neumann extended with his Sacramento Youth Symphony in 2000. It was intended as a one-time event, but when members of the audience requested *Adagio* for the following year, the orchestra obliged and has repeated it on its Veteran's Day concert ever since. Neumann professed, "The knowledge that our young musicians touch [the veterans'] hearts so deeply is a significant reason I continue this concert tradition."[167] He claimed that few people in the audience leave without being deeply touched.

Veterans Day is known in the British Commonwealth as Remembrance Day, and various orchestras have programmed *Adagio* on their concerts, including the Australian Classical Players (2001), the University of Ottawa Orchestra (2005), and the Vancouver Youth Symphony Orchestra (2007). The Ottawa concert was dedicated to the memory of victims of tyranny, oppression, and genocide.[168]

On 7 November 1992 Alex Chadwick reported for NPR on the tenth anniversary of the Vietnam Memorial Wall, followed by a brief sound bite from *Adagio*. Preceding it he commented, "the grievers walk past slowly or sometimes pause, looking inward, looking outward, lost on purpose, gazing across the decades into the stone and then moving on at last."[169] Justification is clear: thanks to *Platoon, Adagio* has become associated with the Vietnam War, and its use within this context is consistent with these associations. A few years later *Adagio* was heard at "Gathered at the Wall," an exhibit of Vietnam War memorabilia at the Museum of Our National Heritage in Lexington, Maryland (October 1994-May 1995). Co-curators Duery Felton and Cara Sutherland assembled dozens of transcribed excerpts from letters left at the Memorial, along with many photographs that "express a range of emotion, from veterans' survivor guilt

[167]Sacramento Youth Symphony press release, October / November 2004. A compact disc of the 2002 concert is available directly from the orchestra: www.sacys.org/Announcements/130.aspx. Other Veterans Day programs that featured *Adagio* were by the New Hampshire Symphony Orchestra (directed by Kenneth Kiesler) in 2001; the Las Cruces Symphony Orchestra (directed by Lonnie Klein) in 2004; the Boca Raton Symphonia (directed by Philippe Entremont) in 2005; and the Wichita Symphony Orchestra (directed by Andrew Sewell) in 2005. Two choral groups have included Agnus Dei on their concerts: the Brisbane [Australia] Chamber Choir (directed by Graeme Morton) in 1998 and the Vocal Arts Ensemble of Durham, N.C., in 2001.

[168]"A Remembrance Day Concert," *University of Ottawa* (31 October 2005), www.media.uottawa.ca /mediaroom/news-details_718.html.

[169]Transcript of Alex Chadwick, *National Public Radio* (7 November 1992).

to sorrowful messages from children to dead parents."[170] *Adagio* was, in addition, the soundtrack to an accompanying video.

ANZAC DAY

In Australia and New Zealand, veterans are honored on ANZAC Day. The acronym stands for Australian and New Zealand Army Corps, an organization that sets aside a day of remembrance each April 25th, the day that their forces landed on the beaches of Gallipoli in 1915. Some version of *Adagio for Strings* has been associated with ANZAC commemorations on several occasions. The Woolston Brass Band played an arrangement of the work at the Grand ANZAC Concert in Christchurch in 1998. In 1999 the Australian Broadcasting Corporation broadcast *Adagio* in an episode of its series, *Encounter*. At one point Brandt Eustice read from the letters of Alec Raws, a soldier who wrote from the front in August 1916 in the thick of the Great War: "The glories of the great push are great, but the horrors are greater. I don't see that we can break down the artillery." At this point *Adagio* began to play. "Before going into this next affair . . . unless I should go under . . . ." Those were his last written words.[171] In 2002 ANZAC day was held in Moscow, where the program also commemorated the September 11 attacks. New Zealand conductor Lygia O'Riordan directed the Ensemble XXI Moscow in a performance of *Adagio for Strings* in recognition of those who died. In 2004 ANZAC Day was celebrated in Melbourne Town Hall: the choir of the Royal Melbourne Philharmonic Orchestra sang the Agnus Dei. The following year the Dawn Service was held on site at Gallipoli's Anzac Cove to observe the ninetieth anniversary of the landings. A "Prelude to the Dawn Service" was held the night before with readings and music including a didjeridu solo (!) alongside the Barber *Adagio* and the one attributed to Albinoni.

TRIBUTES TO VETERANS ON THE INTERNET

A website for the 101st Army Band of the Colorado Army National Guard provides a template for a Veterans Day program with speeches and appropriate music. It does not indicate if or when this program

[170]Patrick Hagopian, "Gathered at the Wall: America and the Vietnam Veterans Memorial," *Journal of American History* LXXXII/1 (June 1995), 162.

[171]The Raws' letters are published in Alec Raws and Goldy Raws, *Hail and Farewell: Letters from Two Brothers Killed in France in 1916* (Kenthurst, Australia: Kangaroo Press, 1996). A transcript of the program is available at "Bugle from Dawn Service, National War Memorial in Canberra," *Australian Broadcasting Corporation–Encounter* (25 April 1999), www.abc.net.au/rn/relig/enc/stories/s23506.htm.

was performed, but other organizations have the right to use or modify it for their own purpose. Near the end, the script calls for the last part of Calvin Custer's woodwind arrangement of *Adagio* to be played while the commander of the group reads parts of a letter written by Second Lieutenant Sidney Diamond in December 1944, in the midst of World War II. The letter is addressed to Stelle, either his wife or sweetheart:

> I would like to fill the air with plans, dreams, hopes—But—'Stelle—all there is, is a choking in the chest—Every once in a while a guy gets himself overcome by despair; despondency overwhelms him . . . I love you darling—whatever happens—be happy—that's my only request . . .[172]

Such tragic lines go well with the sounds of *Adagio*.

The North Texas Chapter of the Texas Association of Vietnam Veterans sponsors a website honoring veterans of the War and "the memory of the more than 58,000 of our brothers and sisters who never came home. We also want to honor and pay tribute to all veterans from all wars [and to] those that paid the ultimate price." As a guest enters the site, a synthesizer arrangement of *Adagio for Strings* starts to play, and if he or she continues looking at information on the site, it begins again.[173]

A webpage honoring veterans of the Marine Corps begins with this announcement: "Because of you the Veterans of our wars, The honor, the pride you have bestowed upon us We Thank-you so very much." Barber's *Adagio* and Lee Greenwood's "God Bless the USA" accompany the page.[174] On another website sailors pay tribute to their shipmates on USS Hancock CV / CVA-19 and USS Indianapolis CA-35. While a certain Stanley [*sic*] Barber's *Adagio* plays in the background, brief tributes and a few Bible passages are posted on the screen. The shipmates hope that "many will visit here, and remember those who made their 'Last Full Measure of Devotion' to our cause of Liberty, where Justice and the Blessings of God will continue."[175]

[172]"COARNG Homepage," *101st Army Band*, www.coloradoguard.com/webpages/band_home.htm.

[173]Dick Crislip, *Texas Association of Vietnam Veterans North Texas Chapter*, www.tavvntc.org.

[174]Glenn, *Veterans, Thank You*, www.glennjustglenn.freeyellow.com/page1.html.

[175]Jake, "Navy and Military Music," *USS Hancock CV / CVA-19 Memorial*, www.usshancockcv19.com/music.htm.

If veterans of twentieth-century wars can be honored, why not servicemen who died during America's bloodiest conflict, The Civil War, or as southerners still prefer to call it, The War between the States? Open the website for the 9th Georgia Infantry, C. S. A., The Army of Northern Virginia, and *Adagio for Strings* in a rather strident synthesized version begins to play. The site contains photographs of members of this infantry along with several quotations including one from a newspaper in 1863: "'Tis with feelings of deepest sorrow that we recount the many who fell upon this stubbornly contested field; yet 'tis with pride that we recall how bravely they fought and nobly fell."[176] The creator of the website concurs: "the men (my ancestors) that fought and died for the South were decent, honorable men that were fighting for a cause they believed in. . . . Sacrifice such as theirs needs to be recorded for posterity, not forgotten."[177] Amen to that!

Postscript: For Miss Alice, Chicca, and Holly Hamster

There is one last scenario concerning the appropriation of Barber's *Adagio* as an expression of grief that should be addressed. It brings together age-old rites of passage and the timely benefits of technology: posting announcements of the death of a beloved pet on the Internet. For some, this behavior may seem frivolous; others who have enjoyed a strong emotional bond with an animal will sympathize with the need to acknowledge publicly the ending of that special relationship. The implication is, of course, obvious: what was meaningful to mark the passing of a President Kennedy or a Princess Grace can be just as consoling at the demise of a Miss Alice, a Chicca, or a Holly. The first example cites a website; the latter two refer to posts on *YouTube*.

She was just twelve years old when she was "taken from this world." Miss Alice was a beagle who died shortly after she celebrated her birthday at the Northern California Beaglefest and "now frolics at the Rainbow Bridge," a place "this side of heaven," where an animal goes when it has

[176]G. 9th Ga., Letter to the Editor, *The* [Milledgeville, Ga.] *Confederate Union* (11 August 1863); reprinted www.9thgeorgia infantry.org/cunion.html.

[177]Neal Griffin, "My Reasons for a Web Page," *Ninth Georgia Infantry CSA*, www.9thgeorgiainfantry .org/reasons.html. In addition to these, the 50th anniversary of D-Day celebrated at Omaha Beach in 1994 includes pictures and texts of speeches presented by former President Bill Clinton, accompanied by a synthesizer version of *Adagio*. Claude and Vivian Corbin, *Omaha Beach–50th Anniversary of D-Day*, www.dday50.com/omaha.html.

been "especially close to someone."[178] After the death of the pet owner, there is a grand reunion at this special bridge:

> you cling together in joyous reunion, never to be parted again. The happy kisses rain upon your face; your hands again caress the beloved head, and you look once more into the trusting eyes of your pet, so long gone from your life but never absent from your heart.[179]

On the website is a photograph of Miss Alice with her owner, Liz Doughty, probably the author of the above passage. Accompanying the site is an unpolished synthesizer performance of Barber's *Adagio for Strings*.

"Requiem per Chicca," a memorial to a pet cat, is devoted to various clips of the gray Italian pussy in different situations near the end of her life. As *Adagio for Strings* concludes, Chicca is displayed in her kitty casket while the owner slowly lowers the lid. At the end is an Italian epitaph: "In ricordo di Chicca nostra compagna per 19 anni."[180] Like the loss of Chicca, "R. I. P. Holly Hamster" is a requiem for a pet with *Adagio* as the soundtrack. The video shows photographs of the hamster prior to her death in March 2008. The videographer admits that, even at the age of thirty-one (the videographer, not the hamster), it was "still upsetting."[181] For some people, pets are like family members and deserve equal respect.

While not everyone agrees that *Adagio for Strings* is a sad work (see Chapter 12), it, nevertheless, functions well in somber situations, such as funerals and memorial services. Some remember the death of Kennedy — or even Roosevelt; most of us had to endure the devastating days of the attacks on 9 / 11; and others have had to deal with personal loss of friends or family members. *Adagio* has been a comfort to those whose lives must go on.

[178]Liz Doughty, "In Loving Memory of Miss Alice," *Beaglefest 2001*, www.nocalbf2k.homestead.com/Alice.html.

[179]*Ibid.*

[180]Translation: In memory of Chicca, our companion for nineteen years. "Requiem per Chicca," *YouTube* (15 July 2007), posted by frgiordano.

[181]Perhaps just as upsetting, this video has been removed.

The Legacy of *Adagio for Strings*

CHAPTER 11

> "We went to the concert, and heard "Adagio for Strings" by Samuel the Barber."
>
> —Charles M. Schulz, Peanuts 1995 © Peanuts Worldwide LLC.

Any serious consideration of the legacy of *Adagio for Strings* would be incomplete without acknowledging the many surprising ways in which it has infiltrated society as a cultural marker. It has served as a point of departure or as a point of reference for a sizable repertory of original works—now the unofficial standard by which slow music for string orchestras is measured. Its nature and its title have been much imitated. It has been harnessed in advertisements to sell products and adopted as a therapy for emotionally troubled patients. It has been employed successfully as a "calming" stimulus in a subway station, a prison, and classrooms. This effect—and other responses—have been studied scientifically in controlled psychological experiments. It has entered the daily lives of many under even less expected circumstances: computer games, wedding ceremonies, telephone ring tones, greeting cards, crossword puzzles, television game shows, and the like. Surely Samuel Barber would have been flabbergasted to learn of the unforeseen functions his *Adagio* was destined to serve.

Its intrusion into pop culture may best be represented by the comic strip *Peanuts* by Charles M. Schulz. Peppermint Patty, clueless in so many matters, is just as confused as ever. Her understanding of "the barber" corresponds to real-life London teenagers cited in Chapter 8 who called the piece Andagio [*sic*] in G Minor. At least Patty got the title right!

Illustration 11.1. *Peanuts* Comic Strip by Charles M. Schulz

Creating Sound-alikes and Wanna-bes

Imitation is the sincerest [form of] flattery.

—Charles Caleb Colton, *Lacon* (1821).[1]

Imitation is the sincerest form of battery.

—Song by the rock group Every Time I Die, from the album *The Big Dirty* (2007).[2]

If imitation is the sincerest form of flattery, then Barber has, indeed, been endlessly flattered—and battered—ever since *Adagio for Strings* was first heard. While later composers seem to steal moments from the work, others merely imitate its measured pace to recreate a similarly serene atmosphere. A number of pieces with the same or a similar title have emerged; various critics have heard a certain influence from *Adagio*, intentional or otherwise. Are these perceptions of critics valid, or are Barber's colleagues and successors simply writing slow music for stringed instruments? Once listeners come to terms with the Barber composition, nonetheless, it tends to become the standard by which all other similar pieces are judged.

WHAT'S IN A NAME? OR NOT EVERY ADAGIO FOR STRINGS IS *ADAGIO FOR STRINGS*

Theoretically any piece of music written exclusively for strings and assigned a deliberate, unhurried tempo has the legitimate right to be called "Adagio for Strings." Inasmuch as this title is so inextricably associated with Barber's creation, any other piece with that name is bound to lead to confusion. I think that this particular designation deserves an exclusive copyright, preventing anyone else from copying it, but that is unlikely to happen.[3] Nevertheless, several compositions bear the same or very similar titles, which may or may not imply a connection.

Consider the Adagio in G Minor for organ and strings of Tomaso Albinoni (1671-1751). Because it was ostensibly written by an eighteenth-

[1]Charles Caleb Colton, *Lacon: or Many Things in a Few Words; Addressed to Those Who Think* VII (London: J. McGowan, 1821), 113. Accessible through *Google Books.*

[2]*The Big Dirty*, perf. Every Time I Die (Ferret Records, ETIDTBDREG-CD00, 2007). The song is Track 12 on the album.

[3]Titles, if considered generic or arbitrary, cannot be copyrighted, but after official consideration they can acquire the status of a trademark with specified privileges.

century composer, surely there can be no mystery concerning the title or the music. Or might there be? First of all, it is a familiar work in its own right, has been recorded frequently, and has been programmed on many concerts. The problem is that it was composed not by Albinoni but by a prominent scholar of the Venetian composer's works, Remo Giazotto. Another expert in Albinoni scholarship, Michael Talbot, has contended that the piece is based on

> an untraced fragment of unconfirmed attribution to Albinoni allegedly reported by [Fausto] Torrefranca to have belonged to an unnamed private collection that eventually passed to an unidentified state library in Leipzig: this is the original source on which Giazotto's very free reconstruction is purportedly based. Need more be said?[4]

The style of the piece, moreover, is totally unlike any music known to have been written by Albinoni. Talbot characterized it as "unashamedly lachrymose,"[5] and critic Alan Rich called it a "latter-day pseudo-archaic fakery."[6] In the spirit of this revelation, author Fritz Spiegl devised the following bit of doggerel:

The Adagio of Albinoni
Is largely phony;
A sort of musical risotto
Cooked up by Giazotto.[7]

He apologetically added, "That is putting it a little strongly."[8] Yet, for circumstantial reasons, it may be stated that this piece resembles Barber's *Adagio*: it is much closer in style to that work than to any other from the eighteenth century, and it was published in 1958, long after Barber's work

[4]Michael Talbot, "About Albinoni's Adagio," [review of *Albinoni–Adagio in G Minor*, perf. by I Musici (Philips, 6580 001, 1968)], *The Music Times* CXIII (September 1972), 874.

[5]Michael Talbot, *Tomaso Albinoni: The Venetian Composer and His World* (Oxford: Clarendon Press, 1990), v.

[6]Alan Rich, "A Lot of Night Music: Is There Sex after Bach," *LA Weekly* (9-15 November 2001).

[7]Fritz Speigl, *Music through the Looking Glass* (London: Routledge, 1984), 8. He also refers to the work as a clerihew.

[8]*Ibid.*

appeared on the scene. Could the mood of Barber's composition have influenced how Giazotto cooked up his confection?

The title itself has led to confusion. For instance, the Albinoni Adagio was featured in the motion picture *Gallipoli* (1983), but reviewer John L. Walters mistakenly recorded that the movie "made memorable use of Samuel Barber's Adagio for Strings."[9] Several years later another film, *Show Me Love* (1998), written and directed by Lukas Moodyson, also featured the pseudo-Albinoni Adagio, but film reviewer Bill DeLapp asserted that "there are a few melodramatic components, such as Agnes applying a razor blade to her wrist while Samuel Barber's mournful 'Adagio for Strings' (from the movie *Platoon*) plays on the soundtrack."[10] Wrong! It was Albinoni. Other reviewers got it right.

In quite different situations this mix-up prevails. Some commentators have reported that Barber's *Adagio* was played at Princess Diana's funeral. This is not true: Albinoni's was performed. (Barber's *Adagio* was heard at a memorial concert for the Princess ten years later, however.) Then, in 2010, to honor Barber on his 100th birthday, one videographer posted a tribute on *YouTube*, featuring lovely cherry blossoms in Washington, D.C., and inappropriately a pop piano arrangement of Albinoni's Adagio. Since then, the video has been removed—this individual may have realized his or her mistake.

While many works are titled "Adagio for Strings," few have little more than a superficial resemblance to Barber's work. A working list of them is given in Appendix 11, but a few may be singled out. Describing André Jolivet's (1905-1974) *Adagio pour cordes* (1960), one reviewer mentioned "lots of divisi, sul ponticello . . . a prevalence of very small note values, and sweeping arpeggiated figures."[11] That description could never be applied to Barber's composition. Gen Louis Parchman's (b. 1929) *Adagio for Strings* (1971) is also totally different from Barber's; in fact, the second theme resembles more closely Alban Berg's treatment of the Bach chorale in the second movement of his Violin Concerto (1935). Rolf Boon's *Adagio for Strings* (1989) adds a tape of electronic sounds, clearly mitigating any concrete resemblance to Barber's work. The composer

[9]John L. Walters, "No Man's Land," *The Guardian* (10 September 2004); reprinted www.bridgeboy music.com/carrothers_Press_Releases.htm.

[10]Bill DeLapp, "Show Me Love," *All Movie Portal*, www.allmovieportal.com/m/1999_Show_ Me_ Love36.html.

[11]Simon Walsh, "French Traditional," *The Musical Times* CIV (1963), 275.

admits that while he did not attempt to reference that work, he did draw on it as an "important model."[12] *Adagio for Strings* (1987) by William Thomas McKinley (b. 1938) is a reworking of the melodic and harmonic materials of his earlier work *SinfoNova* (1985). In program notes for its first performance, given in Cambridge, Massachusetts in November 1987, he wrote that the work is intended to "communicate tragic and dark lyricism," which could easily apply to Barber's *Adagio*; on the other hand, its construction is identified by the composer as "Mahlerian and Gothic," characteristics not usually associated with the Barber work.[13] Critic Victor Carr goes further: "this Adagio for Strings is nothing like the Samuel Barber work of the same name."[14] In his view McKinley explores "the gamut of human emotions in string writing that varies from lyrical to rapturous to harsh."[15] Barber's creation is lyrical and rapturous, but never harsh.

Two works, however, may be more closely tied to Barber's *Adagio*, at least on first listening. *Adagio for Strings* (1989) by Nigel Keay (b. 1955) is a five-minute work with the subtitle "Image of Java." Keay performed in a gamelan orchestra when he was a student, later spent time in Java, and is convinced that the structured music of that society "eventually filtered through" his compositions of the 1980s. Yet I hear a closer affinity to the Western aesthetic of Barber than the Eastern concepts of Indonesia, especially because neither gamelan instruments nor Javanese time cycles are evident in the score.[16] Keay's composition begins with the same 4 - 3 suspension that began Barber's *Adagio*. While this reference might imply a tribute to Barber, Keay admits that "it definitely was not deliberate. It crept in there unconsciously."[17] Nonetheless, when his piece begins,

[12]Rolf Boon, email (6 March 2011) to the author. Boon revised his *Adagio for Strings* (the first version dates from his "formative years"); the new version, premièred 18 November 2013 with the Lethbridge [Alberta] Symphony, reflects "formal and other design aspects" of Barber's original.

[13]Full program notes reprinted in Jeffrey S. Sposato, *William Thomas McKinley: A Bio-Bibliography* (Westport, Conn.: Greenwood, 1995), 44.

[14]Victor Carr, Jr., "Starer and McKinley," *Classics Today*, www.classicstoday.com/review/review-4438/?search=1. The work appears on *Robert Starer and William Thomas McKinley . . .* , perf. Czech Radio Symphony Orchestra, cond. Vladimir Valek (MMC Recordings, 2070, 1999).

[15]*Ibid.*

[16]This work was conceived to be performed alone or to be heard as the centerpiece of Keay's three-movement *Symphony for Strings* (1989). Both the score and a performance are posted at the composer's website: www.nigelkeay.com/adagio.htm

[17]Nigel Keay, email (3 March 2011) to the author. A violist, Keay has played in several performances of Barber's *Adagio.*

some listeners might be reminded of Barber's composition. As the piece progresses, however, it takes on its own character and sounds less and less like Barber. According to Keay,

> I successfully avoided constructing something along the same lines as Barber's work, that is, an "architectural" approach with grand climax. In mine the form was important, but I was more concerned with preserving a similar ambiance throughout.[18]

Keay's is somewhat minimalistic, in the "time is suspended" sense of the word, fairly static, and lacking a climb to a climax. The harmonic language is also somewhat more dissonant than Barber's.

The initial phrase of Jeffrey Gold's *Elegy: Adagio for Strings* (2007), likewise, contains a similar opening pattern as well as the harmonic suspension of the Barber work, but its ending is more like Vaughan Williams's *Fantasia on a Theme by Thomas Tallis.* Because it is more consonant than Keay's *Adagio,* from that perspective it is closer to the aesthetic of Barber's composition. Agreeing with these views, Gerald Elias, concertmaster of the Utah Symphony, observed that *Elegy* unfolded "in the tradition of Barber and Vaughan Williams," conveying a "mood of simultaneous despair and hope,"[19] two terms that some listeners and critics might apply in the description of Barber's *Adagio for Strings***.**

Identifying Rip-offs

FILM SCORES

Of all the film music compared to Barber's *Adagio,* Alfred Newman's main theme from *The Greatest Story Ever Told* (1965) bears the greatest claim of resemblance, as a number of film critics have noticed. Royal S. Brown noted that it starts out "ever so much in the manner of *Adagio for Strings.*"[20] Steve Schwartz concurred that "the most memorable idea, associated with Jesus, may be an unconscious crib from Barber's *Adagio*

[18]Nigel Keay, email (4 March 2011) to the author.

[19]Because this comment is quoted on the Jeffrey Gold website, the composer must approve of his work being compared to those two prominent composers. See www.jeffreygold.com/bio/.

[20]Royal S. Brown, "Film Musings," *Fanfare* XXII/3 (January-February 1999), 320.

for Strings,"[21] and Edwin Black concluded that Newman "directly cloned [it] without credit."[22] It is remarkably close to Barber's piece; in fact, for the first five seconds listeners probably will think it is *Adagio*. It begins with the same single sustained note followed by the first two chords. The melody then wanders about diatonically, but eventually both melody and harmony diverge from the Barber example. This is not a situation where a composer attempted to capitalize on *Adagio*'s success in *Platoon*. That film was not released for another twenty-one years; Barber's landmark composition was almost thirty years old when *The Greatest Story* came out. Even though the music had not been introduced into a film score during this period, Newman may have been directly inspired by it in its concert context and decided to emulate its sound and mood. Banking on the fact that movie audiences, unless they were concert goers, were unlikely to be familiar with *Adagio,* Newman probably did not intend for anyone to make the association. On the other hand, much of the mood and content of the movie's music was more or less dictated by producer / director George Stevens, who insisted on including bits of the Requiem (1874) of Verdi and the "Hallelujah Chorus" (1741) of Handel. Perhaps he asked Newman for a Barber sound-alike. Record reviewer David Aspinall lamented about the soundtrack in general: "We have what feels like two hours of Barber's *Adagio*. Didn't Barber say it in nine minutes?"[23]

The music in one scene of another film that closely imitates Barber's *Adagio* is Alberto Iglesias's score for Pedro Almodóvar's *Hable con Ella* [Talk to Her] (2002). In a bizarre scene Benigno, a nurse infatuated with his comatose patient, "talks to her" about a silent movie he has recently attended. She may or may not be able to comprehend his words, but the audience not only hears his description but sees the scene in a flashback: a scientist swallows what he thinks is a youth potion, but instead it reduces him down to a few inches, an incredibly shrinking man. This movie within a movie is, in fact, titled *Shrinking Lover*. Despite Benigno's own mishap, his lab partner / lover remains full size. One night, while she sleeps naked

[21]Steve Schwartz, "Review of Sound Track Album," *Amazon.com* (2001); reprinted www.classical.net/music/recs/reviews/r/ryk10734.html0.

[22]Edwin Black, "Opinion: Clones, Composites and Composition," *Film Score Monthly* (13 January 1998); reprinted www.filmscoremonthly.com/articles/1998/13_Jan-Clone Composition.asp.

[23]David Aspinall, "Newman Gets His Due: David Aspinall Examines the Film Music Career of Alfred Newman in the Context of Two New Releases on CD," *@udiophilia* (November 1998); reprinted www.audiophilia.com/software.da13.htm. For the background story concerning Newman's music for this film, see Ken Darby, *Hollywood Holyland: The Filming and Scoring of The Greatest Story Ever Told* (Metuchen, N.J.: Scarecrow Press, 1992). Neither *Adagio* nor Barber are mentioned in the book.

in bed, he cavorts all around her breasts and then crawls head first into her vagina. This is surely one of the most surreal sex scenes ever produced—worthy of Luis Buñuel. During this action the music is remarkably close to *Adagio.* As film critic George Wu put it, "Iglesias' music sounds like a variation of Samuel Barber's *Adagio for Strings* and is very effective."[24]

Of the film scores that critics compare to *Adagio,* many were written by John Williams or Hans Zimmer, two of moviedom's most prolific and sought-after composers. One of Williams's earliest scores is *The Eiger Sanction* (1975), released two years prior to his first big hit, *Star Wars.* Kevin Mulhall wrote that in the part of the score labeled "The Icy Ascent" Williams "offers a haunting adagio for strings."[25] Note that Mulhall uses only a generic form of the term, neither mentioning Barber's name nor italicizing the title. As this is five years before *The Elephant Man* and eleven before *Platoon,* I doubt that there is a deliberate reference to Barber's *Adagio* in the scene. Yet Williams is notorious for lifting ideas from classical composers. Over a decade later, after composing music for other films, he wrote the score for *Born on the Fourth of July* (1989), which critic Mike Sutton considered "haunting, poignant and heavily reminiscent of Samuel Barber's Adagio for Strings" and "perfect in establishing the mood of the film."[26] A few years later Williams composed his score to *JFK* (1991). Tom Daish called the track "Arlington" a "gorgeous elegy for strings" that can be "compared to Barber's *Adagio for Strings,* but this is all Williams and has the benefit of not being horrendously overused in other movies."[27] Because his score for *Saving Private Ryan* (1998) is treated in a *Platoon*-like combat situation, it invites the most comparisons with the Barber work. Conductor Erich Kunzel, for example, speculated:

> I presume Spielberg watched *Platoon.* A prevailing piece of music that went through all those terrible battles in Vietnam . . . was the Barber *Adagio for Strings,* and it was so effective. This is purely

[24]George Wu, "Talk to Her" [*Hable con Ella*], *culturevulture.net, Choices for the Cognoscenti*, www.culturevulture.net/movies/TalktoHer.htm.

[25]Kevin Mulhall, liner notes to *The Eiger Sanction*, cond. John Williams (Varese Sarabande, VSD 5277, 1975); reprinted www.jwilliamsmusic.it/eiger-lst.htm. "The Icy Descent" is Track 4 on the soundtrack.

[26]Mike Sutton, "Born on the Fourth of July," *DVD Times*, www.dvdtimes.co.uk/reviews/region2/bornonthefourthofjuly.html.

[27]Tom Daish, "JFK," *The Sound Track Express* (21 February 1998); reprinted www.classicalrecordings.com/johnwilliams/jfk-review.htm.

> conjecture on my part, but perhaps this is what he said: "Johnny, I think we don't want battle music. What we want is something that is heroic or somber whose underlying theme, even though death and carnage abound, should not be the razzmatazz of battle but the pathos of it all.[28]

While this may be conjecture, Kunzel has clearly recognized not only an *Adagio*-like sound and mood but noticed the similarity of context between the two movies. Yet, despite the similarity of mood and the slow tempos of virtually every track, none of the music truly resembles *Adagio*: no little fragments, no diatonic snippets.

Starting with *Pearl Harbor* (2001), several Hans Zimmer soundtracks have been likened to *Adagio for Strings*. As it is a war movie, Zimmer may have tried for the "*Platoon* effect." An Amazon editor suggested that the "December 7th" cue "even echoes *Platoon* and Barber's *Adagio for Strings*."[29] Echoes, maybe, but the main tune is far removed from Barber's original. According to Stephanie Zacharek, during the climactic battle sequence in *Tears of the Sun* (2003), the music is not Barber's *Adagio for Strings*—"but it's pretty damn close."[30] Steve Townsley also concluded, "it has an *Adagio for Strings* feel to it."[31] True, it does bear some kinship, but the descending melodic line owes just as much to the so-called Albinoni Adagio. Regarding Zimmer's score to *The Last Samurai* (2003), one critic observed that "the narrative string melody on top of the heart-wrenching basses is reminiscent of Barber's *Adagio for Strings* and will send chills throughout your body culminating in somber yet powerful and inspiring notes that literally bring tears to your eyes."[32] This relationship must have gotten on reviewer Arthur B. Lintgen's nerves: "The whole thing sounds

[28]Erich Kunzel, quoted in Royal S. Brown, "An Interview with Erich Kunzel," *Fanfare* XXII/5 (May-June 1999), 525-53.

[29]Jerry McCulley, "Pearl Harbor: Original Soundtrack," *Amazon.com* (28 August 2007), www.amazon.com/Pearl-Harbor-Martin-Tillman/dp/B0005JYBD. "December 7th" is Track 7 on the album.

[30]Stephanie Zacharek, "Tears of the Sun," *Salon Palm Computing* (13 March 2003), reprinted www.salon.com/partner/palm/1138727.html.

[31]Steve Townsley, "Smiling through the Tears," *Tracksounds*, www.tracksounds.com/reviews/tears_sun.htm.

[32]Amy "Priori2ude," "Inspiring, Tragic, Powerful, Emotional–A MUST HAVE!," *Amazon.com* (17 December 2003), www.amazon.ca/product-reviews/B0000DZTIW?pageNumber=4.

like Samuel Barber's *Adagio for Strings* on steroids."[33] I cannot vouch for the steroids part, but all the tracks—all extremely slow—suggest the Barber work in some ways. They wind around diatonically, often with a pattern of several pitches that could be matched with notes in *Adagio,* but I doubt if any of this is intentional. The *Adagio* comparison continues with the score to *Batman Begins* (2005), which Zimmer co-wrote with James Newton Howard. Writer Peter Canavese noted that "Barbastella" [Star-beard], the music in the scene in which Bruce Wayne descends into the lower depths of his manor house, has melodic passages with "a searching string line" that are "reminiscent" of Barber's *Adagio.*[34]

TELEVISION SOUNDTRACKS: DRAMAS

Dennis McCarthy has composed music for many programs in the *Star Trek: The Next Generation* series. In "The Dauphin," the second season's tenth episode (aired 5 March 1989), Wesley Crusher (Wil Wheaton) has a crush on Salla (Jaime Hubbart), a young heiress to the throne of the planet Daled Four. During one of their dialogues the music starts off suspiciously like *Adagio for Strings.* Is it a deliberate reference? Because McCarthy appreciates twentieth-century classical music, he might have slipped a quick fragment of the Barber piece into the scene. Earl Green noticed that in another situation the composer "threw the Picard theme" into the music of a particular scene. McCarthy replied, "Ah, you caught me! . . . I did sneak it in there, you know, I like to have fun!"[35] It would be just like him in keeping with his fun-loving spirit to sneak a little *Adagio* into the regular soundtrack. The passage in question begins with the usual sustained tone and proceeds with similar harmonies. The melody wanders in a manner suggesting *Adagio* but not with the exact contour. At the conclusion of the episode, when Wesley ponders this first romance, a few chords from this passage return.

As Jeff Berkwits observed, "in the course of television history, few individuals have been given the opportunity to shape the overall sound of a science-fiction series as fully as *Babylon 5* composer Christopher

[33]Arthur B. Lintgen, "Film/Music Recommendations," *AV.com*; reprinted www.avguide.com.film/music /musicreviews/tas147/147-classical-caps.new.php. [AV is an acronym for Affiliated Vendors.]

[34]Peter Canavese, "Batman Begins Original Motion Picture Soundtrack," *Groucho Reviews* (5 May 2008); www.grouchoreviews.com/features/104. "Barbastella" is Track 4 on the soundtrack.

[35]Dennis McCarthy, interview with Earl Green, "Interview: Dennis McCarthy," *The Log Book* (30 July 1993; reprinted www.thelogbook.com/music/i_dennis.html.

Franke."[36] Amid the music in the episode "Sleeping in Light" is "Dying Station," a segment that Berkwits calls "heartrending"; in his assessment the passage "subtly echoes" *Adagio for Strings* and, in the process, fashions a "truly affecting ambiance."[37] The echoes are, indeed, subtle; the music is simply slow and heartrending.

Innovators: A Musical Odyssey, a concert telecast on PBS stations in March 2000, combines music, narration, and film clips to celebrate the lives of well-known and not so well-known individuals who have taught us something new about the world or about ourselves, such as Albert Schweitzer, Stephen Hawking, and a student leader of the Tiananmen Square uprising of 1989. The soundtrack consists of a variety of musical idioms, notably, traditional African melodies, Bach, jazz, flamenco, and a newly-composed Requiem. The last element in this list, a definite *Adagio for Strings* sound-alike, references that music's opening gestures: the 4 - 3 suspension, moving it around in sequence. The form is almost exactly like Barber's original, beginning quietly, building to a climax, and then settling into a quiet coda. It was presented in memory of an anonymous victim of the seventeenth-century plague, who, knowing he was about to die, buried himself alive so that his young son would not have to contend with his interment.[38]

TELEVISION SOUNDTRACKS: COMEDIES

In Chapter 8 I mentioned the use of *Adagio for Strings* in "Up the Down Steroid" (2004), episode two of season eight of the animated series *South Park*. In addition to this, episode three from season seven contains an *Adagio* sound-alike in "Toilet Paper." After being reprimanded by their art teacher for not taking the class seriously, the boys decide to retaliate by TP'ing her house. While this is taking place, the music gradually turns into a passage resembling *Adagio*'s climb to the climax, with the same winding-around sequential motive. Is there justification for a reflective *Adagio*-clone in this sketch? One of the boys, Kyle, was reluctant to get involved and regrets the caper even while it is happening. Because the script carries the instruction: "Kyle freezes in awe of the vandalism," the

[36]Jeff Berkwits, "The Best of Babylon 5," *Sci Fi Weekly* (2 January 2002), www.scifi.com/sfw/sound/sfw 7964.html.

[37]*Ibid.*

[38]"Innovators–Requiem," *YouTube* (26 March 2008), posted by kurt Bestor. Kurt Bestor and Sam Cardon are the composers of the musical tribute. Later that year PBS produced a DVD of the program.

music probably implies his guilty conscience and his deep psychological need to confess. In some respects the guilt that Kyle feels ("What have we done?!") mirrors the regret Jimmy experienced ("No, God, no") after the steroid incident. Since the sound-alike comes a full season before the authentic *Adagio*, perhaps the producers thought, "Well, we once gave a hint of *Adagio,* let's now try the real thing."

Another *Adagio* sound-alike occurred on the popular CBS sitcom *How I Met Your Mother* during episode thirteen of season five (first aired on 18 January 2010). Robin Scherbatsky (Cobie Smulders) hosts a television interview program that has become popular among college students, not because they like her or her show, but because they are amused at the number of times she hesitates when speaking by saying, "but—um." They turn their amusement into a drinking game, requiring everyone to down a shot every time she utters the expression. One day several students and their teacher, Ted Mosbey (Josh Radnor), go to a bar to watch the show and play the game. Meanwhile, Mosbey has informed Scherbatsky about her constantly annoying expression and the students' response to it. In this day's interview, therefore, she deliberately repeats the phrase as often as possible to get all game participants drunk. Even though Mosbey soon catches on to her plan ("it's a trap!"), it is too late—everyone lies helpless on the floor. Accompanying this moment is a brief musical reference to *Adagio for Strings,* perhaps an allusion to wounded soldiers in *Platoon.* Bodies strewn on the barroom floor may also refer to the results of Marge Simpson's rampage (see Chapter 8): a kind of double parody. This sound-alike snippet reappears near the end of the episode to accompany these same students attending Mosbey's class the following morning—all of them, students and teacher alike—hopelessly hung over. Mosbey tells his students, "we're gonna have a low-key class this morning." Yet they have underestimated Scherbatsky, who arrives with a bullhorn, tormenting the class members with a loud amplified scolding.

ON THE SATELLITE OF LOVE

Mystery Science Theater 3000 is difficult to describe to someone who has never seen it. The human character, Mike Nelson, portrayed by Michael J. Nelson, and his robot friends, Tom Servo and Crow, are imprisoned on a space ship—the Satellite of Love—and are forced to watch "cheesy movies" but make the best of it by mocking them with caustic comments ("riffing"). They turn a sincere but stupefyingly awful film into a comic experience. It is not true parody or satire because the movie itself retains its original form. It is more like an aside in a play where a character gives the audience information that makes the previous serious remark sound funny. Three of the four episodes with references to *Adagio for Strings* are strictly verbal, as the characters comment on music in the movies: "Skydivers" (#609, 27 August 1994), "Jack Frost" (#813, July 1997), and "Prince of Space" (#816, 17 August 1997); the fourth presents *Adagio* (maybe) in a sketch preceding "Invasion of the Neptune Men" (#819, 11 October 1997).

Skydivers (1963), directed and written by terminally inept Coleman Francis, concerns a diver who plummets to his death to solemn music (someone put acid in his parachute). Crow notices people running from the scene and riffs in a stiff, stentorian tone, "and the crowd is fleeing to Samuel Barber's *Adagio for Strings,* it's just fantastic." It is not actually Barber's score, just a sound-alike, but his comment is clearly an in-joke reference, probably mocking the serious use of *Adagio* in movies.

In "Jack Frost," the American title of the Soviet film *Morozko* (1965), Ivan's head has been turned into a bear's head by a mushroom dwarf (shades of Bottom in *A Midsummer Night's Dream*) and has inadvertently frightened some women. As they flee, Mike comments: "Now it'll go into slow motion and you'll hear Barber's *Adagio for Strings* as he tears them apart." Of course, nothing like this happens.

In a similar situation the three watch the embarrassingly hopeless Japanese film *Yusei oji* [Prince of Space] (1959), in which Professor Mackin has been captured by the Phantom of a distant planet and is forced to watch a television transmission of his house back on Earth. He sees his son Johnny coming through the front door looking dejected. Accompanying him is a moment of quiet cello music (again, not *Adagio*) that Mike solemnly describes as "Samuel Barber's Adagio for Young Japanese Children." As Crow exclaimed earlier, "Oh, the Japanity!"

The series also features "host segments," short sketches implemented between scenes of the movie under consideration. Before the beginning of *Invasion of the Neptune Men* (1961), Mike realizes that he has eyelash mites. While Tom Servo plays *Adagio* on his portable keyboard, Crow recites (with a British accent):

> Though Nelson promised a quick return of the Nanite forces, the war for his eyelashes lasted well into December. Thousands were cut down defending a blasted little patch of Nelson's T-zone known as Follicle Hill.

Adagio immediately aborts when Nelson replies, "Would you guys knock it off!" He later recalled, "I played the faux or quasi-Adagio piece for that with my own two hands."[39] Yet it is not just a "sound-alike." It departs from the original piece in only small details, it is instantly recognizable, and it contributes to the general *Platoon* lampoon.

Did the *Adagio* quips in the earlier movies lead to its incorporation in this sketch? And why were there so many *Adagio* references within a few months of each other? It turns out that *Adagio* is one of Nelson's favorite pieces: "In fact, I do love the piece and a lot of Barber's works."[40] He revealed that during 1997 "I listened to a number of different recordings of it, including the original string quartet movement. We probably had 'Adagio on the brain.'"[41] One clever quip easily leads to another; Nelson confessed, "I'm not a terribly complex person."[42] Be it simple or complex, a mind like Nelson's was key to the success of *Mystery Science Theater 3000.*

REFLECTION

Why does an *Adagio* sound-alike—not the real thing—appear in these movies and television shows? Of course, royalties may have been a factor, but there may be other reasons. In most dramas the intent of the music is to underscore the action while not becoming intrusive. Because after *Platoon* this particular piece was always in danger of being recognized on its own, some film score composers wrote their own version of the Barber work to use in much the same capacity. Yet in comedies the opposite may be true: the director and score composer want the audience to associate their sound-alikes with the real thing. In *Mystery Science Theater 3000, South Park,* and *How I Met Your Mother,* they count on recognition of the original and hope that viewers will notice the discrepancies in their versions—a musical spoof within an already comic parody. On the other hand, some do not even hear the difference. In various listings of movies and television shows and in related question-answer blogs on the Internet,

[39]Michael J. Nelson, email (21 February 2006) to author.

[40]*Ibid.* "MST3K-0819–Invasion of the Neptune Men," *YouTube* (2 May 2012), posted by 4youglencoco. The entire show, original movie, and all the host segments have been posted online. Ten years after the show left the air Nelson tweeted about *Adagio*: "it's quite nice" (15 October 2009) and it "easily won an informal 'most beautiful music ever' competition at my home" (2 November 2009).

[41]*Ibid.*

[42]*Ibid.*

viewers often assume that it is the Barber composition, without questioning its authenticity. While they are aware of the dramatic parody, the musical parody completely escapes them.

ADAGIO COMES TO *SESAME STREET* AND ALMOST TO *SMALLVILLE*

While never heard on the PBS children's program *Sesame Street, Adagio for Strings* is featured on an audio-cassette *Soft and Loud* (1988), produced by the show's production team, the Children's Television Workshop. The package includes a twenty-four-page booklet featuring Bert and Ernie's discussion of everyday soft and loud sounds. *Adagio* is never mentioned here; in fact, the only music in the story comes from a parade marching by. An illustration of their room, however, shows a record player with an LP on the turntable. Might it be *Adagio*?

Smallville was the WB (later CW) television series that depicted the teen years of Clark Kent before he took on the persona of Superman. In the final episode of season three (2004), "Covenant," Lex Luthor (Michael Rosenbaum) visits his father, Lionel (John Glover) in prison:

> Lionel: Lex, please don't let me die in prison.
> Lex: Dad . . . (looking Lionel in the eye and suddenly turning cold.) This might have been more effective if you had a string quartet in the corner playing Barber's "Requiem."[43]

Barber's "Requiem"? Did Lex mean *Adagio for Strings?* Did the writers, Todd Slavkin and Darren Swimmer, have a mental lapse when they came up with that line? Or were they trying to make Lex into a pseudo-classical music buff, who occasionally gets confused? Or, more likely, do they simply think they know more about classical music than they really do? Many *Smallville* fans caught this *faux pas*. One pointed out that Lex was a good pianist and ought to know better.

Putting the Ad in *Adagio*

While *Adagio for Strings* has yet to be exploited in the United States to sell detergents or underarm deodorants (but give it time), two British newspapers have introduced a version of it in television commercials, and another company has appropriated it to sell bread. In 1999 the London

[43]Todd Slavkin and Darren Swimmer, "Act 2 Scene 1," *Episode #322–'Covenant,'* www.angelfire.com /rebellion2/smallville/3/smallville-322.htm.

Daily Telegraph played the orchestral *Adagio* in its advertisements, and a year later *The Times* employed Ferry Corsten's remix of the synthesizer version by Ørbit. It is difficult to imagine the directors of the conservative *Times* embracing this trendy version for its publicity campaign, but it likely wanted to add younger, hip readers to its subscription list. These ventures must have succeeded because in both cases record companies marketed compact discs specifically for clientele who associated Barber's music with these commercials.[44] A decade later, in 2010, a passage from *Adagio* accompanied "Burnt Offering," a thirty-second ad for Warburton's bread. In mock seriousness the music parodies all of its tragic associations. A cook has burnt an entire loaf of the company's bread. Others bakers in the kitchen look sad. One even covers over the burnt loaf with a white cloth (a bakery shroud). Another breaks down in tears, soliciting solace from the hug of a co-worker. At the end the title announced "Warburton's: We Care Because Our Name's on It," undoubtedly the bakery's advertising slogan.[45]

Less mercenary is borrowing from the Barber work for public service announcements (PSA), where profit is not the primary objective. In 1999 Tarsem Singh, producer of television commercials and promotional videos, created "Sarajevo," a PSA for the Sarajevo Olympic Children's Fund. It featured *Adagio* in scenes of Sarajevans, intercut with scenes of the 1984 Olympics and the later war, and emphasized today's rebuilding effort.[46] "Spot director" Marshall Vernet produced a PSA called "Jimmy" for the children's cancer research fund of Boston's Dana Farber Institute that blended "intimate thoughts and impressive locations."[47] In a voice-over an elderly man recalls his childhood struggle with cancer, while walking through metal stairways, industrial locations, and mesh screens, much like cathedrals. The brief presentation ends with views of young children

[44]The recording with Ormandy and the Philadelphia Orchestra is associated with the *Telegraph* and on *Unforgettable Classics-Advertisements III* (Classics for Pleasure, 1162745, 2001), but that is not necessarily the recorded performance heard in the ad. Ørbit's version from *The Times* is provided on *Classic Ads* (Universal, 4724162, 2002) and the double compact disc album *Screen Cuts* (Virgin TV, VTDCD 449, 2002).

[45]"Warburtons–Burnt Offering," *YouTube* (8 May 2011), posted by AdvertJury.

[46]"John Hancock / Sarajevo," *YouTube* (13 October 2009), posted by Ernie Schenck. A copy of the PSA is housed at the Paley Center, New York City: AT:52813.009 (1:30).

[47]Justine Elias, "Development Woes: Grooming New Directorial Talent in a Crowded Marketplace," *Shoot* (8 October 1999).

playing on city streets. According to Justine Elias, Barber's music "sets the tone for the spot."[48]

Finding a New Audience

Authors, record company executives, and others have placed *Adagio for Strings* on their lists of pieces of music to initiate the novice listener into the world of classical music. Its immediate accessibility makes it a logical candidate, and its presence in movies and other pop cultural genres gives it an advanced recognition factor.

The website *AMG 50 Greatest Hits for Newcomers* is directed by AllMusicGuide to listeners who are just becoming interested in classical music and seek advice in the purchase of their first compact discs. It is therefore different from the "popularity contest" nature of most of the lists mentioned earlier in this book. The selections are intended to represent a cross section of classical music—from orchestral to opera, from the sixteenth century to the twentieth century. Both Barber's String Quartet and *Adagio for Strings* are recommended. The AMG website introduces the listener to the differences between classical and popular music and suggests "what to listen for" in classical music as well as provides a short description of each specific item enumerated and a brief recorded excerpt from it.[49] While this might be construed as AMG's ploy to sell records, it nevertheless provides a valuable service to the rookie classical listener.

Ted Libby, a commentator on "PT Basic Record Library," a segment of NPR's *Performance Today*, has compiled *The NPR Guide to Building a Classical CD Collection,* identifying 350 "essential works" with brief annotations and a discography of suggested recordings.[50] His commentary on Barber's *Adagio* references the story of Toscanini's request for an orchestrated version of the string quartet movement (see Chapter 2, not exactly true!) and supplies details concerning the music's association with *Platoon*. Libby recommends the recordings with Schippers and Slatkin. At the back of his book are a few special categories such as a "Teenage Listeners' Classical Checklist" with representative works, like *Adagio*. Its immediate appeal to many on an emotional level makes it

[48] *Ibid.*

[49] "The AMG Guide to Classical Music for Newcomers," *AEC One Stop Group*, www.allclassical.com /newcomers.html.

[50] See Ted Libby, *The NPR Guide to Building a Classical CD Collection*, 2nd ed. (New York: Workman Publishing, 1999).

a reasonable choice. In a similar vein the organizers at Common Sense Media contrived for its "Entertainment for Kids and Families" a list of ten classical albums that young people might enjoy, hoping the pieces would represent a good introduction. Some choices, such as Prokofiev's *Peter and the Wolf* (1936), are fairly obvious, but Barber's piece, coming in at a respectable ninth place, is somewhat less expected.[51]

Soothing the Savage Breast

> Musick has Charms to sooth a savage Breast,
> To soften Rocks, or bend a knotted Oak.
>
> —William Congreve, *The Mourning Bride* (1697), Act I, scene 1.

Pronouncements similar to Congreve's about music's charming and soothing properties have been applied to Barber's *Adagio for Strings* on various occasions and in many different contexts. They range from simple situations of casual kicking-back time through induced relaxation to rigidly controlled psychological experiments.

According to writer and public broadcasting personality Fred Flaxman, to relax, to manage stress, or to recover from illness, an individual should select soothing music. Among his "soft, concrete selections" is the Adagio from the String Quartet, "one of the most beautiful, reposing, first class compositions I can think of."[52] For readers of *The Patriot Ledger* Steven Karidoyanes, the conductor of the Plymouth [Mass.] Philharmonic, named the Barber among the works of art he prescribed as "healing" classical recordings.[53] Likewise, Graham Maxey, a licensed professional counselor who perceives beautiful music as a means of "transcendence" and "holistic healing," singled out the Barber piece in this regard:

> Beautiful music has the capacity to stir something within us that has nothing to do with moving the *cilia* within our ear canals. When one listens to *Adagio for Strings* by Barber longing itself

[51]"Common Sense Media Recommended Lists–Music," *Common Sense Media* (4 May 2004), www.commonsensemedia.org/mediaguide/recommended_list_music.php.

[52]Fred Flaxman, "Surgical Selections: Music for Operations," *Compact Discoveries* (1997), www.compactdiscoveries.com/CompactDiscoveriesArticles/SurgicalSelections.html. He suggests the recording by the Manhattan String Quartet (Newport Classic, NC 600330, 1992).

[53]John Delery, "Opening Notes: Whether You Want Balm, Energy, Healing or Laughter, We've Got Tunes For You," [Quincy, Mass.] *Patriot Ledger* (14 November 2001), 14.

> has a voice that pulls on us to respond. When it is played, what is uniquely and permanently us resonates with a harmonics [*sic*] that goes deeper than sound.[54]

In his book *Dealing with Depression Naturally* Syd Baumel offered advice from a patient's perspective rather than the viewpoint of a medical professional. He attempts to provide a wide array of options for treating depressives naturally, usually without antidepressants. His chapter on music therapy begins with an unqualified declaration: "Music's ability to 'heal the soul' is the stuff of legend in every culture. In hospitals and institutions today, music is still used to lift people's moods, ease pain and tension, and break through walls of isolation."[55] For mild depression, cheerful music seems obvious, but "when depression runs deeper in the bone, music that resonates with it may be more persuasive."[56] Among several possibilities he identifies *Adagio* "to second your sadness."[57]

These ideas are not exactly new. In 1975 Mary Priestley disseminated similar views; in *Music Therapy in Action* she cited Barber's composition in two contexts. First, she recommended it for therapists to use in "ward sessions, individual sessions for listening with the therapist and discussion material projected onto the music, and for movement and relaxation sessions."[58] Second, she assigned it to her category of "relaxing music" and encouraged therapists to use it in promoting success:

> Here is an exercise for those who are seeking success in some areas of their lives but dare not think about it openly. This is limiting because the idea of success is a strongly motivating factor in its attainment. This exercise brings to the surface the inner obstacles to success. Barber's *Adagio for Strings,* with its

[54]Graham Maxey, "Longing: The Lure of the Transcendent," *Seasons of the Soul: The Repeating Stages of Life's Inner Journey* [unpublished book]; reprinted www.ehealingtree.com/activecolumns/holistichealing.htm.

[55]Syd Baumel, *Dealing with Depression Naturally*, 1st ed. (New Canaan, Conn.: Keats Publishing, 1995), 244.

[56]*Ibid.*, 244.

[57]*Ibid.*

[58]Mary Priestley, *Music Therapy in Action* (New York: St. Martin's Press, 1975), 49.

> long, slow string tune rising to one magnificent climax, is the most suitable music I have found.[59]

Yet this is not the view of all therapists. This particular music may not be the best treatment across the board because of its intensive emotional profile. For instance, therapist Kathy Irvine Lorenzato described one highly problematical situation:

> When the ontologist asks you to provide directed imagery / relaxation techniques for the highly stressed parents of a child newly diagnosed with cancer, do not use Barber's *Adagio for Strings* for background music. Although it is a truly beautiful piece, it is also the world's saddest piece of music. You might think that using the world's saddest music would "match the parents' mood," but actually it would probably increase their grief a hundredfold, which would not be the ideal response. Be very careful when working with this population. Do not make the situation worse than it already is.[60]

The quandary—"to *Adagio* or not to *Adagio*"—is best left up to the experts.

The record of Barber's *Adagio* as a catalyst for behavior modification has been extended beyond the realm of scientific inquiry and into crime prevention and related social issues. When the Forest Hills subway stop near Boston was a scene of "rambunctious teenagers," Bill Fleming, chief of the area's transit police, decided on a musical tactic. He thought that, if he played loud classical music, students might board trains sooner or at least stop loitering in the station. It seemed to work. There were no fights or arrests at Forrest Hills. He had cops, kids, and patrons smiling. "Maybe they're laughing at me. As long as they're laughing at me, they're not fighting. So I consider it a victory."[61]

Although *Adagio for Strings* is a far cry from "loud classical" music, it was employed in this experiment. While teenagers did not seem to appreciate it, many older patrons did. One woman found the music

[59] *Ibid.*, 255.

[60] Kathy Irvine Lorenzato, *Filling a Need While Making Some Noise: A Music Therapist's Guide to Pediatrics* (London: Jessica Kingsley Publishers, 2005), 124.

[61] Bill Fleming, quoted in Jason Beaubien, "Profile: Using Classical Music to Help Deter Teen-agers from Causing Trouble at Boston Subway Stations," [NPR] *Weekend Edition* (22 September 2002).

"soothing," a good way "to expose teenagers to something other than rap and hip-hop. . . . They're so used to bump, bumpidty, bumpidty, bump, bump, bump. It's nice to hear Beethoven and Chopin and sonatas and put some opera on there too. It's nice."[62] Chief Fleming announced plans to expand this operation to other stations.

Hospital emergency rooms often tend to get overcrowded, and many patients are forced to wait for hours. For years such delays have been tolerated, but one "itinerant emergency physician," Vincent Hanlon, has come up with a possible solution. He has suggested that, in addition to physical sedation for the patients' ailments, "conscious sedation" could be achieved by piping in music, either popular or classical. "I'm not thinking here of intravenous medication but rather intra aural sound, in the form of Samuel Barber's *Adagio for Strings* or Jesse Cook's *Vertigo* CD. Could music in the treatment rooms help to humanize our windowless big box emergency departments?"[63]

Robert Sewak, a clinical practitioner of what is known as "guided imagery," believes that there is a profound relationship between music and the human being, that one must focus when under stress, and that help is often necessary. Columnist Matt Reed experienced a demonstration of these principles when Sewak subjected him to a "visualization exercise" while listening to a recording of *Adagio*. According to Reed, the music "triggers an emotional connection with your mental picture, the way a music score adds drama to a movie scene."[64] He recalled Sewak's instructions:

> Picture the list of all the things you have to do today [pause] now imagine doing the one thing you need to do first . . . now you're holding a mound of cool, wet clay [pause] you're sculpting it, spinning it [pause] and it begins to form a vessel [pause] now you take all the other things on your list [pause] you place them in the vessel [pause] you close the clay over those other things [pause] and you set the clay aside.[65]

[62] *Ibid. Adagio* is mentioned in this segment but there is no sound bite.

[63] Vincent Hanlon, "Humour and Humanity: Music in My ERs," *Canadian Journal of Emergency Medicine* IV/5 (September 2002), 369; reprinted www.cjem-online.ca/sites/default/files/pg369(1).pdf.

[64] Matt Reed, "New Age Music Therapy Might Be the Ultimate Tune-up," *Cox News Service* (1999); reprinted www.healthy.net/library/newsletters/update/musictherapy.htm.

[65] *Ibid.*

When the music ends, the "patient" feels relaxed and focused. He or she has just experienced guided imagery.[66]

Another provocative illustration of *Adagio* as a behavioral treatment occurred in a Maryland prison setting. Five mornings a week fitness trainer B. Good [*sic*!] subjected inmates to a rigorous Navy Seal workout, part of a new wellness program designed to strengthen minds and bodies at the Anne Arundel County Detention Center. The subsequent class each day with counselor Jerry Januszewski began with all participants standing with eyes closed, listening to Barber's Agnus Dei, and taking deep breaths. According to Januszewski, this experience validated his belief that hope and possibility can spring up anywhere.[67]

Experimenting in the Classroom and in the Laboratory

A PBS series for public schools, *TeacherSource*, presents ideas and lesson plans for levels from kindergarten to twelfth grade. One program, "Arts Everywhere," suggests activities that coordinate music and color. In "The Colors in Music," for grades 3-5, students are asked to bring to class recorded music that they think will illustrate or induce the six basic emotions: happy, sad, funny, angry, scared, and sleepy. As students listen to the music, they are asked to describe the emotions they experience. "Some students will differ in their opinions and the class can discuss why it's okay for different people to feel different things when listening to music." In the guidelines *Adagio for Strings* is suggested for the sad piece.[68]

For a similar purpose the International Reading Association published a book devoted to lesson plans for writing activities for use by middle school and language arts (English) teachers and called special attention to "unconventional strategies, competitive games, art and multimedia."[69] In a chapter titled "Adagio" Lawrence Baines, one of the book's editors, presents an activity with the objective to help students "learn to attach

[66]*Ibid. Adagio* may be only one of several pieces of music that Sewak uses for such therapy sessions.

[67]Darragh Johnson, "Discipline's Newest Disciples; Inmates Lament Canceling of Self-Improvement Program," *Washington Post* (12 June 2003), T: 10. The detention center, based in Annapolis, Md., ended the program in June 2003.

[68]Jan Madden, "2. The Colors in Music," *TeacherSource* (September 2003), www.pbs.org/teachersource /thismonth/sept03/index1.shtm.

[69]Lawrence Baines and Anthony J. Kunkel, *Going Bohemian: Activities That Engage Adolescents in the Art of Writing Well* (Newark, Del.: International Reading Association, 2001), 3-4.

images and words to music."[70] After distributing writing and drawing materials, the teacher is instructed to play Barber's *Adagio for Strings.* The students are then asked to write down four to seven images "that the music evokes in their minds" and to create one drawing that "reflects the nature of the music."[71] They are then to show their work to their classmates and discuss it. In the book is provided one such drawing, the center of which is a Hindu symbol for life. Among other results were "the death of a lover" and an "emotional goodbye between 2 friends."[72] To conclude this activity, the teacher shows the first few minutes of the movie *Platoon,* which, of course, features the music. In his experience with this activity Baines observed that "inevitably, a student will have drawn or written about one of the images that [director] Stone devised for the screen."[73] Presumably the Barber example is intended as a model for this activity; other pieces of music may be added to or substituted for it.

In his interesting and controversial book *The Mozart Effect* Don G. Campbell proposes the concept that music—particularly Mozart's—is not only pleasant to listen to but can also enhance and stimulate the learning process.[74] In the chapter "Beyond Amadeus" he outlines what such music could accomplish. By 2005 he had devised an audio library for health care facilities with various categories; he suggested listening to *Adagio for Strings* to ease hypertension. This might be called "the Barber Effect." Researchers at the Windhill School in Mexborough, South York, United Kingdom, tried out some of these ideas in a modified form and found that pupils subjected to background music, whether as a part of lessons or during break times, performed ten percent better than those who were not. "Chopin and Brahms were for assemblies, Beethoven was used as a calming influence, and when pupils are allotted time to sit and think alone, they can listen to Barber's *Adagio for Strings."*[75] Did Chopin and Brahms quiet the students? The exact music of Beethoven must have been carefully selected! Pop music accompanied more active moments.

[70]*Ibid.*

[71]*Ibid.*

[72]*Ibid.*

[73]*Ibid.*

[74]See Don G. Campbell, *The Mozart Effect* (New York: Avon Books, 1997).

[75]*Ibid.*

As a ten-year-old student put it, "Pop gees us up, classical calms us down. Music is better when you are moving and gets you to walk instead of run."[76]

Barber's music might also be useful as a calming effect after physical education classes. After making various recommendations for dance classes, author Pauline Wetton suggested it as part of a "cool-down" to prepare students for re-entry into the classroom:

> Teachers could play a piece of recorded music to calm the children, for example, "Adagio for Strings" (Samuel Barber), and ask them to sit down and listen carefully to the music. Teachers could encourage the children to stretch their arms slowly and smoothly as the music plays, then to move their upper bodies as they move their arms.[77]

This "cool-down" is, indeed, the opposite of a warm-up.

In his classroom Hiram Harrington, a teacher at the Woodland School in East Hartford, Connecticut, puts *Adagio* to good use after lunchtime. This school is part of a Transitional Education Program (TEP) for students who "suffer behavioral problems" and who would "wreak havoc" at regular schools. He does not necessarily coordinate the recording with physical activities as Wetton suggests but lets the music accomplish its calming effect on its own. It is one of several classical pieces he plays because he feels "the kids get too much rap at home."[78]

A favorite type of educational experience for young musicians is the music camp. Several years ago one of my students was a counselor and teacher at the Blue Lake Fine Arts Camp in Twin Lakes, Michigan. She told me of two incidents that took place during a performance of *Adagio for Strings* by the advanced string orchestra (directed by Fritz Stansell). She had asked the students to think about how they felt when they heard the work. Afterwards, a seventh-grade boy confessed that he had started thinking about the time when a certain girl did not like him. But a more

[76]Gabrielle Axe, quoted in Paul Stokes, "Mozart 'Makes Maths Easier,'" *Telegraph* (19 October 2002); reprinted www.telegraph.co.uk/education/main.jhtml?xml=education/2002/10/25/tenmoz19.xml.

[77]Pauline Wetton, *Physical Education in the Early Years* (New York: Routledge, 1997), 131.

[78]Hiram Harrington, quoted in Michael Downs, *House of Good Hope: A Promise for a Broken City* (Lincoln: University of Nebraska Press, 2007), 234.

memorable reaction was the fact that during the performance itself a fifth grader began to sob quite audibly. My student took him aside, so as not to disturb the rest of the audience and asked him why he was crying. He replied that the music made him think of his horse and his dog. She later learned that both of these pets had to be "put to sleep." These events had happened several years earlier, but Barber's music brought them back to the child's conscious mind.[79]

In addition, *Adagio for Strings* has been considered in several clinical studies that test human sadness and depression. In 1993, when Ruby A. Engel conducted an experiment addressing induced depression, she concluded that this piece rated significantly more "sadness-inducing" than Prokofiev's "Russia under the Mongolian Yoke" from *Alexander Nevsky* (1938).[80] (I am not sure if other pieces of music were also rated.) Four other psychologists also used the work in their study of depression, in which fifteen participants were induced to a "sad mood state."[81] In one procedure they were required to read, slowly to themselves, ten "self-referent sentences" such as "I think life is empty and meaningless," or "only bad things happen to me."[82] While they listened to the music, they were asked to pay attention to their emotions and contemplate sentences as though they referred to them specifically. The result: the induction procedure effectively altered the participants' mood in the expected direction. According to these investigators, "the change in the subjective appraisal of their sad mood, measured by means of a visual analogical scale ranging from 0 to 100, was above 15%."[83]

While classical music may stimulate the physical senses, it can also stimulate the "pleasure center" of the brain. Researchers at McGill University, led by Robert J. Zatorre, asked ten students with advanced musical training to identify a composition that elicited the pleasurable experience of "chills" or "shivers down the spine." Each subject selected

[79]Carter Shepherd, conversation (2003) with the author. Shepherd is a former Butler student and Twin Lakes counselor.

[80]See Ruby Ackermann Engel, *Cognitive Vulnerability to Depression and the Mood-State Hypothesis* (Ph.D. dissertation, University of Pennsylvania, 1993).

[81]Myriam Gallardo Pérez, Amparo Belloch Fuster, Rosa Ma Baños Rivera, and Ma Ángeles Ruipérez Rodríguez, "Attentional Biases and Vulnerability to Depression," *The Spanish Journal of Psychology* II/1 (1999), 14.

[82]*Ibid.*

[83]*Ibid.*

a piece that "consistently elicited intensely pleasant emotional responses"; one chose *Adagio for Strings*.[84] While the subjects were listening to their choices, researchers recorded "neural firing, cranial blood flow, heart rate, EMG, respiration and skin temperature . . . sure enough, chills tingled down the students' spines as they heard their favorite choices. Their other vital signs spiked upward during 77 percent of the scans."[85] Zatorre concluded:

> We have shown that music recruits systems of reward and emotion similar to those known to respond specifically to biologically relevant stimuli, such as food and sex, and those artificially activated by drugs of abuse. This is quite remarkable, because music is neither strictly necessary for biological survival or reproduction, nor is it a pharmacological substance.[86]

In the introductory chapter of this book I called attention to how many people get "goose bumps" while listening to *Adagio*. Scientists have now explained the reason for that phenomenon.

If *homo sapiens* can respond to the Barber composition, then how about other primates? In a 2009 experiment headed by Chuck Snowdon, psychologist at the University of Wisconsin-Madison, researchers played several pieces of music for a group of tamarin monkeys that had never heard music before. An observer recorded their behavior for five minutes before and after playing each selection. The monkeys did not respond at all to Barber but became slightly calmer after listening to Metallica's "Of Wolf and Man" (1991).[87] Would Charles Darwin be pleased or disappointed?

[84]Anne J. Blood and Robert J. Zatorre, "Intensely Pleasurable Responses to Music Correlate with Activity in Brain Regions Implicated in Reward and Emotion," *Proceedings of the National Academy of Sciences of the United States of America* XCVIII/20 (25 September 2001); reprinted www.pubmedcentral .nih.gov/articlerender.fcgi?artid=58814.

[85]Paul McKay, "Music and the Brain," *Ottawa Citizen* (18 November 2002); reprinted www.dovesong. com/positive_music/archives/basement/MusicandtheBrain.asp.

[86]Anne J. Blood and Robert J. Zatorre, "Intensely Pleasurable Responses to Music"; reprinted www.pubmedcentral.nih.gov/articlerender.fcgi?artid=58814.

[87]Hadley Leggett, "Monkeys Don't Go for Music–Unless It's Made for Them," *Wired Science* (1 September 2009; reprinted www.wired.com/wiredscience/2009/09/monkeymusic. *The Black Album*, perf. Metallica (Elektra, 61113, 1991).

Infiltrating Daily Lives

In addition to all the appearances of *Adagio* in performances, books, films, and popular music, it has also intruded into many other aspects of daily lives. It often turns up at a time or a place where it is least expected.

WITH THIS RING (AND *ADAGIO*) I THEE WED

Despite its numerous associations with death and tragedy, *Adagio for Strings,* for many, has a romantic outlook. As a result, it has been featured on record albums of music suitable for quiet romantic evenings, such as *Classic Love*.[88] It has also been marketed for wedding ceremonies as in *The Complete Wedding Album*, which designates it among pieces suitable for music during the ceremony, *e.g.*, prelude or processional. The album comes with a booklet designed as a reference for brides offering detailed advice on planning the event and selecting the music.[89] Agnus Dei is also deemed suitable for weddings as on the recording on *Wedding Classics*[90] with David Hill and the Winchester Choir. If playing a compact disc at a wedding is not acceptable, then a pianist could play Lawrence Rosen's arrangement of *Adagio* from the Schirmer *Piano Album of Wedding Classics,*[91] or an organist could play the Strickland arrangement.

Adagio has been played at various wedding ceremonies across the country. The following documented situations illustrate *Adagio*'s versatile nature. Tirzah Firestone, a Jewish renewal rabbi and Jungian psychotherapist, related that it was the processional at her inter-faith wedding ceremony to gentile Evan:

> Our wedding began with the casting of a sacred circle around the room, using water, incense, and flower petals. Then Evan's family walked proudly down the aisle. Evan and I followed, arm in arm, accompanied by Samuel Barber's *Adagio for Strings*. We had

[88] *Classic Love*, perf. Monte Carlo Philharmonic Orchestra, cond. Lawrence Foster (Teldec, 15008, 1996). *Adagio* is Track 11 on disc two.

[89] "The Wedding Album," *Telarc*, www.telarc.com/gscripts/title.asp?gsku=0490. *The Complete Wedding Album*, perf. Cincinatti Pops Orchestra, cond. Erich Kunzel (Telarc, 80490-25, 1998). *Adagio* is Track 12 on disc two.

[90] *Wedding Classics* (EMI, 2002). Agnus Dei is Track 10.

[91] *Piano Album of Wedding Classics* (New York: G. Schirmer, 2004). [HL.50482656]

> chosen this unconventional entry to make up for the fact that no parents were there to "give me away."[92]

Firestone, moreover, confessed that, except for one sister, her family had boycotted the wedding

> to show their disdain for my choice of husband. . . . I learned first hand [*sic*] that whether or not you are a religious person, interfaith marriage presents an ongoing challenge in remaining true to your individual self and roots while simultaneously learning to build the bridges of tolerance and understanding.[93]

Two other nuptial ceremonies with the Barber work were more public spectacles: the wedding of Lynda Bird Johnson, daughter of the President of the United States, to Marine Captain Charles Robb on 9 December 1967 and the June 2003 marriage of Miss America 2002, Katie Harman, to Tim Ebner. A critic described Lynda Bird's descent down the White House staircase on the arm of LBJ:

> The 32-man chamber orchestra of the U.S. Marine Band, its scarlet tunics reflected in the Waterford chandeliers pendent from the 20-foot ceiling, played Bach's *Arioso* and Barber's *Adagio for Strings,* as Yuki, the president's favorite mongrel, trotted outside in new red booties and a matching jacket inscribed "congratulations."[94]

While Barber's music was merely a prelude to this occasion at the White House (the ubiquitous Bridal Chorus from Wagner's *Lohengrin* was the actual processional), it was more significant at the Miss America wedding. What made this event so public was its telecast on the TLC (The Learning Channel) program, *A Wedding Story,* a documentary that featured, in addition to the ceremony itself, discussions by the couple about how they met and when they realized they were in love. During the ceremony at the First Baptist Church in Portland, Oregon, a string quartet played the

[92]Tirzah Firestone, *With Roots in Heaven: One Woman's Passionate Journey into the Heart of Her Faith* (New York: Dutton, 1998); reprinted "Thoughts on My Interfaith Wedding," www.interfaithfamily.com/article/issue7/firestone/phtml.

[93]*Ibid.*

[94]"Captains Courageous," *Time* XC/24 (15 December 1967), 29.

Adagio movement from Barber's quartet as Harman walked down the aisle. Perhaps because she was a former Miss America, the decor took on patriotic colors: the bridal party all wore red, white, and blue (the bride herself, presumably in white). Afterwards the guests threw red, white, and blue paper airplanes rather than the more traditional rice.[95]

Illustration 11.2. The Wedding of Lynda Bird Johnson and Captain Charles Robb, East Room, The White House, Washington, D.C., 9 December 1967

Courtesy of the Lyndon Baines Johnson Library and Museum Photo C7882-22A

Image by Yoichi R. Okamoto

[95]Kara Briggs, "A Heartfelt Marriage Ceremony Unites Katie Harman and Capt. Tim Ebner," *The* [Portland] *Oregonian* (16 June 2003); reprinted (26 June 2003) www.genforum.genealogy.com/ebner /messages/152.html.

One of the most unusual weddings with Barber's *Adagio* was that of Abby and Jeff Robbins, practitioners of a variety of exercise programs known as "gymcraftics," described as "a multi dimensional process devoted to helping individuals discover and explore interest in learning and potential within."[96] They expressed their marriage vows while performing such movements to the accompaniment of Barber's music.[97]

Because *Adagio* is associated with death and other dire circumstances, not all participants consider it appropriate for a wedding ceremony. What if only the groom wants it? In his autobiography *Spiritual Perversion* Steve Sanchez recounts the incident surrounding the selection of music for his wedding to fiancée Amanda. When he told the assistant pastor that he wanted Barber's *Adagio,* she was taken aback and told him, "Steve, I don't think you want to use that." The conversation continued:

> I was completely surprised. "Why not?"
>
> "It's depressing. It's not a wedding song. It's like a funeral march."
>
> "It's not that depressing. It may be solemn, but it's moving and beautiful. I love it. I think it is appropriate."
>
> She fixed me with a disapproving look like I was crazy. "I don't think so, Steve, I'm going to check with Amanda."
>
> The song was nixed.[98]

How many weddings almost included *Adagio*, but other, perhaps, saner views prevailed?

If the orchestral work has too many sad associations to be played during the wedding ceremony itself, then why not a trance version at the reception? A posting on *MySpace* documents such an occasion, beginning with the question, "what do you get when two fans of Tiësto

[96]Abby and Jeff Robbins, "Gymcraftics," *Gymcraftics*, www.gymcraftics.com/Pages/Gymcraftics.html. The site has photographs from the stage routine spanning six decades.

[97]Abby and Jeff Robbins, "Background," *Gymcraftics*, www.gymcraftics.com/Pages/Background.html.

[98]Steve Sanchez, *Spiritual Perversion* (Austin, Tex.: TurnKey, 2005), 142.

get married?" While guests awaited the arrival of the bridal couple, someone (probably the best man) announced, "I need you to get your hands clapping with the beat right now. . . . It gives me great pleasure to introduce to you for the very first time as husband and wife . . . Mr. and Mrs. Mark and Michelle Francisco."[99] They entered to the strains of Tiësto's remix, moved gracefully under the arch of up-stretched arms by the wedding party and started the bridal dance. It looks like a good time was had by all.

MANY A TEAR HAS FALLEN: "BUT IT'S ALL IN THE GAME"[100]

Crossword puzzles are an old-fashioned game for one person, the television show *Jeopardy* is a more modern game for three, but with an audience informally playing along, and *Homeworld* is designed for a whole new generation of computer gamers. *Adagio for Strings* plays at least a minor role in all three.

Adagio for Strings can be found in several crossword puzzles. The clue in *The New York Times* on 5 August 2008 is a no-brainer; for 9-down, simply fill in the blank: "Samuel Barber's _____ for Strings." In two other puzzles the answer is almost as easy, requiring a response to "Adagio for Strings composer."[101] The answer, however, in Arthur S. Verdesca's Puzzle No. 66, entitled "Composerendipity," in *Simon and Schuster's Crossword Treasury #42* requires more contemplation.[102] The clue for 101-across is truly thought-provoking: "Mad about 'Adagio for Strings.'" (I would not dream of giving away the answer.)

The title, *Adagio for Strings*, has appeared three times on the long-running game show *Jeopardy*. On 25 June 2007 champion Matt Corcoran uncovered a Daily Double for which host Alex Trebek read the answer: "The horn players took a break on November 5, 1938 when the NBC Symphony premièred Samuel Barber's 'Adagio for' these." The astute and

[99]Mark and Michelle Francisco, "Wedding of Two Tiesto Fans," *MySpace* (19 November 2007), www.myspace.com/video/marknmichele/wedding-of-two-tiesto-fans/20366506.

[100]This is a reference to the lyrics and title of the 1958 hit song "It's All in the Game" by Tommy Edwards (1922-1969). See "It's All in the Game–Tommy Edwards," *YouTube* (3 October 2011), posted by maumau1968.

[101]The clue is 48-across for Kenneth Haxton's puzzle No. 35, "Arts and Crafts" in *Simon and Schuster Crossword Treasury #42* (New York: Touchstone, 2005) and 89-across in *Simon and Schuster Mega Crossword Puzzles.*

[102]See Arthur S. Verdesca, *Crossword Treasury #42*, ed. Eugene T. Maleska (New York: Simon and Schuster, 2003).

musically discerning young man correctly questioned: "What are strings?" He went on to retain his championship. Then nearly three years later, on 13 April 2010, the writers presented the opposite answer, "______ for Strings" in the category Musical Tempos. An equally discerning young man, Arthur Christy, responded with the correct tempo. He also went on to win the game. Less than a year later, on 29 October 2010, the famed *Adagio* again figured into the game under the category Chamber Music dealing with Toscanini's première, although erroneously attributing to him the request for Barber's orchestral work. "Who was Samuel Barber" was the correct response this time, questioned correctly by Marie Braden, who dethroned the current champion. It seems that contestants familiar with *Adagio for Strings* are winners—lovers of the work undoubtedly would agree! Surely these three occurrences have exhausted the game show possibilities inherent in Barber and his most famous composition, but one never knows. (I wonder if Alex Trebek likes the work. He does have a say in the answer-question format.)

It is of relatively minor importance for the name Barber or the title of *Adagio for Strings* to appear in a word game. Far more significant is for the music itself to play a considerable role in a computer game. *Homeworld* by Sierra Studios is a Real Time Strategy (RTS) game in which a player can control a variety of functions. One reviewer claimed that music is used effectively in the game, "from bellicose battle music to the somber strains" of Barber's *Adagio,* "which adds a very appropriate air of grandeur to the large-scale proceedings."[103] Actually, it is the composer's Agnus Dei that is heard, recorded especially for the game by The Quire of Voyces, a choral group at Santa Barbara City College. Due to the fact that the choir had only twenty or so members, the sound for Agnus Dei was enhanced electronically. According to conductor Nathan J. Krietzer, "in order to achieve the rich sonority called for by the heart-on-the-sleeve Romanticism of the piece, they recorded three line overdubs of the piece to transform the Quire of Voyces into a sixty-voice choral orchestra."[104]

How does Barber's music contribute to the story? Sixty years after discovering an ancient starship beneath the desert sand, the inhabitants of the planet Kharak have completed building a new mothership to return

[103]Ray Ivey, "Homeworld," *Just Adventure*, www.justadventure.com/reviews/Homeworld/Homeworld.shtm.

[104]Nathan J. Krietzer, quoted in Temmo Korisheli, liner notes to *Illuminations*, perf. The Quire of Voices, cond. Nathan J. Kreitzer (Vanity, 1999); reprinted www.sevensouth.com/recordshop/QuireofV/01.php. See "Paul Ruskay–Homeworld," *YouTube* (25 July 2011), posted by ketinadrealista.

600,000 chosen citizens to their home planet, Hiigara. At the beginning of the game Agnus Dei is sung as the ship goes through launch preparations, conveying an appropriate sense of hope and expectation: "all systems green."[105] The music reaches its climax when fleet commander Karan S'jet announces, "the mother ship has cleared the scaffold—we are away!"[106] Throughout this sequence the image of the ship and its launch system move about on the screen in a three-dimensional interface, a spectacular graphics achievement for a game of this era. The joyful mood changes, however, during the third mission of the game, when the mothership returns to Kharak only to discover its fiery destruction at the hands of mercenaries in the Taiidan empire; Agnus Dei now takes on a tragic tone: "no one's left [pause] everything's gone [pause] Kharak is burning!"[107] Agnus Dei reappears near the end of the game, when "the galactic council recognized our claim to this world. The sacrifice of thousands has left a trail of destruction behind us, like a path across the galaxy to Hiigara, our homeworld."[108] Thus, Barber's music is able to reinforce several moods throughout the game: exhilaration at the original launch, sadness at the planet's destruction, and hope at the end, paving the way for the sequel *Homeworld 2*. The music continues as S'jet, "no longer fleet command, insisted that she would be the last person to disembark [from the landing vehicle] and set foot on the Homeworld."[109]

The inclusion of Barber's music in the game pleasantly surprised so many players that Internet chatrooms were filled with questions and answers about it. Some bloggers recognized it from *Platoon* but were confused by the choral sound. One person might ask about it, and another might answer, "I think it is Barber's *Adagio,* except that it is choral rather than instrumental." Yet another, with more musical background, might set both of them straight with accurate information about Barber's choral transcription. One blogger even referred to it as "a vocal cover of the

[105]YessMassterHG, "Homeworld Script," *Game FAQs* (8 January 2006), www.gamefaqs.com/pc/141615-homeworld/faqs/40853.

[106]*Ibid.*

[107]*Ibid.*

[108]*Ibid.*

[109]*Ibid.* Many of the scenes in which Agnus Dei appears have been uploaded by users on *YouTube*. One of the best examples is "Homeworld Intro Cutscene + Mothership Launch," *YouTube* (22 November 2006), posted by CrimsonInquisitor. The Agnus Dei portion begins at 2:50.

song," an ostensibly inappropriate term derived from pop music lingo, but actually not a bad description.

There was universal praise not only for the music's beautiful sound but also for its effectiveness. Paul Ruskay was recognized at *Gaming Globes 2000* with an award for the best score in a video game (presumably Agnus Dei was taken into account).[110] Two fans commented enthusiastically about how it enhanced the game:

> Being a person who played the game to the end a few times, I can tell you that the music definitely works in the given setting. It is very awe-inspiring, and combines well with the endless space surrounding you, creating an awesome atmosphere. It also fits the storyline nicely and completely immerses the player into the game.[111]

> It just blew me away man, just blew me away, it was the saddest piece of music I had ever heard, juxtaposed against the backstory, it was all I could do to blink back the tears. . . . The many ways in which this piece of music was used is a testament to the raw emotion it invokes in anyone who listens to it.[112]

While a falling tear does not necessarily apply to crossword puzzles or to a television game show, this enthusiast proves that it often does relate to *Homeworld*, especially for the users who immerse themselves in it.

An unexpected result from the release of *Homeworld* is that it has unleashed a form of *Adagio* onto an almost entirely new audience. Video game players are often a whole world to themselves, not necessarily the same as classical music lovers or film buffs. It is interesting to hear how some of them refer to the music; just as film fans think of *Adagio* as "the theme from *Platoon*," gamers now think of Agnus Dei as the "theme from *Homeworld*," often oblivious to either its concert hall form, its use in movies, or pop arrangements, as demonstrated in the following comment:

[110]Gestalt, "Gaming Globes 2000 Results," *EuroGamer* (5 April 2000), www.eurogamer.net/articles /gg2000_2. This is similar to the Grammy Awards, but with less longevity and catered to the video game industry.

[111]Kosta, email (4 December 2004) to the author. The special Game of the Year Edition includes a compact disc of the soundtrack, with a complete performance of Agnus Dei.

[112]First Born Egg, "Homeworlds," *Chickens Run Free* (26 April 2005), www.chickensrunfree.blogspot.com/2005/04/homeworlds.html.

> I just saw the movie *Simone* on HBO, and the opening theme music was the opening theme music for the RTS game, *Homeworld.* The person who did the music on the movie wasn't the same guy who did *Homeworld,* so maybe it's a clue that the production crew played the game a few times.[113]

Another blogger believed that Diddy used the *Homeworld* opening choral music for "I'll Be Missing You," in his "United We Stand Concert," which he described as "very fitting with the theme of Homeworld and what happened in America."[114] What convoluted thinking! Because this game was obviously the only experience these two had with Agnus Dei, one concluded that the movie producers heard it in the game and got the idea to use it in the film while the other was convinced that Diddy borrowed the music for his song directly from the game.

When *Homeworld 2* was issued in 2003, instead of repeating Agnus Dei, the producers decided on all original music, but many fans of the first game were disappointed that Barber's music was not repeated in the sequel. One gamer devised his own compromise by taking scenes from *Homeworld 2* and producing a music video for *YouTube* with Agnus Dei as the soundtrack.[115] Less successful, however, is a video produced with scenes from the second game but using the Corsten remix, the sound and ambiance of which clearly go against the concept of Barber's music in the original game.[116]

ADAGIO FOR THE COMPUTER GENERATION: RINGTONES, SCREENSAVERS, JESUS'S IPOD, AND ELECTRONIC GREETING CARDS

Many companies have devised lists of ringtones for cell phones that offer excerpts from *Adagio for Strings,* such as the orchestral version by Academy of St. Martin in the Fields and the Agnus Dei by The Sixteen, both from thumbplay.com. Others range from a simple, mechanical

[113]Codezilla, "S1m0ne Production Crew Plays Homeworld?" *GameDev.net* (30 November 2003), www.gamedev.net/profile/profile.asp?id=50026.

[114]Cammer, "Homeworld Opening Music in United We Stand Concert," *Relic News* (21 October 2001), www.forums.relicnews.com/showthread.php?t=441.

[115]"Homeworld 2 Music Video," *YouTube* (23 August 2006), posted by YessMasster.

[116]"Homeworld 2–(Barbers Adagio for Strings remix)," *YouTube* (1 May 2010), posted by MrSquishy01.

synthesizer melody to full harmonic treatments, including those by Ørbit, Tiësto, and The Skip Raiders. Pixmania.com presents the first few seconds of Tiësto's version intact while Esato has several available renderings in "Moodies" formats: Aggressive, Musical, Romantic, Happy, as well as the original. Some company websites offer previews of the ringtones available for purchase.[117] The Protone Company, for example, encourages the customer to "put an air of classical romance back into your phone" with Barber's *Adagio for Strings*.[118] The artistic quality of various ringtones varies a great deal from one to another. In some instances, the result may emulate a Tiësto-like trance sound but foist on the caller an almost unrecognizable version of Barber's melody. Due to the development of smartphones with video capabilities, some companies offering ringtones have offered video clips in the ongoing effort to entice the consumer. For instance, the "tiësto official" site provides a full-color twenty-five second concert video featuring the deejay's remix.[119]

Several screensavers with *Adagio* are available for the computer, such as the one by La Girffa called "Orange." The ad reads: "intricate mosaic patterns and soothing sounds from Samuel Barber's *Adagio for Strings* makes your desktop a beautiful, peaceful place. Full theme elements are included, and the screensaver is available separately" —in case the purchaser does not want to bother with the music.[120]

In his newspaper column Mark Morford posed the fascinating if irreverent question: what kind of music would Jesus have on his iPod, if he were to own such a device. He maintained that "life is, after all, one giant divine iTunes Party Mix, and that Jesus is nothing if not one of the great . . . mystical DJs of the known universe."[121] He pondered over "what a revelation it would be . . . to see the holy playlists, get an idea of what the savior listens to when he's dancing, or working out, or building a new deck for Mary."[122] He reasoned that, because Jesus was an "agitator, a devoted pacifist[,] and a badassed egalitarian," his iPod would shuffle not

[117]*Esato*, www.esato.com.

[118]"Buy Ringtones: Top Quality Orchestral, Film & TV Polyphonic Ringtones by Protones" (9 December 2004), www.protones.net/home.php.

[119]"Tiësto's Official Mobile Portal–Videos" (28 February 2009), www.tiesto.wapfly.com/videos.html.

[120]*Screen Magnifier Homepage*, www.magnifiers.subportal.com.

[121]Mark Morford, "What's On Jesus' iPod?," *San Francisco Gate* (27 April 2005).

[122]*Ibid.*

only protest songs but gospel songs and classical pieces. "Thusly, there are lots and lots of songs about unity and peace and the shared human experience on the sacred iPod (which is why Jesus is all about the eternal bliss of file sharing)."[123] Morford asked his readers to submit possible titles and comments, many of which he printed a week later. One individual (Tyler M) placed Barber's *Adagio* on his list, contending that, because Jesus was a "supernatural being," he would have something "serious in his personal rotation."[124] Such postmodern secular speculations have probably never entered the minds of Billy Graham or Pat Robertson.

These days it is easy to create personal greeting cards on the Internet. One company, Cards By Mouse, gives a step-by-step process to create a card, with a selection of background images (*e.g.*, scenes from nature or "Old Ted & Edward Bear"), a heading, and a musical attachment, with *Adagio for Strings* as one of the choices.[125] AngelWinks Heavenly Post Card Shoppe presents these same options plus the choice of a "small poem."[126] *Adagio* is likewise a musical suggestion for a "Multimedia Holy Card."[127] Visual possibilities range from "Pentecost" and "The Last Supper" to several nativity scenes, notably paintings by Tintoretto, Botticelli, and Le Brun.

Postscript: A Touch of Class or a Profound Meaning?

What has all this pop culture exposure done to *Adagio for Strings*, or should I say to its "integrity?" Does it glorify the work or cheapen it, or does the Barber original withstand all this bombardment? Critic Dan Cairns has expressed a somewhat cynical outlook:

> It is exalted, but not as a piece of music that lives and breathes and evokes entirely within its own 9-minute parameter and entirely as a result of its shimmering, yearning, ascending strings. No, it is exalted by ad agencies or pop stars or artists or film directors as a

[123] *Ibid.*

[124] Mark Morford, "What's On Jesus' iPod? Pt. II," *San Francisco Gate* (4 May 2005).

[125] *Cards by Mouse*, www.mouse.webby.com/.

[126] "Angel Card of the Day," *AngelWinks Heavenly Post Card Shoppe*, www.angelwinks.net/pod.html.

[127] *Multimedia Card*, www.oempcworld.com/.

> touch of class, a bit of posh to add luster and depth to whatever product or vehicle or message it is that they're trying to push.[128]

At the conclusion of his study of *Adagio*'s popular reception Luke Howard maintains that:

> A defining feature of the *Adagio*'s reception history is that crossing over into popular culture has added meaning to the work, not removed it. While the *Adagio* continues to be performed often in the concert hall, and continues to be recognized as a masterpiece of twentieth-century American music . . . it is the audience—a massive and diverse global pop audience—that has created a new program for this work as powerful and meaningful as anything the composer could devise.[129]

Although Cairns's position is somewhat pessimistic and Howard's more optimistic, many may take a moderate viewpoint and seem willing to accept *Adagio* for what it is, no matter what the context.

[128]Dan Cairns, "Barber Strop," [London] *Sunday Times* (25 June 2000).

[129]Luke Howard, "The Popular Reception of Samuel Barber's *Adagio for Strings*," *American Music* XXV/1 (Spring 2007), 75.

Adagio in Perspective: Final Observations and Speculations

> You have to be a rock in the middle of nowhere not to have your gut wrenched out by this music.
>
> —Ida Kavafian, *The New York Times* (7 March 2010).[1]

Which kind of musical work is *Adagio for Strings*? What are its essential qualities? It has functioned as the slow movement of a string quartet. It has emerged as the pre-eminent string orchestra composition of the twentieth century. It has been transformed into a choral work of proven appeal and many other unforeseen transcriptions. It has been allied meaningfully to new expression in the visual arts, ballet, theater, drama, film, poetry, and literature. It has been transfigured into jazz and pop music icons. But deep down, what is it? How can *Adagio*'s intrinsic character be described? There remain a series of questions to be asked regarding its true essence. Is it American? Is it modern? Is it sad? Is it gay? Is it trite? Such questions may never be answered to the satisfaction of all. The following summations represent at the least a first step.

An American Work?

> I'm not sure I'd be able to recognize it as American. I don't think he had any conscious desire to write music that was immediately recognizable as American.
>
> —Aaron Copland, Interview with Peter Dickinson (11 May 1981).[2]

Charles Turner, long time friend of the composer, once pondered whether *Adagio* should be considered an American work: "It has none of the characteristics usually associated with American music—no hard-driven rhythms, jazz or otherwise, no explosive energy, no dissonance or harmony that Bach might not have used."[3] Which composers did Turner

[1]Iva Kavafian, quoted in Johanna Keller, "An Adagio for Strings, and for the Ages," *The New York Times* (7 March 2010), L: 21.

[2]Aaron Copland, quoted in Peter Dickinson, *Samuel Barber Remembered: A Centenary Tribute* (Rochester, N.Y.: University of Rochester Press, 2010), 96. Dickinson's interview with Copland is dated 11 May 1981.

[3]Charles Turner, "The Music of Samuel Barber," *Opera News* XXII/13 (27 January 1958), 7.

have in mind when he identified these benchmarks? Hard-driving rhythms could refer to Aaron Copland or, if they are connected to jazz, then to Copland, George Gershwin, or Leonard Bernstein. Composers whose music exhibits explosive energy could be Roy Harris or William Schuman; the dissonance factor points toward composers such as Charles Ives, Roger Sessions, and Carl Ruggles. Turner's tone is not pejorative, however; he implied that music can still be American without possessing the more obvious characteristics evident in other American compositions. Menotti remembered Barber's own attitude. He hated the "folksy Americana" of Copland and Harris: "he refused to touch it . . . to be American that way is much too easy."[4] Menotti also remarked: "He has been accused of not being American enough, but Sam did not believe in nationalism, of having to be an American in that sense. One had to be oneself. He said, 'I don't feel particularly American. . . .' Sam never had that preoccupation."[5]

Another musical "Americanism" is the sound of the city, as depicted in John Alden Carpenter's *Skyscrapers* (1926). Barber wanted nothing to do with this. He once told his colleague, Gama Gilbert, "Skyscrapers, subways, and train lights play no part in the music I write."[6] Yet it is ironic that, thanks to *Adagio*'s many performances connected with the 11 September tragedy, a large number of people now associate it with the World Trade Center. Of course, no one truly thinks of it as a musical representation of skyscrapers, surely not in the way Carpenter's work is intended to do. Yet, when some listeners hear that opening phrase, the twin towers may inevitably enter their minds.

Others, however, view Barber's lack of Americanism as a liability. For instance, Goddard Lieberson criticized Toscanini's choice of *Adagio for Strings* for his radio broadcast: "His opinion of American music must be much the same as the opinion of American life held by those Europeans whose only contact with the American scene comes through the movies or the reading of Jack London."[7] As to *Adagio,* he asserted that it falls

[4]Gian Carlo Menotti, quoted in Peter Dickinson, *Samuel Barber Remembered*, 96. Dickinson's interview with Menotti is dated 6 April 1981.

[5]*Ibid.*, 61.

[6]Samuel Barber, quoted in Gama Gilbert, "Philharmonic Plays Youths Work Today," *Philadelphia Bulletin* XXIV (March 1933).

[7]Goddard Lieberson, "Over the Air," *Modern Music* XVI (November-December 1938), 65.

> neatly into line with the other American music which Toscanini has chosen in the past. . . . Toscanini, in whose hands lies the opportunity to vindicate our native music by his good taste and musicianship, has again shown American music to be what it is most often not—uncreative, colorless, and sub-European.[8]

Along similar lines, British writer Harold Rawlinson concluded that the work "reflects modern Europe more than it does modern America."[9] While historian Nadine Hubbs conceded that *Adagio* is "an American classic," it is not primarily received as a "statement about or representation of America. Or, to put it another way: Barber's piece is . . . decidedly American music, but unlike Copland's, it is not 'America' music."[10]

Indeed, which kind of American music are these commentators addressing? If Copland's "tender land" finds its counterpart in the photo-realistic cowboys-and-Indians action paintings of Frederick Remington and the rural Eden landscapes by Thomas Hart Benton, then perhaps Barber's type of America is more akin to the pensive sculptures of Augustus Saint-Gaudens or the calm luminist paintings of John Frederick Kensett. Barber's music—*Adagio* in particular—might also have common expression with Edward Hopper's paintings, which often illustrates a more basic America. In the words of art critic, author, and television personality Robert Hughes, Hopper's paintings have "nothing to do with the rhetoric of patriotism" but go much deeper; Hopper understood that "the frontier had moved inwards and now lay inside the self, in that the American man of action was replaced by the solitary watcher."[11] Barber's composition might be considered the musical reflection of Hopper's scenes of solitude. Because the composer never acknowledged in his letters any particular interest in these artists, conclusions must be regarded as somewhat subjective as they can only be reached through informed speculation. He did, nonetheless, express his appreciation of art in general in a letter to a friend and fellow

[8] *Ibid.*, 66.

[9] Harold Rawlinson, "Famous Works for String Orchestra. No. 20: Adagio for Strings," *The Strad* LX (April 1950), 372-74.

[10] Nadine Hubbs, *The Queer Composition of America's Sound: Gay Modernists, American Music, and National Identity* (Berkeley: University of California Press, 2004), 2.

[11] Robert Hughes, "Breadlines and Streamlines" [Episode 6], *American Visions* (Arlington, Va.: PBS Television Series Documentary, 1997).

Illustration 12.1. *Morning Sun* by Edward Hopper, 1952, Columbus Museum of Art, Columbus, Ohio

Columbus Museum of Art, Ohio: Howald Fund Purchase 1954.031

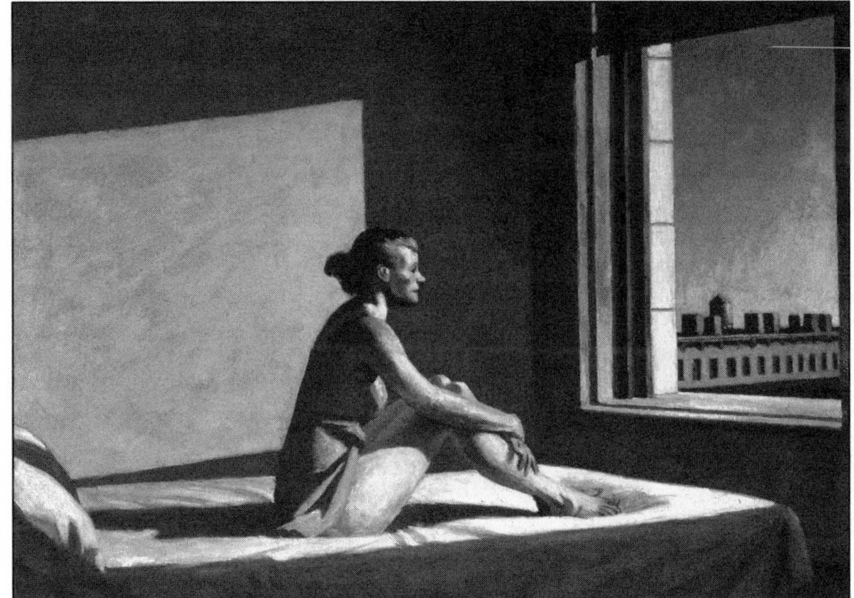

student, Edith Evans Braun: "The more tired I get of music, the more the silence of pictures consoles me!"[12]

Composer, critic, and general curmudgeon Virgil Thomson put the concept of American music into an even more generic category:

> Nobody becomes an American composer by thinking about America while composing. . . . The way to write American music is simple. All you have to do is to be an American and then write any music you wish. There is precedent and model here for all kinds. And any Americanism worth bothering about is everybody's property anyway.[13]

By elevating authenticity, by stressing birthright and geography, and by downplaying raw materials, influence, and intent, Thomson called the entire debate into question.

[12]Samuel Barber, letter (ca. August 1968) to Edith Evans Braun (New York: Edith Braun Collection, New York Public Library). For a general description of this and other letters from Barber to Braun, see Wayne C. Wentzel, *Samuel Barber: A Research and Information Guide*, 2nd ed. (New York: Routledge, 2010), 262-63.

[13]Virgil Thomson, "On Being American," *New York Herald Tribune* (25 January 1948); reprinted *A Virgil Thomson Reader*, ed. Richard Kostelanetz (Boston: Houghton Mifflin, 1981), 305.

Table 12.1. Americana Albums

American Classics
Detroit Symphony Orchestra, cond. Paavo Järvi
Cover: American flag over Brooklyn Bridge
American Classics: An American Salute
Royal Scottish National Orchestra, cond. Marin Alsop
Cover: American flag with torch of the Statue of Liberty
American Dreams: Barber's Adagio & Other American Romantic Masterpieces
Indianapolis Symphony Orchestra, cond. Raymond Leppard
Cover: Bucolic American landscape with farm buildings
American Masterpieces
Philadelphia Orchestra, cond. Eugene Ormandy
Cover: Abstract design
American Music of the Twentieth Century
Scottish Chamber Orchestra, cond. Jukka-Pekka Saraste
Cover: Urban street with taxicab
Bare Essentials: American Classics
Detroit Symphony Orchestra, cond. Neeme Järvi
Cover: Urban bridge
Essential American Classics
London Symphony Orchestra, cond. Michael Tilson Thomas
Cover: Western rock formation
Great American Showpieces
St. Louis Symphony Orchestra, cond. Leonard Slatkin
Cover: Fireworks over bridge
Guido Cantelli Conducts American Masters
New York Philharmonic, cond. Guido Cantelli
Cover: Skyscrapers
Mad about American Music
Los Angeles Symphony, cond. Leonard Bernstein
Cover: Primitive drawing of city and country landscapes

The possible Americanism of *Adagio* is sometimes reflected by its inclusion on "all-American" concerts or its packaging on recordings that group together pieces by various American composers (see Table 12.1). For instance, it can be heard on *American Dreams* (see Illustration 12.2), a 1999 album by the Indianapolis Symphony Orchestra. Although the recording is devoted to slow, contemplative works by composers of the late nineteenth and early twentieth centuries, few of them suggest a conspicuously American sound. A suite by Hoagy Carmichael (1899-1981) and a lullaby by Gershwin, however, might be considered as exceptions. According to the liner notes, the compilation "explores the romantic and spiritual side of the traditionally upbeat American character."[14] The conductor, Raymond Leppard, admitted that, even though he selected the works, he was not responsible for the "dreams" in the title nor for the subtitle, "Romantic Masterpieces." He does agree, nevertheless, that the word "masterpiece" easily applies to *Adagio*: "a remarkable and inspired work for such a young composer."[15] He also agrees that, apart from composers such as Copland or Ives, who quoted traditional folk melodies or hymn tunes, it is rather difficult to discern what constitutes American nationalism (or even nationalism in general). Barber's composition, in his view, does not exhibit that specific type of American character.[16] Yet I concur that it does fit well with some of its companions on the album, specifically the "Noël" movement from George Whitefield Chadwick's *Symphonic Sketches* (1904) and the Adagietto from Arthur Foote's Suite for Strings (1908), both pieces still showing the influence of Edward MacDowell, whose music in general understates an American sound. In such compositional respects, therefore, *Adagio's* contrasting inclusion indicates that it is neither particularly American nor modern (see below).

The bucolic landscape on the *American Dreams* album suggests a relaxed rural scene, as do the covers of several other anthologies listed in Table 12.1. Some also display paintings or photographs of Midwestern or Western landscapes, farms with animals, or more specifically patriotic images such as the American flag. Evidently, record producers assume that *Adagio* fits in with their marketing strategy of American music. Yet the depiction of large steel bridges and particularly of skyscrapers would undoubtedly not meet with Barber's approval.[17]

[14]Byron Adams, liner notes to *American Dreams*, perf. Indianapolis Symphony Orchestra, cond. Raymond Leppard (Decca, 458 157-2, 1997).

[15]Raymond Leppard, conversation (3 April 2013) with the author.

[16]*Ibid.*

[17]See Barber's previous comment to Gama Gilbert on page 516. In addition to those listed in Table 12.1, the album *Copland: Appalachian Spring*, with Bernstein's recording with the Los Angeles Philharmonic on Deutsche Grammophon features a reproduction of "Springtime in Allentown, Pennsylvania" by Missouri Jenkins. The Decca recording, *Barber, Ives, Copland, Creston, Cowell* by Sir Neville Mariner offers a reproduction of "Threshing" by Joe Jones (1909-1963). An album also

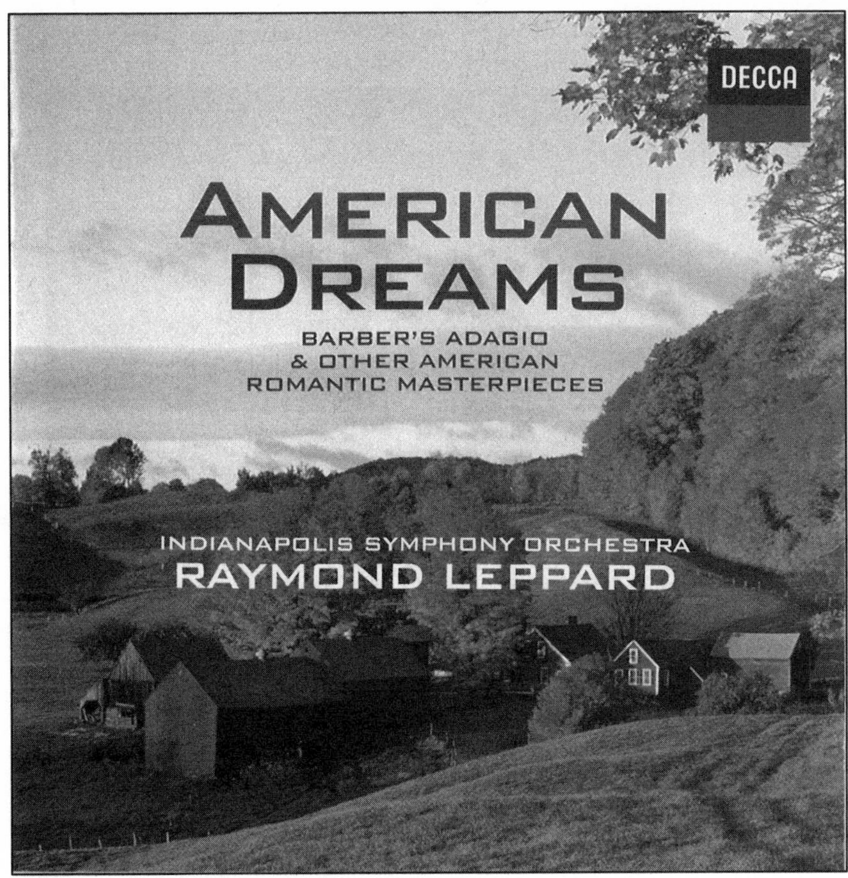

Illustration 12.2. Cover of the Compact Disc *American Dreams: Barber's Adagio & Other American Romantic Masterpieces*, Decca Records, 1999

Courtesy of the Decca Music Group

Art Direction by Conor Brady

A Modern Work?

> Barber writes in a somewhat out-moded fashion, making up in technical finish what he lacks in musical substance. So excellent a craftsman should not content himself forever with the emotionally conventional context of his present manner.
>
> —Aaron Copland, *Modern Music* (1936).[18]

It is impossible to know how much of Barber's music Copland knew in 1936 when he expressed this view. Because Barber was just beginning to compose his string quartet, its slow movement could not have been one of the more "emotionally conventional" pieces Copland had heard. Certainly a year later Copland knew at least his compatriot's *Dover Beach*, Cello

showcasing the Marin Alsop performance has rugged rock formations in the West on the cover. Another album with skyscrapers is *Barber Symphonies 1 & 2* and features Neeme Järvi's performance. There are approximately 200 album covers featuring *Adagio* at the Arkivmusic.com website.

[18]Aaron Copland, "Our Younger Generation: Ten Years Later," *Modern Music* XIII (1936), 10.

Sonata, and *Music for a Scene from Shelley* when he commented: "One cannot help wishing that something or someone would inveigle Mr. Barber out of the safe and sane channels he seems to be content to tread."[19] Ironically, during the mid-1930s Copland himself was turning away from the austere style of his Piano Variations and was embarking on his more popular "Americana" style. Did something—or someone—inveigle him in this direction?

Both Lieberson and Thomson essentially dismissed Barber's music as being rather passé. Lieberson viewed *Adagio* as "contemporary, only in the sense that the composer is still alive."[20] And Thomson later wrote that "certainly, for all its sweetness and fine workmanship, it is no part just now, of our intellectual life."[21] This comment dates from 1965, when Barber's music seemed even less modern than it was perceived when *Adagio* was first composed.

Elliott Carter's assessment is more balanced:

> The question was not whether Samuel Barber's *Adagio for Strings* was good or bad in its reaction style, or whether it was better, say, than Barber's or Roy Harris'[s] *Symphony* and if so why; no the question was, rather, whether *all* American music should be reactionary or *all* should be "modern." This furor disregards the fact that a composer is good not because he is reactionary . . . or advanced . . . but because he has imagination, vitality and other qualities which are always encountered regardless of school or nationality.[22]

Yet some critics are relieved that *Adagio* is not as modern as other trend-setting compositions. Peter Hugh Reed observed: "the thoughtful restraint in this music is rare among modern composers; for Barber's music does not seem to be affected by the restlessness of our times."[23] Gian Carlo Menotti expressed similar views:

[19]Aaron Copland, "Scores and Records," *Modern Music* XIII (January-February 1937), 100.

[20]Goddard Lieberson, "Over the Air," *Modern Music* XVI (1938), 66.

[21]Virgil Thomson, "On Being Discovered," *A Virgil Thomson Reader*, 410.

[22]Elliott Carter, "Once Again . . . ," *Modern Music* XVI/2 (January-February 1939), 101.

[23]Peter Hugh Reed, "Fascinating Novelties of New Records," *The Etude* LXI (January 1943), 31.

> It is time for someone to make a reaction against a school of composition that has bored audiences for twenty years. . . . Isn't it high time that a young David appeared and struck on the forehead that inflated monster which still parades under the anachronistic name of modern music?[24]

Of course, compared to Menotti's music, Barber's seems downright avant-garde! Biographer Nathan Broder justified *Adagio*'s "widespread and abiding popularity" in the following manner:

> [Barber] remained aloof from the swirling currents in which many of his colleagues were immersed. His visions were not of the sort that required the forging of an individual idiom; they could be best expressed in an existing and well-known tongue.[25]

A writer for *Time* summed it up in the most colorful language:

> Steering clear of the dentist-drill dissonances and lurching rhythms with which many other young U. S. composers were trying to pummel their audiences into submission, Barber wooed concertgoers, musicians and critics with more melodic understatement.[26]

Wooing is clearly more effective than pummeling. What is that old adage? "You can catch more flies with honey. . . ."

While critics fret over modernism, composers and other creative artists seem less concerned. Painter Jack Levine participated in FDR's Works Progress Administration (WPA) during the 1930s, when Barber composed and orchestrated his string quartet movement. Levine and other artists working in this project were often accused of turning their backs on recent trends and selling out to the social realism that seemed so relevant during those times. Yet Levine took issue with the idea: "To rally people around the idea of modernism or modernity, is simply silly. I don't know what kind of a cause that is—to be up to date. I think it ultimately leads to

[24]Gian Carlo Menotti, "Drawn from the Mail Pouch," *The New York Times* (20 November 1938), 170.

[25]Nathan Broder, "Music of Samuel Barber," *The Musical Quarterly* XXXIV (July 1948), 331.

[26]"House in Mt. Kisco," *Time* LVII/6 (5 February 1951), 37.

fashion and snobbery, and I'm against it.[27] Had Barber been less reticent about his own music, he might have echoed this opinion. One of the few times he did express himself on the matter occurred during an intermission interview for a radio broadcast of one of his compositions. Interviewer Jay S. Harrison asked him, "Have you ever been chastised by your colleagues for being a romantic conservative?" Barber replied, "I think they all say it, but they don't say it to me." He added:

> I think that it is difficult to know what is conservative and what is advanced; because many times that which appears to us in our time as advanced is actually harkening back to something long before, and, of course, one could also say that both Bach and Brahms were considered terribly conservative by people in their time but they have managed to survive. We all learn from new techniques something, even if we don't use them.[28]

Yet he surely must have read Copland's criticisms disseminated in *Modern Music*, quoted above. Barber had told Gilbert even before composing *Adagio*, "I am not at all concerned with the musical values inherent in geometric cerebrations," clearly deriding the serial methods of Schoenberg and his ilk.[29] Barber continued composing in his somewhat conservative style for the remainder of his life; likewise, Levine continued his social realist paintings long after the movement lost its relevance.

Author Terry Teachout argued that "Barber felt no need to rebel against the musical tradition into which he was born."[30] Since the decline of the musical avant-garde his music has again become popular. This development is, in Teachout's term, "Samuel Barber's Revenge."[31] After years of being accused of being out of touch with contemporary sounds, he has regained stature in the musical world. Record buyers and concert-goers never actually abandoned him. In Teachout's words,

[27]Jack Levine, quoted in "Breadlines and Streamlines" [Episode 6], *American Visions* [PBS Series].

[28]Samuel Barber, quoted in intermission interview at a concert by the New York Philharmonic (10 November 1963). A transcript is reprinted in a program for the Cleveland Orchestra (2-4 January 1964), 393-98.

[29]Samuel Barber, quoted in Gama Gilbert, "Philharmonic Plays Youths Work Today," *Philadelphia Bulletin* XXIV (March 1933).

[30]Terry Teachout, "Samuel Barber's Revenge," *Commentary* (April 1996), 55.

[31]*Ibid.*

virtually all of his music has been re-recorded by a new generation of admiring musicians—and, this time around, it has also been enthusiastically praised by a new generation of critics for whom serialism is of no more interest than Marxism or Freudianism."[32]

As Leonard Slatkin put it, Barber is "not looked at as a throwback anymore but a visionary."[33] Professor Walter Frisch also stressed the importance of the greater context:

> You can make a mistake of mistrusting pleasure. There's a school that concludes, "If it's popular, how good can it be?" The postmodern view is more inclusive. It's the same problem as those who value Schoenberg and discount Samuel Barber because his work wasn't on the trajectory of modernism. But today, you don't have to be ashamed of loving Barber's *Adagio for Strings*.[34]

Although the analogy may not hold up, listening to this piece may be like indulging in the guilty pleasure of a slice of chocolate cake because it is delicious—not because it is "good for us" like a medicinal dose of Schoenberg or Webern.

How does *Adagio* stack up with the music of the more recent "neo-romanticists" such as George Rochberg and Henryk Górecki or the "post-minimalist" music by Philip Glass and John Adams? In an interview with avant-garde composer Pierre Boulez, Jonathan Cott provocatively declared: "sometimes I think that a dyed-in-the-wool conservative like Samuel Barber wrote better 'Romantic' music than most of today's so-called neo-romanticists."[35] Boulez responded:

> Yes, because for him that was genuine—that was his way of thinking, his way of expressing himself. All right, his music wasn't terribly advanced, but at least it was honest. And what

[32]*Ibid.*

[33]Leonard Slatkin, quoted in Scott Timberg, "A Coda for Samuel Barber," *Los Angeles Times* (21 November 2004), E: 40.

[34]Dirk Olin, "Crash Course," *The New York Times* (8 December 2002), VI: 52.

[35]Jonathan Cott, "Pierre Boulez 1984," *Back to a Shadow in the Night: Music Writings and Interviews* (Milwaukee: Hal Leonard, 2002), 142.

I fear in this type of "neoromanticism" is its deep dishonesty—dishonesty with oneself and with the audience—and, ultimately, an avoidance of real musical problems.[36]

What did he mean by dishonesty here? Did he imply such composers secretly wanted to write in an avant-garde style but were pressured to dumb down their music for greater acceptance by the current concert-going public? Or did he feel that they were simply taking the easy way out by not searching hard enough for newer, more original ideas? Even he, perhaps, felt that the music of those modern day neo-romanticists did not reflect authentically on the traditions and ideas of the master composers from that period. Barber did not have to face any of these problems.

Leonard Slatkin believes that, after "a world dominated by academic formalism," the emergence of the neo-romantics helped legitimize Barber's return to favor: "Once more eclectic times came in the '70s and '80s, he came to the fore. We needed to have composers like David Del Tredici and John Adams for Barber to be perceived as an individualist."[37] I doubt that either Del Tredici or Adams ever thought to themselves, "I think I will write this passage *à la* Barber"; yet that composer's approach to romantic values was back in vogue and may have been a subconscious influence.

Leonard Bernstein addressed both the issues of Americanism and modernism. In program notes for a New York Philharmonic Orchestra concert he evaluated the music of the 1930s, such as Barber's, in relation to what he calls the "whoopee" decade of the 1920s:

No more being original for its own sake, no more Indian music, and Negro music as a nationalistic base, no more self-conscious jazz. All these elements had begun to consolidate, and grow together in an unconscious way, producing a new kind of music that began to sound American without even trying: a music permeated by American rhythms and tempos and inflections, solidly grounded in European tradition (mostly French) but still with a decidedly American accent. . . . These composers . . . had a new outlook: to make music that tried to communicate

[36]Pierre Boulez, quoted in *ibid.*

[37]Leonard Slatkin, quoted in Lawrence B. Johnson, "DSO Interprets Barber, Strauss with Precision," [Concert Review] *Detroit News* (2 October 2009).

> with the listener rather than to shock the listener with wild new adventures.[38]

When referring specifically to Barber, he refuted the idea that his music was conservative. He maintained that

> his great talent was fundamentally a lyrical one . . . and he was for years thought by some of his colleagues to be reactionary—old fashioned in his way of making music that sang, that pleased the hearer. We know that there was nothing reactionary about it; it was his genuine expressive self; and his music, year after year, gradually acquired new sophistication and originality in a perfectly normal, un-compulsive way, as he came more and more into the charmed circle of contemporary musical thought.[39]

With such observations Bernstein always revealed his invaluable insights into the many paths of twentieth-century American music.

A Sad Work?

> Écoutez la chanson bien douce
> Qui ne pleure que pour vous plaire.[40]
>
> —Paul Verlaine, *Sagesse* (1881).

The comparison of two musical phrases of *Adagio for Strings à la* Deryck Cooke, presented in Chapter 3, implied an emotional expression extending beyond the simple abstract view that critics and Barber himself have professed. Is there merit to such a viewpoint? Many hear a tragic tone or sadness in this music, which British musicologist Wilfrid Mellers evaluated in the following way:

> Its tender emotionalism goes to the heart because it springs from the heart; if a tear-jerker, it is not a Hollywood tear-jerker.

[38]Leonard Bernstein, Program Notes for a New York Philharmonic Broadcast (29 January 1959), *Thursday Evening Preview Scripts* (Washington, D.C.: The Leonard Bernstein Collection, ca. 1920-1989, Library of Congress).

[39]*Ibid.*

[40]Translation: Listen to the very sweet song, which weeps only to please you.

> The wide arched, finely spun cantilena gives to the harmonic opulence a frail pathos, so that one is involved, but never emotionally bullied.[41]

Yet performers occasionally instill an extraneous pathos into the work. Reviewing a performance by the New York Philharmonic, John F. Majeski admired the "sonorous string sound" but was convinced that Guido Cantelli, its conductor, "delivered the work as if he were directing the *Pathetique*. Every last inch of emotion was wrung out of this music where more simplicity was needed."[42] In a similar vein, critic Lloyd Schwartz found a performance by Boston's Pro Arte Chamber Orchestra "more emphatic" than it needed to be: "This piece is so effortlessly gorgeous, the cooler it's played, the more emotion it seems to have."[43]

How sad is *Adagio*? In 2004 Canadian filmmaker Guy Maddin directed *The Saddest Music in the World*, in which a contest is held to find the best examples of such music.[44] This idea motivated workers at BBC Radio to consider which music *is* the most sorrowful in the world and to mount their own contest. After an initial round of about four-hundred nominations, they narrowed the choices to five, including Barber's *Adagio;* on the BBC 4 *Today* program on 22 May 2004 they announced that it was not only the winner but had received over half the votes.[45] During a short segment on that broadcast an excerpt was played, during which the host interviewed Kazuo Ishiguro, the author of the screenplay for Maddin's film, and music director Leonard Slatkin. Ishiguro agreed that, while *Adagio* was a "very transporting" piece, he, nevertheless, concluded that no orchestral work could fit this description because "sad music is lonely music and orchestral musicians playing together constitute a communal

[41]Wilfrid Mellers, *Music in a New Found Land: Themes and Developments in the History of American Music* (New York: Alfred Knopf, 1965), 196.

[42]John F. Majeski, "Samuel Barber's Adagio Led by Cantelli," *Musical America* LXXV (April 1955), 22.

[43]Lloyd Schwartz, "The BSO, Handel and Haydn, Pro Arte Chamber Orchestra, the Cantata Singers, David Daniels, and Teatro Lirico d'Europa's Tosca," *The* [Boston] *Phoenix* (23 January 2008).

[44]More recently, a book with a similar title has been published. See Thomas Larson, *The Saddest Music Ever Written: The Story of Samuel Barber's* Adagio for Strings (New York: Pegasus Books, 2010).

[45]"Vote for the World's Saddest Music," *Latest Reports*, www.bbc.co.uk/radio4/today/reports/arts/saddestmusic_vote.shtml. The remaining finalist pieces (in no particular order) were Dido's Lament ("When I Am Laid in Earth"), *Dido and Aeneas* by Henry Purcell; Symphony No. 5, Mvt. 4 (Adagietto) by Gustav Mahler; "Gloomy Sunday" by Rezsô Seress, sung by Billie Holiday; and *Metamorphosen* by Richard Strauss.

spirit, the antithesis of loneliness."[46] When listening to this piece, he envisions the orchestra, which detracts from the notion that sadness is a lonely emotion. Slatkin disagreed, pointing out that on that basis no orchestral work could ever be considered mournful and that sorrow was not on the composer's mind when he wrote the slow movement of his string quartet: "It's just a beautiful, haunting, lovely piece of music."[47] Yet he admitted that the many performances during the 11 September period may have added a permanent funereal subtext: "it will now be forever linked in many people's minds with the horrific events on September 11 and to that evening [at the Proms]."[48]

Even if listeners find sadness in *Adagio for Strings,* some actually like to wallow in it. Singer Billy Joel once remarked that this music was "good for you when you really want to feel sad."[49] I think it is significant that he said when you "want to feel sad" rather than "when you are feeling sad," implying that the work has the power to induce such an emotion in the listener. It might even reach a normally stoic audience. Back in 1985, before the fall of the Soviet Union, Joel noted that, when the Russians hear the Barber work, "they cry their eyes out. He's an American, and here's this American music reducing them to tears. That's subversive politics, man. That's infiltration."[50] Joel also imparted a cathartic healing effect to this induced sadness. After the 11 September attacks he confessed, "I listened to the Barber 'Adagio for Strings' and I wept, and it made me feel better."[51]

Listeners may take the same melancholic pleasure as they do with Elizabethan composer John Dowland's "Flow my Tears" or his lute piece "Semper Dowland, semper dolens." Barber's music may not be "always sad," but, when it comes to *Adagio for Strings,* Dowland's motto may well

[46]Kazuo Ishiguro, quoted in BBC 4 *Today* (24 May 2004); rebroadcast on BBC 4 website: www.bbc.co.uk/radio4today/listenagain/zsaturday_20040522.shtml.

[47]Leonard Slatkin, quoted in *ibid.*

[48]*Ibid.* See the discussion in Chapter 10, page 453.

[49]Billy Joel, quoted in interview by David Watts, "Take the Billy Joel Challenge," *Pulse* (24 February 1999); reprinted in www.turnstiles.org/articles/Pulse11-89.html.

[50]Billy Joel, quoted in Phil Dellio and Scott Woods, *Quotable Pop: Five Decades of Blah Blah Blah* (Toronto: Sound and Vision, 2001), 94.

[51]Billy Joel, quoted in Andrew Druckenbrod, "'Piano Man' Composes for Solo Piano as New CD Goes beyond Pop," *Pittsburgh Post-Gazette* (3 October 2001), E: 1.

apply. Psychotherapist and former monk Thomas Moore is convinced that it "speaks directly to the melancholic emotions and depicts the dynamics of grief and sadness. . . . Intuitively people who may or may not know much about classical music immediately sense the melancholic strength of Barber's composition."[52] As a result, it may seem ironic that he advises listening to it as a means of "finding your way through life's ordeals"; rather than listening to upbeat music to try to overcome sadness, he advises the homeopathic approach in which a person, by means of sad music, can "enter further into the darkness and appreciate it through means that are in tune with the dark."[53] If we want to feel sad, we can listen to *Adagio*, but ultimately it can make us feel better. Metropolitan Opera bass-baritone Eric Owens compared listening to *Adagio* to people singing the blues: "They're not singing in order to stay blue. They're singing the blues to get out of it."[54] Some will view this piece in objective, non-emotional terms, while others will always feel a sense of sadness or tragedy when they hear it.

A Gay Work?

> It might be that *Adagio* allows me to listen and love from this [lesbian] *position*, a permission not granted by all the music I hear.
>
> —Suzanne G. Cusick, *Queering the Pitch* (1994).[55]

If music critics—and others—accept the premise that any work by an American composer is "American," then, perhaps, they should accept any music by a gay composer as automatically "gay." Because Barber is a composer welcomed lately by the gay and lesbian community, discussions have arisen about whether his homosexuality is a significant factor in his music. Writer Robert K. Schwartz, for example, has argued that sexuality matters "simply because American society's oppression of gay men and

[52]Thomas Moore, *Dark Nights of the Soul: A Guide to Finding Your Way through Life's Ordeals* (New York: Penguin Books, 2004), 219.

[53]*Ibid.*

[54]Jack Walton, "Chicago Sinfonietta Honors King," *South Bend* [Ind.] *Tribune* (17 January 2013); reprinted www.articles.southbendtribune.com/2013-01-17/news/36401676_1_maestro-freeman-mlk-concert-conductor-paul-freeman.

[55]Suzanne G. Cusick, "On a Lesbian Relationship with Music: A Serious Effort Not to Think Straight," *Queering the Pitch: The New Gay and Lesbian Musicology*, ed. Philip Bret, Elizabeth Wood, and Gary Thomas (New York: Routledge, 1994), 75.

lesbians may have had an impact on the music itself."[56] "May" is the operative word here. Does it matter in this composer's music, and is it significant for *Adagio for Strings*? Sorting out these questions requires turning to members of the gay community.

What about other gay American composers, such as Ned Rorem or Virgil Thomson? Do they sense a "gayness" in *Adagio*, or did their acquaintance with Barber as a gay friend influence their attitude? Even if they detect a gay quality, is it sex or romance? While they have been reticent about any sexual connotation, the two have at least sensed a romantic aspect to the music. Rorem views it "like some forgotten love letter retrieved intact from a cedar chest, penned with vast and tender elegance."[57] He tempers his praise, however, by asserting that such elegance these days is "vaguely irrelevant."[58] It is my impression that Rorem always considered sex more important than romance. Thomson was also a part of the BBC radio interview referenced in Chapter 1. Almost as if he were taking his cue from Rorem, he concluded, "I think it's a love scene . . . a detailed love scene . . . a smooth, successful love scene. Not a dramatic one, but a very satisfactory one."[59] By referring to a love scene in general, was he implying that *Adagio* represents the happy, romantic days that Barber and Menotti spent together in St. Wolfgang when Barber composed his string quartet? If so, then he must have surely accepted the turbulent outer movements as depicting some of the lovers' stormier times as well. Barber would undoubtedly refute such allegations as totally absurd. To him it was just music.

The next aspect to consider is the performance of *Adagio for Strings* in a gay context. These days it is politically correct to devise programs with music written exclusively by black composers, women composers, and, more recently, gay composers. For instance, on 26 January 2010, when the Congregation Beth Simchat Torah, New York City's LGBTQ synagogue, presented its annual Shabbat Shirah concert, featured were compositions by gay and lesbian composers (*e.g.*, Britten, Poulenc, and

[56]Robert K. Schwartz, "Composers' Closets Open for All to See," *The New York Times* (19 June 1994), II: 1.

[57]Ned Rorem, *A Ned Rorem Reader* (Harrisonburg, Va.: R. R. Donnelly and Sons, 2001), 238. Rorem, in fact, may have taken his cue from Thomson, whose remark preceded his.

[58]*Ibid.*

[59]Virgil Thomson, quoted in Barbara B. Heyman, *Samuel Barber: The Composer and His Music* (New York: Oxford University Press, 1992), 175.

Libby Larsen), including Barber's String Quartet. (It is odd, considering he was both gay and Jewish, that no work by Copland was selected.) Does the homosexual community identify with this music's emotional quality? When the String Quartet was performed at this synagogue, when Agnus Dei was sung by The Stonewall Chorale in 1999, or when a wind arrangement was played by The Lakeside Pride Clarinet Choir in 2002, did the participants feel that they were getting in touch with the inner expressions of a gay composer? Likewise, some gay audience members may feel a spiritual affinity, a composer-performer-listener bonding. It may also bring straight members of the audience into the fold through a common musical-emotional experience.

Do individual listeners feel close to Barber because of their sexual orientation? Before coming out, a gay teenager may feel quite isolated, hiding his feelings and believing that he may never achieve happiness in a straight world. The sadness and melancholy of *Adagio for Strings* may reflect this situation. Matt Alber, the openly gay country and western singer and former member of classical vocal group Chanticleer, expressed such a view. The Barber work was one of his responses when he was asked, "if they made a soundtrack to capture your teen years, what are some of the songs that would be on it?"[60]

On the subject of soundtracks, *Adagio for Strings* is found on at least three compact disc sets devoted to the music of gay composers. *Out Classics* (1995), packaged by *Out Magazine* and BMG Records, contains thirteen "seductive classics" by known-to-be or thought-to-be gay classical composers. The author of the liner notes soft-pedaled the issue, however: they are "eight of the world's greatest composers who just happen to be gay."[61] The cover alone might induce some gay record collectors into purchasing the album. Reviewer Anthony Tommasini described it:

> A black and white photo shows the naked upper torso of an impossibly hunky young man, his body glistening with droplets from a recent workout (or shower or sauna—use your

[60]Matt Alber, "Pop Quiz: Matt Alber," *Gay.com* (2007), www.gay.com/entertainment/music/rockout/article.html?sernum=822a.

[61]Robert K. Schwartz, liner notes to *Out Classics*, perf. various artists (BMG Records, 09026-68261-2, 1995). Track 7 features the Boston Symphony Orchestra conducted by Charles Munch.

imagination). Head bowed contemplatively, he surveys his own pectoral grandeur.[62]

Yet he concluded that "Barber's affecting *Adagio for Strings* will probably leave most listeners feeling spent and bereft, not seduced and ready for action."[63]

Illustration 12.3. Cover of the Compact Disc *Classical Erotica*, Rising Star Records, 1996

Courtesy of © Judy Francesconi Photography

Another album, *Classical Erotica* (1996), is aimed more to members of the lesbian community (see Illustration 12.3). It is billed as "a romantic journey to ecstasy," one that highlights the Philadelphia Orchestra's recording of *Adagio*. With the recording are ten erotic photographs of lesbian couples by internationally acclaimed photographer Judy Francesconi. Two additional albums are worth noting. *Club Verboten: Music through the Ages by and for the Gay and Lesbian Community* (1997) contains music from different decades of the twentieth century by various

[62]Anthony Tommasini, "'Outing' Some 'In' Composers," *The New York Times* (6 August 1995), II: 26.

[63]*Ibid.*

composers and performers. Forbidden music? Richard Oliver, the co-producer of the record set, explained, "This particular music is music that comes from or is embraced by the gay and lesbian culture, and in the '30s and '40s and '50s, of course was very verboten."[64] When radio host Susan Stamberg asked him on 30 August 1997 about the presence of *Adagio* in the set, he responded; "[it] has become one of the most popular pieces of classical music . . . its poignancy just grabs everybody so beautifully."[65]

Adagio has also found a receptive ear on *Queer Radio,* a show from 4ZZZ FM (Brisbane, Australia) that presents programs supporting the gay / lesbian / bisexual / transgender community. It is friendly to all, presenting relevant music, guests, news, views, and interviews with discussions of sex, sexuality, and life in general. The show of 24 May 2000 featured, in a varied playlist, William Ørbit's synthesizer version. While several topics were addressed during the course of this particular show, it is not apparent which segment utilized Barber's music.[66] Perhaps it was simply presented without comment as a transition from one segment to another.

As documented previously, gay choreographers, film directors, and (possibly) television scriptwriters have found *Adagio for Strings* appropriate for scenarios communicating their sexual orientation. Choreographer Patrick Scully used this music for his 1992 program *Queer Notions,* in the section subtitled "Too Soon Lost." Edward Morgan and Daniel Scott determined it was suitable for their tribute to Matthew Shephard, a victim of gay bashing. They thought that a same-sex *pas de deux* would illustrate both the spiritual and sexual aspects of a gay relationship.[67] There may as well be such a subtext to both versions of Jimmy Gamonet's choreography for *Purple Bend* (see Chapter 5).

Among the movies in which *Adagio for Strings* appears, two presented gay themes and were supervised by gay directors. In Christopher Larkin's film *A Very Natural Thing* it accompanies a male sex scene. In André Téchiné's *Les Roseaux sauvages*, it enhances the more emotional feelings of one boy for another. The semi-autobiographical story is based on Téchiné's own experiences at boarding school. Even if these directors did

[64]Richard Oliver, quoted in interview by Susan Stamberg, "Club Verboten," *National Public Radio* (30 August 1997), www.npr.org/templates/story/story.php?storyId=1001647.

[65]*Ibid.*

[66]*4ZZZ* (24 May 2000), www.4zzzfm.org.au/.

[67]Daniel Scott, email (11 February 2006) to the author.

not consider *Adagio* to be a gay work, they obviously judged it compatible with gay scenes, either implicit or explicit (see Chapter 8). Another film project planned in the early 2000s was *Love and Taboo*, a compilation of twenty original, short films aimed at the gay / lesbian community. English author and filmmaker Clive Barker contacted numerous directors for contributions, each of whom chose a piece of music by a gay or lesbian composer and were charged to interpret that music through film. Each scenario is intended to deal with some form of forbidden love. Filmmaker Paris Barclay chose *Adagio for Strings*. As of this writing, he has not yet produced his segment nor indicated his plans for the music in this context. In fact, the whole project has apparently stalled.

Adagio as underscoring for a gay storyline on television has occurred on an American soap opera, *One Life to Live,* and on a British comedy-drama, *At Home with the Braithwaites*. (There is no evidence that any of the writers themselves are gay in these cases.) In the soap opera a grieving father reminisces about his gay son, a victim of AIDS, with the Barber score accompanying his sorrowful monologue. In the British counterpart a passionate kiss between two women in a nightclub is accompanied by Ferry Corsten's trance remix as diegetic music. Whoever coordinated the music for these programs clearly felt that, in one show, Barber's plaintive strings ideally reinforced a father's grief and, in the other, a portion of the Corsten remix was appropriate for a passionate same-sex kiss. It is a moot point if anyone in charge considered the music itself as specifically gay.

This discussion may not clarify whether *Adagio for Strings* is gay or not. Many critics spend entire careers trying to determine what is gay, feminist, or black. In the opinion of art critic Robert Hughes, "America is in the business of inventing identities based on narrow conceptions of gender, race and the rest. These have made for narrow, preachy, single-issue arts in which victims' credentials count for more than aesthetic achievement."[68] Barbara Heyman has expressed a similar attitude. When Robert K. Schwartz criticized her for evading the subject of homosexuality in her Barber monograph, she justified her position with the following pronouncement: "in referring to Barber's romantic attachments to men, I treat the composer's homosexuality as a given, a matter needing no label. Would one be obliged, for example, to identify Wagner's relationship to

[68]Robert Hughes, "Age of Anxiety" [Episode 8], *American Values* [PBS Television Series].

Cosima or Liszt's to Marie D'Agoult as heterosexual?"[69] Heyman further argues that, in her book, "Barber's love relationships are discussed as they bear on his creativity" and concludes, "In my view, the current emphasis on discussions of sexuality as obligatory—and the lumping together of creative artists by sex or sexual orientation—tends to obscure rather than reveal the individuality of the composer's voice."[70] This debate seems to be pushing opposing sides further apart and is likely to continue in this way for years to come.

A Trite Work or a Cliché?

Familiarity breeds contempt.

—Aesop, "The Fox and the Lion" (5th Century BCE).

Hollywood sex goddess Mae West once quipped, "too much of a good thing can be wonderful." Unfortunately, that may not apply to *Adagio for Strings*. Ever since Toscanini's landmark première, it has become so popular that it has eclipsed the composer's other works, much to his dismay. In an intermission feature for a CBS Symphony broadcast on 19 June 1949, interviewer James Fassett told Barber that it was the first piece of his that he ever heard. The composer lamented, "I wish you would hear some new ones. Everybody always plays that."[71] Apparently, even as early as the 1940s, its popularity was beginning to frustrate him. Menotti later remarked, "he was a bit bored by [it], always haunted by it."[72] In an interview Arthur Johnson asked tenor Robert White if Barber ever resented the popularity of *Adagio* to the exclusion of most of his other works. White replied:

> I can honestly tell you yes. From his own lips I heard him say it to me, more than once. And I could never quite understand it, I even

[69]Barbara B. Heyman, "Gay Composers: Barber: No Need of Any Label [Letter to the Editor]," *The New York Times* (10 July 1994), II: 2.

[70]*Ibid.*

[71]Samuel Barber, quoted in James Fassett, interview during CBS Symphony Broadcast (19 June 1949) [transcription] (Washington, D.C.: Motion Picture, Broadcasting, and Recorded Sound Division, Library of Congress).

[72]Gian Carlo Menotti, quoted in Peter Dickinson, *Samuel Barber Remembered*, 67.

argued with him, saying: "Sam, no matter what you say, the thing is so outrageously beautiful. Just think if you had never written it!"[73]

White did not supply the composer's response.

Barber was already at risk for being labeled a "one-hit wonder." In fact, the *Wikipedia* article for that subject lists both the composer himself as well as his *Adagio* as examples.[74] Additional evidence for such an assessment takes various forms. For his radio show *Compact Discoveries* Fred Flaxman assigned this composition to a 2003 episode titled "More One-Hit American Composers." Both Deutsche Grammophon and Vox Classical have issued compact discs devoted to such pieces with *Adagio* on them. In New Zealand Listverse compiled a list of one-hit wonders: the Barber piece ranked number two.[75]

Adagio also ends up on lists of "overused" pieces of classical music. It was number six on an Internet list of "Classics Done to Death," coming in behind works that are even more overdone, such as Pachelbel's Canon (first) and the "so-called" Albinoni Adagio (fifth). An editor for the website described the dilemma: "Look, these are fine pieces of music, but they're so commonly played that they've become a part of our genetic code. When cocktailing with those who really know their classical music, don't sigh and remark, 'I just *adore* this piece' when one of these floats by."[76]

While English audiences also loved the piece, by the early 1950s some critics expressed concern that it was performed too frequently. In his review of the recording by the Boyd Neel String Orchestra, Lionel Salter assessed the situation in this manner: "as far as the British public is concerned, Samuel Barber is for all practical purposes the composer of the charming *Adagio for Strings* and nothing more. I doubt whether Mr. Barber . . . is altogether pleased about this."[77] In 1951 a contributor to

[73]Robert White, quoted in Peter Dickinson, *Samuel Barber Remembered*, 147. The last statement was followed by a brief laugh.

[74]"One-hit Wonder," *Wikipedia*, www.en.wikipedia.org/wiki/one-hit_wonder.

[75]"Top 10 Classical One Hit Wonders," *Listverse* (12 December 2007), www.listverse.com/2007/12/12/top-10-classical-one-hit-wonders/.

[76]Playlist Editors, "Classics Done to Death," *Digital Music Playlist for PC & Mac* (15 September 2004), www.playlistmag.com/playlists/2004/09/classicdeath/index.php.

[77]Lionel Salter, review of *The Boyd Neel String Orch.* (Decca, X305, 1950), "Analytical Notes and First Reviews," *Gramophone* XXVIII/325 (June 1950), 15.

The Musical Times with an extreme viewpoint complained that the work was "so overplayed just now that it might be a good thing if it were locked up in the string quartet where it belongs, and not let out for at least three years."[78]

During the next decades few criticized the frequency of *Adagio*'s performances. Orchestras programmed it every few years, interspersed with other Barber works. Nobody seemed to mind. Yet once it found a place in the cinema and in other contexts, the danger of over-saturation became immediate. Oliver Stone's use of *Adagio* in *Platoon* seemed to set off the objections, but not right away. After the movie's release some critics decried its constant presence, but not because of its pervasiveness elsewhere; they only thought it was excessive for that particular film. In later years fans on Internet chat-room forums have perpetuated this view. For instance, blogger "Travis Bickle" on *Movie Forums* characterized the music in *Platoon* as the "best film score ever," but because *Adagio* plays "in nearly every scene, it's so overused it loses its effect."[79] Richard Berger on the *BBC Collective* expressed his strong misgivings more colorfully: "The unrelenting use of Barber's *Adagio for Strings* does get on your tits, mind."[80]

Because *Adagio* is inextricably linked to *Platoon*, its introduction into later movies sometimes makes people consider it trite or redundant. A blogger on *Yahoo* stated, "Unfortunately I think this great piece is used far too often in the movies and on tv. . . . I use to love it and now I have gotten a bit tired of it. Sad how this happens to many great pieces of the classical repertoire b / c they never shake things up."[81] In a review of *Rocky Marciano* (1999) a reporter complained that *Adagio* is "a beautiful musical reference that has been used to death since 'Platoon.'"[82] Noel Megahey, a reviewer for *The Digital Fix*, protested that this music in *Reconstruction* (2003) is "misjudged and overused, having too many

[78]W. S. M., "The Jacques Orchestra," *The Musical Times* XCII/1298 (April 1951), 177.

[79]Travis Bickle, "Best Film Ever," *Movie Forums* (9 January 2006), www.movieforums.com/community/showthread.php?t=11453&page=2. This blogger, from Huddersfield, England, uses the name of the character played by Robert De Niro in the film *Taxi Driver* (1976).

[80]Richard Berger, "What's on TV," *BBC Collective: The Interactive Culture Magazine* (23 April 2004), www.bbc.co.uk/dna/collective/A2553374.

[81]*Yahoo! Blog*, www.blog.yahoo.com/explorer.

[82]"'Joan de Arc' Relies Heavily on Razzle-Dazzle, Star Cameos," *Southcoasttoday.com News Archive* (15 May 1999), www.southcoasttoday.com/apps/pbcs.dll/article?AID=/19990515/NEWS/305159931.

associations with other films."[83] Yet another blogger, Beyond Geography, called *Adagio* "stirring, but after signaling sadness and destruction" in *Platoon* and other movies, "it needs to be banned from films for a while."[84] The work has also resonated on chat-room forum categories such as "Musical Clichés on the Big Screen" and "Recent OverUsed Movie Trends or Devices That We Don't Want to See Anymore."[85]

Even some trance dance fans concede that the various remixes may be wearing out their welcome. One is convinced: "Tiesto's version was way overplayed and overrated," and another thinks that *Adagio* has been "remixed to death over the last 6 / 7 years."[86] A blogger was particularly opinionated: "the tiesto mix is crap" and "Ferry's mix pisses on it from a rather large height."[87]

Barber himself should be allowed the last word on the subject. Thirty years after his previous remark, he still seemed vexed but at least viewed it with his typical dry wit:

> Sometimes I get tired of hearing the *Adagio for Strings*. But I amuse myself during performances because I know there's going to be a mistake somewhere. I just wait for it to happen. It's such an easy work, they never bother rehearsing it. And orchestra psychology is rather funny: When they see whole notes, they think "We don't have to watch the conductor." Invariably a viola or second violin will make a mistake. Happens everytime.[88]

[83]Noel Megahey, "Reconstruction," *The Digital Fix* (26 July 2005), www.film.thedigitalfix.com/content/id/57908/reconstruction.html.

[84]Beyond Geography, "Most Commercially Overused Piece of Classical Music," *Democratic Underground* (28 October 2007), www.democraticunderground.com/discuss/duboard.php?az=view_all&address=105x7080871.

[85]Abiola Lapite, "Musical Clichés on the Big Screen," *Foreign Dispatches* (26 July 2005), www.foreigndispatches.typepad.com/dispatches/2005/07/musical_cliches.html; and The Red Avenger, "Recent OverUsed Movie Trends or Devices That We Don't Want To See Anymore . . .," *Council-of-Elrond* (30 November 2005), www.council-of-elrond.com/forums/showthread.php?t=9035&page=3.

[86]Black Fabio, "Adagio for Strings," *TranceNu Forum* (7 July 2007), www.trance.nu/v4/forum/viewtopic.php?p=1986422; and Makoto, "Tiesto–Adagio for Strings," *The Site* (5 February 2006), www.vbulletin.thesite.org/archive/index.php/t-93825.html.

[87]Miguelinho and dachemicalbro, "Adagio for Strings," *AATWC Forum* (4 August 2004), www.aatwc.com/forum/showthread.php?t=3357&page=2.

[88]Samuel Barber, quoted in Allan Kozinn, "Samuel Barber, the Last Interview and the Legacy: Part 1," *Hi Fidelity* XXXI (June 1981), 65.

Final Thoughts

After reading the views of so many others on the nature of *Adagio for Strings*, I have come to my own conclusions. Is it American? I am still not certain exactly what Americanism is meant to sound like. *Adagio*'s broad sweeping lines may be somewhat like Roy Harris's, but I tend to associate his music far more with the American landscape than Barber's. If I were not told in advance that the composition was written by an American, I am not sure that I would reach that conclusion. Is it modern? Certainly not modern in the Stravinskyan or Webernian sense of the word, but its sense of tonality is well beyond the practices exhibited in earlier music. Many works of Copland are just as tonal, yet few would deny his modernism. Is it sad? Although Barber may not have intended a sad perspective, its melodic and harmonic language seem to point inexorably in that direction. While I may not agree with all of Deryck Cooke's ideas, I acknowledge that his concepts of sadness in music fit *Adagio* to a tee. Its appropriation in *Platoon* and in programs after 11 September, moreover, have altered most people's perspective, including mine. When I now listen to this work, it is difficult to keep the image of Leonard Slatkin conducting it at the Proms concert out of my mind in the wake of that tragedy. Is it gay? Not specifically. The gay population may find a kinship in the music's romantic sound, but so do other representative segments of the listening public. The queer community does not have a monopoly on sensitivity. Have I been over-*Adagio*-ed? After researching this piece of music for several years, I thought that surely I would have wearied of it by now, but that has not happened to me. It still means as much to me—perhaps even more—than when I began studying it and writing about it. Indeed, familiarity need not necessarily breed contempt!

What does *Adagio* mean to us? How can it have such a remarkable and often profound impact on so many people from so many walks of life? George Parker, the author of *The Atomic Kid* (see Chapter 6), conveyed the following thought that truly reaches the heart of the matter:

> What Samuel Barber has done in *Adagio for Strings* is to put the power of deep imagination into music. If one really listens one is swept along on a river of sound with a power and dynamism that involves all the senses. The senses power up the emotions, and the energy produced by those emotions drives the will wherever the imagination wishes it to go. True power exists in the air around us, within us, and without us. Barber must have known

this because it is right there in this wonderful piece of music for anyone with ears to experience.[89]

Many have been swept along this river of sound, experiencing the joys and sorrows of Samuel Barber's *Adagio for Strings* in numerous contexts since its creation. How many more experiences are yet to come?

[89]George Parker, email (27 January 2006) to the author.

Selected Suggested Readings

In the following bibliography I identify sources of greatest relevance to the subject of this book. I have not cited all publications and websites referenced in the footnotes for my text.

Barber Studies

Ardoin, John. "Samuel Barber at Capricorn," *Musical America* V (March 1960), 4-5, 46.

Besedick, Stephen T. *Samuel Barber's Cantilena Slow Movements: A Study of Textural Relationships*. M.M. thesis, Florida State University, 1986.

Broder, Nathan. *Samuel Barber*. New York: G. Schirmer, 1954.

Carter, Elliott. "Once Again . . . ," *Modern Music* XVI/2 (January-February 1939), 100-01.

Copland, Aaron. "Our Younger Generation Ten Years Later," *Modern Music* XIII (May-June 1936), 10.

______. "Scores and Records," *Modern Music* XIV (January-February 1937), 100.

Dexter, Harry. "Samuel Barber and His Music," *Musical Opinion* LXXII (March 1949), 285-86.

Dickinson, Peter. *Samuel Barber Remembered: A Centenary Tribute.* Rochester, N.Y.: University of Rochester Press, 2010.

Dougill, David. "Not All Black and White," *The* [London] *Times* (9 May 2004), 33.

Downes, Olin. "Toscanini Plays Two New Works," *The New York Times* (6 November 1938), 48.

Heinsheimer, Hans W. "Adagio for Sam," *Opera News* XLV (14 March 1981), 30-31.

______. "The Composing Composer: Samuel Barber," *ASCAP TODAY* II/3 (December 1968), 4-7.

Heyman, Barbara B. *Samuel Barber: A Thematic Catalogue of the Complete Works*. Oxford: Oxford University Press, 2012.

______. *Samuel Barber: The Composer and his Music*. New York: Oxford University Press, 1992.

Howard, Luke. "The Popular Reception of Samuel Barber's *Adagio for Strings*," *American Music* XXV/1 (Spring 2007), 30-60.

Keller, Johanna. "An Adagio for Strings, and for the Ages," *The New York Times* (5 March 2010).

Kozinn, Allan. "Samuel Barber, the Last Interview and the Legacy: Part 1," *High Fidelity/Musical America* XXXI (June 1981), 45-47, 89-90.

Kozinn, Allan. "Samuel Barber, the Recordings," *High Fidelity/Musical America* XXXII (July 1981), 45-47, 89.

Larson, Thomas. *The Saddest Music Ever Written: The Story of Samuel Barber's* Adagio for Strings. New York: Pegasus Books, 2010.

McQuinn, Julie. "Listening Again to Barber's *Adagio for Strings* as Film Music," *American Music* XXVII/4 (Winter 2009), 461-99.

Pollack, Howard. "Samuel Barber, Jean Sibelius, and the Making of an American Romantic," *The Musical Quarterly* LXXXIV/2 (Summer 2000), 175-205.

Ramey, Philip. "Samuel Barber at Seventy: The Composer Talks about His Vocal Music," *Ovation* I/3 (March 1980), 15-20.

Schwartz, Robert K. "Composers' Closets Open for All to See," *The New York Times* (19 June 1994), II: 1.

Simmons, Walter. *Voices in the Wilderness: Six American Neo-Romantic Composers.* Lanham, Md.: Scarecrow Press, 2004.

Teachout, Terry. "Samuel Barber's Revenge," *Commentary* MI (April 1996), 55-58.

Turner, Charles. "The Music of Samuel Barber," *Opera News* XXII/13 (27 January 1958), 7, 32-33.

Wentzel, Wayne C. *Samuel Barber: A Research and Information Guide,* 2nd ed. New York: Routledge, 2010.

Wittke, Paul. "Samuel Barber: A Personal Note" [Introduction], *Samuel Barber: Complete Piano Music.* New York: G. Schirmer, 1986.

______. *Samuel Barber: An Improvisatory Portrait.* New York: G. Schirmer, 1994.

Other Relevant Studies

Alper, Garth. "Making Sense Out of Postmodern Music," *Popular Music and Society* XXIV/4 (Winter 2000), 1-14.

Baillargeon, Stephane. "An American Fairy Tale: Cirque Éloize," *Le Devoir* (24 February 2002).

Bewley, John. "Marking the Way: The Significance of Eugene Ormandy's Score Annotations," *MLA Notes* LIX/4 (June 2003), 828-53.

Bogdanov, Michael, and Michael Pennington. *The English Shakespeare Company: The Story of the Wars of the Roses, 1986-1989.* London: Nick Hern Books, 1990.

Cooke, Deryck. *The Language of Music.* London: Oxford University Press, 1959.

Daniel, Oliver. *Stokowski, a Counterpoint of View.* New York: Dodd, Mead, 1982.

Dixon, Kathleen. "The Dialogic Genres of Oprah Winfrey's 'Crying Shame,'" *Journal of Popular Culture* XXXV/2 (Fall 2001), 171-91.

Eichelbaum, Stanley. "Two Impressive Ballet Premieres," *San Francisco Examiner* (7 July 1964).

Fink, Robert. "Elvis Everywhere: Musicology and Popular Music Studies at the Twilight of the Canon," *American Music* XVI/2 (Summer 1998), 135-79.

Fricke, David. "Buried Treasure: The Full Story behind the Beatles Album That Never Was," *Rolling Stone* CMXVI (20 February 2003), 38-43.

Gruen, John. *Menotti: A Biography.* New York: Macmillan, 1979.

Gurewitsch, Matthew. "Dance; Inspired by Dance, A Circus Is Writing the Poetry of Flight," *The New York Times* (17 February 2002), II: 8-9.

Hay, Deborah. *My Body, the Buddhist.* Hanover, N.H.: Wesleyan University Press, 2000.

Heinemann, Lynn. "Janney and Baryshnikov Create Electrocardio-choreography," *MIT Tech Talk* (13 May 1998).

Kennecott, Philip. "Sounding the Right Notes: National Symphony Opens Season with an Altered Program," *Washington Post* (20 September 2001), C: 1.

Kirk, Elise. *Music at the White House: A History of the American Spirit.* Chicago: University of Chicago Press, 1986.

Knight, John. "Lessons in Interpretation from Arturo Toscanini," *The Instrumentalist* XLVIII/5 (December 1993), 16-20.

Lowens, Irving. "Accurate Listing of Funeral Music [for John F. Kennedy]," *Washington Star* (1 December 1963).

Lynch, David, and Chris Rodley. *Lynch on Lynch,* 2nd ed. New York: Macmillan, 2005.

Meyer, Donald Carl. *The NBC Symphony Orchestra*. Ph.D. dissertation, University of California, Davis, 1994.

Parks, Elena. "Lincoln Center and Emerson Quartet Pay Tribute to the Missing and Deceased in World Trade Center and Pentagon Attacks," *Andante* (17 September 2001).

Prasch, Thomas. "Platoon and the Mythology of Realism," *Search and Clear: Critical Responses to Selected Literature and Films of the Vietnam War,* ed. William J. Searle. Bowling Green, Ohio: Bowling Green State University Press, 1988.

Schelle, Michael. *The Score: Interviews with Film Composers.* Los Angeles: Silman-James Press, 1999.

Shapiro, Laura. "Mischa's New Moves: After a Trip Home and with a Solo Tour About to Begin, Mikhail Baryshnikov Is Dancing Past 50," *Newsweek* CXXXI (19 January 1998), 19.

Sulpy, Doug, and Ray Scheighardt. *Get Back: The Unauthorized Chronicle of the Beatles' "Let it Be" Disaster.* New York: St. Martin Press, 1994.

Temin, Christine. "Baryshnikov Makes Himself Modern," *Boston Globe* (10 May 1998), N: 2.

Thomson, Virgil. "On Being American," *A Virgil Thomson Reader.* Boston: Houghton Mifflin, 1981.

Tobey, Cheryl. "White Oak at Dance Center of Columbia College, November 18, 2001," part two of "Bodies of History and Historical Bodies: Baryshnikov and the Judson Legacy," *PAJ: A Journal of Performance and Art* XXIII/3 (September 2001), 20.

Testimonials from Additional Admirers

The following individuals have disseminated their high opinions of Samuel Barber's *Adagio for Strings* as part of the public record.

Pop and Jazz Musicians

Vinnie Colaiuta, jazz-fusion drummer, with Sting, Frank Zappa, and others

Adagio for Strings is "one of my favorite pieces of music and there are no drums on that."

"Vinnie Colaiuta," *Modern Drummer Magazine* (November 1982); reprinted www.united-mutations.com/c/vinnie_colaiuta.htm.

Ari Gold, singer, voice for Cabbage Patch Kids, and former child vocalist

When asked about his favorite piece of music he replied, "When you say piece it sounds like you mean classical. . . . If it's classical I love Samuel Barber's *Adagio for Strings*."

"Interview with Ari Gold," *Gay Youth Unity Project,* www.gyup.org/arigoldinterview.htm.

Nanci Griffith, singer whom Rolling Stone called the "Queen of Folkabilly"

"Samuel Barber's 'Adagio for Strings' is absolutely my all-time favorite piece of music."

Kerry Dexter, "Another Voice for Nanci Griffith," *Barnes & Noble Music–Pop Interview* (2003), www.music.barnesandnoble.com/features/interview.asp?NID=130965.

Mark O'Connor, violinist performing a wide range of musical styles (country, jazz, bluegrass, Celtic and classical) and composer.

"I'll pick out my favorite piece of music as Beethoven's 9th Symphony and Barber's "Adagio for Strings," and of my pieces, probably the "Fiddle Concerto."

AOLiveMC2, "Mark O'Connor Online Chat," *AOL Live Auditorium* (27 May 1998), www.sonyclassical.com/news/oconnor_chat.html.

Michael Stipe, lead singer of R.E.M.

In 1996 producer Steve Singer produced an album of classical music aimed at the popular music audience and asked Stipe for a contribution. He selected *Adagio for Strings*. His only comment in the liner notes says that it "makes good morning music." We have to presume that this is indeed what he meant, and not "mourning" with a "u." If he expressed himself verbally, we may never know which meaning he had in mind.

Michael Stipe, quoted in Steve Singer, liner notes to Sinners and Saints —The Ultimate Medieval and Renaissance Music Collection (L'Oiseau-Lyre / Decca, 448 559-2, 1996.)

Quentin Stoltzfus, member of the group, Mazarin

"I love classical music. . . . Samuel Barber's *Adagio for Strings* is one of the most beautiful and haunting musical pieces ever created—the choral version is my personal favorite."

Daniel Gill, "Mazarin," *Ink 19* (December 2000), www.ink19.com/issues/december2000/inkSpots/mazarin.html.

Lee Jackson, British bass player and singer, band member of The Nice

"I was listening to that piece [*Adagio for Strings*] in particular quite a lot when I was working on 'Watch it Happen.' I think I always have that arrangement of that piece in the back of my mind when writing more ethereal progressions."[1]

Lee Jackson, "Interview," *Broken Face* (Spring 2001), www.mazarinmusic.com/bfi.html.

Naomi Striemer, Canadian / American singer-songwriter

Adagio for Strings "happens to be my all time absolute favorite piece of music ever written. If I had to choose one song to be the soundtrack of my life, it would be that one."

Naomi Striemer, "Journal," *NaomiOnline[dot]com* (7 June 2004), www.naomionline.com/journal.php.

Bekki Williams, English freelance musician and composer

She considers *Adagio* to be one of her favorite pieces, and so does her father. She, in fact, made a version of it on her JV1080 synthesizer for her father's birthday present and it is available on CDR from her. She hates the William Ørbit version, contending, "I just think that some pieces are best left well alone, without being given the 'modernizing' treatment, *Adagio for Strings* being one of them."

Email (4 July 2004) to the author.

[1]"Watch It Happen" is also the title of the album on which that song is found.

Deejays and Producers

Majere (a.k.a. Jard Sexty), deejay in the San Fransico area

When asked, "What CDs are currently making rotations in your home / car stereo," Majere replied that "my all time favorite is the choral version of Samuel Barber's classical masterpiece, 'Adagio for Strings.'" He does not call it Agnus Dei, perhaps just a mental lapse.

Element, "Interview with Majere," *Deciblast* (March 2003), www.deciblast.org/articles/interviews/majere/majere2.php.

U4T4, popular deejay in Belgium

When asked which record (or track) gave you the "biggest kick ever?" (Is it a "play loud" track), U4T4 responded, *Adagio for Strings* by Samuel Barber (not "play loud" at all.) This site contains the only reference to this question / answer dialogue. It also is not clear as to what performance he refers to. However, if "Adagio for Strings by Samuel Barber" is considered a full title, any trance remix of William Ørbit's version is the most likely.

Uzine, "Faves Inquiry," www.dma.be/p/ultra/uzine/0406.htm.

Matthew Dekay, Dutch deejay and composer ("Eyes Wide Shut")

When asked who his favorite classical composer was, Matthew Dekay responded: "Well that must be Barber. I love melodramatic music and feelings, plus his *Adagio for Strings* is still one of my favorite songs. It was given a digital face by William Orbit and that was done really well."

Rob Szepesi, "Interview: Matthew Dekay," *Xpander Interviews*, www.xpander.nl/xpandr/specials_main.cfm?1=1&special=138.

Simon Parkes, producer and remixer in Wales, United Kingdom

When he was asked, "what are your top five all time classic tunes?" (note: "classic" not "classical") he started with Ørbit's version of *Adagio for Strings*. He said, "no matter when or where I hear this tune, it creates a loving far off mood, makes me feel creative."

"Interview: Simon Parkes," *Super Sexy Promotions* (2003), www.supersexypromotions.co.uk/simon_parkes_interview.htm.

Rich Rydell, New Jersey deejay

Rydell includes Ferry Corsten's remix of Barber's *Adagio* among the "most influential records" in either his own style or the scene in general.

Jody Rodd, "Interview with DJ Rich Rydell," *Promo New York–Guide to Nightlife in NYC* (2001), www.promony.com/street/rydell1.html.

Timeline of Selected Performances

The following performances, listed here in chronological order according to medium, were cited in the text of Chapter 2.

String Quartet

1936 December 14. Pro Arte String Quartet. Rome: The American Academy. [Villa Aurelia]

1937 March 7. Curtis String Quartet. Philadelphia: Curtis Institute of Music.

1937 April 20. Gordon String Quartet. Washington, D.C.: Library of Congress.

1938 March 14. Curtis String Quartet. Philadelphia: Curtis Institute of Music.

1938 March 15. Curtis String Quartet. New York: Town Hall.

1938 August. Curtis String Quartet. Philadelphia: Radio Broadcast.

1938 October 3. Curtis String Quartet. *Monday Afternoon Concerts from the Curtis Institute.* Philadelphia: CBS Radio Broadcast.

1938 (Late). Curtis String Quartet. Glasgow.

1938 (Late). Curtis String Quartet. Brunswick, Maine: Bowdoin College.

1943 May 28. Budapest String Quartet. Washington, D.C.: Elizabeth Sprague Coolidge Auditorium, The Library of Congress. [première of the final form]

1945 October 4. Budapest String Quartet. Washington, D.C.: Elizabeth Sprague Coolidge Auditorium, The Library of Congress.

1951 October 25. Budapest String Quartet. Washington, D.C.: Elizabeth Sprague Coolidge Auditorium, The Library of Congress.

1961 April 21. Budapest String Quartet. Washington, D.C.: Elizabeth Sprague Coolidge Auditorium, The Library of Congress.

1995 October 26. Audubon String Quartet. Los Angeles: Wilshire Ebell Theatre.

1997 May 6. Emerson String Quartet. Aspen, Colo.: Aspen Music Festival.

1999 January 19. Shanghai String Quartet. Scottsdale, Ariz.: Scottsdale Center for the Arts.

2001 April 18. Emerson String Quartet. Portland, Ore.: Portland State University.

String Orchestra

1938 November 5. NBC (National Broadcasting Company) Symphony Orchestra, cond. Arturo Toscanini. New York: Studio 8H.

1939 March 3. Los Angeles Philharmonic, cond. Otto Klemperer. Los Angeles: Philharmonic Auditorium.

1939 May 1. Orchestrette Classique, cond. Frédérique Petrides. New York: Carnegie Chamber Music Hall.

1939 June 24. New York Philharmonic, cond. Massimo Freccia. New York: Lewisohn Stadium.

1939 July 14. Chicago Symphony Orchestra, cond. Vladimir Golschmann. Chicago: Ravinia Festival.

1939 July. Federal Symphony, cond. Edwin McArthur.

1940 January 25. New York Philharmonic, cond. John Barbirolli. New York: Carnegie Hall.

1940 March 1. Durieux Chamber Music Ensemble, cond. William Durieux. New York: Town Hall.

1940 May. National Youth Administration Symphony, cond. Edwin McArthur. New York: World's Fair.

1940 June 27. NBC Symphony Orchestra, cond. Arturo Toscanini. Buenos Aires.

1940 July 10. New York Philharmonic, cond. Edwin McArthur. New York: Lewisohn Stadium.

1940 July. Toronto Philharmonic Orchestra, cond. Reginald Stewart. Toronto. [likely first performance outside of United States]

1941 October 20. Havana Philharmonic, cond. Massimo Freccia. New York: City College of New York.

1941 December 13. NBC Symphony Orchestra, cond. Arturo Toscanini. New York: NBC Studios.

1943 June 14. Hallé Orchestra, cond. Louis Cohen. Liverpool, England: Philharmonic Hall.

1943 December 13, 17, 18. Philadelphia Orchestra, cond. Eugene Ormandy. Philadelphia: Academy of Music.

1943. Czech Radio Orchestra, cond. Samuel Barber. Prague.

1945 July 8. New York Philharmonic, cond. Leonard Bernstein. New York: Lewisohn Stadium.

1946 September 13. London Symphony Orchestra, cond. Samuel Barber. Hereford, England.

1951. Cond. Samuel Barber. Berlin.

1951. Cond. Samuel Barber. Frankfurt.

1953 February 27, 28. Boston Symphony Orchestra, cond. Charles Munch. Boston: Symphony Hall.

1953 August 9. Boston Symphony Orchestra, cond. Charles Munch. Lenox, Mass.: Tanglewood Music Festival.

1955 January 13. New York Philharmonic, cond. Guido Cantelli. New York: Carnegie Hall.

1958 June 7. Cond. Leopold Stokowski. Moscow: Moscow State Conservatory.

1958 December 26, 27. Boston Symphony Orchestra, cond. Charles Munch. Boston: Symphony Hall.

1985 November 21. Philadelphia Orchestra, cond. Klaus Tennstedt. Philadelphia: Academy of Music.

2004 January 31. Philadelphia Orchestra, cond. Simon Rattle. Philadelphia: Verizon Hall, Kimmel Center for the Performing Arts.

Linking *Adagio for Strings* to the World

This table displays durations from the shortest to the longest, with the date added if a conductor has recorded the work more than once.

Durations of Selected Recorded Performances of *Adagio for Strings*

CONDUCTOR	ENSEMBLE	TIMING
Mario Bernardi	CBC Radio Orchestra	5:52
Antonio Janigro	I Solisti di Zagreb	5:57
Eugene Ormandy	Philadelphia Orchestra	6:20
Leopold Stokowski	USSR Radio / TV Orchestra	6:25
Leopold Stokowski	Leopold Stowkowski Orchestra (1957)	6:34
Jan Olay Wedin	Stockholm Sinfonietta	6:42
Kurt Graunke	Graunke Symphony Orchestra	7:00
Klaus-Peter Hahn	Moscow RTV Symphony Orchestra	7:02
William Boughton	English String Orchestra	7:03
Richard Owen	Camerata New York	7:03
Richard Hickox	City of London Sinfonia	7:05
Arturo Toscanini	NBC Symphony Orchestra	7:11
Raymond Leppard	Indianapolis Symphony Orchestra	7:18
Erich Kunzel	Cincinnati Pops	7:21
Neville Marriner	Academy of St. Martin in the Fields (1988)	7:25
Eric Hammerstein	London Promenade Orchestra	7:26
Leonard Slatkin	St Louis Symphony Orchestra (1981)	7:28
James Sedares	New Zealand Symphony Orchestra	7:29
Guido Cantelli	New York Philharmonic Orchestra	7:30
Kenneth Slowik	Smithsonian Chamber Players	7:42
Charles Munch	Boston Symphony Orchestra	7:45
(No Conductor)	Capella Istropolitana	7:45
Marin Alsop	Scottish National Orchestra	7:47
Yoav Talmi	Israel Chamber Orchestra	7:50
(No Conductor)	Budapest Strings	8:00
Lazar Gosman	Tchaikovsky Chamber Orchestra	8:04
Thomas Sanderling	Saarbrücken Radio Symph Orchestra	8:07
Yoel Levi	Atlanta Symphony Orchestra	8:12
Lawrence Foster	Monte Carlo Philharmonic Orchestra	8:20
Göran Nilson	Örebro Chamber Orchestra	8:33

Conductor	Ensemble	Timing
Neeme Järvi	Detroit Symphony Orchestra	8:37
David Zinman	Baltimore Symphony Orchestra	8:40
Carl Davis	Royal Philharmonic Orchestra	8:40
Neville Marriner	Academy of St. Martin in the Fields (1976)	8:42
Michael T. Thomas	London Symphony Orchestra	8:42
Leonard Slatkin	National Symphony Orchestra	9:00
Leonard Slatkin	St. Louis Symphony Orchestra (1988)	9:07
Andrew Schenck	New Zealand Symphony Orch. (1996)	9:02
Andrew Schenck	London Symphony Orchestra (1985)	9:18
Lukas Foss	Milwaukee Symphony Orchestra	9:44
Victor A. Feotov	Kirvov Orchestra	9:50
Leonard Bernstein	New York Philharmonic (1971)	9:56
Leonard Bernstein	Los Angeles Philharmonic (1982)	10:03
Leonard Slatkin	BBC Symphony Orchestra (1991)	10:20

String Quartet Albums Containing the Adagio Movement

Alexander Quartet. *Dover Beach.* Analekta / Amplitude, CLCD 2009, 1992.

Borodin Quartet. *Kvartet.* Artia, MK 1563, 1961.

Beaux Arts String Quartet. *String Quartet No. 4.* Epic, LC-3907 / -1307, 1965.

The Chester String Quartet. *The Chester String Quartet.* Koch International Classics, 3-7069-2 H1, 1991.

Cleveland Quartet. *Two American Masterpieces.* RCA, AARL-1-1599, 1976.

Concord Quartet. *String Quartet Op. 11: Dover Beach, Op. 3.* Elektra, N 78017, 1983.

Composers String Quartet. *American Classics for String Quartet.* Musical Heritage Society, MHS 4823 H or DS, 1983.

Dickerman Quartet. *Barber: Streichquartett Op. 11.* Thorofon Capella, MTH-275 SD, 1985.

Duke String Quartet. *Barber: String Quartet, Op.11 / Dvořák: String Quartet, Op.96.* Collins Classic, CDC 1386-2, 1993.

Emerson String Quartet. *AMERICAN Originals: Ives & Barber, String Quartets.* Deutsche Grammophon, D101392 (435 864-2), 1992.

Endellion String Quartet. *Dover Beach Serenade; Songs; String Quartet.* Virgin Classics, 45033, 1994.

The Kronos Quartet. *Winter Was Hard.* Elektra / Asylum / Nonesuch Records, 79181-2, 1988.

The Lindsay String Quartet. *25 Years: Lindsay String Quartet Live.* ASV, DCA 825, 1992.

Manhattan Quartet. *Adagio for Strings: Featuring Music of Barber, Dvořák, Gershwin, Kern and Puccini.* Newport Classics, NCD 60033, 1987; reissued on *The Romantic Approach.* Celestial Harmonies, 13087-2, 2008. [both albums contain Adagio movement only]

Stradivari String Quartet. *Stradivari String Quartet.* Naxos Classical Archives, 9.80942, 1951.

Tokyo String Quartet. *Red Seal Sampler.* RCA Victor Red Seal, 09026-61387-2 9026613872, 1993.

Additional Concerts with *Adagio* as Film Music

Federal Way Philharmonic, cond. A. Brian Davenport. "Champagne Pops Concert." Seattle: 1993. [with music from *Dances With Wolves* and *Star Trek: Deep Space Nine,* suite from the television series]

Croydon Symphony Orchestra, cond. Darrell Davison. "Film Classics Concert." Croydon, England, UK: April 2005.

Additional All-American Concerts with *Adagio*

Chamber Orchestra of Philadelphia. Philadelphia: October 2004. [with Anton Webern's Five Movements for String Quartet, Op. 5]

Rotterdams Philharmonisch Orkest, cond. Jan Stulen. "America: The Good Old Days." Rotterdam, Netherlands: De Doelen Concert Hall, 21 November 2004. [with Morton Gould's *Tap Dance Concerto*]

Illinois Philharmonic Orchestra, cond. Carmon DeLeone. "American Jubilee." Springfield, Ill.: January 2005. [with Morton Gould's *Tap Dance Concerto*]

Middletown Symphony Orchestra, cond. Carmon DeLeone. "American Jubilee." Middletown, Ohio: January 2005. [with Morton Gould's *Tap Dance Concerto*]

Additional Concerts with *Adagio* for the Support of AIDS Victims

Musicians Against AIDS Orchestra. Washington, D.C.: Church of the Epiphany. November 1992.

Positive Music. Memorial Day Concert. 29 May 1995.

Association des Musiciens de l'Orchestre Symphonique de Montréal. Concert in support of the AIDS hospice, La Maison du Parc. Montreal: 30 November 2003. [eve of World AIDS Day]

The Longwood Symphony Orchestra. Concert for AIDS Action Committee of Massachusetts. Boston.

University of North Carolina Symphony Orchestra. Concert to support Project OpenHand. Chapel Hill, N.C.: March 2005. [a non-profit organization that helps feed those living with AIDS and HIV]

Adagio for Strings in Print and on Recording

The following is a list of commercially available transcriptions and arrangements. They are categorized in score order chronologically according to publication date when known. The bracketed number [#] refers to an entry in Wayne C. Wentzel, *Samuel Barber: A Research and Information Guide*, 2nd ed. (New York: Routledge, 2010).

Published Transcriptions and Arrangements

FOR FLUTE

Schmidt, Riё, arr. *Adagio for Strings*. New York: G. Schirmer, 1991. Schirmer 50481502. [quartet, Wentzel #295]

Findon, Andy, arr. *Adagio for Strings*. Available for free download at www.andyfindon.co.uk/Barber.htm, 2006. [choir]

FOR CLARINET CHOIR

Cailliet, Lucien, arr. *Adagio for Strings*. New York: G. Schirmer, 1964. Schirmer 45593c. [Wentzel #269]

FOR WOODWIND ENSEMBLE

O'Reilly, John, arr. *Adagio for Strings*. New York: G. Schirmer 1967. Schirmer 50481483. [Wentzel #272]

FOR SAXOPHONES

Warner, Michael, arr. *Adagio for Strings*. New York: G. Schirmer, 1997. Schirmer G582658. [saxophone quartet]

van der Linden, Johan, arr. *Adagio for Strings*. Viljandi, Estonia: Global Music Facilities (GMF) Baltic States, 1997. [saxophone quartet]

van der Linden, Johan, arr. *Adagio for Strings*. Wormerveer, The Netherlands: Molenaar Edition, 2006. [saxophone choir]

FOR EUPHONIUM AMD TUBA ENSEMBLE

Wilson, Kenyon D., arr. *Adagio for Strings*. Baltimore: Tuba-Euphonium Press, 1999. [Two euphoniums and two tubas, two possible endings, suited for large ensemble]

Spies, David, arr. *Adagio for Strings*. Baltimore: Tuba-Euphonium Press, 2000. [Three euphonium & three tuba parts, twelve players required, nineteen recommended by arranger]

Lindsey, Allyn, arr. *Adagio for Strings*. Salem, Conn.: Cimarron Music and Productions, 2001. [Two euphoniums & two tubas, more appropriate for large ensemble]

Wilkinson, Robert, arr. *Adagio for Strings*. Salem, Conn.: Cimarron Music. CM541. [Two euphoniums and two tubas]

FOR BRASS QUINTET

McNeff, Stephen, arr. *Adagio*. Milwaukee: Hal Leonard, 1986. HL.50488458. (*The Canadian Brass Ensemble Series*)

Zellner, Hans, arr. *Adagio (from String Quartet No. 1)*. Munich, DE: Brass Works, 2004. Munich BW.HBQ-077.

FOR TROMBONE OCTET

DePaolo, Charles, arr. *Adagio, op 11*. Ithaca, N.Y.: Ensemble Publications. ENS 804.

FOR BRASS BAND

Velde, Rieks van der, arr. *Adagio for Strings for Brass Band*. Willebroek, BE: Bernaerts Music. B1.990209-HAR.

Gordon, Bill, arr. *Adagio for Brass Band*. San Rafael, Calif.: SLD Brass. GM 001.

FOR PERCUSSION

O'Connor, G. Allan, arr. *Adagio for Strings*. Akron, Ohio: Panyard. Panyard 7003. [steel drum band]

FOR PIANO

Rosen, Lawrence, arr. *Adagio for Strings for Solo Piano*. New York: G. Schirmer, 1987. Schirmer 50480216. [Wentzel #299]

______, arr. *The Nation's Favourite Classical Music*. London: Chester Music, 2000. CH61798.

Lesley, Simon, arr. *Classic Ads: 22 Classic Themes* and *Music Made Popular by TV Ads*. London: Chester Music, 2002. CH65989.

Classical Chart Hits Gold. London: Wise, 2003. AM976316.

Rosen, Lawrence, arr. *Movie Hits You've Always Wanted to Play*. London: Chester Music, 2005. CH65439.

Long, Jack, arr. *Requiem: The World's Most Moving Music for Solo Piano*. London: Wise, 2005. AM982520.

Great Piano Solos: Classical Chillout Book. London: Wise, 2007. AM989472.

FOR ORGAN

Strickland, William, arr. *Adagio for Strings for Organ*, with Hammond registration. New York: G. Schirmer, 1949. Schirmer 50284770.

FOR VIOLIN AND PIANO

Lanning, Jerry, arr. *Adagio for Strings for Violin and Piano*. New York: G. Schirmer, 1966. Schirmer 50482603. [Wentzel #297]

FOR DOUBLE BASS

Ludwin, Norman, arr. *Adagio for Strings*. Los Angeles: Ludwin Music, 2003. newitem160473031. [double bass quartet]

FOR ACCORDION ENSEMBLE

Brehm, Marc-Oliver, arr. *Adagio for Strings from String Quartet in B Minor*, Nr. 1 [*sic*], Opus 11 Akkordeon-Orchester. Lyss, Switzerland: Akkordeon-Musik-Edition, 2001. AME-7194.

FOR SYMPHONIC WIND ENSEMBLE

Mortimer, John Glenesk, arr. *Platoon: Adagio for Strings*. Crans-Montana, Switzerland: Editions Marc Reift, 1978. MA.EMR-1978.

Jennings, Paul, arr. *Adagio for Young Concert Band*. New York: G. Schirmer, 1991. Schirmer 2248656. [Wentzel #210]

Custer, Calvin, arr. *Adagio for Strings for Band*. New York: G. Schirmer, 1992. Schirmer 50481482. [Wentzel #127]

FOR STUDENT ORCHESTRA

Hoffman, Jamin, arr. *Adagio for Strings*. New York: G. Schirmer, 2005. Schirmer 50485978.

FOR CHORUS

Barber, Samuel, arr. *Agnus Dei: Music of Inner Harmony*, Opus 11. New York: G. Schirmer, 1967. Schirmer GS50313910.

______, arr. *Lamb of God*. New York: G. Schirmer, 1967. Schirmer GS31398.

This discography identifies a spectrum of recorded examples of transcriptions and arrangements. They are categorized in score order chronologically according to release date when known.

Selected Commercial Recordings

FOR VOICES

Dale Warland Singers, cond. Dale Warland. *Cathedral Classics*. American Choral Catalog, ACC 120, 1995.

Choir of Ormond College, cond. Douglas Lawrence. *Music from Heaven*. Move Records, MD3181, 1997.

Oxford New College Choir, cond. Edward Higginbottom. *Agnus Dei*. Erato, 3984 29588-2, 1997.

Denver St. John's Episcopal Choir, cond. Donald Pearson. *Serene Journeys*. Delos, 1608, 1998.

Winchester Cathedral Choir, cond. David Hill. *Lux Aeterna*. Virgin Classics, 45340, 1998.

Cambridge Trinity College Choir, cond. Richard Marlow. *More Tears from Heaven*. RCA Victor Red Seal, 63450, 1999.

Cambridge Singers, cond. John Rutter. *Images of Christ*. Collegium Records, 124, 2000.

Ex Cathedra, cond. Jeffrey Skidmore. *A New Heaven*. Ex Cathedra Ltd., EXCCD002, 2000.

Celtic Tenors. *So Strong*. EMI Records, 724355728425, 2002.

The Sixteen, cond. Harry Christophers. *À la Gloire de Dieu*. Coro, 16013, 2003.

Westminster Choir, cond. Joseph Flummerfelt. *Heaven to Earth*. Avie, 0046, 2003.

London Voices, cond. Terry Edwards. *Choral Adagios*. Decca 000316102, 2004. [trans. Runswick]

Handel and Haydn Society, cond. Grant Llewellyn. *Peace*. Avie, 39, 2004.

The Sixteen, cond. Harry Christophers. *Renaissance: Music for Inner Peace*. Decca, 000453102, 2004.

Accentus Chamber Choir, cond. Laurence Equilbey. *Melancolie*. Naive, 5036, 2006.

FOR FLUTE

Fluteforce. *Pastorale*. Video Artists International (VAI) Audio, 106079350, 1996. [trans. Schmidt]

Flutes Fantastique. *Flutes Fantastique*. The Orchard, 1999. [trans. Schmidt]

Andy Findon. *Andy Findon–Tracked*. Quartz, 2005. [trans. Findon]

FOR FLUTE / SYNTHESIZER

James Galway. *The Lark in the Clear Air*. RCA Victor Records, 61379, 1994. [trans. Fujikake]

FOR CLARINET

Lucien Cailliet. *The Clarinet Choir–Arranged and Conducted by Lucien Cailliet*. Huntington Station, N.Y.: Golden Crest Records, CR 4079, 1979. [trans. Cailliet]

Richard Stoltzman. *Dreams*. RCA Victor, 090266193622, 1994. [trans. Opperman]

FOR SAXOPHONE

Jean Yves Formeau Saxophone Quartet. *The Art of the Jean Yves Formeau Saxophone Quartet*. René Gailly, B0000044YK, 1995. [trans. Warner]

Washington Saxophone Quartet. *Daydream*. Americus Records, 327050, 2000. [trans. van der Linden]

Aurelia Saxophone Quartet. *Blow!–Saxophone Music from America*. Challenge B00005A8DT, 2001. [trans. van der Linden]

FOR TROMBONE

Eastman Trombone Society. *60th Anniversary Celebration*. Eastman School of Music, 1995. [trans. Pugh]

The London Trombones. *The London Trombone Sound*. Cala, CACD 0108, 2006. [trans. Crees]

Muncher Posaunen Quartett (Munich Trombone Quartet). *Ouverture*. Audite, 97533, 2008.

FOR BRASS QUINTET

Gomalan Brass. *Movie Brass*. Naxos, 8.572244, 2007. [trans. McNeff]

FOR PERCUSSION

Hohner Percussion Ensemble. *Lift Off*. Digital Music Prod CD-498, 1993. [trans. Hohner]

FOR ORGAN

Todd Wilson. *In a Quiet Cathedral.* Delos 3145, 1994. [trans. Strickland]

David Pizarro. *Barber's Adagio.* RCA Victor Gold Seal 68758, 1997. [trans. Strickland]

Willibald Guggenmos. *The Grand Organ, Sydney Town Hall.* Motette Records B000051ZMC, 2000. [trans. Strickland]

Carlo Curley. *A Genesis in Harmony.* Svensk Orgelkonsult AB, B005QZAOE6, 2003. [trans. Strickland]

James Devor. *Mystica Rosa.* Herald, HAVPCD 308, 2008. [trans. Cullen]

FOR STRINGS

I Musici. *Concerto per archi.* Philips, 416 356-1, 1986.

Cello. *Cello.* Pro Arte, CDD 500, 1990.

Ryuichi Sakamoto. *Beauty.* Virgin Record, VJD-322 35, 1990. [trans. Sakamoto]

California Guitar Trio. *Pathways.* Discipline Us, CGTCD003, 1998. [trans. Funicelli]

Outer Bass. *Outer Bass.* Outer Bass, 20001114, 1999. [trans. Crantford]

Jenny Oaks Baker & Jenny Richards. *American Tapestry.* Shadow Mountain Records, R 556384, 2001.

FOR SYMPHONIC WIND ENSEMBLE

Brass Band de Wâldsang, cond. Frans Violet. *Simply the Best.* Bernaerts Records BB0535, 1999. [trans. van der Velde]

The Band of the Royal Lancers, cond. J. R. Young. *Summon the Heroes.* Soundline, 4011, 2002. [trans. Young]

The DUT Yorkshire Imperial Rothwell Band, cond. Simon Godfrey Wood. *Beyond the Stars: 16 Fantastic Film Themes.* Chameleon Arts Management Recordings, 101 CAM CD, 2002.

Philharmonic Wind Orchestra, cond. Marc Reift. *Cinemagic 5.* Marcophon, CD 7040, 2008. [trans. Mortimer]

FOR VARIOUS MEDIA

Various Artists. *Barber's Adagio.* RCA Victor Gold Seal, 68758, 1997. [trans. Fujikake, McNeff, Barber, Strickland]

FOR PANPIPE

Andy Findon. *The Best Panpipes Album in the World . . . Ever.* Virgin TV, VTDCD545, 2003. [trans. Findon]

Durations for Selected Agnus Dei Performances

TIME ORCHESTRA, CONDUCTOR (NUMBER OF ENSEMBLE MEMBERS). *NAME OF ALBUM*. LABEL, NUMBER, YEAR.

5:29 London Voices, cond. Terry Edwards (60-85). *Choral Adagios.* Decca, 000316102, 2004.

5:55 Ormand College Choir, cond. Douglas Lawrence (22). *Samuel Barber: Choral Music.* Naxos, 8.559053, 2006; *Eternal Barber.* Naxos, 8.572133, 2008.

6:14 Crouch End Festival Choir, cond. David Temple (ca. 100). *Cinema Choral Classics*. Silva, SILKD6040, 2005.

6:20 Ex Cathedra, cond. Jeffrey Skidmore (14). *A New Heaven*. Ex Cathedra Ltd., EXCCD002, 2000.

7:05 Goeyvaerts Ensemble, cond. Marc Michael de Smet (26). "Goeyvaerts Ensemble, Belgium; Barber: Agnus Dei," *YouTube* (20 April 2007), posted by DolfRabus.

7:11 Accentus Choir, cond. Lawrence Equilbey (32). *Transciptions, Vol. 1*. Naïve, V4947, 2003.

7:13 Handel and Haydn Society Choir, cond. Grant Llewellyn (60). *Peace*. Avie, 39, 2004.

7:36 Cambridge University Chamber Choir, cond. Timothy Brown (41). *Samuel Barber: Choral and Organ Works*. Guild, GMCD 7145, 1998.

7:41 Atlanta Symphony Chorus, cond. Robert Spano (208). *Transmigration*. Telarc, 80673-25, 2009.

7:43 Winchester Cathedral Choir, cond. David Hill (54). *Lux Aeterna*. Virgin Classics, 45340, 1998.

7:57 Oxford New College Choir, cond. Edward Higginbottom (ca. 32). *Agnus Dei*. Erato, 3984 29588-2, 1996.

Time	Orchestra, Conductor (Number of Ensemble Members). *Name of Album*. Label, Number, Year.
8:00	Rundfunkchor Berlin (Berlin Radio Chorus), cond. Simon Halsey (63). *Copland: Simple Gifts.* Coviello Classics, COV40611, 2006.
8:14	The Dale Warland Singers, cond. Dale Warland (40). *Cathedral Classics*. American Choral Catalog, ACC 120, 1995.
8:19	The Sixteen, cond. Harry Christophers (16). *Barber: Agnus Dei.* Coro, COR16031, 2005.
8:30	Mormon Tabernacle Choir, cond. Craig Jessup (330). "Barber: Agnus Dei," *YouTube* (8 March 2007), posted by jrtapia.
8:38	Conspirare, cond. Craig Hella Johnson (91). *A Company of Voices*. Harmonia Mundi, HMU907534, 2009.
9:27	Cambridge Trinity College Choir, cond. Richard Marlowe (30). *The Only Choral CD You'll Ever Need.* RCA Victor Red Seal, 63760, 2001.
9:50	Corydon Singers, cond. Matthew Best (35). *Bernstein: Chichester Psalms*. Hyperion, 66219, 1993.
10:55	Robert Shaw Festival Singers, cond. Robert Shaw (76). *Evocation of the Spirit.* Telarc, 80406, 1995.

By Professional Companies

TITLE	COMPANY	CHOREOGRAPHER
Above	Tom Evert Dance Company	Daniel Job
Adagio for Strings	Kibbutz Dance Company	Rami Be'er
Adagio for Strings	San Francisco Ballet	Gerard Bohbot
Adagio for Strings	Sadlers Wells Ballet School	Antony Dowson
Adagio for Strings	Ballet Theatre Ashtabula	Shelagh Dubsky
Adagio for Strings	Alberta Ballet	Yukichi Hattori
Adagio for Strings	Grant Street Dance Company	Kim Jureckson
Adagio for Strings	Academia de danza la Duncaniana	Mónica Montañana
Adagio for Strings	Ballet Theatre of Maryland	Bryan Skates
Adagio for Strings	Carolina Ballet	Robert Weiss
Adagio for Strings	Toledo Ballet	Kerri Wilde
Adagio for Strings	City Ballet of San Diego	Elizabeth Wistrich
Adagio for Ten and Two	San Francisco Ballet	Richard Gibson
Adagio for Two	New York City Ballet	M. Mahdaviani
Adagio for Two (or *Roblise*)	Humphrey Dance Ensemble	Robert Pachette and Elise Choen
America	Ballet Oklahoma	Bryan Pitts
Angels' Domain	Helios Dance Theater	Laura Gorenstein
Appasionatto	Bay Area Houston Ballet & Theatre	Milena Leben
Ascension	Wylliams/Henry Dance Company	Leni Wylliams
Atemlos, Atme, Los! [Breathless, Breathe, Go!]	Gera Altenburg Ballet	Silvana Schröder
Atom	Diavolo	Jacques Heim
Barber's Adagio	Kirov Ballet Company	Oleg Vinogradov
La Barre Vassili	Nevada Dance Theatre	Veseljko Sulic
The Beloved	Dance Augusta	Andrew Kuharsky

TITLE	COMPANY	CHOREOGRAPHER
Beyond: Portraits of Chinese Women	Ballet Memphis	Lily Cai
Brethren	Las Vegas Contemporary Dance Theater	Bernard H. Gaddis
Bristle	First Feet Contemporary Dance Series	Donald Byrd
Butterfly Print	Hartford Ballet	Victoria Marks
Coercing Virtue	American National Ballet	A. Maldonado
Crossroads	At Marah Dance Theatre	Stephen Wynne
Descending	Whitebird Dance Series	Minh Tran
Dracula	New Mexico Ballet Company	Patricia Dickinson
Earthly Love, Heavenly Spirits	MorganScott Ballet	Morgan / Scott
Earthly Love, II	MorganScott Ballet	Edward Morgan
Ecos	Ballet Argentino	Mauricio Wainrot
Elegy (Sagan's Song)	Philadanco (reconstruction)	Gene Hill Sagan Kim Y. Bears
Ephemeral Possessions	American Repertory Ballet	Douglas Martin
Exit	various	Deborah Hay
Facade	Singapore Dance Theatre	Jeffrey Tan
Futility	Ballet Central	Sara Matthews
Gates of Mercy	Northern Lights Dance Theatre	Paula Thomson
Gift of Passage	City Center Ballet	Ruth Mayer
HeartBeat: mb	White Oak Dance Project	M. Baryshnikov
Hear I am Before You	Chico Community Ballet	Andrew Allagree
Hymn to Man	Sarasota Ballet	Robert de Warren
If Only	DanceDetour	Alana Wallace
Into Rain	Demetrious Klein Dance Company	C. Plunkett
Journey	Chamber Dance Project	Diane C. Bruning
Lament	Australian Ballet	John Meehan
Litany	Concert Ballet of Virginia	Nan Blackwell
Maquette	Monte/Brown Dance	David Brown

Title	Company	Choreographer
Memory	American Ballet Theatre	John Meehan
On the Verge	The Santa Barbara Dance Alliance	Marnie Baker
One	Take Dance Company	Takehiro Ueyama
Pedestal	Rochester City Ballet	Jamey Leverett
Penance	Deja Vu Dance Theater	Barry Martin
Per Sonja	WashAshore Dance Ensemble	Ivan Cavallari
Portinari	Parsons Dance	David Parsons
Prayer	Ballet North	Laura Reinschmidt
Purple Bend #1	Miami City Ballet	Jimmy Gamonet
Purple Bend #2	Miami City Ballet	Jimmy Gamonet
Rusing Angels	North Carolina Dance Theatre	Septime Webre
Sabachthani	Raven Dance Project of Huntsville	Dana E. Nicolay
Scarlet	Canyon Concert Ballet	R. Sher-Machherndl
Silent Night	Susan Tenney and Company	Susan Tenney
A Song for Peace	Saint Anthony Performing Arts Sacred Dance Troupe	Indi Dieckgrafe
Stigmata	Gregory Hancock Dance Theater	Gregory Hancock
Still Life Moving	Northwest Professional	James Canfield
Submerged	Melbourne Ballet Company	Simon Hoy
Suspended Breath	James Sewell Ballet	James Sewell
Thorns	Toronto Dance Theatre	Sharon Moore
Through the Edge	Washington National Ballet	M. Lopuszanski
Too Soon Lost	Solo dance	Patrick Scully
Transcendence	Artisan Dance	Sallyann Mulcahy
Tribute	Kansas Regional Ballet of Overland Park	C. Kierl-Bourman
Trinity	Ballet Bahia	Luis Arrieta
Two Golden Hours	Kansas City Ballet	Robert Mills
Unter Gewitterwolken [Under Thunderclouds]	Stadttheater Bermerhaven, Germany	Jörg Mannes

TITLE	COMPANY	CHOREOGRAPHER
Voices	Brandywine Ballet Company	Nancy Page
Who's Who	Eifman Ballet	Boris Eifman
Yet So Far	Northwest Florida Dance Festival	Todd Eric Allen
Yhteentörmäys [Clash]	Helsinki Dance Company	Arja Tiili
Youth	Harkness Ballet	Richard Wagner

By University Companies

TITLE	UNIVERSITY	CHOREOGRAPHER
Adagio for Strings	Boston Univ. Dance Theatre Group	Miguel Estefan
Adagio for Strings	Boston Conservatory	Julie I. Thompson
Adagio for Strings	Dance Theatre Northwest (Tacoma Community College)	Melanie K-Stauffer
Adagio for Strings	Indiana University Ballet Theater	Jean-P. Bonnefoux
Adagio for Strings	Indiana University Ballet Theater	Laura Colofranson
Adagio for Strings	Princeton Pro Musica	C. W-Marcuard and Janell Byrne
Adagio for Strings	Texas State Univ., Marcos	
Adagio for Strings	Univ. of North Carolina, Greensboro	B. J. Sullivan
Adagio for Strings	Wagner College	Kathy Jo Hubner and Mary Lilligren
Adagio for 13 Music (Stands and a Rope)	Univ. of Arizona Dance Ensemble	Douglas Nielsen
Balet Divertissement	Old Dominion University	Valerij Miklin
Barber Adagio for Strings	Univ. of Wisconsin, Eau Claire	Chelsey Dahm
Before Denial	Butler Ballet	Tommy Lewey
Blue Adagio	Northern Kentucky University	Stephen Mills

Title	University	Choreographer
Broken Off From the Sky	Rice Dance Theatre	Sophia Torres
Burden	Murray State University	Michelle Myers
Dimensions	Colorado University	Nada Diachenko
Duetto	Orange Coast College	Israel "El" Gabriel
Eternal	Univ. of Dayton Dance Ensemble	Lori Weaver
The Faces of Grief	Butler University	Marjorie Harter
In the Dark	Hope College	Jodi H. James
Light in the Shadow	Ballet School Basel	Vitali Safronkine
Memories: A Requiem	Western Michigan University	Edgar Page
My Ascension	University of Tennessee Dance Company	Melinda Brown
". . . only to begin again,"	Western Illinois University	Heidi Clemmens
Permission	Hobart and William Smith Colleges	Kim N. Nofsinger
Refuge	Lane Community College	Bonnie Simoa
Threads	University of Hawaii-Manoa	Kristi Burns
Throughout Sentiment	SUNY Pottsdam	Janet Speranza
A Time to Love	Eastern Michigan University	Lourdes Bastos
Unbow	Emory University Dance Studio	George Staib
Until There's a Cure	University of Iowa	C. Goldman
Verlangen	Case Western Reserve University	R. Dickinson

Other Plays with *Adagio*

Title	Company	Choreographer
Defying Gravity	Robert Merrimack Repertory Co.	Jane Anderson
Humboldt's Current	The Fiji Company	Ping Chong

Title	Company	Choreographer
Huis Clos [No Exit]	Amateur Dramatic Club Theatre Cambridge University	Jean-Paul Sartre
Jacks	Lys Anzia	
Keely and Du	Times Centenary College	Jane Martin
La Maison Suspendue	Actors Theatre / San Francisco	Michel Tremblay
One Night Only	Stella Adler Theatre	Stephen A. Roberts
The Realm of Wasps	National Institute of Dramatic Arts	Steven Dawson
Someone Who'll Watch Over Me	Hempstead Theatre, London	Frank McGuiness

Adagio in Aerial Ballet: Battle of Britain Memorial Flight

Each year at the Leuchars Airshow, planes flown during the Battle of Britain participate in an "aerial ballet." In 2006, *Adagio for Strings*, broadcast over loudspeakers, accompanied their display. Taking part were an Avro Lancaster, the main heavy RAF bomber with four Rolls-Royce Merlin engines (only two planes are still airworthy) and the single-engine Merlin Hurricane. The Spitfire, the usual third member of the trio, could not participate due to last-minute engine problems. (Even a Merlin sometimes fails).[1]

Others

Adagio is the final part of a solo dance in four parts, *Angels' Domain* (1997) that Laura Gorenstein choreographed for Helios Dance Theater. Dance critic Victoria Looseleaf described it as a "potent, near-flawless blend of humor and pathos" dealing with the "heart, soul and stamina of woman."[2] Dancer Diana Mehoudar becomes a fallen angel, clothed in a black costume with skeletal wings. "This heartbreaking solo saw the

[1]See "Lancaster and Hurricane (BBMF)," *YouTube* (23 September 2006) posted by hapgood617. A few nearly inaudible notes of *Adagio* can be heard during the flight display.

[2]Victoria Looseleaf, "Dance Review: Helios Troupe Celebrates the Vital Power of Woman," *Los Angeles Times*, Home Edition (20 December 1997), 5.

dancer scrambling unsuccessfully to rise above her plight" as *Adagio* underscored her will to persevere; "flapping her hands, arms quivering, [she] infused her expressions with piquancy, her dance with valor."[3]

Choreographer Anders Christiansen described *Discussion of the Male Anatomy* (Copenhagen, 1997), as a "dance performance for seven dancers, one choirboy and a pianist." He expressed his intent:

> The performance moves from quiet compositions of images to transvestite-like variety theatre in its uncovering of the male. A strictly subjective examination that seeks to shed light on the nature of masculinity in general by focusing on tendencies associated with the homosexual male.[4]

A statement in the program concerning the choreography implies that Christiansen devised the original concept and most of the movements but allowed his dancers to contribute some of their own ideas. The program does not detail what the choirboy (Søren Birch Plum) sang, but the pianist, Christer-Irgens-Møller, played her own music. *Adagio for Strings* is placed in a group of taped pieces.

Agnus Dei was a piece Stephen Wynne inserted in *Crossroads,* a work he choreographed in 1997 for Philadelphia's At Marah Dance Theatre.[5] His choreographic style draws much from the modern dance techniques of Martha Graham and Jose Limon.[6] The other music for the dance is Bach's Brandenburg Concerto No. 5.

[3] *Ibid.*

[4] Anders Christiansen, quoted in Vibeke Wern, "Discussion of the Male Anatomy," *Berlingske Tildende* (27 February 1997).

[5] "At Marah" is a Biblical reference meaning "where bitterness can be made sweet."

[6] "Mission," *At Marah Dance Theatre*, www.atmarah.org/mission.htm. A video clip of another portion of the work appears on the AMDT website. Other works choreographed to Agnus Dei include Jack Hansen's *Agnus Dei* (2005) for the Sacramento Ballet and *Loveblind* (2004), which James Clouser originally created for the Dayton Ballet and reprised for the University of Arizona Dance division.

By Marching Bands and Drum and Bugle Corps

Title	Location
Adams Central Squadron of Sound	Monroe, Ind.
Arcadia High School Marching Band	Arcadia, Calif.
Blue Mountain High School Color Guard	Schuykill Haven, Penn.
Buccaneers Drum and Bugle Corps	Reading, Penn.
Colony High School Marching Band	The Colony, Tex.
Connecticut Hurricane Drum and Bugle Corps	Derby, Conn.
Donna High School Marching Band	Donna, Tex.
Eagle Marching Band Norristown Area High School	Norristown, Penn.
Friendswood High School Marching Band	Friendswood, Tex.
Govenaires Society of Brass (brass section of the Govenaires Drum and Bugle Corps)	St. Peter, Minn.
James E. Taylor Marching Band	Harris Co., Tex.
James Madison High School Band	Vienna, Va.
Kellam Marching Knights	Virginia Beach, Va.
Lebanon Valley College Marching Band	Annville, Penn.
MacArthur Cardettes, MacArthur High School	Irving, Tex.
Mandarins Drum and Bugle Corps	Sacramento, Calif.
Meade Country High School Band	Brandenburgh, Ky.
Millersville University Drumline	Millersville, Penn.
Mount Pleasant High School Marching Band	Mount Pleasant, N.C.
Northwest Viking Marching Band	Greensboro, N.C.
Oak Grove High School Marching Band	San Jose, Calif.
Portage Northern High School Band	Portage, Mich.
Syracuse Brigadiers Winter Guard	Syracuse, N.Y.
Whitehall High School Infinity Guard	Whitehall, Penn.
Whitesboro (High School) Bearcat Band	Whitesboro, Tex.

Adagio References in Fiction and Poetry

APPENDIX 6

Literary works discussed by the author in Chapter 6 are marked here by an asterisk (*).

Fiction

Ambrose, David R. *Letters From the Nude Lake.* Victoria, B.C.: Trafford, 2001.

*Austin, Alan K. *The Adagio: A Mystery*. Bloomington, Ind.: iUniverse, 2007.

*Baltzell, Karin Bundesen, and Georgianne Nienaber. *Horse Sense.* New York: Authors Choice Press, 2006.

*Bennett, Alan. *The Laying On of Hands: Stories.* New York: Picador, 2002.

Biank, Tanya. *Under the Sabers: The Unwritten Code of Army Wives.* New York: St. Martin's Press, 2006.

Brewer, Wesley C. *Beyond the Sangres: A Tale of Hope, Pain, and Courage*. Lincoln, Neb.: iUniverse, 2005.

Butterfield, Catherine. *Joined at the Head.* New York: Dramatists Play Service, 1993; revised 1998.

Carter, Betsy. *Nothing to Fall Back On: The Life and Times of a Perpetual Optimist.* New York: Hyperion Books, 2002.

*Christie, Valerie. *The Mysterious Affair at Redfield.* Bloomington, Ind.: Xlibris, 2002.

Cohen, Theodore Jerome. *Full Circle: A Dream Denied, A Vision Fulfilled.* Bloomington, Ind.: AuthorHouse, 2009.

Crafton, Barbara Cawthorne. "Before the Last War," *The Sewing Room.* Harrisburg, Penn.: Church Publishing, 1997.

D'Alfonso, Antonio. *Fabrizio's Passion.* Toronto: Guernica Editions, 1995; revised 2000.

Deaver, Geoffrey. *The Bone Collector.* New York: Viking (A Lincoln Rhyme Novel), 1997.

Dent, Grace. *Lbd: It's a Girl Thing*. New York: G. P. Putnam's Sons, 2003.

Dixon, Terence, and Martin Lucas. *The Human Race.* New York: McGraw-Hill, 1983.

Dorfman, Harvey A. *Persuasion of My Days*. Falls Village, Conn.: Hamilton Books, 2005.

Downs, Michael. *House of Good Hope: A Promise for a Broken City.* Lincoln: University of Nebraska Press, 2007.

Eyre, Linda. *I Didn't Plan to Be a Witch and Other Surprises of a Joyful Mother.* Salt Lake City: Publishers Press, 1988; revised New York: Fireside, 1996.

*Fedo, Michael. "The Musicians' Corner in Purgatory," *Whistling Shade: A Twin Cities Literary Journal* IV/1 (Spring 2004); reprinted www.whistlingshade.com/0401/purgatory.html.

Finch, Robert. *The Cape Itself.* New York: W. W. Norton, 1991.

Flesher, Jerry. *Tomorrow I'll Miss You.* Lincoln, Neb.: iUniverse, 2005.

Ford, MacKenzie. *The Clouds Beneath the Sun.* New York: Random House, 2012.

Foster, David. *The Glade Within the Grove.* London: Fourth Estate, 1996.

Fouz-Hernández, Santiago, and Freya Larman-Ivens. *Madonna's Drowned Worlds: New Approaches to her Subcultural Transformations, 1983-2003.* Burlington, Vt.: Ashgate, 2004.

Gatza, Geoffrey. *Black Diamond Golden Boy Takes Bull by Horns.* Kenmore, N.Y.: BlazeVOX Books, 2007.

*Gerrold, David. *Bouncing off the Moon.* New York: Tom Doherty Associates, 2001.

Gildner, Gary. *Nails.* Pittsburgh: University of Pittsburgh Press, 1975.

Gordon, Michael. *Acid Tree Park.* Oxford, Mich.: Monk Press, 2009.

Hayes, Charles D. *Portals in a Northern Sky.* Wasilla, Alaska: Autodidactic, 2003.

*Hickam, Homer H., Jr. *Back to the Moon.* New York: Dell Publishers, 2001.

Huey, Tom. *Mischa, Me, and Wittgenstein.* Bloomington, Ind.: Xlibris Corporation, 2011.

*Johnson, Forrest. *A Parson's Tales.* Bloomington, Ind.: Xlibris, 2000.

Jones, Cindi. *Squirrel Cage.* Raleigh, N.C.: Lulu Press, 2006.

Kastens, Theana. *Green Gold in Jamaica.* Bloomington, Ind.: Authorhouse, 2006.

Kehoe, Denis. *Walking on Dry Land.* London: Profile Books, 2011.

Kiser, John W. *The Monks of Tibhirine.* New York: St. Martin's Press, 2002.

Kuner, Susan, ed. *Speak the Language of Healing: A New Approach to Breast Cancer.* Berkeley, Calif.: Canori, 1999.

Landi, Val. *A Woman from Cairo.* Charleston, S.C.: BookSurge Publishing, 2006.

Lavoie, Karla Lee. *For Time and All Eternity: Love Never Dies.* West Conshohocken, Penn.: Infinity Publishing, 2006.

Leighton, Cecil Donald. *A Divine Comedy: The Sacred and Profane Journey of Tom Spotted Tail.* Pittsburgh: Dorrance Publishing, 2009.

*Lester, Julius. *The Autobiography of God.* New York: St. Martin's, 2004.

Lock, Norman. *A History of the Imagination: A Novel.* Tallahassee, Fla.: Fiction Collective Two, 2004.

Mann, Mark. *Of Greater Value*. Ostego, Mich.: PageFree Publishing, 2001.

Manuel, Dustin. "Adagio," *Musings*. Cary, N.C.: Lulu Press, 2005.

*Martin, Emer. *More Bread or I'll Appear*. Boston: Houghton Mifflin, 1999. [The string quartet is mentioned rather than the orchestral *Adagio*.]

McDermott, Keith. *Acqua Calda: A Novel.* New York: Carroll & Graf, 2005.

*McDonald, Janet. *Project Girl*. Berkeley: University of California Press, 2000.

*McEwan, Ian. *Saturday*. New York: Random House, 2005.

Mentis, Paris. *Plato's Cave*. Bloomington, Ind.: Xlibris Corporation, 2001.

*Moore, Lorrie. "Four Calling Birds, Three French Hens," *Birds of America*. New York: Picador, 1998.

O'Brien, Michael. *Eclipse of the Sun*. San Francisco: Ignatius Press, 1998.

Olden, Marc. *Gaijin*. London: Corgi Books, 1986; revised New York: Jove Books, 1987.

*Parker, George. *The Atomic Kid: Adventures in the Antiworld*. New York: Bookman Publishing, 2004.

*Parrott, M. R. M. "On the Page," *A Bartered Tide*. Columbia, S.C.: Rimric, 2002.

Pearson, John. *Train Doors Slamming*. Oxfordshire, U.K.: Writersworld, 2005.

Powers, Richard. *The Time of Our Singing*. New York: St. Martin's Press, 2003.

*Rakow, Mary. *The Memory Room*. Emeryville, Calif.: Shoemaker and Hoard, 2002.

Renner, David. *Memoirs of a Fool, Volume 1*. Bloomington, Ind.: AuthorHouse, 2007.

*Robinson, Kim Stanley. *Icehenge*. New York: Orb Edition, 1998.

Runholt, Susan. *Rescuing Seneca Crane*. London: Penguin, 2009.

Salinger, Wendy. *Listen: A Memoir*. London: Bloomsbury Publishing, 2005.

*Sebold, Alice. *The Lovely Bones*. New York: Little, Brown, 2002.

Shaw, Ashraf. *Autumn*. Cary, N.C.: Lulu Press, 2006.

*Shields, Jean. *Air Burial.* New York: Carroll & Graf, 2002.

Shriver, Lionel. *Double Fault*. London: Serpent's Tail, 2006.

Singer, Marilyn. *The First Few Friends*. New York: HarperCollins, 1981.

*Smith, Deborah. *Charming Grace*. New York: Little Brown, 2004.

Spencer, Scott. *A Ship Made of Paper: A Novel.* New York: HarperCollins, 2003.

Steinbach, Alice. *Educating Alice: Adventures of a Curious Woman*. New York: Random House, 2004.

*Stephenson, Neal. *Cryptonomicon*. New York: HarperCollins, 2000.

Stonich, Sarah. *The Ice Chorus*. New York: Little, Brown, 2005.

Storm, James. *Domination*. Washington, D.C.: Olympia Press, 2008.

*Talley, Marcia. *In Death's Shadow*. New York: HarperCollins, 2004.

Trofimuk, Thomas. *Waiting for Columbus*. New York: Randon House Digital, 2009.

*Venator, William. *Wither This Land.* London: WritersPrintShop, 2003.

Weir, John. *What I Did Wrong*. New York: Viking, 2006.

Wells, Kellie. *Skin*. Lincoln: University of Nebraska Press, 2006.

Wenner, Kate. *Setting Fires*. New York: Berkeley Trade, 2001.

*Willett, Marcia. *A Summer in the Country*. New York: St. Martin's Press, 2002.

Poetry

Brock, James. "The End of the Age of Irony," *Gods and Money*. Cincinatti: WordTech Communications, 2010.

Chappell, Frank R. "A Note on Values," *An Atheist Who Prays: Paradoxical Poetry*. Lincoln, Neb.: iUniverse, 2004, 27.

Dirr, Robert H., Jr. "Vernal Equinox," 1997, www.wingman.dier.us/poems /dirr.htm.

Freed, Elliott. "Adagio for Strings," *Falling Poems*. Cotati / Venice, Calif.: Cotation Press, 2001, 21; reprinted "Adagio for Strings," *Elliott Freed: Falling Poems* (1999), www.wordrunner.com/chapbook/authors/Freed .htm.

Jarman, Mark. "Adagio for Strings," *Quarterly West* LIII (2001), 18-19.

*Matthias, John. John Matthias, "A Note on Barber's Adagio," *Pages: New Poems and Cuttings* Athens, Ohio: Swallow, 2000).

Perkins, John Brian. "A Little Annoying Night Music," *The Fruit of Falling Down*. Bloomington, Ind.: Xlibris, 2003, 47.

Shepard, Neil. "Listening to Samuel Barber's *Adagio for Strings*," *Quarterly West* XLVII (1998), 14-15.

Adagio for Strings in Pop Culture

The following performances, listed here in order of presentation, were cited in the text of Chapter 7. It is a useful point of departure for understanding the breadth of contexts in which *Adagio* has been played, not a comprehensive performance list.

Live Performances

The Cure. Dream Tour through Europe and North America, 2000. Intro. "Out of This World."

Deep Purple. Various European Concerts, 1996. Royal Albert Tour, 2000. United Kingdom Tour, September 2001. Intro. "When a Blind Man Cries."

Deep Purple with the Romanian Philharmonic Orchestra, cond. Paul Mann. Live Telecast, October 2000. Stuttgart, Bade-Wurtemberg, Germany. Intro. "When a Blind Man Cries."

Joel, Billy. Live Concert, 16 April 1994. Miami, Fla. Intro. "Shades of Grey."

Ørbit, William; The Sixteen. Karlheinz Stockhausen Electronic Festival, October 2001. Barbican Centre, London.

Puff Daddy [Diddy, Sean Combs]; Evans, Faith; and Sting. MTV Music Video Awards, 4 September 1997. New York. Intro. "I'll Be Missing You."

Tiësto. Album Release Concert of *Just Be*, 20 May 2004. Heineken Music Hall, Amsterdam.

______. Opening Ceremony of the Olympic Games, 2004. OAKA Spiros Louis Stadium a.k.a. Olympic Stadium, Athens.

______. *Tiësto in Concert,* May 2003 and subsequent tours. Gelredome Stadium, Arnhem, Netherlands

Recorded Performances

Alexander, Glenn. *Oria*. Palmetto Records, PM-2015, 1 January 1996.

Alkana, Danney. *Rock the Bach*. Four Winds Entertainment, 2006, 6 April 1999.

Atkinson, Dawn. *Adagio: A Windham Hill Collection*. Windham Hill Records, 11648, 2003. Arr. Philip Aaberg.

Bastille. *Other People's Heartache*. [vanity], 27 February 2012.

The Beatles. *Let it Be. . . Naked*. Capitol, 07243-595713-2-4, 17 November 2003. Incl. "Sun King."

Bernstein, Leonard. *Shadows and Light: Ambient Music From Another Time*. Polygram / Deutsche Grammophon, G2-45922, 7 March 1995. Arr. R. Peter Munves.

Bond. *Classified.* Decca Music Group Limited, 2894756161, 15 June 2004.

The Brave. *Classical Spirit.* Higher Octave Music, 13138, 2003.

The Cure. *Bloodflowers*. Electra, 62236-2, 2000. Incl. "Out of This World."

______. *Rarities*, vol. 2. Matrix / Runout, CR 00-2, 2003. Incl. "Out of This World."

Coryell, Larry. *American Odyssey*. DRG Records, 5213, 1990. Arr. Ryuta Suzuki.

Delerium. *Chimera*. Nettwerk, 30306, 24 June 2003. Incl. "Eternal Odyssey."

Direct to Dreams (Bruno Meunier). Direct to Dreams, 2007. "Adagio for Strings Barber Remix."

Escala. *Escala*. Syco Music, 88697474232, 2009.

Hahn, Steve. *sh*. Deep Chocolate Productions, DC980502, 1999.

Hoffman, Holly and Mike Wofford. *Live at Athenaeum Jazz, Vol. 2*. Capri, 106531137, 2007. Incl. "Free Day (for Samuel Barber)."

Il Divo. *Wicked Game*. Syco Music, R 2292085, 2011. Trans. "Dov'è l'amore," by Marco Marinangeli and Savan Kotecha.

Liberation Music Orchestra. *Not in Our Name*. Verve Records, 06024982 92488, 29 August 2005. Cond. Charlie Haden, arr. Carla Bley.

Minimalistix. *Elements*. Mostiko, 22 207002, 2002.

Muse. *Absolution*. Taste Music Limited, 5050466-8587-2-6, 2003. [This is an interlude between "Hysteria" and "Blackout" on Tracks 7 and 9.]

Oakenfold, Paul. *The Goa Mix 2011*. New State Music, NEW2CD078, 2010. [Album includes portion of the Bernstein recording with the New York Philharmonic on Track 18, disc one.]

______. *Great Wall*. Reprise Records, 48558-2, 30 September 2003. Incl. Skip Raider's work, "Another Day."

______. *Perfecto Fluoro*. Warner Music UK Ltd., 0630-16694-2, 1996. Trans. "New Kicks" & "Kabalah."

Oceanlab. *Armada Best of Vol. 1*. Armada Music B.V., ARDI126, 2006. Trans. "Satellite" from Tiësto's "Adagio."

Off Beat, dir. Larry McDonough. *Larry McDonough and Off Beat: Live, Cooking at the Dakota*. [vanity], 2002.

Ørbit, William. *Barber's Adagio for Strings*. WEA International, 247CD, 2000. Incl. Ferry Corsten remix.

______. *Pieces in a Modern Style*. Maverick, 9-47956-2, 2000.

Puff Daddy. *No Way Out*. Bad Boy Records, 73012-2, 1997. Incl. "I'll Be Missing You."

______. *Tribute to the Notorious B.I.G.* Bad Boy Records, R 328134, 1997. Incl. "I'll Be Missing You."

______. *Diana Princess of Wales Tribute*. Sony, C2K 69012, 1997. Incl. "I'll Be Missing You."

Serenata, part of the *Quantic Nature Collection*. Quantic Music Productions, QNC9981CD, 2000.

Snidow, Chris. *Number Our Days*. Cowrind, CSN 3332, 1999.

The Taliesin Orchestra. *Sacred*. Compendia Media Group, 5415, 2002. Arr. Trammell Starks.

Tiësto. *Adagio for Strings*. Nettwerk Records, B00097DX6W, 2005.

Trovato, Steve. *About Time*. Steve Trovato, 1639 [vanity], 7 March 2002.

Urwin, Gary. *Living in the Moment*. Sea Breeze, 2123, 2003. Incl. "Lush Life," Comp. Billy Strayhorn; arr. Gary Urwin.

Songs on Disc by Order of Discussion

"When a Blind Man Cries," *Live at the Olympia '96*, perf. Deep Purple. EMI, 7243 8 57982 2 1, 1997.

"Adagio for Strings," *Other People's Heartache*, perf. Bastille. [vanity], 2012.

"Out of This World," *Bloodflowers*, perf. the Cure. Electra, 62236-2, 2000.

"Out of This World," *Rarities*, vol. 2, perf. the Cure. Matrix / Runout, CR 00-2, 2003.

"I'll Be Missing You," *No Way Out*, perf. Puff Daddy. Bad Boy Records, 73012-2, 1997.

"I'll Be Missing You," *Tribute to the Notorious B.I.G.*, perf. Puff Daddy & Faith Evans. Bad Boy, R 328134, 1997.

"I'll Be Missing You," *Diana Princess of Wales Tribute*, perf. Puff Daddy. Sony, C2K 69012, 1997.

"Adagio for Strings," *Pieces in a Modern Style*, perf. William Ørbit. Maverick, 9-47956-2, 2000.

"Adagio for Strings," *Perfecto Fluoro*, perf. Paul Oakenfold. Warner Music UK Ltd., 0630-16694-2, 1996.

"Adagio for Strings," *The Goa Mix 2011*, cond. Leonard Bernstein, perf. New York Philharmonic. New State Music, NEW2CD078, 2010.

"Barber's Adagio for Strings (Ferry Corsten Mix)," *Barber's Adagio for Strings*, perf. Ferry Corsten. WEA International, 247CD, 2000.

"Adagio for Strings," *Tiësto in Concert* [DVD], perf. Tiësto. Black Hole, BH DVD 02, 2003.

"Adagio for Strings," *Just Be*, perf. Tiësto. Nebula, NEBCD9010, 2004.

"Adagio for Strings," *Parade of the Athletes*, perf. Tiësto. Nettwerk Records, 0 6700 30393 2 1, 2004.

"Adagio for Strings," *Adagio for Strings*, perf. Tiësto. Nettwerk Records, B00097DX6W, 2005.

"Adagio for Strings," *Just Be: Remixed*, three mixes perf. Danjo-Styles, Phynn, and Baker. Nettwerk, 0 6700 30463 5 0, 2006.

"Satellite," *Armada Best of Vol. 1*, perf. Oceanlab. Armada Music B.V., ARDI126, 2006.

"Another Day," *Great Wall*, perf. Skip Raiders feat. Jada, mixed by Paul Oakenfold. Reprise Records, 48558-2, 2003.

"Eternal Odyssey," *Chimera*, perf. Delerium. Nettwerk, 30306, 2003.

"Adagio for Strings," *Classified*, perf. bond. Decca Music Group Limited, 2894756161, 2004.

"Adagio," *Escala*, perf. Escala. Syco Music, 88697474232, 2009.

"Dov'è l'amore," *Wicked Game*, perf. Il Divo. Syco Music, R 2292085, 2011.

"Adagio for Strings," *Oria*, perf. Glenn Alexander. Palmetto Records, PM-2015, 1996.

"Adagio for Strings," *American Odyssey*, perf. Larry Coryell, guitar; Wayne Shorter, saxophones; arr. Ryuta Suzuki. DRG Records, 5212, 1990.

"Adagio for Strings," *About Time*, perf. Steve Trovato. Steve Trovato, 1639, 2002.

"Adagio for Strings," *Rock the Bach*, perf. Danney Alkana. Four Winds Entertainment, 2006, 6 April 1999.

"Adagio," *sh*, perf. Steve Hahn. Deep Chocolate Productions, DC980502, 1999.

"Free Day (for Samuel Barber)," *Live at Athenaeum Jazz, Vol. 2*, perf. Holly Hofmann, flute; Mike Wofford, piano. Capri, 106531137, 2007.

"Adagio," *Not in Our Name*, perf. Liberation Music Orchestra, cond. Charlie Haden; arr. Carla Bley. Verve Records, 0602498292488, 2005.

"Lush Life," *Living in the Moment*, perf. Gary Urwin Jazz Orchestra; arr. Gary Urwin. Sea Breeze, 2123, 2003.

"Adagio for Strings," *Larry McDonough and Off Beat: Live, Cooking at the Dakota*, perf. Larry McDonough and Off Beat. LM Jazz, [demo disc], 2002.

"Sun King," *Let it Be. . . Naked*, perf. The Beatles. Capitol, 07243-595713-2-4, 2003.

"Scene One," *Let it Be* [documentary], perf. Paul McCartney. United Artists, 1970.

"Adagio for Strings," *Shadows and Light: Ambient Music From Another Time*, cond. Leonard Bernstein; perf. Los Angeles Philharmonic Orchestra. Deutsche Grammophon, G2-45922, 1995.

"Adagio for Strings," *Number Our Days*, perf. Chris Snidow. Cowrind, CSN 3332, 1999.

"Adagio for Strings," *Serenata*, perf. Alain Lemay. Quantic Nature Collection, QNC9982CD, 1999.

"Adagio for Strings," *Adagio: A Windham Hill Collection*, perf. Philip Aaberg. Windham Hill Records, 11648, 2003.

"Adagio for Strings (Main Theme)," *Sacred*, perf. The Taliesin Orchestra. Compendia Media Group, 5415, 2002.

"Adagio for Strings," *Classical Spirit*, perf. The Brave. Higher Octane, HOMCD 13138, 2003.

"Adagio for Strings Barber Remix," perf. Direct to Dreams. 2007.

Recordings with a New Age Orientation

William Strickland, arr. "Adagio for Stings," *Wordless Healing: Contemplative Selections for Organ*, perf. Lee Schiring. Kandl / Music, 1000, 2002.

Meeting Angels through Sound and Music. Angel Records, 66347, 1997.

Delta: Unwind and Sleep. Relaxation Co., 3003, 2003. [One disc plus 10-page booklet. This is a separate issue of disc three of the album *Brainwave Symphony* as well as a cassette from the Institute for Consciousness and Music to accompany the book *Music and Your Mind*.[1]]

In utero: Music for My Baby. Virgin Classics, 5 61824 2, 2000. [Not to be confused with the *In utero* Nirvana album]

[1]Jeffrey Thompson, *Brainwave Symphony* (Relaxation, 3000d, 1999). Helen L. Bonny and Louis M. Savary, *Music and Your Mind* (New York: Harper and Row, 1973, revised 1990; St. Louis, Mo.: MMB Music, 2004; Gilsum, N.H.: Barcelona Publishers, 2005).

Adagio in Soundtracks

Feature Films

1974	*A Very Natural Thing*	Drama
1980	*The Elephant Man*	Drama
1983	*El norte* [The North]	Drama / Mexico
1986	*Platoon*	Action / drama
1990	*Soldiers of Music: Rostropovich Returns to Russia*	Documentary
1992	*Lorenzo's Oil* (*Adagio* /Agnus)	Drama
1994	*Les Roseaux sauvages* [Wild Reeds]	Drama / France
1995	*The Scarlet Letter* (Agnus)	Drama
1996	*The Crime of the Century*	Drama
1997	*The Garden of Redemption* (Agnus)	Drama
1997	*Tour of the Inferno: Revisiting Platoon*	Documentary
1999	*Rocky Marciano* (three versions)	Drama
2000	*Kevin and Perry Go Large* (*Adagio*/Trance)	Comedy / England
2001	*Amélie*	Comedy / France
2002	*S1mØne* (Agnus)	Comedy
2003	*Reconstruction*	Drama / Denmark
2003	*Swimming Upstream*	Drama
2004	*ma mère* [My Mother] (Agnus)	Drama / France
2004	*Shake Hands with the Devil*	Documentary
2004	*Peace One Day*	Documentary
2006	*Tenacious D in the Pick of Destiny* (Agnus)	Comedy
2007	*Sicko*	Documentary

DRAMAS

1974 *A Very Natural Thing*, dir. Christopher Larkin. Uncredited recording.

1980 *The Elephant Man*, dir. David Lynch. London Symphony Orchestra, cond. André Previn.

1983 *El norte*, dir. Gregory Nava. Uncredited recording.

1986 *Platoon*, dir. Oliver Stone. Vancouver Symphony Orchestra, cond. George Delerue.

1992 *Lorenzo's Oil*, dir. George Miller. *Adagio for Strings* and Agnus Dei, uncredited recordings.

1994 *Les Roseaux sauvages*, dir. André Téchiné. I Musici.

1995 *The Scarlet Letter*, dir. Roland Joffé. Agnus Dei, Robert Shaw Festival Singers.

1996 *Crime of the Century*, dir. Mark Rydell. Uncredited recording.

1997 *The Garden of Redemption*, dir. Thomas Michael Donnelly. Agnus Dei, uncredited recording.

1999 *Rocky Marciano*, dir. Charles Winkler. *Adagio for Strings* (orchestra), Agnus Dei, and *Adagio for Strings* (organ), uncredited recordings.

2003 *Reconstruction*, dir. Christoffer Boe. Academy of St. Martin in the Fields, cond. Neville Mariner.

2003 *Swimming Upstream*, dir. Russell Mulcahy. Capella Istropolitana.

2004 *ma mère*, dir. Christophe Honoré. Agnus Dei, uncredited recording.

COMEDIES

1997 *S1mØne*, dir. Andrew Niccol. Agnus Dei, Dale Warland Singers.

2000 *Kevin and Perry Go Large*, dir. Ed Bye. *Adagio for Strings*, uncredited recording and "Another Day," The Skip Raiders.

2001 *Amélie*, dir. Jean-Pierre Jeunet. Capella Istropolitana.

2006 *Tenacious D in the Pick of Destiny*, dir. Liam Lynch. Agnus Dei, St. John's Episcopal Cathedral Choir.

DOCUMENTARIES

1990 *Soldiers of Music: Rostropovich Returns to Russia*, dir. Bob Eisenhardt, Susan Frömke, and Albert Maysles. Uncredited recording.

1997 *Tour of the Inferno: Revisiting Platoon*, dir. Oliver Stone.

2004 *Peace One Day*, dir. Jeremy Gilley. Royal Liverpool Philharmonic, cond. Libor Pešek.

2004 *Shake Hands with the Devil: The Journey of Roméo Dallaire*, dir. Peter Raymont.

2007 *Sicko*, dir. Michael Moore.

Television Shows

1973	*The Ascent of Man*	UK-US, documentary
1991	*Celeste*	Argentina, drama
1991	*Soldiers of Music*	US, documentary
1992	*One Life to Live*	US, drama (soap opera)
1994; 1997	*Mystery Science Theater 3000*	US, comedy
1995	*The Oprah Winfrey Show*	US, talk show
1996	*The Fast Show*	UK, comedy
1996	*Seinfeld*	US, comedy (sit-com)
1998	*Daria*	US, comedy (cartoon)
1999	*Red Dwarf*	UK, comedy
2000	*At Home with the Braithwaites*	UK, drama-comedy
2001	*Spaced*	UK, comedy
2002	*Esperança* [Hope]	Brazil, drama
2003; 2007	*The Simpsons*	US, comedy (cartoon)
2003	*ER*	US, drama
2004	*Filthy Homes from Hell*	UK, reality-comedy
2004	*South Park*	US, comedy (cartoon)
2006	*Soccer AM*	UK, sports-comedy
2007	*Boondocks*	US, comedy (cartoon)
2009	*American Dad*	US, comedy (cartoon)
2009	*Big Love*	US, drama

BRITISH AND AMERICAN DRAMA

1992	*One Life to Live*	ABC
2000	*At Home with the Braithwaites*	BBC and BBC America
2003	*ER*	NBC
2009	*Big Love*	HBO

ACTION COMEDIES

1994; 1997	*Mystery Science Theater 3000*	Comedy Central
1996	*The Fast Show*	BBC
1996	*Seinfeld*	NBC
1999	*Red Dwarf*	BBC2
2001	*Spaced*	LWT
2004	*Filthy Homes from Hell*	ITV
2006	*Soccer AM*	Sky

AMERICAN CARTOONS

1998	*Daria*	MTV
2003; 2007	*The Simpsons*	Fox
2004	*South Park*	Comedy Central
2007	*Boondocks*	Cartoon Network

DOCUMENTARIES

1973	*The Ascent of Man*	BBC/PBS
1995	*The Oprah Winfrey Show*	Syndicated
2002	*Frontline: "Faith and Doubt at Ground Zero"*	PBS
2002	*In Memoriam: New York City*	HBO
2005	*Dr. Who Confidential*	BBC
2007	*The Conspiracy Files*	BBC

Selected Catalogue of *YouTube* Uploads

All groupings are organized alphabetically by content. Performers have been listed in cases of certainty. The following set consists of raw performance footage or original recordings accompanied by scenic images.

Raw Uploads

Azusa Pacific University Choir and Orchestra. "Agnus Dei," *YouTube* (28 February 2007), posted by sc0tlas.

BBC Symphony Orchestra, cond. Leonard Slatkin. "Proms 2001–Adagio for String 9-11 Tribute," *YouTube* (28 May 2007), posted by RupertJones.

Berlin Philharmoniker, cond. Simon Rattle. "Samuel Barber: Adagio for Strings (S. Rattle, cond.)," *YouTube* (27 October 2012), posted by firefox142857.

Choir of Trinity College, cond. Richard Marlow. "Samuel Barber: Agnus Dei (Adagio for Strings)," *YouTube* (1 November 2007), posted by lee32uk.

Direct to Dreams, a.k.a. Bruno Meunier. "Platoon–Adagio for Strings Barber Remix–Music by Direct to Dreams," *YouTube* (21 September 2009), posted by Direct2Dreams.

DJ Tiësto. "Tiësto–Adagio for Strings," *YouTube* (18 March 2008), posted by officialtiesto.

Hirano, Gen. "Gen Hirano Performing Samuel Barber's Adagio for Strings," *YouTube* (30 May 2010), posted by komrade666.

Indianapolis Symphony Orchestra, cond. Raymond Leppard. "Adagio for Strings–Raymond Leppard," *YouTube* (24 March 2007), posted by PatriciaHDaly.

Cond. Martínez-Pulgar, Jose Ignacio. "Adagio para Cuerdas–Samuel Barber," *YouTube* (17 April 2008), posted by CamerataExtrema.

Manuel, Juan. "Juan Manuel–Samuel Barber: Adagio for Strings," *YouTube* (23 November 2006), posted by hmariod.

l'Orchestra Jupiter di Mirandola, cond. Stefano Seghedoni. "ADAGIO per ARCHI," *YouTube* (24 April 2007), posted by idyllium.

R.A.F Zone Remix. "Adagio for Strings 2009 / I Feel Love [R.A.F. Zone Remix] nlx78," *YouTube* (22 October 2009), posted by N LX.

San Diego School of Creative and Performing Arts High School Orchestra, cond. Tamara Paige. "Adagio for Strings," *YouTube* (8 June 2007), posted by katroscar.

Savoie, Matt, Figure Skating. "Matt Savoie 2005 Four Continents SP," *YouTube* (24 December 2007), posted by jedellis.

Toine, Kevin. "Adagio For Strings Op.11–Samuel Barber–Electric Guitar," *YouTube* (21 August 2009), posted by Kevin Toine.

The following grouping includes themed images featuring compiled visual material from around the globe that uses *Adagio* as an audio track in the form of a tribute. Offensive or gruesome material is indicated by an asterisk (*).

Tribute Footage

9 / 11, perf. Choir of Trinity College, cond. Richard Marlow. "Agnus Dei," *YouTube* (11 September 2006), posted by PeregrineJohn.

______, perf. William Ørbit. "9/11: Remembering the Jumpers [Edit 1]," *YouTube* (11 September 2007), posted by mindOvermood.*

American Wars. "Adagio Slideshow," *YouTube* (19 April 2007), posted by cellopatrick.

Animal Rights. "Agnus Dei–Liberation," *YouTube* (20 December 2007), posted by RyanRoboto.

______, perf. New York Philharmonic, cond. Leonard Bernstein. "All God's Creatures–*Warning, Graphic Images*," *YouTube* (29 May 2008), posted by raggatt.*

______. "Calf Roping," *YouTube* (24 December 2007), posted by standingatthedoor.*

Environment. "Adagio for Recycling," *YouTube* (9 September 2006), posted by sgtjonson.

Environment Parody. "Plant Cruelty (What Animal Lovers Fail to Mention)," *YouTube* (27 March 2007), posted by Calvolini.

Ferrari, perf. DJ Tiësto. "Ferrari-F360 & DjTiesto–Adagio for Strings," *YouTube* (3 August 2006), posted by taruMutlu.

Gerrard, Steven, perf. DJ Tiësto. "Gerrard the Legend," *YouTube* (18 June 2008), posted by Damian Emanuel.

Hand-to-Hand Combat Demonstration, perf. DJ Tiësto. "Russian Style 1 (Original Russian Style)," *YouTube* (2 December 2006), posted by RedBerkut.

Homeworld Soundtrack, perf. Quire of Voyces, cond. Nathan J. Krietzer. "Paul Ruskay–Homeworld," *YouTube* (25 July 2011), posted by ketinadrealista.

Human Rights. "A Commercial for Compassion," *YouTube* (13 November 2007), posted by Gaiamuse.

______. "Social Change Through The Power of Peace Adagio for Strings," *YouTube* (6 June 2006), posted by sellaseat.

Hurricane Katrina, perf. New York Philharmonic, cond. Leonard Bernstein. "Hurricane Katrina: Return to New Orleans," *YouTube* (2 September 2007), posted by ZouiGJ.

______, perf. New York Philharmonic, cond. Thomas Schippers. "St. Bernard Parish–One Year After the Federal Flood," *YouTube* (13 September 2007), posted by scoutp.

Insult Video, perf. Choir of Trinity College, cond. Richard Marlow. "MOVING TRIBUTE TO YANKEE STADIUM," *YouTube* (22 September 2008), posted by SureShotDC.*

______, perf. Ferry Corsten. "My Loving Tribute to Ayrton Senna," *YouTube* (15 February 2010), posted by ayrtonLOSERsenna.*

Iraqi War Memorial. "Faces of the Fallen–December 2007," *YouTube* (21 March 2008), posted by AsianPolitics.

Jackson, Michael. "Adagio for Michael Jackson," *YouTube* (30 November 2009), posted by mjalbatros.

______. "Michael Jackson–They Broke You," *YouTube* (27 October 2009), posted by TheRaGiTe

Minneapolis Bridge Collapse. "Video Memorial–35W Bridge Collapse, Minneapolis Minnesota," *YouTube* (5 August 2007), posted by drakkar91.

Nature Scenes, perf. Tchaikovsky Chamber Orchestra, cond. Lazar Gosman. "Rosée de Diamant Musique Samuel Barber Adagio pour Cordes," *YouTube* (20 May 2009), posted by frederick292.

Political Advertisement, perf. Milwaukee Symphony Orchestra, cond. Lukas Foss. "It Was 1776 All Over Again," *YouTube* (13 August 2006), posted by 1776Again.

Racecar Drivers. "Tributo a Fernando Alonso y Ayrton Senna–de Todo Sobre la Formula Uno," *YouTube* (16 March 2012), posted by Jesus gonzalez Martinez.

Real Madrid, perf. DJ Tiësto. "Adagio for Strings ft. Real Madrid," *YouTube* (8 June 2011), posted by JayDean74.

Rickman, Alan, perf. DJ Tiësto. "Adagio for Alan Rickman," *YouTube* (25 October 2006), posted by Rickmanlover.

Royal Navy, perf. DJ Tiësto. "The Royal Navy," *YouTube* (11 January 2007), posted by ieuz123.

Sandy Hook, perf. London Philharmonic Orchestra, cond. David Parry. "A Tribute to the Victims of Sandy Hook," *YouTube* (21 December 2012) posted by WellnessNowNetwork.

______, perf. National Symphony Orchestra, cond. Leonard Slatkin. "For the Children," *YouTube* (15 December 2012), posted by tieemiami.

______, perf. New York Philharmonic, cond. Leonard Bernstein. "Newtown and Sandy Hook Memorial" *YouTube* (20 December 2012) posted by Jerry Angelica.

______. "Sandy Hook Elementary School 12/14/2012–RIP 26 New Souls in Heaven," *YouTube* (18 December 2012), posted by John Smith.

______, perf. New Zealand Symphony Orchestra, cond. Andrew Schenk. "Sandy Hook Tribute (Adagio for Strings)," *YouTube* (18 December 2012), posted by MrAugustusfinch.

______, perf. New York Philharmonic, cond. Leonard Bernstein. "We Remember Sandy Hook Elementary School Victims," *YouTube* (21 December 2012) posted by RedKnightTV.

Senna, Ayrton, perf. Capella Istropolitana. "A Senna Tribute," *YouTube* (19 January 2008), posted by sennanumber1fan.

Soccer Showdown, perf. DJ Tiësto. "Cristiano Ronaldo vs. Ronaldinho," *YouTube* (24 January 2009), posted by CR7Ronaldo07.

Space Slideshow, perf. Choir of Trinity College, cond. Richard Marlow. "Barber's Adagio for Strings, Op. 11," *YouTube* (22 February 2007), posted by Lyecoatha.

Sting (wrestler), perf. DJ Tiësto (Phynn Remix). "ADAGIO FOR STING," *YouTube* (26 June 2007), posted by THEBIGSEXC.

Tyson, Mike, Photoshop, perf. Ferry Corsten. "Mike Tyson Ferry Corsten–Adagio for Strings," *YouTube* (3 April 2010), posted by Ir0niClconic.

World War I, perf. New York Philharmonic, cond. Leonard Bernstein. "World War I Deaths–In Memory of the Slain," *YouTube* (18 August 2006), posted by jagorev.

World War II, perf. Moscow RTV Symphony Orchestra, cond. Klaus-Peter Hahn. "Normandy 2012–D Day Landings 06/06/1944," *YouTube* (19 September 2012), posted by lukebuckley1.

______, perf. New York Philharmonic, cond. Leonard Bernstein. "The Holocaust–Pictures and Videos Part 1," *YouTube* (15 May 2008), posted by Arsenal341.*

______, perf. St. Louis Orchestra, cond. Leonard Slatkin. "Adagio For Strings German War Memorial WWII Deutsche Zweiten Welt Krieg Kriegerdenkmal," *YouTube* (3 September 2009), posted by BadgemanDFW.

World War II Concentration Camp, perf. Emerson String Quartet. "Auschwitz," *YouTube* (2 November 2006), posted by Guillermo Gallego Lora.

Yamaha Motorcycles, perf. DJ Tiësto. "Yamaha YDH–Details & Tips," *YouTube* (22 October 2008), posted by SasedaReal.

This set of uploads consists of professional video stock taken from pre-existing sources and united with a commercial recording of *Adagio*. Sources may include television series, films, computer games, or live events.

Borrowed Footage

Battlestar Galactica, perf. Atlanta Symphony Orchestra, cond. Yoel Levi. "Starbuck's Death," *YouTube* (23 April 2007), posted by jsgould.

Football Factory vs. Green Street, perf. DJ Tiësto, "Football Factory 'n' Green Street Fights," *YouTube* (4 August 2008), posted by liamoh7.

General Hospital, perf. Choir of Trinity College, cond. Richard Marlow. "Emily~Agnus Dei," *YouTube* (17 September 2006), posted by NLdotcom.

"Halo 3 Remix," *YouTube* (19 January 2007), posted by DannoHung.

Jackson, Michael. "Stranger in Moscow," perf. William Ørbit. "Adagio Stranger in Moscow," *YouTube* (9 December 2006), posted by angelgijon.

Kickboxing Match, perf. William Ørbit. "Natthapong Thaibox–Weltmeister 1997," *YouTube* (10 July 2008), posted by MrHuman.

Little Match Seller, The, perf. The Choir of Trinity College, cond. Richard Marlow. "Re: What's Your Favourite Quotes?," *YouTube* (13 April 2007), posted by kawthari.

Lost, perf. DJ Tiësto. "LOST.Adagio for Strings (A Nalom Production)," *YouTube* (14 August 2006), posted by Markyz8.

______, perf. Moscow RTV Symphony Orchestra, cond. Klaus-Peter Kahn. "Adagio for Strings Jate / Skate AU," *YouTube* (18 March 2008), posted by NikkiMonique.

"Ma mere (clip)," *YouTube* (23 January 2010), posted by Kinoteatr3z.

"Marilyn Monroe on Samuel Barber," *YouTube* (15 April 2007), posted by durcetcurval.

Marvel vs Capcom video game, perf. DJ Tiësto. "MvC EoH Combos / Bugs," *YouTube* (20 July 2008), posted by BlueDrumV.

"Matrix Revolutions–Battle for Zion," *YouTube* (11 August 2007), posted by LostAngel88.

Metal Gear Solid, perf. Choir of Trinity College, cond. Richard Marlow. "Metal Gear Adagio: Song for the Patriots," *YouTube* (7 July 2007), posted by BigBrotherWii.

______. "Metal Gear Platoon," *YouTube* (5 August 2006), posted by OxoRee.

"Metal Gear Solid 4: Adagio for Strings," *YouTube* (4 July 2008), posted by John Scott.

Metropolis, perf. DJ Tiësto. "Metropolis Laboratory Scene Re-dub," *YouTube* (3 June 2009), posted by JTHawk30.

Naruto, perf. DJ Tiësto. "The Relationship," *YouTube* (24 August 2006), posted by 0kashii.

Obama, Barack. "Barack Obama's Speech on Race, set to Adagio for Strings," *YouTube* (19 March 2008), posted by markus1379.

Pittsburgh Penguins Athletes, perf. DJ Tiësto. "Sidney Crosby & Marc-Andre Fleury Tribute," *YouTube* (8 February 2009), posted by floorballgirl33.

"Platoon Music Video," *YouTube* (10 June 2006), posted by Zicod.

Reconstruction. "Реконструкция (Reconstruction)–Adagio for Strings," *YouTube* (9 March 2010), posted by labrussca.

"Saving Private Ryan / Band of Brothers Mix!," *YouTube* (5 December 2006), posted by ponchoyo.

"Smallville–Lionel Luthor's Funeral," *YouTube* (18 April 2008), posted by japa28.

Stargate SG-1, perf. William Ørbit. "SG1's Amanda Tapping 'Thank You' to William Orbit's Adagio," *YouTube* (2 April 2007), posted by muckypups1.

Stone Cold Steve Austin vs. Bret Hart, perf. Vancouver Symphony Orchestra, cond. George Delerue. "Emotional Wrestling Montage," *YouTube* (18 November 2007), posted by Maverick2212.

Supernatural. "Swan Song | Supernatural 5x22 | Adagio for Strings," *YouTube* (3 May 2011), posted by NorweganWood.

Tyson, Mike, perf. Ferry Corsten. "Mike Tyson Training Highlight Reel from www.mike-tyson.info," *YouTube* (8 June 2007), posted by Steven R74.

"Vietnam War–Adagio for Strings," *YouTube* (6 February 2010), posted by kmcgeachin.

World Record Dive. "Dana Kunze World Record Dive with Barber's Agnus Dei," *YouTube* (5 September 2009), posted by Sloppyorrus.

This section highlights the work of *YouTube* members who creatively employ original video footage coupled with a version of *Adagio*.

YouTube Originals

Addicted to Sugar, perf. Vancouver Symphony Orchestra, cond. George Delerue. "Ultimate Sugar Relapse / Freakout," *YouTube* (6 July 2012), posted by InfamousPlay.

Claymation. "Retrete," *YouTube* (7 September 2006), posted by chibizumi.

Coffee Addict, perf. William Ørbit. "Coffee Noir," *YouTube* (6 August 2006), posted by timbo808.

Couple Fight. "The Interrogation," *YouTube* (20 April 2006), posted by Sefiros.

Dramatic Teenager Falls, perf. William Ørbit. "AdagioforHumanity," *YouTube* (20 June 2006), posted by annoyingidiot.

Environment, perf. DJ Tiësto. "Adagio for the Earth (or Global Warming 101)," *YouTube* (30 July 2006), posted by VaginalMcGruder.

Guy Gets Dumped by Girlfriend, perf. Philadelphia Orchestra, cond. Eugene Ormandy. "The Letter," *YouTube* (12 September 2006), posted by SurgicalSteel.

Guy Makes Sandwich. "Roast Beef," *YouTube* (6 October 2006), posted by Justin Adams.

Guy Mourns Dead Girlfriend. "Adagio for Love," *YouTube* (25 October 2006), posted by heyfreedom.

Harris, Sam. "Sam Harris Recites CRANK THAT Song Lyrics by Soulja Boy Tell'em," *YouTube* (18 September 2007), posted by SamHarrisCOM.

"Lunar Eclipse 2008," *YouTube* (4 March 2009), posted by endlessdream94.

Poker Game Gone Wrong, perf. Philadelphia Orchestra, cond. Eugene Ormandy. "BFM Cheat," *YouTube* (22 March 2007), posted by BandageFaceMan.

Program Demo. "Adagio for Strings Donk FL Studios," *YouTube* (26 October 2007), posted by 02curwda.

______. "Adagio for Strings–Tiësto (Fruity Loops 7)–Juaco," *YouTube* (14 May 2008), posted by oscarva.

______. "How to Create From Scratch, Tiësto–Adagio for Strings on FL Studio (Arron Murray)," *YouTube* (17 May 2007), posted by Arron Murray.

______. "How To Play Adagio for Strings–Samuel Barber on Piano / Keyboard," *YouTube* (26 March 2009), posted by Jordan D.

Sand Dune ATV Jumping, perf. Choir of Trinity College, cond. Richard Marlow. "PPG for Morons: BOOTCAMP Day 4," *YouTube* (1 March 2008), posted by Paul Anthem.

Tae Kwon Do Training, perf. user remix. "Tae Kwon Do–Gurtprüfung AHS 07," *YouTube* (31 March 2008), posted by carbonmusic.

Ten-Minute Sunset. "Sunset Adagio for Strings," *YouTube* (27 November 2008), posted by Coco Esteves.

Tourist Promotion, perf. DJ Tiësto. "5-Minute Short Film on Wellington (New Zealand)," *YouTube* (15 January 2007), posted by mondo34.

Wushu Combat Demonstrations, perf. DJ Tiësto. "Beijing Wushu Team 2005 Tour," *YouTube* (20 June 2006), posted by wushubabe92.

Selected List of Memorial Performances

The following is a list of causes and individuals to whom *Adagio for Strings* has been dedicated in concerts and memorial services.

General Dedications

ANZAC Day, national day of remembrance in Australia and New Zealand to honor servicemen who fought at Gallipoli in Turkey in World War I. Woolston Brass Band. Grand ANZAC Concert, 25 April 1998. Christchurch.

ANZAC Day. *Encounter* radio program. Australian Broadcasting Corporation, 25 April 1999.

ANZAC Day and commemoration of the September 11th attacks. Ensemble XXI, cond. Lygia O'Riordan, 25 April 2002. Moscow.

ANZAC Day. Royal Melbourne Philharmonic Orchestra. Melbourne Town Hall, 25 April 2004. Melbourne.

ANZAC Day. Royal Melbourne Philharmonic Orchestra. Gallipoli Anzac Cove, 25 April 2005. Turkey.

ANZAC Day. Christchurch Symphony Orchestra, cond. William Southgate, 25 April 2008. Christchurch.

Boxing Day Tsunami (26 December 2004), Southeast Asia, fundraiser in support of the victims. Orchestra London, cond. Timothy Vernon, 9 January 2005. London, Ontario, Canada.

Boxing Day Tsunami, Southeast Asia. Musicians from Yale University, cond. Shinik Hahm, 15 January 2005. New Haven, Conn.

Boxing Day Tsunami, Southeast Asia. Heriot-Watt University Orchestra, cond. Steve King, 23 January 2005. Edinburgh, England, United Kingdom.

Boxing Day Tsunami, Southeast Asia. One World Symphony, cond. Sung Jin Hong, 20 & 28 January 2005. Brooklyn, N.Y.

Boxing Day Tsunami, Southeast Asia. St. Luke's Church, 29 January 2005. London.

Boxing Day Tsunami, Southeast Asia. Rochester Philharmonic Orchestra, cond. Jeff Tyzik, 30 January 2005. Rochester, N.Y.

Boxing Day Tsunami, Southeast Asia. Rutgers Presbyterian Church, 11 February 2005. New York City.

Boxing Day Tsunami, Southeast Asia. Norwalk Symphony Orchestra, cond. Diane Wittry, 26 February 2005. Norwalk, Conn.

Children of Chernobyl Relief Fund. Binghamton String Quartet, 25 April 1998. Binghamton, N.Y.

Fairfax County and the cities of Fairfax and Falls Church, firefighters and rescue departments. George Mason University String Orchestra. Tysons Corner Center, 27 May 2002. McLean, Va.

Firefighters who died in the line of duty. Butler University students, cond. Richard Auldon Clark. Fire Department Instruction Conference, 13 April 2005. Indianapolis, Ind.

Genocide victims around the world. Long Beach Poly High String Orchestra, March 2004. Long Beach, Calif.

Gujarat, India earthquake victims. Japan Philharmonic Chamber Orchestra, cond. Robert Rÿker, April 2001. Tokyo.

Holocaust Victims. Texas Master Chorale. The Centrum, 19 March 2001. Houston, Tex.

Holocaust Victims. South Florida Renaissance Orchestra, cond. Richard Fleischman. Horvitz Auditorium, 5 May 2005. Fort Lauderdale, Fla.

Katrina, musicians affected by Hurricane. University of Southern Mississippi Symphony Orchestra, 4 October 2005. Hattiesburg, Miss.

Katrina, musicians affected by Hurricane. University of Texas at Arlington, 15 October 2005. Arlington, Tex.

Katrina, musicians affected by Hurricane. San Obispo Symphony. February 2006. San Obispo, Calif.

Katrina, musicians affected by Hurricane. Sacramento Metropolitan Orchestra, September 2006. Sacramento, Calif.

Katrina Hurricane victims. Plano Symphony Orchestra, cond. Hector Guzman. Plano, Tex.

Katrina Hurricane victims. Baton Rouge Symphony Orchestra, cond. Timothy Muffitt. Baton Rouge, La.

Kelly, Grace, American actress and Princess consort of Monaco. Monte Carlo Cathedral, 18 September 1982. Monaco.

Kelly, Grace. National Symphony Orchestra, cond. Mistislav Rostropovich. Kennedy Center, March 1983. Washington, D.C.

Kennedy, John Fitzgerald, thirty-fifth president of the United States. National Symphony Orchestra, cond. Howard Mitchell. Constitution Hall, 23 November 1963. Washington, D.C.

Kent State University, students killed by National Guard. American Symphony Orchestra, cond. Leopold Stokowski. Carnegie Hall, 8 May 1970. New York City.

King, Jr., Martin Luther, American civil rights leader. Savannah Symphony Orchestra, cond. Chelsea Tipton II. Johnny Mercer Theatre, 5 February 2000. Savannah, Ga.

King, Jr., Martin Luther. Cleveland Orchestra, cond. Thomas Wilkins. Severance Hall, 14 January 2001. Cleveland, Ohio.

King, Jr., Martin Luther. Atlanta Symphony Orchestra, cond. Robert Spano. Atlanta Symphony Hall, 20 January 2003. Atlanta, Ga.

King, Jr., Martin Luther. Philadelphia Orchestra, cond. Thomas Wilkins. Martin Luther King High School, 18 January 2004. Philadelphia.

King, Jr., Martin Luther. Chicago Sinfonietta, cond. Paul Freeman, January 2008. Chicago.

Memorial Day. National Symphony Orchestra, cond. Erik Kunzel. White House on the West Lawn, 28 May 1990. Washington, D.C.

Political-ethnic crimes, victims. Cantate Chamber Singers, cond. Gisele Becker. Bradley Hills Presbyterian Church, June 1998. Bethesda, Md.

Pope John Paul II. Belarussian State Symphony, cond. Charles Ansbacher, April 2005.

Pope John Paul II. Augsburg Philharmonic Orchestra, cond. Rudolf Piehlmayer. Basilica of St. Mary Major, May 2005. Vatican City.

Pope John Paul II. Canticum Novum Singers, March 2006.

Rabin, Yitzhak, fifth prime minister of Israel. Israel Sinfonietta Be'er Sheba, November 1995. Be'er Sheba, Israel.

Rabin, Yitzhak. Israel Philharmonic, cond. Yoel Levi, 4 December 1995. Tel Aviv, Israel.

Rainier, Prince, ruler of Monaco. Monte Carlo Philharmonic. Monte Carlo Cathedral, 15 April 2005. Monte Carlo, Monaco.

Remembrance Day, also known as Poppy Day or Armistice day, the holiday honors the sacrifices of servicemen and civilians since World Wari I. Australian Classical Players, 11 November 2001. Victoria, Australia.

Remembrance Day. Vancouver Youth Symphony Orchestra, 11 November 2007. Vancouver, B.C.

Riverside Cemetery, men and women interred at. Riverside County Philharmonic, cond. Patrick Flynn. Riverside National Cemetery, 2 July 2006. Riverside, Calif.

Roosevelt, Franklin Delano, thirty-second president of the United States. Pittsburgh Symphony, cond. Peter Oundijian. Heinz Hall, February 2005. Pittsburgh, Penn.

Sanielevici, Emil, talented student and victim of school shooting. Anonymous organ performance. Heinz Hall, 7 March 2000. Pittsburgh, Penn.

Smuts, Jan Christiaan, British field marshal in World War II and Prime Minister of South Africa. Broadcast via public radio, 11 September 1950. South Africa.

Taft, Robert A., Republican United States Senator. Broadcast via public radio, 31 July 1953. United States.

Tyranny, oppression and genocide victims. University of Ottawa Orchestra, 11 November 2005. Ottawa, Ontario, Canada.

Veteran's Day. Sacramento Festival Orchestra, cond. Donald Kendrick, 11 November 1996. Sacramento, Calif.

Veteran's Day. Sacramento Youth Orchestra, cond. Michael Neumann, 11 November 2000. Sacramento, Calif.

Virginia Tech (Polytechnic) Institute, students shot. Roanoke Symphony Orchestra, cond. David Wiley, April 2007.

Worcester Cold Storage and Warehouse Company, firefighting disaster. Cond. Doug Weeks, November 2000.

World War II veterans. Duluth Symphony Orchestra, cond. Tauno Hannikainen. Duluth Armory, 18 March 1945. Duluth, Minn.

The following is a brief list of other musicians, or others involved with symphony orchestras to whom concert performances of Barber's *Adagio* have been dedicated.

Musician Dedications

Barber, Samuel. New York Philharmonic Orchestra, cond. Leonard Bernstein. Avery Fisher Hall at the Lincoln Center, January 1981. New York City.

Beck, Jack, violinist with the Reno Philharmonic. The Truckee Meadows Community Orchestra, cond. Jennifer Martin, 15 April 2002. Reno, Nev.

Christianson, Lawrence, former conductor of the West Virginia University Symphony Orchestra. WVSO, cond. David Tang, 10 October 2004. Morgantown, W. Va.

Delun, Li, conductor of China Philharmonic Orchestra. CPO, cond. Long Yu, 21 October 2001. Beijing.

Dickson, Harry Ellis, conductor of Boston Pops and first violinist of Boston Symphony Orchestra. Boston Classical Orchestra, cond. Steven Lipsitt. Faneuil Hall, 21 & 23 August 2008. Boston.

Gilbert, Gama, journalist, musician, and friend of Samuel Barber. New Center of Music Chamber Orchestra, cond. Joseph Levine. Town Hall, November 1940. New York City.

Gilbert, Gama. Primrose String Quartet. Universalist Funeral Chapel, September 1940. New York City.

Gingold, Josef, prestigious violin educator at the Jacobs School of Music. Indiana University students of Josef Gingold, cond. Paul Biss, 1995. Bloomington, Ind.

Hammond, Michael, former Dean of Rice University's Shepherd School of Music, chairman of the National Endowment of the Arts (NEA). Houston Symphony, cond. Christoph Eschenbach, 1 February 2002. Houston, Tex.

Jarvis, Gerald, former concertmaster of the Vancouver Symphony Orchestra. VSO, 20 January 1996. Vancouver, B.C.

Johnson, Bryan, violinist with the National Symphony Orchestra. Guest cond. Giancarlo Guerrero, 20 July 2001. Washington, D.C.

Kellog, Juliet Spangler, member of the Bangor Symphony Orchestra. BSO, 16 March 2007. Bangor, Maine.

Korman, John, violinist with the St. Louis Symphony. SLS, November 1998. St. Louis, Mo.

Kreisler, Fritz, violinist with the New York Philharmonic. NYP, cond. Thomas Schippers, 2 February 1962. New York City.

LaSanke, Geraldine M., violinist with the Knox-Galesburg Symphony. KGS, 24 March 2001. Galesburg, Ill.

Lieberson, Lorraine Hunt, mezzo-soprano. The New York Philharmonic, cond. Branwell Tovey, 6 July 2006. New York City.

McEldowney, Sylvia, violinist with the Bangor Symphony Orchestra. BSO, cond. Xiao-Lu Li, 31 January 2005. Bangor, Maine.

Menotti, Gian Carlo. Quatuor Dell'Arte. Cathedrale de Monaco, 10 February 2007. Monte Carlo, Monaco.

Menotti, Gian Carlo. Ginn Resorts Spoleto Festival USA Orchestra, cond. John Kennedy. Spoleto Festival USA, May 2008. Charleston, S.C.

Rosenthal, Perry, principal cellist with the Rhode Island Philharmonic. RIP, cond. Larry Rachleff, 13 May 2006. East Providence, R.I.

Shaw, Robert. Renowned conductor and Guggenheim Fellowship recipient. Cleveland Orchestra, February 1999. Cleveland, Ohio.

Watkins, Sara, conductor of Annapolis Chamber Orchestra. ACO, cond. Markand Thakar. April 1998. Annapolis, Md.

Weir, Osby L., former president of the National Symphony Orchestra Association and a member of its board. NSO, cond. Howard Mitchell, 25 January 1997. Washington, D.C.

9 / 11 Memorial Concerts

2001

11 September

Colorado Springs Symphony, cond. Leighton Smith. Colorado Springs, Colo.

13 September

Los Angeles Chamber Orchestra, cond. Esa-Pekka Salonen. Hollywood Bowl. Hollywood, Calif.

Winston-Salem Symphony. Winston-Salem, N.C.

Ying Quartet. University at Buffalo. Buffalo, N.Y.

14 September

Cape Cod Symphony Orchestra, cond. Royston Nash. Barnstable, Mass.

Cincinnati Orchestra, cond. Paavo Järvi. "To the Honor and Memory." Cincinatti, Ohio.

Dallas Symphony Orchestra. Dallas, Tex.

Knoxville Symphony Orchestra, cond. Kirk Trevor. Knoxville, Tenn.

Mark Williams, organist. In memory of the employees at Cantor Fitzgerald who perished in the World Trade Center on September 11th. St. Paul's Cathedral, London.

University of Michigan (with the Philharmonic Orchestra). Ann Arbor, Mich.

Oregon Symphony, cond. James DePriest. Portland, Ore.

Richmond Symphony, cond. Eckart Preu. Richmond, Va. (Mark Russell Smith, the orchestra's director, was stranded in Minneapolis, Minn.)

15 September

Alabama Symphony, cond. Christopher Confessore. Birmingham, Ala.

BBC Orchestra, cond. Leonard Slatkin. Royal Albert Hall, 15 September 2001. London.

Memphis Symphony Orchestra, cond. David Loebel. Memphis, Tenn.

Savannah Symphony Orchestra, cond. Chelsea Tipton II. Savannah, Ga.

16 September

Emerson String Quartet. Avery Fisher Hall at the Lincoln Center. New York City.

Philadelphia Orchestra, cond. Wolfgang Sawallisch.

19 September

National Symphony Orchestra, cond. Leonard Slatkin. Kennedy Center. Washington, D.C.

Shanghai String Quartet. University of Richmond. Richmond, Va.

20 September

Denison String Quartet. Denison University. Granville, Ohio.

Seattle Symphony, cond. Gerard Schwarz. Seattle, Wash.

St. Louis Symphony Orchestra, cond. Hans Vonk. St. Louis, Mo.

21 September

Chicago Symphony Orchestra, cond. Daniel Barenboim.

Jacksonville Symphony Orchestra, cond. Fabio Mechetti. Jacksonville, Fla

Florida Orchestra, guest cond. Michael Christie. St. Petersburg, Fla.

Fresno Philharmonic Orchestra, guest cond. Bernard Gueller. Fresno, Calif.

22 September

Madison Symphony Orchestra, cond. John Demain. Madison, Wis.

Syracuse Symphony Orchestra, cond. Daniel Hege. Syracuse, N.Y.

Topeka Symphony Orchestra, cond. John Wesley Strickler. Topeka, Kan.

23 September

Nashville Symphony, cond. Byung-Hyun. "Spirit of America." Nashville, Tenn.

28 September

Baylor University Symphony Orchestra. Waco, Tex.

St. Luke's Orchestra, cond. Christoph Eschenbach. Ground Zero. New York City.

30 September

Atlanta Symphony Orchestra, cond. Robert Spano. "Music of Recovery, Music of Healing, Music of Hope." Atlanta, Ga.

North Carolina Symphony, cond. Rodney Wynkoop. "A Concert in Memoriam." Raleigh, N.C.

8 October

Minnesota Orchestra and St. Paul Chamber Orchestra, cond. Andreas Delfs. Minneapolis, Minn.

13 October

Miró String Quartet. Dumbarton Oaks Concert Series, 13 October 2001. In memory of passenger Bryan Jack on American Airlines flight 77, which crashed into the Pentagon. Washington, D.C.

23 October

Miami String Quartet. Montreal.

4 November

Iowa State University Symphony Orchestra, cond. Mark Laycock. Ames, Iowa.

6 November

Corigliano Quartet. Dickinson College. In memory of the firefighters and police officers who served during the 9-11 crisis. Carlisle, Penn.

Orchestras around the country presented concerts in memory of the terrorist attacks that occurred the year before. The following is a list of most of the concerts that included *Adagio for Strings* as part of their program. Those concerts where *Adagio* appeared as part of an "all-American" program are given an asterisk (*). Concerts that were free are indicated by a plus (+).[1]

Anniversary Concerts

2002

4 July

Boston Pops, cond. Keith Lockhart. Edward A. Hatch Memorial Shell. Boston.

7 September

Tallahassee Symphony Orchestra, cond. Daniel Meyer. "An American Celebration."* Tallahassee, Fla.

8 September

The Woodlands Symphony Orchestra. Woodlands, Tex.

10 September

Russian Chamber Choir.

11 September

Amarillo Symphony, cond. James Setapen. "America Remembers: A Musical Tribute."*+ Amarillo, Tex.

[1]Much of the information below is derived from a list of orchestral commemorative concerts published by the American Symphony Orchestra League, www.symphony.org/911. A few others have been added.

Arlington Symphony, cond. Barry Hemphill. "Arlington County 9/11 Memorial Program."*+ Arlington, Va.

Avila String Quartet. Live broadcast via WFMT radio. Chicago.

Bakersfield Symphony Orchestra, cond. John Farrar. "Concert of Remembrance."+ Bakersfield, Calif.

Cincinatti Symphony Orchestra, cond. Paavo Järvi. Recording broadcast on *Paavo Järvi: Inaugural Concert*, PBS. Cincinatti, Ohio.

Grand Rapids Symphony, cond. David Lockington. "We Remember–September 11 Community Commemoration."*+ Grand Rapids, Mich.

Hamilton-Fairfield Symphony Orchestra, cond. Paul Stanbery. "Presbyterian Memorial Service."*+ Hamilton, Ohio. [presented with slide presentation of images]

Johnstown Symphony Orchestra. Seven Springs resort, 11 September 2002. Seven Springs, Penn.

Juilliard String Quartet. Ground Zero, 11 September 2002. New York City.

Knoxville Symphony Orchestra, cond. Kirk Trevor. "9/11 In Remembrance Concert."+ Knoxville, Tenn.

Los Angeles Philharmonic, cond. Leonard Bernstein. Recording broadcast on *Echoes*, "A Radio Soundscape." 11 September 2002. Public Radio International.

Louisville Orchestra, cond. Uriel Segal. "Memorial Concert."*+ Louisville, Ky.

McKeesport Symphony Orchestra, cond. Bernard Goldberg, "Memorial Concert."*+ McKeesport, Penn.

Mendelssohn Choir of Pittsburgh, cond. Robert Page. 11 September 2002. In support of funds for the Somerset County Flight 93 Memorial Fund.

Münchener Bach-Chor, cond. Gilbert Levine. Church of St. Peter and St. Paul, 11 September 2002. Cracow, Poland.

New Mexico Symphony, cond. Roger Melone. Albuquerque, N.M.

Plymouth Symphony Orchestra, cond. Nan Harrison Washburn. "Honoring the Memory, Embracing the Future: Our Community Remembers."+ Plymouth, Mich.

San Francisco Symphony, cond. Michael Tilson Thomas.+ San Francisco, Calif.

The Toledo Symphony, cond. Stefan Sanderling. "Special Tribute."+ Toledo, Ohio.

The Woodlands Symphony Orchestra, cond. Dagan Chen. "Honoring Our Freedom." Woodlands, Tex.

Virginia Symphony, cond. JoAnn Falletta.+ Hampton Roads, Va.

12 September

Greensboro Symphony Orchestra, cond. Stuart Malina. "A Tribute to the Heroes and Victims of September 11th." Greensboro, N.C.

Orchestra X, cond. John Axelrod. "works of American composers." The Parador, Houston, Tex.

13 September

Alabama Symphony, cond. Christopher Confessore. Birmingham, Ala.

Illinois Symphony Orchestra, cond. Karen Lynn Deal. "In Remembrance, A Tribute to America."* Springfield, Ill.

Omaha Symphony, Victor Yampolsky, music director and Ernest Richardson, resident conductor. "The American Spirit."* Omaha, Neb.

22 September

Queens Symphony Orchestra, cond. Arthur Fagen, and guest cond. Tom Scott. "Salute to Our Heroes."* Flushing, N.Y.

28 September

The Orchestra of Northern New York. "September Tribute." Potsdam, N.Y.

2003

11 September

Orlando Philharmonic Orchestra. Orlando, Fla.

I Musici di Montreal. Montreal.

Orkiestra Symfoniczna Filharmonii Narodowej [Warsaw Philharmonic Orchestra]. Warsaw, Poland.

12 September

Lancaster Catholic High School Marching Band. Lancaster, Penn.

London Musical Arts String Orchestra, cond. John Landor. London.

21 September

Bangor Symphony Orchestra. Bangor, Maine.

22 September

Manila Philharmonic Orchestra, visiting cond. Eduardo Browne. Manila, The Philippines.

23 September

Liverpool Organ Recitals, Liverpool Anglican Cathedral. Paul Gobey, organist at London's Norwegian Church performed Strickland's transcription. Liverpool, England, United Kingdom.

25 September

Belmont Ensemble of London, cond. Peter Gilbert-Dyson. London.

26 September

London Concertante. Wyndham School. Egremont, Cumbria, United Kingdom.

2004
11 September

East Texas Symphony Orchestra, cond. Per Brevig. Tyler, Tex.

Allen Philharmonic Orchestra, cond. Domenico Codispoti. Allen, Tex.

Louisville Orchestra, cond. Steven Mercurio. Louisville, Ky.

Tribute Orchestra, cond. Jeffrey Stirling. Linden Hills, Minn.

2006
11 September

Shanghai String Quartet. Bargemusic. Brooklyn, New York City.

Adagio for Strings by Other Composers

Beath, Betty [Australia]. *Lament for Kosovo: Adagio for Strings.* Wollongong: Wirripang, 1999. Wirripang M-720065-93-9. *Music of Betty Beath*, perf. Camerata of St. John's (Wirripang, WIRR024, 2009).

Boon, Rolf [Canada]. *Adagio for Strings.* 1989.

Borenstein, Nimrod [Israel]. *The Shell Adagio for Strings*, Op. 17. London: Boosey & Hawkes, 2003. Hal Leonard, 48019409.

Dela, Maurice [Canada]. *Adagio for String Orchestra.* Toronto: Hart House, 1956. CTL 477-65137.

Fomitchov, Pavel [Russia]. *Adagio for Strings.* 2012.

Gold, Jeffrey [United Kingdom]. *Elegy: Adagio for Strings* (Corpus Polymedia, 2007).

Hummel, Bertold [Germany]. *Adagio for Strings in memoriam Benjamin Britten*, Op. 62a. Mainz, Germany: Schott Music, 1976. ED 20280.

Jolivet, André [France]. *Adagio for Strings.* 1960. *Jolivet: Works for String Orchestra*, perf. Orchestre des Pays de Savoie, cond. Mark Foster (Timpani, 1143, 2008).

Keay, Nigel [New Zealand]. *Adagio for Strings: Image of Java.* Paris: [vanity], 1989. www.nigelkeay.com/adagio.htm.

Körvits, Tõnu [Estonia]. *Adagio for Strings.* 1995.

Matthews, David [United Kingdom]. *Adagio for String Orchestra*, Op. 56b. London: Faber Music, 1990. 0-571-51928-8. *David Matthews: Complete String Quartets, Volume One*, perf. Kreutzer Quartet (Toccata Classics, TOCC0058, 2010). [The score and the album are two different versions of the same work.]

McKinley, William Thomas [United States]. *Adagio for Strings.* 1987. *Robert Starer and William Thomas McKinley . . .*, perf. Czech Radio Symphony Orchestra, cond. Vladimir Valek (MMC Recordings, 2070, 1999).

Olsen, Carl Gustav Sparre [Norway]. *Adagio for Strings.*

Parchman, Gen Louis [United States]. *Adagio for Strings.* 1971.

Syberg, Franz Adolf [Denmark]. *Adagio for Strings.* 1938. *Franz Syberg Symphonic Works*, perf. Odense Symphony Orchestra, cond. Támás Vetö (SteepleChase Productions, 32088, 1991).

Weigl, Vally [Austria]. *Adagio for Strings.* 1945.

Adagio in a Gay Context

Ensembles

London Gay Symphony, cond. Stefan Hofkes. London, May 1999.

The Stonewall Chorale. New York, 18 December 1999.

The Lakeside Pride Clarinet Choir. Chicago, 2002.

Albums

Various Artists. *Out Classics,* 1995. New York: RCA Victor Red Seal 09026-68261-2.

Various Artists. *Club Verboten: Music Through the Ages By and For the Gay and Lesbian Community*, 1997. Chatsworth, Calif.: DCC Compact Classics, A28552-A28555.

Various Artists. *Classical Erotica*, 1996. Atlanta: Rising Star Records RS0280.

Ballet

Queer Notions, choreo. Patrick Scully.

Earthly Love, Heavenly Spirits, choreo. Edward Morgan and Daniel Scott. MorganScott Ballet. New York: St. Mark's Church, Danspace Project, 30 March 1999.

Purple Bend, choreo. Jimmy Gamonet. Fort Lauderdale, Fla.: Bailey Concert Hall.

Films

A Very Natural Thing, dir. Christopher Larkin. New Line Cinema: 1974.

Les Roseaux sauvages, dir. André Téchiné. Strand Releasing: 1994.

Love and Taboo, dir. Clive Barker. Paris Barclay chose *Adagio for Strings* for her work. [Project stalled], 2000.

Themes in Television Shows

One Life to Live, prod. Frank Valentini. 15 July 1968-present, ABC. United States.

At Home with the Braithwaites, prod. and written Sally Wainwright. 20 January 2000 - 9 April 2003, BBC and BBC America. United Kingdom. Dist. Acorn Media.

Subjects

Names and Titles

For the sake of expedience a number of entries in this index have been organized in the following categories: actors in film and television, dances, documentaries, films, radio programs, recorded anthologies, and television programs. The compositions or works by individuals are noted with their creator's name.

Recorded Examples

All tracks are composed by Samuel Barber.

1 String Quartet, Op. 11, Movement II – Molto Adagio [8:01]
Published by G. Schirmer (1939)
Performed by The Tokyo String Quartet
Mikhail Kopelman, Violin I; Kikuei Ikeda, Violin II;
Kazuhide Isomura, Viola; Sadao Harada, Cello

2 *Adagio for Strings*, Op. 11 [7:17]
Published by G. Schirmer (1939)
Performed by NBC Symphony Orchestra
Conducted by Arturo Toscanini

3 *Adagio for Strings*, Op. 11 [7:42]
Published by G. Schirmer (1939)
Performed by The Smithsonian Chamber Players
Conducted by Kenneth Slowik

4 Agnus Dei [9:29]
Transcribed by Samuel Barber
Published by G. Schirmer (1967)
Performed by The Choir of Trinity College, Cambridge
Conducted by Richard Marlow

5 *Adagio* [5:39]
Transcribed by William Strickland
Published by G. Schirmer (1949)
Performed by David Pizarro, Organ

6 *Adagio* [6:29]
Transcribed by Hiro Fujikake

Performed by James Galway, Flute; Hiro Fujikake, Synthesizers

7 *Adagio* [4:33]

Arranged by Kalmen Opperman

Performed by Richard Stoltzman and The Kalmen Opperman Clarinet Choir

Conducted by Kalmen Opperman

8 *Adagio* [5:57]

Arranged by Stephen McNeff

Performed by The Canadian Brass

Frederic Mills, trumpet; Ronald Romm, trumpet; David Ohanian, horn; Eugene Watts, trombone; Charles Daellenbach, tuba

9 *Adagio* [4:03]

Arranged by Stan Funicelli

Performed by The California Guitar Trio

Bert Lams, Hideyo Moriya, Paul Richards

10 *Adagio* [2:43]

Arranged by Dean Westman and Jim Casella

Performed by The Santa Clara Vanguard

Conducted by Jim Casella

11 *Adagio* [10:24]

Arranged and performed by Antonio MilláN

12 *Adagio* [6:19]

Performed by Larry McDonough and Off Beat

Larry McDonough, Piano; Phil Holm, Trumpet; Jeff King, Tenor Saxophone; Bruce Heine, Bass; Dave Stanoch, Drums